RED ATOM

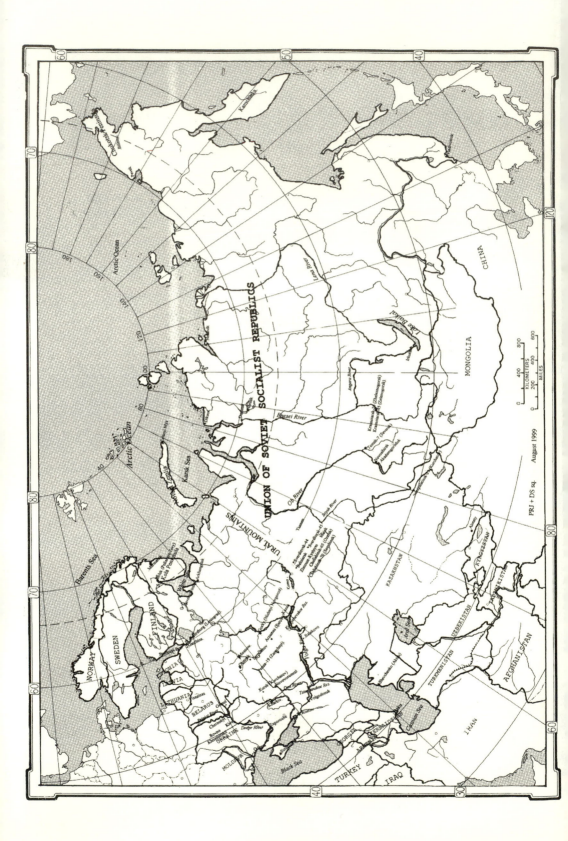

RED ATOM

Russia's Nuclear Power Program from Stalin to Today

Paul R. Josephson

W. H. FREEMAN AND COMPANY
NEW YORK

Text design by Cambraia (Magalhães) Fernandes

Library of Congress Cataloging-in Publication Data
Josephson, Paul R.
    Red atom: Russia's nuclear power program from Stalin today/Paul R. Josephson.
      p. cm.
    Includes bibliographical references and index.
    ISBN 0-7167-3044-8
    1. Nuclear energy—Former Soviet republics—History—20th century. 2. Nuclear industry—
Former Soviet republics—History—20th century. 3. Nuclear energy—Russia (Federation)—
History—20th century. 4. Nuclear industry—Russia (Federation)—History—20th century.
5. Former Soviet republics—Politics and government. 6. Russia (Federation)—Politics and
government. I. Title
TK9085.J67 1999   99–42005
333.792´4´0947—dc21   CIP

Printed in the United States of America

First printing 1999

W. H. Freeman and Company
41 Madison Avenue, New York, NY 10010
Houndmills, Basingstoke, RG21 6XS, England

This book is dedicated to the liquidators of the Chernobyl disaster and to the people of Ukraine, Russia, and Belarus, who must live with its legacy.

Two workers, without respirators, gloves, or heavy clothing, involved in the construction of the "Sarcophagus" for Chernobyl's unit 4. *(Courtesy of Anatolii Diatlov)*

Illustrations

CONTENTS

CHRONOLOGY

ACKNOWLEDGMENTS

Through their advice, critical comments on parts of the manuscript, and above all else their friendship and collegiality, many people contributed to the writing of *Red Atom.*

Kharkiv, Ukraine is a gracious city, largely because of the hospitality of physicists Iurii Freiman at the Institute of Low Temperature Physics and Iurii Ranyuk at the Ukrainian Physical Technical Institute. They invited me into their homes, shared their historical work with me, and facilitated contacts with other scientists.

In Moscow, my first home in the former Soviet Union as a graduate student in 1985, several people in the Institute of History of Science and Technology have always provided a kind word, a historical insight, or a family meal: Vladimir Vizgin, Iurii Krivonosov, Boris Iavelov. Igor Golovin, who was Igor Kurchatov's deputy on the atomic bomb project, warmly facilitated my access to Kurchatov Institute for Atomic Energy archives. During his trip to the United States in 1993, I had the honor of driving him around the Northeast and having him as a guest in my home. Dr. Golovin died in 1998, and I will miss him. Raissa Kuznetsova, head of the Kurchatov Museum, generously shared her knowledge of Kurchatov with me, and made me feel like an honored guest in the museum. Evgenii Feinberg, Pavel Rubinen, Aleksandr Andreev, Lev Pitaevskii, Lev Okun, Vitaly Ginsburg, and Evgenii Velikhov also made it possible for me to do research on *Red Atom*, sharing their intimate knowledge of the history of Soviet physics.

In Obninsk, Vladimir Yarovitsyn and Lev Kochetkov made my stay informative and fascinating. Oleg Kazachkovskii, former director of the Soviet breeder reactor program, was a gracious critic of my chapter on breeders and warmly welcomed me into his home. Bob Simpson also carefully read the chapter.

St. Petersburg was my second home in the USSR, but because of Viktor Frenkel, the leading Russian historian of physics and a member of the Leningrad Physical Technical Institute, it is my home away from home. After Vitya's sudden death, his wife, the biologist Olga Cherneva, has continued to open her home and heart to me and my family. Vitya's friends, Viktor Golant, head of the LFTI fusion program for many years, and Zhores Alferov, director of the institute, have never hesitated to offer good criticism of my work and arrange contacts with other physicists and institutes.

Macy Morse and Vladimir Vashchenko, members of the Portsmouth/Severodvinsk Connection (an organization striving to build a sister-city relationship to assist two nuclear submarine cities convert from military to civilian enterprise), contributed to this work by example and inspiration. Sergei Borsky greeted me in Severodvinsk with professionalism and camaraderie.

I have had four editors at W. H. Freeman and Company: Elizabeth Knoll, Jonathan Cobb, John Michel, and Erika Goldman, whose collective generosity made writing *Red Atom* significantly easier. Still, I hope for no more than three editors for my next book. Jodi Simpson was a marvelous copy editor in every way.

Donna Brown and Mary Vandebogart made it a joy to work at the University of New Hampshire, providing invaluable emotional support to this project. Deep thanks to Anne Fitzpatrick, Ron Leblanc, Edward Josephson (no relation), Rima Apple, Foss Tighe, Iurii Smirnov, Rebecca Herzig, Bart Hacker, and Milo Nordyke, who provided comments, materials, historical overview, or a combination of the three on some aspect of this book.

Without the financial and institutional support of the National Science Foundation, Office of Eurasian Affairs of the National Academy of Sciences, the National Endowment for the Humanities, the Dibner Institute for the History of Science and Technology, the National Council for Eurasian and East European Research, and the International Research Exchanges Board, I would never have been able to finish *Red Atom*.

In Durham, New Hampshire, Cathy Frierson helped this book mature, with the promise of an island retreat as a reward for finishing it. She greeted my return from slightly radioactive sites with only a little consternation. Isaac Josephson has moved from cross-country skiing to baseball, basketball, and soccer. His insistence that I coach his teams or take him to seven different practices or games every week never interfered with writing, because I wanted to be out on the field playing with him. During the book's production, Jamie Calderwood and Sarah Sherman taught me to roof, Deb and Dennie Straussvoge reminded me how to change an alternator, and Roberto Clemente provided inspiration for the map on page ii.

My thanks to Dima Derkach, Boris Malitskii, and Iurii Khramov for all of their assistance during my visits to Kiev, Ukraine, one of the most beautiful cities in the world. Iurii Trofimenko at the Institute of Nuclear Physics educated me about the history of nuclear physics in Ukraine. Igor Egorov, a specialist in science policy, has become a life-long friend through our shared interest in the economics of big science. But the real reason that Kiev is so beautiful is because of Sasha Popov and Tanya Peskhova, who have never failed to invite me into their home and who never forget to send New Year's greetings. Sasha is one of the most generous people I have ever met. He has fed my love for Ukrainian sausage and beer, but not insisted that I eat the delicacy sala (pork fat).

RED ATOM

PROLOGUE

Atomic-Powered Communism

Long live communism—the radiant future of all mankind.
—A slogan of Soviet socialism

Like many Americans, I am a child of the nuclear age. My first memories are of fallout shelters, mushroom clouds, and rockets capable of carrying nuclear warheads as well as astronauts. I grew up in a nuclear family. My father was a nuclear physicist who worked on reactor design. I got my first scar in Oak Ridge, Tennessee, home of the United States's effort to separate the fissile from nonfissile isotopes of uranium, when, as a three-year-old, I fell on a cinder block and cut my right knee. So I have been honored to visit nuclear facilities in Chernobyl, Obninsk, Severodvinsk, Kharkiv, Kiev, Moscow, Novosibirsk, and St. Petersburg to learn firsthand about the Soviet nuclear age.

My interest in Soviet atoms for peace programs grew out of one of the greatest misfortunes of the nuclear era: Chernobyl. Chernobyl touched me directly. As soon as we learned about the terrible accident, Western news media interviewed the experts about what happened. Because of my work in the history of Soviet physics, they broadcast interviews of me on radio and published fragments of my thoughts in newspapers. In various lectures and in the article I wrote over the next few weeks ("The Historical Roots of the Chernobyl Disaster"), I set forth my basic ideas about the unique way in which the Soviet system shaped steel, concrete, water, nuclear fuel, and the careers of scientists and engineers. Over the next few years, while engaged in other projects, I returned to nuclear themes, visiting the glorious sites of the Soviet atoms for peace programs; and I resolved to tell a story about the transformation of symbols of progress, truth, and hope into those of despair and

1

danger. This is a cautionary story of engineering hubris, and how the desire to change the world for the better sent a nation stumbling headlong into calamity.

One of the symbols of hope was Chernobyl. When completed, with ten reactors instead of the four that were built, the station would have powered Ukraine. I have since visited Chernobyl, warming myself on top of one of the reactor units that functions to this day and driving by the sarcophagus that entombs unit 4. That unit exploded because of a foolhardy experiment, ejecting a dangerous cloud of radioactivity into the atmosphere and spewing chunks of glowing uranium onto the ground nearby. I have lived in Kiev and watched friends grapple with the deadly legacy of Soviet nuclear engineering.

Another symbol of hope was Obninsk, site of the first reactor to produce electricity for a national grid in 1954, beating any United States effort to commercialize nuclear power by four years. The Obninsk reactor is located about two hours south of Moscow. A forerunner of the Chernobyl model and still in operation to this day, the Obninsk power reactor was a propaganda coup for the Soviet Union. It demonstrated the peaceful intentions of the nation on the heels of President Dwight Eisenhower's address to the United Nations calling for shared nuclear know-how in medicine, agriculture, transportation, and power generation for the benefit of all humankind. When I visited Obninsk in March 1998, a small leak of radioactive water, hastily mopped up in my presence, immediately canceled any hopes I might have had of warming myself upon that reactor.

This book is about how culture and politics shape the development of such large-scale technologies as nuclear reactors. In this case, these "peaceful" nuclear technologies will have an impact on our lives for decades to come. The Soviet Union has collapsed, but its nuclear establishment lives on in dozens of reactor and research sites, closed military cities, scores of institutes, thousands of scientists and engineers, and tens of thousands of other employees, most of them within Russian borders. Many of the scientists are world-class specialists in radiation chemistry, nuclear physics, and biophysics. Most are narrowly trained, staff members geared to producing the various technologies of the nuclear era: pumps, steam separators, batteries, centrifuges, screens, filters, fuel rods, reactors, isotope separation facilities, accelerators, and radioisotopes.

The founders of the nuclear industry intended it to be no different from any other industry where mass production techniques were engaged to produce standard equipment. They believed they could link together a series of simple technologies through complex processes they had tamed in the laboratory. Mid-level workers, who had mastered supposedly infallible technologies with only a basic understanding of nuclear physics, supervised the technologies. The workers acquired understanding through crash courses provided at technical institutes connected with the industry. This view of technology as infallible and manipulable by the simple worker was standard fare in the USSR for any branch of the economy: Legions of workers armed with rudimentary technology would eventually construct the "material-technological basis of communism." Yet was this the blind leading the blind?

The Soviet nuclear effort, like that in the United States, centered on military technologies. The goal was the mass production of light-weight, miniaturized warheads, several of which could be affixed to missiles or rockets of multikiloton and multimegaton yield. From the early days of the effort, physicists also considered nuclear technologies with applications in the civilian sector, for they wished their legacy to be connected with peace. The slogan was, "Let the atom be a worker, not a soldier." The physicists desired energy "too cheap to meter" through power-generating reactors. They sought new ways to produce nuclear fuel—plutonium—cheaply through liquid metal fast breeder reactors. They attempted to design a factory in which mass production of reactor vessels and components would keep capital costs down. They built small nuclear engines intended to power locomotives, rockets, airplanes, and portable power plants. The power plants would have extensive application in the far north and Siberia, making the USSR's extensive natural resources accessible even in the polar winter. They founded a design institute and factory to mass produce magnets, accelerators, and other tools for use throughout Russia, Ukraine, Georgia, Armenia, Kazakhstan, Uzbekistan, Latvia, Lithuania, and so on. They sterilized various food products with low-level gamma radiation to prevent spoilage and increase shelf life. They pioneered the so-called tokamak reactor in pursuit of fusion power. And they used "peaceful nuclear explosions" for various mining, excavation, and construction purposes. Nuclear technology was at the center of visions of a radiant communist future born in the Khrushchev era, but this technology's legacy of failure and radioactive waste suggests radiance of a different and dangerous sort.

Whether nuclear reactors or food irradiation programs, small powerful nuclear engines or factories spitting out huge concrete forms, liquid sodium or isotope separation equipment, each of these technologies developed significant momentum. As if divorced from human control, the programs expanded, feeding on resources of capital, manpower, institutes, and ore, from the time of their design in the Khrushchev era until the collapse of the Soviet Union after the death of Brezhnev. The reasons for this momentum are not hard to find. The politics and culture of the Khrushchev era contributed to the rapid growth of the nuclear enterprise. Here were men—physicists, Party members, engineers, almost exclusively men—trained under Stalin, committed to socialism, but hoping to avoid any repetition of the inhuman horrors perpetuated in the name of socialism under Stalin.

One way to avoid these horrors was to reform foreign policy to escape one of the dictates of Stalinist Marxism, the inevitability of war with the capitalist countries. What better way to achieve this than to stress peaceful applications of nuclear knowledge? Peaceful nuclear programs grew out of military ones, which already were extensive because of the cold war. The peaceful programs had foreign policy importance, because state leaders and scientists in the USSR, like those in France, the United Kingdom, and the United States, sought to demonstrate the peaceful intentions of the nation. Competition between the two superpowers was especially keen, as each nation strove to show that its scientists were first and best, and its social and political system the most advanced.

There were also domestic policy reasons for the USSR's embrace of "atoms for peace." Most important were the rise of Nikita Khrushchev to leadership and his identification with modern technology with Sputnik and nuclear power. This identification was evidence of the legitimacy of his regime to the Soviet citizen who had suffered through the Stalin era and had paid for Stalin's enlightened leadership with forced collectivization and industrialization, the purges, the labor camps, World War II, and thirty million deaths. The Khrushchev era involved significant political, economic, and cultural changes. Scientists were among the many members of Soviet society who benefited from greater openness during the so-called Thaw. This was still an authoritarian regime, to be sure, but scientists were expected to participate in the construction of communism and to share their great scientific achievements to improve the quality of life of the average citizen. Scientists, and especially physicists, gained great authority in this environment. Many of them, and most of the program and institute directors, were Party members. But whether or not physicists belonged to the Party, virtually all of them shared the view of Party officials that science had an integral role in the radiant future. So scientists were part of a new postwar technocratic elite. Absent a public who questioned the safety or efficacy of their inventions—mobile gamma irradiators for strawberries, reactors that moved around on tank treads—the scientists grew rather arrogant about their ability to use nuclear technology to change the environment.

The notion of autonomous, self-augmenting technology that so well describes the Soviet atoms for peace programs gained prominence in the writings of the French philosopher Jacques Ellul in *The Technological Society* (1964). Many writers have criticized the Ellulian notion of technological determinism for removing agency from human hands. There are ample reasons to present the evolution of Soviet technology from a determinist point of view. There was significant momentum: programs grew larger and larger; institutes expanded to thousands of employees and took on responsibility for building apartments and stores and schools for their workers; new technologies developed and were produced in new institutes. The centralized, bureaucratized, top-down Soviet system of management contributed to the momentum of the institutes and the technologies they designed and manufactured. Clearly physicists were the source of the new technologies. Some of them acquired great power as directors of single institutes that dominated scientific policy making through the centralized Soviet system. But they remained individuals with personalities: Igor Kurchatov, head of the atomic bomb project, who late in life sought atoms for peace because of his horror over multimegaton hydrogen bombs; Anatolii Aleksandrov, his successor at the Institute of Atomic Energy, who gained fame for submarine nuclear propulsion and infamy for the Chernobyl reactor design; Kirill Sinelnikov, Kurchatov's brother-in-law, who presided over the Ukrainian nuclear physics program; Aleksandr Leipunskii, who directed the liquid metal fast breeder reactor program. These nuclear physicists, who were also engineers and institute directors with great authority to command resources in support of still other applications, are central to this story of big technology run amok.

Atoms for peace was crucial to postwar Soviet society on one more count. Peaceful nuclear technologies had great cultural value as symbols of a modern, progressive, industrial nation. From the inception of the USSR, such leaders as Lenin, Trotsky, Bukharin, and Stalin had stressed the importance of technology in building communism and spoke about Soviet leadership in every area. But the citizen knew that claims of leadership were lies or exaggerations. With nuclear power, Lenin's promise that "Communism equals Soviet power plus electrification of the country" seemed to be more than empty words. The 5,000-kilowatt Obninsk reactor was one such major symbol of the communist future, for here was an indigenous technology that produced electricity for the citizen. Unfortunately, rather than Obninsk, the Chernobyl catastrophe has become the cultural icon of the bankruptcy of Soviet nuclear energetics and of Soviet political leadership generally. And rather than building communism, Brezhnev and his cronies had built an empire of large-scale technologies dedicated to increasing the power of the state but providing little to the average citizen in the way of comfort or hope for the future. The tongue-in-cheek slogan symbolizing this disaster, "Chernobyl—the peaceful atom in every home," became the essence of the Red Atom.

Some persons now may scoff at notions of nuclear-powered airplanes, irradiation of food to prolong shelf life of perishable goods, and portable nuclear reactors capable of producing electricity cheaply and safely on demand in the harshest Arctic winters. Others maintain that the goal of building reactor parks of a dozen 1,000-megawatt reactors was always impossible from the points of view of cost, technological know-how, and climate. But this is precisely what Soviet nuclear engineers, like their Western counterparts, strove to do. They nearly succeeded, given the willpower and vision of their leaders, and the nearly unlimited resources bestowed on them by Party officials, who believed with them that nuclear power was a panacea for the economic, social, and geographical obstacles they faced in achieving communism. Whether for poorly performing industry, inefficient agriculture, an undermotivated labor force, inadequate housing and medicine, or inaccessible resources, in the minds of most Soviet citizens the power of the atom was the key to building a modern society free from shortages and wants.

If the standard of living rose, if automation and mechanization freed workers from drudgery, and if electricity illuminated, heated, and cleaned the factory, then communism must be nearly achieved. And if in space with Sputnik and in atomic energy with the first peaceful nuclear power-generating reactors, the USSR had beaten the United States to the punch, what better confirmation that the socialist system truly was better than the capitalist system? Atomic science gave great power to those constructivist visions of future communist society, perhaps greater than any other region of science and technology, for its applications in medicine promised longer life; in light industry, better food and perishable goods; in mining and metallurgy, more exact ways to locate and process valuable reserves; and above all else, in energy generation, the ability to provide electricity, anywhere, anytime, too cheap to meter. This constellation of personalities, economic and political desiderata, cultural factors, and technologies was atomic-powered communism.

1

The Reactor in the Garden

Communism equals Soviet power plus electrification of the entire country.
—A major slogan of early Bolshevik rule

An unspoiled river flows through a nature preserve. People have come down to the river for generations to fish, wash their clothes, wash themselves, and swim. The river has sufficient volume, in the minds of engineers, to provide cooling water for several nuclear reactors. The engineers plan to build four reactors, designing canals for the effluent from the reactors so that it cools and radioactive minerals settle into the silt before the water is discharged into the river. They finally decide to build six, then ten reactors, each at 1,000 megawatts. They build cooling towers to supplement the canals. The cooling towers are significantly more expensive than simple canals. So to keep budgets within projections and somewhat competitive with fossil fuel facilities, the reactors share equipment in common machine halls and employ standard industrial structures, pumps, compressors, conduit, corrugated steel roofs, and piping. In the engineers' minds, the reactors don't spoil the preserve; in fact, the planners refer to it as a "reactor park." And the canals create a "Venice" of nuclear power, where warm-water effluent in the canals attracts geese and ducks, who winter there rather than completing their southern migration.

This is a reactor in the garden, both in the metaphorical sense of showing complete agreement between nature and human designs for huge machines to augment nature, and in the literal sense, because the nature preserve, the river, the reactor, and the park are real. Four reactors were built, and construction was well underway on units 5 and 6 when reactor unit 4 at Chernobyl exploded. On the morning after the explosion, because the authorities had yet to notify the residents of the nearby town of Pripiat about the seriousness of the accident, fishermen downstream from the reactors cast their lines in the river. At dozens of sites throughout the nation, the Ministry of the Fish Industry joined the Ministry of Electrification to seed fish into rivers made warmer by cooling effluent. It had mattered little to Soviet planners that the river, the Pripiat, was a tributary to the mighty Dnepr River, or that the Dnepr flows through the center of Kiev, the capital of Ukraine and a city with a population of four million. Some of the reactor parks employed pressurized-water reactors (PWRs); others a special Soviet design, the channel-graphite model, or RBMK reactor, which gained world attention in April 1986. But the roots of the Chernobyl disaster were to be found in a special mindset central to atomic-powered communism. This was a deep-seated belief dating to the first days of Soviet power in the perfectibility of technology and the ability to place it on any site.

Large-scale technologies have always occupied a major place in Soviet history. Energy technologies, along with steel, concrete, and other heavy industry, occupied the first position. Lenin urged the Bolsheviks to support the modernization of Soviet industry, to take from capitalism its greatest achievements in technology and tie them to socialist "production relations." A technological utopian, Lenin believed that technology was the path to the glorious communist future. He saw electricity as the key to revolutionize backward Tsarist industry. Hence, the slogan of early Bolshevik power, the epigraph for this chapter, was a watchword for all future Soviet leaders. Similarly, the conscious use of such technologies as tractors, light-bulbs, and other machines in propaganda posters as the icons of a new age represented just how completely technology had become a panacea for the great economic, social, and political challenges facing the nation as it embarked on the path of modernization. Many peasants and workers embraced the new technology, naming their sons "Tractor" (*Traktor*), their daughters "Electrification" (*Elektrifikatsiia*) or "Forge" (*Domna*).

Among scientists and engineers, too, great faith was placed in the potential of their work to solve the country's problems. No sooner had Lenin endorsed GOELRO, the State Electrification Plan, in 1920 than they embarked on research into Russia's great energy potential. Through the Academy of Sciences, the Commission for the Study of the Productive Forces (KEPS), the Scientific Technological Division of the Supreme Economic Council, and other organizations, they evaluated different ways of producing electrical energy, the contribution from fossil fuel reserves, even hydroelectric potential as far away from the country's population and industry as the Angara River in central Siberia. They established that fossil fuels—coal, oil, and gas—would power the Soviet Union's burgeoning industry for some time to come. It did not matter that little of the coal was anthracite; low-grade lignites with high sulfur content were easily accessible in the Don Basin (Donbas) of Ukraine and in Kazakhstan. Caspian Sea oil reserves near Baku, Azerbaidzhan were also sufficient for early Soviet industrialization plans.

The Nazi invasion and rapid capture of the nation's industrial and agricultural heartland indicated the need to develop energy resources far to the east, perhaps beyond the Ural Mountains, themselves a natural barrier to potential marauders.

During the war, KEPS scientists studied the hydroelectric potential of Siberian rivers. In the Khrushchev era, they prepared the way for building massive hydroelectric power stations on the Ob, Irtysh, Angara, and Enesei rivers, at the same time identifying the rich oil and gas reserves of Tiumen Province in northwest Siberia and preparing to harvest coal in the Kuznetsk Basin (Kuzbas) in south central Siberia. They deemed these projects necessary because one-third of Donbas reserves had been exhausted, and the rest were of poor quality and hard to extract.[1]

The development of Siberian energy resources brought into full relief a significant issue for long-term investment policy in the nation. The vast majority of industry and population remained in the European USSR, whereas energy resources on which to base future industrial growth and consumer well-being were thousands of kilometers away. The cost of transporting them in their primary form in railroad coal cars or pipelines grew rapidly. Thirty to seventy percent of all freight transported in the Soviet Union was fossil fuel. One alternative, to build power-generating stations near fuel sources and to link those stations by power lines to the European energy grid, was also exceedingly costly; and year by year, open spaces were filled with unsightly towers carrying power lines that measured over 900,000 kilometers in total length (see Appendix, Tables 1–4).

Nuclear energy appeared just at that time when there seemed to be no solution to the problem of geographical maldistribution of energy resources, population, and industry. One radical approach would have been to shift investment to Siberia for new industry and for housing, schools, and stores for the workers and their families. This approach had commenced with Brezhnev's "Siberia" investment program and the construction of a new trans-Siberian railroad known as BAM. But any approach drained scarce investment funds from other important areas such as housing, agriculture, and defense. There seemed to be no way to satisfy the competing demands for investment capital and at the same time ensure resource development. Although exceedingly expensive to build and technologically uncertain, nuclear energy might be the best way to solve the investment problem, for these stations could be built in the European part of the country on the outskirts of major cities. This solution would cut the need to build long power lines, transport fossil fuel, or relocate industry. At least, this was the argument used by nuclear physicists and engineers as they attempted to convince policy makers, economic planners, and fellow scientists of the viability of nuclear power.

As a technology in its nascent stage of development, nuclear energetics could promise little. To be sure, the first military production reactors produced not only weapons material but also copious amounts of thermal energy. The example of a powerful steam engine was prominent in the minds of such physicists as Igor Kurchatov, Nikolai Dollezhal, and Anatolii Aleksandrov. Their ongoing projects to develop nuclear propulsion for submarines suggested that they could harness fission for civilian purposes in the near future. The political environment was propitious for the endeavor, given Khrushchev's rise to power, the revision of domestic and foreign policy, and his personal identification with modern technology.

The problem was how to make nuclear power economically competitive with fossil fuel. Coal and oil were king. Reserves were extensive. New discoveries of gas and oil in Siberia seemed to make a decision to invest in nuclear energy more unlikely. And capital costs for nuclear power stations clearly were significantly higher than those for fossil fuel boilers. So Kurchatov and his associates not only decided to build huge commercial stations but also quickly selected two models to serve as the basis of the program; and they set out to build these stations in reactor parks throughout the European USSR. The first was the channel-graphite model of the Obninsk design, which appeared in two variants, one at Beloiarsk to produce superheated steam and the other the RBMK of Chernobyl infamy. The choice was logical because they rapidly accumulated operating experience with the design, and its multiplicity of channels enabled them to operate it during refueling or repair of individual channels. The second model was a pressurized-water reactor, known in Russian parlance by its initials VVER. This model was also a logical choice because the development of marine nuclear propulsion in both the USSR and the United States had led to the development of PWRs. Within thirty years of the twentieth Party congress, Soviet engineers had embarked on one of the world's most ambitious nuclear programs, constructing more than forty reactors, many 1,000 megawatts and larger, in the European USSR.

The promotion of nuclear power required a well-oiled public relations campaign, because, no matter how diligently they strove to prove that reactors would soon compete with other boilers, physicists had no sound technical or economic basis for their conclusions. Estimates of capital costs of "no more than fifteen percent higher" than those of conventional power stations were based on the assumption that few significant innovations were needed to leapfrog from tiny first-generation reactors newly hatched from military programs to second-generation units of 440 megawatts electric and larger. To keep costs down, they created reactor parks. Like their counterparts in the West, their estimates about the early depletion of fossil fuel reserves and the rapid increase in electrical energy demand turned out to be exaggerated. By using the extensive financial and public relations resources available to them (such as the journal *Atomic Energy,* founded in 1956 and carrying a beautiful photo of Soviet leader Nikita Khrushchev and atomic "Tsar" Igor Kurchatov on a visit to Harwell, England in the second issue), they succeeded in convincing policy makers and economic planners to provide them with adequate resources to commercialize nuclear power even as investments in oil, coal, hydropower, and Siberia increased.

KHRUSHCHEV, INTERNATIONALISM, AND ATOMS FOR PEACE

Three political preconditions had to be met to achieve atomic-powered communism. The first was the ideological thaw that accompanied Nikita Khrushchev's rise to power. Khrushchev launched an attack on many aspects of Stalinism in his so-called secret speech at the twentieth Party congress in 1956. He criticized the arbitrary rule of Stalin's cult of personality; the terrible human costs of the Ukrainian famine, the purges of the 1930s, and World War II; the xenophobic basis of Soviet foreign policy; and the insistence that Russia was the world leader in all fields of culture and science. It was not enough that Khrushchev exposed Stalin's crimes, nor that he triggered a cultural thaw in art, music, and literature, including the publication of Boris Pasternak's passionate tale of the Russian revolution, *Doctor Zhivago,* and Aleksandr Solzhenitsyn's semifictional account of the labor camps, *One Day in the Life of Ivan Denisovich.* Khrushchev promised that the nation would reach communism—that nebulous state of equality, plenty, and happiness for all—by 1980.

To achieve communism, the nation needed the assistance of scientists, engineers, and other experts to bring about a technological revolution in the economy. The Soviet citizen had long heard that communism was just around the corner. But nearly every one had suffered grave personal losses at Stalin's hands and had little to show for this sacrifice. Nevertheless, Khrushchev's promises to improve the quality of life, the Thaw, and successes in science and technology led to the rebirth of constructivist visions of the communist future. Nuclear energetics was central among these visions and was indelibly tied to one of the most important slogans of Soviet life from the early 1920s, a slogan embraced by officials, philosophers, scientists, peasants, and workers alike : "Communism equals Soviet power plus electrification of the entire country."[2]

The second precondition for a nuclear revolution was greater internationalism in science. Under Stalin, Soviet foreign policy was dominated by a belief in the inevitability of war between the socialist and capitalist worlds. When Khrushchev rose to the top of the Party hierarchy, he abandoned Stalinist autarky in the economy, politics, and culture. He promoted the foreign policy doctrine of "peaceful coexistence." This doctrine meant that, in competition with the West, and particularly with the United States, the Soviet Union would win, whether in economic development or in science, by virtue of its superior social and economic system. Under the circumstances, cooperation in expensive fields of big science such as fission, fusion, and high-energy physics was not excluded.[3,4]

Khrushchev's reforms in foreign policy enabled—indeed, required—Soviet physicists to compete openly with their foreign colleagues for primacy in scientific discovery. The Obninsk reactor and Sputnik demonstrated that the USSR was not only the equal of the United States but, in fact, the leader in a number of fields. But to compete with the West, scientists had to reenter the international arena after nearly two decades of isolation. Their renewed activities included sharing reprints through the mail, subscribing to a larger number of foreign journals, and, most important to them, establishing personal contacts. The contacts went both ways. Between 1954 and 1957, over 1,500 Soviet scientists (some 500 "delegations") traveled abroad, far exceeding in number the total of the previous thirty years.[5]

Of course, Khrushchevian internationalism did not mean openness like that which later existed in Russia under Gorbachev. Strict controls on the activities of scientists remained. Foreign journals were censored lest any anti-Soviet sentiment find its way into a research institute; this often delayed issues of Western journals from reaching them by a year. Scientists invited to conferences abroad often were denied permission to go, quite frequently at the last moment. The KGB exercised this control through the "first department," or foreign office, in each institute. In their stead, the Soviet government sent scientists notable more for their devotion to the Communist Party's ideological precepts than for their research interests. Shortly after Stalin died, however, research institutes began to report with pride increasing numbers of foreign contacts.

While breaking sharply with Stalin in foreign policy, Khrushchev retained Stalin's personal identification with large-scale technologies as emblems of his own leadership and legitimacy within the system; and this stance helped the nuclear physicists. Khrushchev had come from a peasant family and had made his name as a Party boss in agriculturally rich Ukraine. His career was tied to the Moscow metro and a never-achieved technological revolution in agriculture. Khrushchev now showed himself to be a twentieth-century man whose visions extended beyond the city and the farm to space—the world's first Sputniks—and the atom. Khrushchev personally promoted nuclear power, recognizing its value both to modernize the Soviet economy and to secure his position as Party leader during the post-Stalin succession struggle—as his visit to Harwell, England, the major British nuclear research facility, showed.

Last, modest reforms in domestic politics enabled scientists and engineers to take an active role in setting the policy agenda, or at least in publicly advancing their new projects. Such vocal lobbying in the Stalin era would have been mistaken for dangerous technocratic aspirations, and met with arrest. Scientists, especially those connected with the nuclear establishment, became near-mythic figures in the pantheon of Soviet heroes. They had access to the inner circles of the Kremlin, where they lobbied for resources and expansion of their programs. Igor Kurchatov was first among them. After speaking at the twentieth Party congress, Kurchatov was a constant visitor at the Kremlin on behalf of these lobbying efforts.[6] How Kurchatov got to the twentieth Party congress and the Kremlin is a story of a great Soviet hero: the disinterested scientist, searching for the truth, in the service of humanity.

THE FATHER OF NUCLEAR ENGINES

Igor Vasilievich Kurchatov stood at the head of the nuclear establishment, from his appointment in 1943 to head of the Soviet atomic bomb project until his early death in 1960. As director of the Institute of Atomic Energy in Moscow, he oversaw an enterprise of nuclear reactor construction and isotope application second to none in the world. Kurchatov was an excellent organizer, strong-willed, and self-assured.[7] He had a penetrating mind and was devoted to causes other than self-promotion. These qualities enabled him to avoid taking on the negative, self-serving qualities of many scientific administrators in his country and to battle the ministerial bureaucracies and Party hierarchy, of which he was a part, with great success.

Kurchatov, the great grandson of a serf, the grandson of a metallurgical factory worker, the son of a land surveyor and school teacher, was born January 8, 1903; and during a life of less than six decades, he built nuclear weapons, reactors, submarines, and icebreakers. He grew up in a small industrial town in the southern Ural Mountains. Kurchatov's father moved in 1909 to Simbirsk, recognizing that, other than a church school, there was nowhere for his children to study in the Urals. Kurchatov attended the Young Men's Public Gymnasium, the school from which Lenin had graduated. He studied hard, displaying an excellent memory and a capacity for mathematics that set him apart from the other students. Soon after the move to Simbirsk, Kurchatov's sister contracted tuberculosis; and on the advice of their physician, the family moved again, to Simferopol in Crimea. Kurchatov entered the finest and oldest gymnasium there, an institution connected with the chemist Dmitrii Mendeleev and the surgeon Nikolai Pirogov. Kurchatov earned top grades in virtually every course except diligence, in which for some unknown reason he received an "unsatisfactory." He read detective stories and science fiction, especially the works of Jules Verne, whose fantasies provided Kurchatov with food for nuclear thought. In 1920, having finished the gymnasium with a gold medal (awarded only on paper because of the current economic conditions), the seventeen-year-old Kurchatov entered Crimea University to study physics and mathematics and become an engineer.

Crimea University was organized in 1917 on the coattails of the intellectual excitement celebrating the end of the Tsarist era and its stultifying educational policies. Kiev professors were the initiators of the endeavor, first establishing the facility as a branch of Kiev University. The noted biogeophysicist Vladimir Vernadskii, then president of the Ukrainian Academy of Sciences, was instrumental in securing resources and convincing other faculty to organize the university. Vernadskii was the rector during Kurchatov's matriculation; N. M. Krylov taught mathematics; senior Leningrad theoretician Iakov Frenkel and future Nobel laureate Igor Tamm taught physics. There were no scholarships, so only a dozen students attended the lectures. Publishing had virtually ceased, so there were no textbooks. After the end of the civil war (1919–1920), economic and political instability persisted through 1923. Some students nearly starved on the ration of 400 grams of bread and watery soup. To make ends meet, Kurchatov found a series of odd jobs. But his time at Crimea University was not all difficult, because there Kurchatov met Kirill Sinelnikov, who became his life-long friend and associate.

In Simferopol, Kurchatov fell in love with the sea. He watched the ships and dreamed of becoming a shipbuilding engineer, a dream he saw fulfilled in the *Lenin* nuclear icebreaker. Although aware of the famine and disorder that gripped Petrograd, Kurchatov nevertheless transferred into the junior class of the shipbuilding department of Petrograd Polytechnical Institute. He worked as an observer in the meteorological observatory in Pavlovsk, where he often spent the night, sleeping on a table under a sheepskin coat. In the winter of 1923–1924, one of his professors gave him the task of measuring the alpha radioactivity of snow, an experience that turned him from engineering to atomic science.

Even though he would have passed the final exams in the shipbuilding department in only two more semesters, Kurchatov threw himself into science. He read everything he could on atomic physics, especially the work of the experimentalists Frederick Soddy and Ernest Rutherford. To earn money, he returned to Crimea at the beginning of the summer of 1924, where he worked in a hydrometeorological station of the Black and Azov seas, carrying out experiments on tides. In the fall, he traveled to Baku, where he worked until the following summer as an assistant in Azerbaidzhan Polytechnical Institute, when he was called to the Leningrad Physical Technical Institute (hereafter, LFTI). The twenty-two-year-old man had entered the center of Soviet physics. Abram Ioffe, the dean of Soviet physics, founded the institute in 1918 with the dream of rejuvenating the Russian experimental tradition and gaining an international reputation for his staff. Ioffe nearly single-handedly reestablished contacts with Western physicists after the Revolution. And he resurrected the practice of publication; physicists at his institution published between one-quarter and three-fifths of all physics articles in the major Soviet journals every year between 1919 and 1939. LFTI gave rise to fifteen other institutes, many at the center of the nuclear enterprise, and trained over six dozen future academicians and corresponding members of the Academy.[8] Nearby, scientists at the Radium Institute under V. G. Khlopin worked on the physics of radioactive elements, nuclear physics, and cosmic rays; and, in 1922, they oversaw the establishment of a factory to produce small quantities of the heavy elements. Leningrad was the place to be for a young physicist.

In 1922, Kurchatov had met Marina Dmitrievna Sinelnikova, the daughter of a country physician and the sister of his best friend, Kirill, who would later preside over the nuclear enterprise in cold war Ukraine. In 1925, Igor and Marina met again in Leningrad. Two years later, they married. They enjoyed listening to music, especially Rachmaninov, Tchaikovsky, and Mussorgsky. Although the couple had no children of their own, they often donated time and money from Kurchatov's books, articles, and prize honoraria to kindergartens and adoption agencies. They also had a network of friends with whom they socialized regularly, gathering at a friend's apartment or in their own to eat, drink, and sing.

Through the 1930s, Kurchatov conducted research primarily in solid state physics, studying dielectrics, semiconductors, insulators, and piezoelectricity with Anton Valter and Sinelnikov. His doctorate, finished in 1934, focused on solid state physics, although he had already embarked on nuclear physics. Some of his colleagues thought his achievements merited membership in the Academy of Sciences;[9] but, as on several subsequent occasions, the Academy leadership did not see fit to admit him, most likely because of his youth. They finally voted him in only on the government's insistence in 1943, after Kurchatov became head of the atomic bomb project.

In Berkeley, Chicago, Berlin, Copenhagen, Kharkiv, and Leningrad, 1932 was the *annus mirabilis* of nuclear physics: James Chadwick, E. T. S. Walton, and John Cockcroft established atomic structure, Anderson discovered the positron, the Joliot-Curies worked on artificial radioactivity, and the Fermi group used slow neutrons to create artificial elements. All these discoveries had a significant impact on the work of Soviet physicists, especially in Kurchatov's laboratory, the Radium Institute, and the Ukrainian Physical Technical Institute, where Leningrad physicists Sinelnikov, Leipunskii, and others had been sent to create a mirror image of the Ioffe institute. By the end of 1932, the physicists had established a nuclear group at LFTI under Ioffe. The real leader of the group, however, was Kurchatov, who gained approval to create a department of nuclear physics and secured 100,000 rubles from

Narkomtiazhprom (the Commissariat of Heavy Industry) to purchase material and equipment.

Kurchatov conducted a nuclear seminar whose activities where known throughout the country and beyond. This group convened the first all-union nuclear conference in 1933; Kurchatov was the chairman of the organizing committee. The 1933 conference and the soon-to-be convened second and third conferences were attended by physicists from around the world. The papers presented indicated how quickly Soviet physicists had moved from the accumulation of data to an experimental attack of the nucleus. Between 1933 and 1935, the Soviet physicists published more than 100 articles in the leading Soviet journals (*Uspekhi fizicheskikh nauk, Zhurnal prikladnoi fiziki,* and *Zhurnal experimental'noi i teoreticheskoi fiziki*). They built cyclotrons and other experimental devices like those in Europe and America.

Then Stalinism reared its ugly head. The Party moved the Academy of Sciences to Moscow, purged Leningrad's intellectual and political elite, and attacked LFTI for its "divorce from practice" and failure to meet the "needs of industry." Party officials condemned what they perceived as ideological deviations in science and sought to limit the extent of this wandering by closing the nation's borders. Until after Stalin's death, Soviet scientists were denied regular international contacts, as the correspondence between Sinelnikov and Kurchatov, between Cambridge, in England, and Kharkiv, in Ukraine, reveals.[10] Sinelnikov was recalled from England in 1930, even before he had defended his dissertation before Rutherford. Physicist Peter Kapitsa faced house arrest. Biologist Nikolai Timofeeff-Ressovsky, physicist George Gamow, chemist Vladimir Ipatieff, and others managed to escape to the West. Somehow, through it all, Ioffe and his colleagues managed to protect nuclear physics.[11]

During the Great Terror of the 1930s, Kurchatov managed to keep his nose clean and write another dozen articles, two monographs, and two university textbooks with future Nobel chemistry laureate Nikolai Semenov and Khariton, who later headed the Soviet bomb design institute at Arzamas. He worked on the Radium Institute cyclotron, and nine of his students defended dissertations. Just at this time, Otto Hahn and Fritz Strassmann proved nuclear fission, an experiment soon repeated by Khariton and Iakov Zeldovich and suggesting the possibility of a chain reaction bomb. Ioffe recognized within all these achievements the practical potential of atomic energy, previously the subject only of science fiction.[12] Unlike Western journals—perhaps because Soviet physicists did not immediately recognize its military applications—Soviet journals continued to publish articles about nuclear physics until 1940.

In July 1940, the presidium of the Academy passed a resolution urging the creation of a uranium commission to tackle this "central problem of contemporary physics." Khlopin was its chairman, Vernadskii and Ioffe his deputies, and Kurchatov, Kapitsa, and Khariton its members. Along with Khlopin, who favored his institute as the center of research, Kurchatov, Khariton, and Georgii Flerov advocated a redoubling of nuclear efforts. But the government hesitated to act on these

Abram Ioffe, the dean of Soviet physics, with Abram Alikhanov and Igor Kurchatov in Leningrad in 1935. *(Courtesy of Raissa Kuznetsova and the Kurchatov Institute)*

Igor Kurchatov and Georgii Flerov, whose letter to Stalin triggered the Soviet atomic bomb project. They are discussing the construction of the Joint Institute of Nuclear Research, a new high-energy physics institute, in Dubna, north of Moscow (1950). *(Courtesy of Raissa Kuznetsova and the Kurchatov Institute)*

proposals. In November 1940, the physicists convened in Moscow the last all-union conference on nuclear physics. Basing his conclusions solely on the works of Soviet physicists, Kurchatov presented a paper on the possibility of nuclear chain reactions.[13]

Under the direction of Kurchatov and Alikhanov, LFTI physicists set out to build a cyclotron. Kurchatov knew the technology well because he had conducted experiments in the Radium Institute—literally a fifteen-minute walk away. But the Nazis invaded the Soviet Union on the very day the physicists intended to start up the cyclotron.[14] Overnight, academy researchers ceased all work on nuclear physics, including the uranium problem, focusing instead on more immediate defense problems and their own survival. They evacuated the institutes to cities in the east. Senior staff and equipment from LFTI migrated to Kazan. Kurchatov and his laboratory moved "voluntarily" to the Black Sea fleet and participated in the effort to protect Soviet ships from fascist mines. Most of the early scientific defense work had little direct application, for the USSR needed tanks and planes more than path-breaking research.

Kurchatov's family was unlucky. In July 1941, Kurchatov's father was gravely wounded. He died at the end of August, and Kurchatov's mother was left alone in Leningrad for several months during the blockade. Although Kurchatov enlisted the help of Ioffe and other Academy leaders to secure her rescue by December, she was so weakened by malnutrition that she died in Vologda in April, en route to Kazan. Sinelnikov and his Kharkiv Institute also had been evacuated—in his case, to Alma Ata. Sinelnikov settled into depression. His family was cold and hungry.[15]

In December 1941, as the Germans reached the outskirts of Moscow, a twenty-eight-year-old student in the air force, Georgii Flerov, speaking at a specially organized Academy seminar attended by representatives of the many institutes that had been evacuated to Kazan, argued that the uranium problem required special attention. Many thought Flerov's ideas were pure fantasy. Ioffe and Kapitsa listened attentively, but the Academy leadership thought in terms of years, not months. So Flerov wrote to Kurchatov, in his capacity as the representative on the State Defense Committee for science; to the chairman of the council of ministers; and finally, in April 1942, to Stalin himself to push the bomb project. In the same way that Albert Einstein's letter to President Franklin Roosevelt gave impetus to the Manhattan project, Flerov's letter convinced Stalin to pursue an atomic bomb. In the spring of 1943, Kurchatov, Khariton, Zeldovich, Isaak Kikoin, Alikhanov, and Flerov gathered in a room of the Moscow Hotel and outlined the research program for the bomb. This meeting led to the creation of laboratories 1, 2, and 3 (later the Ukrainian Physical Technical Institute, the Kurchatov Institute for Atomic Energy, and the Institute of Theoretical and Experimental Physics, respectively).[16] In the fall of 1942, Kurchatov moved to Kazan, and then in early 1943, to Moscow, to head the "uranium" project in laboratory 2.

Until the laboratory 2 facilities were completed in the summer of 1944, some of the physicists worked in a building of the Seismology Institute; others occupied several rooms at the Institute of General and Inorganic Chemistry. Kurchatov requisitioned a number of physicists to the task of the bomb, most of whom were, like himself, "graduates" from LFTI: experimentalists Lev Artsimovich and Flerov, and theoreticians Khariton, Zeldovich, and Isaak Pomeranchuk. Once the building was finally up, they had to equip it—a challenge even in a centrally planned economy because of the ruination of the war. They brought equipment, instruments, and material to the vacant field on the outskirts of Moscow—October Field. The F-1, the first Soviet reactor, was built on this spot and still operates there, on a site between two subway stops.[17]

The physicists' first task was to build an experimental reactor to study fission and establish constants. From this basic knowledge, they could then move to the design of bombs and to plutonium production and power-generating reactors. Containing 50 tons of uranium and 500 tons of pure graphite, the F-1 was no small device. In 1943, Kurchatov convinced the government to organize uranium prospecting on a national scale under the Ministry of Nonferrous Metallurgy. The prospectors found uranium in the most inhospitable regions, in ice-covered mountains accessible with great difficulty, making mining and removal challenging. The reactor came on line, in the usual heroic fashion, on December 25, 1946; the personnel had worked long hours, put up with constant secret police scrutiny, and never complained. The Russians are justifiably proud of several facts concerning F-l: the time required to bring their first reactor on line was a few months shorter than the time the Americans required; F-1 produced 4,000 kilowatts, whereas the American reactor produced only 200 watts; and the plutonium production reactor also was built faster. Without detracting from the significant accomplishment of the Russians, I might defend the skill of the American scientists by noting that it was significantly easier to bring a reactor on line in Moscow because Soviet scientists already knew how to build it on the basis of American engineering experience accessible through open sources and espionage.

As soon as Soviet troops had secured eastern Germany, Kurchatov and Lavrenty Beria deployed scientific commandos, including Igor Golovin, Kurchatov's future deputy director and later fusion specialist, to search through the rubble of the towns, institutes, and universities of Berlin, Leipzig, Halle, and Jena for things of interest to Soviet science, in particular the residue of Germany's bomb and rocket projects. The absence of trucks and automobiles made these scientists' comings and goings difficult. But they returned with 100 tons of uranium, small quantities of radium, spectrographs, pumps, scales, galvanometers, various measuring instruments, hundreds of books, and back editions of such journals as *Die Naturwissenschaften* (1927–1945) and *Physikalische Zeitschrift* (1908–1945), which found their way into the libraries of Soviet institutes. Although the Americans had already taken the choice pickings, the Soviets took the rest, down to professors, docents, assistants, glass and machine shop workers.[18]

The publication of the so-called Smyth report on *Atomic Energy for Military Purposes* in 1946, even more than the actual dropping of atomic bombs on Hiroshima and Nagasaki, Japan, sent laboratory personnel into turmoil, for this document outlined both the power of atomic weapons and the scale of the effort required.

Stalin and Beria realized that time was of the essence. They ordered a rapid increase in the number of personnel in the laboratory and the resources available to them. By 1946, Kurchatov's institute had grown to 650 employees, of whom 110 were Party members. Even though there was a shortage of construction materials, the Party organization managed to command sufficient resources to build forty houses for the scientific elite. Stalin and Beria realized that well-fed, well-housed, and well-coerced scientists worked better than merely coerced scientists. These palatial two-story houses, on a tree-lined street only three blocks from the institute, signaled elitist status in the self-avowed classless Soviet society. In fact, scientists and engineers were the country's elite, and they shared the Party's enthusiasm for science. The houses enabled them to live quietly next door to one another, away from the cramped squalor of communal apartments that were the norm in postwar Moscow. But within the institute itself and for the rest of the employees, problems of adequate heating, repair, storage facilities, construction, and apartments remained.[19]

The cold war years were years of rapid institutional growth and employment of an increasingly well-educated staff. In May 1947, there were 1,500 employees in laboratory 2, with 255 Party members (seventeen percent of employees); by 1956, of roughly 4,000 employees, 1,078 (twenty-seven percent) were Party members (including 169 scientists, 256 technical engineering specialists, 284 white-collar workers, 14 doctors, 2 corresponding members of the Academy, 2 academicians, and 367 persons with higher education). This rapid growth masked the serious problems of finding and recruiting suitable young minds for nuclear research. Many able-bodied men had perished at the front in World War II; and despite specially organized courses in a series of universities and new training centers specifically organized for the nuclear enterprise, there was a significant lag in writing and defending candidate and doctor of science dissertations. This was indeed a serious problem, for the nuclear industry lurched from one program to another, and from one project to another, with inadequate personnel. They always needed more specialists but had no fine-tuned way to train them. In the United States, both electrical and chemical engineers retooled quickly as nuclear engineers. In the Soviet Union, something similar happened as physicists and chemists from the Academy of Sciences joined chemists and metallurgists from the Commissariats of Heavy Industry, Chemical Industry, Ferrous Metallurgy, and Nonferrous Metallurgy to staff the project and train young specialists.[20]

An important gathering in the life of the institute was its second Party conference in August 1952. This meeting was held, like hundreds of other meetings throughout the nation, in preparation for the Party's nineteenth congress, the first national meeting held since 1939. In the intervening years, the Great Terror had ended, World War II had passed, and the cold war had begun. But, in violation of the Party's charter, Stalin failed to call any congress, preferring to act on his own caprices. Some individuals voiced hope in private that the upcoming nineteenth congress meant that Stalinism had a human face; they were unaware that another murderous purge was afoot. The so-called Doctors' Plot had been hatched. According to the secret police, high-level Kremlin doctors, most of whom were Jewish, had tried to poison Stalin and other leaders. A number had already been arrested and shot. The terror machine was gearing up to crush Jews (including a number at the Kurchatov Institute), intellectuals, and long-time Party functionaries, when Stalin, to the good fortune of the nation, died.

Institute physicists tried to ignore the persistence of Stalinism. At the institute's second Party conference, the physicists celebrated significant achievements, the recent award of state prizes to thirty scientists, progress on the hydrogen bomb, the construction of a second research reactor, and the development of an industrial diffusion method of isotope separation. Kurchatov delivered an address referring to the five year plan (1951–1955) and announcing grand plans for the peaceful atom in industry, agriculture, trade, and communications, all uses intended to raise the material well-being, health, and cultural level of the masses. The three major tasks that stood before his scientists were fusion, nuclear power stations, and the construction of the *Lenin* icebreaker. But, he concluded, armed with "progressive Leninist scientific method," talented staff, and nearly unlimited materiel, they would succeed.[21]

Even with their command of resources, physicists grappled with a weak experimental basis for scientific work, especially with regard to research reactors, which had hitherto been used nearly exclusively for military ends, and such modern equipment as computers, of which there was only one plodding first-generation M-20. So tight had funding been for peaceful purposes, that the scientists rarely anticipated the expansion of research that discoveries stimulated. So even though the Soviet scientists were always building new laboratories, many projects had to be scaled back. As soon as a new facility opened, the new space and support services were found to be inadequate to the task at hand. Soviet physicists invited colleagues from Eastern Europe to spend time studying with them in connection with plans to build experimental reactors in the socialist countries. But there wasn't enough room for "fraternal" research either, and they ended up lecturing in noisy corridors.[22]

Stalin's death on March 6, 1953 shook the country. Millions wept openly. Tens of thousands of citizens stood in line to glimpse the leader as he lay in state. The installation of Stalin in the mausoleum that now carried the granite banner "Lenin-Stalin" suggested there would be few changes in policy. His successors worried about how the citizens might react to any sign of instability, and no one wished to offend the evolving collective leadership, especially with Beria still around. Scientists and engineers suffered no less than any other group. But reforms commenced within six months. In July 1953, just after a plenary session of the Central Committee, Beria was arrested, largely because he was feared by the other leaders, but also because he was a murderer and rapist. In the Kurchatov Institute, the Party committee endorsed the arrest without dissent. They had more reason to endorse Central Committee actions than most, for they knew Beria intimately as the overseer of their institute.[23]

In the first days of the Khrushchev era, when success piled upon achievement, when military interest ensured comfortable financing, and when the Party leadership almost unquestioningly supported big science and technology, scientists had no reason to doubt their ability to use nuclear power to solve a variety of problems. One goal was to redress the trick that geography had played on the nation in locating people and fossil fuels so far apart. So when Igor Kurchatov addressed the twentieth Party congress in February 1956, he confidently outlined a long-range program for civilian nuclear energetics. His appearance at the congress was a shock, for Kurchatov had been shrouded in atomic secrecy since 1943; nevertheless, the Party hierarchy permitted this scientist to make bold policy pronouncements. In his address, Kurchatov offered fantastic visions of nuclear locomotives and automobiles that would never appear. But nuclear-powered icebreakers and other ocean-going craft did come to fruition.

Of greatest interest to the assembled delegates were Kurchatov's projections for two million kilowatts of nuclear power capacity within the next four years—even though only one 5,000-kilowatt plant was in operation as he spoke. Construction on other facilities hadn't even begun. Kurchatov promised that two one million-kilowatt stations would be built by 1960 in the Ural region. The size of the projected power plants rivaled that of the Kuibyshev hydropower station, itself the largest power station in the world. Closer to Moscow, a 400,000-kilowatt station would be built. The larger the reactor, the cheaper the electricity per unit, so Kurchatov called for the design of facilities larger than any envisaged in the West. In both reactor size and time of construction, Kurchatov may have been well off the mark. But his speech was important for its daring glimpse of the future, which had already opened at a reactor research institute in the city of Obninsk.[24]

FROM OBNINSK TO BELOIARSK TO CHERNOBYL

Civilian nuclear power engineering began in Obninsk, until recently a closed military establishment. At Obninsk, physicists developed breeder reactors, nuclear generators for satellites, liquid metal submarine propulsion reactors, and the forerunner of Chernobyl, a 5,000-kilowatt channel-graphite reactor. There wasn't much left of the village of Piatkino after the war, just scarred carcasses of buildings, basements, and a few huts. In 1951, the physicists decided to build an atomic reactor there—and the bulldozers came. Where there had been Piatkino now was Obninsk, which quickly turned into a mecca of atomic physics, nuclear energetics, medical radiology, experimental meteorology, radiation chemistry—a city of international reputation after the Geneva conferences of 1955 and 1958 on peaceful nuclear energetics. When Obninsk came into being in 1949, there were three different worlds that existed in the "zone" and, officially, were entirely separate: a narrow circle of German specialists, Soviet specialists, and prisoners from Soviet camps. But after 1951, the authorities had to get rid of the Germans and the prisoners so that they could put the town on the map.

Like any other city, Obninsk grew, despite remaining closed. The authorities ordered an instrument-making factory, kindergartens, schools, libraries, and sports facilities to be built. Young specialists, who had been struggling with the infamous discomfort of dormitories, gained individual, if cramped apartments. Leading physicists made their homes here: Dmitrii Blokhintsev, A. I. Leipunskii, I. I. Bondarenko,

Vladimir Malykh, Nikolai Timofeeff-Ressovsky, Andronets Petrosiants, Oleg Kazachkovskii. They begat other nuclear cities: Bilibino, Shevchenko, Zarechnyi (Beloiarsk), and Melekess. As they had in Akademgorodok in Siberia, scientists assumed they could do no wrong. They used their Scientists' Club to debate philosophy and music—even politics during the Thaw of the Khrushchev era. They contemplated the lyrics of the folksingers Bulat Okudzhave and Vladimir Vysotsky, and they considered the optimism of the novelist Vladimir Dudintsev. Then a young physicist, Valerii Pavlinchuk, spoke too openly, and even wrote to the Central Committee about his belief that there should be no Soviet tanks in Czechoslovakia. The KGB arrested him. He committed suicide. This incident invigorated the City Party Committee to be more vigilant, carrying out a purge of any suspected person. They came down on all perceived dissidents and especially on the internationally renowned radiation biologist Timofeeff-Ressovsky.

Even before the Soviet scientists detonated an atomic bomb in August 1949, Kurchatov and his colleagues decided to build an electric power-producing reactor at Obninsk, two hours southwest of Moscow. Physicists were confident that they could handle all the complexities involved in the search for, mining of, and processing of uranium ore; the various methods for separating the isotopes of uranium; the production of plutonium in reactors from nonfissile uranium; and the design of construction materials needed to build reactors and different apparatuses. No sooner had they successfully detonated an atomic bomb than they set out to show that they were peaceful to the core—unlike the militarist capitalists—and would build a reactor to produce electrical energy. The channel-graphite design selected for Obninsk was the suggestion of one of Kurchatov's close associates, Nikolai Dollezhal. The 5,000-kilowatt reactor played a crucial role in building the scientists' confidence in the belief that the Soviet Union had a nuclear future, for the reactor was seen to operate as intended and tested critical technologies such as fuel rods. It was also crucial for its role in building Soviet identity in the post-Stalin world. Reports on the reactor at the first Geneva conference in 1955 astounded Western physicists, who had assumed that their Soviet colleagues were as backward as the peasants in the collective farms.

AN INSTITUTE FOR WAYWARD REACTORS

At the end of 1952, the government created the Scientific Research and Design Institute of Energy Technology (*Nauchno-issledovatel'skii i konstruktorskii institut energeticheskoi tekhniki,* or NIKIET), an institute whose personnel were destined to acquire a fateful responsibility, the design of the Chernobyl-type RBMK reactor and its forerunners. Under Dollezhal, NIKIET sought to develop reactors with multiple purposes, producing either thermal energy and isotopes or energy and plutonium simultaneously. The creation of the institute indicated the government's conviction that atomic energy had unlimited horizons, even though not one peaceful artifact had as yet been created. Dollezhal himself moved to the top of the nuclear engineering establishment—and before that, the chemical engineering establishment—through a series of fortuitous moves from one city to another and from one bureaucracy to another. During these ascents, he managed to keep out of trouble and earn the reputation of being an all-business engineer. Twice a Hero of Socialist Labor and a laureate of Lenin and State prizes, Dollezhal acquired notable military achievements, including service as the chief engineer for the first Soviet plutonium production reactor and a designer of submarine reactors. Dollezhal's forte was expertise in mechanical engineering, chemical engineering, and thermodynamics. This background prepared him to design reactors, those huge conglomerations of metal, concrete, graphite, and fuel that produce vast quantities of energy and various radioisotopes.

Nikolai Dollezhal had a white-collar background. His father worked on the construction of the first tramline in Moscow, the city where Dollezhal was born on October 27, 1899. His father later moved the family to Podolsk to take a position in a cement factory. Just after the Russian Revolution, Dollezhal attended the Bauman Moscow Higher Technical School, one of two leading technical institutes in Moscow—the other being the Institute of Ways of Communication. Focusing primarily on mechanical engineering, he took classes with some of the leading lights of Russian science, including Nikolai Zhukovskii, the founder of Russian aerodynamics. (When Zhukovskii died, he lay in state in the students' dining hall, and students and faculty from around the city paid their respects. The cooks were not overjoyed.) At Bauman, Dollezhal studied hydraulics, thermodynamics, steam engines, and refrigeration. Dollezhal combined classroom study with hands-on experience. When the Moscow City Council transportation department requisitioned students to rebuild the transport infrastructure that had fallen apart during the Revolution, Dollezhal joined on.

Dollezhal's career took off during the period of the New Economic Policy, when in the mid-1920s the Bolsheviks permitted small-scale private enterprises to prosper and rekindle industrial production. Upon graduation in 1923, he simultaneously taught at the Bauman Institute and joined the heat engineering department of Moscow Coal to design new engines and turbines, their prerevolutionary predecessors having long since ceased to revolve. GOELRO, the State Electrification Plan and forerunner of the massive national projects that characterized Soviet technology, required modern technology and bright, capable engineers like Dollezhal. From Moscow Coal, Dollezhal moved to the joint stock company Heat and Power.

Dollezhal was active in the national organization of heat engineers. But like other scientific and engineering professional societies, this one was disbanded by the Communist Party after its fourth national meeting in 1928. In the last years of relatively open borders, Dollezhal and several hundred engineers were sent abroad by the Supreme Economic Council to study Western achievements and bring its technology back to the Soviet Union. Dollezhal visited institutes and factories in Berlin and Munich. This kind of contradictory behavior, sending scientists abroad yet keeping strict watch on their professional organizations, indicates that the Party both deeply feared the potential technocratic impulses of scientists yet recognized the need for their independent expertise to build a new industrial power. A tense relationship between knowledge and power characterized scientific life from the late 1920s until the fall of the Soviet Union.

In the 1930s, as Stalin's rapid industrialization effort commenced, science, engineering, and production were joined in huge organizations that came to characterize all Soviet industry, including the postwar nuclear enterprise. Joint stock companies such as Heat and Power and newly founded technical institutes representing all branches of the economy were subsumed in massive bureaucracies whose function was to harness the machine to Soviet power. In Dollezhal's case, the bureaucracy was the soon legendary Commissariat of Heavy Industry, known as Narkomtiazhprom in Russian. Narkomtiazhprom commanded the lion's share of chemistry and physics research institutes in the country and lavished them with funding for applied research. Dollezhal was working in the design bureau of Kotloturbina—still a long way to the turbogenerators of atomic power stations—when Narkomtiazhprom tapped him to serve as chief engineer of a new chemical works. His responsibility was to supervise a nitrogen-based (ammonia) factory with applications in fertilizers, medicines, paints, artificial rubber, and, most important, explosives. (The Soviet government recognized that the rise of Hitler in Germany would put an end to their days of close cooperation with the Germans in industry and military affairs.) No sooner was the ammonia factory up and running than Dollezhal was called in by the Deputy Commissar of Heavy Industry to serve as chief engineer of nitrogen machine building in Leningrad. When he hesitated because of teaching obligations at the Bauman, the minister issued on the spot two monthly passes on the luxurious overnight train, the Red Arrow, so that he could be certain to make his Moscow lectures.

Upon arrival in Leningrad, Dollezhal was called to meet with Sergei Kirov, the very popular head of the Leningrad Party organization. (Kirov also had a technical background and was perhaps the last true rival to Stalin. Perhaps for this reason, Stalin had Kirov murdered in 1934 within the Smolny Office Building, instructing the secret police to pin the deed on imaginary Trotskyite conspirators.) Indicating the importance the Bolsheviks attached to heavy industry, Kirov promised Dollezhal and his staff the complete backing of the Party apparatus and access to special rations and other services. Dollezhal had engineers and factory managers at his fingertips because of his good relations with Leningrad Polytechnical Institute, where he had begun to teach, and with the Red Pathfinder, Russian Diesel, and Elektrosila factories in Leningrad, Kompressor in Moscow, and the Kharkiv Turbine Factory. After a brief tour of duty in Kharkiv at Khimmashtrest (Chemical Machinery Trust), he learned second hand, while reading the newspaper *Za industrializatsiiu* in April 1935, that he had been appointed one of twelve members of the new technical council of Narkomtiazhprom; by May, he was back in Moscow. Fortuitous personnel connections, engineering skill, and Stalin's industrialization program brought Dollezhal to the center of action in Moscow.

Dollezhal found the technical council to be an ineffective administrative organization. Each member of the council was supposed to be responsible for a specific area of machine building, but Dollezhal had neither concrete responsibilities nor real rights. At a meeting of Narkomtiazhprom, Sergo Ordzhonikidze, the commissar, spoke about the joys of work at the factory and the raw energy produced by workers and engineers. Looking at Dollezhal, he said, "You, young man, don't you want to be on the shop floor as the head engineer?" Dollezhal responded: "I've written you precisely about that several times." A few days later, Dollezhal was transferred to the Kiev factory Bolshevik as head engineer.

Dollezhal had made inroads in modernizing the laboratory and instrument building departments of Bolshevik when the purges hit. He was unprepared for the news that his mentor back in Leningrad, Aleksei Nadezhdin, one of the founders of Soviet energetics, had been arrested. Then Glavkhimmash, the administration of the chemical machine building industry, replaced the entire directorship of Bolshevik; the previous staff disappeared overnight. Despite the intrigues, which made it virtually impossible to work, Dollezhal became deputy head engineer for science, engineering, and design of the entire Glavkhimmash and was transferred once again into the Moscow bureaucracy. Months later, the bureaucrats were all ready to send him back to Leningrad when war with Finland broke out; so he remained in Moscow, commencing work on a dissertation that he managed to finish in 1944. He was in Dnepropetrovsk, Ukraine on business when the Nazis invaded, and Dollezhal, like other important scientific and engineering personnel, as well as entire research institutes and strategic factories, was hastily evacuated to the east. He was obliged to leave directly from Dnepropetrovsk with only the one suitcase he had brought with him from Moscow.

Facing challenges in administration and research totally unlike those in peacetime, Dollezhal managed to get the Ural factories up and running, simultaneously creating in Sverdlovsk a research institute for chemical machine building, with branches of this institute in Moscow, Leningrad, Kharkiv, and Irkutsk. At the end of the war, he joined a group of engineers sent to Berlin to scavenge anything valuable—material and equipment, even German engineers as prisoners of war. Beyond having read about Hiroshima and Nagasaki, he was totally unaware of the ongoing Soviet bomb project when he and a half dozen members of his staff were summoned to laboratory 2 in January 1946. Kurchatov told him, "Up 'til now, you've worked on the molecular level; now it is necessary to work on the atomic level." Dollezhal and Vladimir Merkin were given the responsibility of building a plutonium production reactor. Kurchatov gave him access to classified literature, but he began by reading the Smyth report, which had been translated and published in 50,000 widely available copies. From the Smyth report, he first gained a sense, not only of what plutonium was, but also of the immense scale of activities needed to produce ^{239}Pu in a reactor.

No longer a public person, Dollezhal disappeared for a decade into the secrecy of the technical department of Main Administration directly under Beria. Working in laboratory 2, Dollezhal was aware of, but paid no attention to, heightened ideological tensions in Leningrad during the so-called Zhdanovshchina, named after Central Committee secretary for ideological affairs Andrei Zhdanov, whose writings triggered a fearful attack on all things bearing the mark of Western influence. Many areas of the philosophy of science, even symphonies of Shostakovich and concerti of Prokofiev, fell beyond the pale. Meanwhile, the Kurchatov conscripts, Dollezhal among them, innocently celebrated the successful design and operation of the first

Soviet reactor (the F-1) with toasts of fine Georgian Tsinandali wine, even though the December 25, 1946 start-up had been delayed by difficulties in producing the 50 tons of uranium and 500 tons of pure graphite required to run it.

As soon as the Soviet's first atomic bomb had been detonated in August 1949, Kurchatov asked Dollezhal to design a reactor to produce heat for turbogenerators—that is, for peaceful purposes. Kurchatov, his colleagues, and the personnel of the Main Administration under Beria debated various proposals to build the electric power reactor. There were three competing groups: the Institute of Physical Problems under Anatolii Aleksandrov (he had replaced its founder, Peter Kapitsa, who remained under house arrest until after Stalin's death), the Physics Engineering Institute under Aleksandr Leipunskii, and a newly formed institute called NIIKhimmash under Dollezhal. Leipunskii's project languished because of his focus on breeder reactors. The Institute of Physical Problems proposed a reactor, the *Sharik* (Little Ball), with a graphite moderator and UO_2 fuel elements. Heat transfer would occur through helium at approximately 800°C. Helium compressors were being developed at the Leningrad Factory. Unfortunately for the Aleksandrov group, Soviet engineers had much greater experience with water-graphite reactors, which were at the center of the nuclear programs at Kurchatov's institute, with its access to resources and political clout.

In February 1950, Boris Vannikov chaired the meeting of the technical council of the First Main Administration at which the council members determined to build AM, an experimental reactor facility with thermal power of 30,000 kilowatts and electric power of 5,000 kilowatts. AM would be in Obninsk under the direction of Dmitrii Blokhintsev. Andrei Kapitonovich Krasin, who had responsibility for scientific issues, and Malykh, with responsibilities for uranium engineering problems, joined Blokhintsev and Dollezhal. (By this time, Kurchatov and laboratory 2 had turned to the superbomb and fusion.) By May 1950, Vannikov's council expanded the decision to include two other reactors on the Obninsk site, one with helium and the other with liquid metal coolant. In August 1950, the laborers imported from the army and prisons dammed the Protva River, built a pumping station, a fossil fuel boiler, an electrical substation, and power lines. Simultaneously, engineering firms joined the project to design buildings and run calculations on neutron physics and on potential moderators, shielding, and coolants (water, lead, bismuth, chromium, cobalt, molybdenum, magnesium, and various steels). Physicists at Scientific Research Institute of Inorganic Materials commenced testing of various fuel rods to establish their short- and long-term mechanical strength. They designed a fuel rod enriched to five percent with a 100-day life that would produce 30,000 kilowatts of energy. The Kalinin Gidromash Factory produced the circulating pumps, and the Podolsk Factory manufactured the steam generators.

Bringing the reactor on line was no simple matter. As director of NIKIET, Dollezhal acquired the authority to requisition personnel with nuclear experience from other institutes. But he was competing now with many other facilities, each of which believed it came first. Worse still, the staff members had no laboratory in which to do the scientific research needed to provide accurate answers to engineers'

queries in a short time. Initially, Dollezhal could not find a building suitable for
NIKIET. Moscow, as Stalin's home and symbol of the Party's greatness, had been
rebuilt more rapidly than any other city after the war, and the supply of construction materials and suitable building sites could not keep up with demand. The chairman of the Moscow Executive Committee finally offered a recently vacated arma-
ture factory building. Over the next six months, NIKIET haltingly came into
existence on this site. Only then was this institute able to begin to solve the problems of constructing the Obninsk reactor in earnest.

The physicists considered themselves fully prepared for the undertaking in
Obninsk. After all, they had built the F-1. Indeed, even before the F-1 was completed, they commenced work on a huge plutonium production reactor, which
came on line in 1948 at Cheliabinsk. At the Kurchatov Institute, they brought the
10-megawatt experimental RFT reactor on line within two years of the start of
work in 1952. Hence, they had sufficient experience with production of pure reactor graphite, metallic uranium, and fuel elements from it. In addition, the training
programs at Moscow University, Leningrad Polytechnical Institute, the Moscow
Energy Institute, Moscow Engineering Physics Institute, and Moscow Physical
Technical Institute were spitting out masses of young nuclear specialists of rote
learning if sufficient skill. Their teachers included Lev Landau, Evgenii Feinberg,
and Leipunskii.

Bringing the Obninsk reactor on line was a learning experience. During 1952,
work in all areas lagged, the work incentives of the Stalinist system such as firing
or arrest notwithstanding. At the end of the first quarter, the plan for the foundation pit for the main building was only ten percent fulfilled; the barracks with a dining hall for the convict-construction workers, seventy-two percent; the power station boiler, nine percent; and the substation, not at all. Although the railroad was
nearly on target, four thirty-apartment buildings nearly finished, and the kindergarten and nursery school ahead of plan, the bakery lagged significantly (convicts,
one supposes, were used to poor food at the hands of the authorities). So Efim
Slavskii took direct control of construction. In 1953, page upon page of project documentation rained down on the Obninsk administrators in the form of government
resolutions. An early one referred to the unsatisfactory work on the 110-kilowatt
power lines, gas pipelines, fuel rods, technological channels, steam generators,
pumps, and so on, with the requirement that the workers be back on schedule by
the end of the year when start-up for the reactor was planned.

Rather late in the construction period, the physicists became aware of serious
safety problems concerning the risk of an explosion and radioactive contamination
from a high-pressure gas bubble that would form if water leaked onto the hot
graphite. Such a leak would also lead to prompt criticality in the form of a stream of
instantaneous neutrons (that is, an uncontrollable chain reaction). They were also
aware that the reactor had a positive void—that is, was inherently unstable at low
power and transitional regimes. Kurchatov, Blokhintsev, Malyshev, and Slavskii put
their heads together. They decided to carry out experimental research on the flow
of water through a broken tube in one of the technological channels. They tried to

design an emergency system to control reactivity and contain potential leaks, another system to contain water that was poured on the core to cool it during an emergency, and so on. They also decided to increase the biological shielding and develop a special system to cool the lower steel plate and concrete foundation. All of this activity led them to postpone the reactor start-up several times.

The goal of producing electricity with the Obninsk reactor assumed greater importance in the growing propaganda battle being waged between the United States and the USSR over the use of the atom for peaceful purposes. The physicists redoubled their efforts to ensure reactor safety before generating steam for turbo-generators. On March 26, 1954, the Ministry of Medium Machine Building (known in Russian as Minsredmash) created a commission to oversee start-up and, manifesting the typical Soviet proclivity to plan to the minutest detail, two weeks later issued an order detailing the first four shifts of start-up. The Ministry ordered specialists who had worked on the plutonium production reactor to be brought in from Cheliabinsk-40, including newly appointed Obninsk facility director N. A. Nikolaev. In March 1954, the physicists began loading the reactor. On the evening of May 9, 1954, with sixty-one fuel rods in place, the physicists confirmed that the reactor had reached criticality. They spent the next month refining calculations. In June, a start-up commission of Slavskii, Alikhanov, Blokhintsev, Dollezhal, and others approved a plan to bring the reactor up to seventy-five percent power over two weeks and hold it there for two days to see what would happen. During that interval, the reactor was in full shutdown for 133 hours, including the time on June 16 when the reactor was shut down in connection with a leak in one of the technological channels. Finally, at 5:30 p.m. on June 26, 1954, the reactor produced steam that turned the turbine and generator, and put electrical energy into the Mosenergo network.

Not everything went as planned, as an extraordinary session of the scientific technical council of Minsredmash learned late in July. There were massive leaks and corrosion in several pipes bringing coolant water to the technological channels; there was insufficient cooling water, as a result of which water was near its boiling point at the exit from the channels, and local boiling was undoubtedly occurring at the exit from the active zone; drainage from the lower part of the reactor reached 350 liters per hour; there was a large amount of steam in the gas (helium) used to protect the graphite from oxidation, as a result of which the temperature of the graphite was significantly higher than calculated; the instruments for control of the coolant through the individual channels seemed to fail constantly; and there were constant false alarm signals. All these problems meant that the reactor was unstable and in need of constant attention.

Especially problematic was a significant amount of oxygen in the reactor core. Whether the source was radiolysis (splitting of water molecules into oxygen and hydrogen) or the result of a reaction between the graphite and steam, a gigantic explosion was possible. Anatolii Aleksandrov argued that it was necessary to resort to a sodium-potassium coolant. Dollezhal suggested turning the facility into a research unit of sorts but closing the reactor after two loadings. But Slavskii insisted that it was a mistake to shut down the facility that was the foundation of future powerful atomic power stations. They decided to carry out repairs and remove all defective equipment, then operate the reactor at only seventy-five percent power. They also decided to create two loops, one of water under high pressure and the other of steam, and to increase the capacity of the heat exchange system of the reactor.

In a surprisingly short time (which indicates a major advantage of the Soviet system of establishing priorities), the retrofitting was completed; and in October 1954, at a power of twenty-seven megawatts, the turbogenerator produced projected power by using steam produced at forty-two tons per hour at 12.5 atmospheres and 250°C. The graphite core reached 720°C, but leakage was less than one liter per hour and there was little oxygen present.[25] Sadly, these difficulties in bringing a five-megawatts electric reactor on line did not impress the physicists as much as a 100-, 200-, or 1,000-megawatts electric reactor might have. Of course, the leading physicists received a Lenin prize for construction of the Obninsk reactor and for its "uninterrupted operation over three years." D. I. Blokhintsev, N. A. Dollezhal, A. K. Krasin, and V. A. Malykh had opened a "new area in the region of technology—atomic energetics."[26]

FROM PROTOTYPES TO PRODUCTION

The first step from Obninsk to Chernobyl, the Kurchatov Beloiarsk Atomic Electric Power Station, was built sixty kilometers from Sverdlovsk in the village of Zarechnyi. This village was chosen because Sverdlovsk and a nascent nuclear industry were already in place. Also, the site was distant from the feared invasion of forces from the hostile capitalist West. Construction commenced on this industrial prototype station in the middle of winter, February 1958—somewhat later than anticipated. In September 1963, Beloiarsk reached criticality; and on April 26, 1964, the reactor sent steam to a standard VK-100 turbine, producing electric power for the Sverdlovsk grid. Extra steam met the heating and other energy needs of the 15,000 persons living in the town near the station. Roughly the same capacity as the Shippingport (Pennsylvania) Westinghouse reactor, the thermal power of the Beloiarsk reactor was 285 megawatts, the electric power 100 megawatts. The second block, twice as powerful at 200 megawatts electric, came on line at the end of 1967. The Beloiarsk reactors were linked to the Sverdlovsk grid by 110- and 220-kilowatt power lines. The station's importance lay in a design employing superheated steam taken directly from the active zone to power standard, serially produced turbines.

At Beloiarsk, experimental work proceeded in two directions: to improve neutron physics of the core zone and to increase the unit power. The Obninsk reactor was tied into this research, for the physicists tested fuel rods with stainless steel cladding there, and the Beloiarsk reactor was designed to produce steam of similar parameters. The Beloiarsk reactor underwent extensive testing over several months before it was brought on line. Physicists focused on confirming that the physical characteristics met estimates, and they rigorously verified the reactor and its components in all stages of operation. The tests convinced them that they could move on to larger units even before the first block was fully operational. Hence, construction had already started on the larger second unit before 1964. And design of a 1,000-megawatts electric unit also was underway.

At Beloiarsk, light winds often blew across the shorelines of the reservoir built to provide cooling water for the station. Fishermen cast lines in gentle waves that pushed rowboats up and down. Willow bushes and trees grew down to the water. This area had been taiga (subarctic conifer forest), but now everyone was comfortable with the reservoir and the water slapping against the shoreline as if it had been there forever. Forest still surrounded the entire site. The main geodesist for the station, Petr Ivanovich Zlobin, arrived in 1959 to figure out how to build a reservoir of thirty-eight square kilometers from a small tributary of the Don, the Pyshma River. This was no problem, because Soviet engineers had experience building similar reservoirs throughout the European USSR. The first Beloiarsk station director, M. L. Kolmanovskii, earned his stars in thirty years of construction on electric power stations in the Donbas, the lower Volga, the Far East, and the Urals. The head of construction, N. A. Rogovin, had built huge boilers throughout the nation. Boilers, reservoirs, electric power stations, there was nothing new here, they thought, although technical difficulties and an inexperienced workforce continually thwarted their efforts to bring the reactor on line.[27]

A few dozen kilometers from Sverdlovsk and the Sverdlovsk-Tiumen railway line is the Bazhenovo station, from which a trunk line goes north. Prior to the beginning of construction at Beloiarsk, the line was the main connection with an asbestos mine. Now machinery, equipment, and boxes of supplies began to arrive from all ends of the country, all marked "BAES" in big, black, block letters. These were shipped north to a newly built station, Muranitnaia. From Muranitnaia, twelve kilometers of service roads—initially mud and gravel, later loosely fitted concrete slabs—led to the construction site. Another concrete highway struck off through the forest to the town where the workers lived. The reactors were built from huge prefabricated concrete blocks, each weighing fifteen tons. The blocks served simultaneously as reactor housing and as biological shielding. The machine hall, too, was built from prefabricated concrete forms. The engineers even used the same blocks to reinforce the dams and levees of the Beloiarsk reservoir.[28]

Viktor Sviridov and other earthmovers who had been recently discharged from army construction brigades drew on their experiences with S-80 and DT bulldozers to plow down trees in advance of the growing reservoir. The directors put the laziest workers and underperforming brigades under the supervision of decorated communist laborers, who were capable of turning these reluctant workers into troops capable of winning the honor "Shock Worker of Communist Labor." Training for workers, good or lazy, took a number of forms: textbook instruction, indoctrination, and experience at the controls of an earth-moving machine—a practice risky for worker and nature alike. Advancement came hard. Many workers who tried to get high school degrees failed their exams and had to take correspondence courses. But even lazy or illiterate workers were rarely dismissed, for the directors believed nuclear reactor construction was no different from any other construction. All workers, even those in Komsomol shock brigades, dreaded the chaotic transportation from the site to lunch and to the barracks. Those persons who worked in the reactor hall itself were the elite. They wore clean white clothes, including white boots, and were known as "men in white smocks." And, after station construction was completed, what did the workers intend to do? They clearly understood that the industrialization of atomic energy was not far off. Said one, "We'll go to another site. There will be enough stations to keep us busy until the end of the century." Yet in the same breath, they called Beloiarsk "a unique industrial experiment," the first of its kind.[29] Given the low level of training of some of the workers and the nature of the experiment, it is not surprising that Beloiarsk came on line years after initially intended. Few persons brought wives and family to the site at first, for they lived in dorms—or worse still, in barracks—only later earning rooms that were built for them after the station took shape. Only the lucky ever gained apartments, let alone such luxuries as televisions or refrigerators.[30]

Soviet nuclear physicists considered Beloiarsk to be "the epitome of perfection" of the reactor type employed at the Obninsk site because the Beloiarsk reactor achieved "nuclear superheating of steam on industrial scale." The active zone of the reactor held 67 tons of uranium enriched 1.5 to 2.0 percent, with 998 technological channels through which water flowed to remove heat; of these channels, 730 were for generating steam and 268 for reheating steam. Water entered the steam channels at 150 atmospheres and 300°C and exited at 340°C. It entered the other channels at lower pressure but higher temperature (115 atmospheres and 320°C), and exited superheated to 500° to 510°C. There were ninety control rods, including sixteen emergency rods and six automatic rods.

The physicists designed Beloiarsk without a containment vessel. It sat in an ordinary, if massive concrete box 12 meters high and 3.5 meters wide, with walls 100 to 150 millimeters thick. This kind of reactor "housing" freed the heavy machine building factories from the problems associated with manufacturing heavy steel reactor pressure vessels, which weighed over 200 tons, a problem Soviet industry never seemed to handle well. The use of a concrete box created other difficulties, however, especially control of reactivity; and this problem created the need for precise operation of various instruments. Another challenge concerned the presence of a multitude of pipes of different sizes under high pressure. Yet even before the Beloiarsk station was operational, the first deputy of the Atomic Energy Commission, N. D. Morokhov, touted its advantages for future "serial production," especially the absence of a containment vessel, "which made it possible in a short time to design and build such a reactor."[31]

Beloiarsk physicists rated their machine highly for many reasons: (1) the possibility of building reactors of significant size with modest changes in the active zone; (2) the ease of using channels for various purposes (for example, for boiling water and superheating steam) yet still using standard turbines; (3) reactor safety—if fuel rods were damaged, fission products could not enter the coolant and hence the turbines; (4) the minimal influence of water on reactivity during different transition processes connected with changes in the temperature and state of the coolant;

The F-1 atomic pile, the first Soviet reactor (1946). The F-1 was built in Moscow on the site of the Kurchatov Institute for Atomic Energy and still operates for experimental purposes at low power. *(Courtesy of Raissa Kuznetsova and the Kurchatov Institute)*

The Beloiarsk Nuclear Power Station, shortly after it commenced operation in 1963. *(Courtesy of Raissa Kuznetsova and the Kurchatov Institute)*

(5) the ability to refuel the reactor without complete shutdown; and (6) the heavy reliance on standard construction factories without having to use unique equipment or create a new industry.[32]

The second Beloiarsk reactor (200 megawatts electric), which came on line in December 1967, had the same measurements and basic design as the 100-megawatts electric unit), but the active zone of the second unit had a simpler configuration and produced steam more efficiently. An increase in the internal diameter of fuel rods (without changing the external diameter) enabled physicists to employ less fuel per unit of power output and ensured an optimal relationship between the quantity of fuel and the moderator. The second unit employed 1,430 kilograms of ^{235}U enriched to 3.0 percent; the first unit required 1,200 kilograms enriched to 1.8 percent. So confident were the Soviet physicists in these early efforts that it should come as no surprise to learn that as early as 1964 they had drawn up the first designs for a 1,000-megawatts electric unit (see Appendix, Table 5).[33]

It seemed that Soviet physicists had succeeded in making their reactors a machine in the garden. The first journalists who traveled to Beloiarsk and Novovoronezh strove to make commonplace new words that had recently entered the Soviet lexicon: "Atomic City," "biological defense," "reactor shaft," "atomic worker." The physicists consciously employed the metaphor of the "machine in the garden" to make nuclear power seem unthreatening. At the same time, they referred to the "unique" atomic "giants" presciently as a "great industrial experiment" on a national scale. No longer could the USSR tolerate the lengthy and expensive path from laboratory experiments to production. In atomic energy, science and production now went hand in hand, joining scientists and *praktiki*, engineers and builders. One of the great advantages of the socialist system was that science and construction, research and production, were joined in scale and energy impossible in capitalism.[34]

FROM LENINGRAD TO IGNALINA

How rapidly they jumped from Obninsk to Leningrad and from apartment buildings to reactors, with Kurchatov's ironic blessings, *"S legkim parom!"* Literally these words mean "with easy steam," and they originated as wishes for a good experience at the sauna; but they came to mean "Have a great time!" The steam at nuclear power stations was anything but easy, and building the stations was anything but a great time. Within twenty years, the power of standard Soviet reactors increased 200-fold from 5,000 kilowatts to 1,000 megawatts electric and from 30,000 kilowatts to 3,200 megawatts thermal, and to dozens of atmospheres of pressure. The building sites at first glance looked like any others, with cranes, bulldozers, and dump trucks, concrete forms, bags of cement, piles of garbage, and the usual noise of a big construction project. Yet somehow designers managed to keep aesthetics in mind. Sosnovyi Bor (Pine Forest), the town with the poetic-sounding name only three kilometers from the station on the shore of the Bay of Finland, basked in the winds from the bay and the glorious scent of fir trees. Nowhere was there the acrid odor of coal. At Sosnovyi Bor, we are told, the Lenin Leningrad Atomic Power Station (LAES), with a glorious snow-white main building larger than four football fields, was erected. The station required a new architecture, characterized by one Soviet writer as "unbelievably beautiful, mighty, as if regulated by mathematics which conceal its scale." This structure was "merely a somewhat complicated samovar." But the writer confessed moments later, after climbing up dozens of steps to the reactor hall, a building that looked like a mine with two-meter thick walls, that perhaps this was not quite a samovar.[35]

They called LAES the "flagman" of atomic energetics, for it was the first RBMK-1000. No doubt Peter the Great would have been angered by the construction of four concrete monstrosities on the outskirts of his "Venice of the North," St. Petersburg. But for Soviet engineers and physicists, this was truly a joyous aesthetic and a monument to socialist ingenuity. You could stand on top of any one of the four 1,000-megawatt reactors, watching safely as they replaced spent fuel rods. To some, the huge station recalled the Moscow Train Station in Leningrad, except that it was five times longer and three times higher, and had 500,000-kilowatt turbines instead of locomotives. In comparison with the Krasnoiarsk hydropower station, which had a capacity of six million kilowatts, LAES seemed modest at only two million kilowatts. But in the best years, when there were heavy rains, Krasnoiarsk produced twenty-four billion kilowatt-hours of power (in average years, only twenty billion); whereas LAES produced twenty-four billion kilowatt-hours no matter what the weather and, in addition, saved 150,000 wagons of coal annually.[36]

The LAES, still in operation today, is a single-loop system: The steam fed to the turbine is directly produced in the reactor as a result of the boiling of the coolant. Ordinary water is used as the coolant and circulates in a closed loop; the turbine condensers are cooled by seawater from the Gulf of Finland. Each power unit includes a reactor with a circulation circuit and auxiliary systems, steam and condensate circuits, and two turbines of 500 megawatts each. One hundred eighty tons of uranium oxide enriched to 1.8 percent fills the core. To ensure radiation safety, engineers developed a highly reliable control and safety system, including about 180 independent absorbers with separate sensors, leak detectors, and dosimeters; emergency cooling equipment to prevent mass rupture of fuel rods; periodic inspection; and steam receivers to prevent large steam releases.

The Soviet engineers have come to view the RBMK as a common industrial facility. But, of course, it is more complex. Each reactor is housed in a concrete pit of $22 \times 22 \times 26$ meters. The reactor weight is transferred to the concrete through welded structures that also serve as biological shielding. The graphite stack consists of graphite blocks (250×250 millimeters) arranged in the form of columns provided with vertical cylindrical holes. The holes accommodate process (steam generating) channels or control and safety channels. To prevent the graphite from oxidizing and to improve cooling, the reactor space is filled with a mixture of helium and hydrogen. The process channels are welded tubular structures designed to house fuel assemblies and circulating coolant.

As soon as two units of the LAES had come on line, its promoters advanced the notion of building 1,500-megawatts electric and 2,000-megawatts electric RBMKs. The 1,000-megawatt units were only "a step forward in the development of channel reactors," because analysis of their thermal characteristics revealed "reserves. A series of parameters that defined the power level of the reactor such as the temperature of the metal construction and graphite blocks in reality turned out to be somewhat lower than calculated." The first block of LAES went on line late in 1973, and loading of fuel into the second block commenced in the spring of 1975; in July 1975, a technical proposal for a 1,500-megawatts electric reactor was issued, leading within another half year to the decision to build a reactor of that size, namely, the Ignalina plant in Lithuania. Leningrad convinced the physicists to "force" the thermal power of the RBMK, first by raising the temperature of the moderator and graphite, and then by raising the steam content at the point where the coolant exited from the technological channels. All this was to be done without risk of a transition into a region of critical thermal load.[37]

The intent was clear: No nuclear construction site should be different from earlier ones, and each subsequent unit must be bigger than the previous one. But try as they might, bottlenecks in construction always arose. "Ribbons of asphalt" bent gracefully from the stations to the towns housing the workers. The towns had dormitories, day care facilities, stores, and sooner or later, apartment buildings. The nation contributed materials, services, and workers to the priority endeavor. But whether Volgodonskenergostroi at Atommash or Donbassenergostroi at the Southern Ukraine station, the Soviets couldn't seem to keep on schedule—for such simple reasons as failure to build enough entrances to the worksite.[38] On the outskirts of Smolensk, the Soviet engineers built a town of 35,000 inhabitants, who worked to bring the 1,000-megawatt RBMKs on line, the first slowly, with great difficulty, the second "significantly more quickly and correctly." Construction belatedly developed the character of a "unitary technological process." Earlier, having finished one unit, workers might sit around waiting for further instructions. They used their uninterrupted pay to consume massive quantities of vodka. Once planners achieved a "unitary process," workers freed from one unit moved immediately to the next unit in an orderly—and, of course, rationally planned—fashion, speeding up the introduction of stations over thirty percent. And, by this time, a nuclear industry existed, with all the appropriate equipment, power, technology, transportation facilities, and other machinery.[39]

The queen of reactors was Ignalina in Lithuania. Lithuanian specialists began preparing for the nuclear era along with other Soviet republics. Lithuania was a "republic" in the loose sense of the word, for a number of Western nations, the United States included, never recognized Soviet military subjugation of Lithuania, Estonia, and Latvia, referring to them instead as "Baltic states." But no less eagerly than scientists in other Soviet republics, Lithuanian physicists greeted Kurchatov's twentieth congress speech with the hope that they, too, could develop an indigenous peaceful nuclear program. Indeed, such a program of applications of isotopes in industry, medicine, and agriculture ensued. So did construction of the world's largest reactor. Jonas Gyys, head of the Thermal and Nuclear Energy Department of Kaunas University of Technology, commenced training engineers for nuclear power plants in 1961. The program was interrupted in 1983 but restarted in 1995 with a bachelor's of science degree in nuclear engineering. It was a logical outcome of independence from Soviet power, for Lithuania required its own specialists to manage thermal and nuclear power plants, and technologies in the food, chemical, oil, and building materials industries.

Each Ignalina reactor is a 1,500-megawatts electric, 4,800-megawatts thermal unit and has a direct cycle configuration: Saturated steam is formed in the reactor itself when light water passes through the core and then is fed to two 750-megawatt turbines at a pressure of 6.5 megapascals. Each unit has its own fuel handling system and unit control room. The turbine room, waste gas purification, and water conditioning rooms are shared. As is typical for the RBMKs, the main structural element of the reactor—a graphite stack with fuel channels, absorber rods, and surrounding metal structures—is housed in a concrete vault. Vertical graphite stack columns contain fuel channels and control rod channels. To prevent graphite oxidation and to improve heat transfer from graphite to fuel channels, the reactor space is filled with a helium-nitrogen mixture. The fuel channels are tubes whose lower and upper portions are fabricated from corrosion-resistant steel, whereas the central part is made of a zirconium alloy. (The welds of the steel and zircalloy may be a weak spot of the reactors.) A fuel assembly bank consisting of two fuel assemblies, each assembly containing eighteen fuel rods filled with uranium dioxide pellets, is suspended in each fuel channel. Light water is fed into the lower end of the fuel channels. From there, it enters separators. A biological shield of carbon steel, serpentine crushed stone and gravel, concrete, sand, and water surrounds the core.

There are 211 carbide boron rods in control channels, each rod moved by individual servomotors mounted on the top of the control channels. The control rods are cooled with water from a special loop. Of these rods, forty are used for energy distribution control throughout the entire active zone, and twenty-four are for use during an emergency and can be introduced into the active zone within 2.5 seconds. Extensive sensor and monitoring instruments supplemented by computer systems ensure reactivity control and safety. These systems log data, measure energy release in the channels, monitor fuel assembly cladding tightness, coolant flow, and temperature; they include various sensors and transducers. Almost ninety-nine percent of the radioactive fuel elements are kept in spent fuel pool storage, which is in the same building as the reactor. A German firm, GNB, won a contract to provide sixty steel containers with at least a fifty-year life to provide safe storage after the radioactive material is removed from the temporary fuel pool storage system.[40] The first Ignalina station came on line at the end of 1983. The second Ignalina unit was delayed for months by construction and safety concerns, but it finally went into operation in August 1987. Two more 1,500-megawatt units were scheduled for 1990 but were not built. To cool the massive piles, they built the largest lake in the country.

Ignalina operated more efficiently and more cheaply in 1998 than in 1997, and in 1997 than in 1996. In 1996, unit 1 operated at a 53.5 percent gross capacity and unit 2 at 16.7 percent gross capacity, with six shutdowns, of which four were for emergencies. By the International Nuclear Event Scale, there were no "accidents," only "anomalies" and "below scale event deviations." In 1997, unit 1 operated at 62 percent capacity and unit 2 at 65.1 percent capacity; there were no shutdowns and no accidents or incidents. In 1998, unit 1 operated at 54 percent capacity and unit 2 at 88 percent capacity, with only one "below scale event deviation."[41]

Despite the below scale event deviations and despite the bad reputation associated with the RBMK, the Ignalina station managers now hold a festival each summer for the International Youth Nuclear Association, "embracing young nuclear plant specialists from Russia, Ukraine, and Lithuania . . . to maintain contacts between the power plants, cooperate and exchange experience in nuclear energy, business, culture and environmental protection." Young plant operators from the LAES, Kolsk, Rovno, Chernobyl, Smolensk, Kursk, and Ignalina stations are represented, as are colleagues from reactors in Hungary, Bulgaria, and elsewhere.

In 1986, Soviet physicists had just begun their dance with gigantomania at Ignalina. The "intensive development of nuclear energetics and the aspiration to larger power units" placed before engineers the problem of "construction . . . of reactors from standard components," that is, the problem of how to build bigger reactors with greater output without having to create a special machine building capacity or a more complex design. After considering a 2,400-megawatts electric unit, they settled upon a project employing sectional blocks, which, when assembled, resulted in 2,000-megawatts electric RBMKs. Dollezhal and Vasilii Emelianov wrote, "The application of uniform sections will permit building reactors of practically any power with the utilization of similar component decisions both for the reactor and for the construction of the building." These sections would be sufficiently autonomous to permit localization of accidents and failures without shutting down the reactor. Unlike the RBMK-1000, in which the upper and lower base-shielding metal construction is supplemented with serpentine fill with a low coefficient of thermal conductivity, the RBMK-2000 would achieve thermal stability simply by filling with water. Furthermore, in the RBMK-1000, the coolant is boiling water; in the RBMK-2000, the coolant is nuclear superheated steam.[42] With only modest changes in construction parameters but significant changes in thermal characteristics, engineers planned to construct reactors much larger than anything the world has ever seen, using only slightly more enriched uranium and a relatively small active zone (see Appendix, Table 6).

The advantages of the RBMK were clear. The units and equipment were made at existing plants in the country and did not require the establishment of a new machine building industry. There appeared to be no limits to the unit power associated with manufacture, transportation, and installation. For a system so heavily centralized that one or two organizations might come to dominate an entire industry, it was a significant advantage for the RBMK not to have to worry about manufacture at some distant, inefficient, yet dominant organization. Physicists remained confident that low pressures and branching in the circulation system eliminated the possibility of an accident caused by loss of coolant. The four Leningrad and two Kursk units operated at full capacity over eighty percent of the time in 1982 and 1983, leading to a net efficiency of nearly thirty percent. Fifty-eight years of total reactor operating experience by 1986 contributed to a sense of security. The economic savings of on-line refueling and shared machine hall facilities were significant. And Soviet experience with the pressurized-water reactor, although limited to 1,000 megawatts, seemed to clear the way for unbridled expansion of the industry.[43]

THE SOVIET PWR: THE VVER

If it is possible to move rapidly at one site from one basic design to larger and larger channel-graphite reactors, then it must be possible with pressurized-water reactors, too. And if the Beloiarsk station was "the epitome of perfection," then the Novo-voronezhskaia Atomic Electric Station was hailed as the "greatest in the USSR." Located forty kilometers from Voronezh, a city of one million inhabitants with vital machine building, chemical, construction, and food industries; on the important Moscow–Rostov-on-Don–Kiev railway line; and on the Voronezh River, a tributary of the Don that provides cooling water, the station grew in power by leaps and bounds. Its first reactor was a 210-megawatts electric unit that came on line in 1964. Unit 2 (365 megawatts electric, 1969), unit 3 (440 megawatts electric, 1971), and unit 4 (also 440 megawatts electric, 1972) followed rapidly. A fifth unit reached the magic number of 1,000 megawatts electric. There was no reason for engineers, shift managers, or workers to question the placement of the reactors in beautiful forests minutes from the peaceful Don.

The village of Novovoronezh arose in the muck among recently planted saplings and precisely planned streets, stores, and apartments. This was a new socialist city. In the frequently foul weather, the settlement didn't look all that nice, and apartment construction lagged fifty percent behind schedule. The hope remained that apartments, theaters, stores, and schools would rise up simultaneously with the nuclear reactors. But the workers had to build fifty kilometers of power lines, twenty-five kilometers of highway, and a railroad trunk line from the Voronezh junction to the construction site first. They added two concrete factories, one with an annual capacity of 150,000 cubic meters, the other producing 35,000 cubic meters of prefabricated concrete forms. The simultaneous construction of 20,000 square meters of apartments is much less impressive when we realize that this is only 1,435 apartments, each at 150 square feet. At least they had modern plumbing and a sewer system, and soon they planned to have a milk factory. They quickly put up a movie theater with 350 seats, a hospital, a nursery school, and a bakery. In September 1959, five years before the reactor produced electricity, they opened a music school. Quiet flows the Don![44]

Novovoronezh is not far from the Donbas. The original plan called for a typical coal-fired station on the spot. But how much good Don coal would they have had to burn to produce the four billion kilowatt-hours generated in the first five years of the station's existence? Almost two million tons! Still, a group of local residents who feared radioactive contamination implored the officials not to build the reactors, and then, after it was already built, not to operate it. With a self-satisfied smile, the deputy chairman of the Soviet atomic energy commission dismissed their worries. Wouldn't the atom pollute the Don's pure (*sic*) water? Wouldn't some kind of radioactive fallout ruin the rich black earth steppe? Within the plant, white coats and hats, synthetic boots that squeaked along the marble floors, automatic dosimeters and badges, thick reinforced concrete walls tested by defectoscopes to prevent any radiation from passing from the reactor into the hall, all reflected genuine concern for the health of workers and local residents. The deputy chairman proclaimed, "Don't worry."[45]

When the first PWR came on line at Novovoronezh, scientists and Party officials celebrated its operation as the symbol of a new age. This 210,000-kilowatt reactor achieved criticality without a major glitch, circulating the requisite coolant—35,000 cubic meters of distilled water daily, "an entire lake"—to prevent 30,000 zirconium-clad fuel rods from melting down. The reactor was fueled by uranium oxide pellets enriched 1.5 to 2.0 percent in 343 fuel rod assemblies, each with 91 fuel rods wrapped in zircalloy. Water in the first loop passed through the active zone of the reactor, serving simultaneously as moderator and coolant. Six steam generators produced 1,400 tons of steam per hour. As the water turned to steam, it was time to extract its heat in the second loop, a heat exchange loop that set three 70,000-kilowatt turbines in motion. With concrete and fuel and steel, the reactor weighed over 400 tons. On September 30, 1967, at 3:45 in the afternoon, the first turbine of the station began to spin; and by the morning of October 2, the first million kilowatt-hours of electric power had entered the Voronezhenergo grid.[46]

Station employees hung the typical banner of the era everywhere. On it was the slogan "Let the atom be a worker, not a soldier." The station was not only peaceful but also safe, or so engineers believed, so there was no exclusion zone and most workers lived no more than 1,500 meters away. Not only was the station an achievement of the new atomic era, but those who operated the station were also youthful in their age and exuberance. Most were hardly older than thirty. It was easier to get young workers, many of whom had yet to marry, to migrate to the atomic cities coming into existence around the European USSR. Persons with families rarely wanted to move. Like each future atomic city, Novovoronezh had its Kurchatov Street, Uranium movie theater, and House of Culture with atomic emblems plastered on the exterior.[47]

The hydroelectric stations on the Volga and Dnepr were decades in development before engineers made the leap in power and scale to the massive, multimillion-kilowatt Kuibyshev, Stalingrad, and Bratsk hydropower stations. But for atomic energy, a huge leap in power generation within a decade well befitted the atomic revolution. Nearly instantaneously, engineers moved from the first station in Obninsk at 5,000 kilowatts in 1954 to 210,000 kilowatts at Novovoronezh—a 42-fold increase. The construction site had become "an arena of engineering art," where problems big and small, and especially "the battle for quality," were solved largely with science. Aleksei Stukalov, director of the inspectorate for construction norms, toured the concrete, reinforced concrete, and steel structures, for a long time unclear about how to verify their quality. He settled on ultrasound methods suggested by scientists in the Academy of Construction and Architecture and on X-ray methods to verify welds. Most of the workers and their bosses came from army projects, or hydropower stations and dams, or fossil fuel plants, and they strove to apply that construction knowledge in Novovoronezh. They figured it out through hard work, combined with rolled-up shirt sleeves, natural talent, and a bit of luck. Their credo: "We create the future today." The workers had an evening school, a construction technical school, and a branch of an evening engineering construction institute. The deputy shift director, Evgenii Bedrinov, attended a higher maritime school, then served on the *Lenin* icebreaker, and now "works on earthly elements, studies himself, and teaches young persons the difficult art of the management of the peaceful atom."[48]

The second Novovoronezh block was 365,000 kilowatts. Even though the reactor vessel was the same size as the first unit, technical improvements in the physics of the core enabled engineers to increase the block's output without significantly enlarging the reactor itself. There were some unsettling experiences with the first unit, however. According to planning documents, the station would undergo shutdown, refueling, and start-up within twenty-three days. But the first refueling operation took forty-three days because the engineers discovered a leak and had to dismantle and replace several safety systems, gauges, and thermometers, overhaul the turbogenerators and pumps, and so on. The lengthy refueling process was declared a victory in any event, because planners retrospectively forecast fifty-three days to finish the repairs. In the third and fourth units, there were two turbines, each at 220 megawatts, and the reactor had become the standard VVER-440 prototype. Power lines of 100, 220, and 500 kilowatts joined these reactors to the central energy grid. The head of the State Committee on Atomic Energy, Andronets Petrosiants, argued that this experience, leaks and all, proved that VVERs ought to become the basis for nuclear energetics (see Appendix, Table 7).[49] Of course, most of the stations came on line at the end of the year, usually in December, as workers stormed to meet annual target plans.

They turned on the fifth Novovoronezhskaia unit, a 1,000-megawatts electric PWR, in 1980, ten years after construction commenced, even though the PWR nuclear industry now had its own machine tool industry. In reality, no amount of direct orders could make centrally planned firms work well together. Teploelektroproekt, the main architects for Russia's many heat engineering projects, was the main engineering firm. Gidropress, seemingly the only trust capable of building a huge boiler, designed the nuclear heart of the unit. Kurchatov Institute personnel supervised the scientific aspects of plant construction. The Izhorsk and Kirov Elektrosila factories and the Kharkiv Turbine Factory manufactured special equipment, which would ultimately be produced in serial form. A major goal of this plant was to test the extent to which huge components and other equipment could be transported to the site by railroad, while simultaneously improving the physical characteristics and performance of the VVER-1000. Railroad transportability limited the size of the reactor vessel to 450 to 460 centimeters (a bit less than 15 feet). The choice of number of fuel rods and their orientation; such components as turbogenerators; and construction materials (steels, concretes, standard piping, and so on) had also reached a stage of standard design, approach, and materials. Engineers intended to pursue further modernization of the VVER through modest changes in the active zone of both fuel and control rods, more reliable equipment, and simplification of the reactor as a whole to optimize thermal characteristics, fuel reloading, and so on.[50]

The 1,000-megawatt unit required a huge concrete containment facility: 76 meters high and 45 meters in diameter, "made of pure concrete of the highest quality," with polyethylene-covered rebar 150 millimeters (0.6 inches) thick. The fifth unit also had its own cooling pond, which had a surface area of 600 hectares. Containment eventually became standard equipment for Soviet PWRs, after much heated debate among the engineers and officials of the various agencies and ministries involved in nuclear power. Those promoting more safety won out, even though this decision added significantly to the cost of nuclear construction. More than safety, a desire to sell these reactors abroad, where they would have to compete with Western PWRs with full containment, was a crucial consideration. A plenary session of the Central Committee in December 1977 seems to have led to the decision to put containment on the fifth Novovoronezh unit and all future VVERs.[51]

To keep costs low on the Novovoronezh station and future 1,000-megawatts electric units, engineers recognized the importance of containing labor inputs in construction on site as well as guaranteeing "mass production techniques" where possible. This approach was to be facilitated by arranging work at any reactor park so that four units could be brought to completion within a few years of one another, with workers gradually joining a site, and with housing appearing only sometime later. In theory, this would keep workers busy and Party officials happy. According to a published plan, work on unit 1 commenced in year 1 and finished in year 5; on unit 2 in year 3 and finished in year 7; on unit 3 in year 5 and finished in year 9; and on unit 4 in year 7 and finished in year 11. Four 1,000-megawatts electric reactors in 11 years! Officials in the construction trust Soiuzatomenergostroi codified specifications with applications for any reactor site. These specifications extended to all aspects of construction: planning; number of workers and their organization; what machinery and equipment to employ, from prefabricated concrete forms and components, to what cranes, excavators, and bulldozers to use in site preparation and assembly. At the Zaporozhskaia reactor park, a Kroll 240-ton crane lifted cylindrical pieces of reactor containment 12 × 34 meters and 100 to 120 tons, and other construction pieces weighing up to 150 tons. For construction of the reactor vessel at 314 tons and steam generators each at 322 tons, a bridge crane was used. Transport from factory to site by truck, barge, or railroad depended on weight and size, with the railroad being best for any item up to 3 × 12 meters. Hence, a factory could produce most of the metal work, including containment.[52]

The Minister of Electrification, P. S. Neporozhnii, acknowledged a few of the problems facing the nuclear industry in 1981. One was the failure of machine building to keep up with the tempo of engineering innovation. For the VVER-1000, for example, they had successfully introduced standard manufacture with special nuclear enterprises, standard assembly and construction using reinforced concrete forms, standard machinery and equipment, all of which in theory permitted assembly of the units within five years—of course, only with strict observance of quality control standards for every component and material of the reactor and every stage of construction. Yet Neporozhnii worried that "stoppages interfere with material technological supply. Frequently, there are insufficient numbers of parts manufactured from special alloy steels, which are used in large number in atomic power station construction. Factories manufacture them without any rhythm, so that Ministry of Ferrous Metallurgy must take under special control delivery for atomic energy, for the development of metallurgy itself, especially electrometallurgy depends to a great extent on the production of electrical energy."[53] The solution was the Atommash nuclear reactor factory (Chapter 3).

The VVER had another application, nuclear heating, because Bolshevism had fatally criticized the individual furnace or woodstove as a bourgeois luxury. Huge boilers would provide heat through massive under- and overground conduits, snaking through cities, each leaving a swath of muddy snow in the winter and parched grass in the summer. Academy of Sciences president Anatolii Aleksandrov pushed nuclear heating plants with vigor. The construction of these facilities, designed "AST" in Soviet parlance, within spitting distance of such large cities as Gorky and Voronezh, raised special safety concerns. Plans were made to build similar stations near Minsk, Odessa, Kharkiv, and Volgograd. But a moratorium on nuclear construction after Chernobyl gave impetus to significant public opposition during the perestroika period and beyond, preventing all but Voronezh from operating. When first promoting ASTs, engineers sought sufficiently lightly settled regions (no more than thirty persons per square kilometer and at least thirty kilometers from large cities). This decision meant that perhaps 100,000 and even as many as 200,000 residents might live in nearby regions. But to lower costs further and maximize efficient use of steam, they moved the AST boilers and their infrastructure closer to city centers, as close as a few kilometers away. The steam pipes were not electric power lines; no matter how well insulated, each kilometer of duct permitted significant loss of heat energy into the ground and atmosphere, so the nuclear furnaces had to be as close to the users as possible. Another challenge arose from the fact that demand for heat was uneven, varying two- to threefold during the day. How could you guarantee safe operation of the reactor with such changing load demands? Furthermore, proximity increased manyfold the risk of radiation exposure of significant numbers of persons in the case of an accident. Engineers believed that if they developed higher quality materials and equipment, highly reliable fuel rods, a new reactor design to isolate coolant of the first loop in all cases from steam heat; and siting to preclude accidents such as a direct hit from an errant airplane or an explosion at a nearby enterprise, there was no reason to delay building a dozen or more ASTs.[54] *S legkim parom!*

For nuclear heating plants and nuclear cogeneration plants to play a role in the USSR's energy future, nuclear engineers had to convince specialists in other industrial ministries that nuclear heat was good heat, that its application in metallurgy, hydrocarbon cracking, and home and industrial heating, was a reasonable and achievable goal. Immodest engineers in Teploelektroproekt were convinced that the plants, each equipped with two 500-megawatt reactors, were safe because they operated on "natural circulation," without the need for cooling water pumps, and generally operated at lower temperatures and pressures. They calculated that a 1,000-megawatt AST would provide heat to 400,000 homes, get rid of 400 smaller boilers, save 900,000 tons of coal or oil, employ at least 100 fewer persons, and operate without fossil fuel pollution.[55] Steam of "technological" parameters, 900° to 1,000°C

and even higher, might be used up to eighty kilometers from the site of its generation. Engineers in several countries carried out design work on fast helium breeder
reactors capable of producing superheated steam.[56]

As a special love of Anatolii Aleksandrov, the AST gained momentum despite
the engineering challenges encountered and moved inexorably closer to deployment near unsuspecting residents. The flagship of the AST was the Gorky station
(GAST), which was located only five kilometers from apartments and stores. As if
to underline the machine in the garden philosophy, or perhaps the disrespect of
engineers for citizen concerns, the plant was located next to a rolling landscape
of fir and birch trees, near a sanitarium, a children's pioneer summer camp, and a
series of private plots and vegetable farms. Construction on GAST was well underway when Chernobyl, glasnost, and democratization put an end to peaceful construction. After Chernobyl, engineers claimed to no avail that GAST would replace
270 small boilers, fill half of the city's hot water demand with a heating grid 60 kilometers in total length, and provide heat for 350,000 out of 1.5 million residents.

No sooner had Gorbachev called for "openness" than every weekend "Greens,"
other informal groups, and ordinary citizens took to the streets. They carried ban-
ners calling for a moratorium on construction of the ghastly GAST. They gathered
the signatures of more than 100,000 persons on petitions calling for GAST to be
mothballed. O. Samoilov, V. Kull, and B. Averbackh, the project engineers, explained
until they were blue in the face that the station was totally unlike a Chernobyl reactor: it was self-regulating, self-circulating, self-cooling, and incapable of exploding.
GAST had a massive containment structure of reinforced concrete, capable of with-
standing an earthquake or a direct hit by a huge airplane. None of this calmed
Gorky residents. "The chance of a hypothetical accident at an AST," said the chairman of the atomic energy commission, was "equal to those of a meteorite striking a
passerby on the head." Fortunately, no engineer could think of an experiment to test
that contention. But in the face of Three Mile Island and Chernobyl, citizens were
not to be bought off.

Even after construction of the station had already consumed 200 million rubles, at least another 100 million rubles were needed to complete it. Its generation
costs, too, were higher than those of fossil fuel stations, although with less ecologi-
cal impact. Still, the rector of Gorky Engineering Construction Institute, V. Nai-
denko, pointed out that it would cost only fifteen million rubles to build a gas-fired
boiler just as powerful as GAST on the same site in a shorter time. In the face of
these convincing cost arguments, the authorities shockingly and secretly planned
instead to add another 500-megawatt nuclear boiler to the site.[57] Soon thereafter,
the Iaroslavl division of the Committee for Saving the Volga succeeded in gaining
the support of local officials to kill an AST proposal for that town.[58] Only one AST
operates today, the one at Voronezh; all others were canceled because of public
opposition.

Questions of siting and safety became more and more pronounced as the nuclear program advanced from electricity production to cogeneration and steam heat;
from small units to serially produced units larger than one gigawatt; and from stations somewhat distant to population centers to reactor parks at the city limits.

Aleksandrov and Dollezhal had led the advance to the glorious nuclear future. Now one of them suggested an alternative development strategy.

SOVIET NUCLEAR WORKERS BECOME ALIENATED FROM THEIR TECHNOLOGY

Even before Chernobyl, several officials in the Party science hierarchy expressed concerns about nuclear power. Most surprising was the fact that in 1979 Nikolai Dollezhal joined senior economist Iurii Koriakin in a prominent article in the Communist Party's theoretical journal, *Kommunist,* to question the entire path for the commercialization of nuclear power. Dollezhal had been in the industry since its inception. There is no question that Koriakin, too, was a child of nuclear power. Koriakin believed that breeder reactors should supplement an extensive network of thermal reactors. He and his colleagues used mathematical models intended to define "the optimal structure of developing nuclear energetics at minimum expense" to arrive at a fast breeder reactor future.[59] Dollezhal and Koriakin promoted many of the standard features of atomic-powered communism: mass production techniques in design and construction of reactors; the deployment of nuclear boilers to produce high-temperature, "technological" steam for chemical, metallurgical, gasification, and other processes; and efforts to lower the labor costs of construction.[60]

The article was right on the mark in many of its criticisms, the haphazard siting of reactor parks near population centers in particular. Dollezhal and Koriakin noted the many achievements in the industry: the shortening time to bring larger stations on line and the important role of nuclear energy in saving precious fossil fuel resources. The RBMK, they acknowledged, had been conceived on the eve of the nuclear era; and a mere twenty-five years later the first one million-kilowatt unit had been built outside of Leningrad. Work was underway to develop units as large as 2.4 million kilowatts. The RBMK was also distinguished by the fact that ordinary machine building factories could produce its basic equipment in serial production. Even though the PWR required special equipment, the construction of Atommash would make the VVER succumb to serial production and lower costs. The reactors had been demonstrated to be not only increasingly powerful but also more reliable, for, according to official data that now seem to have been exaggerated, the reactors were on line much of the time. Physicists in the breeder reactor program had encountered more problems; these reactors would not become viable at least until the turn of the century. But even so, uranium economics favored fission reactors for some time to come.[61]

Still, Koriakin and Dollezhal worried about the fact that no one had recently questioned the economic and technical assumptions on which the nuclear program had been based. Uranium ores were increasingly lower grade, requiring more processing and enrichment, and creating vast quantities of low- and high-level radioactive waste. The authors wrote: "The problem of the external fuel cycle and radioactive wastes has become the main problem of nuclear energetics, and not only from an economic and scientific technical, but also from a social point of view." There was no guarantee that fuel cycle technologies would continue to operate as planned. In fact, they had become increasingly costly to maintain and had created significant environmental problems. Dollezhal and Koriakin admitted that the chance of an accident from nuclear waste transport was small, but with growing quantities of waste and the need to remove it from stations by railway and other forms of transport, the likelihood had grown. Expenditures for handling and safety had to be increased.

Furthermore, virtually all reactors were sited in the European USSR, often at the outskirts of major cities—Leningard, Kiev, Moscow—where sixty percent of the nation's inhabitants lived. The effort to develop a tourist industry, build rest areas, parks, and homes, and expand nature preserves in the same region of the country simultaneously made little sense from the point of view of safety and aesthetics. In addition, nuclear reactors were land-use intensive. Not only was the site itself massive, but the cooling ponds for reactor parks of 4,000 megawatts required at least twenty square kilometers. If officials indeed planned to build another fifty or sixty parks (!), these facilities would consume a huge amount of land better suited for agricultural, recreational, and other purposes. There was only one solution:

> The most radical and apparently the most rational from a series of points of view is the proposal to unify in the future newly constructed AES in huge nuclear energy complexes. Such energy complexes, created at some distance from populated regions, will contain at one site not only a great number of stations with a power of several dozens of millions of kilowatts, but also enterprises and the facilities for the external fuel cycle (radiochemical reprocessing of nuclear fuel, processing, and storage, and perhaps peaceful utilization of radioactive wastes, manufacture of nuclear fuel, and also internal specialized transport of nuclear materials).

We may be stunned at the suggestion that dozens of 1,000-megawatt reactors be built at all, let alone be located in one "park." And we may wonder whence the billions of rubles to build these parks. But Dollezhal and Koriakin had no doubt that this was the path of the future. The "rational and efficient organization of the industry" would facilitate the development of thermal and breeder reactor technology. Siting reactors in regions with vast tracks of open land and copious amounts of water—most likely western Siberia—that were not appropriate for agricultural purposes was merely common sense, they concluded. Furthermore, the creation of these nuclear fortresses would power the Siberian rivers diversion project, providing the 20 million kilowatts of electrical energy needed to pump 100 cubic kilometers of water annually from Siberia to the European USSR.[62] Nuclear energy took, but gaveth back.

NUCLEAR POWER ENGINEERING ON THE EVE OF CHERNOBYL

Atomic-powered communism enabled the USSR to move rapidly from experimental small power reactors to massive units that dwarfed human scale. Even if located in "parks," there was something inhuman and unnatural about these reactors. But Andronets Petrosiants, the chairman of the State Committee for Atomic Energy in the Brezhnev era, had a comfortable explanation. He referred to the sense among some engineers that the Obninsk station, small and relatively simple, was an anachronism compared to the 1,000-megawatt monster now being built. Petrosiants pointed out that, having shown humankind the path to the peaceful assimilation of nuclear power, the 5,000-kilowatt reactor was a kind of "Columbus."[63] The question is whether Chernobyl therefore was a kind of Henry Hudson—bold, courageous, but doomed.

Several factors explain the success of nuclear energetics in the Soviet Union until Chernobyl. One was the cultural foundation for big science and technology in the postwar USSR. The second was the force of personalities who carried great weight within the scientific establishment, an establishment itself of nearly omniscient influence. These mighty personalities included Igor Kurchatov, Nikolai Dollezhal, and, above all, Anatolii Aleksandrov, whose authority extended far beyond the nuclear enterprise to the highest reaches of the Party apparatus. Given these factors, physicists were able to dismiss, overlook, or overcome any obstacles to rapid commercialization of nuclear power. The obstacles centered on issues of availability of fossil fuels, cost, and safety.

Only nuclear energy could save the cities in the European part of the USSR from a growing shortfall of electrical energy and from the tens of millions of tons of ash, sulfur and nitrogen compounds that annually rained down from fossil fuel stations. Nuclear power stations were springing up near the biggest cities, irrespective of population densities and the presence of historical artifacts. Many of the first-generation stations served as "schools" for personnel for other stations. Army and navy personnel, some of whom had engineering degrees, moved from Beloiarsk and Novovoronezh to Gorky, Smolensk, Kalinin, Balakova, and Rostov (especially if they had no families), in search of higher pay and technological challenges.[64] The leaders had become complacent, or else they firmly believed that the technology was safe. As it spread and was built with standard components, the only major requirement was well-trained personnel, a requirement met by the establishment of a new training center for the thousands of specialists needed in the control rooms of the huge reactor parks.[65] By the end of the century, channel-graphite reactors at two, three, even more gigawatts might be built. Standardization of construction required significant expansion of a specialized nuclear industry. But atomic heating, desalination, and electric power production, all near population centers, supported the self-fulfilling prophecy that nuclear energy was clean and safe.[66]

Nuclear power reached its zenith at the twenty-fifth congress of the Communist Party in 1975. Aleksei Kosygin praised the achievements in the area of energy machine building, especially atomic, with the manufacture of 1,000-megawatt reactors and soon construction of 1,500-megawatt units, plus the serial production of turbines and generators capable of producing 500, 800, 1,000, and 1,200 megawatts, at Elektrosila, the Kharkiv Turbine Factory, and elsewhere. By 1980, the country would produce 1,380 billion kilowatt-hours of electrical energy, bringing on line in the next five year plan 70 gigawatts of capacity, including 13 to 15 gigawatts of atomic power. Construction had commenced in reactor parks ranging from Lithuania to the Urals, and from Leningrad to South Ukraine. P. S. Neporozhnii, the minister of electrification, modestly reminded the assembled delegates at the congress of the great steps since the first public works projects of the 1930s to the magnificent parks of reactors.[67] At a November 1979 plenary meeting of the Central Committee, Leonid Brezhnev, taking note of the Leningrad, Chernobyl, Kursk, and Armenia stations, called for acceleration of nuclear construction. He said, "It is necessary . . . to develop atomic energetics more rapidly. This is not only for production of electrical energy, but to meet needs for heat energy—here there are entirely appreciable reserves, and this matter is quite feasible. In future plans the accelerated construction of atomic electrical stations with fast reactors and expansion of work on controlled thermonuclear synthesis should be indicated."[68]

Publicly at least, through 1984 there was high reason for optimism. The plants operated safely even in severe climatic conditions and, according to official statistics, operated at higher than international levels, and in some cases nearly 100 percent of the time. Yet even before Chernobyl, there was reason for concern. Reactors had to be shut down more frequently than planned for the following reasons: equipment repair in the first loop, fifteen to twenty percent; turbines, twenty-five to thirty percent; electrical and control equipment, thirty-five to forty-five percent; and auxiliary equipment, fifteen to twenty percent. In fifteen to twenty percent of the cases, personnel were at fault. According to unreliable official statistics, there was an average of two dozen incidents annually resulting in power outages that led, in 1981, for example, to two percent underfulfillment of nuclear energy plans.[69] Like Brezhnev himself, the nuclear energy program had entered its twilight period. Construction had slipped far behind schedule at every reactor park, from Novovoronezh to Beloiarsk, and from Erevan, Armenia to the Kola peninsula.[70] And Atommash, the atomic machinery factory, had yet to produce a single unit. Because electricity was the key to communism, there must have been real concern among policy makers and ideologues for Soviet power. The Chernobyl disaster left no doubt about the Potemkin park in which engineers had built their two score power reactors.

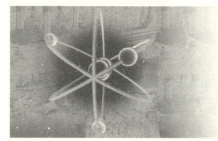

2

Nuclear Breeders:
Technological Determinism

*"Fast" reactors belong to the future. The Phoenixes of
the twentieth century will bring the masses invaluable benefit.*
—Minister of Electrification P. S. Neporozhnii

Enrico Fermi proclaimed, "The country which first develops breeder reactors will have a competitive advantage in atomic energy." Hans Bethe concurred: "Fast reactors are essential to future atomic power." Neither anticipated the tremendous technical obstacles to commercialization of breeder reactors, nor the disaster that befell the namesake of one of these Nobel laureates, the *Enrico Fermi* fast breeder reactor.[1] In October 1966, not far from the center of Detroit, the *Enrico Fermi* melted down. Most of the people living in the area were not aware that Detroit Edison had built *Enrico Fermi*, let alone that the Atomic Energy Commission (AEC) permitted a reactor type at such an early stage of development to be deployed in the nation's fifth largest city.

The AEC endorsed construction of the *Enrico Fermi* even though its advisory committee on reactor safeguards determined that there was "insufficient information available . . . to give assurance that the . . . reactor can be operated at this site without public hazard." They knew that the EBR-1, the United States's first experimental breeder reactor, had suffered a partial core meltdown in 1955. The AEC issued a construction permit anyway, but faced legal battles because several Detroit unions opposed the project. In 1961, however, the United States Supreme Court ruled that the AEC had the right to issue construction permits for reactors with "unresolved safety problems." The *Enrico Fermi* generated electricity for only a few months before its meltdown. After repairs, the reactor began to operate again in 1970, but at low power as a research facility. In late 1972, Detroit Edison announced that it would dismantle the reactor.[2]

Soviet physicists were not patient either. No sooner had they built their first experimental reactor, the F-1, in 1946 than they embarked on the design and construction of plutonium production reactors. They knew that it would be far easier to build nuclear weapons from plutonium than from uranium and that plutonium could be produced relatively inexpensively by transmuting nonfissile ^{238}U into fissile ^{239}Pu in a breeder reactor. Simultaneous with the stockpiling of plutonium for military purposes, an extensive "peaceful" program for the design of breeder reactors began. It was peaceful only on paper, because physicists knew from the start that any separation between military and peaceful uses of plutonium is arbitrary and temporary. Proliferation of weapons-grade nuclear fuel in breeder reactors can only have a destabilizing impact on international relations. President Jimmy Carter recognized this fact and acted on it. He put an end to the United States's effort to commercialize breeder reactors, canceling the Clinch River, Tennessee, commercial prototype breeder reactor project. It had taken government officials a decade to recognize the folly of the *Enrico Fermi.*

France, Japan, and the Soviet Union—none with any great success—were determined to build breeders no matter what their long-term environmental and proliferation costs might be, nor how many technological obstacles to their safe operation might exist. In Japan, sodium fires and leaks of radioactivity from the site of that country's major breeder reactor in the mid-1990s shook the nuclear industry as no previous crisis has. The French program experienced severe technical problems in its breeder program, but no crisis of will. No less aggressively than they had pushed forward with pressurized-water technology, Soviet physicists pursued commercialization of breeder reactor technology. The Soviet Union was much less concerned about plutonium proliferation than the United States was. The assumption of Soviet leaders and scientists was that the stringent political and economic controls characteristic of the Soviet system would prevent terrorists from acquiring plutonium and that their participation in the Nonproliferation Treaty indicated their intention to prohibit the spread of nuclear materials. Yet they simultaneously announced their desire to expand their nuclear trade throughout the world and to sell not only "slow" fission but breeder reactors to Eastern Europe. There was some debate among Soviet physicists about selling breeder technology, but East Europeans greatly desired to acquire it; and the Germans, Czechs, and Slovaks participated directly in its development. According to some estimates, the civilian power reactors of the USSR, Eastern Europe, and Finland would produce 11,000 kilograms of plutonium annually by 1990, raising the specter of Soviet-induced proliferation beyond its borders. The Soviets remained suspicious of the United States antibreeder anti-plutonium-economy nuclear energy policies, attributing American concern to an attempt to protect a projected lead in marketing advanced fuel cycle systems.[3]

The Soviet breeder program commenced in 1948 under the direction of Aleksandr Ilich Leipunskii, an able physicist who managed to escape the Stalinist purges, although he was arrested in 1938. As a Jew and an international traveler, he was doubly suspect. But Leipunskii never lost faith in the ability of the Soviet system to support breeder reactors, a complex technology involving several nascent industries that he nearly single-handedly pushed from infancy to commercialization. (The technology has yet to be perfected and may never achieve widespread application.) Leipunskii brooked no obstacles, moving from small experimental reactors in the 1950s to small prototypes in the 1960s, and immediately to the construction of industrial prototypes in the 1970s. These prototypes included the BN-350, a mammoth machine on the shores of the Caspian Sea that produced both desalinated water and electricity for a burgeoning petrochemical industry, and the BN-600 and BN-800, two units intended to be the templates for a network of serially produced 1,600-megawatts electric breeder reactors.

The history of the breeder reactor program illustrates the major ingredients for the growth of the Soviet cult of the atom and for science in general. First, a strong personality must direct a given program, because the political, economic, and personal obstacles to scientific success would overwhelm most individuals. It was simply safer to learn one's physics, sit quietly through classes and exams, forget the importance of Marxism-Leninism for physics soon after you had passed the exams, strive to be the best within the limits of rote learning, accept any assignment, perhaps join the Komsomol as a young adult and the Communist Party later if asked, but avoid ideology and politics, except insofar as one believed in the superiority of the Soviet social system and its science. For breeder reactors, Aleksandr Leipunskii was such an individual.

Second, a firm institutional basis had to exist. Normally, an institute would be formed to answer a specific goal established by the scientific elite, to reward a scientist after his election to the Academy of Sciences, or to meet a pressing economic or national security need. At first, such an institute might be granted first pick of the most talented recent college graduates. The promise of new apartments (often yet to be built), slightly higher salaries, and relative academic freedom served as incentives to attract the graduates. Young and unspoiled either by success or by the inertia of the Soviet system, they formed a critical mass of excited minds willing to push their new field, and their institute, to the limits of contemporary knowledge. The institute itself would have a small physical plant and a complex apparatus yet to be built or delivered. In this setting, the scientists would have an intimate atmosphere to hash out difficult theoretical questions, unbothered by concerns about experimental apparatus that might require great ingenuity to get operating properly, because there is no hardware store to speak of. Once the typical Soviet institute grew to over 1,000 employees and more, this intimacy and excitement often gave way to ennui— what might be called rote experimentation. The thrill and frustration of equipping the institute and of getting cyclotrons, Van de Graaf accelerators, and experimental reactors to operate as intended had passed. In all these ways, the Physics Engineering Institute in Obninsk was a paradigm of Soviet institute formation.

A finely tuned breeder reactor promises to double its nuclear fuel—plutonium—after about fifteen years of operation, thereby permitting the stoking of another breeder reactor. Breeder reactors would provide additional nuclear fuel after uranium ore reserves disappeared into the first generations of conventional thermal reactors, would offer a use for uranium tailings, and would breed plutonium, in theory both for military and for civilian purposes. The fuel in the first generation of breeders consists of a fertile blanket of uranium, perhaps some spent fuel from thermal reactors, and some plutonium. Breeder reactor advocates stress the utility of their engines for electrical energy production, not for producing plutonium for weapons. They emphasize the environmental safety of breeders in contrast with fossil fuel power generation, with its tons of ash, particulate, and greenhouse gases. They worry about the decline in known reserves of both uranium ore and fossil fuels.

Soviet physicists embarked on an ambitious program in pursuit of an industrial prototype. When Mikhail Gorbachev left office in 1991, they had blueprints in hand and the foundation ready for a massive 1,600-megawatt breeder as the prototype for a network of these machines. In the intervening years, they had experienced several disasters—pipes ruptured, turbines failed, sodium coolant spilled and caught fire— and political disappointments—fossil fuel, fusion, and thermal reactor programs garnered by far the greatest share of resources. Yet the physicists remained certain that they could overcome the scientific uncertainties, safety risks, and political challenges associated with bringing a network of industrial-scale breeder reactors on line by the year 2020. Under the able leadership of scientists such as Oleg Kazachkovskii, Mikhail Troianov, Aleksei Kochetkov, Vladimir Orlov, and patriarch Aleksandr Leipunskii, they remained convinced of the safety and efficacy of breeders until their program disintegrated with the breakup of the USSR. The plutonium is still safe, but many worry it will find a way beyond Russian borders into the hands of terrorists.

ALEKSANDR LEIPUNSKII: BREEDER OF BREEDER REACTORS

Aleksandr Ilich Leipunskii directed the program from its first days in 1948 until his death in 1972. He was a good scientist and a capable administrator. Leipunskii was a socialist patriot. He believed strongly that the science of the twentieth century would, with good leadership, become the technology of the twentieth century. Similarly, he saw science as crucial to industrial development. Leipunskii lacked arrogance and pretense. He was calm, somewhat ironic, affable, and always democratic in relations with staff members and students. He played and worked very hard. His loves included bike riding, mountain climbing, and skiing. He played some tennis to keep his wife, Antonina Prikhotko, a well-known Ukrainian physicist, happy, for she loved to play and was often short of partners.[4] In spite of his love of sport, Leipunskii also smoked constantly, like many of his colleagues, until his first major heart attack in 1955. In those years in the nuclear establishment, they all worked late at night and smoked to stay awake. Leipunskii preferred the *papirosy* (cardboard-tipped cigarettes) and wrote notes to himself on the box so that when a meeting was held he remembered his agenda. He often called meetings that started at midnight and ran until three. He worked long hours, rarely took vacations, and when he did, or when forced to a sanitarium for rest, brought his briefcase with him. After his heart attacks, he increased his exercise until he was able to take a brisk ten-kilometer walk daily—and those who wished to conduct business had to keep Leipunskii's pace. Eventually, there was a line of people waiting to walk with him to talk business. Leipunskii told his brother, "I'll quit work when they carry me out feet first."[5] He did—and they did, after the last of many heart attacks. Leipunskii's authority held sway over all of the groups—theoretical, engineering, construction—involved in breeders, so much so that the credit for the early success of the program falls to him. However, the failures—long lead times, accidents, cost overruns—also occurred under his watch.

Aleksandr Leipunskii lived through the major formative events of Soviet history. Born at the turn of the century, he saw firsthand two world wars, a revolution and civil war, famine in Ukraine, and the other evils of Stalinism. A Jew, he tolerated official and unofficial anti-Semitism, yet rose to the top of his profession. A member of the Komsomol from 1924, and of the Communist Party from 1930 until his expulsion in 1937, he survived arrest during the Great Terror and welcomed the de-Stalinization Thaw initiated by Khrushchev. A representative of the Leningrad school of physicists led by Abram Ioffe, he believed that science should be an international institution and therefore studied abroad. He supported the rapid spread of research institutes throughout the Soviet empire, in part taking from the Western experience. A first-rate scholar, he was at the center of nuclear physics at the Physical Technical Institute in Kharkiv, Ukraine, when it commanded international authority in the field.

Leipunskii was born on December 7, 1903, in the small village of Dragli in the Sokolsk region, the first of six children. After leaving military service, his father worked as a foreman on highway construction, a job that required the family to move from project to project, and place to place; eventually, they settled in Belostok. His mother was a homemaker. In 1914, Leipunskii's aunt died, and his parents adopted her four children. Life was difficult with all those mouths to feed, especially because his father was only seasonally employed. Perhaps because of his father's frequent absences, Leipunskii took the role of man of the house. This experience may explain both his early maturity and his later leadership skills as laboratory and institute director.

When a German zeppelin appeared overhead during World War I and bombed Belostok, the Leipunskii family moved to Iaroslavl on the Volga River. In 1918, at the age of fifteen, Leipunskii found work in a chemical factory in Rybinsk, a town firmly within the cultural sphere of St. Petersburg. Showing a keen interest in modern science, he studied in an evening mechanical technical school. The local authorities recognized him as something of a talent and sent him to the newly opened physics mechanics department of St. Petersburg (soon Leningrad) Polytechnical Institute. Here he fell into the "cradle of Soviet physics" and the school of Abram Ioffe. From the start, he loved physics. He enjoyed conducting experiments, especially those involving some risk. Once he was hospitalized after receiving too much radiation, perhaps while conducting an experiment in X-ray crystallography. This experience may have prepared him for the dangers of breeder research. At the Polytechnical Institute, his first results were in the area of inelastic interactions of atoms. Leipunskii graduated from the Polytechnical Institute in 1926 and moved across the street to the Leningrad Physical Technical Institute. His first research there focused on the processes of elementary atomic interactions. He studied energy transfer by excited atoms and molecules due to free electrons. He was rewarded for his devotion and mastery of his subject with a fifteen-day trip to Berlin in 1928, which he spent listening to the lectures of Max Planck, Otto Hahn, and Werner Heisenberg.

In 1930, Ioffe informed Leipunskii of his transfer to Kharkiv to serve as deputy director and later director of the newly established Ukrainian Physical Technical Institute (UFTI). Until the Great Terror decimated the institute, it was the place to be for nuclear physics in the Soviet Union. Its library was the pride of the institute's researchers. Leipunskii personally attended to it, ensuring that it was well organized and well managed. Young theoreticians like Aleksandr Akhiezer and Lev Rozenkevich hit the library as soon as the doors opened in the morning and stayed until late at night. Each faculty member at Leipunskii's institute had a key and could get into the library at all hours. Leipunskii strove to avoid the bureaucracy, secrecy, and identification cards that were becoming central to Soviet life. And his leadership provided an environment in which theoretical physics experienced a great flowering under Lev Landau and Aleksandr Akhiezer.

Leipunskii managed to survive incarceration during the Stalinist terror. An eighteen-month trip to Cambridge, England in 1934, on the instructions of the Commissariat of Heavy Industry to work in the laboratory of Ernest Rutherford, contributed to his fascination with experimental atomic and nuclear physics. The Cambridge trip, like his earlier visit to Berlin, contributed to the authorities' concerns that within Leipunskii might lurk a Western agent. In 1935, he was elected as a full member of the Ukrainian Academy of Sciences. Leipunskii experimentally proved the existence of the neutrino by measuring the nuclear energy of recoil in beta decay (1936). Over the next few years, he turned to investigations of the interaction of fast neutrons with matter, which led to a series of publications in leading Soviet scientific journals. He was one of the main organizers and the first editor of *Physikalische Zeitschrift der Sowjet Union* (1933–1938), a German language journal out of Kharkiv intended to make the research of Soviet physicists more accessible to the Western audience and secure the priority of their discoveries. Despite his responsibilities as administrator and editor, Leipunskii also managed to lecture on nuclear physics in the physics-mathematics department of Kharkiv State University, a major source of personnel for the growing institute located only a few miles away.

The challenges of securing materials from the Commissariat of Heavy Industry (Narkomtiazhprom) remained in the forefront of the attention of Leipunskii and other UFTI directors. Even if the institute opened with a grand celebration of its new machinery, workshops, and glass blowing equipment, its experimental facilities always lagged behind the needs of the scientists. How Soviet nuclear physics managed to achieve as much as it did before the Nazi invasion, building Van de Graaff accelerators and cyclotrons seemingly out of air and scraps, is a fascinating story of ingenuity, determination, luck, and learning how to play the game with a ministry more concerned with industrial production than with scientific results.[6] Indeed, the Kharkiv physicists often failed to get Narkomtiazhprom to respond with any thing other than glacial speed. So they played their one really major success for all it was worth, sending a telegram to Comrade Stalin to announce that Leipunskii, Sinelnikov, A. K. Valter, and G. D. Latyshev had artificially split a lithium atom. Stalin seems not to have noticed, and funding remained tight.

Leipunskii's own research involved atomic structure and nuclear physics. He participated in experiments to observe the neutrino. After Vladimir Veksler in 1944 discovered the principle behind the phase stability of particles, Leipunskii suggested the idea of a building a ring proton accelerator—the synchrotron, as later named by Veksler—on this principle. Indeed, Leipunskii was given the task of developing a 1.5-gigaelectronvolt accelerator to which Obninsk- and Moscow-based physicists such as A. L. Mints contributed. The accelerator program saw rapid initial successes, and construction began on the UPK-1.5 at Obninsk, but in its place, only a 0.5-megaelectronvolt experimental model was built. Because Veksler was working in the Lebedev Physics Institute on a 1-gigaelectronvolt synchrotron, it was decided to combine the two efforts under Veksler's leadership at Dubna, where a 10-gigaelectronvolt ring accelerator was built. A large number of the Obninsk high-energy physicists then moved to Dubna.[7]

As a member of the second generation of the Ioffe school, Leipunskii knew personally and worked with all the leading figures of the atomic age whose stories are told in this book: Igor Kurchatov, Anatolii Aleksandrov, Abram Alikhanov, and Kirill Sinelnikov. These connections did not prevent Leipunskii from falling victim to the purges. In October 1937, Leipunskii was expelled from the Communist Party, for "aiding and abetting an enemy of the people," and removed as director of UFTI. As the purges grew, it was only a matter of time before Leipunskii was arrested. Leipunskii was one of the lucky few; he managed to survive eight months of constant interrogation. The NKVD (Commissariat of Internal Affairs) released him in June 1938 without any apology except the statement that this is "the end of the matter." Leipunskii was allowed to resume research, eventually rising to the position of director of the breeder reactor program, "Hero of Socialist Labor," and Lenin prize laureate.[8]

Upon his return to the institute, Leipunskii became head of the radiation laboratory. During the war, he served as chairman of the Ukrainian Scientific-Industrial Committee for the Assistance of Defense but was evacuated ahead of the German advance to Ufa with other physicists and whatever could be loaded onto trains in short order. The Kharkiv regional Communist Party organization readmitted him in 1946, although local party organizations had urged his reinstatement from 1939 onward; his renewed Party membership paved the way for Leipunskii to work on the atomic bomb project. From 1944 through 1949, Leipunskii was director of the Institute of Physics in Kiev. He often traveled to Moscow to serve as a consultant to

Kurchatov's laboratory 2 and to head a small experimental group in laboratory 3, where physicists measured the cross section of neutron capture in uranium-238 and thorium-232. In Moscow, Leipunskii rejoined the pulse of Soviet physics. In research, seminars, and pedagogical work, he stood next to Kurchatov, Artsimovich, Kikoin, and others. Leading scientists, especially those associated with the bomb project, believed that the usual norms of Soviet behavior did not apply entirely to them. Under the protection of an atomic umbrella, they met informally. Leipunskii conducted seminars in the sticky, hot summer of 1948, with lecturers and students alike sitting in the waters of the Protva River. This was not unlike the informal atmosphere for Nikolai Timofeeff-Ressovsky's summer laboratory in Miassovo in the Urals in the 1950s, where geneticists heard about recent developments in their field before the fall of Lysenko.[9]

Early in his tenure as director of the Institute of Physics, Leipunskii established the experimental foundations for breeder reactors. Through 1948, Leipunskii conducted a series of investigations employing chain fast-neutron reactions to convert "nuclear ore" (^{238}U or ^{232}Th) into "nuclear fuel" (^{239}Pu or ^{233}U). These experiments moved to laboratory "V," designated by its post office box number 276, in Obninsk. The Obninsk laboratory was a crucial experimental facility in the Soviet nuclear arsenal. Renamed the Physics Engineering Institute in the mid-1950s, it was home to the 5,000-kilowatt reactor, the ARBUS land-based portable reactor, and the Soviet breeder reactor program. At the institute, Leipunskii conducted investigations in nuclear physics, reactor physics, heat engineering, the technology of liquid metals, and nuclear material science. He was the initiator and founder of sodium coolant technologies. And he was the central figure behind the institute's expansion from nuclear physics to other areas of research. Of course, these areas—hydrodynamics, heat engineering, and so on—all had something to do with nuclear reactors because Leipunskii had a feel for what to do when setting forth designs, establishing constants, or selecting materials—for example, for the active zone of a reactor. And even when his intuition failed, he was never off by much.

Before the scientists arrived in January 1948, Obninsk was a small, beautiful, quiet village. The elite such as Kazachkovskii and Leipunskii got three-room cottages. But life was still hard. The electricity was turned off from ten at night until six in the morning, and all day on Sunday. Plumbing had been installed but the water was not running, so tanks of water were brought in. The scientists heated the cottages with woodstoves, and split the wood themselves. Many had gardens, fowl, and a few farm animals. A radio was a luxury. Most used packing crates as furniture. There was one tea service that made its way around town on successive Saturday nights from one social Saturday to the next.

Obninsk residents included three categories of prisoners: Germans conquered by the Soviets and removed to Obninsk, unfortunate Soviet citizens who had fallen behind German lines and were considered tainted, and various Gulag inmates. They all associated freely for quite a while. Within the fences, secrecy didn't exist, as German "colleagues" and the Soviet scientists spoke freely about science, about reactors, about uranium. One idea gave way to another without pause. No one wanted to sleep. Leipunskii was deputy in charge of the German scientists, and he often wore a military uniform, especially when he went to Moscow on business. But after a few "unexpected encounters" and the resulting pregnancies among German-Russian pairs, the slogan "Death to German Occupiers!" returned in full force. Germans were isolated in the south wing of the main building where they worked mostly on reactor physics.[10]

Leipunskii also had a pedagogical career of note. He was the organizer and department chair of reactor physics at the Moscow Mechanical Institute. This did not make life easy on his domestic life, for he had an apartment in Moscow, a house in Obninsk, and a wife and daughter who lived in Kiev. He applied the principles of his own matriculation at Leningrad Polytechnical Institute, which was intended to train scientists capable of pushing recent advances directly into production. The principles included teaching engineers the same amount of physics and mathematics as physicists were taught; involving faculty on the cutting edge of science (in this case, Kurchatov, Artsimovich, Tamm, Leontovich, Pomeranchuk, Kikoin, and Leipunskii himself); and personal contact with students. Leipunskii encouraged democratic relations among students and faculty; the students often dined at their professors' houses. It's hard to understand how students had time to socialize with faculty, however. They had fifty hours of weekly instruction (the Soviet norm being an already excessive thirty-six hours).[11] One wonders whether they had time to eat, let alone sleep.

Moscow Mechanical Institute became Moscow Institute of Physics and Technology, the legendary "MIFI," the reputed Soviet MIT, whose first graduates included one future Nobel laureate, N. G. Basov, and dozens of future leaders of the cult of the atom. Leipunskii taught in the Obninsk branch of MIFI. Other persons who passed through Obninsk included Gurii Marchuk, later head of the Siberian Division of the Academy of Sciences and then the president of the Soviet Academy. Leipunskii's teaching at MIFI included a course on nuclear reactors whose start was delayed when Leipunskii was injured in a skiing accident in the Caucasus. When he commenced lectures a few weeks into the semester—in a heavy cast—the students immediately considered him one of theirs. To catch up, Leipunskii's course initially ran four to six hours per day.[12] By the late 1960s, when nuclear physics had become well established, MIFI became a factory for students in the way that Elektrosila was a factory for magnets or Atommash a factory for reactors.[13]

The initial success of the Obninsk institute, like Soviet institutes generally, in the 1950s occurred when the institute was geographically small scale, when the critical mass of good young minds could meet easily, and frequently did, in the corridors of the one building, the "main" building. Of course, not every advance occurred without tension. The relations between the director of the Physics Engineering Institute, Dmitrii Blokhintsev, and Leipunskii were based on mutual respect, even when Leipunskii expressed misgivings about the Obninsk effort to build the world's first power reactor, which took resources away from his small group of breeder specialists. However, the deputy director, A. K. Krasin, openly expressed his enmity to Leipunskii; and their relations grew worse when Krasin was appointed director. Krasin left Obninsk some years later, when he was fired.[14] Leipunskii died on September 14, 1972, just before his most recent achievement, the BN-350, the world's most powerful breeder reactor at the time, came into service.[15] Despite his devotion to the Soviet cause, after 1934 the authorities never let him travel abroad.

BREEDER REACTORS AS SELF-AUGMENTING TECHNOLOGY

The breeder physicists employed the same approach to the development of reactor technology that their fission reactor counterparts used. First, they hoped to design a prototype fuel rod whose efficiency and reliability would enable them to employ it in advanced reactors simply by making modest improvements rather than radical design changes. Second, they believed that the same "prototype approach" would work for critical components such as fuel rods, compressors, pumps, and heat exchangers, which they tested on critical stands and experimental reactors. Again, they hoped to use these components in industrial reactors with only minimal changes. Third, they dealt with issues of worker and environmental safety almost as an afterthought. They believed that the experimental reactors would operate within design parameters; they did not anticipate severe accidents and therefore provided adequate, but not fail-safe biological shielding and containment. Yet each experimental device raised a new series of technological challenges. The physicists overcame many of them, to be sure, but quickly pressed on toward commercialization of breeder technology even when they encountered difficulties.

Breeder technology appeared to be self-augmenting and autonomous. To function properly, it required the creation of two other extensive, expensive, and dangerous technologies and the industries to support them. The tasks that confronted the physicists were complex, if not insurmountable, but they had no choice in the matter. First, the high concentration—enrichment—of fuel in the core required high fuel burn-up rates to keep the total cost of fuel and the loss of fuel during chemical processing as low as possible. A new fissile fuel processing industry with significant capital costs and health and environmental risks had to be built. Second, the concentration of fuel in the active zone had a very high energy density, requiring the development of heat transfer technology of a new kind. This technology would have to be able to handle liquid metal coolants, because water and organic liquids were inappropriate both as a moderator of fast neutrons and as a heat transfer medium. The physicists had to design systems to keep water and sodium from coming into contact, because that mixture was explosive. The creation of liquid metal technology on an industrial scale was the only solution.

Breeder proponents never doubted their eventual success. Hence, they were guilty of technological enthusiasm. The nature of Soviet science and politics also contributed to the self-augmenting nature of breeder technology. The United States abandoned the Clinch River Breeder Reactor and breeders in general in the late 1970s, while the Soviet Union, France, and Japan just forged ahead. This contrasting behavior suggests that a centralized political and scientific culture contributes to the technological momentum of large-scale, state-supported projects, a suggestion that is almost a tautology.

The United States pursued commercialization of breeder power until the late 1970s. The motivations behind this effort were to lessen reliance on oil imports and

Aleksandr Leipunskii (second from right) who directed the Soviet breeder reactor program from its inception in 1949, with his assistant Oleg Kazachkovskii (second from left) and two colleagues. *(Courtesy of Oleg Kazachkovskii)*

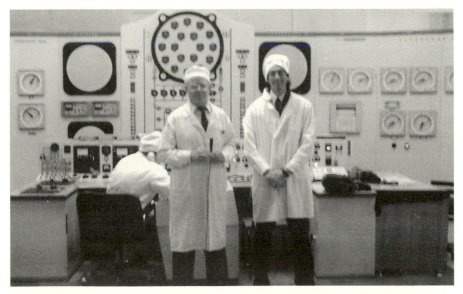

Paul Josephson (on the right) in the control room of the first-in-the-world "peaceful" nuclear power station in Obninsk, Kaluga Province. The station has been in nearly continuous operation since 1954. *(Courtesy of the author)*

to ensure sufficient quantities of nuclear fuel after the (prematurely) predicted depletion of uranium ore reserves. The first United States breeder, Clementine, operated at Los Alamos National Laboratory from March 1946 until December 1953. Its output was 100 kilowatts thermal, later upgraded to 250 kilowatts. It had a mercury coolant and a plutonium core. Physicists at Argonne National Laboratory then built the Experimental Breeder Reactor 1 (EBR-1) at the AEC Reactor Testing Station in Idaho Falls, Idaho and shut down Clementine. EBR-1 operated for a dozen years, through 1963, with an output of 1,200 kilowatts thermal. It suffered a major mishap in 1955, with a meltdown. EBR-1's successor, EBR-2 eventually served as the mainstay of the United States program. EBR-2 should also have served as an indication of troubles to follow. Construction began in May 1957, and physicists projected criticality in June 1959. But supply and construction delays put off criticality until November 1963. Then, after coming on line, leaks and other malfunctions interrupted research several times—but the physicists learned a great deal about reactor materials and fuels.[16]

Officials in the AEC determined by 1960 to embark on an extensive program to develop a liquid metal fast breeder reactor. The program involved industry, national laboratories, and the AEC. In this program, United States physicists built several small breeder reactors, including zero power units; Lampre at Los Alamos; and SEFOR, the Southwest Experimental Fast Oxide Reactor, a joint United States-Federal Republic of Germany endeavor built by General Electric and Southwestern Electric. Gulf General Atomic of General Dynamics, under contract with the AEC, began designing a 1,000-megawatts electric gas-cooled fast reactor in the mid-1960s. Thorium and uranium fuels entered the pantheon of possibilities. The Fluid Fuel Research program at Brookhaven National Laboratory and the Molten Salt and Aqueous Homogeneous Reactors at Oak Ridge were involved. Babcock and Wilcox, Westinghouse, Atomics International, and General Electric joined in. The AEC provided funding for a fast flux test facility (FFTF) as the prototype. This plant was a 400-megawatts thermal high flux fast reactor facility designed to develop fuels and materials and located at Hanford Engineering Development Laboratory. The AEC envisioned demonstration plants by the late 1970s, specifically the 375-megawatts electric Clinch River (Tennessee) Breeder Reactor, scheduled for completion by the 1980s, and several 1,000-megawatts electric breeders some years later. The FFTF and Clinch River facility were waylaid by construction delays, limited alternatives, and cost overruns in the hundreds of millions of dollars.[17]

Similar delays, high costs, and proliferation concerns, which resulted in the cancellation of the United States breeder program, did not deter Leipunskii and his colleagues. Their cause was helped by the fact that the development of breeder technology was linked to the fortunes of Kurchatov Institute physicists and thereby to its leadership, in the form of Anatolii Aleksandrov. He had his mind on plutonium, too—in the RBMK reactor. So long as he kept nuclear power on the Brezhnev administration agenda, the breeder program grew, even when the USSR embarked on the costly construction of dozens of 1,000-megawatts electric fission reactors in the late 1970s.

Oleg Dmitrievich Kazachkovskii was Leipunskii's right-hand man in the development of these technologies and later director of the Scientific Research Institute of Atomic Reactors where the BOR-60, the last Soviet experimental breeder reactor, was built.[18] Kazachkovskii joined Leipunskii's team at the end of 1949. He made his way to the Physics Engineering Institute from Dnepropetrovsk State University and Dnepropetrovsk Physical Technical Institute. His career was interrupted by service in World War II, for which he was heavily decorated. At the front in southern Ukraine, he was wounded and hospitalized; he recovered and returned to the front.

Kazachkovskii, one of only several score individuals who passed Lev Landau's "theoretical minimum" examination, decided to leave physical chemistry, his work on crystallization, and his university mentor Vitalii Danilov for nuclear physics after hearing about Nagasaki and Hiroshima. Danilov urged him to meet with Leipunskii, so Kazachkovskii did, in Leipunskii's room in the Moscow Hotel in 1946. Kazachkovskii expected a stern, distant personage. The first question was about how much he knew about nuclear physics. Kazachkovskii answered honestly, "very little." Leipunskii was impressed with his honesty and accepted him on the basis of his general physics knowledge. Leipunskii had grown interested in measuring the inelastic scattering of fast neutrons from working in Alikhanov's laboratory 3, a subject on which Kazachkovskii was put to work. By 1947, they were ready to move to Obninsk, a place even more secret than laboratories 2 and 3, where Leipunskii finally explained in great detail to Kazachkovskii his view of a crucial task, the problem of plutonium-breeding fast reactors.[19]

At first, Kazachkovskii studied injection of particles into accelerators. He then focused on the determination of the basic nuclear parameters for fast reactors and was involved in the creation of the first Soviet fast reactors—the BR-1, BR-2, BR-5, BFS-1, and BFS-2—on which he based his doctoral dissertation (1958). In 1960, Leipunskii, Kazachkovskii, and the others received a Lenin prize for their breeder research. From 1964 to 1973, Kazachkovskii was the director of the Research Institute of Atomic Reactors, where the focus was reactor physics, material science, reactor components, and reactor technology. After Leipunskii's death, he became director of the Physics Engineering Institute and the main force behind Soviet breeders.[20]

It was a joy for Kazachkovskii to work with Leipunskii in the early days. "AIL," as he was known, carried great authority and was able to push the breeder reactor program despite political or technical obstacles. Most important, AIL possessed deep understanding—as well as an intuitive sense—of a number of fields of science and technology. He had sent a proposal to the government asking that the breeder be designated a priority, with all of the rights and privileges of access to machinery, equipment, isotopes, and personnel. Initially, Kazachkovskii was skeptical of the chances for success, for the safety and reliability of even the much simpler power reactors remained unproved. And then there was the problem of the poverty of the postwar Soviet Union, which needed to invest in virtually every sector of the economy. On the other hand, nuclear programs of any sort always seemed to get funding. The scientific challenge convinced Kazachkovskii to join the breeder program as AIL's deputy. He attended the second Geneva conference, where he met his American breeder counterparts and complemented them on the *Enrico Fermi* project.[21]

The political obstacles to breeder development were many. The program commenced under strict secrecy, like any other nuclear problem. This constraint led to all kinds of curiosities and confusion that were applied in speech and documents alike. For reactor, the Soviet scientists had to use the word "forge"; instead of neutron, they wrote "meteorite"; and fast neutrons were "shooting stars." Of course, the typists weren't allowed to know what this all meant, a further constraint that made corrections a chore. The physicists weren't allowed to read published literature on nuclear science and technology on the subway or bus. Foreign journals were stamped "Top Secret." When someone gave a talk among other persons with security clearance, he still lowered his voice to a near whisper when saying "neutron" or "reactor." Leipunskii was one of a handful of physicists who pushed the Soviet Union to participate more actively in the International Atomic Energy Agency (IAEA), a participation that eventually led to an exchange of information and the breakdown of the Soviet system of controls. From their IAEA colleagues they learned that France, England, and the United States had breeder programs similar to theirs.[22]

EXPERIMENTAL PHOENIXES

Having conducted extensive calculations that indicated the possibility of breeding, AIL and his colleagues set out to establish a firm experimental basis for the push to industrial applications. They built a series of increasingly large and more complex breeders, experimenting with different fuels and coolants. The BR-1, with a concentrated active zone that contained 12 kilograms of plutonium, was their maiden voyage. In getting the BR-1 on line, they were lucky to work with Efim Pavlovich Slavskii, the first director of Cheliabinsk-40. Slavskii and Leipunskii had a good relationship. Leipunskii believed that Slavskii was a smart man and a straight arrow. Slavskii was an outstanding organizer and first-rate engineer and was sensible enough to support the seemingly far-fetched ideas of scientists. Understanding the importance of the BR-1, Slavskii didn't complain about plutonium taken from still modest stockpiles for scientific rather than military tasks. And a year later, Slavskii authorized release of roughly the same amount for the BR-2. Leipunskii's group worried about the possibility that the plutonium would be wasted, because there was not one reactor builder among them. Should they invite someone who had worked with chain reactions to help them in this matter? They decided not to act in ignorance, but to think carefully and slowly through each step. In 1952–1953, the physicists carried out a series of calculations to estimate the heat transfer and neutron-capturing capabilities of a series of coolants—sodium, sodium-potassium, lead-bismuth, helium—with the assumption that the power of a prototype reactor would be about 500 megawatts thermal. All the coolants seemed acceptable, although helium required high pressure, which would be dangerous if pressure were lost in an accident. Lead-bismuth was then rejected because its corrosiveness was higher than those established as core parameters. Sodium-potassium did not require preheating of the coolant loop as sodium alone did. But sodium possessed better heat capacity characteristics, and hence less of it was required. Sodium was the choice. This early decision enabled the physicists to concentrate on the other significant technical problems more intently and to wrestle with the thermo- and hydrodynamics of sodium coolant.[23]

The BR-1 was a "dry" reactor, a zero power critical assembly without coolant. They encountered only modest difficulties in getting it to operate. It achieved criticality in May 1955. As a powerful source of fast neutrons, the BR-1 turned out to be useful for a wider range of experiments than anticipated, so it was kept in operation for a longer time than planned.[24] To gain experience with an experimental breeder reactor, Leipunskii and Kazachkovskii then designed the 100-kilowatt BR-2. The physicists did everything associated with the BR-2 themselves, because engineers were not yet prepared to assist them. This approach set the standard for breeder reactors and established patterns for the nuclear industry generally: Scientists armed with a firm background in nuclear physics pushed experimental and prototype technologies rapidly into the engineering stage, then turned them over to engineers, trained in narrow specialties, whose goal was to meet production, but not necessarily, other standards. This system was an impediment to innovation, because few of the engineers truly understood the physics behind a prototype, and to safety, because the engineers assumed they were working with a proven technology.

In the BR-2, the Soviet physicists made one decision that seemed to challenge their conviction that sodium was the coolant of choice—the BR-2 employed metallic plutonium fuel and liquid mercury coolant. However, mercury would not work in industrial reactors. It had a very high cross section of neutron capture, which lowered the breeding coefficient, and it had a noticeable corrosive effect. It did not require any special pumps or heat transfer devices, as sodium would. The coolant moved through the active zone from the top down, a flow that permitted design of a relatively simple and reliable heat removal schema.

Reactivity was controlled by moving parts of a reflector, which, in such a small reactor, was quite acceptable. But on this and other early reactors, they noticed significant fluctuations in reactivity. They eventually found that some fluctuation occurred because the reactivity control cylinder was not firmly affixed and could experience some "nonsanctioned" movement. One small fluctuation was connected with an earthquake in Bucharest in 1977, which was only three on the Richter scale; this event should have suggested to other specialists that the siting of reactors near active faults was a grave error. (Of course, Armenian and Californian reactors that were built on faults didn't employ this kind of reflector device, nor did the planned Crimean reactor. But even avoidance of mechanical reflectors does not justify their construction in seismically active regions.)

On the BR-2 experimental reactor, the Leipunskii group grappled with the development of fuel rod technology. A. A. Bochvar oversaw design of all fuel rods for fast reactors at his Research Institute of Inorganic Materials; Igor Golovin designed them for the BR-1 and BR-2. The length of operation of fuel rods in fast reactors was determined, not by the loss of reactivity (as usually occurs in power reactors), but by the loss of mechanical strength due to radiation and heat damage. The development of fuel rods with high burn up was therefore a major challenge facing physicists as they strove to make breeders economically competitive with thermal reactors. The 108 plutonium and uranium fuel rods of the BR-2 were 10 millimeters in diameter and 130 millimeters long. They consisted of thick-walled hermetic stainless steel pipes secured in a long stainless steel shaft. The coolant was liquid mercury, which filled seventeen percent of the active zone. A rotary pump with a capacity of six cubic meters per hour circulated the liquid mercury through the active zone to a water-cooled heat exchanger. In the event of a pump failure, natural circulation of the mercury coolant guaranteed a cut in power to twenty kilowatts. The reactor employed a neutron reflector consisting of a layer of uranium and copper. Operators controlled reactivity through the motion of a fifteen-millimeter metallic cylinder that enveloped the core from the outside. During emergencies, the cylinder dropped freely, without the chance of jamming, to cover the core and slow multiplication of neutrons. Several other devices made of copper and nickel also served as control mechanisms. These devices were lowered into the reactor around the active zone, thereby cutting reactivity more than five percent. Biological shielding consisted of a 500-millimeter layer of water, a 400-millimeter layer of cast iron, and a 1,200-millimeter layer of heavy concrete. The reactor had a series of vertical and horizontal experimental channels exposed to various neutron energies, depending on their orientation to the active zone, through which physical, material science, and other experiments were carried out. Mainly, experiments included defining and fixing physical constants necessary for design of energy fast reactors and measurement of the capture energy of fast neutrons.[25]

There was one serious accident with the BR-2. Mercury entered the loop of the discharge tank, significantly increasing the internal gas pressure. The physicists initially decided that the increase was not major and that they should lower the liquid level in the tank through the lower edge of the fence pipe. This action produced a powerful hydroshock, releasing mercury and mercury fumes into several reactor systems and the hall. They later determined that they had not taken into account the possibility that the gas bubble that burst into the loop would increase in volume so quickly as it rose and passed into areas of lower hydrostatic pressure. It was decided in the future not to put the coolant under great pressure, but to pump it continuously. The reactor also had another problem—a small positive void coefficient of reactivity (both Doppler and configurational) that raised the prospect of instability at low power. Nevertheless, start-up always proceeded without a hitch.[26]

For a few months, reactor operation was stable. Then suddenly they noticed that it was losing reactivity; and the more it lost, the more rapidly reactivity fell. They could not detect any configurational change. They began to worry that a serious accident was about to occur. They examined the mercury with a probe and noticed alpha radioactivity. It turned out that in the lower part of the fuel rods, at the hottest point, a large number of fissures had appeared and the plutonium was leaking out. Because of the low operating temperatures, the physicists had not anticipated that this problem would arise. It was a real blow to their confidence. They had no choice but to shut down the reactor and then consider what to do next. Their next decision might now appear to be rash, but it was to be expected, given the environment of heady successes and ample resources in which they had operated up to this time. They decided to build a more powerful experimental reactor, one using sodium, with parameters approximating those in an industrial prototype: a maximum density of heat removal in the active zone of 500 kilowatts per liter and temperatures of the sodium reaching 450°–500°C. The resulting five-megawatt reactor logically received the name BR-5 (it was later reconstructed as the BR-10).

The BR-5, which resembled the BR-2, was located in a modest building next to the renowned 5,000-kilowatt power reactor and was built on the site of the BR-2, saving time and money in construction. In the BR-5, control of reactivity was facilitated by the movement of parts of the reflector, which were suspended on cables from the outside of the reactor vessel. The Soviet physicists realized that this arrangement was risky, especially because of the limited experience with sodium technology and because of the decision to use plutonium oxide fuel rods (because of their higher working temperature). Even so, they moved on to the construction of the reactor with only limited testing on physical stands. Making matters worse, when they disassembled the BR-2, mercury leaked into the air in concentrations that far exceeded even lax Soviet norms. Ultimately, they had to cover the walls of the reactor building with thick layers of paint to prevent mercury poisoning among the workers. Despite all this, the BR-5 commenced operation without coolant in the summer of 1958 and achieved criticality when fully loaded with sodium in January 1959.[27] For their honorable labors, Leipunskii, Kazachkovskii, I. I. Bondarenko, and L. N. Usachev received Lenin prizes in 1960.[28]

The physicists were especially pleased with how well the plutonium oxide fuels functioned. There were eighty fuel assemblies in the core. A nickel cylinder-reflector regulated neutron activity: If you moved it up just a bit, neutrons began to fly about. The cylinder was surrounded by concrete four meters thick. The fuel rods were designed for two percent burn up, reached four percent by June 1961, and ultimately achieved seven percent. Because of the greater compactness and heat conductivity of monocarbide fuels in comparison with oxide fuels, they loaded the BR-5 in May 1965 with an enriched uranium-235 monocarbide core, and by March 1, 1967, had achieved burn up of two percent.

Leipunskii and Kazachkovskii concluded after several years of operation that the BR-5 proved that liquid sodium technology had been assimilated on a fairly large scale, that sodium was better than mercury in many of its properties, especially with respect to the greater corrosiveness of mercury, and facilitated repair of heat exchange equipment without requiring full shut down of the apparatus by allowing the sodium at the point of repair to solidify. Calculations showed that the reactor was stable, with a negative reactivity coefficient. During transition phases of operation, however, there were "very short periods" with a positive power coefficient; but physicists dismissed this concern by saying that "the temperature coefficient of reactivity in and of itself does not exert a significant effect on the stability of the reactor." They were pleased that there had been no case of "overirradiation" of personnel, despite the fact that workers and physicists had had to work with radio-active sodium during repairs.[29] At least mercury vapor was no longer a hazard. The fact that such a small reactor produced 5,000 kilowatts led Kazachkovskii to calculate that a breeder with an active zone of one cubic meter might produce one million kilowatts.[30]

The BR-5 also demonstrated success in handling sodium, especially when austenites of steel (special steels high in carbon) were used and "cold traps" were employed to clean the sodium of any oxides to prevent corrosion. Five cubic meters of liquid sodium with a temperature of approximately 500°C was pushed through the active zone at 250 cubic meters per hour.[31] Leipunskii concluded that reliable equipment for sodium technology—pumps, heat exchangers, measuring instruments, and so on—gave them confidence in handling even sodium that was contaminated with radioactivity when fuel rods developed fissures or cracked. Still, the circulating pumps were unreliable and the source of frequent stoppages—in all, there were forty-five stoppages to repair pumps, although twenty-five of the stoppages occurred in the early days of operation between 1959 and 1961. Indeed, as is clear from official data, only in the second and third years, were physicists able to operate the BR-5 more that seventy-five percent of the time; and for three years running, not once did they achieve full-power operation (see Appendix, Table 8). As with the BR-2, damage of the BR-5 fuel rods occurred. The physicists became worried when they observed radioactive fission products in the coolant. Would it be necessary to moth-ball the reactor? Locate and remove the defective fuel rods? But the damage turned out to be much less than that in the BR-2, and the fuel rods essentially remained intact. From September 1961 through March 1962, they shut down the reactor to repair damage caused by leakage of fuel into the coolant and equipment of the first loop. Another long down time, from December 1964 until May 1965, involved the shift to monocarbide fuel rods. At least they managed to tackle the change of pumps on the first loop in fifteen to twenty days and on the second loop within a week.[32]

Most of the heat of the BR-5 was released into the atmosphere, but they put an experimental steam generator on one of the two heat exchange loops. To avoid the accidental interaction of water with sodium, they utilized doubled piping with a thin layer of mercury between the two layers. The steam generator turned out to be complex, bulky, and not very reliable. Frequently, fissures developed in the pipes, often because of corrosion caused by the mercury. They were engaged in constant repairs, eventually having to disassemble the unit. But even though the steam generator experience turned out unhappily, the breeder specialists did not change their strategy and were confident of creating reliable steam generators in the future. At the very least, the Soviets had more experience in handling sodium and sodium tainted with radioactive fission products and in the cleanup of sodium systems (removal of fission products) than any other country in the world.[33]

Once the publicity of the Geneva conferences enabled them to speak openly of the BR-5, its creators, Aleksandr Leipunskii and Oleg Kazachkovskii, described the technical challenges of breeder reactors in measured, yet confident tones, making light of the challenges of high temperatures, radioactivity, the dangers of handling liquid sodium, and the problems with the fuel rods. They were sure that commercialization was around the corner.[34] The reactor sat in a huge hall served by a control room filled with red lights and bells that would signal even the slightest rise in radiation levels. The fact that the BR-5 was sited in Obninsk, a city like any other Soviet city, with broad thoroughfares and squares and stately pine trees reaching toward the top of ubiquitous multistory apartment buildings, confirmed its safety. Obninsk had become a mecca for foreign scientists, too, even though it was closed to the ordinary Soviet citizen. Delegations from over seventy countries visited Obninsk between 1954 and 1962.[35]

Kazachkovskii, Leipunskii, and their colleagues now sought to produce data demonstrating the economic advantages of breeder technology so that they could move toward the next stage—construction of industrial prototypes. Research on the nuclear physical, chemical, metallurgical, and technological characteristics of fuels and components gave the physicists hope on economic grounds, even though they were bothered by certain physical phenomena such as brittleness and swelling of the steel fuel casings during exposure to high radiation. They developed austenite stainless steels that had sufficiently high mechanical strength and retarded—but did not prevent—swelling and break down; and they achieved burn up to ten percent, with working temperatures up to 700°C.[36] On the technical side, they had indeed made progress; but the economic calculations on which breeder physicists based their optimistic projections were tainted by uncertainties regarding the cost of nuclear fuels, the nature of the fuel cycle, and the absence of industrial experience. When they claimed that breeders were cost effective, they meant that only their theoretical calculations indicated that short doubling times could be achieved. The concentration of the fissile material in the active zone of a fast reactor has to be significantly higher than that in thermal reactors to produce roughly equivalent amounts of electrical energy. So, to keep fuel costs as low as possible, they needed to improve fuel fabrication and increase burn up with better fuels. They believed that pyrochemical and electrochemical methods of fuel processing would permit abandonment of the messier, more dangerous hydrochemical methods largely in use; but these methods were unproven. Simply put, fuel costs could be lowered for fast reactors if the fuels were produced by electrochemical and other simple, but environmentally dangerous methods.[37]

In this environment of technical challenges and economic uncertainties, Leipunskii decided simultaneously to rejuvenate the experimental reactor program and to build an industrial prototype. The former project involved the reconstruction of the BR-5 into the BR-10 (that is, into a 10,000-kilowatt reactor). Although still relatively small in size, the BR-10 was important because it helped breeder engineers learn how to deal with fuel cycle problems, cracks in the cladding of the fuel rods, the presence of radioisotopes and various oxides in the coolant, and the replacement of components while the reactor was on line. They carried out material studies on structural, fissionable, and absorbing materials that were irradiated in the active zone and the channels of the nickel reflector. Because for a large percentage of the time they operated the reactor with defective fuel rods, the first loop became contaminated with radioactive cesium, tritium, and iodine, which were removed primarily in cold traps. The reactor usually operated at 6,000 kilowatts. Physicists undertook extensive testing of a solid plutonium oxide fuel element at a burn up level of nine percent. After they changed the reactor vessel, they examined twenty pieces of piping from the first loop and were encouraged by the discovery that a thin film of sodium had formed and was fifty percent harder than the metal piping itself, while the metal largely retained its mechanical strength (see Appendix, Table 9).[38]

By the mid-1960s, breeder specialists had accumulated years of operating experience and reams of data with the British DFR, the Soviet BR-5, and the United States EBR-2 and *Enrico Fermi*. The BOR-60 would soon come on line in Dmitrovgrad, the FARRET (forty megawatts) and SEFOR (twenty megawatts) in the United States, and the Rhapsodie (twenty megawatts) in France. Whereas American and British scientists had chosen to work with metallic uranium fuel that had an alloy cladding of molybdenum, zirconium, niobium, and other metals (zircalloy), the Soviets worked with plutonium oxide fuels. The French, American, German and even the Swiss and Belgian scientists had begun designing industrial prototypes that had maximum powers up to 1,000 megawatts but a median of 300 to 500 megawatts and used a liquid sodium coolant at 600° to 650°C. For Soviet physicists, the next step was an experimental reactor that also produced electrical energy. Engineers identified several options—for example, a twenty-five-megawatt unit (the BR-25) or a fifty-megawatt unit (the BN-50)—before settling on the BN-350, part reactor, part desalinator of water. Leipunskii supported this breakneck program without reservation; he hated to spin his wheels. He and his associates did not anticipate that fourteen difficult years would pass before the BN-350 came on line.[39]

A July 1964 visit to Detroit and the subsequent *Enrico Fermi* disaster in 1966 served as an important lesson to Leipunskii. He recognized that he had skipped a necessary stage, prematurely wishing to build an industrial fast reactor before the construction of yet one more prototype. Kazachkovskii visited Detroit in 1965, giving a talk on the BN-350 that excited great interest among the Americans. So the breeder physicists decided to jump-start the BN-350, building at the same time a large experimental reactor, the BOR-60 (sixty megawatts). The facilities at the Physics Engineering Institute were becoming overburdened. Hence, another institute, the Lenin Research Institute of Atomic Reactors in Melekess (later Dmitrovgrad), Ulianovsk Province, was plugged into the effort; Kazachkovskii was chosen to be the director of the new institute, where he remained until becoming director of Obninsk in 1983.

Kazachkovskii didn't relish the idea of going to Melekess, where he would have to abandon science for administration. To make matters worse, construction of the BOR-60 was held up by new officials in Minsredmash, who didn't understand its importance. Kazachkovskii and Leipunskii attended a meeting of the collegium of the ministry, where Petrosiants presented the project; Slavskii postponed any decision, leading Kazachkovskii to lose hope. But a few days later, Slavskii gave approval to go ahead, apparently after a Central Committee meeting and Brezhnev's personal approval. Still, for unclear reasons, the Melekess City Party Committee chairman tried to have Kazachkovskii removed from his post. The next challenge for Kazachkovskii was to mediate hard feelings between supporters of the Moscow (Kurchatov

Institute) and the Ural (Cheliabinsk) type of reactors—between scientific and military designs—and still maintain a creative atmosphere for all his colleagues. The BOR-60 was built in four years, over the objections of officials who were concerned with cost cutting and had tried to halt construction when reactor vessel construction was well underway. It required a letter from the Soviet Union's leading nuclear physicists, including Bochvar, Aleksandrov, and Leipunskii, to end an eighteen-month stoppage.[40]

The BOR-60 achieved critical operation with liquid sodium coolant in December 1969 and has operated more or less continuously ever since. The BOR-60 provided crucial experience and information for the BN-350 and BN-600. The physicists who designed the BOR-60 with its own fuel reprocessing facility had three research tasks in mind: assimilation of sodium technology; far-ranging studies of the physics, hydraulics, transitional and emergency periods of operation, and radiation conditions; and testing of various fuel rods, absorbers, and construction materials to exposure to sodium at high temperature. Physicists irradiated various materials, fuel compositions (especially oxides and, later, carbides), and cladding in one of four horizontal and eight vertical experimental channels in the active zone. Their tests on fuel rods enabled them to estimate the reliability of industrial fuel rods for the BN-350 and the rod's resistance to deformation and brittleness. They developed a closed fuel cycle with chemical processing that did not use water. They built a small "industrial" facility with electrochemical and fluoride technology to reprocess irradiated fuel and developed an automated method of producing fuel rods to ensure worker safety.

The initial blueprints indicated an operating temperature of 800°C, but this temperature would have destroyed the cladding. A sodium temperature of 650°C was also too high, because the factories could not manufacture steel that was sufficiently heat resistant within cost and other constraints. Therefore, the physicists established 550°C as the best temperature, although it meant lower efficiency. Most important, they used the BOR-60 to develop new coiled steam generators with the appropriate heat engineering characteristics so that the reactor could operate as an electric power station. Unfortunately, these tests did not indicate the many kinds of outages that they would later experience on the BN-350 and BN-600.[41]

Although no outage, planned or otherwise, exceeded fifty days, the BOR-60 still indicated the problems and challenges that faced Leipunskii and Kazachkovskii in commercializing breeder power. During start-up, they experienced a series of instabilities as a result of faulty control and safety systems. There were faulty welds; and some of the measurements deviated significantly from planned tolerances. Next, the physicists introduced argon into the piping and tested welds through nonferrous and gamma spectroscopy. They used austenite steel in much of the sodium technology—because of its greater strength under high-radiation conditions. Finally, they filled the reactor with sodium and ran critical tests, reaching a power level of five megawatts with sodium at 350°C in December 1969. The sodium seemed to circulate well, although one of the lines of the first loop experienced a powerful hydraulic shock wave as a result of the oscillation of a check valve in a second line. Repeated operator errors also shook their confidence during start-up. In March 1970, the power was raised to twenty megawatts, with the sodium temperature at 400°C; and by August, the power level had reached forty-seven megawatts.[42]

Physicists also used experiments on the BOR-60 to allay concerns about the safety of breeder reactors generally. The stability of fuel rods and personnel safety during repairs were the primary concerns. During operation of the reactor, which reached a maximum burn up of 10.7 percent, the cladding of some fuel rods, which reached a maximum temperature of 700°C, failed and radioactive isotopes including xenon and krypton were released.[43] No more than one percent of the fuel rods actually failed, but any failure of this type was a significant problem because the high radioactivity and chemical activity of the sodium coolant might be hazardous to personnel carrying out maintenance and repairs. So the physicists designed a safety sleeve weighing several tons to ensure hermeticization during repairs. Yet even during minor repairs, a large number of the personnel were exposed to radioactivity. For most repairs, much of the dose occurred, not surprisingly, to the hands rather than the body. Not more than two to three percent of personnel received more than 1.5 to 5 ber. The average dose was 0.3 to 0.5 ber per year. For replacement of cables, armatures, and other work in the first loop, however, the collective dose on personnel was 100 to 500 ber. The physicists therefore concluded that in some cases such work could be carried out only after draining or cleaning the coolant, and in others, only after deactivation. They established that in many cases cooling the sodium to its solid form enabled them to remove entire components without difficulty and that repairs could be conducted safely on breeder reactors even when the coolant was tainted by radioactivity or products of corrosion.[44]

THE SHEVCHENKO BREEDER REACTOR: TECHNOLOGICAL AND URBAN MOMENTUM

Many of the breeder physicists were convinced that it was time to turn to an industrial prototype, and 1,000 megawatts seemed like a good round number. Others believed that it was too risky to build such a massive plant right away. If things turned out badly and they had to shut it down, as they did the BR-2, they would lose time, money, clout, and momentum. In any event, simultaneously with the BOR-60, they set out to build the BN-350, with 1,000 megawatts thermal power. To minimize risks, they decided to limit the physical parameters to those which had been mastered on the BR-5 (temperatures up to 500°C and heat removal density up to 500 kilowatts per liter), to use similar fuel rods, and to test all components carefully on physical stands. Slavskii proposed that the BN-350 be built on the Mangyshlak peninsula, where both electricity and desalination demands existed.[45] Another reason for the selection of this Caspian Sea site, in addition to testing breeder and desalinization technology in a sparsely populated area, was the presence of extensive oil reserves.

Shevchenko itself was an empty expanse of parched land before it became a town. In 1961, geologists discovered huge oil deposits on the Mangyshlak peninsula; they referred to the area as "the peninsula of treasures." Economic planners quickly authorized the construction of the New Uzen and Zhentybai petrochemical factories. The Caspian Mining Chemical Combine was created to mine and process uranium ore. (In the 1990s, the Combine converted some of its military activities to toothpaste manufacture based on local phosphorus mining.) They brought as much water in tankers across the Caspian from the Caucasus mountains as they could. Further development was limited by the absence of water, and only the Caspian could provide more. Diesel desalinators produced 50,000 cubic meters an hour, enough for 80,000 inhabitants and industry. The town fathers built gardens, boulevards, and a 550-acre park, but they could go no further without more water. That's where the BN-350 came in.[46]

Shevchenko, now with more than 150,000 inhabitants, is no longer sparsely populated, and the water finds use not only in the oil industry but also in a Las Vegas-like array of water works. Shevchenko's streets are lined with trees and flowers, and fountains flow twenty-four hours a day. Like Las Vegas, this is an artificial city built on a desert, requiring significant investment to make the environment hospitable to human habitation. Each step in construction and influx in population required more investment and greater interdependencies of man, machine, and nature. Each step led to increased water use and environmental degradation.

To many persons, Shevchenko looked like a mirage. There were sand and camels and the endless sameness of the Mangyshlak steppe, then suddenly fountains, lawns, lights, avenues, and homes. In the early 1970s, Shevchenko grew rapidly, like Los Angeles, in this case facilitated not by canals built with billions of federal dollars bringing water from California's central valley, but by Caspian Sea water, desalinated by the BN-350 liquid metal fast breeder reactor. Completion of the reactor announced "the second stage of atomic energetics," according to Soviet popularizers of the station. Everything else had been "merely a prelude." How quickly physicists had raced from the Physics Engineering Institute to the Mangyshlak peninsula. Dmitrii Sergeievich Iurchenko, the station's first director, proudly explained to anyone who would listen about fuel loading every two months, the accumulation of plutonium in the active zone, the shipping of the fuel rods to separate the plutonium from other isotopes for other "peaceful uses," and the production of 120,000 tons of fresh water daily from the Caspian for the petrochemical industry and the inhabitants of Shevchenko. They produced water at levels per inhabitant that rivaled those of Kiev, Leningrad, and Moscow.[47] Of course, this too was a mirage: The bulk of the water went to the petrochemical industry, not to the consumer.

The desalination of water became a big business in the 1960s—and it was big science, too. In October 1965, in Washington, DC, scientists gathered at the first international symposium on the desalination of water. Soviet scientists, who along with their colleagues examined economical, technical, and heat engineering questions related to desalination, presented twenty-one papers on the subject. Scientists agreed there were two ways to go about the business: evaporation and repeated boiling. Nuclear reactors were suited to both tasks. The question was how best to design a facility to produce electricity and distillate simultaneously. Of course, it is difficult to choose between two uses, electricity and water, and hence to determine true costs. On the basis of analysis of the performance of the Beloiarsk,

Novovoronezh, and planned Shevchenko facilities, physicists were convinced that a dual-purpose breeder reactor was more economical than one producing only electricity. The physicists also recommended the small, portable ARBUS reactor, developed in Melekess, for simultaneous production of electrical energy and distillate. In theory, a 70-megawatt ARBUS could produce 1,500 kilowatts of electricity and 505 tons per hour of distillate at only 42 kopeks per ton.

Because the ARBUS was designed for more limited uses in the far north, physicists decided instead to build a breeder of intermediate size. Two problems faced them: how to insure safe and efficient heat exchange and how to limit corrosion of the desalinating apparatus. They believed they had already solved both problems, the latter through extensive testing of stainless steels of various sorts on site in the Caspian Sea. Beginning in October 1963, they tested a four-stage apparatus with a capacity of 200 tons per hour. They tested another apparatus near Baku, Azerbaidzhan, with a capacity of fifty metric tons per hour. They were set for the push toward the BN-350 and the production of 120,000 tons per day of distilled water. This water, although manufactured with nuclear power, was no different from any other drinking water. The result would be 450 to 500 liters per person per day, an amount about which inhabitants of many European cities can only dream. The reactor itself was nothing unusual to the residents of Shevchenko; they saw it from their apartments across the flat landscape. The cost of desalinated water would be about $1.34 to $3.20 per 1,000 gallons U.S. equivalent, not cheap by any stretch but better than thirst.[48]

The physicists proclaimed BN-350 a success, although continued reliance on mixed oxide fuels and a series of mishaps, including a serious sodium fire, called that evaluation into question. In any event, they doggedly pursued operation of the BN-350, never allowing these difficulties to interfere. Even though the fuel elements occasionally deformed under conditions of high temperature and neutron flux, and did not produce breeding coefficients that might be achieved with future carbide, nitride, and carbide-nitride or metallic fuels, they decided to stay with uranium oxide fuels for the initial loading of the BN-350. Later they would switch to a mixed fuel of uranium oxide and fifteen to twenty percent plutonium oxide. Using only uranium oxide enabled them to avoid the danger of fouling unique untested equipment with plutonium in the event of the appearance of defects in the new fuel rods; plutonium contamination would make any repair work much more dangerous. They also didn't wish to lose time waiting for an industrial-scale plutonium fuel fabrication facility to be built. Industrial production of the highly toxic fuel required at the very least the construction of novel robotic facilities to ensure worker safety.[49]

Before the BN-600 was designed, breeders were based on maximum utilization of standard industrial (nonnuclear) design and manufacturing practices. Components were isolated from one another so that the various component industries could design and build components from performance specifications without space limitations. Designers and construction trusts used more concrete and less steel in building construction than was, for example, United States practice. American physicists who visited the BN-350 said plant arrangement was similar to conventional USSR fossil-fueled plants. The reactor building was not airtight; it was just like any other mill building. Reliance for containment therefore fell on the fuel elements, reactor vessel and plug, secondary containment, and biological shielding.[50] Similarly, they located power plants in any location that had high load demands and enough water to cool the reactor. Town sites were developed conveniently for personal access, including housing for plant workers. Beloiarsk had 13,000 persons within three kilometers of the BN-600; Melekess has more than 200,000 inhabitants within five kilometers of the BOR-60 and VK-50; Shevchenko had almost one-quarter of a million people within six kilometers of the BN-350.[51]

The most crucial issues for the BN-350 concerned the selection of sodium pumps and heat exchangers. As part of what they considered a conservative approach, they designed the BN-350 with six parallel and independent loops for heat exchange; five were always in operation and one was held in reserve so that they could carry out repairs at any time without lowering the reactor's power. Unlike the RBMK design, which allowed refueling during operation, the BN-350, like all breeders, had to be shut down during refueling. In heat exchangers, which are multitudinous modular units of small-dimension pipes, the sodium in the first loop is cooled by the sodium in the second loop. The sodium in the second loop, the heat exchange loop, heats water into steam in the steam generators of the third loop. The sodium in the first loop enters the heat exchanger at one end at 500°C, and exits the other end at 300°C. Nonradioactive sodium in the second loop enters the heat exchanger at 273°C, and exits at 453°C. The heated sodium in the second loop powers steam generators capable of producing 276 tons of super-heated (435°C), high pressure steam per hour.

The pumps for the BN-350 were based on those designed for the BR-5. In the first loop, they circulate 3,220 cubic meters of sodium per hour and have extensive biological shielding; in the second loop, they circulate 3,850 cubic meters per hour and have no biological shielding. The Obninsk physicists designed intermediate heat exchangers, which they believed would be sufficiently reliable to preclude the need for biological shielding. Each heat exchanger consisted of three independent bundles of well over 300 U-shaped tubes with a diameter of twenty-eight millimeters (approximately 1.125 inches) and wall thickness of two millimeters through which the sodium of the second loop circulated. To prepare for possible accidents that unfortunately turned into realities, the physicists conducted a series of experiments on sodium-water interaction during "rupture" of the heat transfer tubes. They concluded that rupture of one pipe would not lead to catastrophic rupture of other tubes and pipes and a dreaded sodium fire.[52]

The complexity of the components and fuel of the BN-350 slowed the completion of construction through 1971; and once construction was complete, the hookup of various auxiliary systems added additional time, expense, and worry. These systems included a sodium-potassium cooling system for the cold traps of the first and second loops, which cleansed the sodium coolant of fission products and oxidants; a cooling system for "freezing" seals of the primary circuit plugs; electrical sodium-heating systems, and a fire safety system. In the fall of 1972, they loaded approximately 700 cubic meters of sodium into the reactor. Then they subjected the steam generators to stress to check their reliability and verified the integrity of what seemed to be dozens of kilometers of sodium circuits (the circuits had a volume of nearly 1,000 cubic meters). Welds had to be solid, seals tight. Then the circuits were evacuated, heated and dried, and filled with nitrogen to prevent the sodium from igniting spontaneously as it came in contact with oxygen in the air during loading. Coolant loading was followed by hydraulic and vibration research, including operating the pumps both at low speed and at rated speed (1,000 revolutions per minute).

Preparation of the sodium coolant itself had not been perfected; it took six months and required still more technical development. The scientists arranged for production of the coolant at the nearby Chechikskii Factory. It was shipped in one-cubic meter barrels in railway cars covered by a layer of argon. There were six electric "ovens" that enabled them to heat six containers simultaneously in preparation for loading the reactor sodium circuits. But trace impurities still remained, until the scientists finally figured out how to filter the sodium further.[53]

In May 1973, the power of the BN-350 reached six percent, a level enabling the physicists to check instrumentation, measure radiation fields, and verify coolant natural circulation. Steam generation reached approximately 100 tons per hour, and approximately 650 tons per hour of distillate for Shevchenko were produced. When, on July 16, power reached twenty percent and steam production increased to 300 tons per hour, the operators were able to switch one of the turbogenerators into the local electrical grid. By the end of 1973, the plant had operated for about six weeks at twenty to thirty percent power levels. They did not observe any leakage of fuel into the coolant; they had redesigned the cladding and increased fuel rod diameter. At 720 megawatts power, the activity of ^{24}Na, ^{133}Xe, and other products of fission remained within established limits. Cold traps operated as intended to ensure purity of the coolant. Desalination equipment also performed admirably. Start-up, in other words, was not a defined moment of achievement of planned parameters but an extended period of complex work and research leading to production of steam.[54] Leipunskii died before the BN-350 came on line. Party activists referred to the BN-350 as "a new victory," the "coming on experimental-industrial line of the largest fast reactors in the world," and a "confirmation of the directives of the Communist Party."

On the ten-year anniversary of its operation, the physicists considered the Shevchenko facility proof of the promise of industrial-scale liquid metal sodium breeder reactors. They concluded that it operated "in correspondence with norms and laws which have been established for the work of atomic electrical stations in our country" and called for the utilization of large power breeders in the near future as an integral part of the country's energy future.[55] They could move ahead because many of the personnel who ran the Soviet nuclear program were no longer the Kurchatov conscripts or their students. The chief engineer for the BN-350, A. E. Timofeev, and the director of the Mangyshlak Energy Factory, D. S. Iurchenko, both worked in the Institute of Atomic Energy. Engineer V. V. Bubanov, a native Siberian, graduated from Tomsk Polytechnical Institute, and A. Z. Zakirinov, a graduate of Kazakh State University physics department, was deputy shift director. The establishment scientists had every expectation that these young men would either move on to fill other new facilities or themselves train dozens of new specialists for nuclear work.[56]

Owing to the relatively low pressure in the first sodium loop, in 1978 personnel carried out what they considered a rather "bold" experiment while the reactor was operating at full power. They closed one of the loops, "froze" the sodium in it, and replaced a part of a pump that had seized.[57] The mindset of considering a nuclear reactor a simple machine on which one could conduct experiments may have been bold; but, in fact, the process was risky because it involved checking out components while the reactor was in operation. This mindset was a precursor to the Chernobyl accident.

In reality, the operation of the BN-350 had been anything but simple. The nuclear establishment downplayed the extensive problems with sodium pumps and steam generators and the danger attending several serious sodium fires. In 1978, there were four such unplanned shutdowns; in 1979, there were two; in 1980, only one; and in 1981 and 1982, there was none. The operating personnel acknowledged several leaks in steam generators, which allowed water to enter the sodium loop; between ten and thirty kilograms of sodium spilled out between October 1973 and February 1975, most of which remained "local." By acknowledging that there also had been "several smaller leakages of nonradioactive sodium that did not lead to fires," they admitted to a more serious accident later described in detail in a report to the International Atomic Energy Agency in Vienna, Austria. This incident destroyed steam generators, caused an explosion, and started a fire that burned for two hours.[58] But, in the opinion of Kazachkovskii, "The factor of huge scale did not present any unexpected events, unless one considers the unpleasantness with the steam generators. At first, they frequently broke down. The repair of the steam generators was a lengthy and time-consuming process, so the reserve loop really did the job. Because of the insufficient reliability of the steam generators, it was even necessary to limit the power of the reactor to seventy-five percent of its planned capacity."[59]

INDUSTRIAL BREEDERS

Sodium fire or no, all of the prerequisites were in place for industrial breeder reactors. Devoted leadership with unquestioned authority had the ear of policy makers in industrial ministries connected with energy production and military applications. A modern industry based on self-augmenting technologies was in place. The few accidents involving sodium and plutonium technology were not too catastrophic. An impending shortage of uranium ore seemed more crucial than a few missteps. Nuclear engineers were dismayed by growing opposition to nuclear power in the West and specifically by the Three Mile Island disaster in the United States in 1981, for they believed it stained their reputations as well. But they remained confident of the efficacy and safety of their designs and gratified that the government would not permit public disaffection with nuclear power.

Breeder physicists decided that in order "not to waste time," they would not await the results of long-term operation of the BN-350 to determine the next stage of development; instead, they would move simultaneously to design a reactor with more advanced heat parameters—"more appropriate, we hoped, for serial industrial utilization," Kazachkovskii said. This reactor, the BN-600, was built at Beloiarsk, the birthplace of the industrial RBMK. Speedy construction was aided by the fact that the BN-600 was built on the Beloiarsk site rather than in some deserted area, because construction workers, equipment, and operating personnel were already in place. It was by now common for economic planners and Party officials to seek out huge projects to keep workers in massive construction organizations busy. In the case of the BN-600, the trusts were Uralenergostroi, Tsentroenergomontazh, Elektrouralmontazh, and Uralenergoproisoliatsiia. They integrated these trusts in the so-called workers' relay. In reality, the workers' relay was little more than constant supervision by the Party's minions of production of advanced components, and they involved several scientific research institutes, design bureaus, and factories. Party officials intended the relays to produce special equipment in a timely fashion. They required the managers, engineers, and workers of the massive trusts to embrace "socialist obligations" in every relay race and, in this case, to bring the BN-600 reactor on line on the eve of Lenin's one hundred and tenth birthday anniversary in April 1980.

The decision to build the BN-600 at Beloiarsk was not made casually. First, the site in the Ural Mountains region remained far from population centers; in the case of an accident, which they would never admit was a motivating concern, fewer persons would be exposed to radiation. Second, the Ural region provided only eleven percent of its own energy needs, so nuclear power was welcome. Third, the Sverdlovsk region had significant atomic machine building capacity. Fourth, the Party apparatus in the Sverdlovsk region had been involved at all levels—regional, city, and local—to ensure that loyal and hardworking communists were involved in that industry. Its propaganda effort extended to the Beloiarsk site, which had fifteen Party groups and twelve Party cells. This organization created a "school of builders and operators of atomic power stations." Hundreds and then thousands of workers were involved in "workers' relays," first to pour concrete, and then to build special equipment. Komsomol shock workers then joined the project.[60]

When Kazachkovskii became director at Obninsk, he worried about the slow progress made on the BN-600. He met with Boris Yeltsin, who at that time was the first secretary of the Sverdlovsk regional Party committee, to explain the importance of the problem and the need for help. Yeltsin immediately agreed, creating a special operating group in the Party committee to coordinate efforts of Sverdlovsk construction and industrial organizations; and Yeltsin himself periodically looked into things. Just as scientists, indeed workers everywhere throughout the country, were called in to help with the harvest on farms, Yeltsin now ordered local collective farmers to the BN-600 site to help in construction.

At 600 megawatts electric (1,470 megawatts thermal), the BN-600 would be the largest breeder reactor in the world. In both the BN-350 and BN-600, the physicists employed enriched uranium, not plutonium fuel. They chose uranium because the technology of uranium fuel elements was fully developed. Furthermore, if an accident occurred, it would be easier to deal with uranium than plutonium fuel rods in a cleanup. A number of technical improvements were also made: burn up was raised from five to ten percent, the sodium temperature raised from 500° to 550°C; the steam pressure, from 50 to 130 atmospheres. Accordingly, reactor efficiency grew from thirty-five to forty-two percent; and the time between refuelings increased from two to five months.[61]

After visiting several breeder sites, United States physicists in 1970 characterized the Soviet program as "aggressive" both in the simultaneous construction of large-scale units of different designs and the philosophy that any deficiencies in design, fabrication, and technology would be "amenable to correction." The Soviets believed that accidents or failures would be highly unlikely. For example, not only did they omit steel containment buildings, the Soviets also did not build meltdown structures below the core, because a total loss of coolant, which would result in a molten core, was not considered credible.[62]

With the BN-600, physicists moved away from conventional industrial practice to components and designs specific to breeder technology. This shift required more design effort and manufacturing skill, and demonstrated a national commitment to liquid metal fast breeder reactors (LMFBRs) in the willingness to pay for major retooling to fabricate fast reactor components on a commercial scale. The BN-600 entered the construction phase at the end of 1968, with a workforce of 450 men pouring 60,000 cubic meters of concrete. Because of uncertainties regarding the component delivery dates, officials initially estimated completion between mid-1973 and mid-1975. The BN-600 was sited next to two channel-type boiling-water reactors, one at 100 megawatts electric, the other at 200 megawatts electric. Cooling for all three units was provided by a man-made lake of ten square kilometers, which was also used for recreational purposes.[63]

The lengthy start-up operation for the BN-600 commenced in December 1978. They started loading and purification of sodium in March 1979, electrically heating the first and second loops and irrigating the pipes and equipment with water and acid. They brought in 1,800 tons of sodium in special railway tankers of 25 cubic meters capacity fitted with an electrical heating system to bring the temperature of the sodium to 240°C; larger container size and preheating made transport and loading much easier than it had been for the BN-350. The reactor vessel itself was gas heated at a rate of 10° to 15°C per day over roughly two weeks, reaching a temperature of 180° to 230°C to avoid thermal shock when liquid sodium was loaded in December 1979. During this time, the turbogenerators were also tested and primed. Assembly, testing, and heating of the steam generators took eight months.

The BN-600 was a complex way to boil water. It had three modular steam generators with a capacity of 660 tons per hour at 140 kilograms per cubic meter pressure and 505°C, plus three turbogenerators each rated at 220 megawatts. Each steam generator had twenty-four modular heat exchangers, each of which had eight sections. Once again, this modular design made the reactor safer in the event of a water leak into sodium, for a section could be closed off without affecting reactor operation. The primary coolant circulated through three parallel loops, each equipped with two heat exchangers and a submerged centrifugal circulating pump. The reactor core consisted of 370 fuel subassemblies with uranium oxide fuel and 27 control rods: 2 automatic, 19 for temperature and power compensation, and 6 safety rods. In December 1979, the physicists commenced loading the fuel elements. On February 26, 1980, after 215 elements of low enrichment and 44 elements of high enrichment had been installed, the reactor reached criticality. On April 2, the power of the reactor raised to 0.5 percent of nominal. Four days later, when it was clear that all systems functioned properly, they raised power to the five percent level, and two days later to thirty percent, when the steam in the steam generators reached 430°C. For the next three months, with short periods of downtime, the engineers cautiously tested equipment and took measurements of basic parameters, reaching eighty percent power in September with sodium temperatures in the range of 520° to 570°C. A final planned shutdown, during which they replaced a few fuel rods and repaired a turbogenerator, occurred in late fall in preparation for a lengthy operational period commencing with the winter of 1980–1981. Late in 1981, the reactor achieved planned power of 600 megawatts and produced superheated steam at 490°C.

Personnel seemed to be prepared for all eventualities because they had been trained on the BOR-60. Brezhnev himself was pleased with their work. He greeted them with these words: "This outstanding labor victory, achieved on the eve of the one hundred and tenth anniversary of Lenin's birth, opens yet another page in the history of the nation's atomic energetics, and indicates that our socialist motherland by all rights occupies leading scientific and technical positions in the utilization of the energy of the peaceful atom for the benefit of mankind. The creation of electric power stations with breeder reactors, which will permit us most rationally to utilize nuclear fuel, is a new great step in the furthest assimilation of the fuel-energy potential of the country, and signifies a radical transformation in energetics."[64]

On the eve of the start-up of the BN-600, Kazachkovskii was in the machine hall of the station. Its clean metal walls gleamed. He felt proud of their achievements. The head of the construction operation, however, worried about a meltdown like that at *Enrico Fermi* and asked Kazachkovskii if the thing would operate as planned. But Kazachkovskii was confident that their work would not be forsaken.[65] Although no "Detroit" occurred, nor a "Shevchenko" sodium fire, the steam generators failed four times in the first year. Unlike similar events in the BN-350, these failures did not significantly affect power levels. And despite the generator failures, operating personnel had been exposed to levels of radioactivity that were 10 to 100 times lower than those established for normal nuclear power stations.[66]

If one could jump to RBMK reactors of 2,000 megawatts without a second thought, why not to the BN-1600 with two 800-megawatt turbogenerators. They pursued the idea of a BN-1600, using standard industrial technologies to produce equipment, components, sodium, and fuel rods, which would serve as the foundation for serial deployment of breeders. Physicists settled on an integral design essentially similar to the BN-600 and with virtually the same heat characteristics. The integral layout made it possible to obtain a more compact design of the first circuit, which was reliable with respect to cooling the active zone and localizing radioactivity. But a whole range of technical problems arose, and so "as not to break the forward pace of ongoing work in all links (manufacture of equipment, construction)," in an abrupt shift they decided to bring into production a series of BN-800 reactors first. The BN-800 was a modification of the BN-600 and required very little new equipment in its inevitable transformation into a BN-1600 (see Appendix, Table 10).

Scientists and journalists strove to demonstrate that the massive nuclear power stations engendered feelings of peace, quiet, and oneness with nature. A tour of any reactor facility revealed that the engines worked without noise; there was no need to raise one's voice, even as the power of nuclear boilers reached 600,000 kilowatts or more power. The director of the Beloiarsk station, V. A. Malyshev, recognized the great challenges placed on the engineers, builders, and workers under his watch in bringing a liquid metal fast breeder reactor on line. But he was confident of their success as they loaded 800 tons of sodium into the reactor vessel and another 900 tons into the three loops of the second loop, sodium that required careful handling, goggles, thick plastic gloves, and safety clothes, lest the metal come in contact with human skin, oxygen or, worse still, water. The real reason for the delay in bringing the industrial breeder on line was the need to create reliable sodium technology.[67] But this technology, too, plastic gloves and all, also fit perfectly with Soviet views of nature and the reactor in the garden.

Leading officials in the Party and the scientific establishment began to object to the pace and scope of breeder deployment. Some of them worried about the cost of moving ahead on any project until each step had been completed. Yet, if the breeder physicists waited for the successful operation of the BN-350 before embarking on the BN-600, and on the BN-600 before attacking the BN-800, it might be years before they achieved the operating experience required to deploy breeders with six- to eight-year doubling capacity. Worse, the engineers and experimentalists would lose incentive and focus, perhaps transferring to more exciting projects. Leipunskii seldom permitted these objections and worries to deflect his energy. He advocated design and construction of the BN-600 from 1967 onward.

When opposition to the BN-600 was revealed, Academy president Anatolii Aleksandrov, Minenergo officials, and N. A. Dollezhal provided support crucial to the decision to expand the Beloiarsk site to include another breeder, a decision about which Leipunskii only later admitted second thoughts. Aleksandrov had been the originator of unrealistically low doubling times. His goal was to promote the technology, but his estimate was based on fuel burn up and reactor temperature parameters that breeder specialists accepted. Aleksandrov's support and the successful operation of the BN-600 in fact gave new impetus to breeder development among leading Party officials. At a plenary session of the Central Committee of the Communist Party in July 1981, Party officials endorsed the physicists' plans for a Soviet nuclear future. Politburo member A. P. Kirilenko gave the major address, announcing that during the eleventh five year plan, twenty-five gigawatts of nuclear capacity would be added, three times more than in the preceding five year plan. When the BN-600, the third block at Beloiarsk, came on line in April 1980, seven years after Leipunskii's death, it seemed to prove that Leipunskii had been correct all along. It has since operated at an average of seventy-five percent of capacity. The operators believe that the primary reactor components (core, pumps, heat exchangers, control and safety rod mechanisms, reactor refueling systems) work as designed. They estimate electricity costs at twenty percent lower than that from fossil fuel plants in the region. The scientists' optimistic view of the potential of breeders was shared among specialists in other countries.[68]

Despite the great inertia of science policy making in the Brezhnev era, ever more grandiose projects issued forth because institute personnel had become adept at harnessing a series of institutes to huge construction projects and thereby linking the livelihoods of thousands of researchers and their families to big science. The projects, in turn, seemed to acquire lives of their own, for no official wanted to derail one aspect of a project for fear the other parts would come unraveled. So it should come as no surprise that breeder physicists managed to jump-start the construction of the design and construction of an 800-megawatt reactor even as operation of the BN-350 and BN-600 remained the source of never ending problems.

They initially intended to build a network of 1,600-megawatt plutonium factories as the final stage of breeder development, each powering two mammoth 800-megawatt turbogenerators that they intended to produce in serial form. They permitted the tedious pace of work on the BN-350 and BN-600 to convince them instead to build a fourth block at Beloiarsk at 800 megawatts, the BN-800. For this breeder, which they hoped to have on line by the early 1990s, they recognized the need to develop more extensive reactor safety systems, including emergency core cooling, and to build more expensive containment to localize radioactive products in case of a hypothetical radioactive leak or meltdown. Swelling, creep, and plasticity of structural steels under high neutron fluxes, corrosion of fuel element claddings at high burn up, and other problems also remained to be investigated. The construction on two BN-800s had just begun in the Urals when the Chernobyl disaster put on hold all further work. This may have been a blessing for the rest of us, because the Obninsk scientists had developed several fascinating, but untested alternative breeder designs that also were nipped in the bud—for example, a "simple" reactor without fuel rods in which the sodium flowed through a liquid active zone of a plutonium-iron alloy.[69]

The breeder specialists intended to site three BN-800 reactors on the site of the Maiak chemical nuclear fuel facility at Cheliabinsk to take advantage of the plutonium produced on site and one at Beloiarsk. But all work was suspended in the 1990s because of lack of funding. Despite the positive conclusion of several independent expert commissions, the deputies and residents of Sverdlovsk region refused to allow resumption of construction on the Beloiarsk BN-800. The government, however, has refused to listen to the popular will. The "Key Directions of Power Engineering Policy in Russia through 2010" includes the four BN-800 reactors. Viktor Murogov, the director of Physics Engineering Institute in the early 1990s, explained that the BN-800 is crucial for its role in closing the fuel cycle, primarily by providing a market for plutonium from the N300 fuel fabrication facility, under construction at Maiak. But the N300 was frozen when the facility was only fifty percent complete. He also proposed the use of plutonium from nuclear weapons in the BN-600 in newly designed fuel rods and the design of a modified version, the BN-600M, which he described as safer and cheaper to operate than a light water reactor, even though capital costs of sodium technology made a kilowatt of electricity fifty percent higher than in a VVER.[70]

Large-scale technologies do not appear out of the ether. A large array of institutes and their personnel contributed to the breeder. Other institutes that required Kazachkovskii's attention included the Scientific Research Institute of Atomic Reactors in Dmitrovgrad; the Gorky (now Nizhnii Novgorod) Design Bureau of Machine Building, which provided much of the early one-of-a-kind equipment for the breeder program; the Special Design Bureau Gidropress in Podolsk, which produced steam generators for the breeders; the All-Union Scientific Research Institute of Inorganic Materials, whose personnel worked closely with Obninsk physicists on fuel rods; and the Leningrad Design Institute, which was the main engineering firm for this and other big technology projects. Soviet physicists did not intend to stop with liquid metal fast breeder reactors. They held as a medium-term objective the N_2O_4-dissociated reactor being developed in Minsk in the Institute of Nuclear Physics, the BRIG-50 (a 1,000-megawatts electric prototype, later rescaled to 300-megawatts electric);[71] as long-range objectives, a helium-cooled fast breeder reactor with a low doubling time of five to six years; and a liquid lead-bismuth or lead-cooled reactor being developed under Kurchatov Institute leadership. All of these programs and institutes required resources. All of them became adept at initiating new projects. But these models were opposed by liquid metal specialists, not because the projects diverted resources, but because, in their opinion, the designs had significant technological shortfalls and had no place in the general energy plan.

Safety precautions could not prevent disaster, as the development of many large-scale technologies has frequently proved. In some cases, exogenous factors not initially included in calculations—for example, the production of hydrocarbons in the ubiquitous internal combustion engines—fall outside safety considerations. In other cases, engineers and scientists fail to take into account issues that clearly are crucial—for example, the handling and storage of radioactive waste—because cost or political considerations divert their attention. This was true for the new physical apparatus designed in Obninsk. In the early years of accelerator technology, the physicists were so devoted to fine-tuning the new alpha particle accelerator that a number of them received extremely high doses of X-rays and later developed sarcomas. Another incident involved a square meter pond of mercury that was being used as an early breeder coolant; mercury fumes sickened a handful of specialists. Accidents and leaks such as these occurred with greater frequency over the next three decades.[72] Then there were the frequent sodium fires. If the meltdown at Chernobyl had not occurred, a massive sodium fire at Beloiarsk might have triggered public awareness.

Breeders were Soviet big science and technology par excellence. Despite the technical challenges, and seemingly despite the cost, Leipunskii and his colleagues at the Physics Engineering Institute created a complex technology—from experimental devices to reactors whose power measured in the thousands of megawatts—whose genesis required the establishment of a half-dozen institutes employing tens of thousands of specialists and the development of other complex technologies to manufacture fuel and coolant and to transfer heat from the reactor active zone to steam generators.

In the early stages of breeder development, before they had encountered sodium fires and steam generator failures in industrial prototypes, Soviet physicists and journalists who publicized their efforts spoke of breeder reactors as the Phoenix. The phoenix, a glorious bird larger than an eagle and with magnificent plumage, had a life span of at least 500 years. As it approached the end of its life, the phoenix built a nest, set it on fire, and was consumed in the flames. Like one breeder reactor producing fuel for another, from the fire a new phoenix sprang forth. The metaphor of the phoenix unfortunately suggested another feature of the Soviet breeder program—only one phoenix lived at a time. For all the achievements of the Soviet program, financial, political, but in particular technical challenges prevented physicists from powering more than one breeder with the plutonium from another.

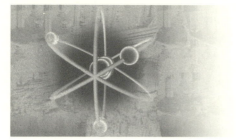

3

Nuclear Concrete

Cement is a mighty binding material. With cement we're going to have a great building-up of the republic. We are cement, Comrades: the working class. Let us keep that in mind. We've played the fool long enough; now we've got to start real work.
— From Fyodor Gladkov's *Cement*

The workers of the South Ural Construction Trust poured only 3,000 cubic meters of concrete in 1954. In 1958, they poured 82,000 cubic meters of the stuff, enough to fill a soccer stadium to a depth of fourteen meters. They used the concrete largely for the construction of plutonium production and experimental reactors for the military establishment, their primary customer. In the trust's first days during the onset of the cold war, the Kremlin exerted direct control over concrete-pouring activities, with Secret Police Chief Lavrenty Beria constantly telephoning General Iakov Rapoport, the first head of the trust, with not too subtle inquiries to move things along more quickly. No one voluntarily came within five meters of Rapoport when he toured the cement factory looking for ways to stretch production even further. Concrete had assumed great cultural significance in the Soviet Union, and they seemed never to be able to produce enough for hydropower stations, canals, apartment buildings, and reactors, even when they employed tens of thousands of soldiers, an equal number of German prisoners of war, and political prisoners requisitioned from the Stalinist Gulag. Of course, prisoners lacked any incentive to achieve higher productivity, for any success would lead immediately to increased norms. Many of them dropped dead on the job; their meager rations and ragged clothing allowing them to waste away in the frigid air. So the secret police resolved to add 100 grams of vodka to their daily ration. Many still died, but at least they died tipsy.

Concrete represented more than its components of mortar, sand, binders, water, and various additives. And the huge construction trusts amounted to more than the thousands of workers who operated excavation, pouring, and pumping machinery and the managers who planned and oversaw each operation. The South Ural Construction Trust, Volgodonskenergostroi, Sibakademstroi, and dozens of other organizations (whose tongue-twisting names grew out of bits and pieces of geographical, machinery, and construction words) were given responsibility for one task and then others, growing rapidly in terms of numbers of employees, scope of activity, quantity of earth moved, meters of scaffolding and forms erected, and tons of concrete poured. The employees of these geoengineering trusts and their families had to be housed and fed, their children schooled, their free time filled with distractions, their illnesses treated. So entire towns were established not far from construction sites.

In theory, the workers' state, as sole employer and owner of all property, gave precedence to the comfort and safety of the worker. In practice, plan fulfillment, often expressed in gross output figures, took precedence; and in virtually every town, the housing, shopping, educational, and other needs of the citizen, what the Soviets called *sotskulthyt* (referring to the social, cultural, and living conditions) lagged far behind the production targets for the burgeoning trusts. Workers were disgusted by the situation. No sooner were apartments finished than they began to crumble; as many as half of the children of trust workers waited for places in schools; roads and sidewalks remained unfinished; mud and garbage filled the neighborhoods. Absenteeism grew; labor productivity fell; worker turnover plagued most trusts. In the Stalin period, the Party identified those responsible for this series of problems and meted out severe punishment. Under Khrushchev and Brezhnev, the guilty often escaped with admonishment or reassignment. But the unwieldy trusts chugged on, providing the state with poorly finished construction projects, the workers with employment—and occasionally *sotskulthyt*.

For the Soviet Union, the concrete produced for nuclear power engineering projects was no different from the concrete used in apartment buildings, in dams and canals, in oil and gas pipelines. If the South Ural Construction Trust managed to build plutonium production reactors in a relatively short time, then a specially created organization, Atommash, ought to be able to produce power-generating reactors in serial fashion. Party leaders, economic planners, and nuclear engineers saw the task of reactor construction as similar to a construction task in any sector of the economy. They believed that lessons learned in one area could easily be applied in another. They sought to make nuclear power economically competitive by adopting commonplace construction techniques and materials. Having met with some success in cutting costs, meeting plan targets, and limiting opportunity for errors in the field through standardization in other areas of construction, they pursued similar ends in the nuclear power industry. They shared the conviction of engineers in other countries that nuclear power would be competitive only if they could turn from one-of-a-kind reactor design and construction to standardized models built largely from ordinary components, forms, and techniques. Given Stalinist tech-

nological style, there were few impediments to leaping from prototypes to serial production, and to treating a complex technology (1,000-megawatt pressurized-water
reactors) as the sum of its standard parts (piping, conduit, prefabricated concrete
forms, uranium fuel rods), to be produced at the Atommash factory on the Volga
River. And like any other sector of the Soviet economy, "nuclear concrete" became
huge construction trusts of dissatisfied workers, standardized techniques, and stag-
geringly large gross output figures, but very little to show in terms of quality control. Nuclear concrete ultimately is a story of devastating technological and economic failure, a story lost only in the radioactive cloud of Chernobyl.

CONCRETE: FOOD FOR SOVIET GODS

From the late 1920s onward, Soviet leaders assembled unskilled workers and peasants into malleable, but only somewhat efficient labor crews to form huge construction organizations. The organizations evolved into the mega-construction trusts
of the Brezhnev era that moved through the vast Soviet landscape looking to apply
the technology of prefabricated concrete forms on a truly large scale and leaving
only dull gray structures and scarred land in their wake.

From the earliest projects, Soviet leaders learned how large-scale technologies
might carry symbolic meaning, but never quite meet their expectations in function:
Dneprostroi was the socialist state's first major hydropower station located on the
Dnepr River in Ukraine and the prelude to future symbols of Soviet economic
might; the Belomor Canal was built by political prisoners with hammers, saws, and
shovels (thousands of these workers perished while cutting through the permafrost); and the Moscow Metro, whose ornate marble stations truly are architectural
wonders. The poorly paid and often illiterate workers frequently, if unintentionally,
destroyed expensive equipment, loading it poorly, getting it stuck in the mud, leaving it to the elements' mercy, or operating it carelessly, losing limb and life in the
process. The concrete itself cured poorly, first bending forms and soon beginning to
crumble. Still, the projects served as forums for the social, cultural, and political
indoctrination of the burgeoning working class in the glories of Soviet power, and
especially its infallible leader, Iosif Vissarionovich Stalin. The projects jump-started
rapid industrialization. In all sectors of the economy—the iron industry, the machine building industry, and the energy industry—Soviet construction was transformed in one generation from one of artels to one that epitomized the industrialized ethos of prefabricated forms and huge machines, an industry whose success
was judged in tons and deadlines, not in aesthetic pleasure or worker safety.[1] For
the nuclear enterprise, even more so, concrete was food for the Party gods.

There were only a few ways to cut the costs of reactors to make them competitive with fossil fuel boilers. In any event, capital costs would be higher. It remained
to cut back on expensive materials to the extent possible. One path was to use less
steel by replacing it with concrete, but only in "stationary reactors," where the
mechanical strength and radiation stability of concrete was not in doubt, even in the

presence of cracks and fissures. Engineers decided it was possible to build the reactor vessel entirely of reinforced concrete, put less steel into thermal barriers, and skimp on steel in biological shielding. A Soviet scientist observed that several thousand tons of steel had been used in Hinckley Point Station in England, but he believed that Hinckley Point could have been built more cheaply with reinforced concrete.[2]

Nuclear engineers determined that, in the final analysis, they could make nuclear power competitive with fossil fuel boilers only by building larger reactors. It would be even better if they succeeded in standardizing reactor construction to arrive in some sense at "serial production." Toward this end, they built the Atommash (for "atomic machinery") factory on the Volga River. Atommash's immense foundries had conveyors and cranes, stamps and extruders, and workers and engineers to make Henry Ford envious, even though his River Rouge (Michigan) Plant had revolutionized the assembly line. Before reaching the Volga River, the nuclear engineers had learned how to use concrete in plutonium production reactors for the military enterprise. They wanted to take what they had learned in Cheliabinsk, Obninsk, and elsewhere to the civilian sector. Quickly they decided that nuclear reactor construction was essentially no different from highway or apartment construction. Concrete made it all possible.

Concrete and reinforced concrete are wonderful stuff. Even without extensive mechanization, it is easy to use because it pours to fit almost any shape, dries quickly, and has great strength. The Soviet Union produced only 6 million tons (metric tons, here and throughout) of cement annually on the eve of World War II, but they made 46 million tons in 1960, 95 million tons in 1970, and 125 million tons in 1980. Portland cement accounted for the lion's share of production until the 1950s. Then they increased output of quick hardening and slag Portland cement. The Russian republic produced sixty-five percent and Ukraine twenty-one percent of the cement. A great jump in production in the 1950s did not mean that concrete lacked importance for Stalin, only that the construction industry remained in its infancy until after his death, because it had been forced to rebuild from the ground up after the Nazi armies retreated, leaving rubble in their wake. Perhaps to mourn Stalin's death, in 1954 the Central Committee of the Communist Party passed a special resolution, "On the Development of Production of Prefabricated Concrete Forms for Construction," expressing dissatisfaction with the rate of diffusion of this new technology and calling for a fivefold increase in the production of forms between 1954 and 1957. This expansion would require building over 400 new cement factories in 1955 and 1956, but it would facilitate the construction in those two years of 14.5 million square meters of apartment space, 6.5 million square meters of industrial buildings, and 8.4 million square meters of agricultural buildings.[3] Not surprisingly, a national convocation of the Workers of Construction Industry, Design, and Research Organizations gathered in the Kremlin to show their support for the resolution.

Under Khrushchev, the effort to produce prefabricated concrete forms expanded rapidly. A few dozen massive factories dominated production for the entire nation, with one located in each major region. In 1955, there were eight factories in the USSR that produced more than 600,000 tons of cement annually; by 1958, twelve; and by 1966, twenty-six prefab form factories. The eighteen largest spit out one million tons annually—nearly three-quarters of all the cement in the USSR. From these factories, finished forms were loaded onto railway wagons for the long trip to construction sites. Planners overlooked the cost and inefficiency of long-distance shipping, for they sought centralized control of production. The "industrialization of construction" was the goal in the eternal "battle for durability and stability" using concrete, "the artificial stone." By 1965, the factories produced 56 million cubic meters of prefabricated reinforced concrete forms; in 1970, 85 million cubic meters; in 1975, 114 million cubic meters; and in 1980, 123 million cubic meters.[4] One unit of the Leningrad Atomic Energy Station alone, the first 1,000-megawatt RBMK to be built, contained roughly 300,000 cubic meters of reinforced concrete in the shape of a ten-story building nearly 500 meters long.[5] Few goods and services achieved such rapid and sustained growth in the former Soviet Union, an achievement that says something about the priorities of the government vis-a-vis the citizens' desires for better food, clothing, and health care (see Appendix, Tables 11 and 12).

So important was concrete that Soviet scientists created a series of scientific research, development, and design organizations to complement the construction industry—their raison d'etre was concrete. They studied various mixtures and admixtures, the better to cure it in weather conditions in the Soviet Union that ran the gamut from the well-known extreme cold of the far north, to the hotter, more arid Central Asia. They studied all kinds of ways to keep production costs low, including tests to determine how much concrete could be watered down and still be used in apartment buildings, dams, and nuclear reactors. To disseminate such ethereal information, they established an international journal, the monthly *Beton i zhelezobeton* (Concrete and Reinforced Concrete). This journal was the organ of the State Committee of the Council of Ministers of the USSR on Construction. Concrete's experience went full circle. At one time merely the foundation of production reactors, it turned into the glue of reactors whose every molecule, resistance, density, and stability were studied by a huge network of institutes. These institutes included the Scientific Research Institute of Reinforced Concrete (encountered frequently in the scientific literature according to its exotic acroynm, NIIZhB) and regional centers where experts gathered over coffee to analyze the glories of concrete, for example, the Novokuznetsk Division of the West Siberian Branch of the Academy of Construction and Architecture of the USSR. In Ukraine alone, there were forty-four research and design institutes for the construction industry, which employed 6,500 researchers, including 100 doctors and 1,900 candidates of science.[6]

Cement is a powder that, when mixed with water, sets and hardens into a solid mass. Limestone, volcanic ash, and clay are the most common materials used as cement. The limestone quarried on the Isle of Portland gave rise to the name Portland cement. Slag cement is produced by slag by-products of blast furnaces. When cement is mixed with sand, it forms the mortar used in masonry construction; and when mixed with gravel or crushed stone, it forms concrete. It is so versatile and strong, and so easily fits the shape desired by builders, that it led to a revolution in construction late in the nineteenth century.

Concrete and reinforced concrete are vital ingredients of nuclear reactors. By weight and volume, they constitute seventy percent of this complex steam engine. They are the foundation, a container for the core of the reactor itself and, at the same time, serve as the biological shielding against radiation and as a containment vessel. As a containment vessel, the concrete must tolerate the very high temperatures and pressures that might be produced in the core of the reactor during an accident involving loss of coolant. Some containment vessels exceed 170,000 cubic meters in volume. As V. B. Dubrovskii, the concrete specialist and later professor of nuclear engineering, wrote, "Like any other nuclear installations nuclear power plants mainly use concrete radiation shields which also serve as load-bearing structures. Concrete is a cheap and rather effective shield material. Among its advantages is also the fact that its engineering and physical (including shielding) properties can be varied at will." The variations include heavy and superheavy concretes, concretes with different binding agents and aggregates (for example, magnetite-aggregate concrete and Portland cement), concretes that can withstand medium-high temperatures and those designed to withstand temperatures higher than 350°C (heat-resistant concretes), concretes with boron or cadmium, and concretes with increased water (hydrated concretes). Prestressed concrete was a major innovation in building engineering. By putting rebar (tensioning steel bars or wire) into concrete, builders put the concrete in a state of compression, thereby strengthening it and allowing less material to be used. In Soviet practice, radiation shields ordinarily used two types of concrete: ordinary heavy concrete and superheavy concrete; but in all cases, the ingredients were locally available aggregates, binders, and admixtures. The standard Soviet PWR—the VVER-1000—used 21,000 cubic meters of ordinary heavy concrete, 1,000 cubic meters of superheavy concrete, and 50 cubic meters of hydrated serpentinite concrete. There would have been more, much more, but the Soviet nuclear energy enterprise avoided using containment vessels until after the nuclear disaster at Three Mile Island, Pennsylvania in 1981, so confident were they of the integrity of their designs and concrete.[7]

The first publications concerning research on the radiation resistance of cements were published in 1944 and were based on experience with the first Oak Ridge National Laboratory reactor. The authors concluded that a moderate flux of thermal neutrons did not have an effect on the strength and stability of the concrete and that the loss of water in the concrete was a result of higher temperatures, not radiation itself. In 1950, however, another series of articles on magnesium cement and cements with boron revealed a significant lowering in the strength of concrete after neutron radiation. Scientists at Harwell, England asserted, on the basis of a series of experiments conducted from 1953 to 1956, that changes in the strength and weight of various kinds of concrete depended both on temperature and on level of irradiation. But Soviet scientists disputed the former contention, believing that neutron activity was the crucial factor. In the BR-5 experimental breeder reactor, they irradiated small briquettes of heat-resistant Portland concrete made with a filler of chamotte clay and sand produced at the Voskresenskii Factory. They determined that the magnitude of radiation damage depended on the age of the cement, stone, and filler, and on the destruction of the bonds between them as the crystals were deformed and ruptured. They also determined that Portland cement with chamotte and sand as filler could be used as biological shielding against a high level of neutron activity.[8]

At first, prefabricated concrete and reinforced concrete forms were rarely used in the construction of biological shielding for reactors, because there was a danger of radiation passing through fissures along the joints of the forms. However, scientists at Brookhaven and Los Alamos National Laboratories applied the prefabricated concrete technology with some success to low-power research reactors, and Soviet engineers gladly followed this example with their own forms in the first steps of the effort to employ standard technologies to keep reactor costs to a minimum. Starting with experimental reactors, engineers used standard series ST 02-01 blocks that were 0.5 meter thick. The blocks could also be used for accelerator biological shielding. It was a simple process to cover the blocks with a layer of concrete, thereby bringing the walls to 0.8-meter thickness. The procedure was used with success on the synchrotron at the Moscow Institute of Theoretical and Experimental Physics. At the synchrocyclotron at Dubna, engineers used prefabricated slabs with concrete blocks in between them to a thickness of 1.5 meters.[9] After another ten years of study, researchers determined that proton accelerators of 100 to 1,000 megaelectronvolts such as synchrotrons, phasotrons, cascade generators, linear accelerators, and meson factories required biological shielding of hydrated material such as concrete; steel alone was inadequate.[10] Although all this experience concerned experimental facilities, it left no doubt among scientists that concrete, including prefabricated concrete forms, could be used in accelerator and reactor construction, serving as good, inexpensive biological shielding and structural material. Were there other savings of materials and time they might find in concrete, at the same time preserving its other functions?

Engineers and builders, working closely with scientists who understood the ability of water molecules to serve as a moderator of neutrons, decided first to focus on concrete itself and then to apply what they learned to standard building techniques. They examined the extent to which water might be added to various concrete mixtures, studying roughly fifty different mixtures and levels of hydration. The goal was the radiation safety of the personnel who operated the reactor. They determined that increasing the quantity of water by itself did not reduce the radiation safety of the cement. Rather, the quality of the concrete, its uniformity, how it was laid, and other issues were crucial. In one study, they concluded that the most economical concrete for reactors had a density of 2,350 kilograms per cubic meter, which, not coincidentally, was the least dense of all the concretes tested.[11]

V. B. Dubrovskii began his distinguished career pouring, curing, and testing various kinds of concrete for their radiation stability. Of various heat-resistant concretes available in the mid-1960s, Dubrovskii and his colleagues determined that chromite concretes were radiation resistant. Using the BR-5 reactor, they irradiated samples of concrete in hermetically sealed steel ampules at temperatures of 200° to

550°C and various levels of neutron activity. The chromite concretes retained their dimensions, their form, and sufficient strength under all conditions, a result suggesting to Dubrovskii that they held great promise for the future of nuclear power engineering.[12] But such scientific achievements anticipate the story of the formation of a construction trust to build the USSR's first plutonium production reactors and isotope separation factories, and its inexorable march toward nuclear concrete.

THE SOUTH URAL CONSTRUCTION TRUST

The South Ural Construction Trust (*Iuzhnoural'skoe upravleniia stroitel'stva,* or IuUS) built Cheliabinsk-40 and Cheliabinsk-65 (first called Base-10, and now called Ozersk, a city with 90,000 inhabitants in 1998). Cheliabinsk was not on any maps, for it was the site of the Soviet Union's first plutonium production reactor, the Soviet equivalent of the Hanford (Washington) reactor. IuUS moved quickly in the cold war. The workers built five reactors in four years, largely using cement and steel to contain the lethal fuel, the boiling water, and the high-pressure steam: Building 301 and the AV reactor (which came on line in June 1950); Building 602 and the AV-2 (April 1951); the OK-180 reactor (October 1951); Building 701 and the IR reactor (December 1951); Building 501 and the AV-3 (September 1952). But they weren't done. The OK-190 commenced operation in 1955 and the OK-191 (Building 401a) in 1966. (On the eve of the break-up of the USSR in 1991, there were five graphite-moderated plutonium production reactors at Cheliabinsk, all of which are now shut down; two light water-moderated reactors for tritium and special isotope production; and two chemical separation plants.) In short order, the workers also built a radiochemical factory to separate fissile plutonium necessary for bombs from other isotopes; it was called the "B" factory and was completed in 1957. They encountered all kinds of critical problems in the operation of that first isotope separation facility, with the majority of those persons who worked on it being buried prematurely because of exposure to excessive amounts of radiation. B had another unique problem: in 1957, it was dusted by fallout from an explosion of a nuclear waste dump located in nearby Kyshtym. Every nook and cranny of B had to be scoured for a year before operation could begin because it was so contaminated by radiation.[13]

IuUS came into existence because of the confluence of the demands of secrecy, the presence of natural resources, and the existence of a nearby machine building industry that was running at full capacity. As quickly as they could following the Nazi invasion, the Soviets loaded entire factories and research institutes onto trains bound for the Urals. From here, slowly and in the worst possible conditions—without heat and sometimes without roofs—they geared up for production of tanks, planes, and other weapons. Kurchatov and Beria agreed to site the plutonium production reactor near a former monastery and sanitarium, a forested 100-square mile area in the southern Ural Mountains. The Techa, Irtysh, and Tobol rivers provided copious amounts of water for the tremendous cooling needs of the massive pile. A powerful wartime machine building organization, Cheliabmetallurgstroi, provided a staff of narrow-minded, but capable engineers. They had thousands of German prisoners of war and Gulag conscripts to excavate and build and pour. In many of the sectors of IuUS, you might find two Russians, a director and chief engineer; the rest of the personnel were German prisoners of war from *spetskomandatura*, a special labor brigade under direct control of the secret police.[14]

Iakov Rapoport, who was a major general of engineering technical services and had headed the White Sea Canal Project and several dams on the Volga, oversaw construction. Kurchatov often found himself on site, during the day moving from question to question and from bottleneck to bottleneck, and at night listening to reports and approving new plans. Boris Vannikov, the head of the First Main Administration (that is, the bomb project enterprise); Avraami Zaveniagin, who had headed the Magnitogorsk Metallurgical Combine and was Vannikov's deputy; and Mikhail Pervukhin, minister of the chemical industry, also frequented the important facility.

There were even scientists in special Stalinist labor camps geared to research and development who were hooked into the nuclear enterprise. They included Nikolai Timofeeff-Ressovsky, known as the "Bison." Timofeeff-Ressovsky was in Nazi Germany at the Institute of the Brain when the war broke out. He decided not to return home. Although he was repatriated after the war, many of his former colleagues refused to have anything to do with him, thinking him a collaborator. He never got a job in an Academy institute, nor was he ever elected to its membership. But Timofeeff-Ressovsky was beholden to no one. Connected with the atomic bomb project to do studies of the impact of radiation on various organisms, he had no qualms about pushing cybernetics and genetics at a time when both disciplines were out of favor. Young scientists flocked to Timofeeff-Ressovsky at his Miassovo laboratory to sit naked in the lake and listen to his lectures on these ideologically suspect sciences.[15]

A town with a monastery and a sanitarium hardly had an adequate infrastructure for a plutonium production reactor, so this was the first task. In an attempt to hide the purpose of Cheliabinsk, Beria ordered the construction organization not to touch the huge tracts of forest nearby. They sent in tanks to pack down the first dirt roads; then they cut down trees for the log roads that had to be used until the cement factory was operational. The heavy traffic required continuous replacement of the logs. In the winter, horse-drawn sleighs were used. In the absence of sufficient cement for the first reactor, they relied on lumber for many of their tasks. By the end of 1947, they had consumed 114,000 cubic meters of timber; in 1948, 117,000 cubic meters; and in 1965, 114,000 cubic meters, not to mention the lumber used in tens of thousands of window and door frames for the ever-expanding weapons material production facility.

Lazar Kaganovich, the member of Stalin's circle who had been responsible for the Moscow Metro, visited the site early on. Recognizing that Cheliabmetallurgstroi could not handle all the tasks at hand, Kaganovich created a new construction administration—Glavpromstroi NKVD, later called Iuzhnouralstroi—with energy, communication, transport, railroad, and machinery and equipment divisions. Even with direct secret police oversight and orders signed by Beria or Stalin himself, Cheliabinsk was built, not by specially requisitioned machinery, but from the ground up with pickaxes, crowbars, shovels, and huge flathead hammers. For electricity, they used portable diesel generators until they built power lines from the Irtiash/Kyzyltash miniature hydropower station. Of course, they got as many soldiers and prisoners as they needed, so there was no incentive to mechanize. Many other organizations were thrown into the task: Soiuzprommontazh, Teplokontrol, Uralelektromontazh, Spetsmontazh.[16]

Excavation and construction commenced with 3,000 unskilled and poorly motivated employees who toiled in two shifts, with bosses patrolling constantly to inspect their work. The bosses blamed the workers for every failure; but, in fact, poor planning, inexact surveying, and constantly changing requirements were the real sources of the problems. For the plutonium production reactor, the workers were required to dig deeper and deeper—at first six meters, then eighteen meters, and finally forty-three meters. They had planned to use forty-eight tons of explosives to loosen things up. But the commandant of a land-locked naval mine base at Tatysh categorically opposed detonation for fear of triggering his mines with the shock waves. A struggle with a gusher of groundwater then commenced; and because they didn't have powerful pumps either, the work slowed to a muddy crawl. They had to build special carts to move around huge finished pieces of concrete, some six meters in diameter and one meter high, which were pushed and pulled by horses and prisoners. Then they discovered the need to go another ten meters down beneath the muck. Because some concrete was already in place, there was the danger of a cave-in. However, they found volunteers to dig down another ten meters by offering to reward them on the spot with cash, bread, and sausages. In April 1948, great joy greeted the arrival of three bulldozers.[17]

With so much activity and so little concern for the expendable workers, accidents were inevitable. The entire scaffolding for the 150-meter chimney for B suddenly leaned sideways, sending hundreds falling to death and injury. The workers were always poorly treated. If they were late by fifteen minutes, their pay was docked by one-fourth for three months. The dining hall was far away and there were no buses to take them there, but no one was allowed to be late returning from lunch. As Vannikov told them, "If you don't do it, you'll get dry bread."[18] The building of Cheliabinsk was a crucible event, for it convinced engineers of the need to adopt standard practices to avoid delays and accidents. Yet all these misfortunes—industrial accidents, problems with groundwater, poorly treated and therefore poorly motivated workers—befell Atommash, too.

Stalin and Beria were obsessed with secrecy. At first, Stalin and Beria simply forbade workers to leave the zone for other work, or even after retirement. Until apartment buildings went up, workers lived first in tents, then in barracks. When Stalin died, internal passports were issued to the "free" employees of IuUS. Internal documents were required for travel within the Soviet Union in any event. But free Cheliabinsk employees were not permitted to travel further than Irkutsk in the east, Tashkent in the south, and Kuibyshev in the west. They could travel as far into the Arctic Circle as they wanted, but there were few takers. For the most part, the administrators kept close reins on the workers, often farming them out to such alluring winter cold spots as Magadan in railway ore wagons for their next job assignments. The workers' only bonus was previewing uncensored films, which the authorities tried out at Cheliabinsk before their release to the rest of the country.[19]

The real problem was not workers, but concrete. They couldn't get enough of it. V. A. Beliavskii, a supervisor at Cheliabinsk, said: "Concrete is the bread of construction workers, its delivery was under special control. The factories worked without pause, even on the weekends. How do you guarantee such uninterrupted work of the equipment at such a pace? We created a rich supply of parts, even entire assemblies, which wore out very quickly." Under pressure from Moscow, Rapoport and Beliavskii complained there still wasn't enough. Over the telephone from the concrete factory, director Tsarevskii complained: "It's a lie that there is no concrete at the site. I'm sending truckload after truckload out there. The factory is working like a clock. Listen for yourself." And he held the phone out the opened vent window of his office, picking up the din of the machinery. The worst crime, of course— even worse than changing plans to meet unforeseen difficulties—was to miss a deadline.[20] Concrete, if not sophisticated equipment, would never be a problem in the nuclear industry again.

Productivity at Cheliabinsk grew significantly after the factory started manufacturing prefabricated reinforced concrete forms. At first, the concrete factory produced only foundation blocks, supports and conduit, highway slabs, hollow concrete slabs for finishing brick apartment buildings, and six-, nine-, and twelve-meter reinforced concrete columns and girders. The production of these prefabricated building materials grew rapidly, from 3,000 cubic meters in 1954 to 19,800 cubic meters in 1955 and 82,000 cubic meters in 1958. The next step was the creation of a new trust, the Apartment Building Combine, to erect series I/119 apartment buildings, one of a half-dozen such designs intended to fill all Soviet housing needs from the late 1950s onward. In the Khrushchev years, as part of something like a general amnesty for crimes committed in the Stalin era (sadly, in many cases posthumously), many political prisoners were released, and "free" workers (in some cases, the very same person) replaced them on the job. Free workers required much more in the way of the comforts of home. Prison food, prison garb, and prison housing would not do. So IuUS acquired the added responsibility of building apartments. They used the same tried and true mass production techniques of military construction. To raise the apartment buildings more quickly, the bosses often put a small orchestra in the center of the site, and it played marches or some other energetic music for the desired inspiration. They built three-story buildings on Beria Prospect in less than six months. By 1958 they had built sixteen buildings with 30,000 square meters of space, including dining halls, kindergartens, a public bath, and a movie theater. Unfortunately, the apartment buildings, stores, and theaters had a life span of only twenty years, sometimes less, before they began to crumble.

IuUS eventually downsized to no more than 800 employees. In the meantime, they had acquired bulldozers and concrete pumps and BK-1000 cranes reaching fifty meters and lifting thirty tons. IuUS activities extended far beyond the Ural Mountains to the newly constructed cities of Navoi and Akademgorodok, to RBMK reactors at Sosnovyi Bor outside of Leningrad and Ignalina in Lithuania, to Tomsk-7, to Minlesstroi for slabs for logging roads, to Minneftgas for roads and supports for oil and gas pipelines, and even to the Angara River for hydroelectric power stations, albeit all under Minsredmash auspices.[21] Its concrete-pouring skills only partially met the nation's growing appetite.

After years of study, scientists, engineers, planners, and construction officials concluded that there was essentially no difference between the concrete used in reactors and that used in apartment buildings, highways, or other applications. The successful operation of special construction trusts involved in construction of apartments, hardened silos for ICBMs, and shielding for particle accelerators (for example, Sibakademstroi in Novosibirsk, Siberia) confirmed this conclusion. The special nuclear construction trusts—created, as it were, out of the tundra and taiga to apply the achievements of scientists and engineers—were huge. And they grew ever larger, moving from one military task to another and then into the countryside in search of other huge construction projects. They built entire towns, the world's largest hydropower stations, and, of course, nuclear reactors. Other construction trusts were hatched from the marauding armies of workers, bulldozers, steam shovels, and concrete pumps. For example, Angarastroi, which ultimately employed 70,000 laborers, was dedicated to conquering Siberian rivers. No matter where they happened to be at the end of April 1986, the workers of these trusts "volunteered" to assist in the liquidation of the Chernobyl disaster. Their association with concrete and nuclear power had come full circle.

Lest the Soviet fascination with concrete appear to be an anomaly, be assured that none of the cold war bomb factories suffered from concrete envy. By the end of November 1944, the British realized they were destined to be second-class citizens in any nuclear alliance with the United States. So they determined to set up their own research establishment and weapons production facilities. For a research facility with experimental reactors and accelerators of various sizes and types, physicists Marcus Oliphant and Sir John Cockcroft selected the 300-acre Harwell site to the west of London. The Harwell reactors discharged between 300,000 and 400,000 gallons of slightly radioactive effluent into the Thames each day; the Metropolitan Water Board claimed never to have detected any unusual radioactivity in their reservoir uptakes. Next, the scientists planned uranium fabrication and plutonium production facilities. Calder Hall and Windscale on the west coast not far from the Lake District and Dounreay, an experimental reactor facility on the northern tip of Scotland, were chosen both for their isolation and for proximity to an excellent coolant, ocean water. Windscale Works in England covers 260 acres on the Cumberland coast ten miles south of Whitehaven. The River Calder runs at the end of the site. Until 1940, the area was farmland, and the beach fronting it was unfrequented. A Royal Ordnance Factory for the production of TNT was built there in 1941. So when the United Kingdom Atomic Energy Authority selected Windscale in 1946 as the site of a factory to process uranium ore from Congo, South Africa, and Australia, all the important elements were in place: clean water, road and rail communications to an industrial facility, and low population density.

The Windscale plant had huge stack chimneys, each 410 feet high and 47 feet wide, so that the slightly contaminated radioactive air used for cooling the atomic piles would be dispersed high into the atmosphere. Radioactive effluent was diffused into the sea through pipes that extended into the ocean 3,000 yards beyond high-water mark. The chimneys are impressive landmarks, visible for miles; they vented BEPO, the first big British experimental reactor. BEPO was a cube with sides each twenty-six feet long, made with 28,000 graphite blocks of 1,500 different shapes and engineered to an accuracy of 0.015 inch. Through these blocks, 1,760 horizontal channels provided access for loading uranium. BEPO was surrounded by a shield that was 6.5 feet thick and made of concrete. The weight of each pile (the graphite and uranium core of the reactor), together with the foundations, fan-houses, and a 3,000-ton chimney, was 57,000 tons. Engineers put each pile on a reinforced concrete mat 200 feet long, 100 feet wide, and 10 inches thick. The fans were so strong that on start-up they caused the great steel doors of the building to belly inward several inches.[22] When pile 1 melted down, radioactive iodine spread throughout the countryside, requiring milk supplies to be withdrawn. Other dangerous radioactive isotopes laced the region. Of course, the nuclear industry played down the danger as unexceptional and controllable, and painted the Windscale Works as important to the tourist trade, "attractively planned and maintained as most modern factories," and successfully blotting out the old explosives factories from the horizon.[23]

SOCIALIST INDUSTRY BEFORE ATOMMASH

"Socialist industry" meant more than vast quantities of concrete. It meant serial production of larger and larger capacity machinery and equipment, replicated across eight times zones. For all of the Soviet Union, there were six basic apartment building styles, a handful of frames with interchangeable bodies for dump trucks, garbage trucks, and troop carriers, a one-volume discussion of the architecture of highways, and a two-volume construction manual for nuclear power stations, yet little sense that construction techniques or components ought to be different for highways, apartment buildings, and reactors. Socialist industry required centralized determination of standards for the entire nation for all building materials—piping, conduit, pumps, turbines—by bureaucrats sitting in the State Committee on Standards, the State Committee on Construction, and other Moscow organizations. In every case, the predominating philosophy was to increase industrial production in terms of gross output. The bureaucrats had an overriding fascination with economies of scale, not only because of the desire to cut production costs, but also because of their proclivity to push Soviet industry to hurtle from modest innovation to prototype to industrial production to fulfilled target plans. One enterprise often produced all the large-capacity machinery for the entire nation; for example, Elektrosila provided huge turbogenerators for the hydropower industry and the Kharkiv Turbine Factory made the 500-megawatt turbines that were powered by the VVER and RBMK reactors. Other massive engineering organizations were the sole source of expertise: for example, Giproproekt directed water melioration projects from the

Volga to the Amur. It should come as no surprise that Soviet economic planners and engineers attempted to create a single enterprise to produce reactors for the nuclear power industry in a serial fashion.

It was a vicious circle. Centralization, premature standardization, and fascination with economies of scale contributed to the domination of an entire industry by one firm. And these giant firms served the huge construction trusts that built the apartments, dams, oil fields, railroads, and highways spreading throughout the Soviet Union. Only the fall of the Soviet empire put an end to the great momentum that these massive systems of technology acquired and removed from them the vast resources they commanded. Take the case of Elektrosila, one of the largest electrical motor and component enterprises in the world. Elektrosila grew from prerevolutionary roots. It manufactured a 500-kilowatt generator in 1923; but, by 1927, it produced a 7,000-kilowatt hydrogenerator for the Volkhovskaia hydropower station. Although its engineers learned a great deal from the experience of building Volkhovskaia, they required technical assistance from General Electric, which included the purchase of technical specifications and four generators as well as training on site in Schenectady, New York. They believed this limited experience prepared them to power up for the Dnepr hydropower station (known as DneproGES or Dneprostroi). DneproGES, the first major construction project of Stalin's industrialization effort, served as a paradigm for melding unskilled workers into capable, but inefficient, construction organizations through coercion, political indoctrination, and exhortation.[24] Rather than General Electric's twenty-two types of turbogenerators ranging in power from 10,000 to 100,000 kilowatts, Soviet engineers suddenly decided to move immediately to the serial production of just four generators, rated at 12,000, 25,000, 50,000, and 100,000 kilowatts. Work with Siemens, Metropolitan-Vickers, and other European firms was also crucial to the development of Soviet turbogenerators.[25]

Stalin then decided to go it alone, to build "socialism in one country." Foreign engineers came under suspicion as spies and wreckers, a large number were arrested, and many fled the country. This left Elektrosila engineers alone in the pursuit of higher capacities and efficiencies, aided only by what documents and information secret police agents who manned the euphemistic "Bureaus of Science and Technology" in European embassies and the United States could steal or acquire through espionage. Stalin's faith in Elektrosila was rewarded. The factory turned out 123,500-kilowatt generators in the 1950s, and 500-, 800-, 1,000-, and then 1,200-megawatt generators by the late 1960s. It supplied virtually the entire Soviet hydroelectric power industry single-handedly. By 1993, fifty-four 500-megawatt and twenty-two 800-megawatt turbogenerators had been built. In a display of gigantomania reminiscent of the Stalin era, engineers hoped to produce 3,000- to 4,000-megawatt turbogenerators based on superconducting magnets. A limit on transportability and efficiency of turbogenerators precluded the development of even larger ones. A special railroad flatbed car with twenty-eight axles and a capacity rated at 360 tons had to be built to carry the massive generators from Elektrosila's foundries into the Soviet countryside.[26]

Just as Elektrosila and its massive turbogenerators were inevitable in the hydro-electric power industry, given this approach to technological development, Atom-mash was the logical step for the nuclear industry. Atommash was intended to pro-duce eight pressure vessels and associated equipment annually for the VVER-1000 reactor. Factory engineers and directors planned eventually to produce 1,500-megawatt PWRs, 800-megawatt breeder reactors, and fusion devices in serial fash-ion at Atommash. Industry on this scale was a huge undertaking, even for the Soviet Union. Situated on the Volga not far from Tsimlianskoe Lake, the site was perfect: close to the Donbas region with its metallurgical and machine building industries; near the Tsimlianskaia hydroelectric power station, a source of cheap energy; on the Volga-Don canal, which ensured easy water transport of the finished product through the Don and the Volga rivers to the Baltic or through the Azov and Black seas to the Danube and the Mediterranean. The 1,200-ton weight of each reactor vessel made truck or rail transport impossible. A special monorail was built to bring the reactors from the factory to the barges. Similar rail facilities would have to be built from shore to whatever final resting places were chosen for finished reactors.[27]

The selection of a site for Atommash near Tsimlianskoe was a decision based on antecedents of history, geography, and technological style dating to the Stalin era. Like the nuclear power industry after it, the hydropower industry employed thou-sands of workers ill-prepared to deal with high technology; it turned prematurely to serial production of components, prefabricated concrete forms, and equipment; and it did not tolerate obstacles to plan fulfillment. For Stalin and the hydropower in-dustry, the obstacles included perceived failings among humans or in nature, which too would have to be crushed like an "enemy of the people." Stalin claimed that cap-italism prevented rational utilization of natural resources. Too many small land-owners each sought to maximize profits from exploitation of land, water, mineral, and other rights. The resulting competition wasted resources, enriched few at the expense of many, and precluded efficient large-scale scientific management. In the Soviet Union, state ownership of property allowed utilization of large-scale tech-nologies that extended to the horizon, not merely to tame, but to transform nature.

Starting from a series of smaller dams and canals, Soviet hydrologists, geolo-gists, and planners designed an increasingly grandiose network of water manage-ment projects with a threefold purpose: connect the major rivers of Russia and Ukraine for inland transport; generate hydroelectricity to power the industrializa-tion effort; and store water for irrigation in the southern steppe regions that have rich soil but low annual rainfall. Exploitation was the name of this Soviet game. The hydroelectric power stations of the late Stalin period resulted in tremendous human dislocation and submerged thousands of square miles of towns, homes, cemeteries, farmlands, and forests, without a thought about their human, cultural, and histori-cal importance. Persons who had lived for generations in one place were moved into unfamiliar, poorly constructed prefab homes and saw their churches and town cen-ters submerged.[28]

The construction of hydroelectric power stations during Stalin's first five year plan of forced industrialization and collectivization was a prelude to geoengineering on a vast scale. Including DneproGES, the party built ten new stations, totaling 345,000 kilowatts of capacity by 1933. During the second five year plan (through 1938), another 745,000 kilowatts of capacity was added; and on the eve of World War II, over ten percent of the country's electrical energy was now generated by hydropower, mostly on the Volga, Don, and Dnepr rivers. The thirty-seven stations built from 1928 to 1941 had a total capacity of 1.5 million kilowatts. The Nazi invasion put an end to this period of uninterrupted growth. The Soviet Union lost twenty million people during the war. Most of Ukraine, with its high concentration of agriculture and industry (including many hydropower stations), fell to the Nazis. The Germans destroyed the stations whenever they could, taking special glee in dynamiting DneproGES to demonstrate what they thought of Bolshevik revolutionary symbolism.

Postwar reconstruction not only was a monument to Stalin but also was consciously intended to utilize dams and canals to transform nature itself. In five years, construction trusts built thirty hydroelectric power stations on the Volga, Don, Dnepr, and Syr-Darya rivers, forever changing the face of European Russia and Ukraine. They began the same transformative process in the Ural, Caucasus, and Central Asian regions. A series of government resolutions in 1950 called for the construction of the massive Stalingradskaia, Kakhovskaia, and Kuibyshevskaia hydropower stations. The Kuibyshev facility, at 1.5 million kilowatts, was the largest in the world at that time, with hundreds of miles of canals and hundreds of thousands of miles of irrigation channels. Each European river would be tamed to serve energy, transport, or irrigation needs.[29] (Siberian rivers fell to hydroengineers during the Khrushchev and Brezhnev eras, their waters driving massive stations that would have made Stalin envious; for example, the 4,500-megawatt Bratskaia station had sixteen 225-megawatt turbogenerators and two 250-megawatt turbogenerators.) In theory, these great projects of the Stalin era served the people; in practice, they served the center. A lion's share of the benefit—electricity generated, goods and services transported, food produced—went to Moscow-region inhabitants and to the central Party apparatus in particular.

This unparalleled postwar reconstruction of nature was known as the "Big Volga" project. Big Volga served as a model both for future large-scale economic development projects and for the overriding interest in "proletarian aesthetics." Proletarian aesthetics grew out of the headlong pursuit of all-union standards to achieve economic ends. At all construction sites, for every kind of technology, regardless of meteorological and geological circumstances, engineers sought standardization to keep costs low and accelerate the pace of construction. If a state committee approved standards for the thickness of pipe or the specific weight of cement, then the local engineer could no longer be held responsible for failure to meet targets. Once a standard had been approved, that item found universal application in dozens of industries—the same piping was used for sewage and for high-pressure gas pipelines that crossed fragile Arctic tundra, for example. Another source of proletarian aesthetics was the ideology of the egalitarian workers' state. There was no need for anyone to live in an apartment with high ceilings and modern fixtures, when mass-produced concrete slabs could serve as building blocks for buildings from Lviv to Vladivostok. To be sure, proletarian aesthetics enabled the state to provide housing for millions of people in a nation that had always struggled with poverty. Unfortunately, proletarian aesthetics was manifested not only in dams, and in more ordinary technologies such as automobiles that had no safety and pollution control equipment, but also in nuclear reactors, with their potential for catastrophic accidents.

Canals were another important cog in the machine of Soviet environmental management; and a Big Volga canal was crucial to the success of Atommash. Engineers built seven canals before World War II, including the infamous Belomor, the White Sea-Baltic Canal, assembled by hand by thousands of political prisoners equipped only with picks and shovels. Many of the workers perished in the exercise. Engineers built another seven canals from 1946 to 1960, and twenty-two more by 1980.[30] The goal of the Volga-Don canal was to unite all the great rivers of the European USSR, primarily through the tributaries of the Volga: the Kama, Oka, Viatka, and Belaia rivers. These canals would join all major ports—Moscow, Leningrad, Belomorsk, Iaraslavl, Kuibyshev, Saratov, Stalingrad—in one giant waterway.[31]

In building the Volga-Don canal, 152 million cubic meters of earth were excavated, 57 million cubic meters of concrete and reinforced concrete were poured, and 45,000 tons of metal devices and mechanisms were employed. Construction was faster, the sources claim, than any effort the West could muster, and more mechanized, too, using 900 graders, 300 bulldozers, and 350 excavators—including several Soviet monsters with a bucket capacity of fourteen cubic meters—three dozen suction dredges, and thousands of trucks, tractors, cranes, and winches.[32] The unitary water transport system once again disproportionately benefited the political elite. Manufactured goods from the Volga; bread, coal, and iron from the Don; Azov fish in newly built freezer carriers, all wound their way to Moscow. On the Don river, the Tsimlianskaia dam was built to keep water high year round for shipping and to serve irrigation needs in the sunny steppe regions located along each bank. By 1951, the "Spark" and "Il'ich's Legacy" collective farms had drawn off the first water some 70 kilometers into the steppe.[33] All the necessary preconditions were in place for Atommash: a head-long rush to serial production of large-scale technologies, a belief that technology should be used to overcome the mistakes of nature, ample quantities of electrical energy, and a well-developed inland water transportation system to carry the finished units away by barge.

"LET THE ATOM BE A WORKER, NOT A SOLDIER"

Atommash consisted of three main buildings and a structure for workshops, machine tools, and experimental facilities for assembling the special machines needed to run the factory. To accommodate uninterrupted material and production flows, the buildings grew to unprecedented size. The main foundry, building 1, was 770×400 meters. It covered over seventy acres and was filled to the brim with presses, stamping machines, and one-of-a-kind equipment. Steel billets up to 160 metric tons would be carried by overhead cranes to some of the largest boring and milling machines ever built, machines used in the manufacture of 800-ton pressure vessels.

Building 2 was 500×350 meters and covered forty-one acres. It was for production of operation and control equipment of high sensitivity and accuracy. "Nuclear purity" was ensured through temperature, humidity, and other controls. Building 3 stretched to a modest 6.5 acres and was filled with various nonstandard equipment for repair of Atommash equipment.[34] In three forty-two-meter bays of the main building, reactors were built; and in two thirty-meter bays, steam generators and separators. The Iuzhstalkonstruktsiia Trust was responsible for building concrete highways that stretched into the steppe. Workers used massive excavators to prepare the foundation pit and giant cement pumps to pour the foundations.

Of course, to build the reactors, unique equipment was required: presses with a capacity of 15,000 tons; steel-bending devices capable of handling steel rods over 250 millimeters in diameter; five-meter diameter forges standing near tanks eighteen meters deep; powerful cranes each rated at 1,200 tons; and dozens of smaller bridge cranes with a total capacity of 12,000 tons. Each of these machines in turn had to be reliable and strong. The goal was to have the factory up and running on the eve of the sixtieth anniversary of the revolution in October 1977, with the first reactor leaving the plant by the end of the tenth five year plan (1980). In theory, each reactor vessel required three years to build, during which time it would move through a factory, itself three-quarters of a kilometer long, over a production path that was nearly ten kilometers long and involved a series of complex operations. Fortunately, Iuzhstalkonstruktsiia had experience in such massive undertakings, having built the KamAZ truck plant in Tolyatti, which was similar in size. The Tolyatti plant required special conveyors and other equipment, employed prefabricated forms, and turned out millions of trucks for military and civilian purposes in the Brezhnev era.[35]

Volgodonsk was one of the first towns of Stalin's great postwar reconstruction effort. It was the site of the equipment park for the Tsimlianskaia hydropower station. In 1958, Volgodonsk experienced its first rebirth in a spurt of growth connected with the construction of one of the largest chemical factories in the south of the nation. This was the period of Khrushchev's insistence on the "chemicalization of agriculture." Then, beginning with Atommash's construction in 1974, Volgodonsk was reborn again with the construction of a massive boiler, a cement plant, a sawmill, and a new city of five-, ten-, and sixteen-story apartment buildings. Next to Atommash itself, all this other construction seemed rather modest. Hundreds of letters poured into Volgodonsk every day from workers who desired employment in this factory of factories. Many were highly qualified metal workers or carpenters, others were young and inexperienced recruits, but saw Atommash as a stepping stone to a new apartment, or a ticket out of the countryside; and the true believers embraced the official line about the glory of Atommash and its role in realizing the great watchword of the Bolsheviks: "Communism is Soviet power plus electrification of the entire country." Atommash attracted veterans and heroes of labor from the Volga-Don canal and the Tsimlianskaia hydropower station. In 1954, there were 2,500 residents in Volgodonsk, and on January 1, 1976, the city had 36,500 inhabitants; but only two years later, there were over 100,000 residents there, placing it beyond the vaunted census category of "small town", with access to higher political and economic organizations and officials. Of the 100,000 residents, 73,000 were workers, the largest number of them in construction; for example, Volgodonsken-ergstroi, a new trust brought together to assemble the city, had 27,000 employees. In 1975, the average age of the residents was thirty-two; but by 1978, it was only twenty-three years.

At one time, a bay sat at the very outskirts of Volgodonsk, and beyond the bay lay the steppe. But the city grew around its shores, so that the bay merely divided the city into two parts. The old part of the city was a mere thirty years old, and the new part, about five years young. The somewhat musty smell of the bay often filled the air. The first apartment buildings of the new town went up along Twenty-Fifth Party Congress Prospect. Along Kurchatov Prospect, apartment construction began to reach into the steppe itself.[36]

Could the "most advanced technology" in the nation be produced in a factory staffed with workers hampered by raw youth, rote education, and middling initiative? Atommash directors strove to build reliable reactors by training workers to be specialists in one of a series of narrower tasks required in their production; for example, workers would be trained in welding and then be designated, no doubt prematurely, "engineers." The directors also sought to improve the workers' skills by bringing scientists, engineers, and workers together in a number of different forums. Since the late 1920s, workers in Soviet factories and scientists in research institutes had been engaged in exchanges of expertise; the goal was to bring modern science, technology, and production together under one roof. Atommash sent many of its employees to the Zhdanov Izhorsk Factory, the Ordzhonikidze Podolsk Machine-building Factory, the Leningrad Metallurgical Factory, and other enterprises of the Ministry of Energy Machinery Building to learn welding and assembly skills needed for manufacturing the huge reactor vessels.

In the effort to inject some kind of youthful thinking and innovative expertise into science and technology generally, the Communist Youth League (Komsomol) established a series of special councils across the nation to assist enterprise managers and institute directors in achieving their goals. For Atommash, the Komsomol's Council of Young Scientists created a special coordinating center that imported specialists from the Bauman Moscow Higher Technical School, the Moscow-based Energiia scientific production organization, the Novocherkassk Polytechnical Institute, the Central Scientific Research Institute of the Technology of Machine Building, and the North Caucasus Scientific Center. During the periodic visits arranged by the Komsomol council, nuclear engineers lectured workers, conducted experiments, and helped solve pressing production problems. Bureaucratic obstacles between educational, scientific, and production ministries often prevented this kind of exchange program from achieving significant long-term results. At Atommash, too, the exchange program had only limited impact and involved too few leading personnel.

In the other direction, about 600 Atommash engineers were sent to study at various technical institutes. One of these sites was the Moscow Energy Institute, where a new field of study, "Materials and Technology of Nuclear Electrical Apparatus," had been created. The caliber of the training was not that of the program offered at, say, the Oak Ridge School of Reactor Technology, which was established in the mid-1950s to fill the ranks of nuclear engineers for America's nascent nuclear industry. At best, many of the new engineers became accomplished metallurgists, because they were always more interested in the production process than in mastering nuclear physics.

A leading fusion specialist from the Kurchatov Institute, Evgenii Velikhov, was central to the activities of the Komsomol coordinating center. With nuclear scientists from the other institutes, he set up special courses to train Atommash engineers. In the late 1970s, the coordinating committee strongly recommended that Atommash engineers develop a computer network with expert system software—known in Soviet parlance as an automated management system—to bring Atommash on line.[37] The drive to create these systems to improve production in enterprises of all branches of industry turned out to be yet another example of failure to bring about reform from above. The desire to control computer hardware and software and prevent any uses that might contribute to freer exchange of ideas precluded the development of anything resembling the vital computer culture that developed in the West.

Because it seemed to be more efficient to train engineers on the premises than to send them to Moscow and thereby lose their labor, Atommash officials set out to establish three technical schools in Volgodonsk. Only one of them had opened by 1979. It trained specialists to use robotic welding machines instead of the hand-operated blowtorches familiar to most employees. Other important specialties included heat engineering, material science, and welding materials (flux and electrodes). Unfortunately, only one institute in the country, Kiev Polytechnical Institute, trained persons in the use of welding materials; and only 100 individuals graduated with this honorable specialization annually. These graduates were coveted by machine building factories throughout the country. But most wished to remain in Kiev, because Kiev was the site of the Paton Institute of Welding, an institute of the Ukrainian Academy of Sciences under the direct rule of Academy president Boris Paton. It was considered to be a relatively plush place to work. Gosplan (the State Planning Administration) and Minvuz (the Ministry of Higher Education) remained to be convinced that other departments of welding science ought to be opened elsewhere. The provincial Communist Party organizations in Rostov and Leningrad joined the Volgodonsk city Communist Party organization in the call to establish regular, evening, and correspondence classes at nearby Novocherkassk Polytechnical Institute in welding. Better still, thought Atommash director V. Pershin, it was time to launch a higher technical school that was closely tied to Atommash, on the model of those connected with the Leningrad Metallurgical Factory or Rostselmash, an agricultural machinery complex. The notion of a welder trained by correspondence to build nuclear reactor vessels apparently never seemed absurd to the party officials. Atommash was extraordinary, not because of what it produced, but because the Soviets had managed to build it. Whatever the successes of turning out highly qualified specialists, Atommash was, in Pershin's mind, "not only a future enterprise, but an enterprise of the future."[38]

In addition to providing special training for workers, the planners wanted the Atommash production lines—if not the foundries themselves—to be put on a "strong scientific foundation." Hence, production would be strictly controlled by using modern defectoscopy and other equipment based on radioactive tracers and sensors. The factory employed X-ray chambers and linear accelerators for detecting the tiniest imperfection or fissure in steel. Atommash managers contended they would dispose of even a forty-ton part that cost 90,000 rubles rather than risk using a weak link in a very crucial chain. Like Soviet citizens near any facility connected with the nuclear energy industry, some Volgodonsk inhabitants worried that the plant must be building some kind of nuclear bombs. But in the minds of managers, planners, and engineers, this was a machine building factory, pure and simple—except with unprecedented power. Were Atommash to meet its targets, then it would produce enough reactors, steam generators, and other equipment to turn out in the eleventh five year plan (1981–1985) alone 24–25 million kilowatts of nuclear power capacity. To show the peaceful intent of their endeavor, the managers hung a portrait of Niels Bohr in the main laboratory. What would he have thought of that?[39]

Atommash had some early successes. It manufactured the vacuum chamber toroidal doughnut for the T-15 fusion reactor at the Kurchatov Institute; at 6 meters high, 11 meters in diameter, and 120 tons, this was no mean feat.[40] Velikhov had gotten something for his efforts. In addition to equipment for the T-15, Atommash directors unwillingly accepted responsibility for building reactor vessels for municipal nuclear heating stations (known as AST). They were reluctant because this job was just more responsibility to handle while they were still struggling to master the first. The directors were told that AST technology was just as important to the country from an economic point of view as the PWRs were. The flagship of AST reactors was built in Gorky. The 500-megawatt boiler was to be manufactured in the Izhorskii Factory, but it became the headache of Atommash when the Izhorskii Factory failed in its charge. That failure to fulfill its task ahead of schedule—the production of a huge airtight vessel with welding and other technological challenges—should have been a hint of the misfortunes that would later befall Atommash. Even after creating a special facility for the AST-500, Atommash managers had to wait repeatedly for technical drawings from their engineering and welding departments. The engineers failed to test prototypes under laboratory conditions. The main problem occurred during fabrication, because the vessel always deformed either in the rolling mills or after anticorrosion treatment. Atommash directors faced criticism for failing to take its production seriously, until the day they floated the reactor vessel up the Volga to Gorky.[41]

Yes, Atommash was ordinary, and its ordinariness was of the Soviet garden variety: high labor turnover, inadequate *sotskultbyt*, failure to come within years of plan targets, and resistance of the directors to accept additional production responsibilities. Beginning in 1978, workers started leaving in droves. The major reason, as usual, was the absence of housing. Housing construction lagged at least three years behind schedule, so almost 20,000 workers lived in shabby dormitories. Volgodonsk had no social services, few stores, or schools—one of three children waited for a place in kindergarten. Atommash workers seemed not to mind working ten days in a row, but they felt shame at having to stand in line for the simplest of things. Another problem was that, given the youth of the workers, many had an interest in the opposite sex and in families, but fewer than thirty percent of them were women. The energy and construction industries remained the domain of men.[42] Worse still, management had to fire over 1,500 workers in 1981, even though hundreds more were needed to fill already open positions. But, we are told, as a factory of the twenty-first century, Atommash could not tolerate imperfection.

Workers also quit because they had nothing to do. Construction lagged terribly. By the summer of 1981, the plant was only one-half complete. The lag, a self-acknowledged Soviet tradition, added to cost and inefficiency. The expensive, unique equipment operated at one-quarter capacity. Not only Atommash, but energy facilities around the country suffered from these labor and production problems. The Ministry of Electrification, already feeling budget pressures of trying to expand oil, gas, hydropower, and nuclear production at once with inadequate resources, refused to add to the *sotskultbyt* fund at any of its sites: Energomash, the Rostov and Balakova atomic power stations, and Atommash. Many Atommash workers could afford cars and motorcycles, and they took long weekends sailing or fishing at the reservoir to ease their boredom. (The reservoir was seeded with fish because pollution and overfishing had removed most indigenous species.) Others enjoyed working on private garden plots. But the lags in factory and housing construction foreshadowed disclosures of mismanagement and then disaster.[43]

Comrade Ivanitskii, the Party secretary of the Rostov province Party committee, had great hopes for the success of Atommash. He noted that the factory would play a crucial role in answering the call of the twenty-fifth Party congress in 1976 to bring thirteen to fifteen gigawatts of atomic energy on line in the new five year plan. His fiefdom now included the largest assembly line in the world. He proudly acknowledged the designation of the project a national Komsomol project, with the result that tens of thousands of young laborers joined senior workers of the construction trusts in "shock work." Teachers, doctors, service and trade people were also needed. So Ivanitskii promised them that in the coming year about 200,000 square meters of housing would be finished, with six kindergartens, two schools, thirty stores, five cafes, a hospital, a polyclinic, and an airport with direct flights to Moscow. This promise flew in the face of his knowledge that the state acquisition agency, Gossnab, had failed to deliver funds for over 150 different presses, furnaces, and bridge cranes—and the shortage of workers had become an epidemic.[44]

A series of articles in the major journal of Party economic and ideological activism, *Partiinaia zhizn'*, underlined the difficult challenges Atommash managers faced in getting the massive plant up and running. The usual proclamations protested success. By 1979, 418 million rubles had been spent. More than 2,500 Party members toiled in the factory, giving its organization the rights and privileges of a district committee (Raikom). Brezhnev himself sent a "letter of greetings" on the occasion of the first deadlines being met in December 1978. The local Party officials acknowledged that Brezhnev's "unforgettable and moving books, *Vozrozhdenie* (Revival) and *Tselina* (Virgin Lands)," enabled them to keep the main goals of the Party and Atommash itself in mind. The books inspired them to adopt two campaigns to hold the workers' attention. One was called "Work without leaving anyone behind," a reasonable, if obvious goal. The other was the "Labor Relay," where the workers of several factories were tied together like a "technological link" in the production of a given product and pledged high quality, ahead-of-schedule fulfillment of plans.[45] Having neither the coercive power of the Stalin era nor any material incentives, the Party's exhortations, campaigns, and relays fell short on all counts.

By the early 1980s, it was clear that the plant was not operating well. Labor productivity remained dreadfully low; new processes and technologies were introduced at a snail's pace, if at all; even the special equipment for the plant, and the special equipment to build the special equipment for the plant, was slow in being produced. According to official sources, the Volgodonskenergostroi trust that had been formed from Iuzhstalkonstruktsiia was systematically violating construction norms and "frequently turned over facilities with major portions unfinished." Paperwork was sloppy, so it was hard to track what had been done, what remained to be done, and where bottlenecks were worst. There were also many accidents,[46] and perhaps even fatalities.

The hallowed place of concrete in Soviet history notwithstanding, they could not even get the right mixture for Atommash. According to technical specifications, Volgodonskenergostroi was supposed to use coarse, not fine sand. The State Committee on Standards forbade the small size, because the quality of concrete is higher if gravel is used. Furthermore, the use of finer sand requires the addition of thirty percent more concrete to the cement. Volgodonskenergostroi ended up using an extra 100,000 tons of cement in three years because they used fine sand. Their motivations for this practice are baffling, because coarse sand was available nearby. All they would have had to do was dig a sand pit; and then they would have had enough of the stuff, not only for Atommash, but for the Rostov atomic power station and other principal construction projects. In fact, Minstroimash of the Russian Republic was supposed to build the pit with funds transferred from MinenergoSSSR. But no one in any bureaucracy could manage to sign the necessary papers. The story remained the same through the mid-1980s at a great cost in rubles and in lower quality concrete.[47]

During the interregnum between Brezhnev's death and Gorbachev's rise to power, Soviet leadership was preoccupied with the problem of "labor discipline," which it saw as the source of the endemic difficulties that plagued even priority industries such as Atommash. In the view of Iurii Andropov, general secretary for a brief fourteen months until his death in 1984, the Soviet Union's stagnating industrial production and the consistent failure of its agriculture were caused by lazy workers and managers, poor labor discipline, and alcoholism. Apparently, they had nothing to do with an outmoded economic system that had successfully turned a backward agrarian economy into an industrial power but now appeared incapable of innovation, stifled initiative, and appealed only to proletarian aesthetics. Andropov and the Central Committee could not admit that the Soviet worker was merely responding as expected to low wages, poor *sotskultbyt*, and a monotonous life. So when Atommash and Volgodonsk continued to lag years behind targets, Party leadership took its managers to task for "gross violations of labor discipline." To be sure, there had been serious accidents, and cables, pipes, and phone lines constantly broke or failed. The directors had lied when they claimed the first reactor was completed in 1981, for in 1982 it was still only partially complete.

Viktor Dolgikh, candidate member of the Politburo and secretary of the Central Committee, attended an *aktiv* of the Volgodonsk city Party committee in July 1983, a meeting publicized in *Pravda* to signal Andropov's approach to lagging industrial production. The selection of Dolgikh to run the operation followed the Soviet tradition of moving successful people out of one industrial enterprise into a new endeavor, as Zaveniagin, Rapoport, and countless others had been. Dolgikh had been a successful manager at Norilsk, the major Soviet nickel and platinum facility in northern Siberia. His arrival at the *aktiv* signaled clearly that some one was on his way out. Indeed, Ignatii Novikov, the chairman of the State Committee on Construction, Gosstroi, suddenly retired. Dolgikh pointed to problems of idle production, confusion, and high turnover and absenteeism (the loss of 7,000 man-days in the first quarter of 1981 alone; the arrival of 5,000 new workers accompanied by the departure of 3,000 others). Furthermore, deliveries of cement, timber, steel, and design drawings had always lagged significantly behind schedule.[48]

The assembled throng followed Dolgikh's lead in criticizing the pace of construction both of Atommash and of the social, cultural, and consumer services including apartments that were supposed to house the burgeoning labor force. Dolgikh made certain each participant of the *aktiv* recalled the comments Andropov made at a plenary session of the Central Committee in June about the central role of fission and fusion in the country's energy future. Atommash had to become the flagship of this vital sector. Dolgikh noted that production capacity lagged well behind plans, new technologies were slow to be assimilated, and training of workers had fallen well short of goals. Worse still, the quality of construction, whether at the factory or in apartment buildings, was inadequate.[49] The *aktiv* concluded by dismissing the director of Atommash and rebuking senior Ministry of Energy officials.

In fact, there were far more serious problems. Slowly, by rumor and word of mouth, the truth leaked out. Soviet officialdom finally had to acknowledge that from its first stages of construction, Atommash was doomed to failure. It had been built too close to the shores of the lake that backed up behind the Tsimlianskaia dam. Engineering organizations employing trained hydrologists had somehow failed to take into account a rise in groundwater associated with Stalin's waterworks along the Volga. Atommash's main foundry was slowly sinking into the muck, and an entire wall of the building had collapsed. Only three pressure vessels were ever produced by a facility intended to spit out eight annually. And that is the story of nuclear concrete.

The authorities learned nothing from the Atommash failures. They had planned to install the first VVERs that rolled off the assembly line at sites located seven miles from Rostov and twenty miles from Volgodonsk. These installations would have given them the opportunity to perfect methods of transport. But like Atommash itself, they built the Rostov atomic energy site on water-saturated, unstable ground. They failed to prepare the foundations adequately to take the multithousand ton weight of buildings, containment vessels, and reactor units. In the years before the Atommash debacle, the walls and floors of Rostov factory and apartment buildings had cracked and settled. The officials overlooked the great costs an accident would have for the fertile black soil regions of the lower Don River basin. They spent millions of rubles on the Rostov facility, then had to close it in the face of public opposition. They could have spent money on refurbishing old fossil fuel boilers. Irrationally, Soviet investment policy always emphasized new capital, not repair and upkeep. When gas and oil from the North Caucasus went into short supply, and other atomic power stations could not meet the demand of the region, the authorities had no choice but to fill such dinosaurs as the Novocherkassk heating station with low grade coal. It puffed along to meet local energy demand, polluting local streams and rivers and killing all the fish and crabs; cows there have a life expectancy of three years. The result of closing the Rostov site and Atommash was rampant unemployment, followed by a crime wave of unheard-of proportions. Yet even when they closed the Rostov power station, thousands labored on. Viktor Mikhailov, the head of MinAtom, had secretly ordered the ministry to spend nearly 200 million rubles on radio, television, and print media propaganda in support of the station; he also ordered construction to continue in preparation for a 1994 or 1995 opening of the station.[50] And like the management at the Seabrook Station in New Hampshire, they subverted established regulatory policy, never implementing an evacuation plan capable of handling the millions of residents near the station who might have to leave in an emergency.

A frightful indicator of the amoral behavior of planners and policy makers is the fact that Volgodonsk was also the center of an ongoing oncological crisis. In the last decade of Soviet power, cancer rates increased twenty percent in Rostov and thirty-two percent in Volgodonsk, versus an already terrifying nine percent increase for Russia as a whole. Of the thirty largest cities in the USSR, Rostov was at the bottom in terms of natural population growth, and in eighth place, exceeded only by Central Asian and Caucasian cities, in infant mortality. Its Temernik River is a lifeless monument to Soviet industry, carrying more than 200,000 tons annually of every kind of filth, garbage, and poison into the Don. Rostov town fathers thought it an inspiration to build an incinerator on the river shore; one can imagine how safely the incinerator operates. In the center of town is a chemical factory. Petrochemical facilities ring the city. Automobiles clog the streets. So now 130,000 persons suffer from cancer in the region.

Who chose the Rostov station site? Eduard Mustafinov, the main engineer for the Armenian station just outside of Erevan (a station built on a seismic fault), was responsible. He arrived at Atommash in 1977. He chose the most economical location on the shores of the Tsimlianskoe reservoir, so as not to waste money on canals and on cooling ponds and towers. His view of nuclear reactors: "A reactor is just a boiler, and the operator is a simple stoker." He had no other considerations, either hydrological or seismic. Like all Soviet economic planners and managers, Mustafinov reasoned that the key to Soviet industrial growth was the growth of electrical energy capacity and production. Over the last decade of the century, Soviet planners intended to add twenty million kilowatts of new capacity, even though they had never added more than ten million kilowatts in any earlier five year period. In Sweden, per capita production of electrical energy was five times that of the Soviet Union. Nuclear energy seemed to be the only way to raise production. Mustafinov ignored the time-honored joke about why the Swedish form of socialism and energy production would not work in Russia: there weren't enough Swedes in Russia.[51]

Atommash was a "project of the century," an "all-union Komsomol shock-work project." The struggle against its "self-destruction" has cost millions of rubles; and its descent into the muck has stopped the factory at fifty percent completion. Nearly one-quarter of a million people were drawn to the great project from around the country. The traditional ministerial tactics of proclaiming a city the next great project of the century, of promising modern infrastructure, plumbing, heating, and new apartments providing everything that every other Soviet city wants in full complement but does not have, and then delivering only the factory resulted in 30,000 single mothers, truancy, juvenile delinquency, homelessness, organized crime, and murders between youth gangs.[52]

QUIET FLOWS THE VOLGA

The impetus to standardize nuclear components is understandable. Constant retrofitting to meet ever-changing safety standards left the American nuclear industry uncompetitive with other forms of power generation. American engineers who worked at Babcock and Wilcox, Westinghouse, and General Electric lamented their inability to standardize construction practices. Having assessed the safety and reliability of reactors built with containment vessels, they were certain that they could employ reinforced concrete forms, turbogenerators, and other equipment of standard production to rejuvenate the industry. Soviet engineers labored with similar concerns but different constraints. They were not required to employ containment vessels; they did not encounter skeptical public scrutiny of their protestations of safety; they had government endorsement of the effort to embark on serial production of nuclear power reactors. Yet the aspiration to produce "nuclear concrete" did not involve merely the determination of safe and reliable components and materials used in power stations. Nuclear concrete comprised entire construction trusts engaged in the building of reactors and the towns to house the workers; it was poor quality construction caused by the same problems that plagued all other Soviet industries; it was engineers, or even skilled workers, employed to push scientifically determined norms into the production process; and it was common technologies and techniques employed in the diffusion of complex technologies.

Not only Atommash experienced this approach—and the infuriating bottlenecks—during the diffusion of nuclear technology. The actions of Dolgikh and the Party elite did little to change the situation. Volgodonskenergostroi had a budget of nearly 200 million rubles in 1984, but an additional 130 to 150 million rubles were needed annually to rectify the low quality of *sotskultbyt*. Volgodonskenergostroi had other things on its mind: construction of three blocks of the Rostov Atomic Power Station, where *sotskulthyt* for the workers was no better.[53] In addition to the *sot-*

The fifth unit of the Novovoronezh Nuclear Power Station, a 1,000-megawatt pressurized-water reactor, completed in 1980. *(Courtesy of Raissa Kuznetsova and the Kurchatov Institute)*

skulthyt problem and the sand-cement problem at Rostov, they had built transport corridors in the reactor blocks thirty-eight centimeters (fifteen inches) lower than specified in the drawings. The corridors weren't supposed to be for dwarfs, one boss complained, and he ordered some workmen with jackhammers to blast the doors and corridors open and do the job over. Worse still, the steel cask for the reactor wouldn't fit. Repairing this error was an expensive and time-consuming endeavor. No one took responsibility for the 136 serious violations of the project turned up during a routine inspection,[54] an inspection that did not include X-ray analysis of welds, which no doubt would have turned up cracks, fissures, and potential leaks of frightening proportions. Could they only produce concrete in the specified quantity in a timely fashion, but not necessarily in the right dimensions?

As grandiose as the plans for Atommash were, it was still only one of dozens of major projects being tackled simultaneously by an industry trying to meet past commitments with outdated equipment and workers who did not relish their jobs. Each year, twenty new Soviet cities and towns arose from the earth, each day one or two enterprises opened, and each day 9,500 families moved into long-awaited homes. Of course, Atommash received special attention, but so did the Tolyatti Lada (Fiat) Automobile Factory, 55,000 kilometers of gas and oil pipelines under construction, the Ust Ilimsk and Nurek hydropower stations, and the Donetsk and Tiraspolsk textile factories. Each project ultimately would suffer the consequences of the effort to solve countrywide large-scale problems with countrywide large-scale solutions.[55]

The stories of Izhorsk and Podolsk, Rostov and Balakova, Atommash and Volgodonsk are not caricatures. Nor is "nuclear concrete" merely shorthand for an anecdote. The Soviet system gave rise to an effort unique to the annals of nuclear power engineering to produce reactors serially. The effort involved typical Soviet scientists, managers, planners, and workers whose activities revolved around a construction trust with the usual foci of activity: excavation, erection, pouring of concrete. Yet in treating Atommash as ordinary in terms of technology to be produced—although glorious in terms of scale—officials and engineers made a fateful mistake. The mistake was understandable considering the genesis of Stalinist technological style. But considering the youthful level of their experience with PWRs, the well-known poor quality of Soviet technology in most areas of the economy, and the weak links that abounded in the production process, there can be no doubt that they hold responsibility for the premature quantum leaps in both the size of reactor units and the effort to produce them in a factory, and for the disaster that befell the massive Atommash foundry. It is a blessing that the Soviet Union collapsed, and the foundations of Atommash with it, before reactor units were loaded onto barges in the Volga and the Don rivers and installed willy-nilly in the European USSR.

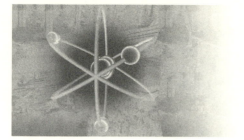

4

Nuclear Engines:
Technology as Panacea

The main part of the engine was a vertical metal cylinder three meters high and a half meter in diameter. Menni explained that it was made of osmium, a very refractory precious metal resembling platinum. It was in this cylinder that the decomposition of the radioactive material took place. Its red-hot, 20-centimeter thick walls gave an indication of the enormous energy being released in the process.
— From Aleksandr Bogdanov's *Red Star* (1908)

Vladimir Aleksandrovich Malykh never formally finished his higher education. He does not have a diploma. Yet the nuclear establishment saw to it that he was given candidate and doctor of science degrees for his work on nuclear reactors at Obninsk's Physics Engineering Institute. He was there when the 5,000-kilowatt channel-graphite reactor came on line in 1954, and he followed this achievement with the design of the TES-3, a 1,500-kilowatt portable atomic electrical power station that could move around on railway flatbed cars or even on tank treads. The prototype of this "small-size, huge block transportable" reactor was first manufactured in Obninsk, Kaluga Province, in 1961. It consisted of four platforms, each 10 meters long and 3.4 meters wide, perfect for barge or railway transport; and it weighed 360 tons in all, most of the weight being due to the lead and distilled, borated-water biological shielding, which was 830 millimeters thick. Once installed at the chosen construction site, the TES-3 moved at speeds of up to eighteen kilometers per hour over terrain with an incline of up to 15°.[1] The TES-3 made possible the production of electric energy at any locale, especially north of the Arctic Circle where Chukchi reindeer herders might take advantage of its portability.

Malykh had come a long way to Obninsk's Physics Engineering Institute. Born in Shurtan, a Siberian village without a school or teachers, he learned physics from hands-on experience as a repair man in a Machine Tractor Station (those equipment parks the Bolsheviks established in collective and state farms in the 1930s, not so much to provide the peasants with tractors and combines as to ensure political control over this element of the population, who so hated them). Malykh found his way from the tractor station to the physics-mathematics department at Moscow University at the beginning of World War II. Like most able-bodied men, he was called to active service. He returned after the war to the university as a laboratory assistant of Aleksandr Savvich Predvoditelev, who became director of the Scientific Research Institute of Physics at Moscow State University, one of the first special centers for training engineers and physicists for the USSR's burgeoning nuclear research establishment. Malykh's other professors included Ilya Mikhailovich Frank, a specialist in high-energy physics and a future Nobel laureate.

In Moscow, Malykh contracted tuberculosis and had to leave the city. He was sent to the Kaluga pine forests that surround Obninsk. And there, he joined the reactor research effort, bringing to physics immodest visions of the application of nuclear power to change nature, from the Kolsk and Bilibino atomic power stations of the far north, to the Shevchenko breeder reactor on the Caspian Sea (which produced electricity and desalinated water), to the TES-3.[2] Enthusiasm for the enterprise was contagious. S. N. Tarkov, a zoologist from Krasnodar, wrote Kurchatov in May 1956 with a design for small (thirty-kilowatt!) nuclear motors for use in the fields of the Soviet Union's poorly performing collective farms.[3] Bolshevik scientists didn't just fantasize about the future; they made it a reality.

From the first days of the nuclear age, scientists touted applications of nuclear steam engines—small reactors in airplanes, jets, ships, hydrofoils and submarines, locomotives and automobiles, and various other mobile power plants. Initially, the railroad and shipping industries were particularly interested, for they dreamed of freedom from reliance on diesel and oil depots. Powerful nuclear engines would enable them to cart freight—ore, coal, oil, and timber—long distances at low cost. The first and most extensive use of nuclear engines, of course, was for military hardware; aircraft carriers and submarines could operate for months without refueling. Submarines would not have to surface for the oxygen needed to burn diesel fuel and would have nearly silent engines, undetectable by the enemy's sonar. From the early 1950s, Academy scientists in the Institute of Complex Transportation Problems also studied technical, economic, volumetric, and weight issues in support of nuclear shipping.[4]

The cold war gave considerable momentum to the military's desire for nuclear engines, and the certainty of the physicists that they could build the devices quickly secured extravagant funding. The physicists confidently poured out chapter and verse on economic and technical parameters indicating that nuclear devices would outperform internal combustion engines in the near future. For Soviet physicists like Vladimir Malykh, nothing seemed more logical than using nuclear engines to overcome the various tricks nature had played on their country, a country with only one warm-water port in the Black Sea and vast natural resources trapped by ice and permafrost in the far north, Siberia, and the far east. Atomic energy would free the country from the difficult task of shipping fossil fuels into the harsh Siberian winter. The paragon of these efforts was the *Lenin* icebreaker, which, in spite of technical problems that delayed its launch, was intended to be only the first of many ocean-going nuclear-powered vessels that would open the Arctic's resources to exploitation. Small nuclear hothouses and power stations would follow the *Lenin* into the far north.

The construction of nuclear engines was as much for symbolic and cultural value as for military and economic purposes. But decades of research and billions of rubles (not to mention dollars, pounds, marks, and francs) have resulted in human and environmental costs, for the lure of the atom's power proved greater than its reliability and safety. There was no public scrutiny of what lay behind the notable technical achievements: the ocean floor was being littered with nuclear reactors and millions of curies of radioactive wastes haphazardly disposed of in the absence of a real solution to the legacy of nuclear engines. And the economic cost was much greater, the performance far less stunning than the physicists had anticipated.

THE REVOLUTIONARY SYMBOLISM OF THE NUCLEAR ENGINE

Lenin could not have imagined that the first Soviet nuclear-powered ship, an icebreaker, would be named after him. But he was a technological utopian, seeing such technologies as electricity, irrigation, and the tractor as panaceas for economic growth and revolutionary change. Electricity would illuminate the shop floor, allowing the worker to toil in a healthy environment to build communism. It would turn Russia's rich, but dry soils into fields of grain. The State Electrification Plan was only the first of many large-scale systems that the Bolsheviks believed would alter both society and nature for the better. Irrigation would enable agronomists, hand in hand with the peasant, to revolutionize agriculture, creating a Soviet garden of plenty. Hydroelectric stations would power agriculture. The tractor would extend furrows—and Soviet political control—to the horizon.

Lenin died before his utopian visions came to fruition. But the Lenin cult that blossomed after his death required that myriad future construction projects bear his name—from the infamous Lenin Chernobyl Atomic Energy Station, which even today goes by that name, to the first atomic icebreaker. No doubt Lenin would have approved of the nuclear engine, which, in the simplest version, was a nuclear reactor to produce heat to boil water to produce steam to turn a turbogenerator to produce electricity to turn an electric motor. Whether he would have approved of dumping three spent reactors from the *Lenin* in the Tsivolka Inlet in the Arctic Ocean is another matter.

By 1949, physicists at the core of the nuclear bomb project had already discussed a number of different peaceful applications of nuclear reactors. Their plutonium production reactor worked admirably and generated huge quantities of thermal energy that might somehow be used to generate electricity. Plans for the Obninsk reactor were well underway. On top of this, in November of 1953, the Council of Ministers approved a project to build a powerful icebreaker that could open a northern ocean route. As with many other projects involving the development of resources north of the Arctic Circle, the icebreaker had prewar roots. In 1932, the Administration of the Northern Shipping Lane was established to look into the potential for a route from Murmansk to Vladivostok. During World War II, several diesel icebreakers, including one called *Lenin*, operated around Dikson north of the Arctic Circle in the Enesei delta. Stalin himself had great interest in developing the Arctic, not the least through the use of forced labor. The Gulag camps dotted the map, and millions of prisoners died opening veins of gold, building dams, and logging trees. Stalin proposed the construction of New Park in the Ob delta to tie the far north together with truck convoys. Sadly, building a road through the tundra was not only expensive but also never-ending because of damage caused by the frequent hard frosts and thaws. So a decision was made in May 1947 to develop a 45,000-horsepower icebreaker, which would allow nearly year-round shipping instead of an overland route. The Leningrad Central Engineering Bureau 15 under Vasilii Ivanovich Neganov took on the design task. In 1948, Neganov's group produced a plan for an icebreaker with four powerful diesel engines. Then the project was placed on the back burner when Bureau 15 was ordered to build cruiser-class warships instead.

In 1953, just after Stalin's death, physicists and engineers found a Communist Party leadership more responsive to their plans to move away from military research toward various peaceful applications. The Party officials especially wanted to show that Eisenhower's Atoms for Peace program was already standard fare in the USSR. In Moscow, the entrenched foreign policy pronouncements about the inevitability of war between capitalist and socialist camps were giving way to the concept of "peaceful coexistence." Enlightened scientists and policy makers recognized the potential propaganda coup associated with the peaceful atom. The *Lenin* had both technological and symbolic meaning: it would demonstrate the scientific hubris and peaceful intentions of the Soviet power. Thousands of workers and scientists joined the effort. By June 1955, the technical aspects of the project had been worked out.[5] Engineers were going full speed ahead on the design of nuclear submarines, for which they were building a land-based prototype reactor. Scientists knew that similar reactors would easily find successful application in other oceangoing vessels, especially broad-bow icebreakers. Neganov, I. I. Afrikantov (the head of the design bureau of Factory 92), and Anatolii Aleksandrov joined forces to build the flagship—or rather flag-icebreaker—of the peaceful atom, the *Lenin*.

In the United States in the same years, Admiral Hyman Rickover forced the pace of development of the nuclear navy through sheer power of personality. With dogged certainty that his way of doing things was the only way, he convinced AEC laboratories and a loose conglomeration of industrial contractors including General Electric, Electric Boat, and, most important, Westinghouse Electric to develop PWRs, first for submarines, and then for civilian nuclear power. The Shippingport (Pennsylvania) 60-megawatt reactor was the first civilian nuclear power station in the United States. In the Soviet Union, because the government was not only contractor but also owner of all industry, any design, testing, construction, and diffusion of the new technology depended on it and on similarly devoted nuclear barons. In this case, it was Kurchatov's right-hand man, Aleksandrov. Rather than waste time creating an industry, he and Kurchatov logically determined that the Kurchatov Institute would sit at the head of the project, carrying out all preliminary research, on one of the newly created BESM Soviet computers. This research included the development of the reactor, the determination of the physical characteristics of the active zone and biological shielding, and the nature of the fuel elements. Using Kurchatov's contacts in the military and in the Kremlin, they got the right mix of industrial firms—Elektrosila, the Izhorsk Steel Works, and naval facilities—to snap to at any request.

MR. ATOM: ANATOLII ALEKSANDROV

Anatolii Aleksandrov rode the engine of nuclear-powered submarines and ice-breakers to the top of the Soviet scientific establishment. He was already well entrenched at the center of that establishment when Kurchatov urged him to take on the task of nuclear propulsion. Aleksandrov was a capable physicist whose fields of interest included solid state and nuclear physics. His career was blessed with the appropriate contacts and proper appointments from the start. He was a devoted communist, reliable beyond doubt concerning his sentiments about the correctness of the Soviet mission. He became corresponding member of the Academy of Sciences in 1943 and full member in 1953. In spite of noteworthy engineering achievements, his leadership as president of the Academy from 1975 until 1986 and as a member of the Communist Party Central Committee from 1965 until 1986, when he retired at the age of eighty-three, is distinguished by the well-known "stagnation" of the Brezhnev era. This stagnation in science was the result of significant support for massive construction projects characteristic of Soviet technological development; the ossification of an old-boys' network controlling scientific resources and decision making; piecemeal attempts to reform the administration of science; and an almost haughty attitude toward the public, which was kept in the dark about the potential dangers of modern science and technology. For all his efforts, Aleksandrov received three Hero of Socialist Labor awards, eight Lenin prizes, an Order of the October Revolution, and several other prizes.[6]

Aleksandrov (1903–1992) was born in Tarashch, Ukraine. His father was a teacher. For a time after he completed Real School in Kiev, Aleksandrov worked as an electrician. Simultaneously studying in the physics-mathematics department of Kiev University, he graduated in 1923. A curious young man, he organized a student circle to discuss current developments in atomic physics and pursued correspondence with Ernest Rutherford, whose Cavendish Laboratory in Cambridge, England stood at the forefront of efforts to understand atomic structure. His letter went unanswered. A letter from the Rostov-on-Don University student physics club to Rutherford provoked quite an outburst. Having confused the English and Russian words for "nucleus" and "cannon balls," they informed the great man that he had been elected an honorary member of their club "for having proven that atoms have balls." Rutherford angrily demanded an explanation from Kapitsa, who happened to be in the Cambridge laboratory at that time and who calmed Rutherford down.

After graduating from the university, Aleksandrov entered the Kiev-based Roentgen Institute, conducting research on the properties of dielectrics. His first work was on "High Voltage Polarization in Resin." This research, and that of his colleagues, came to the attention of Abram Ioffe just before a conference of the Russian Association of Physicists, held in Odessa in 1930, the last such conference before the Communist Party shut down the association. Ioffe sent his colleagues Nikolai Semenov, Iakov Frenkel, and Igor Kurchatov as an advance group to search out young talent among Ukrainian scholars and among the 750 participants at the congress. The congress included a steamship trip to Sevastopol and by car to Yalta and then Batumi, by which time Aleksandrov and several of his colleagues, overwhelmed by stories of the vitality of physics research at Ioffe's institute, had agreed to transfer to Leningrad. Aleksandrov subsequently invited an entire group of Kiev Roentgen Institute physicists back to Leningrad to work with him.

Upon arriving in Leningrad, Aleksandrov discovered a hard life. He was without his family at first and slept in a frigid room in the Scholars' House, shivering under one blanket. The food was so wretched that he preferred to walk around in a state of perpetual hunger. Still, Leningrad was the place to be for a physicist. The city was the center of Soviet culture—its theater, art, and science. Soviet physicists had built up a series of fine institutes in a matter of years, equipping them with new instruments and recent journals, and establishing contacts with their colleagues in the West. There was always something interesting going on. Aleksandrov met Alikhanov, Artsimovich, Sinelnikov, Kikoin—all future leaders of Soviet physics. Here one could engage in cutting-edge research. Nuclear physics commenced under the leadership of Ioffe's physicists and at the Radium Institute, which was building a small cyclotron. At Ioffe's institute, work on a cyclotron had begun under Kurchatov, Abram Alikhanov, and Dmitrii Efremov (the future minister of the electronics industry) when war interrupted their preparations. The cyclotron was hurriedly dismantled and finally installed in Moscow.

Aleksandrov recalled the challenges of physics research in the Stalin era. In 1936, the authorities organized a special session of the Academy of Sciences to criticize Ioffe's leadership in the physics community and the lag in practical applications from physics research, including the seemingly foolish pursuit of nuclear research. This was a stunning blow to the authority of physicists and a slap in the face for Ioffe, for he had resurrected the physics enterprise from the ravages of the war and revolution to international reputation in such fields as solid state and nuclear physics. Aleksandrov wrote: "Today it is difficult to imagine that this occurred only two or three years after the discovery of nuclear fission."

Aleksandrov's own work was in the experimental tradition of LFTI, involving the study of such new materials as polystyrene and other polymers, work that led to his doctoral degree. He then focused on high-molecular compounds, but his research was cut short by World War II. During the war, like many *fiztekhovtsy*, Aleksandrov undertook research with military applications, developing a method for compensating for a ship's own magnetic field to protect it from triggering magnetic mines. Aleksandrov had already tested a few of the antimine devices on several ships when the war broke out. The Navy immediately equipped what few cruisers they could in the Gulf of Riga with the test devices, and this deployment certainly saved ships in the short term. Because the Germans were constantly improving their mines, Aleksandrov worked feverishly to improve the antimine devices, successfully testing his new designs in Sevastopol in the spring of 1941. Subsequently, he inspected their installation under very dangerous conditions: Stalingrad, where the Germans had installed mines in the Volga River, and blockaded Leningrad. He flew into Stalingrad just after the Germans had bombed the airfield; it was a wonder the plane didn't hit a crater on landing. Aleksandrov traveled to Murmansk in the fall of 1941 to inspect the devices on the crippled Soviet submarine fleet; he read in the newspaper in April 1942 that he had received a Stalin prize for this work. Aleksandrov's northward journey introduced the Arctic to him; he would return, or at least his nuclear-powered icebreakers and reactors would, in the 1950s and 1960s.[7]

In 1944, just elected a corresponding member of the Academy of Sciences, Aleksandrov's career was changed forever when he was called by his long-time friend, Igor Kurchatov, to participate in the atomic bomb project. Aleksandrov had not been directly involved in nuclear research, but he was no stranger to the field because of his personal contacts. He knew Georgii Flerov well. Flerov, now at the Ioffe institute, had, with Konstantin Petrzhak at the Radium Institute, discovered the spontaneous fission of uranium. Iakov Zeldovich and Iulii Khariton at Institute of Chemical Physics were also Aleksandrov's friends. Aleksandrov's first assignment was to develop the thermal diffusion method of isotope separation in case other methods—electromagnetic and gaseous diffusion—failed. When Aleksandrov commenced this work, the German blockade of Leningrad had only recently been lifted. The city was in ruins; tens of thousands of persons had starved to death; there was no running water, electricity, or heat. Aleksandrov commandeered a locomotive to power his experiments; it sat on the street next to his laboratory.

In 1946, Kurchatov called Aleksandrov to Moscow, where he became Kurchatov's scientific deputy and worked first on the F-1 reactor project and then at the plutonium production reactor. It was amazing how quickly the physicists moved from experiments that measured minute quantities and produced micrograms of new substances to projects involving huge industrial facilities that produced the kilograms of materials needed for the atomic bomb project. Of course, Stalin had ordered the leading representatives of industry—B. L. Vannikov, M. G. Pervukhin, V. A. Malyshev, A. P. Zaveniagin, and E. P. Slavskii—to facilitate his every need.

Aleksandrov's next assignment was a bittersweet one. Peter Kapitsa was removed as director of the Institute of Physical Problems (IFP) and placed under house arrest because of his incessant criticism of the way Beria was handling the bomb project. Beria selected the reliable Aleksandrov to take over the institute in the middle of 1946, where he served until 1955. After Stalin's death, Kapitsa was allowed to return to his rightful position. Aleksandrov was met coolly, but professionally in this new position, for he counted among IFPers a number of acquaintances. At IFP, Aleksandrov supervised the theoreticians Landau, Lifshits, and others who were working on calculations for the hydrogen bomb. But he spent most of his time in factories connected with the bomb project, especially the plutonium production reactor, where he joined Dollezhal. For all his travels and responsibilities, he remained close to Kurchatov. Some time after the Soviets exploded their first bomb, Kurchatov dropped in at IFP. Aleksandrov reminded him of his promise to shave his beard after the successful detonation. Then and there, they found shaving soap and a straight edge razor. Kurchatov snipped off the beard before shaving; a long piece remains in the IFP museum to this day.

After the successful atomic bomb test on August 29, 1949, Aleksandrov was ordered to work on atomic engines for submarines and icebreakers. The design tasks for the submarine were daunting, but the prospect of developing an engine that did not require huge diesel fuel tanks or oxygen for combustion made this an exciting quest. In 1956, there were successful land-based tests, then the creation of an atomic submarine and surface fleet, and finally such honorable achievements as the conquering of the North Pole by Soviet submarines and icebreakers. Aleksandrov also oversaw the design of prototypes for channel-graphite reactors, starting down the fateful path to Chernobyl.[8]

During the 1950s and 1960s, Aleksandrov often spent as much time in industrial facilities, busying himself with production problems, as he did at the Kurchatov Institute, where he became director after Kurchatov's death in 1960. His visits to factories convinced him of the feasibility of pursuing standardization in many areas of reactor construction, a goal he pursued with vigor. Under his leadership, the USSR created a massive atomic energy industry based on principles of serial production. He displayed great ability as physicist, engineer, and organizer, supervising closely the work of other engineers, designers, and material scientists. He paid attention both to the general aspects of projects and to their details, so that his associates believed he would always manage to avoid "striking any underwater objects." He believed that engineers could design inherently safe technologies. This is clear in his work on the VVR, SM, and IGR research reactors, as well as on the VVER and RBMK power reactors. Aleksandrov prodded physicists, engineers, and industrial managers who fell within his bailiwick to lower reactor capital costs by producing the components serially, increasing the unit size of the reactors, and using standard factory and construction industry materials wherever possible. But he did not avoid hitting one underwater object, the Chernobyl RBMK reactor.

Aleksandrov was the prototypical scientist-administrator of the Brezhnev era. He was an imposing figure, tall and massive, with a perfectly bald head; and he commanded attention in every setting. He espoused the standard view of the role of science in "developed socialist society." During the Khrushchev era, he had shown impatience with the pseudoscience of Lysenkoism, helping to establish the radiobiological department of the institute (later the Institute of Molecular Genetics, next door to the Kurchatov Institute). But his subsequent activities and pronouncements showed a further impatience with novelty and a desire to develop science as stipulated from above rather than by individual initiative, and to reform science by bureaucratic fiat rather than by the true decentralization of scientific policy that is required to invigorate scientific research. He viewed science solely as a segment of the economy, not as an institution that required special efforts to ensure its productivity—including granting greater academic freedom to researchers to choose their own paths rather than laboring under scientific bosses at huge science institutes. In this environment, the big science of river diversion, Chernobyl, space, and metallurgy were paramount, while fields on the cutting edge—computer science and technology, genetic engineering, fiber optics—languished with inadequate support. For the Communist Party, nuclear artifacts were more important than social programs.[9]

By the late 1960s, Aleksandrov had set forth the major outlines of the Soviet energy policy: a gradual decline in the share produced by fossil fuels with a growing percentage produced by thermal reactors; then the construction of a network of breeder reactors to utilize and breed more plutonium; and finally the building of fusion and hybrid fusion-breeder reactors in the early twenty-first century. Aleksandrov pushed two major variants of thermal reactors: the channel-graphite RBMK (based on the plutonium production reactor, with the Obninsk 5,000-kilowatt reactor (1954) and the Siberian 600,000-kilowatt reactor (1958) as forerunners) and the VVER pressurized-water reactor (whose design grew out of submarine and icebreaker reactors and was first utilized at the Novovoronezhskaia atomic power station).[10]

Aleksandrov could refer with impunity to the viability of nuclear power during its early years, for the Third Communist Party Program, promulgated in 1961, promised to achieve the glorious communist utopia by 1980. The program was based in part on the achievements of science and technology, including "the construction of atomic electrical power stations." Like many Soviet visionaries before him, Aleksandrov promoted a utopian vision of heavy industry that would expand rapidly because of cheap and plentiful energy. He never hesitated to recall the roots of his vision in the Leninist GOELRO plan nor how it reflected the concern of the Communist Party for the people and an interest in "the growth of their material and spiritual culture." At the annual meeting of the Academy of Sciences in February 1962, for example, Aleksandrov touted atomic energy based on huge reactors produced in serial fashion as a key to economic development and the growth of "material culture."[11]

Like many Western nuclear engineers, Aleksandrov made a number of erroneous assumptions: that the demand for electrical energy would continue to grow two to three percent, if not more, annually; that known reserves of fossil fuels would be exhausted soon; and that the cost of nuclear power would soon be comparable to that of energy produced by other sources. Believing these assumptions, scientists wanted first to make nuclear energy reliable and then to lower its costs. Aleksandrov claimed that the higher than anticipated costs had nothing to do with insurmountable technical problems but were due to a lag in building huge reactors with standardized equipment. He pointed to the construction of the Novovoronezhskaia station as evidence that physicists had solved many of the technical problems concerning pressurized-water reactors and to the Beloiarskaia station, being built under the supervision of Nikolai Dollezhal, as proof of the reliability of the channel-graphite reactor. However, both were small by present day standards, at only

210,000 kilowatts. Before the monsters of the Chernobyl era would be built, much work remained to be done.

In his last years as leader of the Soviet scientific establishment, Aleksandrov proposed that nuclear power be used not only for electrical power generation (which, in the USSR, would reduce the amount of fossil fuels being used by only ten percent) but also for nuclear "thermalization of cities, heating of homes, providing of heat in technological processes in industrial enterprises, that is, in all regions of demand of energy resources." Aleksandrov proudly recommended the construction of nuclear heating plants within city limits because, although they had higher capital costs, they would turn out to be cheaper than oil or diesel boilers, would pollute significantly less, would save hundreds of millions of tons of fossil fuel annually, and would free freight lines from the burden of coal transport.[12]

Aleksandrov was not content to push atomic energy with geopolitical and economic arguments. He criticized those who failed to sing his tune, including industrial enterprises that insisted upon seeing atomic energy as "rich women who it is a sin not to rob. . . . The matter has become laughable. A standard steel staircase, just because it is destined for an atomic power station, for some reason costs three times more. It is necessary to stop thinking about equipment for atomic energy stations as exotic and to specify costs for them more rationally. This is the essential factor in the struggle for economy. It is time for factories to stop closing gaps in their finances through extortion of atomic energy." At the same time, Aleksandrov had utopian visions for the application of atomic energy. With the atom, "it was possible to consider problems of grand scale about which earlier it was not even possible to dream." Swamps, taiga, ice-blocked rivers, and other impediments to conquering Siberia's great resources would give way. In the empty expanse, "gigantic construction atomic trusts would travel about, leaving in their wake highways, canals to assimilate the swamps, and . . . even agriculture." Engineers were already building a huge station on the shores of the Caspian to desalinate water and create a "fertile paradise" where once there had been desert. With atomic energy, it would be possible to create cheaply "microclimates of Sukhumi somewhere in Norilsk or in Igarka (in the far north)," all within one generation. Whether nuclear engines, pressurized-water reactors, channel-graphite reactors, or breeders, in 1,000-, 1,500- or 2,000-megawatt blocks, for the production of electrical energy or heat for industrial and home-heating purposes, on the Kola peninsula, in Armenia, or in Siberia, for Aleksandrov and the Soviet scientific establishment, atomic energy had become the crucial ingredient of technological progress.[13]

When Alekansandrov referred to geological, industrial, and medical applications of tracer atoms in diagnostics and therapy, Brezhnev interrupted his speech at the twenty-fifth Party congress: "Will there be any kind of 'bomb' against the flu?" Against a background of tittering in the huge hall, Aleksandrov responded, "The flu? Leonid Ilich, I can answer you straight away that the Institute of Nuclear Physics in Gatchina together with an institute of Minzdrav [Ministry of Health] developed a vaccine against flu which has been tested. . . . [T]he question is the industrial production of the vaccine. It is necessary to make it triflingly inexpensive."[14] Like the scientists developing the flu vaccine, Soviet physicists strove to make nuclear power inexpensive, by moving toward industrial production of nuclear engines.

Mr. Atom, Anatolii Petrovich Aleksandrov (in 1984), one of Kurchatov's deputies. Director of the Institute of Physical Problems from 1946 until 1955, deputy director of the Kurchatov Institute until 1960, then director until his retirement in 1983. President of the Soviet Academy of Sciences, 1975 to 1983, and a member of the Central Committee of the Communist Party under Leonid Brezhnev. Designer of nuclear submarine reactors and the RBMK Chernobyl-type reactor. *(Courtesy of Iurii Lavrov and the Mayor's office, Severodvinsk, Russia)*

The TES-3 portable nuclear power station—just like a mobile home. The chimney in the background belongs to another facility. *(Courtesy of Lev Kochetkov and the Physics Engineering Institute in Obninsk)*

The *Lenin* nuclear icebreaker. *(Courtesy of Raissa Kuznetsova and the Kurchatov Institute)*

A RADIOACTIVE *LENIN* SPREADS GOODWILL
IN THE ARCTIC

Nuclear-powered ships had significant advantages over diesel- and steam-powered vessels. The *Lenin*'s reactors could operate for one year between refueling. In contrast, the diesel-powered icebreaker *Moscow*, at 16,000 horsepower, used 110 tons of fuel daily; it had to return to port at least once a month to top off its 3,000-ton capacity tanks. Engineers saw a potential both for powerful 40,000-horsepower engines (and later much larger ones for aircraft carriers) and for "small" 10,000-horsepower engines for atomic-powered river transport. Nuclear icebreakers produced 2.75 horsepower per ton, whereas conventionally powered icebreakers produced only 1.1 to 2.0 horsepower per ton. They moved at eighteen to twenty-one knots, far exceeding the twelve to fifteen knots of conventional icebreakers. They could remain away from base, technically speaking, for a year at a time. The *Lenin*'s small ratio of length to width (134 to 27.6 meters) ensured maneuverability, easy access to dry docks, and stability. It could easily break up ice over two meters thick while moving forward at two knots. Power and maneuverability were the keys to opening shipping lanes and facilitating the assimilation of the great resources of the far north—ore, rare metals, and fossil fuels. The major obstacles to the new technology were forty percent higher capital costs over those of the conventional diesel icebreakers and slightly higher operating expenses.

Engineers proposed several different kinds of reactors for the *Lenin*: one-, two-, and three-loop systems, pressurized- and boiling-water reactors, graphite- and water-moderated, even liquid metal- and helium-cooled units. For example, the advantage of a one-loop reactor with helium coolant is that the helium does not become radioactive, making shielding a simpler matter and also making it possible to build an efficient smaller, lighter reactor. Still, helium itself is expensive; it would have to be heated to 760°C; and Soviet scientists had more experience with pressurized-water reactors that had cheaper, more reliable, standard steam turbines. Abram Alikhanov, of Kurchatov's rival Institute of Theoretical and Experimental Physics, proposed a homogeneous heavy water reactor to increase the engine's efficiency while lowering its cost, but difficulties in hermeticization of the circulating pump and the danger of the possibility of precipitation of the fuel in stagnation points of the first loop, as well as the high radioactivity of the first loop, doomed this variant. Ultimately, Aleksandrov settled on an icebreaker powered by pressurized-water reactors whose water served the dual role of moderator and coolant.[15] The 44,000-horsepower *Lenin* had three reactors with ^{235}U fuel enriched to five percent, two of which powered the ship, the third being held in reserve in case of emergency.

In the fall of 1953, physicists, engineers, and radiation safety specialists set out to build the nuclear steam engine for the *Lenin*, a huge task that involved a number of design bureaus, industrial enterprises, and the Kurchatov Institute of Atomic Energy. The *Lenin*'s reactors had a maximum power of ninety megawatts, but they produced a maximum thrust of 44,000 horsepower in the turbogenerators with all three reactors operating at sixty-five megawatts. The *Lenin* also had diesel generators rated at 200 and 1,000 kilowatts in case of reactor failure. Operating experience showed that the reserve diesel generators produced sufficient power for safety and control when the reactors for some reason failed to operate properly or were down for repairs. The size of the ship allowed sufficiently thick shielding to ensure the safety of personnel. The weight of each reactor with biological shielding was 3,100 tons. Special ventilators allowed radioactive steam to be vented from the first loop, after first passing through filters. Liquid radioactive wastes were temporarily stored in special drums; but more often than not, they were simply dumped into the ocean.[16]

The operating personnel received special training in the Makarov Leningrad Higher Engineering Naval School. Their training was complete only after they successfully passed an examination. They also had to be recertified annually. Many of them later worked at atomic stations. The equipment was so reliable, it was claimed, that personnel set foot in the reactor compartment no more than once briefly every twenty-four hours to check the equipment.[17] The crew had all the comforts of home to ensure the safety and success of the ship's missions. Navigation equipment was up to the minute. The *Lenin* had two radiolocators and radios that operated on ultra-short, short, medium, and long wave, as well as a powerful megaphone to address nearby ships and the shore. The megaphone may have been more to the sailors' liking because they were used to screaming at the top of their lungs to be heard when speaking on poor-quality Soviet telephones. The sailors were grateful for accommodations that were not much smaller than typical Soviet apartments and made the long periods they were at sea much less claustrophobic: one- and two-bunk compartments nearly eight feet tall; hot and cold running water; special lights to suggest the sun during interminable polar nights; bathrooms, toilets, and showers separate from the cabins; spacious refrigerators; a medical and dental facility, pharmacy, laboratory, intensive care facility, and quarantine; dispensary; and gymnasium.

The atomic and space ages overlapped fully. On August 24, 1956, metalworkers at the dry docks of the Admiralty Factory in Leningrad laid the *Lenin*'s keel; the ship itself was pushed from its dry dock on December 5, 1957, less than a month after Sputnik. But unlike Sputnik, which was an unqualified success even if its function was only to "beep" periodically, it took the *Lenin* several years to make waves as intended. In June 1958, N. S. Khlopkin wrote Kurchatov to warn him that all was not well. The central section, a three-reactor vessel, had been built, two of six steam generators were in place, and the biological shielding with steel walls 350 to 420 millimeters thick was installed, but Khlopkin worried about "low quality welding." The Elektrostal Factory manufactured the cladding for the fuel rods, but the scientists initially failed to load all the rods into the reactor because of excess reactivity. The uranium load had to be reduced, and its enrichment was also lessened. Furthermore, instruments to be produced by the Admiralty Factory for the control room, display panels, and dials had yet to be manufactured, leaving questions of electrical safety and stability unresolved. Generator construction lagged. Khlopkin suggested that various enterprises and managers needed a kick in the pants.[18]

Like Sputnik, the launching of *Lenin* was a matter of national pride and political significance. This was not the first time that Soviet leaders used technological feats to legitimize their rule. In the 1930s, Stalin grasped the achievements of Soviet airmen who, in balloons and planes, established distance, time, and altitude records—at the cost of human lives in accidents—as confirmation of the fact that the path he had chosen for technological development was the best—indeed, the only—alternative. Bolshevik leaders initially sought Western technological assistance, purchasing the services of American and German engineers, buying their technology outright, or stealing it through foreign trade offices established in Europe and America and run by the KGB. Once Stalin had assumed power, the nation sought to construct what was called "socialism in one country," showing self-sufficiency in economic matters, eschewing foreign trade for domestic development, and subjecting foreign engineers and any of their intimate Soviet colleagues to harassment, arrest, even execution. The world records in aviation also won support at home and abroad when the regime later came under intense criticism because of purges.[19]

The successful completion of the first tests of the *Lenin* generated a front-page photograph in *Pravda* on December 20, 1959, and a congratulatory declaration from the Central Committee of the Communist Party and the Council of Ministers of the USSR to "scientists, designers, engineers, technical specialists, workers, and sailors of the navy, and to the entire collective who have participated in the creation of the first in the world nuclear icebreaker *Lenin*." This success was a "new huge victory in the matter of the utilization of atomic energy" which "opened new possibilities for the assimilation of the riches of the Soviet Arctic and the furthest development of the economy of the northern regions of the country." The communiqué from the government verification commission on the safety, maneuverability, and quality of the huge vessel accompanied the declaration.[20]

The minimal initial 2,000-mile tests of the *Lenin*'s seaworthiness and safety apparently raised as much suspicion about nuclear ships as celebration of their promise, for the authorities were required to address publicly the concerns raised by an Odessa-based sailor who, like hundreds of other persons, harbored misgivings about the safety of "nuclear passenger ships and freighters" for passengers and inhabitants of ports alike. A certain Ermakov, a scientist at the Institute of Complex Transportation Problems, calmed worries, informing citizens that nuclear-powered ships would be few in number until the 1970s in any event, but that contemporary technology ensured their safe operation, containment of products of fission, and shielding of personnel from radioactivity. Contrary to popular fears, the reactor could not explode like a nuclear bomb. Ermakov acknowledged that there were technical challenges concerning repair and refueling, but these activities would be strictly controlled and away from populated areas. He admitted that the navy would dump certain wastes at sea, but only in agreement with international law. Ermakov soothingly mentioned that the United States, England, Germany, and Japan also had nuclear ship programs. "Sailors should know," he concluded, "that not one person on an atomic ship has suffered from radiation. Residents of ports, too, may be given a guarantee that all activities of atomic shipping in ports present no danger to anyone."[21] Shadowed closely by apprehensive Norwegian, Danish, and American airplanes, the *Lenin* "steamed," or perhaps fissioned, in early May 1960 to Murmansk, the major northern port of the USSR on the Barents Sea. The *Lenin* had "passed the exam," entering the port on a clear sunny day to begin its lengthy service. "The tug-boat *Afanasiev* met the atomic giant which had on board representatives of the Party, and of Soviet and social organizations of Murmansk, and newspaper, radio, and television reporters," the newspapers reported. The *Lenin*'s arrival in Murmansk carried special meaning as a symbol of Soviet power, technological know-how, and peaceful intentions.[22]

Recognizing the potential propaganda coup to be gained by harnessing the peaceful atom, Japan, Germany, Britain, and the United States also pursued nuclear tankers and freighters of various sorts. Take the example of the United States: In April 1955, President Dwight D. Eisenhower called for an atomic ship to be built. Congress quickly authorized the project. In May 1958, at the New York Shipbuilding yards in Camden, New Jersey, construction commenced. The 20,000-ton *Savannah* was launched on July 21, 1959, with but one reactor running on ^{235}U enriched to four percent—but, as Soviet propagandists never failed to point out, it generated only a measly 20,000 horsepower. Delay in bringing *Savannah* on line may have been tied to the fact that resources were diverted to launch the *Enterprise* aircraft carrier and nuclear-powered submarines first. In any event, the *Savannah* was intended "to demonstrate the peaceful uses of atomic energy." The thinking was that if a nuclear ship were only a little heavier than a conventional ship without fuel, then nuclear-propelled ships of the same size could carry significantly more cargo on long voyages at high power and relatively high speed. Promoters of nuclear maritime shipping were confident that they could handle all problems of docking, cargo handling, and public anxiety in existing harbors. However, legal and statutory changes would be required to ensure proper supervision, pilotage, towage, security and access, fire precautions, medical arrangements, and potential leakage of fission products, because harbors tended to be near heavily populated regions.

While the *Savannah* demonstrated the technical feasibility and operational reliability of nuclear propulsion for merchant ships, it was not economical, costing $100 million over fifteen years; oil supplies proved to be adequate and cheaper. After visiting seventy-five ports and entertaining over one million visitors, the *Savannah* was taken out of service. The United States nuclear merchant ship program then collapsed as a result of safety, legal and insurance concerns raised by growing environmental awareness. This experience did not deter the AEC from seeking to develop a standardized 120,000-horsepower compact nuclear propulsion system for use in high-speed containerships, tankers, so-called Very Large Crude Carriers, and icebreakers, like the *Lenin*, to support Arctic shipping and Arctic oil drilling operations. But the launching of the *Savannah* and the next generation of nuclear ships was not about cost, but about technological hubris, display value, and superpower competition.[23]

The Soviets launched the *Lenin* from their Leningrad shipbuilding yards on September 12, 1959. Unencumbered by worries about cost, legal issues, or public safety, the *Lenin* was permitted to spend the next three decades cutting a path thousands of kilometers long through the ice of the Arctic Ocean, opening shipping lanes to the Enesei, Ob, and Lena rivers, and providing access to Siberia's great resources.

By official quantitative measures, the *Lenin* demonstrated both the efficacy of new technologies and the glory of Soviet power. As its first task, the icebreaker opened the Enesei ice dam and the Vilkitskii Straits; then in the Karsk Sea, it facilitated the Norilsk and Dudinsk nickel operations in the dead of winter. In its first three years of operation, the *Lenin* plowed 47,000 kilometers, half of them through ice as thick as six meters. In October 1961, it delivered crucial supplies to the *North Pole-10* floating research station. By the end of 1963, the icebreaker had traversed almost 100,000 kilometers, roughly two-thirds in ice. With the help of other icebreakers, the *Lenin* accompanied more than 300 ships through the northern routes, speeding the delivery of freight, and nearly ending the capture of freighters by sudden Arctic freezes, which had previously left them trapped until the spring thaw. The *Lenin*'s first complete refueling was in the spring of 1963. With their first load, each reactor had operated more than 11,000 hours, having produced 430,000 to 490,000 megawatt-hours of thermal energy. Through 1975, the icebreaker kept the route through the Karsk Sea to Enesei ports open until the end of December. In 1976, the *Lenin* led a freighter and tanker into the Karsk Sea in March, demonstrating the possibility of early spring shipping in the Arctic Ocean. These achievements earned the *Lenin* a Lenin Award, so that the ship became known officially as the Lenin Award Icebreaker *Lenin*.

But the real story was not that glorious. In 1966, a reactor melted down, burning completely through the hull. Of course, they had to repair the *Lenin*. When the ship was finally decommissioned in 1990, its highly radioactive shielding assembly and spent nuclear fuel, with total radioactivity of more than two million curies, was dumped in the Arctic Ocean; perhaps about five percent of this activity remains today. And in the *Lenin*'s stead, dozens of nuclear submarines and icebreakers plowed the ocean waters, occasionally leaving radioactive waste in their wake, if only when their spent fuel assemblies or reactors hit the ocean floor. These and other significant misfortunes did not deter leading physicists and officials associated with nuclear engines.[24] As Aleksandrov and his colleagues put it in a major article on the *Lenin*, "The development of the economy of northern regions requires the creation of a new powerful ice-breaking fleet which is capable of accelerating transit of caravans of ships along the path of the northern shipping route, lengthening the period of navigation, and widening the path in order to utilize higher latitudes." Nuclear ships were the key to the exploitation of the north.[25]

FROM ICEBREAKERS TO WHALERS

Once Brezhnev realized, as Khrushchev had, that he needed technological achievements as symbols of peaceful intentions and political legitimacy, he chose Siberian economic development as his focus. The "Siberia" program, as it came to be known, was intended to subjugate rich natural resources of oil and gas in the Tiumen region, forests, ore, and even water through such massive technological systems as pipelines hundreds of miles long, a new trans-Siberian railroad called BAM (the Baikal-Amur Mainline), and canals to divert the flow of Siberian rivers to Central

Asia and the European USSR. Nuclear-powered ships would assist in these endeavors by keeping the northern route open. Small nuclear reactors would do their share by providing electricity in Kola and Bilibino. Yet two factors seem to have delayed the expansion of the Soviet nuclear icebreaker fleet beyond the *Lenin* until the mid-1970s. The first was the attempt to achieve nuclear parity with the United States and hence to concentrate resources on the rapid deployment of nuclear submarines. The Soviet Navy launched eighty-nine submarines from 1961 to 1971. The second was the decision to focus "peaceful" nuclear resources on civilian nuclear power stations and the effort to increase the unit size of standard RBMK and VVER reactors.

Toward the end of Siberian development, Brezhnev ordered the construction of a fleet of nuclear icebreakers to assist the *Lenin* in keeping a northern shipping lane open all year. Before the Soviet Union—and its nuclear navy—fell apart, it launched eight nuclear icebreakers, and a ninth neared completion at the Baltic Factory in Leningrad. There was even discussion of building one named after Brezhnev himself (but not of the danger of having an artifact called the Lenin Award Icebreaker *Brezhnev*). The monster nuclear icebreakers generated 75,000 horsepower. They operated well; they averaged 7,000 hours at sea annually (roughly eighty percent of the time) and their reactors generally operated more than 400 days between refuelings. Four icebreakers reached the North Pole. Smaller, more maneuverable diesel ships followed them to the deltas of Siberian rivers. But, because of the hardships of transporting diesel fuel and because the huge icebreakers could not enter Siberian rivers, the Soviet Northern Fleet built jointly with Finland two nuclear icebreakers with limited draft—the 50,000-horsepower *Taimyr* (1989) and *Vaigach* (1990)—to replace diesel-powered icebreakers that had to remain on ice—in port—in the dead of winter.

The expansion of the nuclear icebreaker fleet revealed just how short-sighted Soviet planning could be. First, there were few sufficiently iceworthy freighters (with the exception of such ships as the *Norilsk* at 25,000 tons displacement) to carry cargo through the opened shipping lanes. The decision to build icebreakers should have been accompanied by a decision to build freighters to take advantage of the situation. The Northern Fleet had to struggle to build huge nuclear freighters of the lighter class like the *Sevmorput'* (1988), which had a displacement of 61,000 tons and reactors providing 40,000 horsepower of thrust. The *Sevmorput'* could break through ice up to one meter thick. Second, the merchant navy could barely handle the service requirements of icebreakers and freighters. The Russian Northern Fleet opened a series of bases with similar responsibilities for nuclear submarines and surface vessels within this region, including Sevmorput and Safonovo. The nuclear icebreaker base, Atomflot, was built on the Kola peninsula in Murmansk, not far from the merchant harbor on the Murmansk fjord. Atomflot was used for repairs, refueling, fuel storage, and temporary waste disposal. The base was inadequate to handle such a huge fleet. Absent the proper infrastructure, repair facilities, and trained personnel to take full advantage of its size and keep it running safely, *Sevmorput'* operated only fifty-seven percent of the time. A shift to container shipping and efficient use of its holds seems to have made the operation of *Sevmorput'* more economical in its route from the Kola peninsula to Dudinsk. Nuclear freighters half that size never made it off the drawing board.[26]

But Brezhnev's will pushed icebreaker after icebreaker into the Arctic Ocean. They laid the keel for the *Arktika*, the first new nuclear marvel since the *Lenin*, in July 1971 at the Baltic shipbuilding yard. At 75,000 horsepower and 21,000 tons displacement, it was the largest atomic icebreaker ever launched. The *Arktika* left its dry dock in December 1972 and entered regular operation in 1974, a mere three years later, after undergoing testing in the Baltic and Karsk seas. Unlike the *Lenin*, the *Arktika* had two, not three, reactors, which powered two main turbines whose current fed three electric propeller motors. The reactors themselves were largely unchanged. In response to the accidents on the *Lenin*, crew safety occupied a more important position; trained fully, each crew member had a personal dosimeter. The ship had two independent electrical generators, one in the bow and one in the stern; each was capable of powering the ship fully in case of an accident, the former with two and the second with three 2,000-kilowatt turbogenerators. In addition, there was a diesel generator. A sister ship, *Sibir'*, was launched in 1975 to honor the twenty-fifth Party congress. In 1977, *Arktika* led a caravan of cargo-laden ships in deep ice and terrible weather through the Karsk Sea. Five times in the deepest part of the Arctic winter in late February and early March, the *Arktika* cut through to Iamal with the assistance of the diesel icebreaker *Murmansk* to keep shipping lanes open and ensure progress at the Iamal gas field development. Ultimately, it was possible, although extremely costly and challenging, to go from Murmansk to Vladivostok, even in the dead of winter. In August 1977, the *Arktika* reached the North Pole—a first for an icebreaker—in time for the celebration of the sixtieth anniversary of the USSR. The *Rossiia, Sovetskii soiuz,* and *Iamal* nuclear icebreakers were built next (see Appendix, Table 13).[27]

The new generation of icebreakers had a number of safety improvements. Vertical orientation of equipment facilitated repair, maintenance, and refueling. Standard cranes with a twelve-ton capacity could accomplish most heavy tasks in reactor operation. The reactors themselves were more efficient. Engineers claimed to have mastered backup systems and welding to ensure containment of liquid, solid, and gas radioactive wastes in the event of an accident. They employed improved Geiger, spectrometric, and other sensors. The new generation of icebreakers had two independent 2,000-kilowatt diesel auxiliary power plants with five turbogenerators, one in the bow and the other in the stern; a 1,000-kilowatt diesel generator capable of running all systems in the event of failure of either or both of the power stations; and finally two other 200-kilowatt diesel backup generators.

The freedom from refueling made surface nuclear-powered vessels the logical choice for use in regions far from the Motherland, for example, near Antarctica, where in the 1950s the Soviets commenced extensive whaling operations. Engineers in the Leningrad Northern Project Engineering Institute designed an atomic whaling base, in essence a floating atomic-powered factory. Two prototype reactors were built, one of which served as an experimental device on the grounds of the Kurchatov Institute. The design was intended to eliminate the possibility of the entry of fission products into the whale blubber, which was broadly used for the preparation of children's medicines. Yet atmospheric nuclear tests had rained radio-active fallout into the oceans, where flora and fauna accumulated it. Whales consumed huge quantities of fish and plankton. The danger of radioactivity in whale products either from flora and fauna or from the on-board reactor was considered great enough to convince scientists to cancel the project.

One of the reasons for continued faith in the nuclear engine was a finding of a commission in the Dolgano-Nenets autonomous region that the *Taimyr* had not raised the background radiation on the Enesei River and its delta. The *Taimyr* did the Murmansk-Dudinsk run and was crucial to the transport of Norilsk production to Leningrad and Moscow. But in the summer of 1989, local Dudinsk residents refused to allow what they called a "floating Chernobyl" into port. Without imports on which the region's residents were dependent, and without export capability, reindeer and fish harvests in the region plummeted, the decline contributing to significant economic hardship. The residents were even more worried, however, about the collision between the *Taimyr* and the *Sibir'* in heavy ice conditions and the November 11, 1988 near meltdown of the *Rossiia*'s reactor in Murmansk harbor, a result of human error. When the twin of the *Taimyr*, the *Vaigach*, attempted to enter Dudinsk harbor in September 1990, the locals blocked the harbor. But when ice set in, they relented, allowing the small nuclear ships to clear shipping lanes.[28]

NUCLEAR-POWERED AIRPLANES AND ROCKET SHIPS

At the same time as icebreakers and submarines came into existence, engineers also proposed the use of nuclear engines in other vehicles. Visionaries of nuclear-powered aircraft never hesitated to publish artists' renderings of flying nuclear wings gliding over such heavily populated cities as New York, in spite of the tremendous technical and safety problems, not to mention exorbitant cost, that would accompany the launching of such outlandish vehicles. But military concerns—the possibility of long-term, high-speed flight without frequent refueling, and the belief that future wars would be based on massive retaliation with nuclear weapons delivered by aircraft—pushed those issues into the background until after the expenditure of billions of dollars, rubles, francs, and pounds.

In the United States, the nuclear powered airplane, known as the ANP, was born from the program for Nuclear Energy Propulsion for Aircraft (NEPA), dating to May 1946. The ANP was based at Oak Ridge National Laboratory and supported by contracts between the Air Force and Fairchild Engine and Airplane Corporation. Initially, the program set off raging debates over the exposure of the aircraft's crew to radiation, because the crucial technical issue was how to keep the weight of the plane as low as possible so that it could fly; and this constraint required reduction in biological shielding. There appeared to be three alternatives. One was to increase the speed of the plane, so that each mission was more brief. The second was to limit the total number of missions. The third was to find some sort of drug with which to treat crew members or to acquire additional data that might indicate an increase in the amount of radiation crews could tolerate. Despite ethical questions concerning human experimentation, it was not difficult to find vast sums of government money to keep NEPA alive, especially with military planners seeing nuclear planes as the best way to deliver nuclear weapons to the Soviet Union. The Joint Chiefs of Staff endorsed the ANP program, which ran through 1963, costing over one billion dollars and engaging more persons at Oak Ridge than all other laboratory projects combined.[29]

The American nuclear jet program gained great impetus from the Korean War, which inspired the Air Force to let a series of contracts to develop the nuclear plane. One such contract went to Consolidated Vultee Aircraft Corporation, which confidently predicted operation of a nuclear-powered Corvair B-36 bomber sometime between 1954 and 1956, even though it remained unclear whether the aircraft would have turbojet or propeller propulsion. The United States built a 15,000-foot runway at the National Reactor Testing Station in the southern Idaho desert—a length unheard of at that time—to provide enough run-up to get what was expected to be a much heavier than usual jet off the ground.

The Air Force awarded General Dynamics and Lockheed Aircraft millions of dollars, equipment, and laboratories supported by hundreds of engineers and scientists. At its Wright-Patterson Air Development Center near Dayton, Ohio, it built a ten-megawatt nuclear engineering test facility to test aircraft materials and components. The French and British also spent years and millions (of francs and pounds, respectively) on nuclear propulsion, in the latter case with Rolls Royce working on the atomic power units for the aircraft.[30] Yet, by 1958, the closest any country came to flying a nuclear-powered airplane was the nearly four dozen times—at a cost of $700 million—that the U.S. Air Force flew a reactor in a B-36, not to propel the plane, but to determine how to overcome problems of weight, biological shielding, and the like. Officials acknowledged "certain particular dangers" (but not "unusual" ones) related to the possibility of the release of fission products from the reactor in case of a crash.[31] But what was "usual" in any way about flying a reactor around Idaho in a B-36? The nuclear airplane died in 1963, not so much because technical and safety problems remained unresolved, but because nuclear-tipped ICBMs could do the same job of mass destruction of the enemy with greater accuracy and lower costs.

The basic principle behind a nuclear-powered aircraft is that heat from a reactor—say, at 4,000°F, versus 1,300° to 1,500°F in a conventional turbojet—is used to drive a pure jet engine, a turboprop, or even a rocket motor. In a jet, air is drawn in through an intake, compressed, mixed with fuel, detonated in combustion chambers, and released, thus propelling the aircraft and, simultaneously, revolving a turbine that turns the compressor for the air-fuel mixture. In a nuclear airplane, the combustion chambers would be replaced by a reactor whose sole function is the production of heat, which is used to create a flow of gas at high pressure and temperature. Transmitting the heat to the turbines involves more equipment and weight, for example, pumps and heat exchangers. The reactor heat would pass to a circulating liquid metal that would then pass the heat to a heat exchange unit. There, a working fluid, perhaps mercury, would be vaporized to drive a turbine, then cooled in a condenser, then pumped back to a heat exchange unit. If this design were not complex enough, nuclear jets required the development of metals that boil only at very high temperatures. The molten metal used as the primary heat exchange liquid would solidify as it cooled down when the reactor was shut down. Auxiliary heat, perhaps from a small gas turbine, would have to be used to liquefy the metal in the first place. Furthermore, the metal would have to be drained from the reactor, heat exchanger, and piping before shutdown or the whole unit would seize. Cooling the reactor was a significant problem, as was wiping heat instantaneously off the turbines and reactor at jet speed.

None of this would be a particular technical challenge if all this equipment, the liquid metal, the reactor itself, and its shielding only needed to sit in a huge hanger on the ground. But it had to take off, fly, and land. Scientists explored the concept of "unit shielding" of the reactor and propulsion unit to minimize weight, but any shielding—borated water, lead, steel, even concrete—would have added up to fifty tons. Unlike conventional jets, which consume fuel and thus are lighter when they land than when they take off, nuclear jets would lose only a negligible amount of fuel, requiring that the undercarriage and landing gear also be stressed to withstand landings at greater speeds and weights. Scientists and military personnel in the United States and the Soviet Union were not deterred, for one pound of uranium could supply as much heat as the burning of more than 1.5 million gallons of fossil fuel, giving atomic-powered aircraft almost unlimited range and utility as large bombers, ocean-patrolling jets, and long-range troop transports. They confidently predicted an operational plane by 1960.[32]

More is known of the United States's than the Soviet Union's program, for most documents concerning the latter remain classified. There is no doubt that the Soviet's program paralleled the United States's, even if it was somewhat less extensive. The Soviet Air Force attempted the same flying reactor tests. As with other nuclear engine programs of the early 1950s, Anatolii Aleksandrov was the moving force behind the study of flying nuclear apparatuses. Aleksandrov formulated the basic problem as follows: "Our knowledge in the area of atomic reactors allows us to raise the question of the creation of atomic engines in the coming years which can be applied for heavy airplanes. . . . The basic problem here is the design of the reactor itself, air cooled; and the highest temperature possible of exhaust gases to 1,000°C." On August 14, 1952, he wrote Kurchatov that the time had come to work on industrial and transportable nuclear reactors, with most of the work done at the Kurchatov Institute. Initially opposed by government leadership as costly and technically uncertain, the program was eventually approved. The reasons for approval were the same as in the United States. Jet, rocket, and satellite reactors could provide great power for extended periods of time, making exploration of the atmosphere and solar system possible. Many of the earliest ideas for the Soviet nuclear rocket and jet engines program originated among university seniors at engineering departments created specifically to train nuclear specialists. Flights of fancy, rather than circumspection based on past experience in reactor development, were the rule. Their advisors and supervisors then strove to turn flights of fancy into real designs, which they in turn sent to higher levels for approval and funding.[33] When the first group of students defended their projects before a commission chaired by Aleksandrov, they took turns sitting alone at a table before the commission, sharing a sports coat that became increasingly rank on the hot day. Then the students were invited to hear the commission's decision: "Your projects pleased us; we've giving you all A's. But the feeling remains that in all of your defenses there was something similar."[34] It was the coat, not the projects.

Russian physicists claim to have learned about the American ANP programs late in the game and were surprised that the programs had much in common—down to reactor fuels. They quickly discovered that the weight of the required biological shielding for the cockpit and reactor made it impossible to develop an operational flying engine. They learned that the United States had flown reactors in jets; after consulting with Andrei Tupolev, the famous Soviet jet designer, they built an analogous laboratory in a TU-95 by December 1955. They believed it was possible within fifteen to twenty years to overcome the technical problems of shielding, the stability of reactor operation and materials during flight, and the need to stress the landing gear and fuselage because of the weight of the airplane, one-half of which would be reactor, shielding, and engine. They decided in 1960 to build a land-based model of the flying reactor in Polovinka near Semipalatinsk. When experiments began, there were all sorts of problems, including foam in the reactor loop. They called Aleksandrov in Moscow. He diagnosed the problem immediately: "Where'd they get the distilled water? In Semipalatinsk, near the meat factory? Everything is clear. That's bouillon. Bouillon always foams." Ultimately, the Soviet physicists began to joke that there were other reasons to abandon the nuclear airplane: A nuclear airplane could soar unlimited distance and time, but the earth was too small for that. More to the point, risks associated with a crash of a nuclear reactor engine remained real and unconquerable.[35]

Soviet physicists had much greater success in building nuclear power packs of all sorts for use in space. These included small reactors for satellites and nuclear batteries. The program originated in the search for nuclear rocket engines. While ultimately unsuccessful, this latter line of research indicates the unbridled enthusiasm of physicists and the extensive resources they commanded. Physicists throughout the world turned to nuclear propulsion as "inevitable and essential in the exploration and exploitation of space." They had considered the possibility of nuclear rockets since the advent of controlled fission.[36] Nuclear propulsion had many advantages over chemical rocket propulsion, especially for heavy payloads and interplanetary travel. Scientists explored nuclear propulsion with the firm conviction that they could solve all its problems, which they believed fell strictly in the realm of engineering questions: heat generation and removal, fluid (coolant) distribution and flow, material science and structural integrity, and, of course, nuclear physics.

The length of time a rocket engine can operate is limited by the amount of propellant carried. The higher the power produced per pound of propellant consumed (the specific impulse), the better. Rocket engines, like all jet propulsion engines, produce thrust by transforming a working fluid to gas at a high temperature and expelling the gas at as high a velocity as possible through a nozzle. In chemical rockets, the propellants themselves provide the energy source that raises their temperature through combustion. In nuclear rockets, propellant may be chosen without regard to consideration of its combustion characteristics. The heat is supplied by the fission process in a nuclear reactor. Hydrogen in a nuclear rocket may provide a specific impulse three times greater than that of a chemical system that uses H_2 and O_2, because hydrogen has the lowest possible molecular weight. In a popular design, liquid hydrogen is stored in an insulated propellant tank and is replaced by helium as the hydrogen is drawn off to a pump. It flows under high pressure through pipes to the exit end of the nozzle, where it cools the nozzle. It then enters the reactor and flows down through the core and out of the nozzle at 4,000° to 4,500°F.[37]

Scientists acknowledged that safety hazards might be encountered in the operation of nuclear engines, but they concluded that the benefits of these engines, including higher specific impulse and significant military applications, far outweighed the risk. The potential hazards ranged from the remote chance of bombardment by such space debris as asteroids, comets, and meteors to constant exposures to high-energy protons and electrons, solar radiation including X-rays, extremes of temperature as the vehicle passes in and out of sunlight, and ultrahigh vacuum. For example, radiation may cause damage to semiconductor material in the space vehicle, leading to loss of integrity of vehicle and reactor command and of control devices. For astronauts and cosmonauts, the requirements of shielding against the effects of radiation are even more important, because, during solar flares, exposure levels may range from 10 to 100 rem per hour, and radiation from a reactor would be fatal. Passive (bulk) shielding or active (magnetic) shielding is required against such forms of radiation as neutrons and gamma rays.[38] In all of the early literature, few sources, if any, gave thought to the risks to humans of the explosion of the nuclear rocket in the low atmosphere and the spread of fission products throughout the globe.

In the United States, the AEC began exploring the feasibility of nuclear rocket propulsion in 1955. The Department of Defense pushed early research with personnel and funding. Sponsored jointly by NASA (National Aeronautics and Space Administration) and the AEC, the program was called Project Rover. Los Alamos National Laboratory and the Nevada Test Site were the loci of the program. The first tests were conducted in 1959, using a reactor called Kiwi-A, named after the flightless New Zealand bird; the reactor weighed more than its thrust could lift, so the name was appropriate. The test was successful only on the basis of the criterion that the reactor produce high power at a predetermined temperature level. Another aspect of the program was the Air Force's SPUR (space power unit reactor program), a $250 million 300-kilowatt nuclear turboelectric space power system. But disputes that broke out in the early 1960s over who controlled SPUR—the Air Force, NASA, or AEC—and what each organization's responsibilities were slowed progress. The AEC planned to build forty to fifty test reactors, culminating with the NERVA (nuclear engine for rocket vehicle application) for upper stage use. The plan was to install them in the second-stage position on top of a chemical Saturn booster and at an altitude of one thousand miles bring the reactor to criticality by a ground signal. It was hoped that, by 1968 or 1969, NERVA reactors could be used in actual space missions. Other United States nuclear propulsion schemes included 150- to 600-megawatt thermal nuclear ramjets; the SLAM (supersonic low-altitude missile); and ORION.[39]

The Princeton physicist Freeman Dyson and Los Alamos scientist Ted Taylor were the motivating forces behind ORION. They pushed the program with the slogan "Saturn by 1970." Dyson wrote *A Space Traveler's Manifesto* to extol its virtues. ORION was intended to propel large spacecraft by means of nuclear "bomblets," which would provide a force of about ten kilotons when exploded every 0.1 to 1 second at a distance of 100 to 1,000 feet behind the vehicle. The explosions would exert pressure on a pusher plate "made of ablative material that transmits the propulsive impulse to the vehicle proper through water-cooled springs." Dyson built chemical rocket mock-ups, which he launched from Point Loma peninsula in the Pacific Ocean south of San Diego. Dyson calculated in 1958 that ORION would add one percent annually to contamination associated with atmospheric nuclear tests; but he was excited by the project, which was canceled only with the Nuclear Test Ban Treaty of 1963.[40]

In the Soviet Union, projects for nuclear space engines had high-level attention from the start. Leading physicists and engineers participated in the project: Kurchatov and Aleksandrov themselves, Leipunskii, and, from the aeronautics program Andrei Tupolev, Mstislav Keldysh, and Sergei Korolev. They looked at manned and drone jets, direct and jet engines, reactors with air and liquid metal coolants, reactors with thermal and fast neutrons. There is a famous photograph of the three K's—Kurchatov, Keldysh and Korolev—taken at one of the first discussions about nuclear rocket engines; it demonstrates how crucial personal contacts were in securing development. In 1957, Kurchatov began to think about an impulse-graphite reactor called DOUD-3. Kurchatov gave Aleksandrov responsibility to pursue this variant. Aleksandrov approached Dollezhal about bringing his research facilities into the design work for DOUD-3. In March 1958, Kurchatov, Aleksandrov, and Dollezhal approved the project. By 1960, they were testing a reactor whose active zone heated the fuel—hydrogen—to 3,100 K. This reactor is still operating. Some time later, they built another test reactor that achieved parameters unequaled in the West.[41]

Even though nuclear jet engines and rocket ships turned out to be dreams of the distant future, radioisotopic thermoelectric generators played an important role in the Soviet space program from the start. Building on a tradition of world class research in solid state physics, Soviet physicists and engineers figured out how to turn the energy of radioisotopes into relatively small sources of electrical energy. The small power generators were excellent sources of energy for various apparatuses and instruments on both earth-orbiting and interplanetary satellites, as well as at oceanographic and meteorological stations. Designed with a power of 1 to 1,000 watts and with a life of six months to ten years, radioisotopic generators had an energy capacity two to three times higher than that of chemical batteries, and were more reliable. Unlike solar batteries, they did not require special protection from the radiation belts of the earth or micrometeoric dust.

The choice of which radioisotope to use from among more than one thousand known radioactive substances depended on nuclear physical characteristics: the rate of decay of the parent nuclei (the "speed of burning") and the quantity of energy given up in one instance of decay. The best ones for this purpose were isotopes with a half-life between 100 days and 100 years, of which there were approximately 50. The basic advantage of alpha-emitting isotopes was the high quantity of energy, in particular, the amount that transformed into kinetic energy. For several isotopes (^{227}Ac, ^{228}Th, and ^{232}U), one decay produces thirty to forty megaelectronvolts. Radio-active isotopes are potentially biologically dangerous, so they must be handled carefully. It is easiest to handle them in a solid form which is almost insoluble in sea-water or distilled water and will not sublimate or otherwise react with air, water, or the material of the surrounding ampule. Engineers calculated the smallest amount of the isotope needed to produce the required power level and length of service. They designed small "radioisotopic blocks" for maximum transportability, reliability, and safety during operation.

Engineers used ^{144}Ce and ^{90}Sr in earth-based radiometeorological stations, the former operating for up to one year, the latter from one to ten years. The Beta series of isotopic thermoelectric generators for meteorological and high-mountain cosmic ray research was developed between 1963 and 1967 and used ^{90}Sr. Its prototype operated at the experimental site of Gidrometsluzhba in Khimki, a closed research town just outside Moscow.[42] Between 1963 and 1968, they designed an underwater apparatus that used ^{137}Ce. Another device was the long-lived (to 86.4 years), hand-held MIG-67 generator, which used ^{238}Pu. The most effective means of converting energy was thermoelectric: the production of some semiconductor materials that possess sufficiently high efficiency (five to eight percent) and work at all ranges of temperatures—to 300°, from 300° to 700°, and above 700°C. The combination of several different materials—usually molybdenum, selenium, and titanium—enabled them to achieve efficiencies to fifteen percent.

Nuclear physicists early on explored the possibility of transforming thermal energy directly into electricity by using the Ruzh'e thermoelectric generators. In August 1961, Aleksandrov reported on such a reactor, whose power level ranged from 0.5 to 5.0 kilowatts. The next stage of development was the Romashka reactor-transformer built at the Kurchatov Institute, in which a high-temperature reactor and thermoelectric semiconductor converter without any moving parts were joined to transform or transmit the heat. The compact, light, autonomous, and reliable Romashka showed great potential, operating for 15,000 hours at a maximum of 500 watts, and producing a total of 6,100 kilowatt-hours. In 1964, Keldysh and Aleksandrov decided to try out a Romashka in a Sputnik. Such reactors proved to be crucial for the ambitious Soviet program of space exploration.

The Soviets achieved greater successes with cosmic nuclear electrical motors, so much so that American scientists tried to buy them (for example, the Topaz) once the reforms initiated under Mikhail Gorbachev opened military technology to scrutiny and sale. Experiments begun in 1958 at Obninsk on the BR-5 and 5,000-kilowatt reactor led to the creation of a thermoemission nuclear energy apparatus called Topaz. For the one-hundredth birthday of Lenin on April 21, 1970, the first Topaz was operated, and the more advanced Topaz-2 and Topaz-3 soon followed. The first impulse plasma engines were tested in space on the Zond-2. Later volumetric ionization and stationary plasma engines were tested on the Meteor satellite.[43]

Scientists at NASA and Los Alamos National Laboratory enthusiastically experimented with several third-generation Topaz reactors. The sale of Topaz reactors to the United States frightened environmentalists everywhere, despite the claim of American scientists that the Topaz would power "Star Wars" antimissile laser shoot-down technology to the benefit of both. The failure of Kosmos-954, -1402, and -1900 and their reentry into the atmosphere did little to calm fears. The Topaz was costly to launch and, once launched, could not be serviced. "Do we need a nuclear garbage dump in space?" opponents asked rhetorically, and called for the Soviet and American shuttles to bring nuclear satellites down to earth.[44]

Some Western scientists and officials criticized the extensive Soviet use of nuclear power packs in units ranging from reactors to radioisotopic thermal generators. But academician O. Belotserkovskii, rector of the Moscow Institute of Applied Physics, defended the satellite power packs. He pointed out that the power packs had a significant advantage over solar panels in terms of total power. They were also safe. When brought up to full power and used in high orbits, they had a ballistic lifetime (that is, the time before they descend into the dense stratosphere) long enough to allow the radioactive products to decay to a safe level, that is, to one not exceeding the levels recommended by the International Commission on Radiological Protection. When a reactor can be placed in high orbit, one method of ensuring safety is to disperse small particles of the reactor's radioactive materials so widely that, even if they do fall to earth, they will not be dangerous. Indeed, on several occasions, Soviet space officials gave the telemetric order for satellite nuclear power packs to disperse nuclear materials on reentry. For example, Kosmos-1402 was launched on August 30, 1982, with an enriched uranium reactor core surrounded by a beryllium reflector. When it completed its short mission on December 28, 1982, a command from earth shut off the reactor and separated the satellite into three fragments, one of which burned up and dispersed throughout the atmosphere over the next two months.[45] The Soviets were successful in orbiting thirty-three nuclear reactors to power low-flying radar-spy satellites. Yet for all of Belotserkovskii's self-assuredness, flying nuclear reactors have proved to be less than safe. Two of them have already reentered the atmosphere, spreading radioactivity around the globe. A number of others have begun to decay, leaking at least 70,000 detectable particles and perhaps millions of smaller ones into the atmosphere and forming a cloud of nuclear pollution some 600 miles up. Still, United States government officials and national laboratory scientists remain enchanted with these reactors.[46]

THE CHUKCHI LOVES HIS PORTABLE REACTOR ALMOST AS MUCH AS HIS REINDEER

If not space—which in any event was very costly—then why not use the far north as a home for wayward nuclear power stations? Kurchatov was the motive force. His associates knew he was up to something. He'd become pensive but engaged anyone who would speak with him—metallurgists, chemists, food scientists, textile industry representatives—in a discussion about the magic ability of nuclear power to solve problems of automation, management, control, and power. One day Kurchatov suddenly dropped in on Vasilii Emelianov when Zaveniagin was in his office. It was late, and they were ready to go home. Kurchatov excitedly told Zaveniagin, "You know, Avraamii Pavlovich, we can make it easier for construction workers." He set out the idea for a portable nuclear power station. Zaveniagin tried to temper Kurchatov's optimism, pointing out that construction workers in the far north or far east were so far from creature comforts—comforts of any sort in fact—that they were required to become "Robinson Crusoes." Kurchatov merely stated, "Yes, a Robinson Crusoe with atomic power stations—not that Robinson about whom Defoe wrote." Kurchatov then described how blocks of a portable station might even be dropped by parachute right on any construction site for rapid assembly.[47]

Kurchatov's idea for portable nuclear power stations found a crucial application in the development of fuel, nonferrous, rare, and precious metals, minerals, timber, and other raw natural resources of the far north and northeast of the USSR from the 1970s onward. In theory, the "atomic boiler houses" could be used along the shores of the Arctic Ocean and from the Kola peninsula to the shores of Kamchatka. In practice, north of the Arctic Circle, not far from the Chukotsk peninsula in the northeasternmost reach of the Soviet Union across the Bering Strait from Alaska and not far from the small village of Bilibino, Soviet engineers built a nuclear cogeneration plant consisting of four twelve-megawatt nuclear reactors. Although not "portable" in the sense of other reactors they had designed, the BATETs (Bilibino *atomnaia teploelektrotsentral'*) was constructed of components and prefabricated concrete forms produced eight time zones away and shipped by rail and boat to Bilibino for assembly. Like other nuclear boilers, the BATETs complex was intended to open rich far-north resources, not only to Soviet shovels and picks, but also to equipment powered by electrical motors, and to provide heat for agricultural hothouses and domestic home heating for the workers in Chukotsk mines.

During the brief shipping season in the summer, diesel fuel and coal passed through the ports of Zelenyi Mys and Pevek and through the Arctic Ocean in 6,000-ton displacement tankers and 5,000-ton barges. Any development of the region required construction of more such ships, plus expansion of port handling facilities and storage depots. This construction would make already tight supplies of diesel fuel shrink further, for the Soviet Union was trying to sell oil and gasoline on world markets to earn hard currency. Efforts to bring in fuel caravans at other times of the year ran into thick ice. The effort to overcome this problem by introducing nuclear power commenced in the late 1950s. By 1963, engineers and planners decided to apply their first designs at Bilibino in Chukotia, a region characterized by long winters and temperatures down to $-60°C$, impenetrable rivers and lakes (again due to ice), mountainous relief, deep permafrost, and extreme isolation from any industrially developed region. Electric power had to be transmitted over lines strung through swampy tundra. The swampy mess led to accidents and blackouts as poles sank, rotted, broke, or toppled. Atomic energy would overcome all these problems and, according to engineers, would pay for itself within six or seven years in savings on the purchase of fossil fuels.[48]

Chukotia was also home to the indigenous Chukchis, a group of 14,000 people. Roughly half of the Chukchis were nomadic, living in tents and herding reindeer; and other half were sedentary, inhabiting semisubterranean dwellings and living off the sea. The Chukchis also were the butt of many Soviet ethnic jokes because of their psychological distance from the Soviet industrial development paradigm and their unwillingness to succumb to the planners' imperatives. The Chukchis believed that invisible spirits fill the universe. Their shamans made sacrifices to these spirits. This kind of lifestyle and worldview had to give way to state reindeer collective farms and nuclear-powered mining.

The main unit of the BATETs cogeneration plant consists of four identical reactor-turbine "blocks" under one roof and produces twelve megawatts of electricity and twenty-five gigacalories per hour. The station building was constructed with monolithic reinforced concrete panels that were anchored on piles driven into shale and permafrost. Dalstroiproekt engineers were confident of the building's strength.[49] The walls of the reactor hall are aluminum to protect the facility on cold polar nights. The presence of all reactors in one hall and the absence of concrete walls require the use of a hermetically sealed refueling container device capable of disposing of spent fuel assemblies in a storage facility located within the reactor hall. Engineers acknowledge that "the placing of four reactors in one hall presents high demands on the efficacy and reliability of biological shielding of the reactors which must guarantee a normal radiation situation in the station." The reactors, which resemble the Obninsk, Beloiarsk, and Chernobyl channel-graphite designs and use fuel rods virtually the same as those first employed at Obninsk, are distinguished by simplicity of construction, component design, and light weight for ease of transport to any site by rail. The use of a one-loop system with natural circulation lowers cost and simplifies operation. The steam-water mixture leaves the reactor and passes into a drum separator where steam at sixty-five kilograms per square centimeter and 280°C goes directly into a turbine. From a turbine condenser, the condensate goes through several filters and then through a lower pressure preheater and then into an atmospheric deaerator. The water at a temperature of 104°C enters the loop of natural circulation with the help of feed pumps. The heat from the condenser of the turbine is drawn off by water that circulates in a special loop and is cooled by air with radiothorium coolers. Heat produced in the reactor, which is drawn off by water, is channeled through huge pipes to industrial, agricultural, and residential facilities. All the station turbines are of Czech origin. Air cooling is logical because water freezes so quickly in the north, but this Volkswagen air-cooled engine—the radiothorium coolers—originated in Hungary.[50]

When still under construction, the BATETs designers claimed, "That day is not far away when in the ice expanses of the far north of the USSR the first Soviet polar thermal electric central nuclear power station will come on line."[51] They were right. Working around the clock in freezing cold ranging to −50°C, they brought the first reactor on line in December 1973; by January 12, it was producing electricity. The first one of its kind, the reactor underwent extensive testing of its physical parameters, from the fuel rods to the steam separators, from control mechanisms to turbines.

Engineers were relieved to discover that operating levels essentially met the design parameters. By January 1977, the fourth unit was operating. There were only minor changes in each new reactor. Strikingly, the BATETs was designed to allow changes in the power level seven or eight times daily, with winter daily variation of fifty-nine percent and summer of sixty-eight percent. The fluctuating power demand made control of the reactors an even more crucial issue than in standard reactors, where constant operating levels satisfying base load demands and maximum efficiency were the rule. But in Chukotia, there weren't enough alternative sources of energy to allow the BATETs to supply merely base load. BATETs replaced hundreds of shipments of fuel oil and diesel by truck, rail, and barge to small generators and power stations, which had been struggling to survive in the permafrost.

The BATETs was a Soviet-style machine in the garden, an innovation in terms of geography and technology. Within the vast empty expanses of polar forest tundra was a primitive, almost untouched world that extended in all directions. Here a reindeer, there a Chukchi, here a new Soviet settlement. But the feeling of wonder passed when the Chukchi stopped his sledge, got down and scratched the snow with his walking stick, and said, "So that's a little atomic stove," or politely showed surprise, "What a big fireplace!" These same Chukchis now use transistor radios and receive television from orbiting satellites. The regional political center, the outpost of Brezhnev's rule, was only fifteen years old. The Bilibino industry was the youngest in the northeast. Several enterprises were still of elementary school age. And yet the Chukchis had entered the nuclear age. In one generation, Chukchis who used to burn fat in a fire can get power from the atom.

Like many other Siberian projects—BAM (the Baikal-Amur Mainline, the new trans-Siberian railroad), the Tiumen Oil and Gas Pipeline, the Norilsk Metallurgical Combine, and others—Bilibino was delayed by a shortage of skilled workers. After all, who wished to live in the Arctic cold, in Spartan barracks, with few stores, restaurants, or schools for the families and children who accompanied the laborers? Nor did the railroad get close. When construction trusts offered higher wages as an incentive, they attracted workers interested in earning money quickly to buy a car or an apartment back home. Rapid turnover meant that poorly trained workers were responsible for building complex technologies in the most harsh weather conditions imaginable. The Komsomol strove to attract college-age laborers by asserting that it was a great honor to work at one of the Arctic sites. Many students and patriots took the opportunity to show that they were not afraid of "using their bare hands" or of "hard work," and they arrived in Chukotia with little more than the shirts on their backs. In 1967, Bilibino was already an "all-union shock work" site and a Komsomol organization was formed to manage the rough skills of the workers and combat constant turnover. For, despite the high wages offered, few of the workers were willing to live in the desolate north in special villages with fewer creature comforts than even the typically sparsely furnished Soviet town. Few wanted to stay if they had to live in tents; materials and supplies were waylaid by ice and snow; and many lost limb and life in the polar fog. Chukchi children, who had never seen a steam ship and knew how to fish and hunt like their parents, nevertheless made drawings in school of the nuclear power station and expressed disapproval of those people who participated in the annual October Revolution parade wearing no more than light boots. Clearly, the newcomers were a new breed of people—physicists.[52]

To further Chukotia's economic development, policy makers, planners, and scientists agreed to establish the Institute of Physical Engineering Problems of the North. This institute, established in 1970, had as part of its mandate the development of materials—from metals to plastics—for use in machinery and equipment in the far north, for example, reliable welding equipment and cold-resistant polymers. At a seminar held in March 1978, physicists discussed the extensive engineering and organizational problems associated with developing small nuclear power installations, creating equipment parks and special facilities (including refueling apparatus) to serve the installations, and finding and training personnel. But the experience at Bilibino indicated that nuclear cogeneration plants operated well from a technical point of view under severe climatic conditions, providing enough heat for hothouses, an animal farming complex, a school, a hospital, and a sports complex that included a swimming pool. They had begun study of the use of nuclear waste heat to promote a real revolution in agriculture in permafrost regions. Despite an accident that spread radioactivity throughout the machine hall, they still intend to extend the Bilibino plant lifetime from 2005 as originally estimated until 2015 for, other than the accident, the machine has operated as planned.[53]

But it was the Arbus that excited the greatest hopes for nuclear power in the north. Physicists at the Scientific Research Institute of Atomic Reactors in Melekess brought the transportable 750-kilowatt atomic power plant Arbus on line in August 1963. Arbus was intended to be the "prototype of small electrical stations which are being developed for far-off regions of the Soviet Union." What made the Arbus special was its "block," or component, construction, because that design allowed it to be shipped anywhere by train or barge and easily assembled. It consisted of nineteen blocks, each weighing no more than twenty tons. Assembly was supposed to take two to three months. Arbus would fit in a finished building roughly forty by sixty feet. The Arbus reactor was loaded with 22.5 kilograms of ^{235}U and produced 5,000 kilowatts of thermal energy. Fuel rods of ^{235}U enriched to thirty-five percent sat in a reactor vessel 4.4 meters tall and 1.3 meters wide, with walls 20 millimeters thick. Thirty-two control rods of boron steel regulated reactivity. The reactor, steam generators, and piping of the first loop were built from carbon steel. A 135-kilowatt diesel generator powered the station when the reactor was being brought on line. The main piece of special assembly equipment was a twelve-ton crane. Seventeen persons operated the station.[54]

Physicists were convinced that small reactors were economical because of the high cost of transporting fossil fuel or tapping it at any site. Yet atomic energy had high capital costs, especially in small stations. For the Arbus, cost was lowered by using inexpensive construction materials, serially produced equipment and instruments, light biological shielding, and an organic coolant. Physicists worried initially about accumulation of products of radiation polymerization in the organic coolant which boiled at the high operating temperature, produced a film on the surface of the fuel rods, and contributed to a loss of cooling capacity. Melekess physicists succeeded in tackling these problems through the use of a regenerating apparatus attached directly to the cooling loop. They chose a hydrostabilized, kerosine-based, aromatic organic compound such as hydroterphenol and ditolylmethane. By the early 1980s, the Arbus had two variants, an electrical power generator and a heat producer. Because of their low corrosiveness, organic coolants could be used in loops employing common carbon steels. Their high boiling temperature and low vapor pressure allowed the use of equipment in the first loop under a pressure of not more than one megapascal, which practically precluded an accident in which the reactor vessel or piping was breached. In such reactors, the maximum temperature of the surface of the fuel rods was lower than the boiling temperature of the coolant. Consequently, during a loss of pressure in the reactor vessel, the possibility of the boiling of the coolant on the fuel rods was precluded. Yet the formation of products of radiation-thermal creep required constant filtering of the coolant. Physicists ultimately designed the higher power Arbus-AST primarily to produce heat for industry and housing. The AST was brought up to operating power on November 19, 1979 and now heats the Melekess institute.[55] An amazing engine, only three persons per shift are needed to operate it.

But Malykh's TES-3 (transportable electrical station, third option) was the mother of all portable atomic power packs. It, too, was transported in blocks for easy assembly under the difficult meteorological conditions of the far north and far east. Its unit design allowed the reactor to be operated without the construction of any special buildings; the major construction task was the erection of biological shielding. A refueling container that could be moved about by a twenty-five-ton crane allowed refueling to be accomplished in the field without removing the reactor roof. The reactor operated 250 days without refueling. The entire system weighed 310 tons, including 28.5 tons for biological shielding.[56] And Malykh was just one of scores of engineers, university students, and leading physicists who dreamed about the power of the atom and never doubted their ability to tame it for use in any environment. They were convinced it was safe and effective, even as they were shattering the trust of the Soviet people by contaminating the Arctic with the radioactive wastes produced in their nuclear engines. The Obninsk physicists built one TES to put on display in 1962 at an international fair in Brussels, Belgium, to power the Soviet exhibition. But this TES was never used. Fearing accidental irradiation of the Belgian king, they thought better of it, instead cutting the TES into pieces and burying it on the grounds of their own institute.

From the Arbus and TES, engineers moved to the design of floating reactors. If relatively small reactors could turn turbines to power icebreakers and submarines, couldn't they also be used to produce electricity and heat to run the small company towns popping up north of the Arctic Circle, where Soviet workers searched for oil, gas, platinum, and other valuable commodities? And, like the reactors in icebreakers, couldn't they also float? Soviet engineers believed that they could construct floating nuclear power stations at existing shipbuilding factories by using previously developed naval reactor technology. The stations would have significantly lower capital costs than land-based stations. Because the costs and the effort to prepare a site or remove the reactor from operation would be lower—it floated, after all—

attention could be focused on the integrity and quality of the reactor unit. Engineers claimed that service, including refueling, would also be a simple matter.

Engineers tested a 6,000-kilowatt floating station that produced sufficient electricity to power exploration, drilling, and housing needs. They claimed it would produce electricity twenty percent more cheaply than traditional sources of power. The station's small size made it perfect for maneuvering in small rivers, inlets, and bays. On the basis of their experience with a 14.5-megawatts thermal reactor assembled from block components in the portable heat and electric power station Sever (North)-2, engineers decided to move on to integrated reactors that had naturally circulating coolant and generated up to 200 megawatts electric. A special engineering firm subordinate to Minsredmash carried out the Sever project in the far north. Sever was basically a ship with two pressurized-water reactors, two turbogenerators, a 400-kilowatt diesel generator, a 100-kilowatt emergency generator, a workshop, other equipment, and quarters for supervisory personnel. The ship was 83.6 meters long and 21 meters wide. Once on site, the Sever reactor provided electricity for construction, not power for the ship. Biological shielding was a simpler matter. It consisted of lead and borated water weighing 200 tons. Once in a good location, protected from ice and wind, workers would lay six- and thirty-five-kilowatt cable extending from the reactor as much as thirty kilometers to a drilling site. After a site had been exploited, the Sever could be moved to another region. Engineers forecast an eight- to ten-year lifetime and relocation every two to three years, even in such harsh climate.[57]

The end of the Soviet Union has not stopped the genesis of nuclear engines. In 1992, Khabarovsk design institutes announced "floating river atomic power stations" with the first to be built on the Amur near Amursk. The reactor, based on "reliable" submarine models, would be placed on an icebreaking platform with significantly strengthened biological shielding to prevent any radioactive release. The St. Petersburg-based Krylov Central Scientific Research Institute, the far eastern Scientific-Production Association, Energiia, in Khabarovsk, and the atomic Lenin Komsomol Factory in Komsomolsk were involved in the project. The floating station would consist of four reactors, each producing several dozen megawatts and costing only a few hundred thousand dollars.[58]

Ideas for nuclear applications were not limited to engines, nor were engineers always the source of their inspiration. In October 1958, N. I. Titkov, the director of the Institute of Oil, thanked Kurchatov for his institute's efforts to build a reliable, easy-to-use, and portable neutron generator for oil site analysis.[59] A patriotic citizen apologized for bothering Kurchatov but suggested that the physicists should think about building atomic batteries. His suggestion received a polite "thank you" from Aleksandrov, who failed to acknowledge that physicists were engaged in this very research.[60]

Today, as the nuclear establishment struggles to retain any semblance of its former power and authority as Russia's Ministry of Atomic Energy (MinAtom), its elder statesmen continue to advance problems for nuclear engines. These engines are often based on previously classified military research. One plan suggests employing nuclear icebreakers as floating desalinators. The advantages of this application have not changed: Floating power stations of any sort can be built more quickly than stationary ones; they require less site preparation; they are easy to move into remote areas; and, owing to their component construction, they arrive at the customer's door, or rather shore, ready to plug in. Emergency or routine repair and refueling can be accomplished by a ship sent out from Russia's northern fleet.

The engineers designed one floating seventy-megawatt cogeneration atomic energy station to power oil and gas exploration and production on the continental shelf. Platforms used in northern seas must be massive (and therefore expensive) to withstand the harsh climate, which includes drifting ice and occasional icebergs. Another proposal called for design of submersible stations, submersible up to a depth of six kilometers, for various oceanographic research and economic purposes such as oil exploration; thirty percent of oil and gas reserves are located on the continental shelf. Russian engineers claimed that submerged atomic power sources might be a very effective way to provide energy for exploration, repair, transport, and inspection of drilling equipment. But they recently acknowledged that submersible devices would be expensive, and hence it would be best to develop them with international cooperation. No longer secret, Russian design bureaus and industrial enterprises that developed applicable technologies for the Soviet Navy are looking for Western partners and capital in the post-cold war world.[61] One scientist complained that this application hadn't been explored only because "no one has agreed to dig [that deep] in Moscow" to test its feasibility. Despite high safety, reliability, and utility in the far north, no country will employ this technology, not just because of cost, but because these vessels often are not welcome in foreign ports. This situation must be rectified through "international standards, laws, criteria, and codes."[62]

The Soviet Union was not the only nation whose nuclear establishment pursued the development of small, transportable nuclear engines; they were only the most aggressive in its pursuit. Physicists in the United States designed and built dozens of test apparatuses and prototype nuclear engines for space, atmospheric, surface, and ocean transport, including floating devices.[63] The most extensive applications, of course, as in the Soviet Union, were engines for submarines and aircraft carriers. Even when there was no pressing military or economic reason, the AEC moved to support the hubris of American engineers, for example, in the development of a nuclear locomotive. Lyle Borst, a professor of physics at the University of Utah, completed the first design in 1954—a 7,000-horsepower atomic locomotive with a cost estimated at $1.2 million, or roughly twice the cost of diesel power. The 360-ton X-12 locomotive could accelerate a 5,000-ton train from a standing start in three and a half minutes. Questions of high capital costs, safety, and refueling doomed Borst's nuclear locomotive.[64]

In the USSR, these problems receded into the background. The desire to demonstrate peaceful intentions and the need to develop Arctic resources gave scientists and their government funders every reason to ride the nuclear engine to the end of the twentieth century. They were so confident of their successes—they had, after all, mastered nuclear weapons production a decade earlier than Western experts predicted—that they moved prematurely from experimental devices to applications in space, in the far north, and in the oceans. They believed that they had achieved safe operation in all areas: shielding, fuel handling, hermetic sealing, removal of heat from the reactor active zone, control of the reactor during lengthy periods of subcritical operation. They designed highly reliable components, from fuel rods to pumps and generators. Even with prefabricated and block construction, they were certain that they could manage the reactor during an accident involving loss of coolant and contain all fission products in event of any accident. But this was not the full story. For years, Soviet physicists, and in particular officials of the Russian Northern Fleet, deceived the people of the world about how safe their reactors were and what they had done with the high- and low-level radioactive waste and spent fuel associated with their operation.

THE LEGACY OF NUCLEAR ENGINES

Of course, civilian applications of nuclear engines took a back seat to military ones.[65] The United States and the Soviet Union in particular were consumed by the desire to build nuclear-powered submarines. But a description of the first stages in the development of the Soviet nuclear navy shows how difficult it is to separate military from civilian applications. One application served as the justification for the other. The technical challenges were the same. The personnel involved overlapped significantly. And the symbolism of peaceful applications was important as a counterweight to military ones.

No sooner had design work for the Obninsk reactor ended than Kurchatov thought about reactor applications in transport; not an airplane, and certainly not an automobile, but some kind of ocean-going vessel, whose size allowed adequate biological shielding—surely a submarine would capture military interest, Stalin's fancy, and the funding needed to pursue civilian applications simultaneously. Aleksandrov and Kurchatov were engaged in lobbying the government to develop nuclear submarines from 1952 onward. Stalin himself approved a crash program in September. Kurchatov called an acquaintance, Admiral Petr Ivanovich Aleshchenkov, from the Navy's engineering division. Aleshchenkov and Kurchatov talked informally on the phone about basic parameters, reaching the conclusion that a graphite-water reactor would be too heavy and need a huge containment vessel. But Aleshchenkov drew a picture of a submarine that had a reactor as its heart and excited Kurchatov's imagination. Kurchatov brought the drawing to Nikolai Dollezhal's attention. Dollezhal developed a first approximation, which he sent up the chain to the bureaucrats in Minsredmash. Contrary to the image of an all-powerful and all-wise bureaucracy at the pulse of the nation's defense needs, those bureaucrats waited months before responding and did so at a most inconvenient time: In August 1952, while Dollezhal was on vacation near the Black Sea in the Sochi resort reserved for Kremlin elite, he received a telegram, calling him back to Moscow immediately. On arrival, he learned of the decision to build a nuclear navy, starting with submarines. Aleksandrov was the scientific director of the project, with Blokhintsev as his deputy and Dollezhal as chief head engineer. The challenges of creating a power plant with shielding light and compact enough to fit in a submarine were the same as those of the *Lenin*. The physicists explored a variety of different reactors, agreeing ultimately that the most logical choice was a pressurized-water reactor, designated VVR-2, which had been built within two years and operated within the Moscow city limits.[66] The Physics Engineering Institute and NIKIET worked hand in hand on the project. Obninsk scientists later designed liquid metal reactors that were in fact much more reliable for submarines than were the PWRs.[67]

The director of the thermal physics section of the Physics Engineering Institute, Valerii Ivanovich Subbotin, and his staff carefully followed through on all calculations. One difficulty had to do with a problem new to shipbuilding—trying to fit so many crucial technologies into the limited space of a submarine and still ensure complete radiation safety of the personnel. On the other hand, building an engine that did not use oxygen or require fuel tanks solved two other normally serious problems. Late in 1955, they finished construction of a land-based prototype that reached full power in March 1956 and produced atomic steam and turned turbines in April. However, persistent leaks and shoddy welding scared a few physicists. Next Dollezhal brought two shipbuilding engineers, Vladimir Nikolaevich Peregudov and Genrikh Alievich Gasanov, on board. They built a full scale, fully equipped *wooden* model submarine, then invited top Navy brass to have a look. The brass were impressed.[68]

The physicists and engineers had to teach sailors about nuclear power, basic nuclear physics, and the operation of a reactor. The crew got hands-on experience on board the wooden prototype. Construction on the submarine shell began in 1954 at a factory in Severodvinsk; the reactor was assembled in the ship by September 1956; and the submarine was launched in August 1957. Over the next year, tests revealed not only the promise of submarines but also the challenges in control reactivity, the need for new instrumentation, and the difficulties in containing radioactivity. On July 4, 1958, the *Leninskii Komsomol* commenced operation under nuclear power, with final testing completed in December. And so, the *Leninskii Komsomol* was commissioned in late 1958.[69]

If only the successes of the *Leninskii Komsomol* and the *Lenin* were the end of the story. The extent to which the Soviet Union used the ocean as a dumping ground has only recently become clear. Soviet scientific literature has long referred to the utility of the ocean as a resting place for the hundreds of tons and billions of curies of high- and low-level radioactive waste. Referring to the experience of France, England, and the United States, two scientists from the Polar Scientific Research Institute of Fishing and Oceanography in Murmansk suggested that discharges of radioactive solutions into the open sea ought to be permitted up to a limit of 500 curies. The growing number of nuclear ships and submarines worried these scientists, because such disasters as that which befell the U. S. S. *Thresher* (1964) seemed to be unavoidable and would inevitably result in toxic fuel contamination of the ocean. The solution was to design reactors that would remain isolated and intact even if the ship or submarine sank. Officials at the World Health Organization asked in February 1963 that ocean dumping of radioactive waste be prohibited, because they feared that radioactive products might be transported biologically to humans. They noted the absence of any kind of controls to ensure that oceans remained radiologically clean. But the superpowers continued to dump for many years, with the USSR denying its activities until the late 1980s.[70]

It was impossible to avoid accidents on a fleet with such a large number of reactors. Their number and years of operation exceeded by an order of magnitude those of atomic power stations. Most accidents occurred not during operation but during downtime for repair and refueling, and often when people were new on the job. But for military officials these were minor risks because Soviet submarines rivaled the best the West had to offer in terms of speed and maneuverability. Some models could exceed forty knots by 1970, and Soviet engineers succeeded in making the submarines quieter by inventing better pumps, improving coolant transport, and extending the depth at which they could operate beyond 1,000 meters.[71]

Unfortunately, terrible disasters befell the Soviet Navy. A reactor exploded during refueling in Chazhma Bay near Vladivostok. The Soviets also lost vessels to the ocean floor; some experts estimate that perhaps a dozen Soviet submarines, equipped with fifty nuclear warheads, sank and were not recovered. Soviet scientists maintain that their reactors remain intact and constantly monitor their radioactivity. In the worst tragedy, the result of a fire on April 7, 1989, the nuclear submarine *Komsomolets* sank in 1,700 meters of water. The ship carried two nuclear-tipped torpedoes and 116 kilograms of enriched uranium in its single 190-megawatt reactor. All personnel were lost. If the nuclear material leaks, it will pollute waters from the Kola peninsula and Scandinavia to St. Petersburg and Helsinki. The reactor was switched successfully to a stable cool-down mode before the submarine was lost, and the structural integrity of the reactor seems to be intact. However, the two torpedoes, with six to ten kilograms of Pu and an activity of 430 curies in the warheads, may be leaking, and the efforts made to seal holes in the torpedo section of the submarine to slow seawater corrosion may work only in the short term.[72]

More than disasters, Soviet storage, refueling, and waste management practices showed that engineers overestimated the safety and efficacy of nuclear engines. In spite of the threat to people of the far north—Alaskan natives, Russians, Swedes, Norwegians, and Canadians—the Soviet northern submarine and icebreaker fleets dumped sixteen reactors (six with spent nuclear fuel) into the Arctic Ocean. They also dumped one shielding assembly with spent nuclear fuel from the *Lenin*. In addition, in the Barents and Karsk seas near Novaia Zemlia and the Kamchatka peninsula and in Vladivostok near Japan, the USSR dumped liquid and solid nuclear waste, beginning in 1959. Containers, barges, ships, and submarines were sunk at a depth of 20 to 300 meters, and some of the 22,000 curies of radioactive waste were dumped at less than twelve meters. The Murmansk Shipping Company's Atomflot facility is supposed to take spent nuclear fuel for reprocessing by railroad to Maiak, but often they merely store the fuel "temporarily" on site. They can't afford to pay the railroad shipping fees. Floating reactor compartments from decommissioned Russian submarines also are temporarily stored in bays and inlets near Vladivostok and Murmansk.[73]

Today, Russia has 235 nuclear submarines, ships, and icebreakers, 228 of which serve the military and 7 the fishing industry. These vessels have 394 reactors, or sixty percent of the total number of reactors in the entire world. Each year, the operation of these reactors creates 20,000 cubic meters of liquid and 6,000 tons of solid radioactive waste. The Northern Fleet alone has 62 nuclear submarines with 940 ballistic missiles and 2,804 warheads. There are between thirty and fifty reactors in dry dock on shore, and another eighty await safe, final storage. Over 100 submarines (between 6 and 8 annually) have been taken out of service in compliance with the provisions of START II. But storage and decommissioning costs have become a burden to the few facilities such as those at the four Severodvinsk factories that are equipped for this task, and the military has received only about ten percent of the funds allocated for decommissioning. That a Severodvinsk submarine dry dock is leaking radioactive waste is no surprise. Four other military radioactive waste facilities (two in the north and two in the far east) can't store any more waste.[74]

There are twenty preliminary designs on the drawing board for railway, barge, truck, and small stationary reactors, with the last transported in modules; with channel-graphite, PWR, BWR, organic liquid, and liquid metal models, from 1.5 to 12 megawatts electric; for use in cogenerating and electric power plants; and for municipal, river, or ocean use. Scientists justify them for the same reasons they have always used: the high cost of transporting fossil fuels, the energy density of nuclear fuel, and the small local power grids that don't demand much more than a few megawatts.[75] So the engineers who succeeded Malykh and Aleksandrov continue to dream of new applications for nuclear engines to tame Russia's vast northern lands.

5

Nuclear Chickens:
Out of the Frying Pan,
Into the Ionizing Radiation

I have just finished congratulating Comrade Babichev for creating a salami
that does not go smelly in one day. Otherwise I would not have congratulated
Comrade Babichev. We shall eat it today. Put it down. Never mind the sun.
Don't be afraid, it will have the aroma of a rose.
—From Yuri Olesha's *Envy*[1]

Sergei Eisenstein, an early advocate of proletarian culture, immortalized one of
the crucible events of the Russian Revolution—mutiny aboard a Tsarist naval vessel, the *Potemkin*—in a film by the same name (1925). The sailors turn against their
officers when the captain insists that a hanging slab of maggot-infested meat is fit
to eat. The Bolsheviks promised "Bread, Land and Peace!" The bread had religious
significance for the orthodox believer, but it meant much more: Never again would
Russia's citizens go hungry or eat unfit food. Yuri Olesha's *Envy*, while about many
things, is about the building of a sausage factory and the need to feed the masses.
In addition to modern lighting, electrification, and public health, the Bolsheviks
promised a modern food industry and scientifically based nutritional norms. A revolution in the preparation of food had to accompany political revolution, especially
because the new leaders promised no more *Potemkin* food, and because they controlled and had centralized all food production and sale, from the collective and fish

farms to the bakeries and sausage factories. How would atomic power continue this revolution?

Mikhail Ivanovich Bryksin provided one answer. He oversaw the development of a small nuclear bird town in the early 1960s for three-quarters of a million chickens. His staff zoologist, Lydia Shershunova, operated a series of instruments and apparatus in the incubators that showered the chickens with ultraviolet rays, infrared light, electrons, and gamma rays and lowered infection rates. They treated eggs, too, with small doses of radiation to accelerate the process by which the embryos "breathed" oxygen through the shell. They conducted hundreds of experiments with various doses at various stages of development. The results indicated that ionizing radiation and infrared light could stimulate appetite. "Atomic chickens" produced five percent more eggs than nonirradiated birds; irradiation allowed chicken farmers to produce healthier birds and secured safe handling of chicken meat. But it was costly and unfamiliar to simple chicken farmers, so the pilot program was abandoned.[2]

Each year, tens of thousands of persons throughout the world get ill after eating food contaminated with bacteria. *E. coli* and *Salmonella* outbreaks associated with tainted hamburger, chicken, and other foods have killed hundreds of people. Botulism continues to be a risk. Canned goods are almost one hundred percent safe because food processors long ago abandoned lead solder and learned how to package food. But the food is not fresh. Fumigation with pesticides and herbicides, and the addition of such preservatives as sulfites, nitrates and nitrates, and BHT and BHA also have their opponents. Many foods continue to spoil between harvest and delivery to the consumer, a loss costing billions of dollars. To combat these problems, why not use the power of nuclear energy—low-level ionizing radiation—to preserve foods? Since the dawn of the nuclear age, physicists have explored this possibility because of their conviction of the safety and efficacy of radiation preservation.

There have been many setbacks in scientists' efforts to commercialize food irradiation. The process often produces olfactory discomfort associated with organoleptic processes (that is, processes affecting the sense organs; for example, sensations stimulated by a putrid smell or a green, rotten appearance). Modest doses of radiation can ruin the taste and texture of fruits and vegetables. Some scientists have also produced data (which are dismissed by most food scientists) that show a higher incidence of tumors in laboratory animals that have been given a steady diet of irradiated food. Consumers raised during the cold war tend to associate radiation with danger, concluding that irradiated products must be unsafe. They may fear fluoride treatment of the water for similar irrational associations. Finally, cost considerations, especially capital start-up costs, have blocked more widespread adoption of the new technology; traditional methods of preservation, with improvements in vacuum packaging, packaging materials, and refrigeration, are both familiar and cheaper. Yet nearly seventy countries had significant radiation sterilization programs, and forty have approved the sale of irradiated products.

All methods of conservation of food products (sterilization by heat, salt, and smoking) call forth changes in organoleptic characteristics and chemical makeup. Proponents of food irradiation were convinced that they could master the new technology in such a way as to produce the fewest of those changes. The promise of mass production of food products that could be shipped anywhere without the danger of spoiling, putrefaction, and infestation intrigued them. The allure of the mighty atom and the ease with which ocean-going fishing vessels or even tractor trailers could be fitted with portable gamma radiation sources helped overcome lingering doubts about the feasibility of food irradiation. And once again, the race among the superpowers to be first in commercializing food irradiation, both for economic and ideological reasons, led proponents to underplay uncertainty about cost, efficacy, and safety, even in the face of data that indicated all was not well. To the disbelief of Westerners, Khrushchev himself claimed in 1958 that the Soviet Union, that most progressive of nations, was the first to approve irradiation of potatoes.

The Soviet food irradiation program was extensive by the early 1950s, although how extensive—and how early it commenced—is hard to pin down. Owing to the cold war umbrella of secrecy, Soviet scientists were unable to publicize their achievements widely until after the Geneva conferences. Beginning in the 1960s, articles appeared regularly on the subject in such journals as *Voprosy pitaniia* (Issues of Nutrition), *Radiobiologiia* (Radiobiology), *Gigiena i sanitariia* (Public Health and Sanitation), *Rybnoe khoziaistvo* (Fish Industry), and *Konservnaia i ovoshchesushil'-naia promyshlennost'* (Canning and Vegetable Processing Industry). The content of these articles indicates that policy makers and scientists decided early on to apply radiation preservation on a broad scale to deal with waste and rotting of foods between the time of harvest or slaughter and the time of purchase in stores. Soviet scientists irradiated potatoes to prevent eyes from forming. They disinfested dried fruit and grains with radiation produced from industrial electron accelerators. Those working in the meat packing industry even studied the possibility of irradiating live animals prior to slaughter to prevent proteolytic deterioration (the breakdown of proteins) in meat later preserved by gamma radiation. These scientists worked primarily in research institutes of the Academy of Medical Sciences, the food industry, and the Academy of Sciences. Researchers in mirror institutes in almost every republic joined the massive effort to promote food irradiation as cheap, safe, and effective. Despite significant attention from Soviet leaders, and a substantial share of national annual investment capital, agriculture remained undercapitalized. Most roads were dirt or gravel and therefore nearly impassable during the spring thaw and fall harvest seasons. Refrigeration equipment was scarce. The mighty atom would bring agriculture, the sore spot of the Soviet economy since its early days, into the modern era.

In many respects, the Soviet food irradiation program resembled that in the United States.[3] Military concerns about the difficulty of providing soldiers in the field with unspoiled food, even in the most inhospitable circumstances (such as distant jungles or deserts) or in situations of difficult supply and resupply (such as space) gave impetus to early research. In both countries, enthusiasm among scientists who were connected with the weapons programs and wished to see good come from the peaceful atom grew quickly. And in both countries, grain, fruit, and vegetable growers and fish and meat producers were intrigued by the idea. But neither the Americans nor the Soviets seemed able to resolve conclusively questions concerning the safety and efficacy of irradiated products. A major difference between the two countries was the lack of consumer awareness of food irradiation programs in the USSR. The Soviet citizen was raised to believe that science and technology were inherently safe and that one who stood in the way of progress was either an ignorant Luddite or an obstructionist enemy. In any event, the government didn't tolerate opposition. Hence, opposition, or at least the admonition to go slowly, would have to come, if it came at all, from within the scientific sphere—in this case, from radiation safety experts in the Soviet Academy of Medical Sciences.

BACTERIA BEWARE: THE MOBILE GAMMA IRRADIATOR IS COMING

After initial results showing that ionizing radiation was effective in killing bacteria or significantly slowing its growth, governments around the world underwrote the development of prototype food irradiators. These came in many forms. Some were mobile, small enough to fit in a semitrailer for use in the field after picking berries, tomatoes, and other fruits and vegetables. Larger irradiators might sit in the hold of a ship, making longer fishing runs possible. The developers of the technologies stressed their safety, cost effectiveness, and ease of operation; these devices also could be operated by even unskilled field-workers. This was a technology that would not only irradiate food but also solve broader social problems. Researchers forecast the significant cost benefits of centralized retail meat cutting over conventional, in-store meat cutting, even though labor union contracts, meat merchandising, and meat shelf-life limits remained as obstacles to implementation.[4]

The technology itself was rather simple. Radiation sources might be ^{60}Co and ^{137}Cs for gamma rays, cathode ray tubes (electrons), Van de Graaff accelerators for direct use of electron radiation, linear electron accelerators, and X-rays. There were positive and negative features of each. Scientists understood X-ray technology quite well, but the process was too expensive. They were attracted to the low cost and widely available gamma radiation from fission products in spent uranium fuel rods from reactors. Spent fuel elements caused significant problems, however, because hot fuel elements with an activity of hundreds of thousands of curies had to be transported safely to appropriate facilities in shielded transport containers that weighed five to six tons. The facilities included special remote handling apparatus and good biological shielding, and installation of these components led to high capital costs. Cobalt-60 has a half-life of 5.25 years and must be replenished annually, but it is cheap. Cesium-137 has a half-life of thirty years, but it is expensive and difficult to handle, having to be encapsulated in stainless steel because it is easily soluble and also is stigmatized as a weapons by-product. Food scientists were confident that valuable fission products could be separated and concentrated under conditions of large-scale production. The advantages of accelerators was that they could be started up and shut down at any time; maintenance and repair were simple because no shielding was required when a facility was down; and transport of radioactive material was eliminated. Also electron beams were of high intensity, so their dose rates exceeded those of isotope sources by a factor of several thousand; hence, objects could be irradiated for a very short time. However, the penetrating capacity of electrons was much lower than that of gamma radiation, so the beams could be used only for treating thin objects or product surfaces; or the electron beam could be converted to X-rays by allowing the electrons to hit a heavy metal target. The resultant X-rays could be used to treat foods of a thickness similar to that of foods treated by gamma rays.[5]

Many foreign countries looked to the United States for leadership in food irradiation and had done so since the Geneva conferences of the mid-1950s and the establishment of the International Atomic Energy Agency (IAEA). Early basic research was centered in Europe. Then the United States took over much of the developmental work. Now England, Germany, the Netherlands, Canada, Japan, Sweden, and the Soviet Union moved quickly ahead. In 1971, twenty-three countries organized the International Project in the Field of Food Irradiation, cosponsored by the Organization for Economic Cooperation and Development (OECD) and IAEA, to produce experimental data on the wholesomeness of irradiated foods, and to save costs and develop data of internationally recognized quality. The program was located at the Institute for Radiation Technology of the Federal Research Institute for Food and Nutrition, at the Karlsruhe Nuclear Research Center in Germany. As of February 1966, the United States had loaned or agreed to loan irradiators or radiation sources to seven countries: Israel, Iceland, Argentina, India, Pakistan, Venezuela, and Chile.[6]

By the mid-1960s, over fifty nations had scientific staffs conducting research and another twenty-six had begun programs; and twenty international organizations were actively involved in research, development, and coordination of irradiation activities. In 1966, there were only twelve pilot irradiation plants and experimental facilities in the world. By 1975, there were seventy pilot plants, of which eight were in the United States, five were in the Soviet Union, five in Eastern Europe, and twenty-eight in developing countries (see Appendix, Table 14).[7] The World Health Organization had convened an "expert committee" on the wholesomeness of irradiated foods. In 1970, the committee gave clearance for five years to irradiated wheat and potatoes for human consumption. In 1976, the committee recognized five irradiated food items (potatoes, wheat, chicken, papaya, and strawberries) as "unconditionally safe" for human consumption. Three foods (rice, fish, and onions) gained "provisional" approval. Of course, the USSR, which by this time had the most active program, directed its early attention to the potato.

A BRIEF HISTORY OF SOVIET POTATOES

In contrast to the food irradiation program in the United States, where the government only belatedly permitted mass marketing of radiation-treated foods, the Soviet program moved beyond research to broad application by the late 1950s. The Soviet scientists followed the progress of their American colleagues in "cold sterilization" closely. In the early 1950s, M. N. Meizel at the Institute of Biophysics in Moscow examined what doses were sufficient to eradicate harmful organisms in meat, fish, fruit, vegetables, and juices. They used cobalt sources and Van de Graaff accelerators. At the Scientific Research Institute of Grain, scientists explored disinfestation.

The USSR became the first country to clear irradiated foods for human consumption when it approved the sale of irradiated potatoes in March 1958; this approval was followed a year later by an approval for the irradiation of grain to eliminate insect infestation. And the USSR brought the world's first irradiation pilot plant on line. Its facilities included the Experimental Gamma Irradiator EGO-2 and the EGO-20, the GUBE facility developed at the Institute of Biophysics, the canning and vegetable industry's processing high-intensity gamma irradiator (which used a 240-kilocurie ^{60}Co source), the grain industry's gamma irradiator (which used a 35-kilocurie ^{60}Co source), and a series of reactor irradiation loops such as that at the IRT-2000 nuclear reactor at Georgian Academy of Sciences in Tbilisi.[8] The Soviet official hoped that ionizing radiation would save Soviet agriculture from its traditional stumbling blocks of poor transportation and limited refrigeration infrastructure. There would no longer be hungry Communists waiting in line for spoiled food.

When he came to power, Khrushchev renewed the Soviet industrialization and urbanization efforts of the 1930s. He focused his appeals to the worker to toil harder for the glorious communist future with promises of a shorter work week, higher salaries, more housing, and more wholesome food. But comfort came with a price. The food industry had gained increasing responsibility for feeding millions of persons daily in dining halls whose assembly lines were capable of mass-producing only small portions of soup, bread, potatoes, and fatty, unidentifiable meat chunks. Anyone who has eaten in a Soviet factory, school, public cafeteria, or dining hall will testify to their low standards of hygiene: filthy countertops, inadequately cleaned utensils and plates, shared glasses, and unhygienic and often undercooked meals. Those with an iron stomach survive; the bowels of mere mortals quake when confronted with the choice of "vinaigrette" with rancid sunflower seed oil or room-temperature white pork lard (*"bakon"*). Open-faced sandwiches, slathered with butter, anointed with hard-boiled eggs and cold cuts, and displayed at room temperature all day were hardly a safe alternative. How would officials deal with the potential for food poisoning in an increasingly mechanized and overly centralized food industry? Officially speaking, industrialized, scientific food production was the answer. Indeed, the modern food industry contributed to fewer outbreaks of food poisoning in the postwar USSR, even though the absolute number of cases continued to rise (so much so that the Central Statistic Administration ceased to publish statistics).[9] Once again, as with mining and electrification, the hope was that nuclear technology would solve the problem.

By 1957, the food industry had thirty different branches with 22,000 employers and three million employees. The production of fish, meat, sausage, animal and vegetable oils, and milk products had doubled since the beginning of World War II. There were major meat factories in Moscow, Leningrad, Baku, Sverdlovsk, Kuibyshev, and Dnepropetrovsk. Nearly 500 industrial meat combines processed 12,000 tons of food products per shift, supplemented by 245 chicken combines, 300 slaughter houses, and 500 sausage factories. The largest meat factories turned out 150,000 cans of what was called "meat" in one shift. The largest sausage factories squeezed out 200 tons of smoked products weekly. To meet the major goal of surpassing the United States in per capita production of meat, milk, and butter by the mid-1960s, the industry would be modernized with assembly lines and freezers.[10] There was also a place for food irradiation in the modern Soviet factory.

The fishing industry had grown even more rapidly, ranking second behind Japan by 1960. The number of fishing vessels grew nearly fourfold between 1940 and 1957, with an increasingly large portion of the catch coming from the oceans. The fish industry had modernized ports at Murmansk, Arkhangelsk, Kalingrad, Riga, and in the far eastern cities of Nakhodka, Petropavlovsk Kamchatka, and Vladivostok. New refrigerator and freezer ships trawled the seas. Whales were nearly ten percent of the catch.[11] Couldn't on-board ship irradiators ensure that a larger, fresher catch made it to the consumer?

Soviet food scientists were no fools. They began to explore irradiation with the noble potato as their experimental subject. The potato has long been an important source of nutrition in Russia and Ukraine. Through the 1980s, the USSR produced an average of seventy-five to eighty million tons annually (one-quarter ton per person per year). Russian cookbooks hold dozens of recipes for the ubiquitous, eternal potato. Yet potatoes cannot be stored easily all year long. In contrast to most vegetables, potatoes do not take well to freezing temperatures, for their taste, consistency, and culinary properties deteriorate. They become unnaturally sweet and soft as a result of changes in their carbohydrate composition, they turn dark when cooked, and they lose vitamins. They also decay considerably faster when temperatures rise in the spring. Anyone who has visited a "vegetable-fruit" store in the Soviet Union in March or April before new produce appears is familiar with the earthy odor of overripe and spoiled potatoes. The preparation "M1," a dust that contains 3.5 percent alpha-napthyl methyl acetate, applied to potatoes at a rate of 3.5 kilograms per ton, delays sprouting. But it must come into contact with each tuber; and after dusting, the potatoes must be kept covered with paper or straw matting, which interferes with ventilation and allows them to become wet. For Soviet food specialists, irradiation of tubers was the solution to this problem. The government approved the process in 1958; by 1965, food scientists had developed what they called "industrial radiation processing."

Scientists at the A. N. Bakh Biochemistry Institute in Moscow first set out to irradiate tubers. They encountered a series of problems but solved each one. Irradiation decreased the natural resistance of potatoes to plant parasites, so losses from diseases were greater than in unirradiated tubers. Potatoes whose disease resistance has been lowered by some other cause—for example, bumps and bruises caused by rough handling during storage and shipping or exposure to moisture—were further weakened by irradiation. After studying the effects of ionizing radiation on the chemical composition of potatoes and other vegetables—on the starch, monosaccharides, sucrose, vitamin, and protein and nonprotein nitrogenous compounds—scientists determined that potatoes should not be irradiated immediately after harvest but should be treated later, after being stored for at least two weeks at room temperature and at relatively high humidity. These were conditions favorable to rapid formation of wound periderm (a protective layer of secondary tissue). Unfortunately, the collective farm peasant did not always cooperate with efforts to prevent damage during harvest, shipping, and storage of the tubers.

By the end of 1961, Bakh Institute scientists designed the world's first full-fledged irradiation pilot plant to simulate industrial production conditions for potatoes. It began operation in 1964 at the Dzerzhinskii Base for Moscow Fruit and Vegetable Procurement. For their industrial-scale experiments, scientists acquired potatoes from a nearby Moscow state farm, where the potatoes had been stored under ordinary, uncooled conditions for a month. They were delivered in containers with capacities of 300 and 500 kilograms to the irradiation facility, where they were irradiated with doses of 5, 7.5, and 10 kilorads. The facility had a capacity of 20,000 tons per season, but only 200 tons were irradiated the first year. These tubers sat for the winter, then were examined in June and July of the next year. Six percent of the potatoes in the control group had sprouted by June, and these unirradiated potatoes were unfit for sale or consumption in July, whereas only two percent of the tubers irradiated with 5 kilorads had sprouted by July, and spoilage rates were significantly reduced. The irradiated potatoes were then shipped to the Transpolar, Transcaucasian, and Central Asia regions of the country for further storage and, as far as I can tell, then sold to consumers. By November, those that had been irradiated with 7.5 kilorads had formed sprouts, but those irradiated with 10 kilorads remained edible.

Larger amounts of potatoes (thirty to forty tons annually) were also irradiated at the Bogucharovo branch of the All-Union Research Institute of the Canning Industry (VNIIKOP, near Tula) over a three-year period. Stored for six months after irradiation, the potatoes could be used satisfactorily as chips, flour, or dried products. Soviet potato chips, of course, hardly made up in shelf life what they lacked in taste and texture. But specialists at the Institute of Economics added their seal of approval to radiation processing by calculating that the cost of irradiation was economically justified, based on the assumptions of large supplies of potatoes and vegetables and low transport costs.[12] Despite this success, the Dzerzhinskii and Bogucharovskii plants were clearly too small to handle a large supply of potatoes, and their high capital costs convinced officials not to pursue a larger program. As was often the case in the Soviet Union, the high-level attention ensured local success but not extensive diffusion, and most fruit, vegetables, and tubers continued to spoil between field and store.

As in the United States, the first steps in food irradiation in the USSR were taken in military research institutes and first reported in their journals. Early results indicated that Soviet scientists were aware of the significant impact of ionizing radiation on vitamin C and carotene in several different food products. In one set of experiments carried out under military auspices and published in the *Military Medical Journal*, researchers used a gamma source of ^{60}Co on pickled cabbage, tomato paste, vitamin C in the form of syrup, and a carotene preparation. The authors claimed that there was very little change in the nutritive value of these foods, even after large doses of gamma rays; in fact, losses of thirty to sixty percent of the vitamins were experienced.[13] In follow-up experiments, G. M. Egiazarov continued to examine the degree of destruction of vitamins A, B_1, B_2, C, and E, and carotene in a variety of foods: beef liver, milk, cheese, carrots, tomato paste, roast beef fat, grains, fish, liverwurst, potatoes, and sauerkraut. The products were irradiated in the dark at 5°C at 18,000 rads per hour at an energy of 1.17 mega-electronvolts and doses of 50,000, 100,000, and 150,000 roentgens. Vitamins B_1, B_2, and A were retained virtually unchanged in all products, whereas vitamin E in milk, butter, and sunflower seed oil and carotene in beef fat were destroyed.[14]

Early cold sterilization efforts focused logically on dairy products for two reasons: the importance of milk to children and its short shelf life even after pasteurization. Soviet scientists followed foreign research on cold sterilization of milk, cheese, cream, and butter with interest, commencing their own programs in the early 1950s. They were convinced of the complete safety of the process for many foods. The only drawbacks seemed to be that cold sterilization intensified natural processes of autooxidation and organoleptic deterioration, especially in foods with a high fat content. To put it in simple terms, irradiation preserved milk but gave it a strong sulfur odor and an unpleasant taste, which made the product unpalatable. The addition of antioxidants and the heating of the product to 30° to 35°C during irradiation often countered these undesirable side effects. Food scientists turned to irradiation of sunflower oil, subjecting it to a dose of 180 kilovolts of X-rays. This, too, led to undesirable effects, but they were completely removed by irradiation at higher temperature and the addition of ascorbic and citric acids. Such treatment allowed storage at a low temperature (3°C) for up to 240 days.[15]

This research raised a series of questions. One was whether foods sterilized by ionizing radiation at such high doses as were then standard called forth any radioactivity in the food products themselves. In some foods, radioactive isotopes of oxygen, nitrogen, and carbon were formed and, although all had short half-lives of several minutes (^{13}N, ten minutes; ^{15}O, two minutes; and ^{11}C, twenty minutes), their presence raised concerns of artificial radioactivity. Studies showed that if neutrons or other radiations have an energy of less than ten megaelectronvolts, then the energies are too low to convert stable chemical elements in food products into radioactive ones. Holding the products for fourteen hours ensured that the induced radioactivity did not exceed natural radiation levels of the food. Most food specialists recognized the need for lower levels of energy. Others remained unconvinced, especially because long-term feeding tests of mice with irradiated food products had inconclusive results, some showing no impact, others indicating impact on growth and sexual function.[16]

Leningrad was a logical setting for early food irradiation research. The USSR's nuclear navy was based in Leningrad, where a series of military-technical institutes, design bureaus, and construction trusts contributed to its development. In the late 1950s, in Gatchina outside of Leningrad, physicists established a special institute for nuclear physics. The Sosnovyi Bor nuclear power station with four Chernobyl-type RBMK reactors was nearby. Military scientists in one Leningrad establishment, the Kirov Military Medical Academy, were extensively involved in various aspects of radiation safety, including human exposure studies. An early study dealt with the advantages of ionizing radiation for sterilization of food products over such traditional methods of conservation as heating, which led to undesirable changes in color, flavor, texture, and smell, and loss of vitamins. These changes were particularly undesirable in fruits and vegetables, which have a much more fragile constitution than meat. Kirov Academy scientists touted cold sterilization for its efficacy, simplicity, and low cost. The major problem was to determine a level of radiation low enough to destroy microfauna but not produce organoleptic changes. They determined that ^{60}Co, ^{137}Cs, ^{109}Pd, and ^{182}Ta were effective sources of gamma rays that penetrated more deeply than X-rays up to ten megaelectronvolts and therefore were good for cold sterilization. Cathode ray tubes and Van de Graaff accelerators that produced beams of high-energy electrons might also be used, but the accelerated electrons did not penetrate as deeply as gamma rays did. Linear accelerators would be better. In any event, various bacteria, yeast, and molds all showed resistance to the impact of ionizing radiation, especially in such dangerous bacteria as *Clostridium botulinum,* which continued to grow for hours after irradiation with lethal doses. Unfortunately, doses of one megarad and higher killed them outright but provoked organoleptic changes in the foods themselves. It remained to find ways to lower the dose, yet still kill microorganisms, perhaps in concert with food additives or modifications in the entire process.[17] Like their colleagues in the United States, they determined that blanching the food product at 60° to 80°C to inactivate various enzymes, vacuum packing to exclude the atmosphere, freezing to −40°C, and then irradiating would solve all their problems. But the process had just become longer and more expensive.

A logical application for Soviet agriculture was radiation disinfestation of food products such as grains, groats, dried fruits and vegetables, and dry food concentrates. Chemical and thermal methods of disinfestation have many drawbacks. It is nearly impossible to entirely remove from food products the fumigant and other residues that might hurt the consumer if ingested. Moreover, the chemicals cannot reach the interior of the fruits and vegetables. And some foods cannot readily be treated by fumigants or hot air. Soviet scientists at the All-Union Research Institute of Grain (VNIIZ) and VNIIKOP turned therefore to the study of the action of ionizing radiation on insects. Using a cobalt source, scientists applied either lethal doses or small doses that sexually sterilized the insects. Generally, depending on the dose, radiation slowed insect respiration and food consumption, prevented reproduction by preventing development of eggs, larvae, and pupae, or killed the insects outright. Scientists were happy to discover no evidence that irradiation led to the development of insects with significantly greater radiation resistance, nor did they mutate into more virulent eaters. The studies also demonstrated that carbohydrates, proteins, and, to a certain extent, fats in various grains were not changed significantly by irradiation. It was quite important for the Russian diet and psyche that bread-baking properties changed very little.

SILENT AUTUMN

Radiation sterilization was an important technology for a country with significant problems in both harvesting grain and delivering it to mills and bakeries before spoilage and infestation. On the basis of early studies, the USSR Ministry of Public

Health in 1960 authorized the use of food products made from wheat irradiated with 100 kilorads. In the United States, authorization was granted in 1963 for commercial use of grain irradiated at doses ranging from twenty to fifty kilorads. Tests at a VNIIZ pilot plant constructed in 1963 showed that irradiation of grain at doses ranging from eleven to eighteen kilorads completely destroyed pests and allowed grain to be stored for at least four months without damage or deterioration in quality. VNIIZ researchers developed a gamma irradiator capable of handling 400 kilograms of seed per hour, and scientists at the Institute of Biophysics designed a two-ton, portable, cesium irradiator of grain with a capacity of one ton per day.[18] Once again, the Institute of Economics provided its cost imprimatur by showing that radiation disinfestation was cheaper than chemical disinfestation.

Scientists in the United States, England, Canada, France, and the USSR put two and two together (isotopes and trucks) to manufacture portable irradiators that followed the farmer into the field.[19] In the early 1960s, Soviet specialists affixed an irradiator with a capacity of twenty kilograms of grain per hour to the chassis of a standard ZIL-131 truck. A 3,500-curie ^{137}Cs source powered the Kolos irradiator. It permitted doses of 750 to 1,000 rads and processed one ton of grain or fodder hourly. Researchers recommended serial production of the Kolos for installation on fleets of trucks. In 1968, workers processed 760 hectares of grain on Moldavian farms; in 1969, 1,250 hectares; in 1970, 4,000 hectares or a total of 102 tons. They expanded the Kolos's operation to Kirgizia for sugar beets and sunflower seeds, but that operation was only a small, demonstration program.[20]

Because irradiation causes changes in the biochemistry of the grains (partial oxidation of carbohydrates, destruction of fats with consequent formation of peroxides, changes in the quantity of vitamins and in some cases their destruction), researchers turned to an investigation of whether consumption of these products might impair sexual function and growth and development of progeny or increase mortality. By the early 1970s, Soviet researchers were divided on the issue of the safety of irradiated products, despite their agreement on the efficacy of cold sterilization. In one study, researchers examined three generations of rats and six generations of mice fed irradiated grain over eighteen months to see whether any essential differences developed between control and experimental animals in weight, physical development, natality, morphological blood picture, and activity of the oxidizing blood enzymes (peroxidases and catalases). They concluded there was none.[21] But in another experiment, rats were fed beef, cod filet, green peas, rye bread, and oats that had been sterilized by using a ^{60}Co source. In these animals, sexual function was inhibited, as was growth and development of progeny. The progeny also had increased mortality rates. Daily introduction of a vitamin E oil concentrate seemed to reverse these phenomena almost entirely, a result leading the researchers to conclude that the unfavorable effects of the irradiated food products were associated with the reduced nutritive value of the products.[22] The question that no one seemed to ask was whether a modern technology that destroyed an essential nutrient, therefore required the addition of that same nutrient at another stage of the process resulted in a more wholesome product, let alone whether it was worth the cost and effort.

Industrial accelerators could also be used for disinfestation. Physicists at the Budker Institute of Nuclear Physics in Akademgorodok took the lead in the development of this technology. In 1966, the State Committee for Science and Technology approved their proposal to set up a small-scale serial production facility for high-power accelerators that ran on 220-volt current and, when turned off, were no more dangerous than a typewriter. The institute gained control over the profits earned in the sale of the accelerators money and pumped that money back into its research program. The parameters of the industrial accelerators covered an energy range from 0.3 to 2.5 megaelectronvolts and a power range from hundreds of watts to hundreds of kilowatts. There were three kinds of these machines: the ELIT accelerators were based on high-voltage pulse transformers and were primarily used for experimental studies; the ELV operated on the commercial frequency, and the ILU-type accelerators were based on RF (high-frequency) resonators. The latter two machines found broad application in industry, agriculture, and medicine. One such application was irradiation of grain to destroy insects. Introduced experimentally at the Novosibirsk Grain Elevator of the Siberian branch of the All-Union Grain Research Institute, this type of accelerator was installed at the Odessa port elevator and in five other installations on the Volga and Don rivers. The accelerators were also used for the preparation of animal feed by radiolysis (chemical decomposition by the action of radiation) of inedible plant material, disinfestation, sterilization, pre-sowing radiation, and radiation-induced mutations for breeding.[23]

Once research left the shield of military secrecy, much of it was carried out in the division of food safety of the Institute of Nutrition of the Academy of Medical Sciences under I. I. Shillinger, who first studied the potential carcinogenicity of additives, pesticides, and herbicides. Although no Soviet Rachel Carson publicized the dangers of these chemicals, scientists were concerned about their overuse because of the new food program promulgated under Khrushchev that called for the "chemicalization" of agriculture to increase yields. Soviet agriculture was intensely chemical, with amounts per hectare of herbicides, pesticides and fertilizers anointed per acre ultimately exceeding those used in the United States by threefold, and even fivefold, by the 1970s. The goal of Shillinger's research was to protect the inhabitants of the Soviet Union from additives—including radiation—that were carcinogenic. He called for food specialists in leading institutes in the USSR to carry out work on the subject in first-rate laboratories staffed by qualified personnel.[24] With researchers in the F. F. Erisman Moscow Scientific Research Institute of Public Health, Shillinger and his colleagues showed that irradiation did not affect the wholesomeness of dried fruits, potatoes, and other vegetables, and that there were only minor changes in vitamin, carbohydrate, and protein content.

Each branch of the food processing industry had its own laboratories for examining the promise of this new technology. Specialists at VNIIKOP found it difficult to manage ionization sterilization of fruit and vegetables, especially of fragile fruits such as raspberries, which have a short shelf life and serve as a fertile home for microfauna. Like scientists at the University of California Davis, Soviet food specialists experimented on berries by using rather low doses. Kudriasheva and Medvedskaia, who worked in the laboratory of microbiology and entomology at a branch of the canning institute in Bogucharovo, used a ^{60}Co multipurpose irradiator for raspberries in standard containers at two levels of power, 23 and 150 rads per second, and three different gamma-ray doses: 300, 400, and 500 kilorads. When irradiated at the higher level, the raspberries could be stored at 20°C for one to two days longer; and at 5°C, they lasted for three to four days longer.[25] This was hardly a monumental increase in shelf life and did nothing about the heavy hands of shippers and packers in the Soviet food industry. The average citizen rarely saw a fresh raspberry in any event.

Other VNIIKOP scientists conducted experiments in preparation for building an industrial pilot plant for dried fruits with a throughput of 1.5 tons per hour. They forecast that it would be ten percent cheaper to use than chemical methods. The experiments showed that there were no "nutritionally significant losses" in most fruits—for example, of ascorbic acid—under modest doses of radiation. The Ministry of Health gave approval for use of these products as food. Then VNIIKOP scientists ran into significant problems. When fresh fruits were treated with irradiation sufficient to destroy microorganisms on the surface of the fruit, the fruits themselves became soft, altered in color, changed taste, and lost natural microbial resistance, especially if the skin of the fruit had been damaged. Further, the microorganisms were quick to return in large numbers. Irradiation technology turned out to work better with fruits that are harvested partially or fully ripe and thus have a relatively short postharvest life. Yet with those that "ripen" on the way to market and on the table, even treatment with ethylene could fail to trigger ripening after irradiation. In some fruits (tomatoes), irradiation provoked anomalous ripening. Furthermore, one could not expect to make good fruit out of bad by the irradiation process: If infection was related to endemic handling and transit injuries, and the presence of pathogens such as fungus spores was high, then the dose required to kill the infection was too great and destroyed the fruit. Said V. I. Rogashev, of the All-Union Scientific Research Institute for Canning and Vegetable Drying in Moscow, "It is clear that the irradiation of fresh fruit and vegetables is not as simple a matter as it appeared initially."[26] Soviet scientists seem to have been unable to lick the difficulties of irradiating fruit, especially given the poor state of their harvesting and handling equipment and the poorly paid workers who lacked any incentive to operate it well.

VNIIKOP researchers determined that they needed to understand fully the characteristics of cells of irradiated microorganisms to determine optimum conditions for irradiation of food products and stifle the growth of microflora and microorganisms such as *C. botulinum*. The most radiation sensitive species are the Gram negative bacteria, especially *Pseudomonas aeroguinosa*, *Escherichia coli*, *Salmonella typhosa*, and *Serratia marcescens*, where from 25 to 250 kilorads are required to destroy 10^8 per milliliter. To inhibit growth of botulinum type A spores at a concentration of 10^{12}, a dose of about five megarads is needed. Other studies showed that radiation resistance decreases in the presence of oxygen. To be certain that all activity of microorganisms has been suppressed, a dose of four to seven megarads is needed if the pH of the product is higher than 4.5, but a dose of only one to three megarads is required if the pH is below 4.5, because *C. botulinum* spores do not germinate to the vegetative stage (when they secrete their toxins) if the pH is more acid than 4.5. However, such large doses cause changes in the organoleptic properties of many products, the most obvious of which was a sulfur odor, and this unwelcome outcome limited high-dose applications to the production of canned goods.[27]

TRIM WITH AN AXE, HANDLE WITH CARE

Naturally, another goal of irradiation was to increase the shelf life of meat. An increase of a few days of shelf life would be of great economic value, especially because in the modern world, the distances that meats travel from point of slaughter to market is often hundreds of kilometers. Think of the international sale of New Zealand lamb. Think of the changes in the United States since Chicago became its meat capital and grain elevators and stockyards dominated the landscape. Railroads contributed to Chicago's preeminence, allowing most shippers to send their meat and other products eastward through the city. Eventually the packers and the railroad owners consolidated their operations in the huge Union Stock Yard. Once they had introduced refrigeration into the process, they were able to market western beef, already dressed, at prices that eastern producers could not match because production in the West was cheaper. Butcher shops displayed the trimmed, dressed meats in an attractive fashion, harnessing impulse buying in the consumer.[28]

In the Soviet Union, several of these items were present: centralization, railroads, and long distances from slaughter to market. But much else was not: refrigeration, high-quality beef, and attractive displays. Irradiation promised a solution. When meat is refrigerated, cooled on dry ice, or even frozen, transport works well; but when food is defrosted, its quality declines. Irradiation would make cheaper transport possible, with only cooling and thicker stacking of dressed and undressed carcasses. Soviet scientists determined that irradiation with 0.5-megarad doses increased the storage time of meat at 3°C up to six months. Raw pork vacuum-packed in plastic wrap and irradiated with a 0.9-megarad dose kept four months at the same temperature. Scientists at VNIIKOP produced cut-up beef, pork, rabbit, and chicken packaged in film in vacuum. It kept seven to ten days at 20°C or eight weeks at 5°C when irradiated with doses of 500 to 600 kilorads. The meat dishes, according to "professional taste panels and consumers," had good taste properties and were used with the approval of the USSR Ministry of Public Health in train dining cars and with no complaints from patrons or chefs.[29] Having eaten in many of these dining cars myself in Ukraine, Russia, and Siberia, I have strong doubts about the quality of these products, let alone their ability to make up for the filthy conditions in the kitchens.

Meat products gained considerable attention both because vegetables and fruits turned out to be far more susceptible to damage from ionizing radiation and because fresh vegetables were available only in the summer months. Like their colleagues in the West, the Soviets had another reason for their interest in meat products. They had come to believe that rapid increases in production and consumption of meat were a sign of the higher culture of the modern industrial world. They built a special pavilion to the meat industry at the Exhibition of the Achievements of Agriculture in which glorious sausages and hot dogs, trimmed meats, and other delights were displayed in cooler cases rarely seen in stores. Ionizing radiation would propel these food products to a higher level of being: They would acquire a long shelf life and would need only to be heated before use in restaurants and stores. With irradiation of meat products, the salesperson or butcher in the store would no longer be able to sell hamburger like that offered to me with the claim, "It's not spoiled. It only smells. When it's spoiled, it's green."

Citing the approval of the FDA in 1963 to permit the sale of bacon irradiated with a dose ranging from 4.5 to 5.6 megarads from a ^{60}Co source, Soviet scientists set out to duplicate the effort. Using both gamma and electron radiation, scientists succeeded in extending shelf life three- to fourfold for products that normally perished relatively quickly at room temperature. They were concerned, however, about changes in the proteins, fats, and carbohydrates in the products. For example, under the action of gamma rays, a series of radiolabile vitamins (that is, those readily destroyed by radiation), such as tocopherols (various antioxidants), ascorbic acid, thiamin, vitamins E and K, both water- and fat-soluble, were partially lost. In some experiments, doses for the pasteurization of meat products (600 kilorads for beef and 800 kilorads for pork) partially destroyed vitamins B_1, B_2, K, and E.

Another extensive study dealt with the impact of ionizing radiation on the quality of beef. In one experiment, fresh, chilled, and frozen beef samples were trimmed of fat, then ground and put in glass jars, both vacuum-packed and not, and sometimes wrapped in plastic. The GUT-Co-400 served as the source of gamma radiation. The samples were irradiated at room temperature, at $0°C$, and at $6°C$ for eighteen hours. I. M. Buznik, who carried out the experiments, also conducted an extensive literature search to compare his results with those of American, British, and German scientists. He noted that irradiation of fresh meat changed the color to a brown or brownish-silver hue and imparted a disagreeable, foreign smell, described by several unfortunate sniffers as "unpleasant," "a smell that reminds me of joiner's glue," "boiled potatoes," or "steamed pumpkin." American food scientists did not encounter these olfactory surprises in their samples, leading them to speculate that Soviet technology was unsophisticated and perhaps too powerful. Buznik also presented startling results at the thirteenth scientific session of the Institute of Nutrition in 1959, showing that all animals fed these products in one of his experiments had no offspring and died in four to five weeks.[30] To the American specialists, again, the cause of mortality was most likely anything but radiation. Perhaps it was Buznik's culinary virtuosity.

The All-Union Scientific Research Institute of the Meat Industry (VNIIMP) in Moscow was also engaged in wide-ranging experiments intended to demonstrate how best to make tasty Soviet meats more long lived. They conducted experiments on the effect of gamma rays and thermal processing on the destruction of antioxidants in lard. Generally, antioxidants retarded oxidation of fats and the rapid spoilage of meat. The action of heat on lard results in the accumulation of peroxides and in simultaneous dissociation of antioxidants. Using a gamma source from the Institute of Biophysics at a dose of 2,000 rads per minute, they irradiated fat with doses of 300,000, 600,000, and 1.5 million rads. Increased doses of gamma-irradiation tended to accelerate the destruction of antioxidants, so that an awful smell was observed almost immediately in the higher doses samples.[31]

Two other problems occur with extended meat storage: rancidity of the fat and exudation of meat juice. But studies at the VNIIMP showed that irradiation with the addition of antioxidants worked against the first of these problems. The second problem could be treated with a mixture of sodium chloride, tripolyphosphate, and ascorbic acid; this treatment also increased the retention of natural color. Another treatment was partial cooking (blanching) in vacuum pouches at 80°C after irradiation. In addition to beef, scientists also obtained good results with bacon, smoked and cooked cured pork, and smoked Ukrainian sausage, with no deterioration in quality after forty-five days of storage at room temperature, three times the storage time of nonirradiated products.

Chicken was a greater problem. Chicken meat is a breeding ground for *Salmonella*. Rad-pasteurization of chicken increases its shelf life four- to fivefold over untreated chicken stored at 0°C. Is irradiated chicken safe for human consumption? Over six months, Shillinger and Kachkova examined the impact of chicken that had been gamma-pasteurized on the health of albino rats; during the experiments, the chicken meat was sixty percent of the protein and fifty percent of the fat in their daily diet. The scientists concluded that there had been no harmful effects on the rats.[32]

Fish, also, were important subjects of irradiation tests. Scientists of the All-Union Scientific Research Institute of the Fish Industry (VNIIRO) extended storage times of flounder, cod, salmon, crab, oysters, and shrimp up to fivefold with irradiation. But few Soviet consumers ever saw unfrozen fish, irradiated or otherwise. They saw frozen slabs of fish mass. Nevertheless, irradiation was a technology with great possibilities in the fish industry. Along with the United States and Japan, the Soviet Union was a major commercial fishing power of the late twentieth century. The Soviet maritime fishing industry applied large-scale technologies in the name of efficiency and economies of scale, but the huge fishing vessels and mechanized drift nets trapped everything, including dolphins and nonfood fish. The massive floating factories used on-board freezers and canners to deliver large blocks of frozen and canned fish to stores. This enterprise overcame the problems associated with poorly developed railroad and trucking industries, but still lost one-third of the catch to spoilage. The fish industry sought on-board irradiators to deal with the need to deliver more of the growing catch to the consumer before it spoiled.

To supplement the efforts of the Soviet fishing fleet to deliver products to port, VNIIRO scientists conducted extensive studies on radiation preservation of such products as cooked cod, shellfish, carp, and perch, vacuum-packed in tomato sauce in glass containers. This process kept the product essentially sterile for more than two years, even in tomato sauce, which retains its "bright color . . . and has a pleasant aroma and taste."[33] At a United Nations symposium in 1966, A. V. Kardashev presented results of experiments in which various vacuum-packed fish products (boiled, fried and stuffed fish, fried fish filets, hot-smoked fish) were subjected to irradiation. Unfortunately, sterilization was accompanied by significant organoleptic changes, for the vacuum seal was not tight. During storage, the fat in many irradiated products turned putrid. Kardashev attempted to prevent the changes by lowering the pH of the products and adding carotenoids, ascorbic acid, and commercial tomato sauces. Pieces of fish were cooked until ready for eating, placed in glass jars, and vacuum-sealed; other samples of the products were autoclaved. The fish received 0.2 to 2.0 megarads of gamma radiation from a ^{60}Co source; a dose of 1.5 megarads was found to be sufficient to sterilize them. Even though adding vitamins and sauces made the microorganisms more resistant to radiation, lowering the pH and cooking countered that problem. This product was popular and widely consumed in the Soviet Union.[34] Best of all was the tomato sauce, for it covered the "off flavor." Rather than endure a gnawing feeling in my stomach, I have eaten dozens of tomato sauce-laden tins of these fish to the horror of my family and friends. But fish was one product not approved for irradiation, because freezing it into blocks and storing it in the holds of refrigerated ships was cheaper (see Appendix, Table 15).

THE EYES (AND NOSE) HAVE IT

The process of irradiation produces food with a wide variation in quality and in length of storage life. Reduced quality includes unpleasant texture, flavor, and smell. Undesirable side reactions that often accompany irradiation include higher processing temperature, removal of free-radical scavengers, and synergistic radiolethal effects on food additives such as nitrites, nitrates, sodium chloride, and antibiotics. Scientists at the Institute of Nutrition and the Erisman Institute were responsible for carrying out studies on these changes. They identified a host of problems.

Water is the principal constituent of all living organisms and of most food products. When it is exposed to ionizing radiation, radiolysis occurs; that is, free radicals—atomic hydrogen, hydroxyl (OH) groups, or fragments of molecules—are formed. Even though they exist only a short time as free radicals, they are very active chemically and may react to form various compounds, including hydrogen peroxide (H_2O_2). They also react with substances dissolved in the water and thus affect or bring about various reactions. Oxidation-reduction processes are intensified, complex organic substances are decomposed to simpler compounds, and new substances are formed. Different organisms, organs, and tissues react differently to the action of ionizing radiation, as do different metabolic processes. For example, in meats, chicken, and fish, unappetizing smells are due in part to degradation of muscle protein.

Scientists quickly turned from a realization of the change in the food products themselves to a study of the influence of products with degraded proteins, new substances, and insufficient vitamins on such laboratory animals as dogs and rats. Several studies showed the prevalence of often fatal hemorrhaging in rats. Yet Bondarev's work, in which he fed laboratory dogs a diet of irradiated foods (hamburger meat, fish filet, rye, and peas), indicated no danger to the animals. Nor had long-term studies of irradiated grain indicated danger. Considering the contradictory nature of the data on this subject, Soviet scientists at VNIIKOP, the Institute of

Nutrition, the Erisman Institute of Health, and the Institute of Experimental Pathology and Therapy examined the impact of a diet, largely meat, in which thiamin, vitamin K, and other important nutrients had been destroyed by ionizing radiation. In one experiment, using two groups of six dogs (one control, one experimental), they measured the amount of thiamin and other vitamins in the urine and blood, the morphology of the blood cells, the phagocytic reaction of leukocytes, and the changes in some aspects of metabolism. Over an eighteen-month period, they found little difference in the health of the animals, and certainly "no toxic effects." On the other hand, an experiment in which monkeys were observed over an eleven-month period showed the negative health effects of reduced amounts of vitamin C and folic acid in the irradiated foods.[35]

Soon, too, evidence accumulated about the impact of irradiated products on the reproductive system. A ten-month study carried out at a series of food industry research institutes on five successive generations of white rats, which were given a diet of meat, oats, grits, and potatoes treated with different doses of gamma radiation but supplemented by other products, failed to indicate a measurable influence on the organism of the animals. However, gestation period was lengthened in many of these animals, and the survival rates of the progeny in the first month decreased. Some disease rates in the experimental animals (pneumonia, for example) also exceeded that of the control animals.[36] Indeed, as early as 1962, Indian researchers had demonstrated that cytological aberrations occur in plant embryos that had been cultured in irradiated potato mash.[37] Conversely, a study conducted at the National Institute of Public Health in Bilthoven, The Netherlands, indicated that there was no effect on the reproduction of rats given a diet of irradiated mushrooms. Similarly, there were no significant changes in organ weights or histopathology.[38]

Unlike their colleagues at Academy of Sciences and Minsredmash institutes who tended to ignore many safety issues, a number of food scientists reached the conclusion that laboratory animal studies indicated that irradiation posed health hazards serious enough to warrant delay in approval of many products. In the mid-1960s, Kamaldinova, in the laboratory of food safety and standards of the Institute of Nutrition, conducted experiments intended to clarify which products were safe and what doses of radiation were permissible. She noted that high doses (three to twenty megarads) were clearly unacceptable for both vegetable and animal products, causing reproductive and metabolic disorders and nonspecific growths. Using a dose of 0.8 megarads on beef, she determined that, in both the control and experimental groups of laboratory animals, weights remained relatively the same, as did blood cell morphology. However, there were significant differences in organ function (for example, the liver and metabolism of lipids) as well as earlier noted vitamin deficiencies, which were significant enough to recommend against human consumption.[39]

Were irradiated food products mutagenic and cytotoxic? Many food scientists remained convinced of their safety and efficacy. An experiment conducted jointly by specialists at the Erisman Institute and the Central Institute of Advanced Medical Training in 1972 answered "No." They fed thirty-two mice a diet containing eighty percent irradiated products, then looked for cytogenic action by using a test for recording chromosomal aberrations of the bone marrow. The tests showed the absence of any marked untoward effect of the experimental ration: Chromosome aberrations were roughly the same in controls (0.75 percent) and test animals (1.0 percent).[40] Shillinger and his colleagues, who had a kind of seniority in resolving the matter owing to their fifteen years of research, were more direct. They had grown tired of delay, of overreaction, and of what they believed was excessive caution. Like their colleagues in the United States, they observed that the only thing holding back widespread use of ionizing radiation in the food industry was the absence of a complete guarantee of the safety of the products, and such a guarantee was impossible. But it was clear that they were safe enough. They pointed to the fact that in many countries (the United States, the Netherlands, and Israel) government approval had already been given for their use.

In the early 1970s, however, evidence mounted throughout the world that several products with carbohydrates and raw plant products, when irradiated, possessed mutagenic characteristics. As a result, the Joint Committee of Experts of the IAEA recommended further study of these products and verification of the safety of already approved products. One problem was that irradiation occasionally created unusual compounds or higher than usual concentrations of metabolites. Some of the toxic or mutagenic agents caused by irradiation of carbohydrates included formaldehyde, formic acid, and hydrogen peroxide. In addition, twenty-four hours after irradiation, some mutagenic and toxic compounds of a quinone nature appeared in potatoes. Another mutagenicity study focused on extracts taken from raw and cooked potato, with the tubers being stored for various periods of time after their gamma irradiation at a dose of ten kilorads. Extracts obtained from the potato directly after its irradiation (within twenty-four hours) were found to exert a mutagenic effect on the sexual cells of male mice. But either cooking or storage of irradiated tubers for forty and ninety days abolished the mutagenic activity of the extracts. Hence, safety of irradiated food products depended on a wide range of factors: dose, power of irradiation, temperature, concentration of oxygen, humidity, packing material, pH, and storage time. There were many variables, and the data were contradictory.[41]

Scientific uncertainty, growing awareness of the high cost of irradiation, inadequate facilities, and filthy conditions stopped the Soviet program dead in its tracks by the end of the 1970s. Leonid Ilich Brezhnev, secretary of the Communist Party, set out to rectify the situation. The so-called Brezhnev food program, with huge investments in agriculture and the creation of a Ministry of Agricultural Industry, was intended to provide inexpensive wholesome food. But the increased investment in agriculture had a limited impact, given the lack of incentive for collective and state farmers to work hard. There were no products to irradiate. The stores in the countryside had empty shelves. The rural diet was high in sugar and fat, and low in fresh fruits and vegetables, which were distributed largely among urban residents. Outmigration from the countryside to the cities accelerated. The small private plots that the government tolerated remained the most productive sector of agriculture. Not even the mighty atom could change this situation. Economic and political reform were required.

Ionizing radiation has found limited application wherever it has been adopted. Health authorities in over thirty countries explored the new technology, experiencing a number of successes. Food scientists have determined at what level to irradiate a series of products while preserving the foods' nutritive value and ensuring their wholesomeness. But while promoted as a panacea in the 1940s and 1950s to increase the shelf life of fruits and vegetables, grains, meat, chicken and fish, the process failed to win broad application. The major reason appears to be economic, for pilot plants turned out to be far more costly than initially estimated. To ensure competitiveness with traditional means of preserving foods, the new facilities had to include huge shielded buildings fed by complex conveyor systems, capable of handling tons and tons of food products hourly. These facilities had high start-up capital costs; and despite detailed cost-benefit analyses that promised otherwise, the operating costs still exceeded other methods, even when spoilage and rotting were taken into consideration. Often processors had to add nutrients destroyed during irradiation. The private sector in market systems proved unwilling to follow through on pilot programs when the governments cut funding. In terms of safety, there is scientific uncertainty. Several food scientists have publicly spoken about the potential problem of producing new strains of bacteria more resistant to sterilizing processes because of radiation-induced mutations.

In such countries as the USSR, where the government underwrote all expenses as the only player, the costs remained noncompetitive with canning, salting, heating, and freezing. Even though agriculture remained the sore spot of the economy for the entire Soviet period, radioactive isotopes on their own were incapable of rectifying the situation. Agriculture lacked dedicated farmers with the incentive to toil hard in the field and the technology to do their job well. Radical reform of the entire organization of the food industry, from field to shelf, was the only solution. The Soviet citizen was relegated to "four basic food groups" of a new sort: sugar, salt, fat, and alcohol. The image of the mighty atom joining us at the dinner table was no more a reasonable hope than that of other images promoted during the glory days of atomic energy: the atom and nuclear engines, the atom as excavator, and the atom and unlimited electric energy.

The final straw—or irradiated chicken, for that matter—was consumer reluctance to purchase these products. Nuclear fear played a role in this rejection. Some persons equated irradiated food products with radioactive food. They knew of the health dangers of exposure to radiation. In the Soviet Union, when the Ministry of Health approved irradiated foodstuffs for public consumption, it did not require any kind of labeling. Hence, scientists did not have to worry about consumer awareness and approval. The Soviet consumer of the 1950s through the 1980s therefore had little choice in the matter. Because economic and scientific factors limited the spread of the technology, it is doubtful that many persons suffered any long-term health consequences from eating irradiated foods. But we will never know, for records are poor and it is nearly impossible to establish causality. What is left are wonderful acronyms and brute-force technologies.

In September 1986, in the aftermath of the Chernobyl disaster, the Central Committee of the Communist Party of the Soviet Union secretly ordered the Ministry of the Agricultural Industry to facilitate the sale of sausage produced with meat tainted ever so slightly with radioactivity in all regions of the Soviet Union, excluding, of course, the Moscow region where they sat.[42] The meat was frozen and held in storage for several months before being used, so that its radioactivity had fallen below acceptable norms. In Briansk region, they made sausages tainted with cesium. Then they restocked the Briansk Meat Factory with another fifty tons of slightly radioactive meat. The first batch used nine tons of lamb, which had been sent to the factory by the order of regional agricultural industrial powers-that-be. Those powers claimed the authority to use tainted meat, asserting that "there is absolutely nothing dangerous in this." The new batch was five to ten times more radioactive than established norms, but the factory lacked the authority to ship it back and had to hold it in cold storage. So they mixed sausage in portions of four or five to one, carefully cleaning it, washing as much as they could down the drain, paying workers extra for their low-level exposure. The directors of the meat factories merely followed orders.[43] Most likely, Chernobyl sausage was safe for humans to eat. But this is not what scientists had in mind when they began to advocate radiation sterilization and pasteurization of food products in the postwar years. In the aftermath of Chernobyl and the painful transition to a market economy and consumer awareness, it is certain that Russians and Ukrainians today would prefer their potatoes with eyes and their sausages with extra salt.

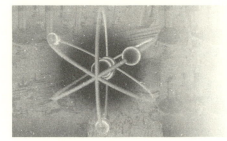

6

A Stellar Promise: The Display Value of Fusion Power

I had never stopped thinking about nuclear power and how to ensure its safety . . .
The solution I would favor would be to build reactors underground.
—Andrei Sakharov, *Memoirs*

Soviet physicists were pioneers in fusion. In 1950, Andrei Sakharov and Igor Tamm proposed a model for magnetic confinement of a plasma under high temperature. Tamm and Sakharov were at Arzamas, the center of Soviet bomb design efforts from that year onward. They received a letter through Beria's secretariat from Oleg Lavrentev, a young sailor in the Pacific fleet, who somehow conceived of the potential of fusion for energy production. Lavrentev proposed electrostatic confinement of plasma. But there was no way to keep the very hot plasma needed for a fusion reaction away from electrostatic grids around the reactor volume. The advantage of magnetic confinement was that the force lines of a magnetic field can be imposed from the outside of a reactor vessel, keeping the plasma from touching the interior walls. In 1950, when Tamm returned to Moscow from Arzamas, he quickly grasped the importance of magnetic confinement and set forth a proposal for what they called the magnetic thermonuclear reactor, or MTR. Over the next four decades, theoreticians and experimentalists in Moscow, Leningrad, Akademgorodok, and Kharkiv made a series of stunning advances, notably with the tokamak reactor, that left little doubt that sometime in the twenty-first century fusion power will become a reality. Lev Artsimovich and Mikhail Leontovich stood at the forefront of these efforts through the 1970s. Evgenii Velikhov, Boris Kadomtsev, and others ably replaced them when the effort turned toward building industrial prototypes in the 1980s.

Fusion was important to atomic-powered communism on several counts. First, developments in fusion were inextricably linked to those for the hydrogen bomb. Peaceful applications grew out of military ones, and they were always subordinate to those intended to produce more powerful bombs or manufacture more weapons-grade fuel. Second, as pioneers in fusion, Soviet scientists had shown that they were ahead of the West in a major area of modern science. For many of them, especially in the post-Stalin era as they reentered the international arena, it was crucial to be accepted as equals by their western counterparts, especially those in England and the United States. Big science and technology had "display value," that is, ideological and social significance that in some ways was just as important as any technical accomplishment, for fusion research demonstrated that the Soviet social system produced scientists and engineers at the cutting edge of knowledge and that this knowledge served the ends of world peace, not war. Third, fusion (controlled thermonuclear synthesis) promised to generate virtually unlimited quantities of energy. If all had worked as planned, by the year 2020 fusion reactors would have dotted the Soviet landscape, at first augmenting and then replacing thermal (slow neutron) and breeder (fast neutron) fission reactors. Unfortunately, physicists encountered many more difficulties in realizing the promise of a fusion reactor than they initially anticipated, perhaps because their first successes in fission had come so quickly. And fusion was also far more technologically challenging and costly than expected, leading governments around the world to cut back on funding in the mid-1980s, to the great dismay of the scientists. For the physicists in the Kurchatov Institute, this loss of funding was a blow, for they were not used to having any program cut.

Like the development programs for thermal fission reactors, programs at the Institute of Atomic Energy received priority in funds, resources, and manpower. The institute focused on the tokamak model, perhaps the most promising of various approaches. But this meant that physicists in other institutes who wished to conduct research had to focus on various alternatives or conduct research that fed into Kurchatov Institute programs. Evgenii Velikhov is a plasma physicist who replaced Anatolii Aleksandrov as director of the Kurchatov Institute. He was a member of the Central Committee of the Communist Party and to this day serves as one of eleven vice presidents of the Academy of Sciences. Velikhov's advent made the national commitment to tokamaks all the stronger. His closeness to Mikhail Gorbachev secured national support for an international fusion reactor when the commitment of the Soviet government to fusion seemed to waver. Gorbachev saw international cooperation in fusion as a way to involve President Ronald Reagan in discussions on arms control through confidence-building measures such as joint research in science and technology.

But fusion was important in Soviet foreign policy from the very beginning. The reentry of the Soviet Union into the international arena after the death of Stalin under the banner of peaceful coexistence received a tremendous boost from fusion. Khrushchev and Kurchatov seized on fusion as a diplomatic tool, employing Soviet advances to meet the foreign policy ends of various arms control agreements and cooperation in science and technology to share the costs and challenges of research. And they would do so as equals of the West, not as technologically backwards, poorly dressed second cousins.

Fusion specialists had to navigate a series of minefields to achieve results. One was political interference, as manifested in Beria's decision to remove Jewish scientists from projects, meddling of ideologists in philosophical matters, and Sakharov's exile to Gorky (which triggered a boycott of collaborative efforts by Western scientists). A second was the dominance of the Kurchatov Institute, which stultified scientific competition among centers of physics excellence. But at the start, because of the force of the personalities of Lev Artsimovich, an experimentalist, and Mikhail Leontovich, a theoretician, the commitment of Kurchatov to fusion diplomacy, and the identification of Khrushchev with achievements in big science and technology, the Kurchatov Institute made significant strides in fusion research.

FUSION'S AMBASSADORS

Lev Andreevich Artsimovich (1909–1973) was a product of the Ioffe school.[1] His family belonged to Polish nobility. As punishment for participating in a Polish uprising against the Tsar in 1863–1864, his grandfather, a professor of statistics and economic geography, was exiled to Siberia, married there, and moved to Smolensk after being freed. His father was born in Smolensk and graduated from Lviv University. Artsimovich's mother attended finishing school in Switzerland. She filled her home with piano music. There was a huge library, and paintings hung everywhere. In this environment, Artsimovich learned to read early and to love art, music, and culture. The family moved to southern Russia in connection with his father's involvement in the first Bolshevik census; during the civil war they were evacuated to Gomel, where Artsimovich educated himself by working his way through the *Brokhaus-Efron* encyclopedia. In 1923, the family moved to Minsk, where Artsimovich entered the eighth grade of the Cherviakov Railroad School; and as a fifteen-year-old, he entered the physics-mathematics department of Belarus University. He read all the modern physics he could get his hands on, including Einstein and Lorentz. Although he rarely attended lectures, he passed exams easily and graduated from the university in 1928. In the meantime, his family had moved into a beautiful small house on Arbat Street in Moscow, a street where many of the intellectuals lived.

Artsimovich gravitated to the center of physics, entering the Leningrad Physical Technical Institute as a staff scientist. He worked in the laboratory of Artem Isaakovich Alikhanov, who became his closest and life-long friend; in later life, Alikhanov frequented Artsimovich's apartment to tell stories about his friends the satirist Mikhail Zoshchenko, the poet Anna Akhmatova, and the composer Dmitrii Shostakovich. Artsimovich relied on Alikhanov for his daily routine, settling into the latter's apartment on Vasilevskii Island, near the center of the city but quite a distance from the institute. They took turns sleeping in the bed—but the one on the floor got the blanket. Artsimovich didn't pay much attention to his appearance; in fact, Alikhanov often washed his clothes for him. The authorities held a small-scale "purge" in the institute in 1930, but Artsimovich passed without any damage, perhaps gaining security in an unkempt appearance. The young physicists listened to Fock's lectures on theoretical physics and were surprised when Ioffe himself occasionally showed up. But this inspired them. With Alikhanov, Artsimovich conducted his first independent research on the full internal reflection in the X-ray region of the spectrum and published the results in *Zeitschrift für Physik*.

Like many other young scientists, the *annus mirabilus* turned Artsimovich's attention to nuclear physics. In the mid-1930s, he studied the properties of slow neutrons. In 1936, with the Alikhanov brothers, he proved experimentally the correctness of the law of conservation of energy and impulse during annihilation of positrons. Artsimovich was mostly interested in the processes of the interaction of fast electrons with matter, an area in which he showed his experimental skill and the rigor of his results. But work in this area became more difficult after Artsimovich was denied access to high-voltage generators at other institutes, apparently because their own scientists used all available research time on them. He defended his master's thesis ("Absorption of Slow Neutrons") in 1937 and his doctoral dissertation ("Brehmsstrahlung of Fast Electrons") in 1939. Despite little involvement in social and political organizations at the institute beyond membership of the editorial collective of the bulletin board newspaper, Artsimovich received a written endorsement from the institute's Party cell for his scientific degrees.

During the war in evacuation with the institute in Kazan, Artsimovich conducted research on electronic optics. His small "laboratory" was set off from others in the same small room by a wall of laboratory file cabinets and workbenches. Next door was a children's dental clinic. How they got work done with children crying from early morning until nine at night is anyone's guess. In 1945, Pomeranchuk and Artsimovich succeeded in measuring Brehmsstrahlung of electrons in a betatron (that is, the braking character of electromagnetic radiation that arises during the motion of electrons in a magnetic field). Artsimovich was determined to accomplish as much as possible during the war so that "we won't be ashamed of what we have accomplished after the victory."

In 1945, Kurchatov picked Artsimovich, whom he had known for fifteen years, to join the bomb project in laboratory 2 and put him in charge of developing the electromagnetic method of isotope separation. But this method proved more costly and less efficient than radiochemical and gaseous diffusion methods. The Soviet Union couldn't produce the equivalent of America's Oak Ridge or the electricity needed for it, so Beria removed Artsimovich as deputy director of the bomb project, replacing him with Igor Golovin. From 1950 until the end of his life, one problem consumed Artsimovich: controlled thermonuclear reactions using magnetic devices to isolate hot plasmas. This was a logical field of study for him, considering his long-term experiments with ions, electrons, and gas discharge. Whereas Artsimovich's previous war tasks involved the creation of specific equipment, the fusion program demanded the creation of an entire new field of science: high-temperature plasma physics.

Sakharov and Tamm had just set forth the notion of a controlled thermonuclear reaction in a plasma heated to 100 million degrees in a powerful, yet practically realizable magnetic field.[2] Sakharov proposed the conception of the reactor that led to the tokamak design—tokamak referring to the Russian words for "toroid (that is, doughnut shaped) current and confinement." Kurchatov realized the potential of fusion for peaceful applications and energetically began to propagandize it within the government.[3] He created a commission that included Artsimovich and Leontovich. The commission's first responsibility was to listen to presentations by Tamm and Sakharov. These two scientists enthusiastically predicted that a fusion reactor would be operating within ten to fifteen years. Kurchatov sent the commission's report to the Council of Ministers, which passed a resolution giving the Kurchatov Institute responsibility for developing a fusion reactor, with Artsimovich as executive director of the project, Mikhail Leontovich in charge of theory, and Tamm and Sakharov as standing consultants. On May 5, 1951, Stalin signed an order officially establishing the fusion "program MTR," a peaceful but nonetheless top secret program because scientists believed the reactor would be a good source for tritium, plutonium, and uranium-233. Sakharov said that the theoretical research rapidly surpassed the level of his understanding, but he remained in close contact with Artsimovich and Leontovich's group at the institute for some time.[4]

By the middle of 1951, institute scientists had already built on Tamm and Sakharov's theory with their first grudging steps toward experimental devices. At one meeting, Artsimovich presented results of the early stages of research on a magnetic toroidal device. They had begun to run current through plasmas to test the impedance. These experiments gave them a better understanding of the resistance of the plasma and the transmission of energy from the electrons to the ions. The theory of the MTR was still in such an early stage that any conclusions were only rough approximations. Any attempt to measure processes, temperatures, and vacuum in the vessel (a field that came to be known as diagnostics) fell short, because measurement affected the behavior of the plasma. This difficulty prevented better comprehension of the laws of heat exchange, particle diffusion, and plasma dynamics in the reactor "container."[5] At another seminar, Vitaly Ginzburg, who also had been central to the conceptualization of the hydrogen bomb and who worked with Tamm and Sakharov at the Physics Institute of the Academy of Sciences, called for expanding research on the magnetic thermonuclear reactor to clarify processes of heat transfer and conductivity, Brehmsstrahlung, and photoionization and photodissociation.[6]

A plasma is matter at a temperature of thousands of degrees. At this temperature, the kinetic energy of the atoms is so great that they cannot be confined at a distance small enough to form a liquid or a solid. During collisions of atoms within the plasma, some electrons are pulled off and the atoms that have lost one or more electrons become positive ions. Hence, a plasma is a gaseous mix of electrons, ions, and atoms. It is almost neutral, but electrical forces that act between the charged particles of the plasma give it elasticity. Thermonuclear synthesis occurs when two lighter particles—say ions or atoms of deuterium—fuse into heavier particles—for example, lithium. The fusion process releases tremendous energy. A fusion reactor attempts to hold those particles away from the walls of the reactor with electromagnetic energy. The temperature sufficient for overcoming the electrical repulsion of opposite charges is around 100 million degrees.[7]

If you put a plasma in a magnetic field, then the charged particles (electrons and ions) move freely along the force lines of the magnetic field. Physicists control the motion of the particles by several means: a system of magnetic pinches; magnetic mirrors; and such toroids as tokamaks and stellarators. Stellarators differ from tokamaks by the fact that within a stellarator a plasma may be confined by a magnetic field of a spiral configuration without exciting in the plasma an electrical current, which is the source of a whole series of instabilities.

The tokamak has the advantage of a simpler construction, within which it is easier to create a "thick" plasma of larger diameter that interacts with the walls of the vessel to a lesser degree. In addition, in a tokamak, the electric current simultaneously supplements the powerful toroidal magnetic field to confine the plasma and heats it, thereby eliminating the need for additional sources of heating (injectors of charged particles from high-energy, high-frequency generators). For these reasons, scientists at the Kurchatov Institute decided to focus on tokamaks. They developed ohmic heating (electric current passed through a resistant medium), cyclotron heating, and laser heating of the plasma. The first tokamak was built in 1955 at the initiative of Igor Golovin and N. A. Iavlinskii.

GENEVA, ATOMS FOR PEACE, AND FUSION ENVY

If Artsimovich was responsible for experimental aspects of fusion, Kurchatov was its publicist. In March 1954, Kurchatov forwarded an article written by a handful of his closest associates to Georgii Malenkov, then first pretender to Soviet leadership, in which they argued that the use of hydrogen bombs in war would mean the end of world civilization. They asked the government to seek agreements to ban atmospheric testing because of the dangers of radioactive fallout. Kurchatov urged the publication of this article in the open press and the declassification of fusion research as a way to promote international understanding and lessen cold war tensions.[8]

Kurchatov asked to be relieved of responsibility for bomb design after the November 1955 test of a massive, fifty-megaton, air-dropped hydrogen bomb. This test indicated that strategic weapons could be mass produced and delivered thousands of miles by jet.[9] Kurchatov realized that the arms race was a dead end for the United States and the USSR, and that nuclear war was simply mad. From this point on, essentially all bomb design tasks fell to Arzamas-16 and Cheliabinsk-70 scientists, and Kurchatov focused on peaceful technologies and on the reestablishment of international scientific contacts. For the rest of his life, in public presentations and in private discussions, among Party loyalists or foreign visitors, Kurchatov emphatically spoke, not about the inevitability of war, but about peaceful coexistence between the capitalist and socialist systems. He urged his fellow scientists to use various nuclear applications to surpass capitalist countries in industrial production. He referred to great achievements of peaceful nuclear programs in agriculture, medicine, and industry and to the construction of experimental reactors in Kazakhstan, Uzbekistan, and Georgia as examples of what might be achieved. But above all the other technologies, Kurchatov promoted fusion as a panacea for the problems of human civilization.[10]

In his last years, Kurchatov, weakened by worsening health and a series of small strokes, was unable to provide leadership in the areas of arms control. Andrei Sakharov stepped into the breach as one of the leading spokespersons of this effort. Sakharov was both a product of the Stalin era and the Khrushchev thaw. As a patriotic physicist, he willingly devoted his talents to the development of the hydrogen bomb. Yet, in response to the twentieth Party congress and Khrushchev's attack on the cult of personality, he began to question his role in the military industrial complex. He recognized the cynical attitude of the authorities toward scientists. To them, scientists were mere tools, or "productive forces." Sakharov decided to enter the public sphere. He published an article in *Atomnaia energiia* that called for a comprehensive test ban and circulated other arms control papers in the Kremlin. He approached Khrushchev directly about a unilateral test ban. But when he sought modest political reforms, he was told to mind his own business.[11]

Like their counterparts in the United States, the most savvy nuclear physicists recognized that they could hardly remain divorced from the international scientific arena from either a political or a scientific point of view. Their political contributions consisted of protracted debates over arms control, confidence building measures, and verification. Yet the authorities controlled scientists' political activities. They prohibited the creation of organizations like those springing up in America: the Federation of American Scientists, which had centers in Chicago, Boston, and Berkeley and pushed the consideration of the moral aspects of nuclear weaponry, or Pugwash organizations, named after the site of their initial meeting place at the estate of philanthropist Cyrus Eaton in Pugwash, Nova Scotia. But even though Soviet physicists were limited to closely monitored behavior, many of them sincerely desired frank and open discussions with the West. Hence, they welcomed "Atoms for Peace" programs.

President Dwight Eisenhower jump-started "Atoms for Peace" programs when he addressed the delegates of the United Nations General Assembly on December 8, 1953. He wished to redress the failure of the world's governments to establish international control over atomic energy. Eisenhower proposed the establishment of an international agency to make expertise, information, and fissionable material available under strict guidelines to countries wishing to engage in peaceful applications—isotopes, fertilizers, reactors. This international research effort was intended to build trust among the nuclear powers. Eisenhower embellished his proposal with the call for an international conference on the peaceful atom to be held in Geneva, perhaps in 1955. Because the United States and the Soviet Union had engaged nearly fruitlessly in arms control negotiations since the dawn of the nuclear age, no one was surprised that the Russians initially rejected Eisenhower's proposals as empty propaganda. But within sixteen months of Stalin's death, the new leadership showed a willingness to negotiate with the Americans on arms questions and to participate with the West in some kind of international atomic energy agency, kicked off symbolically with a conference in Geneva. Now, nations of the world faced the difficult task of rapidly declassifying thousands of documents concerning dozens of peaceful applications that had previously been withheld from public scrutiny.[12]

Soviet leaders and scientists recognized immediately that they could derive significant political capital from atoms for peace. For the leaders, the peaceful atom showed that a nation whose citizens had been illiterate and agrarian less than forty years earlier, had become a leading scientific and industrial power. The achievements of science and technology, with nuclear energy at the summit, were symbols of the legitimacy of the regime both to Soviet citizens and to citizens of the world.[13] The peaceful atom also allowed the USSR to score points with the conquered countries of Eastern Europe, Hungary, Poland, Czechoslovakia, Romania, and Bulgaria, each of whom had a nuclear program based on Soviet isotopes, technology, and training programs and, in part, its largesse. The Joint Institute for Nuclear Research in Dubna, north of Moscow, gave the "fraternal" countries access to a seventy-gigaelectronvolt accelerator.[14]

For scientists, the peaceful atom gained them respect from disbelieving counterparts in the West, who had hesitated to treat these "backward" researchers as equals. At every forum Soviet physicists appeared. They stunned audiences with revelations of significant achievements in fusion and fission reactors, and of applications of isotopes in industry, medicine, and agriculture. Soviet physicists, and the scientific establishment in general, prepared feverishly for the Geneva conference, intending to score a propaganda coup with these achievements. At the beginning of July 1955, the Soviet Academy of Sciences brought together scientists from all ends of the empire and all disciplines in a trial run for Geneva. Leading physicists rehearsed a series of papers on reactor physics, focusing mainly on uranium-graphite systems, but also on pressurized-water/enriched-uranium and heavy water reactors. They also touted their achievements with particle accelerators: for example, Vladimir Veksler and his associates at the Lebedev Physics Institute and the Joint Institute at Dubna were well on the way to building a synchrotron.[15] Soviet scientists were ready to use Geneva to celebrate internationalism in nuclear physics.

The spirit of internationalism permeated the Palace of Nations in Geneva, Switzerland during the two conferences on the peaceful atom in the 1950s. At the first, from August 8 through August 20, 1955, there were 1,400 delegates from 73 countries and perhaps as many observers, who delivered 1,067 scientific papers at 8 plenary and 52 scientific sessions. The Soviet Union sent one of the largest delegations other than the British or Americans—seventy-eight delegates including physicists, engineers, graduate students, government officials, and the usual KGB staffers. They delivered 102 papers (26 by Kurchatov Institute physicists). Soviet scientists were overjoyed at seeing old friends, many of whom they had not seen since before World War II: Niels Bohr, Hans Bethe, Ernest Lawrence, Otto Hahn, Glenn Seaborg, John Cockcroft, Georg Hevesy, and others. They found the exchange of opinions fruitful and were surprised but gratified to find that the solutions to problems connected with the utilization of atomic energy in England and the United States were similar to those discovered in the USSR.[16] For the Soviet delegation, the conference was mainly an opportunity to showcase achievements in fission and high-energy physics.[17]

On August 24, at the invitation of the British government, many of the Soviet delegates to Geneva, including Kurchatov and surprise guest Nikita Khrushchev, continued on to Harwell, England, the research center of the British nuclear effort. Nobel laureate John Cockcroft, director of the center, welcomed them. In a talk reminiscent of his twentieth Party congress speech, Kurchatov spoke at length about the development of atomic energetics in the USSR and the economic and geographic reasons behind its development in the European USSR.[18] Kurchatov nearly single-handedly tore the cover off "top secret" reports when he related the work of the Artsimovich group—even though he did not provide extensive classified details. Kurchatov said he hoped that British and American physicists would join the Artsimovich group in tackling the fusion problem.[19]

The Harwell meeting, following on the heels of the first Geneva conference, led to the opening of the Soviet scientific community to visits from foreign scientists. A delegation from the Swedish Academy of Sciences arrived in Moscow in April 1956, and for most, it was their first visit to Moscow, and to its institutes and scientists. One day they were presented with the opportunity to visit the "Moscow Institute of Physics" (that is, the Kurchatov Institute) but at first they refused because the scheduled sightseeing activities seemed more interesting. "Don't you want the opportunity to meet Artsimovich, Budker, Golovin, and Leontovich?" They didn't know who these people were, but were thrilled at the chance, even though the laboratories they saw were not on the level of those in the West. [20]

The second Geneva conference on the peaceful uses of nuclear energy was also a victory for Soviet physicists. Held in the first two weeks of September 1958, it drew 5,000 persons, including 2,000 delegates from 66 countries.[21] The Soviet delegation consisted of more than eighty persons, including Anatolii Aleksandrov, Igor Golovin, Mikhail Leontovich, Georgii Flerov, Roald Sagdeev, Boris Kadomtsev, Igor Tamm, Vladimir Veksler, and Abram Alikhanov. This was a "who's who" of Soviet physics, the likes of which was never again seen abroad. Of the 2,500 papers, the Soviet delegates presented 229 (forty-six of those by Kurchatov Institute physicists, with seventeen on fusion, including a series of papers on the stabilization and dynamics of plasmas in magnetic fields). There were thirty-four papers on energetics and reactors, including Aleksandrov's speech on the *Lenin* icebreaker, launched in September 1959. But there were some notable absences: Sinelnikov, Artsimovich, and Gersh Budker, the first because of his British wife, the second because he was the head of Soviet fusion research, and the third because his bold personality and sense of humor inspired mistrust.

The head of the delegation and chairman of the State Committee for the Utilization of Atomic Energy, Vasilii Semenovich Emelianov, created quite a stir when he referred to the achievements of Soviet scientists in the three years since the last conference, especially in the construction of large and experimental reactors at Novovoronezh, Beloiarsk, and Ulianovsk. Furthermore, two experimental breeder reactors had been brought on line. And there was also the striking news of the *Lenin* icebreaker. But it was the presentation of declassified research on fusion that had the greatest impact. Kurchatov had promised at Harwell that Soviet research would be made available. Now, on behalf of the Soviet delegation, Emelianov presented the congress with a four-volume collection of 100 articles on theoretical and experimental aspects of fusion. Many of the papers had been written in the early 1950s but were only now published. Their authors included Sagdeev, Spartak Belieav, Tamm, Budker, Kadomtsev, Sakharov, Leontovich, and Artsimovich, all of the leading lights of Soviet fusion. The secret of Soviet success was out of the bag.[22]

Geneva and Harwell led to more regular scientific exchanges. When Khrushchev subsequently visited the United States, he changed forever American impressions about the USSR. He instructed members of his delegation to establish long-term contacts on the basis of "peaceful coexistence." In private meetings with Atomic Energy Commission chairman John McCone, Emelianov (McCone's Soviet counterpart, who had accompanied Khrushchev) proposed that American specialists visit Soviet facilities. Subsequently, American and Soviet officials agreed to visits and discussions in eleven areas of the physical and biological sciences, including high-energy physics, fusion, and power reactor development. Visits to Obninsk, the *Lenin* icebreaker, the Institute of Atomic Energy, the *U.S.S. Savannah* in Camden, New Jersey, the Shippingport (Pennsylvania) reactor, the *Enrico Fermi* fast reactor in Detroit, the nuclear facilities at Oak Ridge, Berkeley, and other sites followed.[23]

THE ACCELERATION OF THE KURCHATOV INSTITUTE FUSION PROGRAM

International contact gave great impetus to the Soviet fusion program by leading to head-to-head competition between the British "Zeta" apparatus and the "Alfa" copy in Leningrad. The British claimed to have made a breakthrough on the Zeta in 1958 by producing a thermonuclear reaction. Artsimovich called the results "dog shit," which, if impolite, turned out to be the case. Kurchatov gave the British their due for the Zeta because of its important early results in temperature and time of containment, even if they were less than initially claimed, for he was convinced that atoms for peace diplomacy was just as crucial as the science itself.

But the science *was* crucial. Before learning that the Zeta results were off, "it became clear to us," Kurchatov said, "that it is necessary to strengthen our work on all fronts." There was only one division of the institute working on the subject. So Kurchatov decided to make fusion a general problem of the institute. They organized the "T" seminar in which 270 physicists from a series of departments took part. Another two dozen persons attended from outside the institute. A second step, Kurchatov announced, was to free Golovin from his administrative responsibilities to work solely on fusion. Five or six other sectors joined the effort. In two months, they succeeded in doubling the number of engineers and scientists attacking fusion.

When it seemed in 1957, as Kurchatov informed his audience at an institute Party cell meeting, that Soviet physicists might lose the race with American and British physicists in fusion, the Politburo immediately agreed to commit resources to expand the institute's program. By 1957, three facilities had been built: T-2 and OGRA in Moscow and Alfa in Leningrad. And Western visitors to the facilities, including Gottlieb and Freeman of the Princeton stellarator and Cockcroft and oth-

At the tokamak T-3 (from left to right): Lev Artsimovich, Igor Tamm, Niels Bohr, and Anatolii Aleksandrov. *(Courtesy of Raissa Kuznetsova and the Kurchatov Institute)*

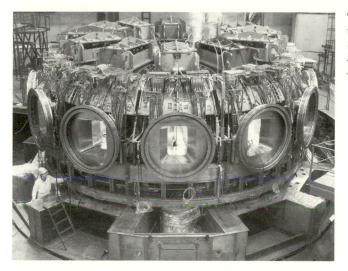

The tokamak T-15, under construction. *(Courtesy of Raissa Kuznetsova and the Kurchatov Institute)*

ers from Harwell, were impressed. Kurchatov met with Khrushchev on January 2, 1958. He explained that "the institute worked as never before," but it needed more money to compete with the Americans and the British. Khrushchev enthusiastically approved the expansion of fusion research, on the next day bringing up the matter in the Politburo, and again securing additional funding on the spot.[24]

But most of the early Soviet fundamental and experimental research was completed in Artsimovich's department of plasma physics: discovery and research on plasma focusing, experimental proof of various plasma instabilities and the stabilizing action of magnetic traps with mirrors (Ioffe's research), and the development of tokamaks, which produced relatively stable high-temperature plasmas. Artsimovich's *Controlled Thermonuclear Reactions* had two editions and was published in several foreign languages.[25] His students included Kadomtsev and Velikhov. In 1958, for a series of experiments on phenomena that occur in powerful discharges, Artsimovich, A. M. Andrianov, S. I. Braginskii, O. A. Bazilevskaia, Leontovich, Iavlinskii, and Golovin received a Lenin prize. But whether there could be a sustained, confined fusion reaction remained unknown. Artsimovich joked that plasma physics was not science, because the subject of natural science was objects created by nature and the subject of plasma physics was objects created by the experimentalist.

In a paper at the second Geneva conference on peaceful uses of atomic energy, which a colleague read for him, Artsimovich summarized the theoretical and experimental achievements since the early 1950s, including the work of Moscow and Kharkiv physicists. He celebrated the declassification of fusion work and the end of the isolation of physicists of different countries from one another. The scientific foundation had been created in the USSR, in the United States, and in England, Artsimovich said, "on which the solution of the problem of controlled thermonuclear synthesis will be based." But he warned his audience not to underestimate the difficulties that remained and prevented physicists from producing a stable plasma. Avoiding a pessimistic tone, he expressed the firm belief that international cooperation would speed the achievement of valuable results.[26]

There were three directions of research in Artsimovich's department of plasma physics, all of them to see how to heat a sufficiently dense plasma and contain it in a heated state before significant instabilities ruined things: (1) pinches (powerful impulse discharges); (2) tokamaks under Iavlinskii, who replaced Artsimovich after the latter's death; and (3) mirror traps, so-called open systems, first proposed by Budker and developed in the Kurchatov Institute under Ioffe. Ioffe presented the results of some of his early work at the second IAEA conference of fusion in Salzburg, Austria in 1961, the first international meeting at which Artsimovich took part. Ioffe's results gave powerful impetus to further research on magnetic confinement, for they not only challenged American interpretations but also developed a way to correct instabilities.[27] In Salzburg, foreigners became familiar with Artsimovich's erudition, oratorical talent, broad knowledge, and subtle wit when he criticized the optimism of the American physicists over early successes. Artsimovich was convinced that many effects in question were connected with apparatuses, not with laws of physics. In his summary at the conference, Artsimovich acknowledged that they had made few steps toward high-temperature plasmas, but there was no doubt in his mind that the problem of fusion would be solved. Indeed, from 1962 to 1972, the temperatures of plasmas rose from several hundred thousand degrees to ten million for ions and thirty million for electrons.

From this point on, Artsimovich served as international ambassador of fusion, visiting the United States and Europe to promote cooperation. He spoke about improvement of plasma parameters on various tokamaks and other signs of success, not to brag but to stress the need to cooperate. Artsimovich loved to travel; he enjoyed even more making a big splash with his lectures at conferences and symposiums, including Pugwash meetings. In 1963, Artsimovich visited the United States at the invitation of Glenn Seaborg and the Atomic Energy Commission. The delegation, which included A. M. Petrosiants and other dignitaries, flew from New York (after a site visit in Brookhaven) to Oak Ridge in a jet provided by the vice president. Suddenly, the captain announced that one engine had shut down and

Theoretician Mikhail Aleksandrovich Leontovich, at a seminar at the Kurchatov Institute in 1975. *(Courtesy of Raissa Kuznetsova and the Kurchatov Institute)*

the other had begun to smoke, so they were going to make an emergency landing at a military base near Washington. The American and Soviet physicists became quite unsettled until Petrosiants asked what one ought to drink in such a situation and Artsimovich replied without blinking, "Good cognac."

The true danger of international contacts was not air travel, nor the secrets that xenophobes, generals, and spies obsessed about. According to Artsimovich, the danger was that scientists would pay too much attention to foreign programs and mistakenly go down the wrong path, the one chosen by others, rather than finding their own way. Artsimovich was convinced that significant instabilities would disappear, contrary to classical theory, with improvement in thermal confinement of the plasma. But mastering the instabilities would require more advanced experimental devices. So, in his last years, already gravely ill but refusing to quit smoking, he pushed the T-10 tokamak to completion.

From the early 1960s, the tokamak stood at the center of research, nowhere more than at the Kurchatov Institute. At the second international conference on thermonuclear synthesis and plasma physics at Culham, England in 1965, Artsimovich presented results that suggested great progress on tokamaks since Salzburg. Three years later, he reported to the astonishment of Western participants at the third conference in Novosibirsk that T-3 experiments had achieved ten million degrees, with confinement thirty times higher than before.

Over 700 physicists, representing 20 countries, gathered in Akademgorodok in August 1968. There had been a national crack-down on dissidents in the Soviet Union in the spring, and the scientists in Akademgorodok had felt the wrath of the KGB and Party apparatus for behaving outside of social and intellectual norms dictated in Moscow. Soviet tanks were rolling in Czechoslovakia. But the plasma physicists were permitted to behave as if nothing had changed. The Akademgorodok social clubs were opened one last time for the honorary international visitors. Artsimovich revealed results that demonstrated the advantages of the T-3: vacuum down to 10^{14} particles per cubic centimeter and temperature up to three to five million degrees. Spectroscopic methods of measuring the speed of neutral particles in plasma allowed the researchers to define the average life of particles, which turned out to be fifty times larger than predicted by Bohm diffusion. Physicists reported on stellarators at the Physics Institute of the Academy of Sciences; on a second direction of work involving adiabatic, corkscrew traps that confined plasmas with minimal magnetic fields; on magnetohydrodynamic instabilities; and on various fusion devices at Princeton, Livermore, and Oak Ridge and in England. A. A. Galeev, Sagdeev, V. D. Shafranov, Marshall Rosenbluth, and Bruno Coppi presented papers that expanded theoretical underpinnings of plasma behavior, and Ioffe reported on the use of the PR-5 and PR-6 of an ion magnetron. At the final session of the conference, Budker said that a large number of questions had, in principle, been solved, and it was time to build a real reactor.[28]

In 1969, Artsimovich toured the United States giving lectures on the tokamak. He often encountered skepticism, which hurt his pride. But after the publication of results of Anglo-Soviet experiments that confirmed the results presented in Novosibirsk, all the major countries of the world turned to the tokamak—for example, the Princeton C-Stellarator was transformed into a tokamak—and the Russian word became the standard of the field.[29]

Despite deep concern about being diverted from experimental work, in his last years Artsimovich worked as an administrator, as scientific secretary of the division of general physics and astronomy of the Academy of Sciences, and as a member of its presidium, from which positions he supported not only fusion, but also high-energy physics and astrophysics. He astounded his colleagues with his support of bigger, more expensive telescopes and other equipment. But he believed that the study of the structure, origin, and evolution of galaxies and stars was crucial, even though no immediate applications were apparent. On one occasion, Mstislav Keldysh, then Academy president, called Artsimovich at home to inquire about a speech the latter would give the following day about the future of astrophysics in the USSR and abroad. Artsimovich declared, "When I speak, I don't prepare texts earlier, so you will hear what I have to say tomorrow." Thirty minutes later, Keldysh called again to learn more about the talk. "If it interests you so much, get a bottle of cognac and come over tonight." Keldysh heard Artsimovich's thoughts that evening.

Artsimovich fought the move to turn the Academy into a kind of "ministry of science." He believed that applied science should be turned over to appropriate ministries, with the Academy focusing on fundamental tasks. Of course, this approach encouraged the formation of ministerial barriers between discovery and innovation. But most of the bigwigs supported his endeavors, especially such authorities as Peter Kapitsa. Artsimovich found time to support biology and medicine, and wished there had been greater emphasis on fundamental scientific research on organ transplants and skin grafts to overcome rejection. He was disturbed about the growing role of purely bureaucratic impediments to science—although he himself proved to be a brilliant and far-sighted administrator. He wrote, "A few years after the beginning of his scientific work, a capable and energetic physicist climbs up organizational rungs and becomes the head of a separate group or laboratory. Then the amount of purely organizational activities he has grows, which is spent on a series of small operations of an administrative character necessary to guarantee normal conditions for carrying out scientific research. Each year the amount of time consumed by such functions increases and the possibility to take part in directing experimental work becomes more restricted." Young researchers, those not yet beholden to authority, should do what was necessary to conduct research in search of truth, while those who had become inured to the Soviet system needed to show some respect to the administrator. Artsimovich often said that "a good researcher after a year in my department should consider all administrators, including me, to be fools. But if he thinks this about me in five years, that's inappropriate."[30] He mistrusted those academicians with scores and hundreds of publications; clearly they had not completed the research to achieve those ends. He was a product of the Soviet system, yet clearly understood the impediments to its smooth operation.

A brilliant extemporaneous speaker, Artsimovich also wrote articles off the top of his head, only later consulting the scientific literature. When he offered scientific-popular lectures, the halls were packed, even the great hall of the Physics Institute of the Academy of Sciences (FIAN). He was a great popularizer. His sober personality enabled him to penetrate to the heart of the matter, and his great story-telling ability motivated those around him to action. He believed that if you could not explain an idea fully, or at least the significance of what it was you were doing, to the first person you met on the street, you had no right being in the business. Artsimovich strove to be in the thick of things, not to follow the fashion. He used a similar style in a teaching career that spanned forty years in Moscow and Leningrad. In 1955, Artsimovich presented a project proposal for a new department of atomic physics at Moscow State University. The project required the appointment of twelve new professors, fourteen laboratory technicians, and the assignment of fourteen rooms. The department grew into one of the leading conduits of students for the nuclear enterprise, attracting over 500 matriculants in a few years. His university lectures, too, filled the hall. He began each lecture by lighting a cigarette, interrupting his lectures only to light another. He was a true patriot, devoted to the Soviet system and not at all your typical academician. His definition of science was "the method of satisfying your own curiosity at the expense of the government." A corresponding member of the Academy from 1946 and a full member from 1953, a hero of socialist labor who won four orders of Lenin and two Orders of the Red Banner of Labor, Artsimovich died of heart disease, encouraged by heavy smoking, on March 1, 1973. His death was a loss for Soviet and international science.

MIKHAIL LEONTOVICH NAVIGATES TREACHEROUS PHILOSOPHICAL PLASMAS

There was someone to fill the void. The theoretician Mikhail Leontovich worked side-by-side with Artsimovich for over twenty years. They were a good pair. Leontovich recognized Artsimovich's grand ability to select the correct experiment and then determine how to proceed with the results. Leontovich often recalled the occasion in July 1952 when two of Artsimovich's lab assistants, N. V. Filippov and V. I. Sinitsyn, first detected neutrons in a fusion pinch apparatus, a sign of synthesis of deuterium. The physicists in the department were so excited that they broke out the champagne. It seemed the path to thermonuclear synthesis had been found.

Igor Tamm was an incorrigible optimist, so one couldn't really rely on him to be a naysayer.[31]

Even the experimentalists were certain of the results. Only one person remained sober in all senses of the word: Artsimovich. He put an end to the celebration, set forth a series of experiments to test the results, and determined that the neutron flow was a result of a break in the plasma column. Many people thought that Artsimovich was too critical of others. But he reminded those who gravitated toward him: "Remember, an experimentalist, in contrast to a theoretician, will be mistaken only once, and then they will no longer believe him."

In the same way that Artsimovich was not a typical experimentalist, Leontovich was not a typical theoretician whose thoughts were often far from experimental physics. His broad-ranging interests drew him to optics, molecular physics, and radiotechnology. Leontovich may not be well known in the West because his list of publications was not very long, but every work was a fundamental contribution, for Leontovich abided by the rule of publication he urged on his students and colleagues: Seek not priority, but understanding in published works. Like Artsimovich, he was skeptical of those scientific administrators who managed to publish twenty articles a year merely by signing their names to the institute's work. His distinguishing feature was skepticism of authority.

Leontovich was born in 1903 in Petersburg into a family of the intelligentsia. His father was a professor of animal physiology at Kiev University, taught at the Timiriazev Agricultural Academy, and was a full member of the Ukrainian Academy of Sciences. His mother was a doctor. His grandfather on his mother's side was the well-known Russian mechanician V. L. Kirpichev. Leontovich shared his parent's love of knowledge, studying history, literature, and art; and he learned to speak French, German, and even Latin with some fluency. His family moved to Moscow in 1913. Leontovich entered the physics-mathematics department of Moscow University in 1919 to follow his childhood interest in the natural sciences. A year later, he began work as a junior laboratory assistant at Petr Lazarev's Institute of Physics and Biophysics, becoming a senior assistant in the laboratory of the Kursk magnetic anomaly. He became friends with Sergei Vavilov, later president of the Academy of Sciences, at the institute. In 1925, Leontovich joined A. A. Andronov, A. V. Vitt, and S. E. Khaikin as the first group of students of Leonid Isaakovich Mandelshtam, the leading Moscow theoretician. All of them would suffer in the Stalin era—in the case of Mandelshtam, posthumously. In the next three years of graduate work, Leontovich published ten works, one in the newly developed field of quantum mechanics. With Mandelshtam, he published a pioneering work on the tunnel effect. His major interest was experiments on dispersion of light in liquids. When he finished his studies at the university, he became docent, then professor. With Vavilov, he taught a practicum on optics.

At the end of 1934, Leontovich joined others at the newly formed FIAN and the oscillation laboratory of N. D. Papeleksi, Mandelshtam's close friend and associate. Leontovich conducted research on optics, molecular acoustics, hydro- and thermodynamics, and electromagnetism. Leontovich's originality and breadth quickly earned him a place among the leading physicists. He continued to focus on the dispersion of light and sound in various media.

Even before the crucial postwar philosophical disputes over alleged idealism in the new physics of quantum mechanics and relativity theory, Leontovich joined other physicists in attacking the efforts of the so-called Mechanists to achieve hegemony in the physics enterprise. The Mechanists sought the endorsement of the Communist Party to promote anachronistic views of physics. On several short-lived, but damaging occasions, they won Party approval to attack the new physics. The Mechanists embraced a Newtonian, mechanical view of the universe in which they advanced discredited notions of a materialized ether that permeated the universe to explain the transmission of electromagnetic waves. In 1937, Leontovich signed an article with the country's leading theoreticians—Mandelshtam, Blokhintsev, Iurii Rumer, Tamm, Vladmir Fock, and Frenkel—that criticized the rejection of relativity theory by one such Mechanist that had somehow been published in a leading Academy of Sciences journal.

One of the most important centers of research for controlled thermonuclear synthesis was the Lebedev Physics Institute of the Academy of Sciences (known in Russian as FIAN). This is not surprising, given that Sakharov, Ginzburg, and Tamm worked in its theoretical department, had been trained by Mandelshtam, and advanced the theoretical underpinnings for the hydrogen bomb within its walls. The surprise is that the institute was so young, founded only in 1934, and that its physicists had been subjected to the withering criticism of Marxist scholars pushing ideological orthodoxy over physics, yet had managed to remain at the cutting edge of science.

Even more, during the last years of Stalin, a virulent anti-Semitic campaign threatened the careers and lives of Ginzburg and Evgenii Feinberg. Feinberg, a talented theoretician in his own right, was denied direct participation in the atomic bomb project because of his American-born wife; but he managed to survive with his career intact, although he was limited to instructing young physicists at MIFI for entry into the project. Leontovich was honest, open, and forthright at a time when many scientists remained silent as the anti-Semitism grew, and others refused to defend the new physics from Marxist attacks. He was always willing to speak out against the abuses of the system. As a result, the authorities and even physicist colleagues often treated Leontovich as an outsider.

FIAN was a child of Stalin's industrialization effort and the transformation of the Soviet Academy of Sciences into a communist institution at the end of the 1920s. The major physics and chemistry institutes in the USSR such as Ioffe's fell under the jurisdiction of the Commissariat of Heavy Industry. Those in the Academy, both communist and noncommunist, and physicists and nonphysicists, recognized that the future of the Academy might reside with its ability to meet the desiderata of Stalinist economic development, and that a physics institute must be created along those lines.[32]

The authorities ordered the evacuation of FIAN to Kazan after the Nazi invasion in 1941. But Leontovich returned to Moscow within a year to direct a factory laboratory, transferring in 1944 into one of the institutes of the Commissariat of the Electrotechnical Industry. Not surprisingly, given his research interests, from the first days of the war Leontovich worked on radionavigation and radiolocation, and managed to explore theoretical issues of radiophysics. In 1945, he returned to FIAN where he became head of the oscillation laboratory in 1947, after the death of Papeleksi. In November 1946, Lev Landau, Grigorii Landsberg, and Tamm were nominated for membership in the Academy of Sciences. The day before the vote, Leontovich's name replaced Tamm's in a newspaper article about the elections. Leontovich, as a student of Tamm, couldn't stand this affront to Tamm's reputation, and he spent the night calling every academician he could find to get Tamm elected instead. As a result, Leontovich received the largest number of votes. But to his great disappointment, Tamm was not elected.

Leontovich joined the atomic bomb project in the late 1940s as a professor at the Moscow Institute of Physics and Technology, where he headed the theoretical physics department from 1949. At Tamm's initiative, Leontovich moved into the Kurchatov Institute in 1951 to supervise theoretical research on the fusion problem. He undertook the endeavor with great joy. Recognizing the difficulty of the problem of producing a high-temperature plasma, he used his various teaching positions to identify students capable of joining the effort. The scientists worked under the direct scrutiny of secret police chief Beria, who had brought to Moscow secret police Major Makhnev, formerly the director of the Kolyma labor camp. Makhnev once handed Beria a list with Leontovich's name on it. Beria glanced at the list, then declined to send him off with his signature, saying, "We'll keep a close eye on this one."

Leontovich was one of the few individuals who courageously fought the rise of quack science in biology and physics under Beria and Stalin. He did not hide his abhorrence of Lysenko and other "people's academicians." He openly opposed individuals inclined to similar ends in physics. On one occasion, Leontovich was dining in the Academy of Sciences dining hall, around the corner from FIAN's front door on Lenin Prospect. When the hostess seated Lysenko at his table, Leontovich gesticulated, expressing grotesque dissatisfaction, whereupon she seated Leontovich at another table. When Leontovich inquired why she had moved him and not Lysenko, she sweetly replied, "Because people usually ask to be moved away from *him*." When Tamm, P. A. Cherenkov, and I. M. Frank got the Nobel prize for physics in 1956, everyone rejoiced. But the reactionaries condemned the Nobel committee for awarding the prize in literature in 1958 to Boris Pasternak. One physicist complained publicly that the Nobel prize committee clearly did not know what good literature was. Having read *Doctor Zhivago* and enjoyed it immensely, Leontovich set out for the writers' colony in Peredelkino outside of Moscow to explain to Pasternak that not all physicists were such Stalinist toadies. Leontovich called fools—fools, no matter their titles, do-nothings—do-nothings. He hated especially those bureaucrats who stood for secrecy. He was one of the few who voted against Academy membership for all those nominated by that very bureaucracy, especially Lysenkoists and narrow engineers. During the Brezhnev era, he stood up for dissidents, for Yuli Daniel and Yuri Galanskov, and against the use of psychiatry to "treat" dissidents. Perhaps that is why the mainstream Brezhnevite Anatolii Aleksandrov found it possible to devote only a half page to a childhood memory for inclusion in the *Reminiscences* of Leontovich, but why Sakharov spoke of Leontovich as the one individual in the physics establishment of unquestioned integrity.

Moscow University physicists saw the conference held at the Lenin All-Union Academy of Agricultural Sciences (VASKhNiL) in 1948, which proclaimed Lysenko and the Lamarckian biology of the inheritance of acquired characteristics as orthodoxy for the entire Soviet Union, as a model to secure their own political aspirations and scientific hegemony in physics. Leontovich sprang into action with colleagues Tamm and Fock of Leningrad. They recognized that the critics of the new physics intended to see their bureaucratic supervisor and patron, the Ministry of Higher Education, sponsor a conference in which their attacks had a central place. Vavilov struggled to include the Academy of Sciences in any endeavor to prevent a repeat of the tactics of the Lysenkoists and their allies in VASKhNiL, who ran the entire show while excluding the Academy from deliberations. The university dominated the three-month investigation of "idealism," but the presence of the Academy ensured that mainstream physicists did not suffer the fate of the biologists.

The university physicists and their allies had had a number of successes in the previous months that had convinced them of their growing invincibility. One was their posthumous battering of the memory of the revered theoretician and former head of the theoretical physics department at Moscow State University, Leonid Isaakovich Mandelshtam. Mandelshtam (1879–1944) came from a middle-class Jewish family. After being expelled from Novorossiiskii University in 1899 for participation in student demonstrations, he went to Strasbourg where, with several other Russian physicists, he studied with Carl Ferdinand Braun, a 1909 winner of the Nobel prize in physics. He returned to Russia after the war broke out, ending up at Odessa University in 1918 as an ordinary professor. He was one of the organizers of Odessa Polytechnical Institute and head of its physics department. He invited Tamm to work with him. In 1925, Mandelshtam moved to Moscow State University and became the central figure of the physics department. He worked jointly at FIAN after its founding in 1934.[33]

A specialist in the physics of the radio, propagation of light, and other phenomena of oscillation, Mandelshtam possessed deep theoretical insights, as revealed by his five-volume collected works, which included many of his lectures and were published posthumously. His lectures on statistical physics (1927/28), wave mechanics (1929/30, 1938/39), and relativity theory (1928/29, 1933/34) were published in volume five of those works. They provoked a fire storm of disapproval among Mechanists and Party philosophers for reputed "positivism, conventionalism, and operationalism." At a special FIAN conference in 1949, Mandelshtam was condemned for idealism; and the entire fifth volume, which was printed, bound, and ready for release, was expunged. At Vavilov's urgings, a new fifth volume with cosmetic changes was prepared under Mikhail Leontovich and published in 1950.

Not even the growing effort in peaceful and military applications of fusion derailed constant attacks on physicists' integrity. The winter of 1952/53 was cold and hard both in weather and in ideological pandering. Publications spoke of "reactionary Einsteinianism" in physics. Nimble young scientists under the influence of

the Mechanists asserted that the use of quantum mechanics to explain molecular behavior was idealism, equal to the Copenhagen view of indeterminacy. Party authorities warned about the danger of cosmopolitanism, that is, the danger of Western
influences, particularly from Jewish quarters. At FIAN, the authorities and their
Mechanist allies orchestrated further attacks against the Mandelshtam school. They
expelled his students from Moscow State University and set out to do the same at
FIAN, where his most successful colleagues remained. But it was difficult to find a
physicist to drag Mandelshtam through the mud in "open" discussions. The Leningrad mathematician Aleksandr Danilovich Aleksandrov, a communist to the core,
willingly took on the task. Scientists filled the main auditorium of FIAN to listen to
Aleksandrov pontificate about ideological deviations in physics among Mandelshtam and his followers. Aleksandrov, using a series of references to volume five of
Mandelshtam's posthumously published collected works, proved without a doubt
the existence of idealism, positivism, conventionalism, operationalism, and other
isms. After the talk, three more speakers came to the lectern to endorse his oration.

Then Tamm stepped forward. He used the very same citations to prove the
commensurability of Mandelshtam's work with dialectical materialism. Just when
support for this position seemed to whither away, Leontovich took the floor. Leontovich was the editor of volume five. Knowing his principled character, those in
the hall grew silent. Leontovich condemned the tendentiously organized character
of the whole discussion. He categorically declared that the question at hand—was
the new physics "idealist" and hostile to the proletariat?—could not be resolved
by proclamation, and therefore the entire meeting was a farce. He added that
Mandelshtam had written his lectures fifteen years earlier and that, of course, they
would not satisfy everyone. But it remained for his critics to write a new book that
treated relativity properly, not to sully the reputation of a dead colleague. Leontovich left the lectern and walked quietly and slowly down the main aisle and out
of the auditorium to total astonishment. But amid mumblings and murmurs, the
gathered throng voted to censure Leontovich and to condemn the "idealism" inher-
ent in Mandelshtam's works. This decision was in keeping with the resolutions of
the recently held nineteenth Party congress, which had placed before the Soviet scientist the task of greater vigilance in the struggle with various manifestations of
hostile ideology and vulgar misinterpretations in science. Who knows what would
have happened to Leontovich if Stalin hadn't had the good grace to die on March
3, 1953?

But before Stalin's death, the academic council of the institute held a session to
present the results of an investigative commission, where leading scientists with
the exception of Leontovich lined up behind the condemnation of Mandelshtam's
"Machist, subjective idealist, and reactionary" views. By Machist, they meant that
sensations, not matter itself, were the foundations of knowledge. Leontovich took
another position entirely: He proclaimed his disagreement with the conclusions of
the commission. He used the occasion to describe science as "that product of the
human spirit which at its roots is totally opposed to any dogmatic canonization of
any one point of view or any other fetishization." He refused to hear that the new
physics could be in any way inconsistent with dialectical materialism.[34] Yet the con-

clusion of the investigation was that the institute physicists were obliged to recognize Mandelshtam's ideological errors, paying only lip service to his significant contributions. Those who had defended Mandelshtam, like Tamm and Leontovich, were criticized for trying to cover up Mandelshtam's errors. A resolution censuring his work was published in *Uspekhi fizicheskikh nauk*.[35] Mandelshtam's lectures were republished again in 1972, but without mention of the reasons for which volume five of the previous edition had become a collector's item.

The attack on Mandelshtam coincided with the "Doctors' Plot," the arrest of prominent Jewish physicians on trumped-up charges of having tried to poison Kremlin leaders. No doubt thousands of others would follow them into the Gulag. Anti-Semitism was already a major force in Russian history. It needed no assistance from the Communist Party. The Tsarist regime made entrance into universities difficult for Jews. Whole disciplines were essentially proscribed by spoken and unspoken rules. So Jews gravitated to mathematics and physics as two relatively young disciplines with fewer obstacles for entry. This situation continued during the early Soviet period until entrance requirements for Jews were introduced to keep their numbers from growing. Over the next fifty years, Jews faced many barriers, in particular in mathematics. Jews rarely were voted membership in the Academy of Sciences in mathematics. There were unspoken quotas for admission to universities, and in many cases they were prevented from defending theses. Yet in a number of physics institutes, they were disproportionately represented and may had been a target of the growing intrigues. At FIAN in 1951, one of four academicians, two of six corresponding members, seven of twenty-four doctors of science, and eighteen of fifty-one candidates of science were Jewish, and nearly half of the Jewish personnel were Party members.[36] The problems that these persons faced because of the Doctors' Plot were not nearly as horrendous as those facing Jewish physicists in Nazi Germany, but they were potentially as threatening.[37] Anti-Semitism tinged the campaign against the new physics as Frenkel in Leningrad; Feinberg, Ginzburg, Khaikin, Mandelshtam, Zeldovich in Moscow; and many others faced the ire of great Soviet patriots.

Theoreticians in Moscow and Leningrad realized that they needed to present a united front against the harsh personal and anti-Semitic attacks they faced. Fock, a specialist in quantum mechanics who rejected the Copenhagen interpretation and a firm believer in the contribution that dialectical materialism could make to theoretical physics, was the front man in the defense of the new physics. Fock was a survivor. He survived the first years of the revolution in Leningrad as a student with a special "atomic ration" when it became clear to his mentor, the optical specialist Dmitrii Rozhdestvenskii, that Fock was wasting away during the famine that took dozens of other leading scientists. (Rozhdestvenskii himself committed suicide in 1940, despondent over the death of his wife and unable to tolerate the growing criticism of his institute, the State Optical Institute.) Fock endured the purges. He was arrested and interrogated by the NKVD for a week.

From positions at Leningrad State University and at FIAN, Fock threw all his strength into the battle to save the new physics. In a series of public forums at physics institutes in both cities, he bluntly presented the same text and message:

The fundamental tools of contemporary physics were the relativity theory and quantum mechanics, both of which had been experimentally proved, enriched our understandings of matter in motion and the properties of space and time in connection with matter, and confirmed dialectical materialism. He acknowledged that several bourgeois philosophers and physicists had succumbed to idealistic tendencies, but he berated Soviet philosophers for accepting without a fight the notion that the new physics was so permeated with idealism that it should be returned in essence to pre-Einsteinian and pre-quantum views. More reprehensible, they carried out this reactionary attack in the name of dialectical materialism. At FIAN, Leontovich joined Fock in defending the new physics, for he recognized its importance to the bomb project and fusion.[38]

Leontovich's real contribution to fusion was as a plasma theoretician.[39] His work was directed toward overcoming the many obstacles to controlled thermonuclear synthesis: the slightest impurity in the plasma, any weakness in the vacuum, any instability in the special traps designed to hold the plasma. But even though the challenges were many and the construction of a prototype reactor far off, the notion of producing millions of kilowatts of electricity from a virtually inexhaustible supply of deuterium intrigued Leontovich. He worked for nearly thirty years at the Kurchatov Institute, solving a series of theoretical problems and training the next generation of fusion specialists—Velikhov, Kadomtsev, Sagdeev, Shafranov, and their students—who directed fusion efforts to the end of the century.

KURCHATOV'S LEGACY

Artsimovich and Leontovich provided the correct balance between experiment and theory. Kurchatov ensured that fusion was well connected politically. The arms race with the United States guaranteed more than adequate financial support. Communist Party and economic organizations made certain that machinery, equipment, and supplies arrived at the institute's gates according to schedule. The institute's prominence secured continuing predominance over other programs when physicists in Leningrad, Kharkiv, and Akademgorodok wished to expand their own research, enabling Kurchatov's physicists to build nearly a dozen major devices. The major effort at the Kurchatov Institute focused on plasma heating and confinement in toroidal magnetic fields, and dates to 1954 when Igor Golovin put the first tokamak, the TMP, into operation. Since 1960, Soviet physicists brought a variety of tokamaks of different parameters on line, from the TM-1 and -2 to the T-15, a superconducting tokamak that was designed for the production and analysis of a plasma with thermonuclear parameters but has yet to operate as planned because of shortages of manpower, funding, liquid nitrogen, and equipment.[40]

At the end of the 1960s, when Artsimovich's colleagues produced results for heating and containing a plasma that suggested a breakthrough, the toroidal tokamak design spread rapidly throughout the world. They had achieved a crucial result in plasma temperature, confinement (ten meters, a record-breaking value), and density (5×10^{13} particles per cubic centimeter) on the T-3. (Currently, hydrogen ions can be heated to millions of degrees and hot plasma can be maintained for tenths of a second.) In the 1970s, two other tokamaks of middle parameters were built, including the T-10 at the Kurchatov Institute and the Princeton Large Torus, which achieved a "spectacular" maximum ion temperature of sixty-five million degrees, or ten times the results achieved less than a decade early. On the T-10, physicists succeeded in heating and confining hydrogen and deuterium, with fewer instabilities and impurities interfering with its performance. The T-10 research program had three basic directions: research on heating and transport mechanisms in a plasma; research on the makeup of the plasma and the behavior of impurities during discharge; and supplementary high-and superhigh frequency heating of the plasma.[41] Also on the T-10, physicists achieved a world record in electron-cyclotron heating. Experimental devices that complemented the T-10 were the TM-3, on which magneto-acoustic plasma heating was studied; the T-4 with which high parameters of deuterium plasma were obtained; the T-6, which demonstrated the stabilizing effect of a copper shell on the magnetohydromagnetic instability as the boundary of the plasma column approaches the surface of the shell; and the TO-1, on which Golovin studied the equilibrium of plasma using feedback control systems.

Between March 1977 and March 1978, Kurchatov Institute physicists had a number of glorious achievements. The nuclear-powered icebreaker *Arktika* reached the geographical North Pole, for which N. S. Khlopkin received a Hero of Socialist Labor award; the first block of the Chernobyl station came on line; Aleksandrov won an Order of Lenin award; Velikhov became vice president of the Academy of Sciences; Leontovich had his seventy-fifth birthday; the OGRA had its twentieth; the T-7 operated using superconducting materials; and Kurchatov Institute physicists defined the parameters of the T-15 in conjunction with NIIEFA personnel. The period was the peak of fusion research for the institute. The physicists had four major tokamaks at their disposal: the T-10, T-4, T-11, and TM-3; at the same time, testing with superconducting windings on the T-7 was being carried out; and the T-10 was being updated into the T-15.

Kurchatov Institute physicists established two goals with the operation of the T-7: design and operation of equipment essential to fusion reactors of the future, and greater simplicity and effectiveness of experimental efforts in plasma physics on contemporary machines. Operation of the T-7 was based on several years of experience with superconducting magnets on the OGRA-3 (from the 1970s) and the baseball configuration of the OGRA-3B. In geometry, the T-7 differed little from the T-10, a design similarity that enabled the physicists to use the latter in conjunction with startup experiments on the T-7. Nitrogen screens surrounded the superconducting magnet system. When first tested, they cooled the T-7 system to 50 K over five days, so that there was no thermal deformation or leakage of the vessel.[42] In March 1978, for the first time in the world, physicists used the superconducting magnets on a tokamak. Because they were not superconducting, the windings of the T-10 had to be cooled for fifteen to twenty minutes between impulses, an experimental constraint that made it difficult to achieve consistent results. Soviet scientists claimed that their path to fusion power, pushing the limits of available technology, was a more rational and certain path to fusion than long and expensive experimentation on powerful windings, the so-called American path.[43]

These successes masked growing problems in financing fusion devices. Each step brought physicists closer to believing that the time had arrived to build an industrial prototype fusion reactor. Yet their optimistic promises made government funding agencies increasingly skeptical, for new technical and theoretical challenges accompanied each new achievement. In 1973, at an international conference on the device held in Dubna, the participants nevertheless decided to press their governments for increasing funding for prototype tokamaks. They secured substantial initial support for the TFTR in the United States, the JET in Europe, the JT-60 in Japan, and the T-15 in the USSR.[44] Just at that time, however, the OPEC oil embargo created a world crisis that called for rapid improvements and alternatives in energy production, not those the plasma specialists promised in more decades to come. Budget pressures in each country came from other quarters as well, for example, from growing military expenditures in the United States and the Soviet Union. This situation required physicists to pare back research on such alternatives to tokamaks as stellarators, while working hard to keep tokamaks alive, a process that has led to cuts for fusion research since the early 1980s.

It was a roller-coaster ride of experimental successes, renewed government interest and financial support, increased expectations, the failure of physicists to deliver as rapidly as promised, and loss of support. At the twenty-fourth Party congress in 1971, the Minister of Power and Electrification, P. S. Neporozhnii, spoke about thermal reactors, breeder reactors, and the rapidly expanding nuclear power industry in the USSR, while Anatolii Aleksandrov, president of the Academy of Sciences and a member of the Central Committee, referred to fusion only in passing. In discussions held on the eve of the twenty-fifth Party congress at the Academy of Sciences, fusion had somewhat recovered its position. Scientists stressed the central position of Soviet scholars in the world fusion community, as well as its importance for the development of the Soviet economy. Just before the congress, Velikhov and Kadomtsev announced a series of studies conducted on the newly constructed T-10 and plans for a hybrid fission-fusion demonstration reactor, for which they and the Kurchatov Institute were praised. At the congress in 1976, Neporozhnii and Aleksandrov reiterated the place of fusion research as a small, but integral part of the program for expanding the network of thermal and breeder reactors.[45]

By the twenty-sixth Party congress in 1981, however, financial pressures connected with the construction of VVERs and RBMKs had intruded on the fusion program. In a major speech in 1979, Aleksandrov tried to restore fusion to its rightful position. His institute stood to benefit directly. He argued that thermonuclear power engineering had excellent prospects. He promoted a hybrid fission-fusion tokamak that produced plutonium fuel for fast reactors, not to mention bombs. But it took four years of lobbying, during which time the research program chugged along slowly, before the Politburo increased funding at a plenary session in June 1983—a move that was reflected in the USSR's Long Term Energy Plan, with conservation and nuclear power intended to begin to replace gas and coal by the turn of the century and industrial tokamaks to be built early in the twenty-first century.[46]

Superpower competition, which had been such a critical engine of fusion research in the 1950s and 1960s, no longer served that role. The Soviet Union had achieved parity in nuclear weapons, which was more important to Leonid Brezhnev and his cronies than parity in science. The future promise of fusion no longer carried the weight of economic or geopolitical arguments it had at first. And even though the physicists who replaced Leontovich and Artsimovich were first-rate scientists, they certainly lacked the clout of their predecessors, and were forced into administrative positions by the deaths of Leontovich and Artsimovich.

Boris Borisovich Kadomtsev was a member of the Leontovich school and sought to parry his government's vacillating interest in controlled thermonuclear synthesis. Kadomtsev, a theoretician, focused on instabilities in plasmas that prevented the achievement of the parameters necessary for fusion. He remarked in the late 1960s that the lack of knowledge surrounding the nature of those instabilities and the processes occurring with them naturally led to experimental and theoretical focus on their study. At one time "it seemed as if we might never achieve complete account of them," Kadomtsev said. But things had improved. It appeared that only a few of these instabilities presented real obstacles to achieving confinement of a high-temperature plasma. The real tragedy would be failure to support the development of appropriate "concrete experimental conditions" to study them—that is, newer, more powerful tokamaks.[47]

In the view of some Soviet and Western scholars, Kadomtsev may have contributed to the uncertainties regarding fusion research in the USSR in its last years. Apparently, a Soviet nuclear engineer caught Kadomtsev's ear some years earlier and convinced him that an attempt should be made to build an industrial prototype fusion reactor as quickly as possible. As a theoretician, he may have underestimated the experimental difficulties and promised results that could not be attained. Perhaps Kadomtsev was taken in by the enthusiasm of officials in the Atomic Energy Commission and the Department of Energy in the United States for the idea that commercialization of fusion reactors would soon be possible. Or, perhaps, his own enthusiasm reflected the optimism that existed among fusion specialists throughout the world.

Kadomtsev's close relationship with Evgenii Pavlovich Velikhov, and in turn Velikhov's central role in the politics of Soviet science, secured the stability of the fusion program in any event. Velikhov was an active Party member, a deputy of the Supreme Soviet of the USSR, and a member of the bureau of the Central Committee. After the death of Artsimovich, Velikhov became director of the Soviet fusion program and deputy director of the Kurchatov Institute. As vice president of the Academy of Sciences, the major figure in Soviet participation in international fusion programs, and a close associate of the leading physicists and policy makers, he was the most important figure of the Soviet fusion program until the end of the empire. Velikhov began graduate work at the Kurchatov Institute in Leontovich's laboratory in 1958, where, under the tutelage of S. I. Graginskii, he commenced research on magnetohydrodynamics (MHD). He turned to fusion after completing his graduate studies and, with Sagdeev and others, investigated the stability of hot plasmas. With academician M. D. Millionshchikov, he organized MHD research at the Kurchatov Institute.[48] Eventually, the Soviets built an experimental MHD station, with a capacity of 20,000 kilowatts and used gas from a fossil fuel as a plasma and an intense magnetic field to produce heat energy for steam power. They used this experimental station to test the parameters and equipment for the Riazan 500-megawatt MHD power station.

At one time, Velikhov shared Kadomtsev's optimistic views of the promise of fusion power, predicting the demonstration of a controlled thermonuclear reaction before the end of the 1980s. Velikhov saw tokamaks as the solution to the USSR's energy problems. In the previous decade, he and his colleagues had experienced both great hopes and dashed hopes that the tokamak might some day work. But by 1981, his confidence was renewed, for they could contain a plasma for seconds. It didn't matter that it might be fifteen years before they could produce energy. They were close to achieving the appropriate pressure and temperature needed for the plasma to ignite. The fact that Princeton physicists had achieved good results was a manifestation of the "international division of labor" and cooperation, not of the USSR falling behind. The T-15, an industrial prototype with superconducting magnets capable of reaching 100 million degrees, would surely secure the leadership of the USSR again, especially in the area of superconducting systems. The achievement of thirty million degrees on the T-10 and work on the T-15 also inspired hope. The T-15 corresponded to the JET (Euratom), JT-60 (Japan), TFTR (United States), and Torus-2 (France). Like them, the T-15 was being built to produce a thermonuclear plasma for research and for solving a series of engineering problems. It differed from the T-10, the largest in the USSR, by the large volume of its plasma, the presence of several supplementary systems for heating, and superconducting windings.[49]

Under Velikhov's leadership, Soviet fusion physicists also advanced the notion of the hybrid tokamak to produce plutonium. This technology was attractive to military planners, for it provided yet another source of weapons fuel. A uranium blanket for a fusion reactor would "multiply the power level and make it possible to produce large amounts of plutonium, thereby sharply reducing the cost of producing a unit of electricity," and would help solve the problem of limited resources of fissionable nuclear fuel. Breeder reactors might produce enough plutonium to fuel one more reactor, whereas a hybrid tokamak could provide enough fuel for five to ten reactors. These hybrid fission/fusion reactors were no shrinking dwarf stars. Typical of Soviet gigantomania, they were designed to produce 7,000 megawatts thermal and 2,500 megawatts electric, with a 1,000-ton uranium "blanket," capable of producing 4,200 kilograms of plutonium per year to power dozens of gigawatts of thermal fission and breeder stations over the decades.[50] Physicists could not have guessed that the Soviet Union would soon wither away, creating great uncertainty in the management of nuclear fuel, where once they could rely on a police state to control the plutonium, uranium, and other strategic materials.

Perhaps the major obstacle facing Soviet fusion efforts was a big lag in computer power, diagnostics, and modeling. Computers made understanding, modeling, and controlling superheated plasmas in magnetic fields more manageable. But the T-15 struggled with a series of outdated Hungarian computers, somewhat like PDP computers from a generation earlier; they even used the same serial numbers. Hewlett-Packard minicomputers assisted physicists in complex plasma calculations, but they were underpowered, leaving the experimentalists bogged down in numerical computations. This was surprising in view of Velikhov's devotion to the computer. But to many of his plasma physics colleagues, Velikhov seemed to be more interested in the Strategic Defense Initiative ("Star Wars") and the ongoing computer revolution than in fusion itself.

In an effort to overcome a growing computer gap between the USSR and the West, the Academy leadership appointed Velikhov chairman of a new division of Informatics, Computer Technology, and Automation, where he took "the initiative to found several institutes to develop advanced computational automation and facilities." As a product of the Soviet system, Velikhov believed in computerization from the top down. His vision was based on his faith in government resolutions to bring about the production of millions of computers through the investment of billions of rubles. He promoted a fifteen-year national plan, approved by the Politburo and announced in January 1985, to introduce computer technology throughout industry and society. But the computer was merely a means to raise economic productivity by enhancing the ability of managers in industry and agriculture to control labor and capital inputs. This was a mechanical view of scientific progress that saw diffusion of technology through exhortation and slogans, not reality. Social receptivity was less important in Velikhov's mind as a key to computerization; he merely saw increased production and distribution as the key.[51]

For other Soviet physicists and for Velikhov, the Chernobyl disaster was a crucible event. He saw first hand the impact on persons and on the environment; he led or participated in several government commissions to investigate the causes and to suggest tactics for cleanup and health care. He recognized that the Kurchatov Institute leadership might be tarred with the brush of blame, because his predecessor as director, Anatolii Aleksandrov, had developed the RBMK and pushed its replication into larger and larger units. He was genuinely apologetic for the role of physicists in the tragedy. But the accident itself barely put a dent in the Soviet fusion program. Rather, initially it was a boon to fusion research for a number of reasons. First, plasma specialists argued that tokamaks were inherently safer than fission reactors and fewer fission products were produced in the reaction. Of course, this ignored the fact that the "hybrid" fusion reactor would produce plutonium for breeder and other fission reactors. Plasma researchers used concerns raised by Chernobyl to bring their technology to the forefront again. The notion that one could substitute one large-scale unproven technology for another large-scale but failed technology indicates that the Chernobyl crisis did little to shake the faith of most Soviet physicists in technology as a panacea for social and economic problems, and reflected a widespread ingrained belief that human error, not technological fallibility, was the real danger.

FUSION ALTERNATIVES IN LENINGRAD, KHARKIV, AND AKADEMGORODOK

Because of the predominance of the Kurchatov Institute in fusion research, other institutes turned to alternatives to the tokamaks or subordinated their programs to theirs. Kurchatov had recognized the importance of spreading program resources more widely in the race to controlled thermonuclear synthesis. But after his death, the absence of anyone with his authority in the higher echelons of the Party and the growing resistance of the scientific bureaucracy to expensive research outside a few major centers ensured that this was not to be.

In 1957, Boris Konstantinov, the director of LFTI, became interested in fusion.[52] The question was the rapid construction of the Alfa toroid to compete with the British Zeta. They designed the device at the Scientific Research Institute of Electrophysical Apparatus (NIIEFA). In addition to Konstantinov and his laboratory, N. V. Federenko, Viktor Golant (then at the Polytechnical Institute and later head of fusion programs at LFTI), V. V. Afrosimov, V. A. Glukhikh, A. N. Zaidel, N. A. Monoszon, and E. G. Komar took part in the effort. Konstantinov organized an informal seminar to discuss the work on Alfa. The participants soon realized that the temperature of the hydrogen ions achieved on the Zeta, on the order of millions of degrees, had to do with their speed, not true temperature. This was an important finding for the LFTI group, because there was every chance that their work on the Alfa might produce better results. After work on Alfa ceased in 1962, and realizing the scope of the problems ahead, these physicists established a series of laboratories to continue research in this area: physics of nuclear collisions (Afrosimov), optics of plasma (Zaidel), and physics of plasma (Golant).

Golant first had contact with Konstantinov just after the war as a student in the physics mechanics department of the Leningrad Polytechnical Institute. Golant and the other students were excited about the news of the bomb in the United States. There were rumors that Konstantinov had something to do with the Soviet atomic bomb. He did: isotope separation. Golant excitedly sat in on Konstantinov's lectures. When he graduated, Golant moved on to the "Svetlana" Factory and then commenced graduate work in the electronics department at the Polytechnical Institute, where he studied gas discharge. Once, in 1958, he dropped in on Konstantinov's lecture on thermonuclear synthesis, a project that had just become public knowledge. Konstantinov talked about Zeta and the British optimism about fusion. During the question period, Golant asked whether anyone was working on fusion at LFTI. Because Konstantinov's answer was rather vague, Golant approached him after the lecture and Konstantinov invited Golant to his office to talk about the subject at length. Golant was so intrigued by their discussion that he agreed to transfer to LFTI on the spot. For the next several, years he worked on fusion in Konstantinov's laboratory.

The first task was the verification of British results. With Kurchatov's full support, they built Alfa at NIIEFA in the unbelievably short time of six months. Of course, the parameters of Alfa were similar to those of Zeta. They turned next to the development of diagnostics for research on hot plasma. The diagnostic methods were applied broadly on the tokamaks at the Kurchatov Institute, especially the corpuscular method, but they also used high-frequency, laser, X-ray, and other methods. Diagnostics at that time was a weak spot. The problem was that it was difficult to measure a broad spectrum of parameters of a heterogeneous plasma in disequilibrium with sufficiently good spatial and temporal resolution, because the act of measuring would inevitably cool the plasma. Golant and the others developed super–high-frequency wave measurement methods; Zaidel came from Leningrad University to develop spectroscopic techniques; and at Konstantinov's suggestion,

V. M. Dukelskii and Fedorenko looked at the fruitful technique of using neutral particles. In their study of the interaction of high-frequency waves with plasma, LFTI physicists used the FT-1 and FT-2 tokamaks and investigated plasma compression in the Tuman-2, -2A, and -3. The former research included lower hybrid heating tests and electron cyclotron heating (similar experiments were initiated at the Kurchatov Institute).[53]

In getting Alfa to operate, Konstantinov, Golant, and the others had the vital assistance of Dmitrii Vasilievich Efremov. Efremov, who founded the Scientific Research Institute of Electrophysical Apparatus that now carries his name (NIIEFA), was instrumental in ensuring that the early fusion effort during the 1950s received what it needed to win the competition with the West. Efremov was a thoughtful and capable man, an electrical engineer, a professor at the Leningrad Electrical Technical Institute, and the chief engineer at Elektrosila. His ability in physics made him known to Ioffe and his colleagues. He was a logical choice for help in design and construction of the first cyclotron in Leningrad. Like so many others, Efremov was arrested in 1938 but was released shortly thereafter without a word. He himself never talked further about his experience in the Stalinist oppression, except for claiming that a letter he wrote to Stalin while in the prison hospital, about his full devotion to the dictator and his indignation over the mistake made in connection with his arrest, must have done the trick. He returned to Elektrosila, where he praised Stalin's wisdom and greatness. Efremov spent the entire blockade period in Leningrad at Elektrosila. The Germans nearly reached the factory's front door, and their bombs tore the roof off. Even in frigid cold and snow, Efremov kept at it. Kurchatov and Alikhanov involved him in the bomb project in 1943, more specifically, in the effort to build the powerful cyclotrons and other devices needed for separation of isotopes. He was so successful at this task that Kurchatov, who of course had direct contact with the Council of Ministers, recommended his appointment as deputy minister of the electrical technical industry. After two years, he was appointed minister, because his predecessor couldn't seem to handle atomic problems. Even as minister, Efremov continued to work as chief engineer on atomic projects, mainly on the increasingly massive electromagnetic apparatuses needed for isotope separation. Later, he was centrally involved in the design and manufacture of the synchrotron at Dubna. He had in mind a program to manufacture accelerators serially for the entire Soviet Union. He pushed this program throughout the 1950s, but it did not become a reality. Over the initial opposition of some physicists who feared dilution of resources, he insisted that an independent design bureau, which became NIIEFA, be split off from Elektrosila and built outside the city in Metallostroi, where there was a metallurgical factory next door and space for expansion.

In April 1951, Efremov arrived at Kurchatov's office with a copy of a western publication that announced that the Austrian Richter had tamed fusion on Juemuel in a secret laboratory for Juan Peron. He couldn't sleep, for they had just sent a project proposal to the government to organize fusion work at the Kurchatov Institute. Although they soon discovered that Richter's announcement had been a charade, this discovery did not prevent Efremov from securing all the materials necessary to ensure Soviet priority and no more surprises. Despite needs in every other sector of the economy, Efremov secured roughly one-third of the annual output of copper from the nonferrous metallurgy industry and about as much electricity as the Kuibyshev hydropower station put out for the various projects of NIIEFA and the Kurchatov Institute. As he lay in a hospital recovering from a heart attack, he dreamed of the first tokamak (then called the TMP) and how to harness NIIEFA to the effort. Artsimovich came to visit him and plot strategy. The OGRA and the T-3 came on line with his help, and the tokamak program took off. He was the initiator of the Alfa, the copy of the British Zeta, which was built in less than a year.[54] Kurchatov's death in 1960 shook Efremov; he lived only two more years himself. But the fusion program moved ahead under Artsimovich, Leontovich, Golant, and others.

Today, research at the Ioffe Institute on fusion research lags. Golant and other plasma physicists were strong in theoretical pursuits, but Golant was more dominant in the LFTI program than any one figure at the Kurchatov Institute, and his work on plasma formation and heating by microwaves in magnetic traps dated to the mid-1960s. Furthermore, LFTI tokamaks had aged considerably, and there was little prospect of gaining new results from them. To keep the equipment in operation, three to four physicists were assigned to each piece of machinery; Western observers agreed it would have been best to concentrate researchers and efforts on one tokamak.

There are several alternatives to tokamaks: stellarators; mirrors, or open confinement systems with magnetic mirrors; composite apparatus using electromagnetic confinement; and reverse field pinches. The most important of the "alternative" centers of fusion research in the USSR were the Lebedev Physics Institute of the Academy of Sciences (FIAN), the Sukhumi Physical Technical Institute, the Efremov Institute (known mostly for design and construction of apparatus, not the theoretical underpinnings for them or experiments on them), the Ukrainian Physical Technical Institute in Kharkiv, and the Budker Institute of Nuclear Physics in Akademgorodok, Siberia. FIAN was important in stellarator research, in laser-controlled fusion (an idea advanced in the early 1960s), and Z-pinch apparatuses.[55]

THE UKRAINIAN HURRICANE

Given the close, family friendship between Sinelnikov and Kurchatov and the overlap of their scientific careers, it is not surprising that a long-term cooperative research program on the problem of controlled thermonuclear synthesis developed between their two institutes. After the second Geneva conference in 1958, at Kurchatov's instigation Sinelnikov's institute embarked on research on stellarators. Kurchatov played a decisive role in the development of the UFTI program, visiting the institute to push things along just weeks before his death. The stellarator that they set out to build at the beginning of the 1960s was just as large as the T-10 and the Princeton Large Torus. But for reasons of cost, technology, and personnel, it was not built, and in its place they designed the smaller "Uragan."

Like Konstantinov, Sinelnikov turned to plasma physics and controlled thermonuclear synthesis relatively late in life. In 1957, Sinelnikov initiated a series of experiments on powerful discharges in a plasma and investigated the topography of magnetic fields with the help of miniature magnetic probes in a Theta apparatus. Within a few years, UFTI physicists had made enough progress to convene late in June 1959 an all-Ukrainian conference on fusion. The main subjects covered included the application of low-temperature technologies to the problem of fusion, high-frequency properties of plasma, magnetohydrodynamics, shock waves in plasmas, magnetic traps, and gas discharge.[56]

Kharkiv physicists were known mostly for their "alternative" research using stellarators. A stellarator, like a tokamak, has a system of toroidal magnetic surfaces that act to confine a plasma. However, the system of surfaces is produced, not by a current excited in the plasma, but by an external multipole magnetic field, which rotates with distance along the system. Its advantage over the tokamak is that the magnetic configuration is a steady-state configuration, so it may be possible to avoid the undesirable alternation of heating and cooling of structural elements. A stellarator, however, contains groups of particles that are not confined within a closed volume. As a consequence, the fluxes of heat and particles across the magnetic field may prove too high during operation with infrequent collisions.[57]

The Kharkiv plasma physicists investigated confinement and heating of hot and dense plasma in a series of machines: the Uragan-1, -2 (for MHD ohmically heated plasma), and -3 (on which a new method for configuration of magnetic field was studied, but which never operated properly), the Sirius, the Saturn, the Jupiter (a composite electromagnetic trap for electron cyclotron heating), the torsatrons Vint-20 and Mini-100, and the Kristall-2. The first task was to determine whether magnetic surfaces could exist in real systems. For example, on the Sirius, built in 1964, the existence of closed magnetic surfaces was shown with the help of electron beams, and several critical magnitudes of gas-kinetic pressure of a plasma contained in a stellarator were determined. Experimental research on confinement of ohmically heated plasmas revealed a series of anomalies with respect to neoclassical theory.[58]

Whereas in the 1950s and 1960s, the main thrust of thermonuclear research was the study of different physical processes (stability, diffusion, thermal conductivity, heating, and so on) in a high-temperature plasma, in the 1970s and later, the main direction of research on tokamaks was the production of plasmas with parameters approaching those of a fusion reactor. Among those who participated in the first experiments on electromagnetic containment was the very same Oleg Lavrentev who first proposed the fusion idea to Beria. In 1969, these experiments entered a new phase with the Jupiter program, whose goal was a fusion reactor with electromagnetic traps. The Jupiter-1A and Jupiter-1M apparatuses with their powerful impulse magnetic fields were created toward this end. For over thirty years, the scientists at UFTI also participated in research on plasma electronics.[59]

The Siberian division of the Academy of Sciences was also active in fusion research at its internationally renowned Budker Institute of Nuclear Physics in

Akademgorodok.[60] Gersh Budker, a brilliant scholar whose flights of scientific fancy and grating personality created professional obstacles to his advancement in the Kurchatov Institute, migrated to Akademgorodok to head up a new institute in 1958. He pioneered the idea of colliding beam accelerators. Budker conceived of an early experimental device, what came to be known as OGRA in 1952 or 1953, by creating plasma traps with magnetic mirrors, so-called open thermonuclear systems (suggested by Herbert York and Dick Post in the United States around the same time). His concept first saw light in a fundamental article that was published in 1958 just before the second Geneva conference. Kurchatov gave Golovin his own department in which to build the OGRA (*odin gramm neitronov v sutki,* one gram of neutrons per day) device. The OGRA-2T and OGRA-3, -3B and -4 followed, with the latter using superconducting coils. The successful operation of these devices gave Golovin the confidence to predict the operation of a thermonuclear electrical power station within a few years.

When Budker and his associates moved to Siberia, they pursued research on open traps in keeping with his general rule to work in areas unexplored by other scientific collectives. Using open traps, his plasma specialists would focus on areas of plasma physics less studied. They worked with supercold plasmas (less than one million degrees), superhot plasmas (at temperatures greater than five billion degrees, also known as relativistic plasmas because particles in these plasmas move with speeds approaching that of light), and superdense plasmas. The strength of the Siberian plasma program was in theory under the leadership of Sagdeev, Gennadi Dimov, and Dmitrii Riutov. In practice, as for all fusion programs in the world, the plasmas subjected to study in experimental apparatuses experienced great instabilities, failing to follow the predictions of the theorists.[61] But these setbacks did not cause physicists to give up their study. Physicists at the Institute of Nuclear Physics (IIaF) focused on various open trap, multicell, multimirror machines where the plasma is created by the injection of fast molecular ions into a chamber.

Because Budker Institute experimentalists first focused on high-energy physics, most of the early achievements in plasma research came from the theoreticians under the leadership of Roald Sagdeev, then a young plasma specialist. Sagdeev made great strides in understanding the capricious plasmas. His career is one of the great early success stories in Akademgorodok. He was born in Moscow in 1932 and graduated from Moscow University in 1956. For the next five years, he worked in the Kurchatov Institute of Atomic Energy, then transferred to Siberia in 1960. At the age of twenty-nine, he headed the laboratory of plasma physics. At thirty-two, he became a corresponding member of the Academy of Sciences. Sagdeev then moved to the Institute of High Temperatures for three years, before becoming director of the Institute of Space Research in 1973. He resigned this post in 1989 to take a position at the University of Maryland in the physics department. His research concerns controlled thermonuclear synthesis, magnetohydrodynamics, and space science, including the theory of stability of plasma, the physics of nonlinear oscillations, and the turbulence of plasma.[62]

With Alberg A. Galeev, Sagdeev developed the neoclassical theory of plasma containment in tokamaks and stellarators. This theory showed that the loss of containment in mirror machines resulted from the anisotropic properties of plasmas, which promote kinetic instabilities. (At the Kurchatov Institute, Mikhail Ioffe showed how to suppress this instability.) Galeev and Sagdeev then built a small stellarator. Budker was against further stellarator research, because this kind of machine had already been built at Princeton, Kharkiv, Oak Ridge, and the Physics Institute of the Academy of Sciences in Moscow. Budker's opposition to stellarator research may have encouraged Sagdeev to leave for Moscow.

When Sagdeev left the institute in 1971, leadership in theoretical plasma research fell to Dmitrii Dmitrievich Riutov. Riutov, too, moved from the Kurchatov to the Budker Institute, although somewhat later in 1968. A charming, erudite, and attractive man, Riutov brings wit and determination to the problem of controlled thermonuclear synthesis. He was born in Moscow in 1940 and graduated from Moscow Physical Technical Institute in 1962. He worked at KIAE for six years. He was introduced to Akademgorodok by Margarita Kemoklidze Riutova, a theoretician specializing in solar physics who is now his wife. Attendance at the third international conference on plasma physics in Novosibirsk in 1968 convinced him to leave the Kurchatov Institute for Siberia. Riutov's works focus on the theory of plasma turbulence, the physics of nonlinear waves, the physics of powerful electronic and ion streams, and the theory of the processes of transfer in thermonuclear devices. With Budker and others, he proposed a series of novel ideas for plasma containment. Riutov supports fusion for a variety of reasons, including the threat of the greenhouse effect arising from continued reliance on fossil fuels for power generation and an understanding that fusion reactors are significantly safer than fission reactors. He fought hard for funding for fusion research after the breakup of the Soviet Union and for international cooperation. Eventually, economic circumstances required Riutov to settle in Livermore, California, where he continues theoretical research.[63]

WILL THERE EVER BE A REAL MOSCOW TOKAMAK?

In January 1980, just after the Soviet invasion of Afghanistan, Andrei Sakharov and his wife, Elena Bonner, were banished to Gorky (formerly Nizhnyi Novgorod and now a decrepit industrial town) and placed under virtual house arrest. The government he had served so patriotically deprived him of his titles and state awards, but surprisingly, they left his Academy of Sciences membership untouched. The Brezhnev regime had tired of his human rights activities. Almost seven years later, KGB officials suddenly arrived at his door with an order to install a telephone. On December 16, 1986, Gorbachev, pushing further the policies of glasnost and perestroika, called Sakharov to invite him back to Moscow. Three days later, Academy president Guri Marchuk met Sakharov at the Gorky Physics Institute, read him a decree from the Council of Ministers ending his exile and pardoning Sakharov and Elena Bonner, for all imagined crimes. Sakharov could not wait to talk with Moscow and American scientists about Star Wars, disarmament, nuclear safety, and fusion. On December 23, his train pulled into Moscow's Yaroslavl Station, and Sakharov reentered Soviet political and scientific life. Miraculously, Sakharov returned to the birthplace of nuclear weaponry and fusion on October 20, 1987, when he attended a meeting of the scientific council on plasma physics of the institute. He discovered that all was not well in fusion.

The number of working machines in the USSR was declining, thus preventing research. The T-7, the world's first tokamak with a superconducting toroidal field winding, and the OGRA both went through long periods of down time. The T-10, the largest operating tokamak in the USSR, also experienced weeks and months of inactivity to free funding and researchers to support other research projects such as the T-15. Planners intended to shut down the T-10 entirely in December 1985, which would have left experimentalists with virtually no apparatus for their tests. This situation led younger scholars to petition Kadomtsev to get the T-10 on line for continuation of their experiments, a decision apparently approved by the Central Committee or Presidium of the Academy of Sciences. But research was hampered by a shortage of liquid helium and nitrogen for experiments. Over the previous year, researchers had about two weeks in which to run tests.[64]

The T-15 was intended to be the mainstay of the Soviet program. It is "designed for the production and analysis of a plasma with thermonuclear parameters." Although originally scheduled for completion in 1982, the plasma physicists had to postpone scheduled operation because such equipment as a vacuum vessel was delivered five years late. The T-15 suffered from equipment shortages, poor welds, and a shortage of personnel, problems leading to a suggestion that it be transformed into the T-20, a 300-megawatts electric experimental (hybrid) power reactor with a uranium blanket, to demonstrate the prospects for and safety of fusion reactors. But today the T-15 sits idle, and the T-20 has become a dream.[65]

In an attempt to overcome bottlenecks, all young physicists were asked to do manual labor for one month. At one time, the institute counted on the help of the Moscow City Party Committee in securing resources, and in declaring the tokamak a "Komsomol Shock Work Construction Site." In a seeming reflection of the lower priority of fusion research, the Kurchatov Institute Komsomol refused to assist in construction. Indeed, personnel problems had intruded on Soviet fusion efforts. Velikhov worried that a shortfall of young persons plagued many Academy institutes; in 1982, in all the institutes, there were only two workers with doctorates who were younger than thirty-three years old. Significant ossification occurred in the Brezhnev era because of increasingly formalistic requirements for degrees and a larger number of social and political rungs to climb on the way up the scientific hierarchy. A visitor to the Kurchatov Institute in the 1980s observed "the total absence of researchers between the ages of thirty-two and forty-five. During the seventies, almost no new graduate students or researchers were assigned to fusion by the government," although there is a large number of young theoreticians.[66]

This was a shocking revelation, considering the long-term, high-level support for fusion in the USSR, which had been reborn under Mikhail Gorbachev. At the Geneva Summit in 1985 and in a speech before the Supreme Soviet earlier that year, Gorbachev threw his weight behind international cooperation in the field.[67] The close relationship between Gorbachev and Velikhov led to this rebirth of interest. Velikhov had long pushed to make fusion research an international endeavor. In

1978, the USSR proposed that the International Atomic Energy Agency coordinate the efforts of highly developed countries to design and build an experimental thermonuclear reactor with the aim of developing a commercial reactor. Beginning in 1979, a working group of United States, Japanese, European (Euratom), and Soviet physicists had met three or four times annually at IAEA offices in Vienna, Austria. The cost of the international thermonuclear reactor (INTOR, a small reactor of fifty megawatts intended to test all main subsystems of a thermonuclear power plant) was high, but its construction would enable each participant to have access to a reactor at one-third to one-half the cost of building it on one's own. In 1986, INTOR gave way to ITER, the international thermonuclear experimental reactor, which is an industrial prototype to be built by 2003 on the basis of the results of experiments conducted on each country's home reactors. This plan gave Kurchatov Institute physicists hope that the USSR might renew its efforts in fusion, even as the T-15 stumbled along.[68]

But the Brezhnev period had been unkind to fusion for too long. Several other major investment projects, notably fission power, Siberian river diversion, agriculture, space, and the military, diverted funds from fundamental research on fusion. Growing pressure to conduct research that was "cost effective and economic" might have been appropriate for industry and agriculture, but, as Kadomtsev fretted, that approach "was absolutely inapplicable to basic science." As the Soviet Union unraveled, science dried up for want of government financing.

Kurchatov Institute physicists never lost faith in big science. They worried about growing public mistrust over the risks associated with modern science, mistrust most clearly raised by Chernobyl. But government support for big science was essential, a necessary expense, they argued.[69] In his last years, Golovin worked tirelessly to promote fusion to meet growing energy demands and declining fossil fuel reserves and to reduce greenhouse gas emissions. Solar energy cost too much to develop. Fission power done correctly, as in France and Japan, met only base demand, but it was environmentally risky. Fusion power was the key, even though it still presented complex problems. Golovin's idea was to use a mix of deuterium with helium-3, which solved the problem of too many neutrons produced in a deuterium-tritium reaction. If only the earth had more ^{3}He. Fortunately, the moon has one million tons of ^{3}He, so the only remaining problem is how to mine it. You could meet the USSR's energy demands (300 gigawatts) on merely forty tons annually.[70] How he intended to transport the ore, Golovin never explained.

Even in the economic disarray that bedevils Russian science, fusion research remains alive, barely, because of the long-term visibility and stability of institutional programs and the role of several individuals in the Party and science policy making apparatus. The overlap between Communist Party and Academy leadership remained until the last days of the Soviet Union. In October 1989, O. D. Baklanov, a secretary of the Central Committee, visited the Kurchatov Institute for talks with Velikhov, Kadomtsev, and others about the importance of the T-15 for the country's scientific and economic future. The minister of Minsredmash, L. D. Riabev, accompanied Baklanov.[71] Seven fission reactors continue to operate on the grounds of the institute (although not the T-15), to the dismay of antinuclear activists. It is too impossibly costly and time consuming to move the facilities beyond the city limits. Dosimeters throughout the territory of the institute confirm that radiation levels did not exceed normal background. Some of the more powerful reactors have to be closed in any event.[72]

The Kurchatov Institute maintains its position both nationally and internationally as the preeminent Russian physics institute. As a newly anointed "national laboratory," it commands resources that many other deserving basic science centers cannot acquire. But its officials attract attention because of the nuclear legacy of Chernobyl, the fear of brain drain, and the need to manage Russia's nuclear arsenal, not because of world-class research in fusion. In this environment, petty personal disputes among its personnel have risen to the surface—and not only petty disputes but historical disputes. Fission reactors are under attack from antinuclear activists; fusion reactors can't operate because of funding shortfalls; accelerators can't operate without more electricity. So the old-timers have been relegated to arguing heatedly about who really took part in the start-up of the first Soviet reactor, the F-1. They complain that the historical literature excludes some participants, and talk about how appeals over the years to Aleksandrov, Brezhnev, and the director of the atomic publishing house, Atomizdat, fell on deaf ears. They protest the fact that the atomic pavilion at the Exhibition of the Achievements of the Socialist Economy, VDNKh, and reminiscences of a series of scientists and officials in a Kurchatov volume don't tell the full story.[73] Velikhov worries that political candidates have won seats in the Russian parliament, not with good ideas, but merely by saying, "I oppose atomic energy."[74] Every January 11th, on the anniversary of Kurchatov's birthday, the older physicists make an annual pilgrimage to his gravesite in the Kremlin wall to lay flowers at his memorial. And the F-1 (which still operates), not an industrial prototype tokamak, is Kurchatov's legacy.

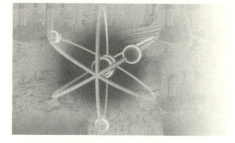

7

Reactors for the Republics

Chto to fiziki v pochete
Chto to liriki v zagone.
(Physicists are held in high esteem,
while humanists remain in the background.)
— Boris Slutskii (1965)

For atomic-powered communism to be more than a slogan, peaceful nuclear programs would have to spread throughout the fraternal republics of the Soviet Union. Not only Chukchi reindeer hunters of the far north, but nomadic and sedentary Turkic people of Central Asia would have to be supplied with nuclear reactors before rhetoric matched the reality of communist construction. Great Russian nationalism and military conquest during the civil war (1918–1920) and World War II had led to the reestablishment of an empire more extensive than that of the Tsarist era. In addition to the classics of Marxism-Leninism, tractors, and inexpensive vodka, what had the peoples of the multinational Soviet Union gained through conquest? Georgians, Armenians, Azeris, Kyrgyz, Tajiks, Kazakhs, Turkmens, Uzbeks, Estonians, Latvians, Lithuanians, and, of course, the other Slavs (Ukrainians and White Russians), perhaps even the grape growers and pig raisers of Moldava, would benefit from isotopes and energy from the peaceful atom. Russification, the official policy of political control through the spread of Russian language and culture in the form of educational, media, cultural, and scientific institutions, required a peaceful component. How better to show the beneficent intentions of the Russian-dominated Communist Party than with nuclear power?

There was a kind of imperialism associated with the spread of science through the Soviet empire. The Party used science and a materialist philosophy generally to combat religious fervor among the Moslems in Central Asia and the Christians of Armenia and Georgia. They used new calligraphy associated with new written and oral conventions to spread the modern language of science. They employed higher educational institutions and then Academies of Sciences for each of the fourteen union republics (excluding Russia, which, when the empire disintegrated in 1991, had neither its own Academy of Sciences nor a Communist Party, but inherited the Soviet Academy and the national Party apparatus as its own) to disseminate Marxist ideology and scientific knowledge as approved in Moscow and Leningrad. In Moldava, Uzbekistan, and other republics with low literacy rates, science and universities created an educated elite that owed its existence, and hence its loyalty, to Soviet power. In the Baltic states and Caucasus, with higher literacy rates and stronger ties to the Western scientific tradition, the peaceful atom molded elites whose pursuit of science submerged feelings of local nationalism in a sea of communist ideology and isotopes. Like the British and French empires, the Soviet empire used Western science as a tool of colonization. Atomic energy was international, even within the borders of the USSR.

Kurchatov died in 1960, but not before setting out to create peaceful nuclear programs in the union republics. In speeches before and after the twentieth Party congress, he preached his belief that Moscow and Leningrad ought to share these programs with the hinterlands. Physicists and political leaders in the union republics took this as a veiled promise to provide them with their own programs, and hence scientific parity with their Russian brothers. Kurchatov was deeply disturbed about nuclear weapons, especially after the creation of the hydrogen bomb, and he wanted his legacy to be the peaceful atom. He himself did not see the reactor as an colonialist tool, but as a key to achieving the communist future. Before he died, research reactors were being built in Ukraine, Uzbekistan, Georgia, and Latvia, with units to follow elsewhere. Sending physicists from his institute as advance agents for the atom, he saw to it that Azerbaidzhan, Belarus, and Moldava had begun to explore how radioisotopes could be used in medicine, industry, and agriculture. Owing to the highly centralized nature of the Soviet system, one facility (the Efremov Institute or NIIEFA, located outside of Leningrad) produced accelerators, magnets, vacuum chambers, and other standard equipment for shipment to the other republics. Atomic-powered communism was multinational.

Out of all the republics, radioisotopes, accelerators, and reactors found the most comfortable home in Ukraine. This is not surprising, given Ukraine's physical proximity to Russia, a strong tradition of nuclear physics, and significant personal, scientific, and political ties. Today Ukraine is a nation of fifty million people, and half of its electrical energy is produced in nuclear power stations. Sadly, Ukraine is known largely for Chernobyl, which is a symbol for many Ukrainians of bankrupt Soviet rule and exploitation, perhaps even a deliberate attempt to risk the lives of non-Russians. But at the start, in the 1930s, Ukraine was the center of Soviet nuclear physics under the leadership of Aleksandr Leipunskii, the father of breeder reactors, and Kirill Sinelnikov, who rose to be head of the Ukrainian Physical Technical Institute (UFTI) in Kharkiv. Sinelnikov's close personal and family ties to Kurchatov helped ensure a Ukrainian nuclear future.

THE RUTHERFORD CONNECTION

Kirill Dmitrievich Sinelnikov, academician of Ukrainian Academy of Sciences, head of the Ukrainian contribution to the atomic bomb project, leader of the Ukrainian fusion project, delegate to the Geneva peaceful atom conferences, and not only close friend, but brother-in-law of Kurchatov, arrived at UFTI in 1930 by way of Crimea, Leningrad, and Cambridge, England. An accomplished musician, a devoted scientist who kept out of politics, an able administrator, Sinelnikov led the institute through the difficult war years to become a leading fission, fusion, and high-energy research center in the Khrushchev era.

Sinelnikov was born on May 29, 1901, the fourth child of a doctor.[1] His family lived in Pavlograd, a village of the western Don coal basin and the site of an important railroad connection with a mill. Like many Ukrainian villages, Pavlograd suffered through two world wars, the second under Nazi rule, and was at the epicenter of civil war between the Whites (monarchists), Reds (Bolsheviks), and marauders. Sinelnikov's father was a stern man who forbade his children to play games with other children or to go down to the Volchia River that flowed through town. This isolation may have contributed to Sinelnikov's slight, fragile constitution; he was sickly throughout his life. The children had few friends. But the house had a wonderful library to distract them, including the Russian classics, translations of Western writers, richly illustrated children's books, encyclopedias, and a large collection on music history.[2] Sinelnikov loved classical music and became an accomplished pianist. He serenaded gatherings of his fellow students in school and fellow physicists in the institutes. The young Sinelnikov also loved to read about physics and engineering, and he was an inveterate tinkerer in his father's workshop, which was filled with various milling machines, scales, glass tubing, magnets, electrical devices, solenoids, and optical glasses. He also played tennis, chess, and croquet.

Sinelnikov's early schooling was interrupted by World War I, revolution, and civil war. The constant comings and goings of soldiers and the confiscation of food, heating wood and oil, and objects of any value contributed to a famine in which Sinelnikov's weakened father caught typhus and died. In 1919, the family fled to Crimea, which was somewhat more stable. In their haste to depart Pavlograd, Sinelnikov was unable to secure his school records; and unlike workers, peasants, and demobilized soldiers, he was not permitted to enter the university because of his middle-class origins and absence of records. A year later, a revolutionary diaspora of scientists and scholars seeking solace from the hardships of life in Moscow, Petrograd, and Kiev had gathered in Crimea. There they organized a university under the temporary leadership of Hungarian communist Bela Kun. They represented both the political left and right, and most merely wanted to avoid politics for work. Sinelnikov fortuitously found himself among such talented scientists as physicist Iakov Frenkel, biochemist A. V. Palladin, metallurgist A. A. Baikov, professor of mechanics N. M. Krylov, and future Nobel laureate Igor Tamm. The Crimean capital, Simferopol, housed the Nikitin Botanical Garden, the Sevastopol Biological Station, the Institute of Physical Therapy, a division of the Pulkovo Astronomical Observatory, and many scientific societies and clubs. Vladimir Vernadskii, a professor of mineralogy of Moscow University and recently elected first president of the newly founded Ukrainian Academy of Sciences, arrived in Crimea in the spring of 1918 and became rector of Tavricheskii University, initially a branch of Kiev University. The Peoples' Commissariat of Enlightenment of Crimea decided to keep the physical-mathematical and medical departments of the university open but to close the juridical, historical, and philological departments, whose students and faculty in the humanities and social scientists seemed to be hostile to Soviet power and Marxism generally.

Although Sinelnikov began his university study under trying conditions, he established life-long patterns of study, friendship, and play. Kirill and his sister Marina took a room with a dirt floor. Tuition was free, and there was also a free dining room for students, but the food was miserable and even with the student's ration it was necessary to work on the side. Sinelnikov managed to get a position as pianist in a movie theater, where he accompanied silent films, playing the Charleston, tangos, and fox-trots. During the first weeks of school, he met Kurchatov, who became a constant visitor to his apartment. In the 1921/22 academic year, things calmed down, and Kurchatov and Sinelnikov both took jobs in the universities. Abram Ioffe symbolically headed the Crimean physics department, but in fact he was thoroughly occupied in Petrograd, organizing his own institute. From time to time, he visited Crimea to deliver a cycle of lectures. More important were the marvelous lectures that Frenkel delivered, for he had the ability to inspire young physicists to intellectual independence. Tamm ran the laboratory that accompanied Frenkel's lectures.

With the return to Bolshevik normalcy elsewhere in the empire, the outstanding faculty departed Crimea University for their home institutions. Kurchatov, who had grown up in Crimea and loved the sea, transferred into the third year of the shipbuilding department at Petrograd Polytechnical Institute; but the move cost him his funding, because the government believed one degree was sufficient. Sinelnikov, having graduated, took a position in the physics department of Azerbaidzhan University. At the suggestion of the department chairman, he commenced study of the properties of dielectrics and became familiar with Ioffe's work. At the fourth congress of the Russian Association of Physicists in Leningrad in 1924, Sinelnikov delivered a paper on some of his research. Ioffe sought him out and invited him to join the staff of LFTI. Within the walls of Ioffe's institute, Sinelnikov met many of the future leaders of Soviet physics. Over the next six years, Sinelnikov worked with Kurchatov and Anatolii Aleksandrov in the area of solid state physics. Kurchatov, who had moved to Baku, was invited to join the staff of LFTI by Ioffe in response to the incessant urgings of Sinelnikov. Kirill and Marina rented an apartment in Leningrad. It had an extra room that served as a living room, where they put a rented piano and where many of the *fiztekhovtsy* gathered in the evenings to talk about physics, listen to poetry, dance, and perform concerts. Frenkel, now the head of the theoretical department at LFTI and an accomplished violinist, often joined Sinelnikov in classical performances.

In 1926, Anton Karlovich Valter, who later worked side by side with Sinelnikov in Kharkiv through the 1960s, also appeared in Leningrad. He was a handsome man, decisive and quick thinking, and a lover of sports, games, and pranks; his sketches and jokes were passed down from generation to generation in Leningrad and Kharkiv. This twosome, as deputy director and director of UFTI, respectively, conducted early nuclear experiments, built a three-megaelectronvolt electrostatic generator, then led the institute into its great postwar years and the construction of a series of powerful linear accelerators of electrons, protons, and charged ions. Valter was born in December 1905. His parents were members of the nobility. Valter's great grandfather emigrated from Germany and served as a surgeon in the Crimean War (1854–1855). His mother's father was director of the St. Petersburg Telegraph. His father, also a surgeon, died in 1919; his mother, a nurse, died during the Leningrad blockade. Valter entered Leningrad Polytechnical Institute in 1922, graduating in 1926 with a degree in engineering. He married in that year and was divorced in 1930; like his mother, this wife later died in the Leningrad blockade. Valter joined Ioffe's laboratory in 1925, where he conducted research on the electrical and mechanical properties of dielectrics; he also joined Sinelnikov's circle of friends and scientists. In 1930, Ioffe sent Valter, along with I. V. Obreimov and Sinelnikov, to Kharkiv. At UFTI in Kharkiv, Valter served as director for science, academic secretary (1935–1944), head of the high-voltage laboratory, and then deputy director of the entire institute from 1944. In 1932, Valter moved from solid state to nuclear physics and was involved in building a number of electrostatic generators, including a three-megaelectronvolt generator for electrons. On the basis of this research, Valter received his candidate of science degree in 1937 without defense and defended his doctoral dissertation entitled "Electrostatic Generators and Their Application" in 1938.

The war interrupted the further development of electrostatic generators when the institute was evacuated to Ufa and Almaty, but Valter's work on new vacuum technologies connected with various accelerators enabled the USSR to introduce crucial new pumps during World War II. As the war wound down, Valter was designated deputy director of UFTI and returned to Kharkiv. A Party member from 1941 on, Valter was secretary of the institute's Party organization in evacuation and a "propagandist-agitator" of the Frunze district Party committee in Almaty. In his last years, he was a Communist Party "agitator-discussant." Valter earned an Order of the Red Banner of Labor and two Orders of Lenin for his classified nuclear research. With such an impressive political and scientific resume, Valter finally became a full member of the Academy of Sciences in 1951. In official documentation in his personnel folder, colleagues and Party officials described Valter as "energetic, devoted and principled." Yet even such a decorated and devoted scientist was permitted abroad only twice, first as a delegate to the Geneva conference in 1956 and again in 1963 to a high-energy physics conference in Poland. Valter died in July 1965 after a long career of research and publication.[3]

Before the xenophobic isolation of Soviet society under Stalin in the name of "Socialism in one country," Ioffe and other leading scientists succeeded in establishing fairly regular scientific contacts with the West. These included opportunities for publication and travel abroad. Even the Rockefeller Foundation underwrote sabbaticals of Soviet scientists in Europe and America. In 1928, Ioffe suggested that Sinelnikov join Kapitsa, Obreimov, and Gamow, already in the Cavendish Laboratory, by securing a Supreme Economic Council Fellowship. Ernest Rutherford apparently had no interest in Sinelnikov's dossier, only in his photograph. There was some doubt among the Russians in Cambridge whether Rutherford would be pleased when he saw a photograph of the young Sinelnikov in a leather coat and cap, smoking strong cigarettes. Surely, this was a grifter, not a physicist. But Rutherford, remembering Kapitsa's initial appearance at the laboratory in his leather coat, cap, and pipe, looked at the photo and exclaimed, "Send him along!" Only when Sinelnikov played Stravinsky or Prokofiev at the piano did Rutherford regret the choice, claiming, "That's not music. But Handel, that's another matter."

During his two years at the Cavendish Laboratory, Sinelnikov was totally consumed in engineering tasks that would have importance for his future career in nuclear physics. He built an electric motor that could turn at 3,000 revolutions per minute in a vacuum and presaged the development of an ultracentrifuge. He followed the work of Cockcroft and Walton in nascent nuclear physics closely. He wrote a doctoral dissertation, which, unfortunately, he was unable to defend before being called back prematurely to Kharkiv. In the meantime, he had met Andrea ("Eddie") Cooper, the sister of his dissertation editor, fallen in love, and proposed marriage. He returned to the USSR with her. Although he asked permission a number of times, Sinelnikov was not permitted to visit England again until 1956, when he traveled there as part of a Soviet delegation to Harwell.[4] Eddie meanwhile had returned home from time to time, visiting her mother in 1934 to give birth to their first-born, a girl they named Jill. Eddie and Marina (Sinelnikov's sister and Kurchatov's wife) became life-long friends one evening while sharing Russian and English language lessons.

THE UKRAINIAN PHYSICAL TECHNICAL INSTITUTE

UFTI was founded in October 1928. It grew out of Ioffe's plan to establish a network of research centers throughout the country. Ioffe first announced this plan publicly in a slogan to the sixth congress of Russian physicists in Moscow in 1928: "Physics to the Provinces!" The idea was that by using core LFTI personnel as the kernel of a new research center, they would attract promising young local talent to a series of physical technical institutes established throughout the country. In each case, these institutes would be located in or near new or planned industrial centers; and in each case, the research focus would be connected with the major industrial tasks of that city. Centers were founded in Siberia (in Sverdlovsk and Tomsk) and in Ukraine (in Dnepropetrovsk and Kharkiv). It was hard to attract young, promising scientists to go to the provinces, for the brightest physicists wanted to be nearer the cutting-edge—and dreaded daily life in provincial backwaters. It was risky to subordinate new institutes to applied tasks because fundamental research suffered, innovation lagged, and interference from local Party and economic bosses who wanted results today was constant. Apparently, the planners asked Kapitsa to become the institute director, but, fearing boredom and poor research conditions, he refused. Mostly, he wanted to stay in England, so he agreed only to be a consultant for solid state specialist Ivan Obreimov, who was designated director. From the start however, the Ukrainian Physical Technical Institute was the epitome of everything that was good about Ioffe's plan.

Even with bureaucratic meddling to ensure that the institute's tasks somehow conformed to Kharkiv's intended status as a big machine building center, the level and quality of the physicists and the panache and originality of their research were world class. Sinelnikov, Valter, Lifshits, Landau, Obreimov, Leipunskii, Akhiezer, and many other talented persons worked at UFTI. The foreigners Fritz Houtermanns, Alexander Weissberg, and Rudolph Peierls contributed to research programs. Viktor Weisskopf passed through, as did Niels Bohr, Paul Dirac, Paul Langevin, P. M. S. Blackett, Robert Van de Graaf, George Placzek, Paul Erenfest, and Boris Podolsky. UFTI physicists were pioneers in nuclear physics, in fusion, in the design of the Romashka nuclear battery, and in linear accelerators. They published extensively, won Lenin and Stalin prizes, and the institute earned a coveted Order of Lenin.

When foreigners passed through, the Kharkiv physicists often were embarrassed, for the institute could not provide enough beds or comfortable quarters for them. When Weisskopf was first in Kharkiv, he brought with him all sorts of things because he had heard how hard life was in the Soviet Union. After a few days, he returned to his apartment and found it barren. Weisskopf reported this to Obreimov, who told the NKVD. The network of informers and secret policemen was so widespread that the very next day everything was back in the apartment just as it was before. When Russian scientists visited, they often stayed with the Sinelnikovs. Eddie liked Kapitsa's visits, for he taught her one dirty Russian word every day.

Although there were special flats for elite scientists, the living conditions were dreadful. Cockroaches and fleas infested them. Hot water and electricity service often failed. There was not enough coal for heating. The furniture was old, broken down, and second hand. Worse still, the food consisted of potatoes, eggs, milk, and not much else. They were often close to starvation, especially in the famine of the early 1930s, which Stalin provoked to subjugate the Ukrainian peasantry. The institute could not secure notes for money in the bank, because the government had to use all of it to buy grain from the peasants. The meals in the dining hall at UFTI were "foul," even when foreign guests visited. The authorities constructed Potemkin stores with displays, but no food. Fortunately, they awarded Sinelnikov a "shock worker's" card, and he was entitled to a ton of coal. But he still had to wait five years to have a telephone put in.[5]

When Sinelnikov returned from Cambridge to Leningrad in 1930, the authorities awarded him a candidate of science degree without defense and sent him to Kharkiv two weeks later. Sinelnikov hesitated to rejoin the Party upon his return from England, so at first he did not have access to the special stores and facilities available to Party members; he even had trouble buying train tickets for Kharkiv. He arrived in Kharkiv in June 1930 and joined Obreimov and Leipunskii at an institute still under construction. Only a few apartment buildings had been completed. Staff physicists carried out experiments in the partially completed shell of the main building. Four months later, Valter arrived and moved in with the Sinelnikovs. But the noise and crowding got on Eddie's nerves. And much to her dismay, Sinelnikov, assuming that Kharkiv was a temporary posting, frequently traveled to Leningrad for business, where he kept up a research program. Fortunately, Kurchatov and Marina frequented Kharkiv, along with Kobeko, Shalnikov, Ioffe, Gamow and Semenov. Sinelnikov quickly settled down to research on crystals, photoelements, and brittle rupture at UFTI, and to running the rest of the institute's business. One of his first tasks was to gather all twenty staff members to help install a two-ton transformer on the second floor. It took the men all day to get the job done. Sinelnikov worked long hours, coming home late and exhausted. He worried about the wild-west aspect of Kharkiv as it underwent rapid industrialization. He insisted that Eddie stay home. His doctors consigned him to bed for nervous exhaustion. He had false teeth at thirty years old.[6]

Personal problems also interfered with research. It seems that Georgii Latyshev (later to transfer to the new Kazakh nuclear facility) had established a club on the premises, and there a circle of drunken physicists spent much of their spare time. There was also constant unpleasantness with Leipunskii over who would lead and who would follow. They fought and swore at each other. Valter and Sinelnikov labored "in isolation" while the drunkenness continued. At last Latyshev left for points beyond, but other laboratory directors refused to be subordinate to Sinelnikov's direction as scientific director of the institute. He desired only to return to Leningrad, but the Commissariat of Heavy Industry would not permit him to go.[7]

Still, Kharkiv was a place to be for young physicists. Ioffe's solid state physics program dominated research decisions in Leningrad, even though other scientists were able to build on the *annus mirabilis* of 1932 with their own research on nuclear structure. The brilliant young theoreticians Akhiezer and Landau soon settled in Kharkiv (the former as the latter's post-doctoral student). As with any recently founded institute, great intellectual excitement accompanied the drudgeries of putting an institute together, equipping it, and dealing with government officials and funding agencies. Until equipment was up and running, daring theoretical pronouncements were likely to dominate the landscape. This was certainly true with Landau and Akhiezer on the spot, especially in such areas as low-temperature physics. Away from Moscow and Leningrad, there were openings for émigrés from the anti-Semitic and Red Scare politics that forced Jewish and socialist physicists hastily to abandon their homelands. Alexander Weissberg arrived from Austria, Rudolph Peierls and Fritz Houtermanns came from Germany, and Viktor Weisskopf, from Austria, was in Kharkiv for a short time. Kharkiv physicists got enough money to publish a German-language physics journal, *Physikalische Zeitschrift der Sowjet Union*, through which they strove to compete with European physicists for priority. *Physikalische Zeitschrift der Sowjet Union* appeared in twelve volumes of nearly ten thousand pages over six years and contained first-rate contributions to world physics by all of Russia's leading lights—Ioffe, Kurchatov, Landau, Leontovich, Mandeltsham, Frenkel, Fock, Leipunskii, and Ivanenko—and by foreigners who happened to be in Kharkiv—Peierls, Podolsky, Weissberg, and others. In a forward to the first issue, Ioffe informed the reader that dialectical materialism guided the work of Soviet physicists and would help make their new journal the central publication of their discipline. He expressed the hope that the journal would involve the cooperation of physicists from all countries.[8]

Within a few years, intellectual excitement had given way to the Stalinist emphasis on heavy industry, the purges that devastated the institute, and finally the invasion of Nazi armies, who destroyed virtually everything. Stalin's intention to turn his country into an industrial power required increased investment, not only in heavy industry, but also in research and development to support that industry. Surely some science and technology could be bought or stolen from the West. The Commissariat of Heavy Industry, under whose jurisdiction most physics and chemistry institutes fell, had sufficient funds to allow them to embark on new research programs, even in areas where applications appeared to be some years away. The UFTI five year plan adopted in 1929 did not refer to any "nuclear theme," but a report to the commissariat about results in 1930/31 noted work on creation of high-voltage apparatus in connection with a study of the breakdown of dielectrics and preliminary research on the production of "very fast ions" and the tracking of these ions in a Wilson cloud chamber. At the beginning of 1932, the plan included a new theme, "the study of the atomic nucleus with the help of collisions of fast particles," achieved through two high-voltage machines and a Tesla transformer. In 1933, the institute added the theme "research on the neutron—a new type of matter." To produce the neutrons, they bombarded beryllium with artificially produced alpha particles or deuterons. Leipunskii led the group investigating the scattering and capture of neutrons in a large group of elements.[9] The physicists defended their work as vital to industrialization.[10]

One of the major foci of research—not surprising, given the tradition of LFTI personnel—was solid state physics. At UFTI, low-temperature physics and material science grew out of this tradition. Under L. V. Shubnikov, they founded the first cryogenics laboratory in the USSR in 1931, working first with liquid hydrogen and soon with liquid helium. Studies of superconductivity logically followed, with Landau creating the theoretical foundation for a series of advances in the mid-1950s. On the basis of this laboratory, they established the world renowned Institute of Low Temperature Physics. Physicists studied electronic, magnetic, and thermal properties of a series of metals. They turned to the physics of isotopes of matter in a condensed state and other related topics.

But it was nuclear physics that soon occupied Sinelnikov's attention. Not one article by his Cavendish colleagues got to the institute's library without him reading it, especially after Cockcroft paid a visit in 1931. When, in 1932, Walton and Cockcroft used charged particles of high energy to promote a nuclear reaction, Leipunskii, Valter, and Latyshev repeated the experiment, splitting a lithium atom with accelerated protons on October 19, 1932. They "worked almost twenty-four hours a day, remembering about what time it was only when [their] wives entered the laboratory in order to give their distracted husbands something to eat."[11] They excitedly sent a telegram to the Central Committee and Stalin announcing their "shock work" in honor of the fifteenth anniversary of the revolution, and they earned a Stalin prize for it. The experiment was more smoke and mirrors (or rather a fluorescent screen of zinc sulfide that revealed helium atoms born during the splitting of a lithium atom) than a true discovery. The experiment was not the result of spontaneous radioactive decay nor did it utilize natural radioactive elements, but it garnered wide coverage in the Soviet popular media, as had other technological displays of the 1930s in aviation. Like dielectrics in 1924, nuclear physics may have been the second area in which Sinelnikov was the initiator of research; Kurchatov, however, moved quickly ahead—in dielectrics with the discovery of piezoelectricity and in nuclear physics with the solution of the uranium problem. But Kurchatov's achievements never created hard feelings between the two life-long friends.

The successes in nuclear physics spread from Kharkiv and Leningrad to national prominence. This led to the first all-union conference on the nucleus in Leningrad in 1933. Attendees Frederic Joliot-Curie and Paul Dirac found the conference to be an indication of the high level of Russian theoretical work. Ivanenko, Skobeltsyn, Tamm, and Gamow all presented important papers. Sinelnikov described the methods developed at UFTI to produce beams of artificially accelerated particles and talked about the high-voltage apparatus at the institute. Leipunskii spoke about research on splitting nuclei with protons. In 1934, the Kharkiv physicists hosted an international conference on theoretical physics that Niels Bohr attended. Tamm presented his musings about nuclear forces. Frenkel attempted to link laws of relativistic quantum mechanics to a description of nuclear processes.[12]

Like their colleagues in Cambridge, England, in Cambridge, Massachusetts, and in Pasadena and Berkeley, California, Sinelnikov, Valter, and the others pushed accelerator technology to penetrate deeper into atomic structure. At first they used charged ions, and then followed the work of Enrico Fermi in Rome, who had used neutrons obtained from radioactive beryllium to irradiate various elements, inducing artificial radioactivity in them. Fermi proceeded to uranium, the last element on the periodic chart at that time, but did not observe the formation of transuranic elements. In 1936, Joliot-Curie proposed that elements that absorbed neutrons in fact broke into two fragments, releasing energy. In 1935, in *Physikalische Zeitschrift der Sowjet Union,* Sinelnikov, Valter, and two other colleagues published two works on the absorption of neutrons in iron and selective absorption of neutrons, and proposed looking at absorption over a range of energy. Eventually, Leipunskii took over as the leader of this direction of research.

Not yet the focus of vigilant attempts to ensure secrecy, nuclear physics entered the public sphere rapidly as an example of the achievements of a proud young Soviet science. Valter and the Kharkiv physicists engaged the atom in battle both in metaphor and in the laboratory, with the aid of the most modern devices available. In *Atomnoe iadro* (1935, an updated version of *Ataka atomnogo iadra* (Attack of the Atomic Nucleus, 1934), both of which were published in runs of 10,000 copies, a huge number for a scientific book at that time), Valter covered recent nuclear physics up to October 1934. He pointed out how Soviet scholars had followed the lead of the Cavendish Laboratory, setting up their own research programs in Moscow,

Leningrad, Tomsk, and Kharkiv, and bombarding the nucleus with protons and electrons, neutrons, and alpha particles. They studied radioactivity, spin and magnetic moments, isotopes and their creation in the laboratory. They employed Wilson cloud chambers, ionization chambers, cathode ray tubes, Tesla transformers, and Van de Graaf accelerators. The UFTI facilities included a 750,000-volt Van de Graaf accelerator, with a 6 megaelectronvolt machine under construction; a 1.5 million-volt impulse generator; and a 1.7 million-volt Tesla transformer.[13]

A measure of the increasing importance of this field is provided by a leading Soviet journal, *Zhurnal eksperimental'noi i teoreticheskoi fiziki*. From 1932 to 1941, the annual percentage of articles on nuclear physics grew from roughly four to eighteen percent. These articles represented a total of eleven percent of all articles for the entire period, with over one-quarter of those based on research conducted in Ukraine. In *Physikalische Zeitschrift der Sowjet Union,* the percentage of articles on nuclear physics grew from around five percent in 1932 to twenty-four percent in 1937 when the journal was shut down. Again, nuclear physics articles represented nearly twelve percent for the entire period, of which twenty-eight percent were produced in Ukraine. In many of them, there was close cooperation with scientists in Leningrad.

By 1940, work in the Ukrainian Academy of Sciences on nuclear physics was carried out under twenty-four topics covering virtually all aspects of nuclear physics; the research was done in close cooperation with institutes in Leningrad and Moscow. The topic "study of uranium fission" was added in 1939, when the effort to find ways to tap nuclear energy began. They bombarded uranium with slow neutrons and analyzed the half-lives of the fission products. Leipunskii recognized early that a chain reaction was virtually impossible unless enriched ^{235}U was used; he calculated the critical mass of enriched uranium at about one ton. None of this would have been possible without the presence of some of the finest theorists in the world in Kharkiv.[14]

LANDAU AND THEORETICAL PHYSICS

The foundation of scientific excellence at UFTI was the Landau school of theoretical physics. Like UFTI itself, this school was formed as the result of the convergence of a scientific diaspora of local, regional, and national talent, a chance coming together possible perhaps only in the USSR, because in other countries, written and unwritten prohibitions against Jews and foreigners would have prevented it. The areas of interest of the brilliant young specialists who gathered around Landau, many of whom would lead Soviet physics into the 1960s, were solid state and low-temperature physics, the theory of conductivity of metals, quantum electrodynamics, and neutron physics. Theoreticians contributed significantly to the nuclear enterprise, proposing improvements not only in weaponry but also in such peaceful applications as reactors and accelerators.

With Evgenii Lifshits, Landau wrote a multivolume course of physics that gained worldwide recognition. Lifshits was a man with a great breadth of knowledge, especially on the theory of condensed state of matter. He was born in Kharkiv in 1915, worked at UFTI from 1933 until 1938, and finished his career at the Institute of Physical Problems. With Evgenii's older brother, Ilya, who was a specialist in solid state physics and the theory of gravitation, Landau examined the formation and annihilation of electron-positron pairs. Lifshits examined collisions of deuterons with nuclei of heavy elements and the dependence of such processes on the energy of the deuterons. Aleksandr Akhiezer and Isaak Pomeranchuk, both of whom worked with Landau, considered elastic scattering of fast charged particles. Pomeranchuk examined the probability of capture and elastic and inelastic scattering of slow neutrons in crystal lattices, publishing a paper on the subject with Akhiezer in 1946.[15]

Lev Davidovich Landau was brilliant, irascible, and energetic, and led a full, yet ultimately tragic life. He came into adulthood when it was briefly possible in the USSR to be Jewish, brash, and outstanding. During the Stalin years, as anti-Semitism was fashioned into a not-so-subtle art, other persons who shared Landau's Jewishness and intellectual gifts were often denied admission to the best schools and programs, and were required to adopt gray personalities lest they perish in the labor camps of the Stalinist maelstrom. Landau couldn't curb his acerbic tongue with students, colleagues, officials, or women. Eddie Sinelnikova initially disliked Landau for his constant musings on sex, love, and relations of husbands, wives, and lovers. She admitted feeling that "Dau" (as he was known by everyone) was "such a darling," but worried about his moodiness and how he "carries on luridly sexual conversations on the telephone when he thinks Kira's [Sinelnikov] out."[16]

Landau was born in 1908 in Baku, Azerbaidzhan, a city built on the profits of the petrochemical industry and the rich reserves of oil on the western shore of the Caspian Sea. Both of his parents were doctors. The family tradition of faith in education carried over to Landau, who entered school early and graduated when he was sixteen. He had a keen interest in both physics and chemistry, and ultimately used mathematics as the key to a deeper understanding of physical processes. Landau attended Baku University and then moved to Leningrad University in 1924. He graduated in 1927 and joined Ioffe's Physical Technical Institute as a graduate student. As a graduate student and then postdoctoral fellow in Leningrad, Landau exhibited a penetrating mind and was quickly recognized as one of the most promising of the many young men, and a few women, who hoped to become physicists in the Soviet Union.

Landau fell in with the "Musketeers" and their "Jazz band" in Leningrad. They were called the Jazz band, not for their love of quantum and relativity physics, but most likely because of the brief popularity of jazz in the USSR before it was forbidden. The Jazz band were George Gamow, or "Johnny," who as an expatriate in America worked on the hydrogen bomb and developed the Big Bang theory; the brilliant theoretician Matvei Bronshtein, "Abat"; and Dmitrii Ivanenko or "Jimmy", who was well known for his work on the quantum field theory, nuclear theory, and synchrotron radiation. The Musketeers were an irreverent group, known equally for their outrageous social behavior and their cutting-edge physics. Both brought them fame but also the attention of stodgy Marxist scholars who saw the danger of idealism lurking in the new physics and who resented everything about them personally, from their attire to their naked satire of Soviet social norms, especially its communalism. When Gamow drew cartoons that ridiculed the attempts of Marxist scientists to comprehend the new physics through anachronistic mechanical concepts of ethers, the know-nothings in the Communist Academy of Sciences attacked them viciously. Each of the members of the Jazz band paid for real and imagined transgressions against the state. Gamow was able to emigrate, ending up at the University of Colorado; Ivanenko was briefly arrested; Bronshtein was shot in 1937; and Landau was in prison for a year before being released. Landau brought some of the enmity of officialdom on himself. He was an outspoken Trotskyist, with whom he shared first name and patronymic. Yet he wore a red blazer to signify his affiliation with the Soviet cause. And surely none of the crimes of the Musketeers justified such harsh punishment.

Landau's reputation for breadth of physical knowledge and penetrating insights was such that he was often invited to the European centers of physics for study. In all, Landau spent eighteen months in Cambridge, Copenhagen, Berlin, Göttingen, and Zurich, before moving to Kharkiv in 1932 as head of the theoretical department at UFTI. He also taught at Kharkiv State University at the Mechanical Machine Building Institute. Again in 1934 and 1935, he visited Niels Bohr in Copenhagen; the two had deep mutual respect built upon real friendship.

As head of its theoretical department, Landau contributed to the rapid growth of UFTI's reputation. With an international reputation himself, he easily attracted an impressive circle of young men who were anxious to work with him. They arrived from all ends of the country to prepare for the "theoretical minimum" (*teormin*). Landau personally interrogated each applicant, posing a series of questions intended to indicate depth of understanding. Candidates were forewarned of the challenges of passing this examination by the sign on Landau's office door at the end of the corridor: "Rue du Dau": "Warning. He bites." Attached to his office ceiling was a green crocodile puppet. Landau's reputation extended to his colleagues in part because of his refusal to lose at tennis in spite of horrendous form. Only with the insistence of Leipunskii was Landau made a member of the UFTI academic council.

Personality, foreign contacts, and Trotskyite inclinations made Landau a likely target for the intrigues that characterized the Stalinist USSR. Recognizing this, Landau left quickly for Kapitsa's Institute of Physical Problems in 1937 when the purges enveloped UFTI, hoping to avoid danger. Although less vigilant in Moscow than in Kharkiv, the NKVD easily identified Landau as a menace to proletarian values and arrested him and his mentor, Vladimir Fock. Fock was released in a week, but Landau was saved from death only by Kapitsa's protestations. Kapitsa wrote Molotov and Stalin, arguing that any missteps had been the result of Landau's personality, difficult temperament, and sharp tongue, not true political errors. Further, Landau was talented, perhaps the most talented theoretician in Russia, and was needed for the success of the revolution. Kapitsa promised to keep an eye on Landau and to take personal responsibility for his actions, and won Landau's release. The first thing Landau did upon his return was scold his students for having done so little in his absence. The secret police continued to keep a close eye on Landau until the late 1950s, never trusting his political sympathies. Landau worked on the hydrogen bomb; but as soon as Stalin died, he quit weapons research. Who informed on him from Kapitsa's institute remains a matter of speculation.

Among the most original and productive theoreticians in the Landau school was Isaak Iakovlevich Pomeranchuk, whose premature death from cancer in Moscow in 1966 at the age of fifty-three deprived the world of a gifted physicist. "Chuk," as he was known to his colleagues from his university days, worked at the center of the nuclear establishment in Leningrad, Kharkiv, and then Moscow, where he was employed at the Lebedev and Kurchatov Institutes before transferring to the newly established Institute of Theoretical and Experimental Physics (laboratory 3, later ITEF, site of the heavy water experimental reactor for the bomb project). Pomeranchuk founded ITEF's theoretical department, heading it for twenty years. He also taught a generation of nuclear theoreticians at Moscow Institute of Physics and Technology. Chuk was known as much for his appearance as for his physics, so sharp was the contrast between the two. He was a slovenly dresser, habitually lost his galoshes and gloves, shaved every third day or so, and seldom combed his hair. His eyes burned when he spoke, and he gesticulated wildly. Everyone who came in contact with Pomeranchuk recognized his enthusiasm and uniqueness. He recited the poetry of Pushkin and Saltykov-Shedrin freely. He kept simple, informal relations with friends, but easily lost his temper, once threatening to quit ITEF over a scientific dispute with Alikhanov.

Pomeranchuk was born in Warsaw. In 1918, his family moved to Rostov-on-Don; and in 1923, to the Don coal region of southern Ukraine. His early schooling included a stint in the Rybezhansk Chemical Factory. In 1931, he entered the Ivanovsk Chemical Technical Institute, transferring to Leningrad Polytechnical Institute in 1932. In Leningrad, he studied with a group of young physicists who were being groomed to staff another physical technical institute in Sverdlovsk in the Urals, an institute to be led by Isaak Kikoin. At first, Pomeranchuk was nearly invisible. He was small, very thin, and wore simple, metal-framed glasses. His demeanor was asocial to the point that many thought he was pouting. In fact, he was uncommonly serious and one of the most capable of the group; he seemingly mastered the lectures even before they were given. His questions anticipated the central issues of theoretical physics of the 1930s. The lectures of Iakov Frenkel on analytical mechanics confused everyone, even Pomeranchuk, who grew downhearted about his own confusion. Then it turned out that Frenkel was reading from his own translation of Max Born's *Atommechanik*, but was making up all the calculations, which were absent from Born's book, during the lectures. From that point on, Pomeranchuk and the others knew they could handle the material, and Pomeranchuk was well on the way to becoming a theoretician. This thrilled the experimentalists, for he often broke instruments when on assignment in A. I. Shalnikov's laboratory.

Pomeranchuk was placed in the group studying chemical physics at the Leningrad Institute of Chemical Physics under Nikolai Semenov, a future Nobel laureate, where he came into contact with Iakov Borisovich Zeldovich, from then on Pomeranchuk's life-long friend. Zeldovich and Pomeranchuk worked in neighboring laboratories. They were bachelors and hard working, so it is not surprising that they fell in together. Zeldovich knew Landau. Whenever Landau came to Leningrad to talk with the theoreticians, Zeldovich made all the arrangements, meeting him with a car, taking him around, and so forth. He told Landau about the talented young physicist. Pomeranchuk was sent in 1935 to Kharkiv for his senior thesis, thus falling into Landau's hands.

At UFTI, the young physicists lived in spartan accommodations: a room fifteen by twenty feet, whose four cots left only enough space for a huge teakettle. Having only six months to spend in Kharkiv, Pomeranchuk initially ignored his senior thesis to take Landau's *teormin*. He worked fourteen-hour days, exhausting the library staff and his roommates, with whom he wished to share his daily catch of physics. No sooner had he passed the *teormin* than Landau changed over to the informal "you" and set him off on independent work. Pomeranchuk finished his candidate of science degree within two years, with his first works on the theory of liquid ^{3}He and low-temperature physics. When Landau was removed from his teaching at Kharkiv University at the end of 1936 as part of the growing intrigues in the institute, the young instructors under him such as Pomeranchuk and Kikoin signed a petition of protest. As a result of this action, they were called to explain their actions before the Commissar of Education of Ukraine, V. P. Zatonskii. They did not suffer Landau's fate. But Kikoin lost his "chief," Landau escaped to Moscow, and Chuk determined to return to Leningrad.

Pomeranchuk bounced between Moscow and Leningrad, then transferred to FIAN, where he defended his doctoral dissertation, "Thermal Conductivity and Absorption of Sound in Dielectrics." He was evacuated to Kazan at the start of the war, in 1942 moving to Armenia to study cosmic rays with Alikhanov. He remained less than a year, first joining Kurchatov in laboratory 2 and then transferring to the other side of Moscow and laboratory 3, where he remained until the end of his life in 1966. From this station, he was active in elementary particle physics and high-energy physics, and supported the construction of the still unfinished "UNK" accelerator in Serpukovsk. For most, Pomeranchuk was simply the best Soviet nuclear theoretician.[17]

THE PURGES AND THE WAR

Not all was joy and increasing energies for accelerators. When the Communist Party leadership unleashed the Great Terror, it hit UFTI with greater force than any other institute in Ukraine. By 1935, the institute was full of intrigues, first scientists against administrators, then scientists against scientists, "using dirty methods to obtain their own ends."[18] The fact of the matter was that the Party's minions in the institute wanted research to focus nearly exclusively on defense topics. The institute wasn't ready for this, nor did the physicists wish to abandon their cutting-edge experimental and theoretical research for it. Significant programmatic differences of opinion fed the intrigues, bringing the wrath of the NKVD down on the scientists. Dozens of its very best physicists were arrested: Ivanenko, Shubnikov, and Leipunskii, the foreigners Houtermanns and Weissberg. More were interrogated by the secret police. In a matter of months, what had been the leading center of nuclear physics in the Soviet Union was a shell of its former self.

In an environment of plots and schemes, simple disagreements about how best to channel the institute's activities generated gossip and innuendo typical of small liberal arts colleges. In the winter of 1935, Sinelnikov complained that the so-called physics association of the Commissariat of Heavy Industry, to which UFTI was sub-ordinate, "hinders the work of the institute" by needlessly diverting his attention to less important tasks, so that "Anton [Valter] and I have forgotten how to work or don't work at all, and now all kinds of dogs (both in Moscow and here, so-called social Party organizations) are after us." Sinelnikov's position was made no easier by the "swine" who headed the technical department and had written in the institute's bulletin board newspaper that Sinelnikov was responsible for the loss of over 30,000 rubles.[19]

Alexander Weissberg and Fritz Houtermanns were arrested and imprisoned, but they were eventually exchanged with the Nazis for Russian prisoners in April 1940. Houtermanns was interrogated fourteen times after his arrest in Moscow in November 1937, three days after the order was issued in Kharkiv. They returned him to prison in Kharkiv. Irina and Frederic Joliot-Curie and Jean Perrin protested the arrests of Weissberg and Houtermanns to the state procurator, but without effect. Lev Shubnikov was arrested in early August of 1937. His wife, Trapeznikova, had just given birth to a baby boy. Because her last name was different from Shubnikov's, she had to get a declaration from Shubnikov attesting to the fact that he was the child's father and approved of having the baby named after him. The NKVD permitted her to secure the necessary documents with great difficulty and then disconnected her phone. Soon they came to arrest her and told her, "Well, he'll just grow up without you." Like so many other children, the baby had to be cared for by distant relatives. Other children had to survive by their wits on the street. How many UFTI physicists were arrested or killed is unknown. These were very difficult circumstances in which to conduct physics research, and it is surprising that those who remained untouched had the stomach to continue working.

A second serious blow to the position of the institute as a center for nuclear physics was World War II. When the Nazis invaded in June 1941, the Kharkiv physicists evacuated what they could just ahead of the onslaught. German bombers hit apartment buildings visible from the institute grounds. The physicists quickly disassembled equipment and packed it away with valuable instruments, books, and so on. They were then sent to Kazakhstan, arriving in Almaty only in the winter of 1941/42 (by which time Kharkiv had fallen). Staffers drove dump trucks east in a convoy headed for Ufa. In September 1941, Sinelnikov, Valter, their families, and other employees arrived safely in Ufa, coming by train through Penza and Saratov. They met many other personnel of Ukrainian Academy of Sciences institutes who had been evacuated. Sinelnikov's family moved to a five-story apartment building crowded with other families. Then in the summer of 1942, they suffered a personal tragedy when Sinelnikov's four-year old son, Patrick, fell to his death from the top of the building while playing.

The Kharkiv physicists organized their physics laboratory and library in two rooms at Kazakh State University. Things were not only cramped, but dangerous. In peacetime, the place would have been closed as a safety hazard. Sometimes they cooked porridge on one table while they filtered mercury for manometers on another nearby. For Sinelnikov, it was hard to live on one salary, even with access to a special dining room and other Academy perquisites, and fuel oil was in short supply. Somehow the physicists managed to continue their research. Beginning in 1944, they worked on problems of nuclear physics at the order of Kurchatov and on theory of moderation and scattering of neutrons in crystals, especially in graphite. Akhiezer and Pomeranchuk completed the first Soviet monograph on nuclear theory and investigated the interaction of particles with matter. A. I. Brodskii of the Institute of Physical Chemistry in Dnepropetrovsk (created in 1927) had a long-term interest in isotopes and was the first in the Soviet Union to produce heavy water (in 1934). He also conducted research on thermal diffusion techniques of uranium separation. At the twenty-fifth anniversary of the Ukrainian Academy in 1944, Leipunskii delivered a plenary speech, "Problems of Nuclear Physics," that summarized their activities. But most of the prewar momentum was gone. The department of nuclear physics created in the Kiev-based Institute of Physics under Leipunskii had only three persons in 1944 and only eleven in 1945, because many colleagues had been lost at the front.

In 1943, Kharkiv was freed from Nazi rule, with the Sinelnikov family sent first to Moscow with some discussion of transferring the institutes of the Ukrainian Academy of Sciences from Ufa to Moscow. Eddie remained with the Kurchatovs, but Sinelnikov returned to Ukraine to head UFTI's resurrection and to participate in the atomic bomb project. Eddie worried that Sinelnikov's weak constitution might suffer the consequences of the hard work, not only at the institute but in the day-to-day struggle for food, clothing, and housing. Kharkiv was empty. Bridges had been blown up. There were no apartments suitable for habitation. The institute's main building had been bombed. All the windows were broken. One could gain access to the second floor only through scaffolding on the outside. The building had been ransacked. There was no heating fuel. The plumbing and sewer systems were destroyed. Only one building remained fully intact, and only a small group of physicists had been sent to Kharkiv to clean up the mess. Even worse, Sinelnikov had "daily unpleasantness" with local Party officials regarding rationed materials.

Sinelnikov found their flat absolutely empty and filthy. His beautiful Steinway lay on the road near the garage, having been used by the Germans as a platform for washing lorries. They had taken all of Sinelnikov's scientific books to Munich. Sinelnikov's first inclination was to get the electrostatic generator running, for it was crucial in measuring nuclear constants for chain reactions. Valter, who had become deputy director of the institute, was appointed head of the accelerator department. Sinelnikov and Valter reported to Kurchatov that the electrostatic generator could be repaired with materials at hand. Unfortunately, the Nazis had carted off almost all the spare parts, electric motors, generators, oils, and lubricants. Sinelnikov asked Kurchatov to authorize funding and materials needed to reestablish a fully operable workshop to repair or replace this equipment, provide orders to reestablish normal supply of gas, and repair a neutron generator. Problems in securing the early release of several physicists from service in the Red Army and the special rations for them delayed the completion of repairs for some months.[20] Even with Kurchatov's intervention, long hours of work and of pleading with local officials accomplished little. Through the spring of 1945, Sinelnikov worked twelve-hour days, and there was no break in sight. He had barely survived a harsh winter, existing without electricity and water in January and February, and he was tired of having to call on Party officials "to intercede with the Academy over every 'trifle.'" They hardly got any work done. "Anton just shows his nose in the morning," Sinelnikov lamented.[21]

Eddie returned to help Sinelnikov in that spring of 1945, until such time as physicists serving at the front were released from the armed forces. As problems mounted, there was some discussion about throwing in the towel, closing the institute, and transferring all personnel to Kiev. But Kurchatov came through, insisting on the central importance of UFTI for the atomic project and on supplying the necessary resources to the institute. From this time forward, Sinelnikov's office was always filled with the comings and goings of officials and scientists. Sinelnikov arrived at work promptly each day at nine. The first half of the day was absorbed with discussions of institute business; during the second half, he completed institute business by himself. He went home late at night, only after having devoured the contents of newly arrived journals before they were sent to the library. Hence, he was always prepared to start the next day with a discussion of the most recent achievements. Depending on who dropped in during the day, his office became the site of either a theoretical seminar, the scientific technical council, or a philosophical dispute. Even when ill, he went to work every day.

As if the difficulties of recovering from the war were not bad enough, the authorities chose the postwar years as the time to renew the call for ideological vigilance in science. In every scientific discipline, in every region of the country, Marxist philosophers and scientists of firm Stalinist conviction asserted their authority in science. In physics, this meant interest in how the new physics of relativity theory and quantum mechanics, of accelerators and electrons, was commensurate with the Soviet philosophy of science. Sinelnikov took a pragmatic position, for he wished to be left alone to do his work. He assisted Akhiezer and Valter in developing readings in the philosophy of science for examinations for the candidate of science qualifying examinations. Sinelnikov actively defended the new physics in a series of meetings in Kharkiv in the late 1940s and early 1950s. He admonished warring philosophers and physicists to find some middle ground in the interests of modern science.

The flavor of the struggle against ideological transgressions differed by republic. In Ukraine, beginning in 1946 on the initiative of Nikita Khrushchev, then first secretary of the Ukrainian Party organization, scientists produced a book series called "university at home" intended to give workers a way to complete their education through middle skills in an easy-to-read and interesting format. There were eighteen components in the series, including one in physics. A. I. Leipunskii was its editor until he moved to Obninsk. Then academician V. E. Lashkarev took over. Several Kiev University professors, including N. D. Morgulis, an experimentalist, criticized the physics series in 1952 for "kowtowing" to the West, failing to recognize the priority of Soviet science in all disciplines, giving an important 1948 Central Committee resolution on ideology, art, literature, music, and science short shrift, and ignoring the brilliance of such leading lights as Lysenko in biology and Stalin in linguistics. Lashkarev was required to defend the physics contribution in the series in the presidium of the Ukrainian Academy of Sciences. He called the criticism petty and personal, precisely because of the fact that it was four years after the fact, superficial, unqualified, and dishonest.[22]

Like scientists in Leningrad and Moscow institutes, leading scholars in Ukraine prepared position papers that defined what was permissible in quantum mechanics and relativity theory in light of the Central Committee resolution. The papers embraced quantum mechanics fully, but trod carefully where the epistemology underlying quantum mechanics suggested a kind of subjective idealism. One group of physicists emphasized the point that "laws of the microworld are objective laws of nature that exist independently of our cognition, and to a greater or lesser degree are reflected in our consciousness. The microworld is material and cognizable."[23] They knew this, of course, from their bombardment of elementary particles with a series of increasingly powerful accelerators.

ACCELERATORS AND STELLARATORS

Most of Sinelnikov's immediate postwar research was connected with the atomic bomb project. But Sinelnikov had two other interests during the 1950s: high-energy physics using large linear accelerators and, an alternative to the Moscow standard of tokamaks, fusion research using stellarators. In 1931, Sinelnikov had already set out to achieve higher energies for accelerated particles needed to split atoms. He estimated that a seven million-electronvolt device would be sufficient. He first built an apparatus capable of producing 1.3 megaelectronvolts. Next he and his associates built a 7.5-megaelectronvolt Van de Graaf electrostatic generator, at that time the largest in the world; Van de Graaf himself visited the facility for a week in September 1935. A working model of a one-megaelectronvolt electrostatic generator built by Kharkiv physicists was erected at an exhibition in honor of the seventeenth Party congress of the Communist Party. They put up a new building twenty meters tall to hold a generator that had a conductor ten meters in diameter. In September 1937, Sinelnikov presented a paper at the second all-union conference on atomic energy in Moscow about an electrostatic accelerator that reached 3.5 megaelectronvolts, a device fifty times more powerful than the sixty-kilovolt apparatus they had built in 1930. In 1938, Valter defended a doctoral dissertation that discussed the construction of the accelerator and the results of experiments on it. Kharkiv's central place in nuclear physics made it the logical site for the second conference on nuclear physics in 1939. Discussion centered on the fission of uranium by slow neutrons, discovered just prior to the conference, but also on the work of the Sinelnikov group on accelerators.

Having at hand an electrostatic generator with a discharge tube in which it was possible to produce electrons with energies higher than two megaelectronvolts, Sinelnikov set out to study the nuclear photoeffect for beryllium, research he published in *Zhurnal eksperimental'noi i teoreticheskoi fiziki* in 1938 with Valter and others. Before they were able to accomplish much more, the Nazi invasion forced them hurriedly to disassemble their large Van de Graaf accelerator, Tesla transformer, cyclotrons, and electrostatic generators, including those under construction. Of the three co-authors of the 1938 article—Ivanov, Abramovich, and Taranov—only Taranov returned from the front. Abramovich, the youngest and perhaps the most gifted, was killed while defending his city.

Returning to Kharkiv in 1943, Sinelnikov recognized the need to raise the power an order of magnitude to billions of electronvolts. In 1947, a two-megaelectronvolt horizontal accelerator injector for a linear proton accelerator was put into operation. A four-megaelectronvolt accelerator followed shortly thereafter, as did a series at 1.2 and 3 megaelectronvolts. They commenced building a proton linear accelerator at twenty megaelectronvolts in 1947. But the physicists encountered a series of problems connected with the choices of optimal construction, stability, and operation, so they did not bring the so-called LUP-20 on line until 1951. On the basis of its successful operation, they were ordered to participate in the design and construction of an injector, dubbed the LUP-9, for the Dubna synchrophasotron. They built a series of electron accelerators at 0.7 megaelectronvolts (1951), 3.5 megaelectronvolts (1952), and 30 and 90 megaelectronvolts (1954 to 1955), then set out to build huge accelerators at 300 megaelectronvolts and 2 gigaelectronvolts in 1955. But these accelerators were not completed until 1963 and 1968, respectively. UFTI was one of the few institutes in the country with a tradition in accelerator technology; hence, it was a logical choice as the site for continued research in this area. They also had compact electrostatic generators at 1.5 and 2.5 megaelectronvolts. By the end of the 1950s, the stable included proton linear accelerators at 2 and 5.5 megaelectronvolts, a 5.5-megaelectronvolt Van de Graaf accelerator, and a 10-megaelectronvolt "linear accelerator of many charged ions" (the LUMZI-10). The physicists designed and built a series of linear electron accelerators in close cooperation with specialists at NIIEFA: 2.4 megaelectronvolts (1953), 30 megaelectronvolts (1956), 90 megaelectronvolts (1960), 360 megaelectronvolts (1963), and 2 gigaelectronvolts (1966), one of most powerful linear accelerators in world. UFTI was clearly the leading research center in the country.[24] The 2 gigaelectronvolt and 300 megaelectronvolt accelerators operated 4,500 hours annually, facilitating extensive isotopic research and generating experimental information about electromagnetic interactions, the structure of exited states of light nuclei, and the properties of very short-lived nuclear isomers.

By the late 1950s Soviet industry produced standard 2.5- and 5-megaelectronvolt compact electrostatic accelerators. The small power of sources of ionizing radiation (electron, proton, X-ray, and gamma ray accelerators) limited their applications. But the successful development of accelerator technology of charged particles and the production of artificial radioactive isotopes in large quantities led to the creation of powerful sources of ionizing radiation with applications in industry and agriculture. One of the foremost applications was gamma spectroscopy with electrostatic generators at two megaelectronvolts, which was used for packaging in plastic (for example, of sterile hospital supplies) at five to ten megaelectronvolts. Based on UFTI designs, NIIEFA produced a series of electrostatic generators at energies of 0.5 to 5 megaelectronvolts (the EG-1, developed in 1954, the EG-05M, EG-1M, EG-2M, EG-2.5, and the EG-5).[25]

Sinelnikov did not live to see the most significant artifact of his legacy come to fruition: nuclear power stations that dotted the Ukrainian landscape and produced

Kirill Sinelnikov, his wife "Eddie," and Anton Valter (on the left) in Kharkiv at the beginning of the 1960s. *(Courtesy of Iurii Ranyuk and the Ukrainian Physical Technical Institute)*

fifty percent of its electrical energy. The Chernobyl nuclear park, with its ten projected 1,000-megawatt electric reactors, would verify the slogan that "Communism is Soviet power plus the electrification of the entire country." Nor did Sinelnikov see civilian power stations go up in Lithuania and Armenia. But he had seen peaceful nuclear programs come to fruition in Central Asia, in the Caucasus, and in the Baltic states. From research reactors capable of irradiating various organic and inorganic substances to isotopes used in industry, agriculture, and medicine, Soviet power was the peaceful atom.

BUILDING NUCLEAR CITIES: ALMATY, SALASPILS, TBILISI, TASHKENT

During the Khrushchev era, the Communist Party approved the construction of dozens of new cities of science at all ends of the empire, including the renowned Akademgorodok in Siberia, which sprang up in a handful of years with dozens of institutes staffed by thousands of scientists. No longer fearing, as Stalin had, a dispersal of loci of power and knowledge far from Moscow's reach, and recognizing the importance of science for economic, public health, and social ends, the Central Committee endorsed the calls of the scientific community to bring science to the republics, finally acknowledging Abram Ioffe's slogan "Physics to the Provinces!" Many of the cities were closed military national laboratories involved in designing weapons of mass destruction. But there were a number of leading centers devoted to the peaceful atom as well.

Khrushchev had become enamored of what he thought was the American way of doing things in science and education. He perceived cities of science in American university centers. He was not loathe to admit that American science had in fact outdistanced Soviet science in most regions. But he was also a proud leader, and he believed that the Soviet economic and social system would enable the USSR to take advantage of science as the United States could not—for the benefit of all the people and guided by a strictly materialist methodology. Sputnik and Obninsk confirmed this belief.

According to leading nuclear scientists, the construction of research reactors in the republics represented "the Leninist national politics of the Communist Party of the USSR, directed toward raising the economy and culture of all nations and

peoples of the USSR . . . and to the flowering of science in all fraternal republics."
Each republic had its own academy of sciences, most of which were founded after
World War II. The academies were dedicated both to supporting Soviet, and hence
Russian, economic development and to assisting the development of indigenous sci-
ence and national culture.[26] Shouldn't every republic have its own 2,000-kilowatt
reactor and 150-megaelectronvolt accelerator?

Given the nature of the highly centralized Soviet system, it should not be surprising that machinery and equipment for particle accelerators and tokamak fusion
reactors came from one institute, the D. V. Efremov Scientific Research Institute of
Electrophysical Apparatus (NIIEFA), located just outside Leningrad. When physicists designed the first accelerators for basic research purposes and then for various
tasks associated with the bomb project, they built what they could in workshops of
their own institutes. But more often, they turned to engineers at Elektrosila to meet
their growing needs for powerful magnets, engines, generators, and motors. Eventually, the appropriate Elektrosila facilities were gathered in NIIEFA in 1945 to supply the burgeoning nuclear program with electrophysical apparatus.[27] When the
decision was made to expand the nuclear enterprise, Kurchatov called on specialists
at NIIEFA to produce standard accelerators and other equipment for the nuclear
physics institutes being established in the union republics. The institute's staff—
5,000 employees at its high point in 1988, including 800 designers and technologists
and 1,400 engineer-scientists—designed, manufactured, and shipped serially produced accelerators made from standard components, as Atommash had for the civilian reactor industry.

In Russia, the major NIIEFA customers were the Kurchatov, Lebedev, and Ioffe
Institutes, the Institute of Experimental and Theoretical Physics, and the High-
Energy Physics Institute near Serpukhov. In Ukraine, the customers were UFTI
and the Institute of Nuclear Research in Kiev. NIIEFA also shipped to Kazakhstan,
Armenia, Uzbekistan, and Tajikistan. Only a toll-free phone number for twenty-
four-hour service seems to have been lacking. NIIEFA produced resonance linear
accelerators, induction accelerators, boosters for accelerators, small-size cyclotrons,
superconducting coil electromagnets, and electromagnetic pumps for liquid metal,
including those used in the main reactor loops of the BR-10 and the auxiliary reactor loops of the BOR-60 and BN-350. NIIEFA's most important products were huge
linear accelerators and large cyclic charged-particle accelerators, which it manufactured for domestic ends and for the socialist countries in Eastern Europe. These accelerators were used for nuclear and high-energy physics research, for applied purposes such as isotope production and activation analysis, and for medical-biological
purposes. One of the first cyclic accelerators was the 120-centimeter (pole diameter)
cyclotron developed in 1947. Later models were 150, 240, and 310 centimeters in
diameter. The 310-centimeter pole diameter cyclotron installed at the Joint Institute
for Nuclear Research in Dubna was designed for transuranium element fusion and
produces accelerated argon ions at 300 megaelectronvolts. In the 1960s, NIIEFA
physicists designed the isochronous U-240 and MGC cyclotrons.

Among major facilities designed and manufactured at NIIEFA are the 680-
megaelectronvolt proton synchrocyclotron (1949) and a 10-gigaelectronvolt weak-
focusing proton synchrotron (1957, installed at Dubna), and a 76-gigaelectronvolt

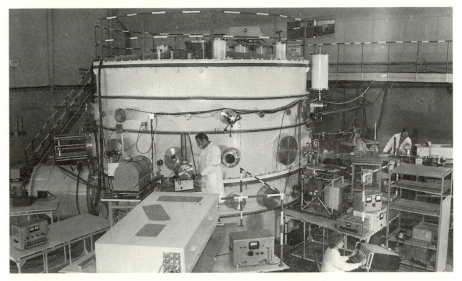

The Uragan-3 torsatron fusion device at the Ukrainian Physical Technical Institute. *(Courtesy of Iurii Ranyuk and the Ukrainian Physical Technical Institute)*

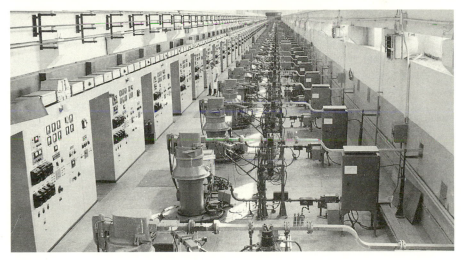

The klystron hall of the two-gigaelectronvolt linear electron accelerator at the Ukrainian Physical Technical Institute. *(Courtesy of Iurii Ranyuk and the Ukrainian Physical Technical Institute)*

strong-focusing proton synchrotron at the High Energy Physics Institute in Ser-pukhov, 150 kilometers southeast of Moscow (1967). The physicists also designed a booster to make possible a tenfold increase in the particle beam intensity. Next to follow at Serpukhov was the machinery and equipment for colliding proton and proton-electron beams, for a new accelerator four kilometers in diameter with ener-gies up to three tetraelectronvolts based on a superconducting ring magnet. This facility may never be finished; funding has been slashed, tunnels for the ring have collapsed; and many scientists have left the institute for other facilities abroad. The completed one-gigaelectronvolt synchrocyclotron at the Gatchina Institute of Nuclear Physics (1967), and a six-gigaelectronvolt strong-focusing accelerator at the Institute of Physics in Erevan, Armenia (1967) also carried the NIIEFA label (see Appendix, Table 16).

NIIEFA was the main organization developing linear accelerators in the USSR. In the late 1950s, its physicists developed several universal accelerators: 400 and 2,000 megaelectronvolts at UFTI, 50- to 100-megaelectronvolt accelerators for the Lebedev Physics Institute and the Erevan Institute of Physics, and a 25-megaelectronvolt accelerator for medical purposes. NIIEFA designed, manufactured, and fine-tuned these machines on site. A number of the linear accelerators were for industrial facilities such as the Izhorsk Steel Works, for quality control of atomic reactor units at Atommash, and for sterilization, medical purposes, insect disinfestation, and quality control. Finally, NIIEFA was the main designer of large thermonuclear installations for the Russians, Ukrainians, and Georgians, servicing, it would seem, all but the Chukchis.

Despite its status as the supreme electrophysical apparatus maker and its command of resources, NIIEFA could not satisfy the demands of the burgeoning high-energy physics research industry. Until 1960, the leading institutes in the country had themselves guaranteed scientific independence by producing most auxiliary equipment on site in their own workshops or with help from Elektrosila, NIIEFA, and other major firms. But as more and more institutes began to need equipment, including those in the countries of Eastern Europe, the production capacity of industry could not keep pace. The Union Scientific Research Institute of Instrument Building (SNIIP), which was subordinate to the State Committee of Atomic Energy and created to assist the institutes, was overwhelmed by orders. Production lagged two to four years behind the orders as SNIP slogged through design tasks with outdated computers and experienced cost overruns. Not only nuclear physics, but also biology and chemistry institutes had embarked on nuclear research. The demand for higher quality, more complexity, and greater exactness of instruments had grown substantially. The Lebedev Institute, Gatchina, and the Institute of Physics in Kiev had been relegated to producing their own equipment again, but the product was often less reliable.[28] Centralization avoided duplication of effort, but it created an overburdened industry unable to meet demand.

Demand grew in leaps and bounds as Lithuanians, Latvians, Armenians, Georgians, and Kazakhs sought to be graced by atomic power. Kazakhstan is almost twice the size of Alaska, and it borders the Caspian Sea, on whose shore (on the Mangyshlak peninsula) the Soviets built a breeder reactor. Kazakhstan's 16.5 million people make their living mining fossil fuels, iron, and manganese and growing grains, cotton, wool, and meat. There were two reasons why one might have expected the Kazakh peaceful nuclear program to commence earlier. One was the fact that, of all the non-Russian republics, the percentage of Russian inhabitants in Kazakhstan was the highest: forty-two percent Kazakh, thirty-seven percent Russian, five percent Ukrainian, and five percent of German descent. In the capital, Almaty (now a city of 1.1 million residents), Russians had a large majority. Surely these Slav colonizers merited a reactor or two. Second, Kazakhstan held the major nuclear polygon, Semipalatinsk, the test site for hundreds of weapons tests and stored wastes. As a symbol of the peaceful intent of the nation and as a reward to the republic for its dubious honor of being the birthplace of Soviet fallout, surely the peaceful atom deserved a home on the outskirts of Almaty.

Moreover, growing out of the postwar effort to promote science, the Central Asian republics each had received great Russian advice and funding to establish or expand an Academy of Sciences. As science had served the British and French empires, so it would serve the Soviet, bringing the appropriate scientific worldview to combat deeply entrenched Moslem customs among Kazakhs, Tajiks, Uzbeks, and Kirgiz, not to mention Uigurs and Urdmurts. Kazakhstan's Academy of Sciences had the longest history among all those in Central Asia.

In the least developed regions of the Soviet Union such as Central Asia, which had the fewest number of indigenous persons educated in the Western scientific tradition, Party officials and scientists focused early education, research and development, and scientific expeditions on cataloging flora, fauna, and natural resources. Kazakhstan and other Central Asian republics presented a special problem in the effort to promote science: the absence of universal education and a low level of literacy. There were few elementary and higher educational institutions, and strong cultural impediments to training women. Given the paucity of native scientists and scholars, the government ordered specialists from other republics to evaluate the natural resources of Kazakhstan for the industrialization effort. Under Stalin, a series of institutions was founded: pedagogical, veterinary-zoological, and the Kazakh State University. All came into being between 1929 and 1931. Simultaneously, 240 Kazakh teachers were sent to Ukraine for advanced study, while Ukraine sent 250 teachers to Kazakhstan. These teachers and native scientists served as the core staff of the Kazakh Branch of the Academy of Sciences of the USSR. Over the next few years, thousands of Kazakh students journeyed to Moscow, Leningrad, Saratov, Omsk, and other cities for advanced study in physics, soil science, and geology. By 1941, sixteen percent of scientific personnel in the branch were Kazakh.[29]

World War II gave special impetus to the transformation of the branch into an independent Kazakh Academy of Sciences with the influx of scientific personnel, their equipment, and industries that were escaping the Nazi armies. These personnel expanded existing programs, especially astronomical observatories in the Altai Mountains, and founded an Institute of Astronomy and Physics in 1941. Three other institutes quickly followed: Chemistry and Metallurgy, Soil Science and Botany, and Zoology. Simultaneously, the Kazakh ministry of higher education established graduate education. By 1945, 68 of the 125 graduate students in Kazakh Academy institutes were Kazakh, as were one-quarter of the scientific personnel. Unfortunately, the success rate for thesis defense among Kazakh students remained low through the end of the 1950s, so that while the Kazakh Academy grew, the percentage of native personnel actually declined, especially among doctors and candidates of science. Their absolute number also fell, most likely in connection with the purge of Jewish scientists during the "Doctors' Plot" and the return of non-Kazakh scientists to the European USSR. Soviet equal opportunity was not working.[30]

In the Khrushchev era, training of scientific personnel expanded fourfold. In 1947, there were only 487 Kazakh scientific personnel in the entire republic. By 1963, there were 3,423, a sevenfold increase. Nevertheless, in 1950, only 2 percent of all scientists in the USSR worked in Kazakhstan. And in 1970, although Kazakhstan had over 5 percent of the nation's population, only 27,000 of 927,000 scientific workers (2.9 percent) worked in Kazakhstan. Of Kazakhstan's 13 million inhabitants in 1970, 33.3 percent were Kazakh, 42.4 percent were Russian. In Almaty, of 729,633 persons, only 12 percent of the inhabitants were Kazakh, and 70 percent Russian. What reason was there to build a reactor, given the dearth of scientific personnel?[31]

The first research in the area of nuclear physics commenced in 1946 at the Kirov Kazakh State University in the department of experimental physics (later the department of radiation physics). Taking advantage of clear skies and high altitudes, Astrophysical Institute scientists organized a laboratory of cosmic rays in 1950, but not without the significant self-interested help of Sergei Vavilov, Dmitrii Skobeltsyn, and Igor Tamm, whose Lebedev Institute colleagues in Moscow had long been engaged in cosmic ray research. Physics research received a boost from important geographical circumstances: In 1958, at the instigation of the Moscow physicists, a cosmic ray research center that was 3,340 meters above sea level was created at Tian-Shan and equipped with a Wilson cloud chamber and other equipment. Polish, Czech, Bulgarian, and Hungarian scientists frequented the Tian-Shan center, along with their brothers from the union republics. Several institutes eventually grew out of the small group of young Kazakh physicists in the laboratory as new directions of research developed: A Physical Technical Institute, which begat the Institute of Nuclear Physics in 1957, and in 1970, on the basis of its laboratories, an Institute of High Energy Physics. The pride of the high-energy physics institute was two underpowered BESM-4s and a BESM-6 IBM clone computers.[32] (Tian-Shan scientists now find themselves isolated from Russian and world science, without infusions of funds for research, and they struggle even to keep the station heated in the harsh alpinelike conditions.)

Beginning in 1957, the Institute of Nuclear Physics was built on a 450-hectare site; as usual, the "picturesque site" included apartments, a park, and a nearby swimming pool to contribute to a campus-like atmosphere. Laboratories of cosmic rays, spectral analysis, radioactivity, electronics, and physics of metals were transferred from the Physical Technical Institute. The two big-ticket items at the institute were a reactor and various accelerators. In 1959, engineers from the Efremov Institute of Electrophysical Apparatuses and a group of Kurchatov Institute specialists under L. M. Nemenov developed a 1.5-meter cyclotron for use by union republics. This device was designed to produce protons, ions, deuterons, and alpha particles. Such a cyclotron was installed at the Institute of Nuclear Physics in Kazakhstan in 1963. The Kirov Kazakh State University installed a U-10 linear accelerator in the same year that scientists used to irradiate seeds for the Institute of Botany and other higher educational institutions, for experiments with various catalyzers, and for radiation therapy at the Institute of Oncology and Radiology of the Kazakh Ministry of Health. In 1971, the physicists updated the cyclotron to increase the power of the protons, deuterons, and alpha particles produced.[33]

More crucial to Kazakh feelings of atomic brotherhood was the gift of a research reactor from Moscow. On October 30, 1967, in anticipation of the celebration of the fiftieth anniversary of the Great October Socialist Revolution, the research reactor of the Institute of Nuclear Physics, a ten-megawatt VVK-K model, reached criticality. Members of the Central Committee of the Kazakh Communist Party organization and the president of the Kazakh Academy attended the event; M. B. Beisebaev, chairman of the Kazakh Council of Ministers, operated the controls to bring the reactor on line, then congratulated the gathered scientists on a job well done and gave them various awards. The water-moderated, enriched uranium reactor produced neutrons and gamma rays to carry out a broad range of research in radiation physics, material science, physical chemistry, and other problems of applied nuclear physics. The reactor had several advantages: It had an intense neutron stream; long-term experiments could be conducted without shutdowns for refueling; its forty experimental channels were large and easy to load; and both low- and high-temperature loops in the active zone of the reactor could be used in experiments.[34]

The Uzbek Academy of Sciences also had an Institute of Nuclear Physics located in Kibrai, near Tashkent, the capital of the republic. Uzbekistan is all deserts and steppe. Sufficient water is provided by irrigation for growing cotton, vegetables, grain, grapes, and potatoes and for mining fossil fuel, gold, copper, tungsten, and aluminum. Textiles and food processing also are major industries. The republic has 23,000,000 inhabitants, 2,000,000 of whom live in Tashkent. The ethnic mix is eighty percent Uzbek, six percent Russian, five percent Tadjik, and three percent Kazakh. The Ulugbek Institute was named for a medieval astronomer. It was established in July 1956, eight months after Kurchatov had arrived in Tashkent and familiarized himself with Uzbek physicists and their work with radioisotopes in various regions of science and the economy. He gave his typical speech on the peaceful atom and promised to support them any way he could. By 1957, a reactor building had started to go up, along with apartments, stores, and schools for the scientists and their families. The center commissioned its reactor in September 1959. It was a 2,000-kilowatt VVR-SM, the first reactor of this type, and was the first of any kind in Central Asia.

In 1980, physicists under the direction of V. V. Goncharov of the Kurchatov Institute, reconstructed the unit at 10,000 kilowatts. The rebuilt reactor had forty vertical and nine horizontal channels, and a unique gamma source with a total activity of 470 curies. The main areas of research were nuclear physics, nuclear reactions, electronics, mass spectroscopy, radiation physics, and radiation chemistry. Between 1960 and 1964, the physicists installed a 150-centimeter A U-150-II Efremov cyclotron that produced protons up to 20 megaelectronvolts, deuterons to 24 megaelectronvolts, alpha particles to 50 megaelectronvolts, and ^{3}He nuclei to 35 megaelectronvolts. Later they added a radiochemical laboratory for isotope production and a 40-megaelectronvolt U-250 cyclotron. The institute eventually grew to twenty-four laboratories employing 300 scientists. Two firms, Radiopreparat (for isotope production) and Tezlatgich (for isotopes produced on cyclotrons), grew out of the institute. The physicists conducted research for the Central Asian division of VASKhNiL (the Lenin All-Union Academy of Agricultural Sciences) on plants, seeds, and polymers for geneticists; the experiments were mainly in support of the growing cotton and silk industries. They developed a device for cutting and splicing cable that was manufactured at Tashkentkabel Factory, and they were engaged in material science, including irradiation of carbon-graphite materials for a new generation of fission and fusion reactors. In keeping with the efforts of Brezhnev-era geophysicists and a Tashkent-Moscow cotton mafia, Ulugbek physicists were hooked into an effort to bring more water to cotton plantations. They came up with various ways to determine the specific gravity and moisture content of earth (soil) at great depth; and with scientists at the Institute of Water Problems and Hydrotechnology of the Uzbek Academy of Sciences, they worked on a series of practical problems to tame the resources of the Golodnaia Steppe: the dynamics of groundwater, the control of settling of the slopes of canals, and the diffusion of water and salt solutions.[35] The atom touched everyone, everything, every product, and every improvement.

LENINGRAD WANTS ITS OWN REACTOR

LFTI physicists by now envied not only their counterparts in Moscow but also those in Kazakhstan and Uzbekistan. At the Kurchatov Institute, the physicists had several reactors to play with, a fusion program second to none, and first priority in most funding decisions. How could the *fiztekhovtsy* be a greater part of the peaceful atom and contribute to its unfolding in the nation, as they had to physics generally? Not so much safety concerns as aesthetic ones led to the decision to build a branch of LFTI south of the city limits near Gatchina, where there was an astrophysical observatory. The LFTI physical plant was filled to the brim, especially after the assembly of the Alfa fusion facilities under Boris Konstantinov and Viktor Golant; they simply couldn't find a place to put a research reactor on its grounds. Perhaps not even the Soviet authorities would approve of operating a 10,000-kilowatt reactor in the Sosnovka Park, two kilometers from the institute's door. Gatchina had the advantages of open land far from residential areas and the presence of underutilized construction trusts.

While in Gatchina, the branch developed a close relationship with the Leningrad Polytechnical Institute, drawing students from the department of experimental nuclear physics. In 1960, a short-sighted decision to forbid scientists to work in two or more places at once and earn several salaries nearly destroyed the pedagogical relationship, but Gatchina physicists continued to teach without pay. At first, the workers commuted from Leningrad, but eventually fifty percent of the Gatchina employees moved into newly built apartments nearby. The third director of Ioffe's institute, Boris Pavlovich Konstantinov, saw to it that Leningrad had its own research reactor.

Konstantinov was a much beloved son of Leningrad. His career took a rather circuitous route from abrasives and musical instruments to high-energy physics and from an acoustic laboratory to the vice presidency of the Academy of Sciences in charge of nuclear energy research.[36] Born in St. Petersburg in 1910, he, his six brothers and three sisters, and his parents left for the countryside around Kostroma in 1918 because of the famine that had begun to grip the city; they remained there until 1924. His father, a construction foreman of peasant roots, died in 1919 of typhus; his mother, a housewife, died in 1930. All his brothers and sisters had advanced degrees and worked as scientists or engineers in Moscow, Leningrad, or Sverdlovsk. Konstantinov audited courses in the physics-mathematics department at Leningrad Polytechnical Institute from 1926 through 1929, simultaneously working as a laboratory assistant in the Physical Technical Institute, where his older brother, Aleksandr, worked on various alarm systems for state banks and museums. Aleksandr simultaneously worked in L. S. Termen's radiophysical laboratory, where Termen had developed an early orchestral synthesizer whose concerts drew huge Leningrad crowds. Boris's friends, who included Kikoin, Flerov, Kurchatov, and Aleksandrov, called him "Bobik." They were young, idealistic, and enthusiastic about physics, working long hours, often into the night.

From 1930 through 1937, Boris Konstantinov was senior laboratory assistant, engineer, and researcher at the Leningrad Electrophysical Institute (that had separated from LFTI into an independent facility). There he turned to problems of acoustics, ultrahigh frequencies, and architectural and musical acoustics, simultaneously working as a consultant for the Leningrad "Ilich" Abrasives Factory and a laboratory of the Baku-Shellarskii Water Main. He published his first article at this time on the breakage of turbine blades. Although lacking higher education, Konstantinov found friends among such leading young physicists as Iakov Zeldovich, whose first wife was Konstantinov's sister. In 1937, Konstantinov accepted a position as head of the laboratory of musical instruments. From 1940 until his death in 1969, he worked in the astrophysical department of the Leningrad Physical Technical Institute, defending in 1943 a doctoral dissertation entitled "Hydrodynamic Sound Formation and Propagation of Sound in an Organic Medium." From this time on, however, Konstantinov no longer studied acoustics, turning largely to plasma physics and isotopes. In 1947, he commenced teaching at the Polytechnical Institute and headed departments of experimental nuclear physics and physics of isotopes, becoming dean of the physics-mathematics department in 1962.

The students respected Konstantinov for his erudition, devotion, friendliness, and effervescent smile. The postwar years were particularly difficult because shortages of food, clothes, and housing hit students particularly hard. The students in the department lived as one family, and some of the leaders turned to Konstantinov at times for financial assistance. He would ask, "How much do you need?" and fork over the money. Because of his involvement in the isotope industry, the authorities provided an airplane for his frequent trips to sites. The students referred to his behavior as the "Konstantinov tunnel effect," for he might enter the room and leave through another door on a business trip. In spite of his frequent scheduled and unscheduled trips, he rarely missed a lecture. He assisted students in securing positions at the new institutes arising in Kazakhstan and Uzbekistan, signing travel blanks as required so that a student might freely consult on site.

From 1957 until 1967, Konstantinov directed the Ioffe Institute, simultaneously serving as editor of *Zhurnal tekhnicheskoi fiziki*. Konstantinov was the third director of LFTI. (Most scientists refuse even to utter the name of the second, A. P. Komar, because of his role in the removal of Ioffe.) Several physicists behaved rudely toward Ioffe after his removal. But Konstantinov always turned to him with deep respect. While thereafter refusing to set foot within the institute's doors, Ioffe himself approved of the choice of Konstantinov. Konstantinov, for his part, frequently visited Ioffe in the latter's new Institute of Semiconductors to ask for advice. Under Konstantinov, LFTI rediscovered its tradition and grew in several directions: nuclear physics, astrophysics, fusion, and theory. Eventually, its nuclear physics division became the independent Gatchina institute, the Leningrad Institute of Nuclear Physics (LIIaF).

In his last years, Konstantinov served in the upper reaches of the Academy of Sciences, the State Committee on Science and Technology, and other administrations. Trusted as a Party member from 1959, he frequently traveled abroad. He served in the Leningrad Party committee, the Supreme Soviet of the Russian Republic, and other Party positions. He won several high awards, including a Hero of Socialist Labor and a State prize. Unfortunately, these responsibilities took a heavy toll on Konstantinov. He smoked heavily and rarely exercised, having long since abandoned skiing. (After once seeing Igor Tamm engaged in water skiing, however, Konstantinov ordered the Gatchina branch of the institute to provide this distraction for staff members.) He could hardly handle a flight of stairs. He suffered from arrhythmia. A heart attack killed him in 1969.

Konstantinov's postwar research was connected with the atomic bomb project and the separation of heavy and light isotopes, including the development of industrial methods. He established a laboratory of research on physical and chemical properties of isotopes. In the last ten years of his life, Konstantinov turned to another basic task: controlled thermonuclear synthesis and the problem of methods of measurement of high temperatures arising in plasma apparatuses. He propagandized the peaceful atom and fusion, seeking international collaboration in this area of research.[37] Other fusion specialists like Iakov Zeldovich loved him dearly, not the least for his interest in their work. Konstantinov had also turned to astrophysics, having long been interested in the physics of comets and meteor showers. Under his direction, the institute formed a department of astrophysics; and he used his positions in the Academy to order experiments on airplanes, high-altitude balloons, and satellites. A final area of interest was holography and television.

But even a bigwig like Konstantinov had trouble overcoming standard barriers to research, with his requests for equipment sometimes falling on deaf ears. As academic secretary, Konstantinov had to solve all sorts of questions: difficulties providing long-promised modern computers to institutes, the purchase of copying machines abroad for the Academy of Sciences library in Leningrad, purchases of scientific instruments with hard currency, an inconclusive investigation into the fact that one S. P. Grinevich, pilot of the flight of a TU-104 from Kiev to Leningrad, saw a UFO in September 1968, challenges in setting up the Tian-Shan cosmic ray station.[38]

Konstantinov, like his nuclear mentor Kurchatov, was on the spot when the VVR-M came on line in Gatchina. K. A. Konoplev, later deputy director of LIIaF, was barely thirty years old when he was appointed chief engineer for reactor operations. The rest of his crew were equally young. They waited for the Kurchatov Institute reactor start-up brigade to arrive, and nobody came, and no one gave the order to bring the reactor on line. Further confusing the issue, virtually everyone had gotten permission to go on vacation right after start-up. Konstantinov gave the order to wait only a little longer for the Kurchatov brigade, then "Start it up yourselves." They did, on July 5, 1960, but it did not reach full power until half a year later, well after their vacations had ended.

Konstantinov saw to it that LIIaF grew into a nuclear center with radiobiological, radiochemical, and astrophysical divisions. Ultimately, there were three major sectors: a laboratory of high-energy physics, molecular and radiation biophysics, and neutron research. In 1963, the physicists developed a ten year plan for the branch, including in it a new experimental workshop, buildings for control-measuring instruments and for the manufacture of deuterium bubble chambers, a building for the synchrotron, a machine shop, and a pool for staff. All this cost ten million rubles, but Konstantinov signed off on the plan without hesitation.

In 1965, they commenced construction on a big one-gigaelectronvolt synchrocyclotron in Gatchina. But having a vice president of the Academy of Sciences as its director did not guarantee LIIaF success in scientific matters. In December 1967, leading officials from the division of nuclear physics, the Lebedev Institute, and NIIEFA gathered to address the problem that a new synchrotron, designed for 1,000 megaelectronvolts, would never surpass the 750-megaelectronvolt level achieved the previous month because of persistent technical problems. Significant redesign and recalibration was called for.[39] By the end of the Soviet era, the accelerator was more a "stand," for other accelerators had surpassed it in power and luminescence. LIIaF physicists awaited the opening of the UNK-3 in Sarpukov or traveled to other facilities in Siberia, Geneva, or Batavia for research. They used the high-energy protons for medical purposes, treating aneurysms and tumors, with a self-proclaimed eighty to ninety-five percent success rate for tumors, and a seventy to seventy-five percent success rate for aneurysms.

FROM THE BALTIC STATES TO THE CAUCASUS

Estonia, Lithuania, and Latvia had experienced only two decades of independence when they were conquered by Soviet armies in World War II. This happened after the signing of the Hitler-Stalin "non-aggression pact" in 1939, through which the two dictators agreed to divide eastern Europe. The Baltic states were considered republics of the great socialist motherland by Russian chauvinists in Moscow, but they were never recognized as such by Western democracies, who retained embassies in these nations until they gained freedom in 1991. The Baltic states were always European looking in terms of culture and science, and had among the highest literacy and educational attainment rates of all the peoples in the former Soviet Union. A number of its educated elite recognized what Soviet power might do for the development of various branches of science and technology, and they pushed for a recasting of the national academies of sciences into the Soviet form and the expansion of the physical sciences. Therefore, when Kurchatov promised to promote the peaceful atom in the union republics, Baltic scientists clamored for their share of investment and for indigenous training, research, and power generation programs. The major artifacts of the Soviet program are the IRT-2000 research reactor in Salaspils, Latvia and the largest RBMK reactors in the world, two 1,500-megawatt units at Ignalina, Lithuania. Other RBMKs were promised, but fortunately they were never built.

Latvian physicists proudly observed that Latvia had been an agrarian country only two decades earlier, but thanks to the help of the "multinational family of Soviet peoples," not only had Latvia repaired the great wounds of World War II, but it had also developed into an industrial power, the center of which was electrical, instrument, agricultural, and transportation machine building industries. Of the three Baltic states, Latvia had the largest percentage of Russian citizens: of 2.4 million inhabitants, fifty-two percent were Latvian and thirty-four percent were Russian. And, although Latvia has limited natural resources, it had a productive agricultural sector (grain, potatoes, sugar beets, vegetables, and animal husbandry) and metalworking and chemical processing industries.[40] As part of the emphasis on the mechanization and automation of all processes during the Khrushchev period, radioisotope apparatuses (such as those designed to control the manufacturing process) were first introduced into Latvia in 1955, somewhat later than in other republics. The Latvian government established a committee to speed up the assimilation of radioisotopes, work that it coordinated with various republican and national planning and atomic energy commissions. The Riga Electrotechnical Factory manufactured some of the first Soviet instruments for industrial control processes. In 1959, Latvian industrialists organized a design bureau, Avtoelektropribor, to manufacture various radioisotope devices to automate the control of thickness and strength of steel alloys. But most isotope devices in Latvia came from the Tallinn, Estonia factory "KIP" and were used in the Sarkandaugava Glass Factory, Liepaisk Linoleum Factory, Riga Butterfat Combine, Blazma Leather Shoe Combine, and Sloka Cellulose-Paper Combine.[41]

The Salaspils IRT-2000 boiling-water research reactor was located twenty kilometers from Riga, the capital of Latvia. Sitting in the picturesque countryside, it was the result of a multinational effort. Enterprises from Moscow, Leningrad, Belarus, and Ukraine provided material and equipment for the reactor. Kurchatov Institute physicists joined those from the Georgian Academy of Sciences in its assembly. It came on line in the first months of 1962. A part of the Institute of Physics of the Latvian Academy of Sciences, the reactor also served researchers at the Riga Polytechnical Institute in an extensive program of radiochemistry and material science, biological research, and nuclear physics. This IRT-2000 had two hot chambers, one of which was served by a liquid-metal radiation loop. The liquid metal, an indium and gallium alloy, circulated through the active zone, became highly radioactive, and provided gamma radiation equivalent to 20 kilograms of radium, ten times cheaper than irradiation using cobalt-60. The physicists determined that irradiation produced such valuable materials as heat-resistant polyethylene, a concrete-polymer stronger than regular concrete (with ninety-five percent less water absorption and three times greater frost strength), tires with fifteen to twenty percent longer life, and softwoods that mimicked hardwoods in strength and beauty (for example, the parquet used in the "Kiev" Moscow Metro station). How they planned to irradiate more than a handful of items at a time without building dozens of hot chambers and what the chambers would cost were topics rarely discussed, although the Latvian Institute of Chemistry of Wood planned to build an experimental facility to demonstrate the possibilities of nuclear parquet.[42]

In Georgia, as in Latvia, physicists acquired an IRT-2000 reactor, which came on line in 1959, not far from Tbilisi. It was used for low-temperature and solid state physics research connected with the Georgian Institute of Physics. They also irradiated proteins, heavy elements in human blood, and nucleic acid. In Belarus, a third IRT-2000 reactor opened in May 1962 not far from Minsk in the Institute of Nuclear Research of the Belorussian Academy of Sciences. The institute staff then added an accelerator, radiochemical, isotope, and several other laboratories. They also had various gamma sources (equivalent to more than 40 kilograms of radium) for research in nuclear energetics, radiochemistry, solid state physics, nuclear spectroscopy, biology (selection), and physiology. Later they built the "Roza" and "Liliia" critical stands (1965) and a complex apparatus to study the thermal characteristics of chemically reacting gases. This latter device was part of the effort to use nitrogen, helium, and carbon dioxide in breeder reactors. Aleksandr Krasin, who participated in the start-up of the first Obninsk station and gave a paper on the Obninsk reactor at the second Geneva conference, had good connections with Blokhintsev and Dollezhal. These ties gave him access to resources and authority when he moved back to Belarus and the new institute. He was convinced that thermal and fast fission reactors were the key to the energy future of USSR and Belarus.[43]

By 1970, Soviet-designed research reactors had spread across ten time zones of the Soviet empire and into eastern Europe. There were forty-two reactors in all, in such far-flung places as Tashkent, Kiev, Tbilisi, Riga (Salaspils), Minsk, Almaty, Tomsk, Obninsk, Arzamas, Norilsk, Moscow (with ten), Khimki (just outside of Moscow, with four), Lytkarina, Leningrad (with four), Sosnovyi Bor (with four at the Scientific Research Technology Institute, which specializes in reactors for submarines, and is near the Leningrad "Lenin" set of four RBMKs), Gatchina, Dmitrovgrad (Melekess, with seven), and Semipalatinsk (with three). Between 1957 and 1961, Minsredmash also built research reactors in "countries of peoples' democracies" (see Appendix, Tables 17 and 18).

Perhaps the Armenian brothers and sisters felt some kind of inferiority toward their big Russian brothers. They had a tradition of cosmic ray research connected with the Alikhanov brothers, and a six-gigaelectronvolt accelerator. But they wanted more, perhaps a reactor or two—in particular, they wanted power-generating reactors. They had a bigwig to go to bat for them, another representative of the Ioffe school, Viktor Amazaspovich Ambartsumian. He was a specialist in astrophysics and head of the Biurakanskaia Observatory. Author of *Theoretical Astrophysics* (published in English in 1958), he promoted the atom in Armenia, even as he focused on the heavens. The Armenians were Christians of an ancient culture who talked about their contribution to world civilization in smelting in the third century at the same time that they mentioned their achievements in cosmic research, nuclear research, high-energy physics, quantum electrodynamics, and the physics of crystals. Although at the time of the revolution, there were few higher educational institutions, and before World War II, there was little modern physics in Armenia to speak of, by the mid-1970s there were 150 different science institutes and the desire for a reactor.

To sell the reactor to the Armenian public required considerable effort, judging from the press reports that explained the difference between a nuclear bomb and a reactor, and the difference between the military designs of the United States and the peaceful ones of the Soviet Union. On the thirty-first anniversary of Hiroshima, to show their true feelings about atoms for peace and American hypocrisy, the Central Committee of the Armenian Komsomol held a contest among welders at the construction site for the two Armenian VVER-440 reactors at Metsamor. A "highly qualified professional," a twenty-nine-year-old laborer finished his weld on a ninety-millimeter pipe in thirteen minutes and won, acetylene torches down. Even with welders racing to completion, nuclear power was safer than automobiles, cleaner than fossil fuel, and less risky to a citizen's health than fire, explosion, earthquake, hurricane, and dam failure. Plant personnel lamented only the fact that these were tiny 440-megawatt stations, hardly competitive with the now standard 1,000-megawatt units, but still necessary because of the growth in electrical energy demand—from 9.15 billion kilowatt-hours to 11.5 billion kilowatt-hours from 1975 to 1980—and the absence of oil, gas, and coal in Armenia.[44]

Only when they spoke about construction practices did the Armenian station promoters foreshadow the real problem with the station. It was built on an active earthquake fault. And they acknowledged that in 1974, of 328 apartment houses built in Armenia (and what's the difference between concrete apartments and concrete reactors?), only 12 were rated "excellent," with half "satisfactory," and the rest below standard. So they would require real Komsomol shock work. Indeed, when an earthquake struck Armenia in December 1988, killing 25,000 persons, one of the major causes of death was the collapse of apartment structures. After the 1988 earthquake, there was no choice other than to close Armenia nuclear reactors 1 and 2. In January 1989, they were shut down, at a loss to the country of 5.5 billion kilowatt-hours annually. (There had been accidents at the site even before it shut down. In October 1982, a fire ravaged 500 meters of safety systems. On another occasion in 1982, pumps to keep cooling water circulating over the reactor core failed. Many of the personnel ran from the station to their cars and didn't stop driving until they had reached Erevan. The handful of employees who remained managed to get reserve pumps circulating water again before a catastrophic core meltdown occurred.) They estimated that it would take at least three years to replace the nuclear station with a fossil fuel plant. But the fossil fuel plant was never built, and, because of the cost to the economy of the resulting shortfall of energy production (37 percent of the electrical energy of the republic), there was no choice but to restart the reactors in the mid-1990s.[45]

When the Armenian station was closed in January 1989, the minister of atomic energy, N. Lukonin, said that any rumors about restarting the reactors at some time in the future were totally unfounded. "It will never happen." Yet as soon as the Soviet Union disappeared, talk began about restarting Metsamor. This, of course, required Russian assistance, the assistance of MinAtom, the delivery of fuel, and the return of waste and spent fuel rods for processing, disposal, and storage. A group of Armenian physicists, part of the great diaspora of Armenians across the globe—in this case, Moscow—signed an "agreement" that gave Russia the responsibility for operating the station and its consequences. Even though President Boris Yeltsin and President Levon Ter-Petrosian of Armenia declared their support, stumbling blocks appeared because Armenia could not guarantee safe operation of the outdated VVER-440 reactors and had not signed the IAEA and nonproliferation treaties. Evidently, Armenian engineers never had any doubt about reopening the station. It remains in pristine form, with the exception of toilets stolen from the living quarters.[46]

THE KIEV REACTOR

But all of the programs in all of the other republics were nothing compared with the program that was moving forward in Ukraine. In 1956 in Kiev, the Ukrainian Academy of Sciences held a special session that was attended by 800 persons. They heard over one hundred talks on potential applications of nuclear power. The highlight of the meeting was Blokhintsev's lengthy speech about the Obninsk reactor. It was a foregone conclusion that the Ukrainian Academy would earmark additional funds for research in nuclear and high-energy physics. Within a year, fifteen different Ukrainian research institutes were carrying out research on general questions of nuclear physics, the utilization of radioisotopes, and nuclear radiation on more than fifty projects seen as vital to agriculture, industry, mining, and metallurgy programs. In 1958, Kiev University added a department of nuclear physics. The Academy's presidium then created two special scientific councils, staffed with scientists, planners, and Party officials to coordinate basic and applied research throughout the republic, one on nuclear physics and one on nuclear energy. Soon they established commissions on radiochemistry and radiobiology. Ukraine became a member of the International Atomic Energy Agency. From the end of the 1950s on, Ukraine hosted a series of international congress on high-energy physics, nuclear physics, and fusion.

The Institute of Physics in Kiev, unlike UFTI, was an academy institute and hence not so completely tied to military tasks or bound by classified research. It was a leader in basic nuclear research. A reactor, electrostatic generator, low-voltage neutron generator, and several cyclotrons stood at the center of their experimental efforts. M. V. Pasechnik, director of the institute, intended to establish the equivalent of a Kurchatov Institute with all of the perquisites and prestige associated with nuclear know-how. Between 1958 and 1965 alone, the Institute of Physics grew nearly threefold. In that period, the total number of employees increased from 344 to 843; and the number of scientists grew from 48 to 172, including an increase in the number of candidates of science from 32 to 48 and doctors of science from 7 to 12. Their annual operating budget swelled from 1.1 million to 2.7 million rubles.[47]

The construction of the VVR-M 10,000-kilowatt research reactor at the same time as similar reactors were being built at Gatchina and Almaty was part of Pasechnik's master plan. Kurchatov personally supported the construction of the reactor and the acquisition of isotopes for research. In fact, the last business trip of his life was in January 1960, when he traveled to Kiev and Kharkiv. These visits led to the last publication of his life, an article in *Pravda* in which he praised the achievements of his Ukrainian colleagues. As a sign of the reactor's importance, builders from all the major Ukrainian construction organizations—Glavkievstroi, Ukrpromstroi, Kievspetsstroi, Kievotdelstroi, and Stroimekhanizatsii—and researchers at secret Ukrainian post office boxes were put to work on it. The reactor required 40 kilometers of cable, 25 kilometers of piping, and 570 instruments produced by more than 80 different organizations. If only apartment housing had merited as much attention, Ukrainians would not have lived three and four to a room—in many cases, without hot water and gas.

Dozens of bigwig national and republican Party and Academy of Sciences officials were invited to the start-up of the unit, including USSR Academy president A. N. Nesmianov, Prime Minister N. V. Podgornyi, and N. A. Nikolaev, a leading official of Minsredmash. In his remarks before the assembled luminaries, A. V. Palladin, president of the Ukrainian Academy, said that the reactor symbolized the fraternal help of the Soviet Academy, design bureaus and factories of MinAtom, and all the other union republics, and represented one more step on the path to the creation of a communist society.[48] The reactor went critical on February 12, 1960. Testing and calibration of the equipment, meters, and control devices was carried out from February through June, and in August, the reactor reached an output of 5,000 kilowatts. From September through the end of the year, the physicists did not exceed this power as they mastered operation. Beginning in 1961, they commenced a systematic study of different materials and biological subjects (cells, mice, rats, rabbits) by using the reactor's various horizontal, biological, and isotope channels. These studies were conducted under contracts with Academy institutes of biochemistry, microbiology, metal physics, sheet metal production, and mineral resources, and UFTI.

As soon as the reactor came on line, a joint government-scientific council to coordinate nuclear research and promote atomic energy was established. The council met first in March 1961 to discuss how to bring dozens of applications to socialist Ukraine—from biomedicine to agrophysiology, theoretical nuclear physics to fossil dating, high-energy physics to nuclear structure and solid state physics. But, in order to achieve these ends, the participants in this meeting recognized the need to train more physicists, offer more university courses, build more equipment (especially accelerators), expand the manufacture of standard apparatuses, and popularize peaceful applications.[49] They opened an "Isotope" store in Kiev like those in Moscow and other cities. This store provided isotopes and simple equipment to enterprises, factories, and universities (and to individuals only after they completed large amounts of paperwork). Departments of experimental nuclear physics were established at Kharkiv and Kiev State Universities in cooperation with UFTI and the Institute of Physics, respectively. At subsequent meetings, physicists called for broader applications in industry and agriculture, and for the development of nuclear engineering for potential electrical energy production. The Ukrainian State Committee on Science and Technology had a standing committee on applications to support all of these efforts.[50]

From this time forward, periodic meetings were held in Lviv, Donetsk, Kiev, and Kharkiv to promote peaceful applications throughout Ukraine. At a meeting in Donetsk in April 1963 of the commission for application of radioisotopes of the Donetsk economic region, the participants indicated their pleasure at the assimilation of instruments based on isotopes in the coke, coal, and coal mining machine building industries. But they criticized a significant lag in the introduction of similar instruments in general machine building, owing in part to poor "propaganda" efforts of the Central Bureau of Technical Information. The commission sent workers from Ukrainian laboratories to enterprises in Estonia and Latvia to learn from their greater success. And there was another problem. In many cases, factories shipped out instruments, but (as was typical for the USSR) there was no money for installation and no on-site instruction on how to operate them. Somehow, there had been savings of 1.2 million rubles from the 408 instruments installed at 58 enterprises connected largely with metallurgy and mining such as Giproniselektroshakht in Donetsk and Luganskugleavtomatika in Lugansk.[51] In real terms, however, the savings were only one and a half man-years of labor per factory.

In June 1963, physicists, industrial managers, engineers, Party officials, and representatives of the Ministry of Health gathered at the second republican conference on nuclear physics and nuclear energy. Valter was chairman of the organizing committee. There were 175 delegates from nearly three dozen organizations, including 41 individuals from industrial enterprises in Kharkiv, Kiev, Donetsk, Dnepropetrovsk, Krivoi Rog, Makeevkka, and Zhdanov. The participants heard reports on the two years of research conducted on the VVR-M reactor, on construction of a 100-megaelectronvolt proton cyclotron at UFTI, and on establishment of a laboratory of nuclear physics at Dnepropetrovsk State University. But most of their attention focused on the efforts to apply nuclear know-how in industry and agriculture through improved production of various instruments and control devices. A lag in the introduction of radiobiological techniques in agriculture suggested not only production bottlenecks in the manufacture of new instruments but also continued challenges in overcoming the Lysenkoist legacy in biology.[52]

In a fifteen year plan set forth at this time, physicists noted a wide range of research tasks utilizing the reactor's ten experimental channels. These included irradiation of blood proteins and types to determine the impact of neutron radiation on blood's electrophysical qualities; the insertion of rabbits and rats into experimental channels of the active zone at high doses two to three times weekly; irradiation of various pathogenic bacteria; irradiation of DNA and other proteins to produce mutations and determine changes to their structure; irradiation of embryos for the Institute of Zoology; and various other programs for the Institutes of Physiology and of Microbiology. They used the reactor to produce short-lived radioisotopes. A series of other material science, spectrographic, neutron physics, thermal exchange, and quantum liquid topics complemented this research. By 1966, personnel had turned to tasks closely associated with the development of atomic energetics (power stations, submarines, icebreakers): fuel rods and composition, safety, control mechanisms, and fast neutron research. Much of this work involved the burgeoning Ukrainian nuclear energy program and the safety and stability of the RBMKs going up at Chernobyl, especially concerning creep, brittleness, corrosion, and other technical defects of the channels of the RBMKs. The physicists were involved in the search for applications in a series of programs of the Ukrainian Academy of Sciences including "Atomic Energetics," "Production of Light Alloys," "Potato," and "Food."[53] No matter what the plans of the institute physicists were, the various commissions, committees, and economic organizations pressed them to produce an immediate economic impact from any activity.

These programs and the natural growth of the institute led to the natural decision to form an independent institute based on the accelerator and the reactor facilities. Because a road ran between the Institute of Physics and those facilities, in 1970 it was a simple matter to create the Institute of Nuclear Research just across the street. The main directions of research at the new institute continue to be fundamental and applied research in the area of nuclear physics of middle and low energies, nuclear energetics, radiation physics and radiation material science, solid state physics, neutron spectroscopy, and plasma physics and fusion. At its founding, there were 915 employees in the new institute. Of the institute's 193 scientists, only 59 had advanced degrees. By 1975, there were 1,141 employees. Of these, 210 were scientists (11 doctors and 90 candidates of science). The institute grew even more by the mid-1980s, at which time it had two cyclotrons from NIIEFA (a U-240 and a U-120), the VVR-M reactor, an EG-5 electrostatic generator (also from NIIEFA), and an M-30 microtron. Physicists conducted research jointly with scientists in Dubna, Gatchina, Troitsk, the Kurchatov Institute, Moscow State University, and the Khlopin Radium Institute.

Roughly four-fifths of the new institute's budget came from state line-item appropriations, with the rest coming from contracts with various industrial, medical, and agricultural organizations. Some of these contracts involved manufacture of tritium targets for nuclear generators with higher thermal efficiency for Obninsk, protein mutation in grain, instruments to measure changes in materials and weld joints in technical channels of RBMKs (to improve their reliability in the event of a leak), irradiation of potatoes to increase shelf life (using an experimental cobalt-60 source), ion generators, and electrostatic neutralizers. The Iagotinskaia Bird Factory had forty-five unipolar ion generators at work, and the Stavropol Factory of Chemical Reagents employed radioisotopes to neutralize static electricity. A contract with Ukrgidroproekt and the South Ukraine Atomic Power Stations supported an investigation of ways to utilize water from cooling ponds for irrigation of arable land, even while it was radioactively and thermally somewhat "hot."[54]

Indeed, much of the institute's work from the mid-1980s onward focused on research and the safety and reliability of atomic power stations that had begun to spread throughout the Soviet empire's southern tier. In cooperation with the Ukrainian ministries of higher education, energy, and the Academy of Sciences, O. F. Nemets, then director of the institute, established a large working group involving several laboratories whose activities included development of control mechanisms for the VVER-440 being installed in Armenia (together with the Kurchatov Institute) and comparison of calculations with actual operating parameters in the Chernobyl reactors. Physicists claimed that reactivity instruments they had designed assisted the engineers at the Rovenskaia station to cut start-up times in half, saving 110,000 rubles. They developed various software programs to ensure radiation safety around Chernobyl. They were working with the Institute of Technical Heat Engineering on problems connected with boiling water in heat channels. With specialists at the Institute of Hydromechanics, they worked on a new method of determining the nature and use of thermal pollution from huge atomic energy stations. With the Institute of Hydrobiology of the Academy, they estimated the impact of the hot effluent of the South Ukraine station on reservoirs. The institute mixed physics and pleasure on the occasion of the sixtieth anniversary of the formation of the Soviet Union by fulfilling before its target date the research on "dynamics of heating of plasma in tokamaks" and "strengthening the patriotic and international upbringing of youth on the revolution, military and labor traditions of the Communist Party of the Soviet Union and of the Soviet people."[55]

Much of the correspondence of the directors of the institute involved demonstrating to higher instances that their research had an immediate economic effect, usually measured in the hundreds of thousands of rubles. They created new laboratories to focus on how to use waste heat, and new laboratories of radiation material science, nuclear safety, radiobiology, and the theory of perspectives of nuclear energetics. Toward these ends, the institute had grown to 2,200 employees (including 190 with advanced degrees) and 22 departments covering all aspects of nuclear physics, radiation material science, and plasma physics. Twenty academy institutes used the VVR-M, which operated consistently at ten megawatts. The U-120 operated for an average of 500 hours monthly, or about eighty-five percent of the time in a six-day week.[56]

UKRAINE: NUCLEAR CAPITAL OF THE EMPIRE

Ukraine bore the brunt of nuclear power engineering in the former Soviet Union. Of forty-four reactors (excluding Bilibino), thirteen were in Ukraine and the Smolensk RBMKs were not far from Ukrainian borders. There would have been more at Chernobyl, and in Odessa and Crimea and at Khmelnitskaia, had the breakup of the Soviet Union not allowed antinuclear activism to grow into a national independence movement. Still, on the eve of the breakup of the USSR, Ukraine produced fifty percent of electrical energy from atomic energy,[57] and the authorities planned to build another six units in the Chernobyl park (see Appendix, Table 19).

If few grasped the long-term implications of the Gorbachev revolution for the Soviet Union itself, they understood immediately its implication for nuclear power. Anatolii Aleksandrov had aged and could no longer provide the leadership that he had provided for two decades, even though his institute remained at the pinnacle of the scientific establishment. Elsewhere, from Obninsk to Leningrad, from Ignalina to Arzamas, scientists wondered aloud about problems of radioactive waste, the absence of containment in older reactors, and the feasibility of expanding RBMKs beyond their present size. Even in Obninsk, you could hear a few voices of concern. The real turning point was the following April and Chernobyl, when even the most avid supporters of nuclear energy had to support a moratorium on RBMK construction. A series of reactors from Armenia to Lithuania were subsequently shut down.[58]

The physics research centers in Kiev, Kharkiv, and Tbilisi had begun to age even before the Chernobyl disaster. The cost of research in Latvia, Kazakhstan, and Uzbekistan was too much to bear. The government could ill afford to upgrade facilities everywhere. The glory days of the 1950s and early 1960s had given way to the economic pressures of the arms race, Siberian development, and housing and food programs. Well-trained physicists with dozens of publications had replaced Sinelnikov, Valter, and Leipunskii, but few of them commanded their predecessors' authority. Aging concrete nuclear boilers stand where there were once mighty power reactors. Vital research institutes are now empty corridors. Physicists continue to gather in the control room of the linear accelerator at UFTI, but not to run experiments, for they cannot buy electricity. Instead, they watch bad American kung-fu and pornographic films. At Gatchina, plans to build a new experimental 100-megawatt reactor, the PIK, were put on hold, first by citizen opposition, and now by lack of funds. In the spring of 1993, the U-240 accelerator at the Institute of Physics in Kiev was closed down because the institute couldn't pay for electricity. The head of the cyclotron department, Aleksandr Valkov, explained that the apparatus was one of the most energy-consuming in the institute. If it operated normally, they couldn't afford to pay any salaries. The most they could do was run the machine a week or two per month, but they finally shut it down.[59] Reactors to the republics! The slogan now breeds fear. The remnants of atomic-powered communism—Ignalina, Chernobyl, and Beloiarsk—will be with the Lithuanian, Ukrainian, and Russian citizens for centuries to come, and the excitement of path-breaking discoveries of decades past has become a painful memory.

8

Nuclear Explosions:
Peaceful and Otherwise

*An increasing volume of resources went to the creation of facilities that had no
direct relationship to nuclear power engineering. Capacities for the manufacture
of fuel elements were established, capacities in metallurgy, a vast majority
of construction resources went to setting up facilities unrelated to [original tasks]
. . . Scientific organizations which were at one time the most powerful in the
country became weak, the share of . . . modern equipment began to decline,
the personnel aged, new approaches were rejected. The rhythm of work became
a habit, as did the approach to the solution of this or that problem . . . A
generation of engineers matured who were skilled at their own work but who did
not perceive in a critical fashion the very apparatuses and systems themselves.*
—Academician and Chernobyl liquidator Valerii Legasov,
shortly before his suicide on April 27, 1988

The Soviet nuclear energy establishment intended the Lenin Chernobyl Nuclear
Power Station to be the paragon for nuclear energetics. Four reactors opened by
1985, another two were under construction, and planners expected to use the construction brigades who lived in nearby Pripiat to erect four more. At 1,000 megawatts each, the fantastic complex would symbolize for Soviet leaders and physicists
precisely the essence of atomic-powered communism: mighty concrete palaces,
energy too cheap to meter, the freeing of citizens from manual labor by wondrous,
electrically powered machines, mastery of modern science and technology indicating the superiority of the socialist system over the capitalist one, and the taming of

nature to serve the interests of society—as defined, of course, by the political-scientific leadership. But the atomic-powered communism that Chernobyl embodied was something else: institutional momentum, absence of public science that precluded the formation of a safety culture, the premature rush to standardization of still developing and not entirely understood large-scale technological systems, and above all else, technological arrogance. Atomic-powered communism created the preconditions for the terrible accident of April 26, 1986, an accident that killed thirty-one persons outright, ejected ninety million curies of radioactivity into the atmosphere (xenon, krypton, iodine, cesium, strontium, and other radioisotopes), effectively destroyed the homes of hundreds of thousands of people (who were belatedly evacuated, although many of the elderly returned to abandoned shacks to live out their lives), ruined productive farm and forest land, exposed vulnerable children to radioisotopes of iodine, strontium, and cesium that will raise levels of leukemia and thyroid cancer, and led to the premature deaths of up to fifty thousand persons.

The Chernobyl catastrophe was the decisive event in modern Soviet history. Mikhail Gorbachev had unleashed the forces of glasnost (openness) and perestroika (restructuring). There would be no way to keep the true meaning of Chernobyl from the citizen, even though self-serving officials initially tried to underplay the dangers, hesitated to order the evacuation of nearby residents, and then obscured many of the details of the accident. Chernobyl led citizens to recognize that technology, which they had seen as a panacea for Soviet social, economic, and political problems, was not inherently safe, nor were its operators infallible. The benefits of living in modern industrial society came with certain risks. Newspapers, journals, television, and radio were engaged in cleansing revelations about the many accidents that had befallen Soviet workers as they built dams, flew into the cosmos, and powered the factory with the atom. They learned of myriad fires and explosions at waste facilities and in reactors, accidents that had gone "underreported." They now understood that the Soviet bus, the automobile, the airplane, too, had frequently crashed and burned.

But it was the "peaceful profession" of the nuclear engineer that lost the greatest luster of technological infallibility. Having touted applications in medicine, industry, and agriculture, mining and metallurgy, the engineer had to admit publicly that the rush to commercialization of nuclear technology in its Soviet form had been a mistake. That the nuclear establishment of Russia, as symbolized by the powerful Ministry of Atomic Energy, MinAtom, continues to promote nuclear energy as a panacea for Russia indicates only an unwillingness to confront crucial issues that have plagued nuclear engineers throughout the world since the dawn of the nuclear age. These issues include the failure to deal adequately in any way with the vast quantities of low- and high-level radioactive waste produced during fifty years of peaceful and military adventure; the high-risk, low-benefit nature of many applications; and the indefatigable search for problems to be solved with the power of the atom when traditional ways of engineering and science are more than adequate, and when nuclear engineers ought to be searching, not for problems to solve, but for solutions to problems that already exist. Unfortunately, Chernobyl was not the only explosion at a facility geared to peaceful applications. There were other peaceful explosions, and not so peaceful ones, which must be considered as a piece if we are to understand the need to refocus resources and efforts toward other areas of modern technology where benefits can be found more cheaply, the risks are not as great, and the confluence of superpower politics, military interests, so-called national security, and technological arrogance are not so central to the genesis of applications.

CORRECTING THE MISTAKES OF NATURE

Scientists have long studied how to use explosives for various peaceful purposes: mining and prospecting, excavating, leveling, and landscaping. The power of nuclear blasts and the ability to direct them in a controlled way toward specific purposes both suggested the desirability of conducting research on their safety, efficacy, and reliability in nonmilitary projects. No sooner had physicists designed and detonated hydrogen bombs than they turned to peaceful applications. Some, such as Kurchatov and Sakharov, sought peaceful applications because they regretted their involvement in the design of weapons capable of destroying world civilization. Others found it difficult to divorce one application from another, whether military or industrial, but recognized peaceful nuclear explosions, so-called PNEs, as a means to continue studying the properties of nuclear devices, including how to make them cheaper, better, and "cleaner." In early discussions, the minister of the industry of nonferrous metallurgy, Petr Fadeevich Lomako, raised the prospect of using PNEs to mine ore. His geologists had identified a molybdenum site whose low-quality ore made traditional mining techniques too expensive. He proposed that engineers use a nuclear explosion to rip open the mountain sitting on top of the ore deposit. Kurchatov, when told by Emelianov of the suggestion, replied, "That's marvelous! Why didn't I think of that!"[1] This conversation led to more than 120 "underground nuclear explosions for industrial and scientific goals" and a special exhibition at VDNKh, the fantasy park in northern Moscow showing achievements of the socialist economy.

Before glorifying PNEs, physicists had to deal with the legacy of military tests that, until 1963, had been conducted in water, on land, and in the atmosphere. These explosions had spread radioactive fallout throughout the globe and endangered the health and safety of the globe's residents in the name of defense. By the time of the collapse of the Soviet Union, there had been over 2,000 nuclear detonations, with a total power of 629 megatons of TNT. The tests spread at least twenty-six million curies of ^{137}Ce, twenty million curies of ^{90}St, and five tons of plutonium into the environment. The declared nuclear nations found themselves in the weak position of condemning nuclear wanna-bes and nuclear have-becomes (most recently, India and Pakistan) from a position of less than moral superiority, for some of them desired a return to the glory days of big yields and more efficient bombs (see Appendix, Table 20).

Until recently, it was difficult to get direct confirmation of the extent of the Soviet PNE program. Officials, military personnel, and scientists were understandably reluctant to describe an experimental program involving nuclear explosions with risk to health and environment, even though it was dubbed peaceful. It was also difficult to decouple military from peaceful tests, not to mention to detect blasts of less than two kilotons with national technical means such as satellites and seismographs. Then there was the matter of the Limited Test Ban Treaty (1963) signed in Moscow, which prohibited tests in the atmosphere, space, and underwater, but permitted underground tests if radioactive debris remained within the territorial limits of the state under whose jurisdiction the test occurred. Although carefully designed, the first post-treaty PNEs released small amounts of fission products into the atmosphere in both the United States and the Soviet Union.

There were six major areas to which Soviet physicists applied PNEs: stimulating gas and oil fields; mining ore; putting out runaway oil and gas well fires; incineration of nuclear and chemical waste; underground storage for hazardous waste or gas condensate; and geophysical engineering ("correcting the mistakes of nature" with nuclear dams, canals, harbors, and reservoirs). In keeping with the traditions of Soviet science, once PNEs became a theoretical possibility, scientific, engineering, and economic organizations piled onto the bandwagon. Hundreds of young specialists received advanced degrees in such hypermodern disciplines as nuclear hydrology and nuclear geophysics. Said Iurii Smirnov, a scientist connected with the PNE program, "Our program as opposed to that of the United States had a great chance for success: we have a great land mass and one political party. Special design institutes came into existence to bridge differences of opinion between scientific and government bureaucracies like PromNIIproekt, which was especially active from 1967 to 1982." The scientists in these institutes were unrestrained in the pursuit of applications. They rarely addressed safety, health, or environmental issues in any systematic fashion. They had few qualms about carrying out a large number of PNEs, even in populated regions of the European USSR.

What do you do when oil production at a field drops? How do you increase recovery of carbonate-type oil deposits? Typically, geophysicists and engineers have tried water and gas injection, fire or hot-water flooding, hydrofracturing to increase the permeability of the formation, and the introduction of gas into the oil to reduce viscosity. The Soviet "Nuclear Oil Project" had the goal of "forcing the depths to give up their riches" through nuclear explosions to increase fracturing. Soviet experiments showed that PNEs increased production twenty-seven percent to sixty percent, at the same time dropping the gas to oil ratio significantly. Calculations made by Lawrence Livermore PNE-niks at the National Laboratory (LLNL) showed that nuclear fracturing would be economically effective, and they envied Soviet tests, for they could not generate interest among American oil companies. In the Tiumen region at Ust'Balyk, in eastern Siberia, and in Bashkiria, Soviets experimented with the transformation of nonindustrial sites of low penetrability and temperature into industrial ones, increasing production up to sixteen times and turning wells that did not exceed 5,000 cubic meters per day into 80,000 cubic meters per day.[2]

Similarly, mining applications were widespread. Nuclear geophysicists conducted thirty-nine explosions for the Ministry of Geology for so-called seismic prospecting. One mining technique was overburden removal. This application was indicated for nonferrous metal deposits, often in areas of difficult climate and geography of the far north—difficult on miners, that is. In one case, engineers calculated that they could remove 900 million cubic meters of the total 2.3 billion cubic meters of overburden with one explosion, at a savings of one billion rubles over conventional costs. For purposes of comparison, the huge Kennecott mine near Bingham, Utah removed about that much over sixty-five years, not in an afternoon.[3] There were also PNEs in the coal regions of the Donbas and Kuzbas. In September 1972, specialists from the Skonchinskii Moscow Mining Institute and Arzamas, and generals from the Ministries of Defense and Medium Machine Building appeared at a mine in Enakievo, Ukraine under conditions of strictest secrecy. They placed a nuclear charge of 3.3 kilotons one kilometer below the town and evacuated the local residents before the blast. Not long after, miners were sent back to the mine. The officials never warned the returning residents aboveground or miners underground about the potential danger of radioactivity or suggested that they watch for signs of illness. To this day, hotspots of radioactivity still show up in the surrounding region.[4] There were two PNEs in the Kirovsk region of the Kola peninsula at the Kolpor Mine near Khibinsk in 1974 and 1984, intended to increase ore mining. Both released radiation and required workers to mine in unsafe conditions.[5]

Another important use of PNEs was liquidation of runaway oil or gas well fires in cases when traditional explosives could not do the trick. Specialists calculated that PNEs did the job faster and two to four times more cheaply than conventional explosives did, at the same time increasing the recovery of oil and gas. The PNE was a "trustworthy helper in the struggle with the elements." In one case, a 2.3-kiloton explosion closed a well; and in another, an 8-kiloton charge set off at a depth of 1,050 to 1,500 meters put an end to the daily loss of millions of cubic meters of gas in smoke and flame. The nuclear method also increased vertical penetrability of the deposit and guaranteed effectiveness of its recovery when there were "gas caps." At Urtabulak in Central Asia in December 1963, oil workers lost control in a gas well at a depth of 2,450 meters, subsequently losing 1.5 million cubic meters daily. Over the next three years, they tried several times to cap the well at the surface, reduce the flow, or extinguish the flame; all such efforts failed. The H_2S content of the gas was also a danger to gas rig personnel. So they drilled a slant well to within 35 meters of the original well at a depth of 1,500 meters and detonated a 30-kiloton nuclear explosive. Twenty-six seconds later, the flare went out and the well was sealed. No radioactivity above background levels was detected.[6]

Given the appropriate geology, PNEs could be used to create underground caverns for storage of hazardous waste or of liquified natural gas. This was another case where physicists sought a technological solution for a technological problem, that is, the disposal of industrial waste whose production annually increased, especially from the petrochemical industry. The cost of storing these wastes in steel and reinforced concrete containers or of processing them had grown exorbitant, and there was also the problem of spoiling valuable farmland and forest with the huge storage facilities. With PNEs, they created underground storage facilities. In one site, they dumped 5.6 million cubic meters of industrial wastes over three years, at a proclaimed savings of 400,000 to 500,000 rubles per year.[7] They argued that the rubble formed in the PNEs served as a good medium for the waste, preventing waste from leaching into groundwater. But there is no evidence that they carried out a long-term study of this phenomenon. In fact, there is evidence that Soviet waste facilities have always leaked hazardous chemicals into the environment. But, to my knowledge, similar techniques were never employed to destroy tactical nuclear warheads. At one time, someone suggested that the military create "atomic crematoria" for chemical weapons. In both cases, scientists believed that intense heat and pressure at great depth would destroy the weapons safely.

Engineers built storage underground for oil and gas condensate in salt domes. They built a 50,000 cubic meter cavity (equivalent to about 300,000 barrels) with a 15-kiloton nuclear explosion. By 1980, they had accumulated enough experience to make it a simple matter to create caverns 100,000 cubic meters and larger in salt domes, using detonations from 1.1 to 25 kilotons. Economists and engineers calculated that underground storage was three to five times cheaper than aboveground oil and gas tanks and used ten to twenty times less metal. The time of construction also was cut by one-half. They learned from experience that the formation of still larger caverns was limited by seismic phenomena connected with the explosions—that is, nearby buildings collapsed. So larger explosions could be used only in sparsely settled areas. After explosions, they flushed and filled the caverns with air, and found them to be pressure tight. Later gas sampling found only background levels of radioactivity.

The most audacious use for PNEs was "to increase man's control over the environment," correct "mistakes of nature," create "winter suns" to melt Arctic snow and turn deserts into lush gardens. Discussed first in literary and popular science journals, these PNEs were intended ultimately to build canals that extended over 2,000 kilometers as part of the Siberian rivers diversion project. They planned to divert water from the Ob, Irtysh, Lena, and Ensei rivers into the Amu- and Syr-Darya rivers to benefit Central Asian cotton, fruit, and industrial programs. The diversion project, the epitome of Brezhnev era gigantomania, was canceled after the breakup of the Soviet Union, but not before "atomic hydrologists" carried out cratering and excavation experiments for canals in the Pechora-Kama (just west of the Urals), the Udachnyi (in Iakutiia and Sakha), and the Shagan River valley (in Semipalatinsk). Interested foreign partners also used these methods (the Orinoco-Negro canal in Venezuela and the Kra in Thailand).

Deserts occupy a large part of the Soviet Union. Their assimilation through irrigation was a problem of the first order. So a "scientific-industrial experiment for the creation of a large reservoir" with a volume of twenty million cubic meters was conducted. Atomic hydrologists chose a parched Central Asian riverbed that had large flow during the spring run-off period. A 100-kiloton explosion in the river bed created a reservoir 410 meters in diameter and up to 100 meters deep, simultaneously "building" a dam at one end from the thrown earth. Now the reservoir has a surface area of three square kilometers and a capacity of eighteen cubic kilometers. The explosion was far from inhabited areas, not dangerous from a seismic point of view, and, referring to radiation, "did not call forth any damaging consequences."[8]

The next step was to dig a huge canal to divert water from the Pechora River through the Volga and south. Hydrologists, botanists, and fish specialists worried that the level of the Caspian Sea had fallen disastrously after World War II, two, three, even four meters in a few decades. This drop in water level had a significant impact on the fish industry, the ports, and other regions of the economy. It was connected not so much with climatic changes, as with rapid development of industry in the Volga and Kama regions, construction of hydropower stations on the Volga, and the filling of reservoirs, all of which reduced the amount of water flowing into the Caspian. Atomic hydrologists determined that the reasonable solution was to transfer water from northern rivers that have "extra" water, in particular, from the Pechora into the Volga, through a canal 112.5 kilometers long. They planned to use nuclear explosions to cut through rock, earth, and permafrost. To gain data on cratering and stability, they detonated three 15-kiloton PNEs simultaneously at a depth of 128 meters, creating a trench 700 meters long, 350 meters wide, and 10 to 15 meters deep. This experiment "provided rich scientific information for future hydrotechnological work." With respect to both radiation and stability of the trench, scientists concluded that they could build future canals safely. They determined that roughly 250 nuclear charges would be needed to create a canal capable of diverting at least twenty cubic kilometers per year from the Pechora into Kama, the Volga, and thence the Caspian. They estimated that the cost would be at least three times cheaper than conventional excavation (see Appendix, Table 21).

Iurii Smirnov was closely connected with the Soviet PNE program. He began work on thermonuclear theory in 1960, when the Kurchatov Institute and Arzamas had first pick of the best physics students. Smirnov entered Leningrad State University to study physics. In March, two KGB agents assigned to the nuclear ministry arrived at the university, went to the dean's office, and asked to look at all the student folders. Within a week, they asked to speak with 6 of the 250 students. They interviewed students all day and selected two. One was Smirnov, who asked what his job would be. It was a dream come true: a fat salary, new apartment, and freedom to do theoretical physics. The devil was in the details, as he found out later.

At the beginning of June, Smirnov received a large wad of rubles and was told to report to Old Money Square in Moscow. He spent some of the money on a big party, bought a train ticket to Moscow, and followed the instructions to the Minsredmash building, where he encountered dozens of other youngsters like himself. They were told about their jobs at Arzamas, given documents, receipts for more money, and put on a special train. For the time being, no one asked for their documents. After they passed the Shatki station their impressions of privilege changed to worry. They crossed moats. At a series of control points, armed guards with dogs scrutinized their papers and belongings closely. The train entered the Arzamas compound through a narrow break in the forest, no more than sixty meters wide and surrounded by barbed wire. Was this a theoretical physics institute or a prison?

Smirnov's assignment was to work with Andrei Sakharov on the design of hydrogen bombs. At their first meeting, Sakharov asked Smirnov, "How do you build a hydrogen bomb?" Smirnov quickly gave some pretty good answers, and Sakharov soon gave him the independence to pursue his own direction. In 1963, Smirnov transferred to the Kurchatov Institute. From 1968 until the moratorium on testing in the mid-1980s, Smirnov worked on PNEs, devising experiments on science, safety, and effectiveness, and seeking ways to turn swords into plowshares.

Nuclear fantasy outlived the breakup of the Soviet Union. The Soviets had already conducted tests in populated areas, developed prototypes, and prepared to move into broad applications through commercial sales, when the country commenced middling steps toward market capitalism. No sooner had the USSR collapsed than representatives of the nuclear enterprise set out to sell PNE technology through the International Chetek (*Ch/T/K*, from the Russian words for "Man/ Technology/Capital") Corporation in Moscow. Chetek officials wanted to sell nuclear blasts to incinerate toxic wastes. They would consider any commercial or peaceful explosion. The corporation seemed unconcerned about the prospects of a charge falling into the hands of a rogue nation or of potential environmental dangers associated with PNEs. How delightful that the purveyors of nuclear war were the first to recognize the ability to profit from their nuclear devices in the post-cold war world. They had help in this endeavor from their counterparts at United States weapons labs, who had always felt cheated because they were not permitted to blow up mountains, harbors, or oil wells themselves. LLNL weapons expert Dr. Ray Kidder endorsed the Chetek program as having "technical merit" and PNE incineration as cheaper than other ways to handle wastes.[9]

The United States PNE program was not as extensive as that in the Soviet Union. It amounted to only twenty-seven blasts. But this was not for lack of desire or a prominent spokesman. Edward Teller was one of the driving forces behind the hydrogen bomb. Teller, a brilliant theoretician and émigré from Hungary, was a cold warrior who so hated communism that he worked tirelessly to scuttle many potential arms agreements for fear the USSR would find ways to cheat. Yet Teller found optimism in the nuclear age, citing the science fiction of Jules Verne to suggest "fantastic and good" achievements even from this powerful weapon. One such fantastic and good application was Project Plowshares for PNEs, which many physicists at LLNL came to believe could be "thoroughly useful." Planning began in 1956, and the first Plowshares test was a 1.7-kiloton detonation in the Nevada desert in September 1957. The test seemed to confirm the notion that deep underground explosions would "imprison" radioactivity in the earth and that useful information about processes occurring in the core would be provided. Over the next months, LLNL scientists drilled into the test site in search of the results of the explosion: a cavern, radioactivity, crumbled rock, and hardened molten rock. There was water-permeable rubble, but the scientists concluded that the radioactivity would decay to harmless daughter nuclei before it reached any living thing. Still, they sought to make Plowshares tools "cleaner."

Plowshares experiments taught physicists how to make big holes at a fraction of the cost, they claimed, of traditional methods. They created a new discipline: geographical engineering. They would change the earth's surface to suit humanity, creating harbors, digging deep and smooth canals, opening rivers to navigation. Plowshares planners identified a series of sites that were not yet heavily populated for their harbors and canals. These waterways would stimulate future development of rich ore deposits, for example, oil and coal in Alaska. They plotted against Ogoturuk, Alaska. As a Plowshares harbor, it would be connected to the ocean at a cost of under $10 million. Four 20-kiloton explosions would produce a harbor 250 to 300 yards wide. Teller suggested pushing mountains near Rampart (northwest of Fairbanks, Alaska) into the Yukon River to create a huge reservoir that would improve the climate of the entire region and allow engineers to create a power plant larger than that at Grand Coulee Dam. Teller put it simply: "If anyone wants a hole in the ground, nuclear explosives can make big holes." The Panatomic Canal across the Isthmus of Panama would have been such a big hole.[10]

Teller worried that Communists might develop Plowshares before the capitalists. The first cause of his fears was a matter of virility and penetration. The Soviets had claimed to raze mountains, irrigate deserts, and clear-cut jungle and forest. By 1958, they had built diversion canals and uncovered deep-lying mineral deposits with PNEs. Teller wrote, "The time may be near when the Russians will announce that they stand ready to help their friends with gigantic nuclear projects. The consequences of such aid would be an economic penetration a hundred times more extensive than those following the Soviet offer to help Egypt construct the Aswan dam." Teller's second concern was fear of losing a propaganda war, for "if the Soviet Union has surpassed America in the peaceful uses of the greatest force on the earth, Russia certainly must be ahead of the United States in military applications. As a propaganda weapon, Plowshares could finish the work begun with the launching of Sputnik."[11]

The nuclear impotence Teller feared was a reality. PNE applications were limited in the United States, owing to worries about of radioactive contamination, a failure to interest industry in purchasing the technology, and the frequency with which experiments failed to meet expected results. Milo Nordyke, one specialist on PNEs at LLNL, lamented that the United States scientists spent ten years on excavation and gas stimulation experiments with some success, but the government handicapped efforts to go further when it demanded that industry pay ninety percent of the costs. This limited the input of LLNL scientists to theoretical design, because industry was unwilling to take the financial and publicity risks of a failed experiment.[12]

In practice, both the vision of the enthusiast and the designs of the hands-on experts fell short of expectations.[13] The Ranier test in Nevada in 1957 suggested that the enormous heat of nuclear explosions could be used to generate power. Could molten salt store that heat to produce electricity via steam-driven generators? But the next salt dome test ("Gnome," near Carlsbad, New Mexico) resulted in a geyser of steam that rose 300 feet into the air. Radioactive venting did not dampen the allure of PNEs, however, for the safety teams reported that both contamination of local personnel, equipment, and vehicles and offsite exposure were well below "prescribed limits."

Plowshares engineers next designed "Chariot" to blast a harbor on Alaska's Arctic coast—after studying fragile ecosystems, of course. This test was canceled because of cost, public fears, and Department of Interior designs on the land. Not wishing their planning to go for naught, the physicists moved onto "Sedan," an inland cratering shot. But Sedan, which took place in mid-1962, not only lifted 6.5 million cubic yards of earth and rock, leaving a hole 1,200 feet in diameter and 320 feet deep, but also ejected radioactivity 12,000 feet into the atmosphere and

spread fallout along a 150-mile path across Nevada. The AEC had to ask milk producers to use dry feed for their animals until the levels of ^{131}I in plants exposed to
fallout fell to safe levels. Milk producers also were asked to focus on making cheese
and powdered milk, so that radioiodine could decay in those products before it was
released to consumers. A subsequent test, "Sulky," excavated poorly; and "Palan-
guin," whose charge shaft was filled with gravel to prevent venting, blew a cloud
of dust and that same gravel 8,000 feet into the atmosphere. Officials of the AEC
claimed that there was no health hazard as the debris drifted toward the Canadian
border, in violation of the test ban treaty. In keeping with the tradition of their
Soviet counterparts, LLNL scientists also conducted experiments in heavily populated regions of the South, for example, the "Salmon" 5.3-kiloton seismic experiment in a salt dome 32 kilometers southwest of Hattiesburg, Mississippi.[14]

By now, the United States Arms Control and Disarmament Agency had entered
the fray, arguing that such PNE tests violated the test ban treaty. A series of small
tests nonetheless followed. Several three- to five-kiloton detonations produced little
off-site radioactivity, culminating with a thirty-five-kiloton test in December 1968
in Nevada. The only active Plowshares program was a sea-level canal study, which
was projected to cost $200 million more than it would if built with conventional
technology. Passage of the National Environmental Protection Act and the requirement that Plowshares warriors produce environmental impact statements put further tests to rest. This left the Soviet physicists to carry the banner of deeper and
wider applications. But it was an explosion at a nuclear power station in Ukraine
that focused international attention on atomic-powered communism.

THE PEACEFUL ATOM IN EVERY HOME

Almost inevitable under atomic-powered communism, the Chernobyl disaster nevertheless stunned Soviet and Western officials and citizens. It will have a significant impact on the lives, health, and offspring of citizens of large regions of Russia,
Belarus, and Ukraine for decades to come. Officials, of course, had intended something quite different: a nuclear-powered future. The forecasted ten reactors would
provide half of Ukraine's electricity. The Pripiat River provided the copious amounts
of water needed to cool the massive units. The location was only one hundred kilometers north of Kiev and guaranteed low transmission costs to the industrial and
population heartland of the nation. All these things also ensured that the disaster
would have an impact on millions of people, their land, and their water supply.

The impetus for the development of nuclear power in Ukraine came from well-
connected scientists, economists, and Party officials in Moscow. Established in
November 1962, the Ministry of Energy and Electrification of Ukraine had the
juridical and titular right to order the construction of atomic power stations. But
Moscow set the agenda for nuclear power and for the location and type of stations.
Ukrainian officials took their cues from Moscow, using arguments developed in the
nuclear establishment on the economic rationale for nuclear power. They also
desired nuclear power as a symbol of modernity and progress. On January 28, 1965,

the chairman of the Council of Ministers of Ukraine sent the Central Committee of the Ukrainian Communist Party a report that forecast a grave energy shortfall and proposed building reactors over the next ten years in the Odessa region, in western Ukraine, and in a third location that could serve the Kiev grid. As a first step, he proposed opening departments in various higher educational institutions to train reactor operators. In June, the Ukrainian Party secretary, Shchelest, turned to the Central Committee in Moscow with a request to approve construction of 2,600 megawatts of nuclear capacity for the next five year plan (1966–1970). Of course, Moscow approved. On September 29, 1966, the Ukrainian Communist Party approved a top secret resolution "On the Plan for Construction and Operation of Atomic Energy Stations, 1966–1975" in the Kiev region, perhaps near Kopachi. They called it the Central Ukrainian Atomic Power Station. The first unit (1,000 megawatts) was to be built by 1974 and the second a year later. Like other nuclear construction trusts, the organization to build Chernobyl grew inevitably from hydropower to fossil fuel to nuclear power, seeing nary a difference in principles of construction, operation, or technology. The Khakhovskii Electric Repair Yard for the Hydroelectric Construction Trust, which was incarnated for work along the Dnepr in 1953, gained responsibility at the Tripolskaia hydrostation and was transformed into the Chernobyl Construction Trust in 1966.

There was no such thing as temporary approval or licensing boards to delay reactor construction progress. In November 1966, a government commission was established to select a site for the reactors. Within a month, the commission considered sixteen potential sites, whose geological, hydrological, land-use, and other characteristics were obviously given superficial treatment. When they discussed reactor plans, some advocated using a VVER pressurized-water reactor because they had heard criticism of the four hundredfold greater maximum radiation design-based discharges from the RBMK. But Anatolii Aleksandrov had praised the latter as cheaper. So who were they to question the Academy president?[15] On the commission's recommendation, the state planning administration (Gosplan), the Council of Ministers, and a raft of communist organizations quickly approved construction of two RBMK units at a site on the Pripiat River, just upstream from the Dnepr and Kiev's water supply. In a document dated February 2, 1967, officials already referred to the fateful concrete monument as the "Chernobyl Atomic Regional Electrical Power Station." The fact that a report was circulating among Party, government, and economic officials at that very time, in which officials detailed growing numbers of accidents at electric power stations in the country, the low level of training of station directors, and poor workmanship, caused no pause. There was no turning back.[16]

In January 1970, P. S. Neporozhnii and K. K. Pobigailo, the ministers of electrification of the USSR and Ukraine, respectively, arrived at the Chernobyl site for groundbreaking ceremonies. Officials of various construction and engineering organizations were also there. The designers had selected this site because the region's farmland was relatively unproductive and thinly settled. The Ural division of the Teploproekt Institute, a public wing of the Cheliabinsk plutonium establishment, and the Zhuk Gidroproekt Institute, the father of Soviet gigantomania in water resource management projects, were responsible for design, architecture, and planning. In 1971, Minenergy officials increased the projected power from two to four reactors to take advantage of the growing number of workers and equipment on site. In May 1971, construction on the unit 1 foundation pit commenced. Six years later, they began loading fuel; and in August 1977, the first unit reached criticality. At the end of September, a turbine connected to the Ukrainian grid was switched on. Units 2 through 4 followed more quickly, with seven workers receiving special certificates for their efforts and two the title "honored energy worker of Ukraine." In 1979, Vlad Tsybalko, the Kiev Party secretary, visited Pripiat and asked why they couldn't build twelve or even twenty reactors near the beautiful town. At the same time, unit 5 construction was hindered by lack of documentation and special hardware. The Communist Party affixed Lenin's name to the station's front door in honor of his one-hundred-tenth birthday. The name "Lenin Chernobyl Atomic Energy Station" remains to this day.

In terms of nuclear concrete, what was Chernobyl? It was 65,000 cubic meters of earth moved and tens of thousands of tons of concrete and reinforced concrete. It was a complex increasingly put together by the factory method, with prefabricated columns, walls, and panels, some of which were 700 millimeters thick (28 inches). It was 52 kilometers of railroad; 180,000 square meters of asphalt roads; 574,000 square meters of apartments; one day care facility and numerous kindergartens with 2,660 places; 3 schools with 4,052 places; 7 dining halls with 1,200 places; and of course, 2 Kharkiv Turbogenerator Works K-300-65/3000 turbines and 2 TVV-500-2UZ generators per reactor. The Chernobyl Construction Trust averaged six years and nine months between commencing site preparation and production of electricity for each of the units.[17] Of course, not everything went so swimmingly. Despite the "highly qualified workforce" and the growing tempo of construction, there were persistent problems of disorganization, waste, failure to meet targets, and poor quality of work. But they still moved on to work on blocks 5 and 6. The panels were poorly produced and poorly put in place. The workers seemed unable to learn from one unit to the next how to improve the quality of their labor, move more efficiently, and raise the quality of concrete poured. Perhaps they didn't care or had come to take reactor construction as commonplace. Even before the explosion, there were constant and numerous leaks totaling almost fifty cubic meters of water per hour. And there was a partial core meltdown on unit 1 in September 1982. But it failed to serve as a warning. Even an exposé on these problems, which was published in a Ukrainian literary weekly a few weeks before the 1986 disaster, was not a prophecy that a terrible accident would occur, but only a summons to work harder and faster on blocks 5 through 10. The plant director, Viktor Brukhanov, had good credentials for presiding over the accident: He came from the Balakova station, where under his watch as chief engineer, fourteen men were boiled alive during a start-up accident in June 1985.[18]

On April 25, 1986, operators in the control room of Chernobyl's unit 4 reactor were about to embark on a safety experiment.[19] They wished to see how long a spinning turbine could continue to provide electric power to the plant during an emergency reactor shutdown. The shutdown reactor obviously could no longer provide electricity for its own operation. If other reactors or sources of power simultaneously failed, for how long could the engineers ensure control in the interval before emergency diesel generators turned on? Perhaps twenty to thirty seconds? The spinning turbine would be one source of electrical energy. The experiment was designed to see how long the turbine would power the main pumps of the RBMK that kept cooling water flowing over the hot fuel and through the graphite core. This test had been conducted on unit 3, but power had fallen off very quickly. So the engineers improved the electrical equipment for a second attempt.

Some of the personnel in the control room that evening had just met for the first time, but they had no qualms about the experiment. They had reduced the power output to one-half its normal output so that all the steam could be put into one turbine. This remaining turbine was to be disconnected and its spinning energy allowed to power the main pumps for a short time. The operators felt pressure to conduct this test at that very moment, because the reactor was up for scheduled maintenance and any postponement would mean waiting for another year. This mindset of testing at any cost contributed to the accident. The operators believed that they could handle the time pressure, for unit 4 was the most modern of the RBMKs and the crew considered itself "elite." Because this was just an electrical test, how could there be a problem with the reactor itself?

Beginning at 1:00 a.m. on April 25, the operators slowly reduced the power output of the reactor to fifty percent as planned. Twelve hours later, they had achieved that level and switched off one turbine. The next stage would be to reduce power to about thirty percent. But electrical authorities at the central grid needed electricity for another few hours, so the reactor stayed at half power until 11:10 p.m., at which time the operators got permission to continue with power reduction. But an operator mistakenly forgot to reset a controller, so the power dropped all the way down to about one percent by 12:28 a.m. on April 26, too low for the test. As happens in all reactors, the sudden reduction in power caused a quick buildup of radioactive xenon, a neutron absorber, which pushed the reactor toward complete shutdown. The reactor was at such low power that the water in the pressure tubes was not boiling but liquid, which further absorbed neutrons. So the operator pulled out almost all the control rods and managed to get the power back up to seven percent. Unfortunately, once pulled, the control rods could not quickly be dropped back into the reactor for an emergency shutdown. At the time of the accident, there were only 6 to 8 of the nearly 200 control rods in the core. Furthermore, the control rods were intended to control power, not to shut the reactor down suddenly. They moved in and out of a channel filled with water (a neutron absorber), so the effect of moving the rods was small. To enhance their effect, there is a graphite rod attached to the bottom end of each control rod. Graphite is a moderator, not an absorber, so the initial effect of inserting a control rod is to increase reactivity near the bottom of the reactor.

Now other problems interfered with the test and, fatefully, with reactor operation. The reactor was so unstable that it was close to being shut down by the emergency control rods. The shutdown would abort the test, so the operator disabled a number of emergency shutdown signals, because, with those signals on, if the remaining turbine were disconnected (as it would be in the test), the reactor would shut down automatically. It was now two minutes before the explosion. The operator was ready to continue the test. Most of the shutdown signals had been disabled. Most of the control rods had been removed. Power was abnormally low. Liquid water almost at the boiling point filled the core. If it boiled it would absorb fewer neutrons and the power output would go up sharply, especially since the shutdown systems were slow or disconnected. And dropping in the control rods would only contribute to a rapid power surge.

At 1:23:04 a.m., the turbine was disconnected and its energy fed to four of eight main pumps. As the turbine slowed down, so did the pumps; and the water in the core, now moving more slowly over the hot fuel, began to boil. Fewer and fewer neutrons were absorbed. Twenty seconds later, the power started to rise because of the effect of the boiling coolant. So the operator pushed the button to drive in the rods and shut down the reactor; and when they moved in, there was a further massive and rapid rise in power. Within four seconds, the power rose to perhaps 100 times full power and destroyed the reactor.

The power surge put a sudden burst of heat into the uranium fuel, and it broke into little pieces. The heat from these pieces caused a rapid boiling of cooling water. A number of the pressure tubes burst. The graphite in an RBMK operates at high temperature, and its heat is removed by boiling water in 1,600 pressure tubes. Graphite burns, so it must be isolated from oxygen in the air. The RBMK core is sealed in a container surrounded by inert gases. The container can withstand the bursting of a pressure tube, but not an explosion. The reactor itself has no containment; it is merely surrounded by water, sand, and concrete for biological shielding. Steam escaped from the broken pressure tubes, burst the metal container around the graphite, which was red hot and now suddenly exposed to oxygen. The lid (upper biological shield, called *piatachok* for its resemblance to a five-kopek piece), which consisted of 2,000 several-hundred-pound concrete cubes, "began to bubble and dance." The steam lifted the concrete shield on top of the reactor, broke all the remaining pressure tubes, and destroyed the top half of the reactor core. Burning fragments of fuel and graphite spewed forth. They landed on the roof of the adjacent turbine building and caused about thirty fires, including the turbine oil and cable insulation. Local firefighters who first arrived on the scene put out all these fires by 5:00 a.m., but most died then or soon after from radiation exposure. The firemen who did not die on the spot from acute radiation poisoning were rushed to Moscow for futile treatment. Their radioactive bodies were buried with heroes' honors in lead-lined coffins.

Pripiat was a town of 35,000 at the time of the accident. Twenty-five percent of the area was forest, thirty percent of the land was unused, hay and pasture took up another twenty percent, with the rest serving as farmland for rye, potatoes, and forage grasses. There were 36,000 cattle and 16,000 hogs in the area at the time of the explosion, many of which were evacuated along with 135,000 persons from

Pripiat and surrounding regions in Ukraine and Belarus. Many persons packed lightly, for they were under the impression that they might soon return. Later, some were allowed to return briefly for important papers, or for automobiles, which had to be washed down thoroughly. On April 27, 1,216 buses and 300 trucks arrived from Kiev and began the evacuation of Pripiat. The surprisingly efficient process took only a few hours. Policemen without respirators were posted at each building. The evacuees were farmed out around the country, some to other nuclear power stations. Some people had already left on their own. These official and unofficial convoys carried radioactivity into the empire on trucks, buses, automobiles, clothing, and animals. At the end of May, the Politburo committee approved permanent resettlement of some "zone" residents into 7,500 apartments and 1,000 dormitory spaces in Kiev and 500 apartments in Chernigov. They also approved the construction of 7,000 modular ("standard") homes in the Kiev region by October and 4,500 individual cottages in Belarus.[20] None of the construction, housing, feeding, or schooling programs came close to meeting targets. In Ukraine, over 150 towns and villages, with a total of 3,000,000 residents, and over 40,000 hectares (square kilometers) of arable land were directly affected by Chernobyl.

Upon arriving, firemen, police, and workers saw a crimson glow, something like a metallurgical plant or major chemical factory blaze. Those who first rushed to the zone—the thirty-kilometer-diameter evacuation area around the reactor—stopped at the checkpoints to down a bottle of vodka. Said one, "It will prevent your testicles from getting fried." In the absence of safety equipment, vodka would have to do. Clearly, something terrible had happened. But those who were in charge in the control room and survived the initial explosion refused to understand that the reactor had blown up. Like radioactivity, this denial clouded the information they sent through intermediaries to Kiev and Moscow, delaying appropriate actions locally and nationally by at least twelve hours. Those on site not fighting the fire ran units 1, 2, and 3 as before, even though the radioactivity was a mortal blow. Reactor 3 shares the same simple factory building as unit 4; units 1 and 2 were contaminated because of a failure to turn off their ventilation systems, allowing contaminated air to circulate everywhere. Even before helicopters circled overhead, it was obvious that the reactor in unit 4 was fully destroyed. Adjacent roofs and ground were littered with metal and glowing graphite blocks, and a constant white column of smoke—burning graphite and products of fission—filled the air. All these objects were evidence of a huge explosion. The reactor poured out radiation for days to come. They knew that the 2,500 tons of graphite in the reactor unit would continue to burn for weeks unless they could put out the fire. They tried flooding the reactor, but this approach produced huge amounts of steam and spread water to the other units through the corridors. They consulted with Anatolii Aleksandrov and other specialists in the Kurchatov Institute and Minsredmash about how to put out the fire with "nontraditional methods." They decided to dump in lead and dolomite to stabilize the situation. Only then, finally sensing the seriousness of the situation some twenty-four hours after the accident, did officials make a decision to evacuate Pripiat.[21]

Any belief that an authoritarian garrison state was prepared for nuclear war or any other disaster ended on the spot. Confusion reigned. The authorities did not have enough protective equipment, including respirators. They did not have enough external radiation meters capable of monitoring exposures. They had no radio-controlled aircraft to measure radiation, and no basic standards for public safety. There were no instruments, no dosimeters, and therefore no available accurate measures of the radiation. Consequently, everyone thought the danger was less than what it actually was—lethal. There was no ready-made literature or medicine such as iodine tablets to distribute; no explanation of what was harmful or how to behave; no pamphlets or leaflets to read. For days after the explosion, people continued to drink and consume the local water, juice, sausages, and cucumbers, all of which had been irradiated. People got "nuclear tans," but few imagined its source. A few unfortunate sunbathers even went up on the roof to get an extra dose. Children played and bicycled even as the authorities sent out trucks to wash down the roads.

The Soviet army, especially its chemical corps, was engaged in dangerous work almost from the first; and no soldier shirked his responsibility. But few of them were dressed appropriately. The helicopter operators, too, faced mortal radiation, dumping hundreds, then thousands of tons of sandbags into the reactor until finally, on May 2, the reactor had been almost fully covered. They calculated how long they could hover in the radioactive plume safely. But there was no "safety," no lead shielding underneath, no respirators on board the helicopters. One official suggested dropping forty tons of lead into the core. But coming from a height of 200 meters, it might punch a hole through the pool beneath the reactor, driving the core into the water, and forcing everyone for kilometers around to flee from radioactive steam. In all, the heroic pilots dropped 5,000 tons of sand, lead, and dolomite into the core in one week, putting out the graphite fire. On May 10, they had stabilized the situation and realized that unit 4 had to be entombed.[22]

For several hours after the accident, government officials had no accurate information about what had happened. Fearing for their jobs, local and regional officials downplayed the extent of damage. Even as firefighters challenged the blaze, some officials scurried about securing train tickets for their family members. Some Pripiat residents were at the river fishing, totally unaware of what had happened. Only twenty-four hours later did the extent of the disaster become clear. In Moscow, after three days of dealing with the international disaster through ad hoc arrangements, the Politburo established a special standing operations group to evaluate the extent of the explosion and deal with its consequences.

Nikolai Ryzhkov chaired the operations group. Personnel regularly invited to attend the meeting included Aleksandrov, Velikhov, Petrosiants, the heads or their deputies of the ministries of health, defense, foreign affairs, middle machine building, and, of course, electrification. The deliberations were a mix of secretive and xenophobic behavior, surreal unwillingness to grasp the gravity of the situation, and the refreshing openness that was one of the foundations of the Gorbachev era. After the third meeting on May 1, 1986, Soviet leaders openly courted medical and technical assistance from the West. At Velikhov's urgings, American specialists provided equipment that enabled a closer study of the disaster and experimental medical treatment. The Soviet government turned down offers of help and expertise from such private firms as Bechtel. At the end of July, embassy personnel abroad received instructions on how to present the disaster in the best light to the foreign ministers of countries of the socialist fraternity (East Germany, Bulgaria, Romania, Vietnam, China, North Korea) and to assure them of the safety of the remaining RBMKs in light of new operating regimes.[23] Much of the remainder of early discussions, shocking as this may seem, centered on getting the remaining reactor units back on line as quickly as possible. The Soviet system proved incapable of forcing the pace of recovery and cleanup, and showed less than complete concern for public health—electricity remained king.

Ryzhkov and Yegor Ligachev represented the Politburo on a visit to the disaster area on May 2, one week after the explosion. Only after listening to Kurchatov Institute scientist Valerii Legasov and other scientists at ground zero did they finally understand that this was not a local incident but a large-scale accident with decades-long global consequences. Virtually all available Soviet heavy industry and military personnel were now to be conscripted to the effort. Minsredmash construction trusts in Cheliabinsk, Krasnoiarsk, Novosibirsk, and Arzamas were among the first to send "liquidators." Many persons patriotically volunteered. Institutes from the Ukrainian Academy of Sciences were enlisted in liquidation. On May 19, Minsredmash gained responsibility for coordinating all aspects of liquidation. Ministry of Electrification personnel had been hobbled by their attitude that nuclear power stations were no different than any other stations under their jurisdiction, and they didn't understand what needed to be done. By midsummer, Ryzhkov and others recognized that shoddy welding, cracks in piping, falsified documents, and poor valves were standard operating procedure. And even if these weaknesses were not the direct cause of the explosion, they reflected endemic shoddy workmanship, lax safety standards, and misplaced faith in the infallibility of Soviet technology and its creators. The plan was everything, the machine must operate, and people with rudimentary training sat at the controls.[24]

Officials initially blamed operating personnel for the disaster. In public forums in May and June 1986, they asserted that the design features of the station "fully correspond to the norms of the country and those generally accepted in international practice," construction had proceeded properly, installation was correct, and only a series of improbable malfunctions had led to the accident. They dismissed Western grumbling about a Soviet lag in technology as a possible cause, for there had been a large number of accidents in Western stations, too, not to mention the recent *Challenger* disaster. As if to underline the infallibility of technology, the Politburo ordered the creation of an independent ministry of nuclear power from the electrical power ministry, appointing as its head Nikolai Lukonin, director of the Leningrad RBMK network at Sosnovyi Bor from 1976 to 1983 and then at Ignalina for three years. Even as the liquidators toiled in inhuman conditions, officials insisted publicly that units 1, 2, and 3 would be back on line, according to plan, by October, even as the difficult work to entomb deadly unit 4 in a "sarcophagus" dragged on. Said one, "Our main job is to restore the damaged reactor unit as soon as possible and get it back on the grid."[25]

Aleksandrov's actions, and those of the commission, were dying efforts of the Party-scientific bureaucracy to hold on to the remnants of atomic-powered communism. They had dismissed growing evidence of the significant technological failings of RBMKs. The only advantage seemed to be that they could be built in bigger and bigger units merely by adding bits and pieces, prefab forms, turbines, and generators to the mix. In terms of reliability and safety—the two most important characteristics of nuclear power stations—they didn't measure up. Why hadn't performance of the Leningrad station at thirty percent efficiency suggested that units 2,400 megawatts in size would waste 2.4 times as much energy as a 1,000-megawatt unit? Efforts to raise the effectiveness of RBMKs at Leningrad caused a series of accidents that resulted in fires and radioactive venting. Overall, in the eleventh five year plan (1981–1985), there had been 1,042 emergency stoppages at stations, including 381 at RBMKs (of which 104 were at Chernobyl). Mikhael Gorbachev inquired at a July 1986 Chernobyl emergency meeting why the United States hadn't built Chernobyl-type reactors nor sited them on reservoirs feeding big cities. The answer, that the United States found the reactors lacking in safety and stability, did not sit well with him. The combination of Gorbachev and Chernobyl led to a change. By the end of the summer, the Soviet Union's policy makers finally agreed that there would be no more RBMKs. They couldn't afford to redesign the reactor. It didn't meet international standards. It couldn't operate at its designed capacity. The Soviets would continue to run them at lower power (and therefore lower efficiency) and eventually take them all off line. Prime Minister Ryzhkov concluded, "If the accident hadn't happened now, then it would have happened at some time."

When it came to health and safety during the cleanup, the Soviets failed on every front. The Ministry of Public Health came under constant criticism for diagnosis, treatment, and follow-up on persons evacuated from and working in the zone. Soviet planners never anticipated a disaster of such a scale, and apparently they never accumulated the medicines and equipment needed for nuclear civil defense purposes, except perhaps for the elite in capital cities. The system that proclaimed its devotion to the simple worker stumbled when its citizens needed help. On May 5, nearly 3,000 persons had been hospitalized, of them 569 children. Nine hundred had radiation sickness, eighteen of whom were in serious condition, and thirty-two, in critical condition. On May 6, nearly 3,500 had been hospitalized; on May 8, nearly 5,500 persons; on May 16, nearly 7,800. Beyond cleaning, shaving, and hydrating the bodies, there was little treatment; and sometimes patients lay in the linens left radioactive by previous patients. By the beginning of June, the number of persons hospitalized had dropped significantly. Only in late June, after tens of thousands of residents, patients, and liquidators had been dispersed throughout the country did officials of the Ministry of Health and the Academy of Medical Sciences realize the importance of tracking their health and establishing a well-equipped medical research center in the zone. Soviet medical personnel eventually concluded that, over the next seventy years, there would be 40,000 deaths in the European territory of the USSR that were caused by the Chernobyl accident.[26]

On May 3, a group from the Central Military Medical Administration of the Ministry of Defense arrived in the zone. Within 24 hours, its leaders claimed, the group was capable of offering medical help through 5 individual medical battalions, 4 sanitary-epidemiological divisions, 20 medical inspection points, and 300 additional medical personnel on loan from other organizations. Within a week, they had examined 78,000 local residents and completed 36,000 blood work-ups in ambulatory conditions, and, in mobile and regional hospitals, they had examined 454 persons. In fact, these were perfunctory examinations of 10,000 persons daily in impossible working conditions.[27]

Valerii Legasov, a product of the nuclear enterprise, a graduate of the physical chemical engineering department of Moscow Mendeleev Chemical Technical Institute, lost faith in his science because of Chernobyl. He led ground-zero efforts at eradication, came to the conclusion that the entire mindset of nuclear engineering must change, and was summarily blackballed by his colleagues for suggesting new approaches. Legasov completed his senior thesis at Kurchatov Institute in the field of nuclear fuel processing. His adviser, Academician Isaak Kikoin, asked him to stay on, but Legasov wanted practical experience in a nuclear plant, so he went to Krasnoiarsk to participate in the start-up of a radiochemical plant. He returned to the Kurchatov Institute two years later, writing candidate and doctoral dissertations on technological processes, winning state prizes, and securing membership in the Academy of Sciences. Appointed deputy director of the institute, he worked in physical chemistry, radiochemistry, and nuclear and plasma sources for technological purposes. His graduate students entered the nuclear industry in areas of isotopes and fuel properties and handling. Chernobyl forced Legasov to recognize that big, conceptual questions of nuclear power were raised frequently (How many reactors should be built and where?), but technical and engineering aspects were rarely discussed (How safe is safe enough? What are the advantages of one reactor over another? What fuels are best and why?). Once they had picked a machine, they stayed with it, even when there were alternatives. The result was reactors that were weaker than Western ones in safety, control, and diagnostics. No one in the USSR seemed to be conducting probabilistic risk assessment. Safety meant organization and documentation, itself often shoddy, not technical improvement. The number of facilities had increased, but not first-rate personnel; and the standard of expertise of personnel had fallen. Yet for those in the Kurchatov Institute at the pinnacle of technological and scientific expertise, it appeared that Legasov's anxiety about safety at nuclear stations was contrived. Legasov and others had acknowledged before the accident that the RBMK was a poor design from the economic point of view because of its great fuel consumption, capital cost, "nonindustrial" basis of construction, use of great quantities of graphite, zirconium, and water, poor safety and regulatory systems, and manual and slow-operating scram systems. When Legasov therefore turned after Chernobyl to the study of inherently safe reactors (for example, high-temperature gas reactors or salt water-cooled ones), it outraged the reactor designers who'd staked their careers on the RBMK. They claimed that he knew nothing and was interfering where he oughtn't. Legasov claimed that he had learned that the system prevented "serious, objective scientific analysis of the real situation." No less than Atommash, Chernobyl was young people, poorly trained, rushed to build an important industrial facility, doing it poorly, with no one paying any attention. And it was like this at all the nuclear power stations.[28]

THE "LIQUIDATORS" IN THE "ZONE"

The encounter with burning radioactive graphite, pieces of uranium, steam, and smoke surely frightened those "liquidators" who rushed to the zone to put out fires and contain radioactivity. They grasped soon enough, even if they were not told, that they faced death. Those who dropped dolomite and sand from helicopters and airplanes into the burning core; those who picked up the radioactive debris, wearing nothing more than gloves and masks, sometimes with shovels and wheelbarrows; those who hung from scaffolding as they built the sarcophagus; all faced radiation doses of 300, 400, 500 roentgens per hour and more. But they courageously stood their ground. Nameless soldiers, volunteers from all ends of the empire, and concerned scientists were the true heroes of atomic-powered communism, and also its most direct victims. The Army ordered 142,000 soldiers and 6,500 officers to the front; many were from the reserves. They came from all republics. The lower the rank, the higher the average radiation exposure.[29] They felled trees and buried them; they plowed grass and dirt under; they searched the thirty-kilometer exclusion zone, shooting pets and wild animals to keep them from carrying radioactivity outside it. Over two weeks in mid-June, 7,300 workers from the police department and Ministries of Defense and Middle Machine Building used 750 machines of various sorts to erect a 196-kilometer fence around the zone.[30]

Armenia sent thousands of soldiers to the zone, giving them no choice but service in "liquidation." One Armenian private resented the fact that their commanders hung back, only showing up in armored carriers. Like liquidators from Estonia, Siberia, and Central Asia, the soldiers were young and raw. They first poured concrete to hold the concrete pumping machines. They worked twelve-hour days, sometimes using tractors but more often their hands and shovels, to clear the debris and level the land. Then they worked on the columns of the sarcophagus. Even when equipment arrived to take over many of the onerous tasks, the size of the brigade grew, and some soldiers stood around with nothing to do but get a nuclear tan.[31] A new construction headquarters was built next to the radiation-spewing reactor hall to direct operations. On its instructions, the workers who had come from Erevanstroi, Sosnovyi Bor, Sibakademstroi, and elsewhere poured 250,000 cubic meters of concrete, erected thousands of tons of girders, and built 53 "villages" with some 8,000 houses at some distance from ground zero.[32]

After they had put out the fire and pushed debris back into the core, they needed to entomb the unit 4 reactor. Constructing the tomb (or sarcophagus, as it is called) was dangerous work for many reasons, not the least of which was the 185 tons of fuel that remained in the destroyed reactor. The radioactivity of this fuel reached 8,000 roentgens per hour, with spikes to 50,000 roentgens per hour. Observation, study, and stabilization were lethal tasks.[33] Once entombed, the reactor became the temple of "suicide scientists" who studied the core at great risk to themselves and

Chernobyl unit 4 after the explosion. *(Courtesy of Anatolii Diatlov)*

The construction of the Sarcophagus to entomb the reactor. *(Courtesy of Anatolii Diatlov)*

with inadequate equipment over the following years. The workers on the sarcophagus avoided using their hands, so there are few welds. The concrete flowed where it would, for they could not build forms.

Life has been hard on the liquidators. As the economies of Russia, Belarus, Kazakhstan, and Ukraine spiraled downward, the governments lost the ability to pay for promised pensions, apartments, and rations. Medical and psychological problems abound. According to the Kharkiv regional and municipal councils of the Chernobyl Union, 300 liquidators died between 1986 and 1990; of these, forty-seven percent committed suicide or drank themselves to death. More than 100 veterans of the "liquidation" ended up in Kharkiv hospitals after a hunger strike to demand that laws providing for the medical care, housing, pensions, and telephones be enforced. Forty-two liquidators from Kazakhstan fasted to protest the fact that they had not received any of the benefits of their hero status as required by law. Specialists at the Ukrainian Scientific Center of Radiation Medicine believe that many who suffer post-traumatic stress syndrome are too embarrassed to turn to psychiatrists for help. Others believe post-traumatic stress syndrome is exaggerated.

Housing shortages for evacuees are an ongoing problem. In St. Petersburg, there are 5,000 liquidators, and in the surrounding region another 5,000, plus 300 families evacuated from contaminated regions of Belarus and Ukraine. With a worsening housing and food situation for residents generally and unforeseen medical problems, what will happen to them? There are a series of first-rate local hospitals and medical centers in St. Petersburg, but there is no financing to treat patients or provide needed rations. Specialists offer psycho-, physio-, and other therapies at centers in Odessa, Kharkiv, Dnepropetrovsk and Lviv, but there is no effort to coordinate their activities or employ a systematic therapeutic doctrine.[34]

But the liquidators would be rewarded. In one form or another, one-half million persons had helped in the liquidation. Without considering levels of heroism or service, the government arbitrarily assigned the number of 5,400 special medals and awards (approximately one percent of those who served in the zone in one form or another), with those 5,400 medals distributed by fixed number to ministry, state committee, Party, Komsomol, and Academy organizations. What of meritorious service and heroism? This was truly Soviet equal opportunity—award by ministry.[35] Surely, virtually everyone who served deserved commendation.

The rush to finish the sarcophagus was not only for safety's sake. On May 11, less than two weeks after the accident, the Politburo instructed the Ministry of Electrification to draw up plans to bring units 1 and 2 on line in short order. At the end of July, officials of the Ministry of Electrification impatiently reported that deactivization of the reactor halls, roof, and territory of the station, repair of the components, and rebuilding of fuel storage units lagged. Until the sarcophagus and biological shielding were finished, much of the work to get the other reactors back on line was impossible. By the middle of May, the government commission had considered twenty different designs for the sarcophagus. Once they selected a design, thousands of workers joined the construction team, equipped with surgical masks but little else—and many removed the masks to smoke. Hence, only 8,000 cubic meters of concrete had been poured by midsummer. By the end of August, 8,200 persons were busy on the huge structure, and 135,000 cubic meters had been poured—sometimes 6,000 cubic meters daily. "Comrade," posters urged, "Give us 120,000 cubic meters of concrete by August 29th!" Fuel rods had been removed to Sosnovyi Bor; they would be shipped back in September. Thirty-five special air conditioners with filters were installed in the facilities of units 1 and 2 to ensure safety; Minsredmash provided 1,200 filters for them just in time for start-up.[36]

The encasement was finished in November 1986. It consisted of a monolith wall 2.3 meters thick and nineteen meters high, from which spread concrete buttresses. Metal tubes and girders supported the roof. The whole structure was covered with steel plates. Special robotic equipment that was used to monitor and repair the sarcophagus suffered painful electronic death in the heat and radiation. In all, they used 220,000 cubic meters of concrete in the sarcophagus, 15,000 tons of metal, and a specially constructed wall to shield unit 3 from radiation. This was self-proclaimed, grade A, first-quality "Sredmash concrete." In their hurry to build the sarcophagus but allow for venting, they left roughly 700 square meters open. They had to build directly on top of debris from the explosion. It was so radioactive that they could not move pieces or inspect the site closely before pouring cement on it for the sarcophagus's foundation. Consequently, a number of weight-bearing structures are weak, and their premature age shows in cracks and fissures.[37] Given the instability of the structure and the radiation hazard, any repairs have been temporary in nature. Were there to be structural failure, radioactive dust would rise into the atmosphere again and spread far beyond the zone. An earthquake of four on the Richter scale in May 1990 fortunately did no damage.

Thinking only about lost electricity even as the liquidators dealt with burning graphite, Party officials and economic planners rushed though a plan to restore units 1 through 3 to operation as soon as possible, fixing October 1986 as the target date for resumption of service. Restoration of operation would indicate that Chernobyl was a tragedy but not the death knell of nuclear power. So officials pontificated about increasing the reliability of RBMKs with new rules of operation and downplayed the danger of exposure to radioactivity in the zone. They spoke hopefully about the decay of strontium-90 and cesium-137 to safe levels in all areas except a few hotspots within a few decades. But some scientists were not so sure. They worried about the accumulation of 414 kilograms of plutonium-239 and 34 kilograms of plutonium-241 in the reactor at the time of the explosion. The activity of plutonium-241 exceeds that of plutonium-239 by 100 to 200 times, and some of it will decay into americium-241, a highly toxic and long-lived isotope that requires significantly increased expense to remove and store. Furthermore, even more thousands of persons at risk might have to be resettled. These isotopes had spread as far as Crimea.[38]

By 1990, it had become clear that a new sarcophagus with a lifetime of at least 100 years was already needed to encase the old one. A study indicated a steady deterioration of the original structure as a result of settling. Acids had been produced by boron carbides, dust suppression solutions, and potassium metaborate injected periodically to provide nuclear safety. All these chemicals and water sped up the corrosive processes. Hamstrung by its own financial crisis, the Ukrainian government held an international competition to generate support for a new structure, a "technological solution" to make the encasement "ecologically safe." Those who desired to enter the competition received extensive technical information on the meteorological, hydrological, seismic, thermal, and radiation conditions at the site.[39] In the summer of 1993, the jury picked one second place winner, a joint French-Ukrainian consortium, Campenon Bernard SGE, which immediately gave its $10,000 prize to the "Children of Chernobyl" fund. The design, one of ninety-two that organizations in Russia, Ukraine, Germany, France, Japan, and the United States had submitted, included tasking of robotic demolition bulldozers to pull down the old enclosed sarcophagus inside once the new facility was built. There was no first prize, nor any fixed cost or date of completion for the new sarcophagus. The reason was that no one knows how many billions of dollars it will cost or who will pay for it.[40]

For energy officials and old-style Party bureaucrats, the most important thing was that units 1 and 2 did commence "normal" operation again in November 1986, and unit 3 in December. The stations had a thirty-year life span, so they could operate until 2007, 2008, and 2011, respectively, before decommissioning. Without replacement of fuel channels, the lifetime of each unit would be reduced by ten years. They closed unit 2 in October 1991 after a fire in its machine hall. There are still 3,800 employees there, running reactors 1 and 3. Ninety percent of those persons working at Chernobyl at the time of the accident are gone; but seventy percent of the current employees have been working three or more years, lured by promises of new apartments in Slavutich, free daily transport to work (thirty-five kilometers each way by train), and employment through 2011. Ignoring such issues as reproductive health, ninety percent are men younger than forty-five years, and ninety percent of the women are under forty. Chernobyl support towns have the highest birth rates in the former Soviet Union. Even with growing evidence that small doses of ionizing radiation have a negative impact on health, employees in the zone work away, with the only benefit being a threefold Chernobyl salary premium. This benefit, of course, makes the cost of running Chernobyl higher, while its efficiency remains low. And the human factor remains obscured, for the government refuses to release for study the medical records of atomic personnel. The Ukrainian parliament (Rada) has voted on several occasions to close the station permanently. But the need for electricity to power the stumbling economy has kept it open. Even some liquidators believe that the Chernobyl stations should remain open until the end of their operating lives, for they fear for their jobs.[41]

After the evacuation of Pripiat, many personnel were moved to Kiev, from whence they worked fifteen days on, fifteen days off. Then many of the workers were sent to live in Zelenii Mys, sixty kilometers away, where they lived in 3,000 hurriedly built apartments and traveled by bus to the reactor and back everyday. Eleven hundred persons received housing in eight moored riverboats; and five more boats soon floated in. A summer drought left the region parched. The heavy trucks and buses used to transport workers kicked up highly radioactive dust. Roads had to be washed down; drivers followed a roundabout route to work sites to avoid dust and hotspots. The construction of Slavutich would make things easier on them. But with Slavutich, they were given a choice: leave Kiev and get a new apartment or look for new a job, and consider leaving Party membership behind. Initially, new young workers arrived from other power stations, military establishments, and secret institutes, replacing those thousands who had suffered Chernobyl's consequences. But Zelenii Mys and Slavutich remained poorly equipped, with inadequate stores and schools; and Russia's atomic power stations offered more pay, safety, and better living conditions, benefits that attracted the cream of the Chernobyl crop.[42] So the Chernobyl plant managers are having a hard time attracting and keeping qualified operating personnel.

Officials of the Ukrainian Ministry of Environment strongly oppose continued operation of the station for two reasons. First, the electricity from Chernobyl powers an outdated, heavily polluting industry, especially a metallurgical industry, itself in need of renovation. The officials argue it would be better for Ukraine to produce less electricity, close that industry, and avoid the exogenous costs of pollution to health and the environment that were never considered in Soviet budgets. Second, even though the station runs better, its principle design flaws remain and, despite modifications, the reactors violate international safety standards.[43] Those officials had every reason for concern. On one occasion, the pools holding spent fuel rods for unit 2 leaked about two cubic meters per hour for a few days before the leak was noticed. Repair required the removal of the rods and a hazardous search for the leak.[44]

LIFE WITHIN THE ZONE

The authorities created the Pripiat Scientific Production Association (NPO) and "Kompleks" to supervise liquidation and research activities in the zone, including what must be suicidal forays into the sarcophagus. To track the radionuclides, they brought in experts from Obninsk and Cheliabinsk who had studied the Kyshtym 1957 disaster. There was a big difference between the two events. At Kyshtym, there was no fire, the sky wasn't filled with chunks of steaming graphite, and the area affected fell entirely within the Soviet Union's borders. At Kyshtym, year after year, flowers come up and birds fill the air as if nothing serious had happened, even though everyone knew it had. People were evacuated, they plowed the ground under, and police patrolled the region. Chernobyl was not a secret, but a national and international incident known to all, with both more immediate and more long term loss of life.

At Chernobyl, disorder interfered with establishing the appropriate scientific protocols, confusion contributed to the failure to maintain documentation of individual medical histories, and an effort to keep information secret dominated investigations, whereas open discussion was called for. Despite what had been easily learned by American satellites and was covered in the open press, Kompleks required its employees to sign a declaration in 1987, agreeing not to divulge any information. Radiophobia—public fear of any kind of radiation large or small—grew in conditions of ignorance, for there was extensive information about the health of flora and fauna, soil and water, but only rumors about individual health.[45] In spite of glasnost and perestroika, the Soviet way of doing things persisted.

No matter the critical state of health care within the zone and no matter the centralized system of health care in the Soviet Union, the authorities simply could not manage to provide adequate medical treatment—diagnosis, medicine, and so on—for the liquidators, operators, and employees in the zone. Fluoroscopes, X-ray machines, and blood-testing apparatus were old and crowded into small, dirty rooms. The ambulances frequently broke down, and the repairmen couldn't get parts for them. Levels of illness and especially alcoholism climbed rapidly, even though the zone was a "dry county." Part of the blame rested with the workers themselves, for unfortunately they quickly became accustomed to the danger of radiation they could not see, relaxed when vigilance was called for, and stopped wearing respirators, masks, head cover, or any other safety clothing. Many liquidators had taken to trapping, shooting, and eating wild animals within the zone, in particular boar, and even fish and mushrooms (which were most laden with radioisotopes).[46] The authorities regularly allowed rules to be broken. Many young men and women of childbearing age worked in the zone. They ate local products. Their children played under radiation danger signs. Many doctors, out of ignorance or frustration, refused to treat patients, claiming that the mass symptoms of physical or psychological disorders could not be the result of exposure to radioactivity but came from some radiophobic hysteria.[47]

Outside the zone, the authorities were no more successful. The authorities put up an automatic dosimeter at an outdoor market in Lviv. For fifteen kopeks, it would determine the level of radioactivity in fruits, vegetables, meat, and fish purchased from local venders. Lviv scientists built the automat from scavenged pieces of dosimeters and such.[48] What impact can one device have on the health of millions? In May, 1992, the Ukrainian enterprise "Isotope" advertised at long last an affordable dosimeter, which is being produced at nuclear instrument factories that until recently had produced products only for the military industrial complex and had no interest in such small devices as dosimeters. In pursuit of conversion and rubles, the factories changed their focus.[49] But few Ukrainians have bought the devices, and fewer still know how to use them.

The editors of the *Chernobyl Herald,* the organ of Pripiat NPO, were powerless to ensure worker safety, try as they might. Beyond answering queries from those seeking workmen's compensation under national law, yet denied it because of shortfalls of funding or intransigent bureaucrats, the paper's journalists were relegated to reminding workers to be careful because radioactive waste would threaten life for thousands of years. The newspaper provided food preparation advice from cleaning to cooking; urged citizens to avoid frying and not to use soup bones in simmered stock; and told them which foods were high in potassium (as a natural enemy of Ce-137) and vitamins. Across the masthead ran the slogan "From the Epicenter of the Atomic Catastrophe" instead of "All the News That's Fit to Print."

And what an epicenter it is. The liquidators washed down, cleaned, and buried as much as they could. They scraped the top soil and filled tens of thousands of barrels with it, and felled trees. They established an off-limits graveyard of machinery and equipment made radioactive during liquidation. They built dams and filters to keep radiation from entering the Dnepr. They have talked about building a processing plant in the zone to transform radioactive wastes into a glassified substance that is easier to handle. For the time being, they continue to store waste and fuel rods underground and in cooling pools.

At the same time, the Ministry of Forestry of Ukraine has its eyes on the zone, because eighty percent of the radionuclides are concentrated in the bark and roots. The wood itself is "almost clean." Researchers have shown that the pine forests in the zone were hit hard by the radioactivity. Many trees were killed outright, of course, especially those closest to the accident; but many more survived and are showing tremendous resiliency. After six years, sixty percent of the trees had died, thus creating a fire hazard. One of the ways to fight forest fires was to resurrect scientific forestry management techniques. Chernobylles, a forestry trust, was created in 1993 by informal groups of foresters and firefighters with the goals of creating firebreaks, protecting the soil, preparing for replanting, and identifying stands of trees in areas of low radioactivity for use as lumber in window and door frames.[50]

Mosses, lichens, and the slightly decomposed litter in the pine forests have a high retention capacity for radioactive matter; therefore these substances confine and preserve radioactive materials at levels higher than the soil in meadows or arable land. What could possibly be worse? In August 1992, grass, peat, and forest began to burn, producing radioisotope-laden smoke that spread far beyond the thirty-kilometer zone. Levels of radioactivity in the air reached 50, 80, even 180 microroentgens per hour (primarily from cesium-137). The fires engulfed the homes of returnees, about 2,800 hectares of meadow, 700 hectares of forest, and 12 hectares of peat. In the first eight months of 1993, there were 199 fires in the zone, a five percent increase from the same period in the previous year. Most of the fires were in the town of Chernobyl itself and a lesser amount were in the village of Zalese, including some in the dormitories of plant personnel. Yet the fire department had difficulty getting the construction trusts responsible for the new facilities to install alarms and sprinklers, as required by law.[51]

We have only recently learned the extent to which fire plagued Soviet nuclear power stations. Fires in October and November 1991 led the government to vote to close Chernobyl by the end of 1993. Then things got even worse. In eighteen months from July 1992 through November 1993, there were eleven fires at Ukrainian nuclear power stations, including some in the machine hall of Chernobyl and in the sarcophagus. The officials of the atomic ministries, the national fire department, and other organizations debated what to do. But it seems that financial constraints and the break with Russia prevented acquisition of fire safety equipment and renovation of components, especially fire-resistant cable.[52]

The large number of fires at nuclear plants finally led the authorities to produce a handbook on fire prevention for nuclear power stations. The author of the handbook, apparently a great believer in progress, asked the reader not to permit a few fires to stand in the way of the ongoing scientific and technological development, especially for atomic power stations. There were many dangers involved in nuclear power to be sure, but understanding where fires had occurred and how to prevent them would enable society to continue down the nuclear road. Generators, cable and conduit channels, and electrical equipment and pumps were the main sites of fire. Cable insulation was one of the most insidious fuels and also formed highly toxic aerosols when burned. Turbine oil and sodium were other flammables, the latter almost exclusively the concern of Russian stations because Germany, the United States, and France had already or were currently abandoning their breeder reactors. (The Japanese have had a series of recent sodium mishaps, with one fire in the autumn of 1997 convincing nuclear policy makers to put a moratorium on the breeder.) In addition to new cable and components, Soviet-inspired reactors require modern containment facilities and workers equipped with reliable firefighting equipment, especially accessible respirators. But vigilance apparently was the key to progress.[53]

NUCLEAR STORKS

Chernobyl continues to operate as a symbol of the bankruptcy of atomic-powered communism. It is part concrete monstrosity, part nuclear mausoleum. It is dangerous to operate the plant, yet its operation is seemingly vital to Ukraine's energy future. To Moscow's nuclear energy establishment, the Chernobyl explosion was only a small detour on the road to omnipotent nuclear power. Its design institutes and construction bureaus, physicists and engineers, policy makers and architects have no desire to rein in the momentum of the plans, operations, and machines.

Into the late 1980s, the authorities in Moscow floated the idea of expanding Ukraine's nuclear energy capacity. This plan provoked protest from Ukrainian writers, similar to the protest among Russia writers over the Siberian river diversion project. In *Literaturna Ukrainy,* seven Ukrainian writers demanded that the construction of a new station at Chigirin in Cherkassy on the Dnepr cease. They asked: Why did the Dnepr and Central Ukraine deserve yet another technological assault? Opposition to the station grew also among Ukrainian scientists. Officials in the USSR Ministry of Nuclear Energy attempted to avoid the issue, acknowledging only that they were discussing whether to put the construction on hold. In the thinking of some Ukrainians, Chernobyl and Chigirin became symbols of Russian exploitation of Ukraine and continuation of Ukraine's status as a scientific colony of Russia, perpetrated first under Lavrenty Beria and now his legacy, MinAtom. A nascent environmental movement that drew heavily on these feelings and on Ukrainian nationalism was born from the Moscow plans and disappeared only with the cancellation of the Chigirin and Crimean atomic power station projects and, most important, with the achievement of Ukrainian independence.[54]

When Ukraine got independence, it gained only partial independence from Russian atomic energy. Although five different nuclear parks in Ukraine produce over one-third of its electrical energy, all aspects of the fuel cycle remain with Russia. The wastes and spent fuel from the Rovenskaia station in Kuznetsovsk (two VVER-440 and one VVER-1000 reactor) belong to Cheliabinsk-40, whereas the ten reactors of South Ukraine, Zaporozhskaia, and Khmelnitskaia stations go to Krasnoiarsk-26.[55] As it is, the five reactor parks in Ukraine that consist of fifteen reactors are located in an area comprising only three percent of the former USSR. The reactors are in poor repair and at risk. To make matters worse, with two blocks of Chernobyl shut down and the others running at partial power, with oil and gas deliveries from Russia on decline or held up by inability to pay, and with Ukrainian coal of low calorific value, energy shortfalls and brownouts plague the nation.

But Chernobyl is not reactors nor radwaste nor dosimeters nor fuel. It is an entire nation whose history will forever be linked to technogenic catastrophe. It is individuals who are denied the ability to assess the risk of living with radwaste and to make informed choices about health and safety. It is liquidators. It is roughly 800 persons who live in the zone without official permission. They are elderly men and women (mostly women) who have returned to live out their lives there. The authorities have given up trying to force them out. It is millions of people who pretend their food and water are clean. It is men and women of reproductive age who must worry about birth defects and childhood leukemia as perhaps no other people in the world do. It is a government incapable of meeting their needs or providing them with adequate information to make informed choices. And it is a nuclear establishment unable to change its ways.

An enterprise capable of setting off peaceful nuclear explosions in populated areas was also capable of siting nuclear power stations close to major cities and waterways. It was capable of downplaying dangers and dragging its feet on cleanup. It knew no better than to hope for a return to "normal conditions" when none could be found, whether the causes of radioactive contamination were peaceful and intended or peaceful and unintended. There are signs of normalcy. Dogs and cats once again inhabit the zone. A few farms animals and elderly folks have come back. And storks, a symbol of health and prosperity in Russian and Ukrainian tradition, have returned after an absence of six years to nest in the electric power towers leading from the station out of the zone. Unfortunately, their return reflects only the resilience of storks, not a resolution to the legacy of atomic-powered communism.

Atomic-Powered Communism Reconsidered

*Our country, having fulfilled Lenin's behest and provided opportunities
for the independent development of science and technology, has
created a dependable fuel and energy complex . . . There are no scientific or
technical problems which would be too difficult for us to resolve.*

Atomic power engineering has become common place.
—Academician Anatolii Aleksandrov

The same engineering culture that existed in the peaceful nuclear industry also held sway in the military industry. Technological hubris, unnecessary risk, and technological momentum combined in a cold war world to create an ethos where issues of health, safety, and environment received inadequate attention. This dangerous situation grew worse because of the total secrecy that covered the nuclear industry. When citizens of any country in the world read that some nuclear program, institute, or industry exists "in the interests of national security" and that its activities must be kept secret from enemies at home and abroad, they should worry that laws concerning occupational and environmental health and safety have been violated, injuries and deaths have occurred, and the costs of rectifying the situation will be great, perhaps approaching those of creating it. Especially in the two major nuclear powers, the United States and the Soviet Union, the secret institutes and industries of the nuclear-military complex were responsible for haphazard storage of low-, middle-, and high-level radioactive waste. Personnel justified the decision to store waste temporarily in huge metal tanks destined to leak by calling them temporary measures. This tautology of inaction remains in force.

The nuclear waste produced during the arms race—hundreds of millions of gallons of liquids and hundreds of thousands of tons of solids—has entered the environment and is slowly, inexorably polluting the water and land. For years, liquid waste has leached into the groundwater and rivers near Hanford, Washington and Cheliabinsk, Russia. A series of devastating accidents has also led to loss of life and limb and to death from exposure to radioactivity. Because of the absence of public scrutiny in the closed Soviet system, the transgressions against safety and environmental protection laws will have consequences significantly more grave than those in the United States. The managers of production facilities in the closed nuclear cities of the Soviet Union never worried unduly about the exposure of workers to radiation. But this behavior should be seen as a call to action to clean up Hanford and Fernald, Ohio and Aiken, South Carolina, not to gloat about victory in the cold war.

There were nuclear guinea pigs in the Soviet Union. Some of them were soldiers sent in to reclaim ground zero after a nuclear test. Others were the object of experiments with questionable ethical standards. Unfortunately, the archives on these tests and experiments have not been opened, so there is no way to judge fully either their extent or their justification. But most of the people who fell prey to cavalier attitudes involving the growing presence of radioactive substances in the country were ordinary citizens, persons whose lives were needlessly endangered by premature utilization of tracers, poorly designed and operated nuclear facilities such as power reactors, and haphazard disposal of nuclear waste. Any number of encyclopedic accounts of the Soviet nuclear establishment, the "polygons" (closed nuclear cities and testing grounds), will provide the reader with chapter and verse about their establishment, functions, and current fate. Both at the polygons and in the civilian sector, atomic-powered communism was technology run amok with the full endorsement of the political and scientific leadership. These practices ran counter to the spirit of Soviet law and public health practices dating to the first days of the revolution. Radiation safety existed on paper, not in reality.

PUBLIC HEALTH BETRAYED

Soviet leaders envisaged revolutionary changes in public health and safety as part and parcel of radical transformations in all areas of life. Officials defined public health broadly to distinguish themselves from their Tsarist predecessors, to include communal and individual responsibility for health, safety, and welfare, and to stress social factors in the spread and control of disease. Many medical practitioners embraced Soviet rule and the support of the new leaders as a way to push programs that had languished in the Tsarist era owing to lack of government interest. The result was an activist state in this area, and not a little interference in the practice of health and safety experts. Struggling mightily to overcome a legacy of Tsarist inattention, policy makers and scientists faced a litany of problems from high infant mortality and communicable disease rates to poor standards of hygiene in homes, hospitals, libraries, schools, restaurants, and stores. Once they embarked on the huge program to industrialize the nation, the focus shifted to include the factory. The Ministry of Health, determined to show that modern practices of hygiene and safety were commensurate with the goals of the regime, set out to alter the health and safety habits of Soviet citizens, so many of which were tied to folk practices, whether at home, at work, or in public.[1] Of course, Russian cultural traditions played out in the Ministry's programs, so one sees, for example, significant efforts to avoid draughts even while windows in public buildings were opened twice daily even in the dead of winter to air them out, the use of heated jars attached to the patient's skin and painful mustard plasters to treat flu, and the persistent overuse of fat and salt in cooking alongside the avoidance of vegetables.

More significant in restricting advances in safety was the importance the regime attached to increasing industrial production at any cost. Industrial hygiene, psychotechnics, and other fields of study of worker health and safety had recently come into their own throughout the world, advanced in part by technocratic movements. But the fields were anathema to Stalinist planners, for they placed concerns about the worker ahead of those of the state.[2] Workers equipped with crude hand tools and inadequate clothing were forced to work inhuman hours to build dams, canals, and roads. Prison laborers fared worst. Many perished from exposure. Even the modern, Soviet shop floor was a source of danger to limb and life, for the electric factory that Lenin envisaged—clean, well-illuminated, and quiet—never came to pass. Bad enough were moving parts, flying debris, grease, dirt, and fires. Rampant alcoholism made factories truly unsafe. It did not help that the authorities put beer kiosks on the street near factories so that the workers could have a little bit of the hair of the dog that bit them the night before. Throughout all of this, electricity remained the panacea for the ills of society, with the reactor to become its most modern producer.

The Ministry of Health and its growing network of research facilities entered a postwar world still firmly in Stalin's grip. It was charged both with assisting in rebuilding industry and agriculture and with modernizing medicine. Through such journals as *Gigiena i sanitariia* (Public Health and Sanitation) and *Voprosy pitaniia* (Questions of Nutrition), the policy makers and researchers in the ministry proselytized modern public health measures. Topics that fell under scrutiny necessarily touted the glories of science and technology as cure-alls (hence, they resemble those in most industrialized nations): clean air and water; ventilation and filtration; fluoridation; the wondrous applications of DDT and hexachlorophene; advances in refrigeration; control of the sources of pneumoconiosis and silicosis; the alleged "self-cleansing" properties of soil that might remove impurities from groundwater. There was some awareness of the risks associated with modern life: the presence of pesticide residues on food; the failure to establish and enforce norms for pesticide use; pollution associated with industry and agriculture; and the persistence of food poisoning connected with unsanitary conditions in restaurants, dining halls, and food stores. Whenever progress in health and safety interfered with the rebuilding of heavy industry, however, it was pushed onto the back burner.

For many scientists connected with the atomic bomb project, the magical elixir of tracer atoms and ionizing radiation sources would contribute to the solution of many of just these health and safety problems, for example, through radiation sterilization of food or through isotopic quality control instruments—and at low cost. Applications abounded. In the late 1940s, the Soviet Union embarked on an increasingly ambitious effort to dam Russia's and Ukraine's many rivers to tap hydroelectric potential. They planned to build reservoirs everywhere as part of the "Stalinist Plan for the Transformation of Nature." And while geophysicists plotted the construction of Stalin's reservoirs and dams on the Volga, Don, and Dnepr, in 1946, with the F-1 reactor in operation less than six months, health officials used radioactive tracers to track the flow of industrial and domestic effluents down those same rivers. Scientists discovered that the tracers were much more effective and reliable than salts and dyes used for the same purpose.[3]

But for scientists involved in public health, the peaceful atom brought with it too much baggage in the way of radioactive waste. After first applying atomic materials willy-nilly to their tasks, they became increasingly cautious and pushed a series of ever-more-strict safety standards for their use. As Stalin's massive waterworks projects gained momentum, several public health professionals voiced concern about the potential danger of the spread of radioactive waste into waterways and reservoirs, as happened at Chernobyl. Beyond the vast quantities of waste entering the ecosystem from poorly constructed storage facilities at weapons production laboratories or at nuclear power stations, there were a number of other ways the atom might pollute: airborne wastes in the form of steam or gas; solid wastes, including laboratory animals and safety clothing; and liquid wastes such as laboratory solutions and those from cleaning equipment and containers and rinsing the workers. Scientists offered measured, yet optimistic reports on their ability to handle the problem. They downplayed the danger by pointing to the small but significant natural background radiation. They added that there were a number of ways to treat wastes to avoid contamination of reservoirs. For example, industries could add various salts to liquids to cause radioisotopes to precipitate, and they could carefully pack and store solid wastes. But the presence of so many isotopes with relatively long half-lives made even minute amounts a great concern. Rapidly expanding research programs in medicine, agriculture, and industry, and poor handling of wastes made it likely that Soviet citizens would come in contact with radioactivity.

Throughout the 1950s, scientists accumulated evidence that chronic exposure to even low-level ionizing radiation was dangerous and that radioactive isotopes all too easily entered the food chain. In light of this evidence, one physician urged in 1956 that norms for exposure to a series of isotopes be revised downward, at the same time as health and safety inspections had to be upgraded. Pointing to the property of isotopes to increase in concentration in organisms, he argued that any discharge had to be prevented.[4] Unfortunately, over the years it became clear that isotopes of strontium, cesium, radon, radium, and uranium had entered both open water and groundwater used for drinking, in part from fallout. In addition to regular physical-chemical and bacterial analysis by the State Epidemiological Service, it was now necessary to check water for radioactivity.[5]

In all countries, the increasing use of radioactive materials and the growing knowledge of their pathways in flora and fauna led to a steady, downward revision of maximum permissible exposures for any period of time. Nowhere worse than in the USSR, there was a significant disjunction between the discussion in scientific journals about the problem of radioactive safety and waste disposal, the letter of the law, and the practice of scientists and engineers, workers, and managers who worked with radioactive isotopes. Each downward revision of maximum permissible exposure levels was accompanied by efforts to circumvent the law. Supervisors underplayed the danger. Workers were also to blame for this state of affairs. They were quick to remove their cumbersome lead-lined gloves as soon as their supervisors left the room. They never gave a second thought to putting a snack on the laboratory table next to some gamma-emitting source. The absence of adequate equipment did not help. "Spetsodezhda" (individual, hermetically closed plastic suits with respirators for workers of the nuclear industry) were not widely available despite Soviet pride over the development of the "pneumo-suit" LG-1 in 1955. High cost and production problems prevented its broad dissemination.[6]

Two of the leading figures of radiation safety were A. N. Marei and N. V. Timofeeff-Ressovsky. By the late 1940s, they had established how radioisotopes migrate from air, water, and soil into biological structures and how these elements moved in the food chain. They studied ^{131}I, ^{90}Sr, and ^{137}Cs, which were especially dangerous because of the body's need for isotopes of those elements. Timofeeff-Ressovsky, an outcast because of his tardy return from Nazi Germany where he had been studying and because of his open support of modern genetics, nearly died in the Stalinist Gulag before being rescued by the secret police to work on the atomic bomb project. He was relegated to a kind of scientific exile in Obninsk, close to the center of nuclear energetics but isolated from mainstream biologists. Dr. Marei established the first laboratory for a field of research known as "municipal radiation safety" at the beginning of 1952 in the Institute of Occupational Safety and Disease Prevention of the Academy of Medical Sciences. Soviet researchers connected with Marei and Timofeeff-Ressovsky were among the first to show that both alpha- and beta-emitting isotopes led to carcinoma.[7]

Scientists knew that tracers were not only elixirs. They were poisons if wrongly used. Researchers in institutes of the Academy of Medical Sciences, under the umbrella of the Ministry of Public Health, gained responsibility for ensuring that they were handled with the utmost care. The institutional foundation of radiation safety accompanied the growth of peaceful atomic programs. In 1956, the Institute of Radiation Hygiene of the Ministry of Health of the Russian republic under N. F. Galinin was formed, as were departments in the F. F. Erisman Moscow Scientific Research Institute of Hygiene, the Institute of General and Municipal Hygiene of the Academy of Medical Sciences, the Kiev Institute of Municipal Hygiene, and a series of special radiological groups in health and safety organizations. At the same time, the Central Institute of Advanced Medical Training organized a department of radiation hygiene, with Leningrad and Kiev counterparts. In these institutes, scientists conducted fundamental research intended to formulate the basic principles of radiation safety. The field had a highly experimental character and involved extensive field studies. Among them were the impact of liquid radioactive wastes on reservoirs and other bodies of water; the migration of isotopes in different soils and geological formations; the study of atmospheric discharges, including those from atomic power stations, experimental reactors, and submarines; and efforts to control the spread of radioactive materials into the food chain.[8]

In 1953, with the approval of the government, radiation specialists in the Institute of Occupational Safety and Disease Prevention set forth the first in a series of public standards for working with radioactive materials. The standard was 100 millicuries, which, they claimed, even with long-term exposure, would be safe. Alluding to the many ways by which radioactive materials might spread throughout a laboratory (from the operation of screens and sifters, grinders, and pulverizers or by evaporation of radioactive solutions), researchers Gorodinskii and Parkhomenko proposed measures to ensure safe use under the rubrics of isolation, separation, and dilution. Any laboratory using the materials had to be isolated from other facilities in a given institute. Work with isotopes in quantities of less than 0.1 milligram radium equivalent for gamma-emitting isotopes and up to1 millicurie for beta-emitting isotopes could be carried out on separate tables as long as the laboratory itself was no smaller than 15 cubic meters and had floor space of at least 4.7 square meters. For ease in cleaning accidental spills, ceilings, flours, walls, and doors had to be smooth, without any cracks. Paints had to be oil or nitroemulsion. Vessels and containers for handling the isotopes had to be stainless steel or china. Once a month, the entire laboratory had to be washed down. Drinking water had to be handled carefully. Radioactive liquids of no more than 10^{-7} curies per liter could be washed down the drain. Any substance capable of producing gaseous radioactive substances obviously had to be held in hermetically sealed containers. Personal care was also a must; the worker had to avoid any contamination of hands, body, or clothing by wearing smocks and boots. Sleeves and pants legs had to be closed tightly. Dosimeters and Geiger counters were to be used frequently to confirm standards of cleanliness.[9]

In 1960, following logically upon increasing evidence of the dangers of working with radioactive isotopes, the government issued "Sanitary Regulations of Work with Radioactive Materials and Sources of Ionizing Radiation no. 333" to improve worker safety and waste management. The standards are noteworthy as much for what was not covered as for what was. The new laws did not establish maximum allowable exposures for different categories of persons and organs exposed (by age and sex), different kinds of radiation (and again combinations of organs exposed), different pathways into the human organism (air, food, and water), or threshold versus acute exposures, nor did they consider how each of these categories was affected when accompanied by other actions on the body (chemical agents, noise, and vibration).[10] The regulations forbade the dumping of wastewater into the sewer system or any body of water. But the application of radioactive isotopes for research, medical, agricultural, and industrial purposes had become so widespread that levels of activity of 1×10^{-6} to 1×10^{-8} curies per liter were common in many laboratory and industrial effluents. The storage of low-level waste in local conditions cost between 60 and 120 rubles per cubic meter of waste. Because a small laboratory might produce two cubic meters daily, the cost quickly exceeded 36,000 to 72,000 rubles annually.[11] Most laboratory managers were loath to spend so much on storage or safe disposal (for example, on decontamination and coagulation), so they resorted to illegal, surreptitious, and dangerous alternatives, including dumping wastes directly into the sewage system.

This picture stands in sharp contrast to the pride Soviet radiation safety specialists displayed when sharing their expertise in the international arena through the World Health Organization, the International Atomic Energy Agency, and other organizations, symposia, and publications. Despite their international reputation as safety specialists, researchers in reality faced a radioactive waste problem that grew without solution, especially in the major cities where most of the industrial and scientific research organizations that used radioactive isotopes were located. One attempt to deal with the problem was the creation of centralized points for receipt of wastes. Such a system would to put an end to temporary on-site storage. One such storage facility outside of Moscow was easily accessible by highways, but the location left the question of the trucks' safety unresolved. Organizations that daily accumulated more than 200 liters were responsible for their own processing and storage, a tall order that many of them failed. Radioactive isotopes with a half-life of fifteen days or less were not accepted but were stored in special facilities from which they were removed for processing along with other municipal wastes. Concerning transportation, the new regulations stipulated standards for labeling, packaging, and handling, which assumed but did not guarantee safe passage, given the poor state of Soviet barrels, forklifts, trucks, and roads. The regulations gave too much responsibility to the organization that produced the waste and intended to get rid of it as cheaply as possible.[12]

The problem of storage and handling of wastes has only grown in the aftermath of the breakup of the Soviet Union because governments have had to close a number of facilities, and the others lack equipment and the ability to pay workers (see Appendix, Table 22). Military wastes fell outside the purview of regulations. But they shouldn't have, given that there were 11,000 containers of radioactive waste and 15 reactors from atomic submarines and the *Lenin* icebreaker (five of which held fuel) at the Novaia Zemlia polygon of 82,600 square kilometers alone.[13]

Waste begat strange radioactive bedfellows. At Obninsk, birthplace of the peaceful atom, of the Chernobyl-type reactor, and of liquid metal technology for submarines and breeder reactors, radiation specialists founded the so-called World Organization of Health for Radiation Medical Problems in 1991. Radiation medicine began in Obninsk long ago, in connection with exposure of its workers to radiation. The organization has on file a registry of 550,000 persons exposed to excessive radiation in connection with Soviet programs, including 220,000 who participated in liquidation of the Chernobyl disaster. Most of the others probably were exposed to radiation in the Kyshtym explosion or during nuclear tests. The director of the organization, A. F. Tsyb, was a curious choice. Tsyb was the head public health official in the Semipalatinsk region who once asserted that the "influ-

ence of radiation on the health of people [in this region] has not been established."
It was standard operating procedure to promote "downplayers" of danger to high
positions in the nuclear enterprise. The head of the All-Union Scientific Center of
Radiation Medicine in Kiev and the former Minister of Health of Ukraine, was A.
Romanenko. He urged his fellow countrymen and women over radio and television
to remain calm in the face of the Chernobyl disaster, for the dangers of the radiation
plume were minimal.[14]

KYSHTYM: THE PRELUDE TO CHERNOBYL

Two events led the Soviet government to pass new regulations concerning radiation
safety. The first, although not acknowledged until 1989, was the explosion of a
nuclear waste dump near Kyshtym in the Urals in 1957. More even than Lysenkoism, the Ural disaster brought atomic physicists and persecuted geneticists together,
for they needed to consider the long-term public health, genetic, and environmental
impact of an accident that spread more than 2,000,000 curies over 20,000 square
kilometers, killed a number of persons, and required the evacuation of thousands.
American and British nuclear spokespersons initially dismissed the 1976 report of
Zhores Medvedev, an émigré radiobiologist in England, that there had been such an
accident. Oak Ridge and British physicists had analyzed the event and confirmed its
occurrence, but they refused to announce that publicly because they feared growing
opposition to nuclear power in their own countries. The CIA claimed that the accident was the result of a neutron (plutonium production) reactor explosion for the
production of plutonium. Of course, many persons knew of the accident. The local
hospitals were filled with the injured. The authorities posted signs along roads that
ran through the highly contaminated regions, urging drivers to travel at high speed
and not to stop. Later still, scientists from various institutes including Obninsk studied the impact on flora, fauna, soil, and water of the radionuclides and their pathways through the environment.

The explosion involved concentrated waste produced by military reactors and
stored somewhere in an underground concrete bunker. It brought radioactive fission products that had accumulated for years to the surface of the earth to be carried by wind and precipitated dozens of kilometers away. But, although there were
a great number of civilian and military laboratories connected to issues of radiobiology, radiochemistry, radiogenetics, and radiotoxicology, issues of secrecy and
national security prevented any systematic study of classified materials and precluded publication even when there was a study. Timofeeff-Ressovsky refused to
participate in the Kyshtym study because every aspect was made top secret. The scientists who conducted research had to publish under the screen of an agricultural
institute or university and to refer obliquely in obscure publications to "scientists at
an experimental station," at "state farm B," or at "pond 2." In 1964/65, with the
ouster of Khrushchev and the removal of Lysenko, some articles could be published
on those subjects more widely. Embarrassment prevented any direct mention of the
Kyshtym explosion. Rather, Medvedev painstakingly assembled a picture of the explosion by gathering articles on radioactive contamination of lakes, water plants,

and fish; mammals; birds; soil; trees; and field plants. Medvedev worked back from the variety of radioisotopes being discussed in the literature to construct a thorough picture of the disaster.

Once they figured out how to produce sufficient plutonium in a reactor to make bombs, they had to separate the various isotopes of uranium and plutonium in the fuel rods. Modern procedures based on years of trial, error, and experimentation allow for nearly complete recovery of plutonium and the production of less high-level radwaste. But, at first, the pressure to produce materials rapidly led the physicists to dissolve fuel rods from the reactor (with original uranium) in nitric acid. Most of the waste at the bomb factories at Hanford, Washington and at the Maiak facility near Cheliabinsk, Russia was stored in large steel tanks and concrete trenches. There was a lot of waste, heat, and acid, and it accumulated rapidly.[15] In the United States, the best documented leak of this dangerous waste occurred with tank 106-T, involving 435,000 liters of liquid radwaste. At Hanford, nine reactors and the plutonium separation process led to the production of more than seventy million gallons of concentrated liquid waste by 1970, with evaporation and precipitation leaving forty million gallons. There were tens of millions of curies in the wastes. At Kyshtym, the problem was this warm, volatile waste. In September 1957, a cooling mechanism failed in an 80,000-gallon storage tank, thereby allowing an explosion that sent 70 to 80 tons of radioactive material into the air. Nearly 11,000 persons had to be evacuated.[16] Thirty-five years later, on May 20, 1993, the Russian Federation passed a law providing for the social, medical, and political rights of individuals who suffered direct or indirect personal health losses during the liquidation of the accident in 1957 at the Maiak facility or who worked near the Techa river in the period 1949 to 1955, including those who voluntarily or otherwise left the area.[17]

A more irresponsible practice involved the dumping of radioactive wastes in lakes, holding ponds, and reservoirs that were separated from rivers only by dams. This practice led to the second major event. In the river basin near the confluence of the Techa and Misheliak rivers, there is an area of 40 square kilometers containing 200 storage sites, 25 of which remain open. Roughly 500,000 tons of solid wastes of unknown total radioactivity, up to 20,000 cubic meters of liquid wastes with a total activity of 150 million curies, and no less than 900 million curies in liquid wastes are stored there in tanks. Between 1949 and 1956, highly radioactive waste entered the watershed at the source of the Techa. The Maiak facility includes a series of reservoirs with a total capacity of 380 million cubic meters. The reservoirs are separated from the Techa by a dam. Beginning in 1951, near Lake Karachai, Soviet nuclear authorities began to pump billions of curies of cesium- and strontium-laced radioactive waste into the bottom of that 100-acre lake. The resulting reservoir held twenty-four times the radioactive content of the debris released in Chernobyl. The summer of 1967 was hot and dry, Lake Karachai evaporated, and winds blew radioactive dust to areas more than fifty miles away, affecting 41,000 people.[18]

In the early Khrushchev era, many hydrologists and radiation geneticists joined nuclear physicists in pushing arms control endeavors and in raising an alarm about the many dangers connected with the headlong rush into nuclear power. Atmospheric tests were not the only concern. The oceans and seas faced a terrible threat. At Geneva, some specialists proposed disposing of radioactive waste in the deep ocean trenches. Others suggested bodies of water even closer to populated regions, for example, the Black Sea, which is 2,300 meters deep and is bordered by Bulgaria, Russia, and Turkey. In both cases the argument was that there was little mixing of deep water with the upper layers of water, and so currents would not stir up or spread the radioactivity. But scientists in Crimea at the Sevastopol Biological Station rejected these contentions out of hand as irresponsible and unfounded, providing evidence that organic matter in the depths was part of the upper layer food chain and that water exchange between "layers" was significant. Even special containers provided little hope of keeping radwaste in the deep. Sooner or later, deep-water dumping would lead to "significant harm for humanity."[19] Nor, of course, were ocean nuclear explosions permissible. Yet for all this public concern and for all the public health measures, the truth was that the Soviet Union's nuclear polygons were public health disasters.

CLOSED CITIES, FREELY FLOWING RADIOACTIVE WASTE

Peaceful nuclear programs were only a small share of the effort to use nuclear power. In atomic-powered communism, military applications predominated in all aspects: manpower, financing, material, and equipment. Many ideas for peaceful applications originated within military research and development establishments; but because of secrecy requirements or concerns about dual military-civilian uses, these ideas withered away. So if the greatest benefits from various atomic research programs were primarily in preventing war among the superpowers, then the costs were equally significant from the perspective of the diversion of resources from other programs that merited greater attention (housing, education, and health) and from the perspective of the legacy of nuclear waste. That waste has now become the major icon of the nuclear age and, like Chernobyl, it cannot be made to go away.

From Arzamas-16 to Pensa-19, from Tomsk-7 to Krasnoiarsk-26 and the Maiak plutonium separation facility at Cheliabinsk, the nuclear establishment grew, thrived, and prospered as part of the cold war. These facilities employed over one million people to produce fuel, separate isotopes, dilute substances, and build nuclear warheads (see Appendix, Table 23). The quantity of radioactive waste from the military sector is an order of magnitude larger than that from the civilian sector. Maiak alone manages 1 billion curies, of which 120 million is in decrepit and decaying storage tanks. Lakes and holding ponds are filled to the brim with radioactive wastes on the sites of the polygons and production facilities. No one knows how to estimate the legacy of radioactivity from PNEs. There are at least 15,000 tons of spent fuel and twenty tons of plutonium. A final resting place remains a solution of the distant future.[20]

The Siberian Chemical Combine, or Tomsk-7 (now Seversk), had five nuclear reactors. Two still operate, providing plutonium for the nuclear industry and heat and energy for the more than 100,000 residents of Tomsk-7 and Tomsk proper. The combine occupies 200 square kilometers. The reactors were buried hundreds of feet underground, both for purposes of safety and to protect them from a direct hit by a nuclear warhead. The combine has one of the most advanced isotope separators in the world. Throughout its many buildings flow radioactive liquids laden with various isotopes, sometimes in pipes under great pressure, other times through concrete "canyons" to which are added various acids and other chemicals to separate the various isotopes. Biological shielding for workers is inadequate. Tomsk-7 has a special "orphanage," where a growing number of deformed children born to employee and resident parents have been left. Some staff worry that the operation of the reactors or the uranium separation plants of the combine might lead to another Chernobyl disaster. There has been no full-scale disaster yet, but there has been loss of life and limb. The combine has also misplaced uranium and plutonium from its inventory. Its instruments to monitor the huge quantities of radioactive waste and fuel are outdated, inaccurate, and unreliable.[21]

On April 6, 1993, the inevitable happened. There was a large explosion at the chemical combine. As in the case of Chernobyl, foreign specialists first announced the accident—in this case, Swedish scientists. And just as for Chernobyl, information about the extent of the accident was withheld for some time from the citizens at risk. The explosion destroyed a huge part of a uranium waste separation building, including its walls, windows, and girders. The level of gamma radiation was 100 to 200 milliroentgens per hour, so that one day in the area would expose you to more than the yearly norm. There were direct signs of plutonium waste in the explosion. Plant operators were slow to minimize the spread of radioactivity, in part because there was no automated system for control of accidents. Radiation levels reached several hundred millicuries per hour especially in the villages of Georgievka and Chernaia Rechka nearby. President Boris Yeltsin was required to respond with an executive order, criticizing the operation of the combine for endangering the life of local residents and calling on all organizations in the military nuclear complex to adopt measures for "safe" future operation. Ultimately, the minister of atomic energy, Viktor Mikhailov, admitted that they would have to build a sarcophagus for the building, even as a government commission concluded that there was no need for radical intervention. Fortunately, most of the waste was contained locally and consisted of short-lived radionuclides. Because the wind was flowing to the northeast that day instead of to the southwest as it usually did, the most populated areas nearby were not endangered.[22] Fearing another accident, local Tomsk scientists and ecologists have called for a medical-biological commission like that functioning at Hanford to evaluate Tomsk's future. They have encountered obfuscation from regional officials, who have downplayed their concerns and have refused to answer questions about the extent of radioactive waste in the immediate environs and its pathways into the flora, the fauna, and the human beings, and into the snow and soil in the region.[23]

This behavior is par for the course. Krasnoiarsk-26, a town of 90,000, is the site of plutonium extraction facilities and three underground graphite-plutonium production reactors (the oldest of which is forty years old). The facilities also store fuel elements from the South Ukraine, Rovenskaia, Khmelnitskaia, and Zaporozhskaia atomic power stations. Krasnoiarsk-26 is the only place in the former USSR that processes used fuel rods from RBMKs and stores their wastes. Its sister city, Krasnoiarsk-45, is a town of 63,000 inhabitants and several uranium enrichment factories. The Krasnoiarsk Mining Chemical Combine has refused from time to time to accept waste from Ukraine, on one occasion because Ukraine failed to deliver sugar and sunflower oil to regional authorities as part of a barter agreement. The same problems of underground reactors, isotope separation canyons, thousands of tons of highly radioactive waste, unpaid salaries, and poor labor discipline that plague Tomsk-7 now plague Krasnoiarsk.[24] The quiet, isolated city has begun to fray around the edges as its leaders begin to understand the great social and environmental costs of cleanup.

At Arzamas-6, Cheliabinsk-70, Cheliabinsk-65, Cheliabinsk-40 and the infamous Maiak facility, Sverdlovsk-44, Sverdlovsk-45, and Semipalatinsk-21 (also known as Kurchatov), the story is the same. Now that the Soviet Union has fallen apart, the formerly privileged status of scientists and workers in the closed military cities has changed for the worse. No longer can they command high wages, well-stocked stores, and good municipal services. Like other state employees throughout Russia, they go months without pay, eking out an existence. They are still responsible for running reactors and separation facilities, and for processing and storing waste. They are supposed to dismantle rockets and warheads according to the START treaty, but programs lag behind because the facilities lack the proper equipment or financial incentives. Like miners and bus drivers, nuclear workers have threatened to strike. In this environment, the handling of radwaste has become lax.[25]

At the world-renowned Arzamas, scientists created a production facility, the "Avangard" factory, capable of serial production of nuclear warheads. Its theoreticians from Andrei Sakharov on down the line were among the best and brightest in the world. Experimentalists verified their thermonuclear calculations on the BIGR reactor and the "Iskra-5," the most powerful laser in world. But Arzamas cannot live on past laurels alone. At a meeting on June 24, 1993, Vladimir Lapin, president of the Union of Science Cities, lamented the catastrophic situation of specialists. Even after President Yeltsin visited Arzamas and promised to expedite wage payments, nothing happened.[26] The financial difficulties extend far beyond Arzamas to other science cities. Attendance at the dining halls of Cheliabinsk-70 (now called Snezhinsk), the same Cheliabinsk where half of Soviet nuclear warheads were built, including the largest in the world, has been cut in two, because 15,000 workers can't afford to buy the cheap fare.[27]

As conditions decline, dangers increase. On July 17, 1993, according to members of the regional commission of MinAtom and specialists of the Maiak Chemical Combine, there was a partial release into the atmosphere through the ventilation system of alpha particles in an aerosol. However, the specialists claimed this release was several thousand times smaller than the maximum allowable norm, and hence no danger to people or environment. On August 2, 1993, they reported another incident in "Factory 22", when 2 cubic meters of radioactive pulp (a water solution of waste materials) containing 300 millicuries contaminated 100 square meters of the factory floor. Constant accidents threaten the health and safety of plant operators, local residents, and the environment far and wide.[28]

Employees of the military establishment expect accidents to happen with increasing frequency. Even highly qualified workers and skilled technicians become lax when they are not paid. One said, "Safety culture is unthinkable without the undivided attention of the government to nuclear production, and the leaders of the country, who have accumulated mountains of military plutonium, should not forget about that inheritance." But the politicians indeed have forgotten about the employees because they no longer need weapons with plutonium. The workers have gotten tired of appealing to their own government, so they have turned to the international community, raising the specter of brain drain and of problems with the nuclear inventory. "You can't just close this place like a macaroni factory," the workers point out. Labor discipline lags; drunk workers stumble around the place. Robbery, delinquency, even murder have begun to creep into the oases of plutonium production.[29]

Although crime has only recently penetrated formerly safe nuclear cities, radioactivity has long seeped out. There are many areas outside of the military domain with an activity of 1 curie per square kilometers and higher, including 12 regions with 119 administrative centers, 4,281 towns, villages, and cities, and nearly 3 million inhabitants. In the Kaluga region, just outside of Moscow, 6,700 square kilometers of land, including 1,615 square kilometers of agricultural land, are radioactive. There are 235 inhabited areas (with 171,200 residents) that have levels of radioactivity up to 5 curies. There are 63 towns and villages with more than 5,000 inhabitants each, where the levels of radioactivity are between 5 and 12 curies. In Orlov, 22 of 24 administrative centers (with a total population of 363,000) are polluted: an area of 910 square kilometers has radiation levels of 1 to 5 curies and an area of 210 square kilometers has radiation levels of 5 to 15 curies (see Appendix, Table 24).

Even major cities, where the country's scientific and political elite live, are vulnerable. In the Moscow region, there are three to four score sites with dangerous levels of radioactivity—from 600 different sources of radiation. The sources include instruments, old dosimeters, and powerful gamma and beta sources (400 to 1,000 roentgens per hour) produced at various factories. The Kurchatov Institute has seven reactors and their associated radwaste on a site located between two subway stations in the middle of a city of ten million people, surrounded only by a concrete and brick wall. The Institute of Theoretical and Experimental Physics had a heavy water reactor and radwaste on the old Chernomyshkin estate in southern Moscow until the Chernobyl disaster triggered a public outcry that pushed officials to close the reactor. Some waste remained behind. The Elektrostal factory produced fuel rods for atomic power stations. In the 1950s, there were several releases of radioactivity from the factory. The releases included gamma radiation of up to 1,500 milliroentgens per hour. The higher educational establishments connected with the nuclear enterprise, including Moscow State University and the Bauman Moscow State Technical Institute, are also riddled with radwaste. In the St. Petersburg region, things are no better. From 1987 to 1989 alone, state environmental officials observed 1,400 radioactive anomalies, including many with dangerous beta radiation. A concrete storage facility for the *Lenin*'s various wastes located on the Bay of Finland has background radiation of 1,500 milliroentgens per hour.

Just outside of Kiev is a low-level radioactive waste facility that receives about thirty tons of waste annually. The waste, which consists of medical supplies, irradiated experimental animals and plants, and chemicals, is buried under mounds of dirt. Many of the buried containers are already leaking. There are no guards and no alarm system, only a concrete fence made of prefabricated concrete forms. There are five other such facilities in Ukraine. All are located near densely inhabited areas. Worse is the fact that many organizations ceased shipping their waste to the storage sites rather than pay the newly established higher fees. In Kharkiv, in the first half of 1994 the amount of radwaste received by "Spetskombinat" was twenty-five times less than in the same period the previous year. Much of that unshipped waste is now stored in common tanks and drums, and buried in railway embankments or even under asphalt. The facility near Lviv, which accepts wastes from enterprises throughout Ukraine, was closed for three years as a result of local protests. However, when various radioactive isotopes began to accumulate at enterprises throughout the country (of which forty were in the Lviv region), there was no choice but to reopen the facility. Of course, the problem of safe transport of wastes from western regions to Lviv remains. Only the Lviv and Kharkiv Spetskombinat have any more space to accept waste. The entire thirty-year-old system is in disrepair.[30]

Not only the land but the ocean is at risk. The first dumpings of radioactive waste in the White Sea and the Bay of Finland were connected with the testing of nuclear submarines and the *Lenin* in the late 1950s. Since that time, the Soviet nuclear establishment regularly dumped liquid and solid wastes, adding the North and East Siberian Seas as dumping grounds in the early 1960s. The waste included 38 ships, 6,868 containers, and more than 100 large objects (such as cut up reactor carcasses) with a total activity of 19,000 curies. In the Barents Sea, the activity level is 319,000 curies, and in the Karsk Sea, 241,900 curies. All this dumping occurred after the government had signed the 1976 London convention, which prohibited dumping. Despite continuing criticism of the Western practice of ocean dumping, the amount of waste disposal grew over the years. From 1946 through 1982, 600,000 items or containers of radioactive waste were jettisoned into the ocean (a total of 170,000 tons).[31] In 1991, they dumped 2,000 tons; in 1992, more than 1,700 tons. More than twenty barges, seiners, and tankers have been scuttled to the bottom of the ocean. As late as October 1993, the Russian Navy dumped 900 tons of low-level radioactive water from scrapped submarines into the Sea of Japan and abandoned plans to dump more only after protests by Japan and the United States. However, the Russian government expected to receive millions of dollars from those nations so that it could build the appropriate facilities for storage.[32]

The personal side of the military atom is no more uplifting. Nuclear veterans in the Soviet Union, those officers and soldiers who handled warheads and their components for assembly did much of their work by hand, wearing "special" equipment that protected them from radioactivity on paper only. The main benefit of their labor was almost unlimited access to alcohol, which they used for "decontamination." The soldiers knew that they were handling uranium with their bare hands, but they worked under such strict conditions of secrecy that many never figured out why they got ill. Manual assembly of warheads ended only in 1961. When they observed nuclear explosions at test sites like Semipalatinsk throughout the 1950s and early 1960s, few of them wore respirators, which were in short supply in any event. They unwittingly breathed the radioactive dust spreading across the steppe toward the observation points while they took photographs as personal mementos. On Novaia Zemlia, soldiers lived in huts left behind by Nenets natives who had been resettled out of the nuclear testing ground. Like the Bikini islanders moved by the United States military before their weapons tests, the Nenets will never go home again. The soldiers observed huge blasts, fifty-megaton tests, and more. A few men died during the "observations," having been exposed to fatal doses of radiation. If the dosimeters, sensors, and other equipment they used in a test survived the experience, the officers sent the soldiers out to gather them for use in the next test. The men gathered souvenirs—watches, compasses, and so on—any debris from the tests. Of perhaps 44,000 such nuclear veterans, 1,000 survive and most are ill. Only after the breakup of the Soviet Union could nuclear veterans form groups to push for their rights.[33]

At the Kazakhstan polygon, there were 124 atmospheric and surface blasts between 1949 and 1963, and another 343 underground tests between 1963 and 1989. Roughly one-half million persons were exposed to excessive amounts of ionizing radiation as a result of these tests. In the Semipalatinsk region, between 1975 and 1985 the death rate from leukemia grew seven times and from lung cancer, two times. In the surrounding regions, the levels of Down syndrome, schizophrenia, and chromosomal aberrations are now significantly higher than normal. When there were blasts, the military moved people out temporarily, then brought them right back home, without any kind of prophylaxis or deactivation. When people got sick, the military doctors lied about the diagnosis or put "top secret" on their medical folders. Even when diagnosed with cancer, the official death certificates might read "arterial sclerosis."[34] After examining data concerning families of subjects exposed to chronic occupational irradiation at atomic energy enterprises during the period of its establishment (1948 to 1954), researchers recently established that these families had both lower fertility rates and greater numbers of early neonatal mortality, perionatal mortality, infant mortality, and mortality in the prereproductive period.[35]

The legacy of atomic-powered communism should frighten even the most convinced advocates of nuclear power that the future development of technology must be contingent upon a solution to the radwaste problem. They also need to abandon the desideratum of industrial approaches. They must see technology as fallible, and the key to its safety must be based on redundancies of technological and human control. They must humbly swallow their arrogance by recognizing the importance of public participation in the development of nuclear machines. Unfortunately, atomic-powered communism holds sway even today. Nuclear specialists wear historical blinders, thinking of the Obninsk achievement in 1954, not of Chernobyl in 1986,

In the tokamak laboratory (from left to right), Anatolii Aleksandrov, Prime Minister Aleksei Kosygin, unknown, Evgenii Velikhov, Boris Kadomtsev, and others. *(Courtesy of Raissa Kuznetsova and the Kurchatov Institute)*

of food irradiation, not of cesium-tainted sausages, and of a future resolution of difficulties, not of the need for action now.

MINATOMIC-POWERED COMMUNISM

All these leaks, cracks, exposures, explosions, gallons, and tons would seem to have a simple solution: Spend more money on research and cleanup. It is not that simple, for the mindset of atomic-powered communism remains ingrained. Veniamin Skvirskii, engineer and academician, is the founder of RosEkoAtom, a consortium devoted to promoting sales of environmentally safe nuclear technology abroad. He informed government authorities about the danger of the continued operation of the Lenin Leningrad Atomic Power Station. This complex of four RBMKs is located outside the city that was founded by Peter the Great, a city called the Venice of the North. Skvirskii determined after lengthy study that the fourteen million kilowatts of thermal energy produced at the station, some of which is released into the water of the Bay of Finland as cooling effluent, warms the wastewater that is produced by St. Petersburg's five million inhabitants and flows into the bay. The result is a different kind of chemical-biological reactor, which produces a mix of hazardous waste and microorganisms that threaten the inhabitants of both the city and the bay. These concerns, delivered in a report to the municipal government, hit the nuclear industry hard, for Skvirskii was not an antinuclear activist but a product of atomic-powered communism, a designer of nuclear ships, and a supporter of underground and floating power stations.[36]

But Skvirskii's concerns were the tip of the reactor pile. The nuclear industry is in disrepair. Accidents, releases, and incidents continue to occur. Consider a few examples. When Russian troops left Estonia, they left behind two nuclear reactors that had belonged to the Russian Navy submarine training unit in Paldiski (dating from 1968 and 1982). The reactors were shut down in 1989, but the physical units remain, along with 600 cubic meters of liquid and 80 cubic meters of solid radwaste. Because the total weight of the units and associated equipment is eight thousand tons, transport to Russia seems impossible. A bank in Lithuania found in its safe deposit boxes twenty-three lead containers emitting radiation that was eighteenfold greater than background levels. The containers held beryllium, not, as first thought, from Ignalina but from someone holding a Ural post office box. The post office box was owned by a Moscow firm. In 1987, near Sakhalin, a twenty-five-ton load, including six kilograms of strontium-90 in an isotopic generator, the IZU-1, was lost by the Soviet Coast Guard when a helicopter went down in heavy winds and fog about three kilometers from the shore. It seems that no one is actively looking for that item.[37]

At the end of July 1993, one of three VVERs of the Balakova nuclear power station was shut down because of a failure of one of the automatic controls. This shutdown came at a time when the Russian government was considering the construction of two more blocks on the shores of the Volga near Saratov as part of its "complex" energy plan to 2010. Locals are upset because they learned of the plan to build two more reactors from the central press, not from the local authorities as required by current law—even though the Volga Center of the State Nuclear Inspectorate is located in Balakova. The residents are also bothered by the fact that the authorities have yet to build a bridge over the canal. The bridge would facilitate the evacuation of inhabitants from a thirty-kilometer zone in case of an emergency. Nor have the authorities built an emergency control center.[38]

In as much as Lithuania was forced by domestic fuel shortages to stick with the operation of the huge Ignalina RBMK facility, civil defense officials worked with atomic specialists and the public to develop emergency evacuation and other procedures.[39] The Ignalina stations run at 1,250 megawatts to ensure stability. But problems of another sort remain. First, the reactors are RBMKs. Second, the usual problems of poor-quality concrete abound, so bulkheads built to protect the earth from slightly radioactive cooling-pond water are leaking. A third, unique challenge concerns the disposition of the citizenship of the Ignalina staff, ninety percent of whom, from engineers to janitors, are Russian. This situation created tension with Latvian officials and employees. At least the emergency safety system at Ignalina works well: One of the turbogenerators of the second block was tripped when a crow's nest built on a tower shorted out a 330-kilowatt power line. The fried bird and the tower fell to the ground.[40]

The Ignalina power station had been the rallying point for Lithuania's independence movement in the late 1980s and early 1990s—as a symbol of Soviet technological imperialism and the effort to place dangerous reactors far from Moscow. Lithuania's leaders therefore rejected completion of construction of a third RBMK-1500 and commencement of construction of a fourth reactor. Yet by 1998, the re-

The Mironova Mountain Radioactive Waste Dump, Severodvinsk. The Russian government declared the decrepit facility a "state secret" in the late 1990s to avoid facing legal battles to force its cleanup. It is as easy to enter the Mironova facility, only four miles from the city center, as it is for wastes to leak out. The sign reads, "Entry Forbidden. Danger Zone." *(Courtesy of the members of the "Rodnik" environmental organization)*

maining two RBMK-1500s, the world's largest single reactors, continued to operate, while representatives of the European Community insisted that they be closed as a precondition the country's entry into the European Union. Lithuanian leaders are in a quandary, for the reactors provide eighty percent of Lithuania's electrical energy and the country, with little fossil fuel or hydropower potential, has few other options. The Lithuanian people are no more comfortable with dictates from Europe than they were with dictates from Moscow. Many individuals who live near Ignalina, a region where the vast majority of residents are of Russian descent, fully support the continued operation of the reactors and lament the mothballing of the other two. They worry about the loss of 10,000 jobs should the station be closed more than they do about the spent fuel rods which must be stored on the site, for they cannot afford to ship them to Russia for final disposition. In a paradoxical way, atomic-powered communism lives on in Lithuania.

The industry has performed no better after Chernobyl than before, despite a heightened interest in safety. Required by law and common sense to provide monthly report cards on "incidents" and to alert local, regional, and national officials immediately in case of a significant accident, MinAtom and power station personnel were embarrassed repeatedly by accidents that revealed Potemkin safety. In June 1989, radioactive water leaked from the Kursk station during repairs. In May 1991, the Bilibino reactor hall and other facilities had to be decontaminated after a leak. In July 1991, three persons were injured by a radiation leak at Ignalina. In March 1992, a fire forced the closing of the Balakova station. Also in March 1992, radioactive gases leaked into the atmosphere at the Leningrad station. A hydrogen fire at the Zaporozhskaia station's fifth block was ignited during repairs on a turbine and killed one worker, injured another seriously, and released radioactivity. In a New Year's Eve accident, flames engulfed several sections of the Beloiarsk station. Communications failed, lights went out, clouds of smoke filled the area, and 1,200 people eventually took part in dousing the fire.[41] It's not much better at "clean" sites of stable VVERs. Research based on 4,000 different samples taken from near the Novovoronezh site beginning in 1987 revealed spots of high-level concentrations of ^{137}Ce and ^{134}Ce radiating 36 to 40 microroentgens per hour, or three times the norm. In some "industrial" sites radiation was up to 500 microroentgens per hour. In 1991 alone, there were 270 emergency shutdowns of reactors at all 15 stations. Of forty-five reactors on the territory of the former USSR, sixteen were RBMKs; and all forty-five are located in heavily populated regions.[42]

Six thousand tons of spent fuel have filled temporary storage facilities at the Leningrad and Kursk stations. The three Smolensk station RBMKs, near Desnogorsk, may have to be closed down, according to main engineer Iu. Dorosh, because of waste-disposal problems. They built the units without storage facilities and have filled the temporary on-site pools with spent fuel. After Chernobyl, Soviet engineers commenced construction on a storage facility, but they ran out of money before it was completed. Plans to transform the wastes into a stable, easy-to-handle glasslike substance and to build a fuel fabrication facility to use spent fuel in breeder reactors have lagged because of inadequate funding. The plan for fuel fabrication worries Washington's nonproliferation specialists.[43]

Belatedly, like the Department of Energy and the military establishment in the United States, MinAtom requested several hundred million dollars to solve a multibillion dollar radwaste problem that requires the participation of a dozen other ministries and organizations. MinAtom has promised to clear holding ponds, ensure the safety of groundwater, and drain the worst facilities, like Lake Karachai. Areas where PNEs were conducted would be surveyed and, if possible, stabilized or cleaned. The legacy of atomic-powered communism at civilian power stations—more than 150,000 cubic meters of liquid, 12,000 cubic meters of sludge, and 100,000 cubic meters of solid wastes, and 6,000 tons of fuel in storage at RBMK sites, with Cheliabinsk and Krasnoiarsk in no shape to process spent fuel—remains.[44] Will the fuel cycle remain unbroken?

For many nuclear scientists, the Chernobyl disaster drove home the point that they could not claim to be "first in the world" in anything, achievements in fusion notwithstanding. Chernobyl indicated that the level of their scientific knowledge at the time of design and building of the reactor lagged behind that level necessary to ensure health and safety. The scientific elite had blindly turned away from applied science and away from proper supervision of the transformation of the results of their research into socially appropriate applications and had abandoned standards of health, safety, and true "workers' democracy."[45] No one spoke when Kyshtym exploded. In hushed tones, they belatedly learned that the *Lenin*'s reactor had melted down in 1966 and thirty people had died. They learned that nuclear submarines had had fires and meltdowns here, there, and everywhere. Only the courageous scientists spoke out, even after Chernobyl.

Valerii Legasov learned from Chernobyl that similar accidents were possible. But poor construction practices, the absence of fail-safe emergency systems, a lack of containment, and the philosophy of the gallop toward nuclear power remained in place. After he published a lengthy article in *Pravda* that eloquently laid bare his concerns, he was blackballed by the Kurchatov Institute leadership, where he was deputy director. In the spring of 1987, 100 voted for, 129 against electing Legasov to the institute's scientific and technical council. Then he was bypassed for a Hero of Socialist Labor award. His evil action was to propose setting up interdisciplinary councils of young scientists who could challenge the establishment and promote a vital relationship to understand risk, progress, and knowledge. The old farts rejected him and his plans.[46] Having pushed Legasov out of the way, the engineers in the Kurchatov Institute and government bureaucracies dealing with nuclear energy tried to take the wind out of the opposition's sails by creating a system within which the regulators will be the regulated.[47] Legasov, unable to carry the burden of Chernobyl, committed suicide on April 27, 1988, on the two-year anniversary of the disaster.

But a "green movement" was engendered by Chernobyl. At one station after another, local opposition led to the mothballing of a number of nuclear reactors. Many of the green movements that appeared in the late 1980s, much to the consternation of the nuclear establishment, were connected to independence movements in countries (Ukraine and Lithuania) and "autonomous" regions such as Tatarstan. The antinuclear sentiment abated once Ukraine and Lithuania had independence, but local opposition to reactors remained strong. The sixth Zaporozhskaia VVER-1000 unit was ready to commence run-up in the summer of 1994. But public opinion prevented its operation. A referendum of residents of the regional centers Nikopol and Kamenka-Dneprovskaia revealed that they wanted neither the sixth unit to operate nor an authorization to draw down the Kakhovskoe reservoir to cool the monster. When physicists connected with the industry and at Cheliabinsk sought approval for the South Ural station and proclaimed the safety of fast reactors, the local residents wondered out loud at public meetings whether nuclear power was necessary at all. Physicists' arguments that an energy shortfall required the development of nuclear energy fell on deaf ears. Claims that the new reactor could safely evaporate much of the radioactive water stored in reservoirs in the region (some 300 million cubic meters) made little sense to the citizens.[48]

Officials of Energiia, an all-union scientific research institute to promote nuclear power that shared personnel with the Kurchatov Institute, countered the greens by preparing compendiums of the central press on nuclear power, with the hope of identifying and neutralizing opposition to nuclear power. They have dismissed the opposition as ignorant. Once they have the financial backing to fight back or sense a weakness in the greens, MinAtom officials order nuclear construction workers to pick up their tools and march toward the nuclear future. Just as they did in the Brezhnev era, they avoid discussion and refuse to complete environmental impact statements. Nuclear power advocates refuse to recognize that opposition arose because of twenty years of inadequate safety, siting, and waste-handling practices that remain largely in force.[49]

MinAtom's engineers have not for a minute given up the nuclear ghost. Industry leaders are unmoved by the Chernobyl disaster or the greens. They postpone repair of defective equipment. They do little to attract and retain qualified workers. Labor turnover is high and living conditions poor, and station sites are a confluence of mud and debris. Officials push ahead with an ambitious nuclear energy program as central to the country's economic development through the year 2010. They maintain plans to finish eleven stations under construction and to commence construction on perhaps another two or three dozen; they initially planned to build another fifty stations. The Russian nuclear industry intends to advance at least five new reactor models of 1,000 megawatts and larger for electrical energy production and thermal district heating. Those physicists whose designs had fallen by the wayside because of the omnipotence of Aleksandrov and his institute have rushed forward with proposals for alternative breeders and thermal reactors that they claim are inherently safe. The director of the Institute of Theoretical and Experimental Physics, Vasilii Vladimirskii, has proposed a heavy water reactor with gas coolant, building on the heavy water traditions of the institute.[50]

Some engineers rightfully argue that it makes no sense to deploy new reactor technology until all the shortfalls in existing reactors are overcome in the first- and second-generation pressurized-water reactors and all RBMKs are shut down. Other specialists call for stations to be built underground, far away in the Siberian tundra, or both. Industry spokesmen rejected siting far from cities because of the loss of eight percent of the power generated per 1,000 kilometers of transmission lines. Others worry that the nuclear industry has stagnated with the decline of orders. It has been years since machinery was upgraded, and therefore equipment produced would not meet contemporary standards in quality and reliability. From an economic point of view, nuclear power remains more expensive than fossil fuel power. From the point of view of safety, the government and industry have yet to work out standards, responsibilities, or oversight. The fuel cycle remains open and unstable. There is no conception of how to solve the growing problem of radioactive wastes. Finally, MinAtom has no sense of where to build reactors.[51]

Connected with the problems of the persistance of MinAtom world view and programs is the fact that producers, regulators, and operators remain the same as during the period of Soviet power. This situation has a dangerous effect on the operation of nuclear power stations. The Ministry of Energy of the USSR disappeared, but in its place almost miraculously rose up a company known as "EES Rossiia," whose stock is held by former Communist bureaucrats. It is even housed in the same quarters as Minenergo. EES Rossiia controls, through fees, charges, and regulations, the power lines that crisscross Russia. Depending on Byzantine understandings of profit, supply, and demand, it has ordered nuclear power stations to reduce production or to operate at lower levels, (a practice that increases the cost per kilowatt hour) rather than sell surplus energy to Armenia, Belarus, or Estonia, perhaps at a lower profit margin. For reasons of safety, cost, and efficiency, nuclear energy should meet base load demand.[52]

Nuclear specialists and policy makers have only begun to think about the costs and uncertainties of another serious problem: shutting down and mothballing reactors that will soon reach the end of their operating lives. To put this massive task in perspective, remember that the average 1,000-megawatt reactor provides enough heat and electricity for a city of 700,000 inhabitants. It sits on hundreds of acres of land, contains 8,000 tons of steel and 100,000 cubic meters of concrete, and it is filled with more than 1,500 kilometers of various cables, wires, and pipes. Removing spent fuel, cutting piping, detaching pumps and steam separators, breaking up walls, cutting up the reactor housing itself into chunks small enough to be handled safely by cranes, packing anything radioactive, and transporting these tons of dangerous materials by barge to some secure storage site, and leaving behind a secure, slightly radioactive shell, is no small matter, especially when Russia and Ukraine run deficits of billions of rubles and hrivnias. Decade after decade, perhaps for 100 years, specialists will need to monitor the shell to ensure public health and environmental safety.[53] Physicists and policy makers postponed decisions in all nuclear nations about how to meet the exogenous and ignored costs of the glorious nuclear future.

The light of atomic-powered communism refuses to go out. When we try to sleep, we have constant nightmares: unemployed or underemployed Russian nuclear specialists, or perhaps former KGB agents, trot around the globe, selling plutonium or highly enriched uranium-235 to bidders from so-called rogue nations. The United

States government has spent over $1.5 billion to help Russia manage its nuclear materials, comply with START and other treaties, and keep specialists actively engaged in research within the closed cities of atomic-powered communism. Owing to a breakdown in procedures, uncertainty of responsibilities, loss of qualified personnel, and failure to pay salaries, mishandling of radioactive materials occurs with increasing frequency.

Unfortunately, this nightmare is the least of the problems. The nuclear enterprise in the former Soviet Union consists of rickety technologies that have outlived their usefulness, many of which should never have been built in the first place; scientific bureaucrats who continue to view nuclear technology as a raison d'etre if not a panacea; millions of gallons and thousands of tons of high- and low-level radioactive waste, solid waste, and weapons-grade fuel. Even today, when the Russian economy shows few signs of life, the government and scientific community continue to pour resources into a few costly space and nuclear physics projects, while leaving basic science to suffer with inadequate support; MinAtom eats up more funding than that allotted for all other civilian research and development programs (for example, through its ITER fusion reactor).[54]

Born of cold war competition for parity and ideological competition intended to demonstrate the superiority of the Soviet social order and its science through a series of technological "firsts," the Soviet nuclear establishment grew, according to some estimates, to 1.5 million employees, 47 top secret, closed and open research, development, and production cities, and scores of engineering and physics institutes. Whole cities were created in the name of nuclear research, but their purpose often had more to do with national security than with the peaceful atom: Dubna, north of Moscow, site of a joint high-energy physics institute for "fraternal" physicists from Eastern Europe; Obninsk, home of the Physics Engineering Institute where many thermal reactors were designed; Arzamas-16, home of the hydrogen bomb effort; Krasnoiarsk-26, Tomsk-7, and dozens of others.[55]

The cold war provided impetus to the growth of the establishment, while secrecy and disregard for health and safety contributed to the operation of its facilities with inadequate attention to the problems of radioactive waste storage and disposal. Encouraged by the now time-bound practices of party officials and economic planners who embraced mass production as a way to minimize the chances for assembly or construction errors, cut costs, and save on materials and equipment, nuclear physicists sought early standardization of fundamental components in many nuclear technologies. Buoyed by their initial successes and convinced that they could do no wrong, technological arrogance and momentum came to dominate their programs. High hopes existed for the power of the atom.

These hopes were dashed in atomic-powered communism. Whether the fear of the enemy postponed decisions about how to store the waste properly, or the conviction that a solution to waste would at some time in the future be found, physicists connected with the military research and development apparatus bear the responsibility of knowing that they have created a environmental and health problem second to none for all the citizens of the world. There are no other technological systems that have had such great human and environmental costs, or where so little has been done to attack the problem. Years pass, officials make policies, and physicists, engineers, and management personnel at nuclear facilities make stop-gap decisions. Waste accumulates at civilian reactor sites and seems to have no place to go. It will take hundreds of years and billions of dollars to clean up hazardous nuclear waste and ensure the safety of future generations. It is no consolation to know that the policy makers and the personnel making the decisions about nuclear waste at Soviet facilities were the most irresponsible of any in the world.

The civilian and military cultures of nuclear physics were mutually reinforcing. Technological arrogance and technological momentum held sway in both cultures, leading to the creation of technologies that were costly in every sense, from exploitation of human and financial resources to impacts on the environment and public health. The cold war pressure to achieve parity with the United States understandably required physicists to master nuclear fuel production rapidly. Unfortunately, they adopted tried and true industrial approaches in reactor construction, waste handling, and other practices when more circumspect and sound approaches were required. Whether Atommash or Sosnovyi Bor, Cheliabinsk or Bilibino, Novaia Zemlia or Chernobyl, Obninsk or Kharkiv, technological style was of a piece. We should not be shocked by images of fishermen standing downstream from Chernobyl on the shores of the Pripiat or downstream from Maiak on the shores of the Techa.

What images does the notion of a nuclear power station provoke among impressionable schoolchildren? A Soviet newspaper published selected drawings from France and the Soviet Union. In France, where power stations have operated thus far without disaster and government technocrats have succeeded in presenting them as a machine in the garden, children portray power stations in their drawings as simple buildings in bright colors. The sun shines down, smiling faces dot the windows (!), trees and flowers grow alongside, and people walk to work in ordinary clothes. But the dangers of the Soviet style of nuclear power engineering have penetrated the consciousness of Soviet schoolchildren. In their drawings, dark clouds cover the sky, armed men in hard hats guard the entrance, and nuclear missiles ring a fortresslike structure.[56]

Nuclear technologies were a prominent postwar example of how the Soviet Union had successfully used science for social, economic, and political purposes to transform an agrarian, illiterate society into an urban, highly educated one; to create an industrial giant on a weak foundation; and to establish viable national defense in the face of what was perceived to be "hostile capitalist encirclement." Physicists developed broad political and cultural support for an expansive research program that involved application of nuclear knowledge throughout the economy for peaceful purposes. This program, which included research, military, and power-generating reactors, peaceful nuclear explosions, and applications of radioisotopes, truly reflected society-wide enthusiasm in science and technology as a panacea, and contributed to a rediscovery of constructivist visions. It was not a Potemkin effort to deceive the Soviet public or international audiences about middling achievements nor an attempt to mislead them about the extensive environmental and health hazards that came to be associated with nuclear power. Rather, nuclear culture reveals the deeper political and administrative structures and research processes that were paradigmatic for science and technology in the Soviet Union.

Because of the presence of a one-party system that tolerated no dissent and excluded the public from the policy process; a centrally planned economy that was intolerant of innovation but treated failure to meet targets as a punishable offense; a fascination with certain aspects of the American system of mass production; and a state-sponsored economically determinist ideology, these technologies developed a particular aesthetics. The Soviet nuclear power effort shows the extent to which technological arrogance dominated program decision-making. It shows the danger of unquestioned faith in large-scale technology. It shows the roots and pitfalls of the blind pursuit of premature standardization. And it demonstrates what happens when scientific and engineering tasks—understanding nature and applying that knowledge for human purposes, respectively—become blurred in a society infused with a xenophobic and omniscient ideology.

APPENDIX

TABLE 1

Oil, Gas, and Coal Production in the USSR, 1940–1980

Year	Oil	Gas (billions of cubic meters)	Coal
1940	31.1	3.2	165.9
1950			261.1
1955			389.9
1960	148.0	45.3	509.6
1965	242.9	127.7	577.7
1970	353.0	197.9	624.1
1975	490.8	289.3	701.3
1980	603.2	435.2	716.4

SOURCES: *Narodnoe khoziaistvo SSSR v 1975 g.* (Moscow: Statistika, 1976), pp. 240–242; *Narodnoe khoziastvo SSSR v 1980 g.* (Moscow: Finansy i statistika, 1981), pp. 156–157.

TABLE 2

USSR Energy Derived from East of Urals, 1940–1972

Fuel	Percentage in One Year			
	1940	1960	1970	1972
Oil	6.3	7.2	18.1	25.3
Gas	0.5	2.4	29.8	33.5
Coal	28.7	35.9	43.2	45.6

SOURCE: Division of Research Research and Development, U.S. ERDA, *Soviet Power Reactors—1974* (Washington, DC: U.S. Government Printing Office, 1974), p. 11.

TABLE 3

Capacity of Electric Power Stations and Production of Electrical Energy in the USSR, 1940–1985*

Year	Capacity of All Stations	Production	Hydroelectric Capacity	Hydro-Production	Nuclear Capacity	Nuclear Production
1960	66.7	292	14.8	50.9	Negligible	Negligible
1970	166	741	31.4	124	0.9	3.5
1980	267	1,294	52.3	184	12.5	72.9
1985	315	1,544	61.7	215	28.1	160

Capacity in millions of kilowatts, production in billions of kilowatt-hours.

SOURCE: *Narodnoe khoziaistvo SSSR za 70 let* (Moscow: Finansy statistika, 1987), p. 161.

TABLE 4

Electrical Power Lines in the USSR with Power of 35 Kilowatt and Greater

Power Rating (kW)	Length of Line (in thousands of kilometers)			
	1960	1970	1980	1985
35	36.7	175.7	303.7	345.0
110	64.6	185.8	309.1	368.9
154	2.0	5.8	9.7	11.0
220	15.6	50.2	92.8	115.0
330	1.1	14.2	24.3	28.4
400–500	4.4	12.2	25.5	34.7
750	—	0.1	2.9	4.2
800	—	0.5	0.5	1.4

SOURCE: *Narodnoe khoziaistvo SSSR za 70 let* (Moscow: Finansy statistika, 1987), p. 162.

TABLE 5

Basic Parameters of First Reactors at Belioarsk Atomic Power Station

Parameter	First Reactor	Second Reactor	Planned Reactor (not built)
Thermal power, MW	286	560	2,220
Electrical power, MW	100	200	1,000
Tons of uranium	67	50	51
Power density, MW/t	4.3	11.2	43
Uranium enrichment, %	1.8	3.0	5.0
Working channels	998	998	1,270
Size of active zone			
diameter, m	7.2	7.2	8.9
height, m	6	6	6

SOURCE: P. I. Aleshchenkov et al., "Beloiarskaia atomnaia elektrostantsiia im. I. V. Kurchatova," *Atomnaia energiia*, vol. 16, no. 6 (June 1964), 493.

TABLE 6

Parameters of High-Power Channel-Graphite Reactors

Specifications	RBMK-1000	RBMK-1500	RBMK-2000
Electrical power, MW	1,000	1,500	2,000
Thermal power, MW	3,200	4,800	5,400
Efficiency	31.3	31.3	37
Number of evaporating channels	1,693	1,664	1,744
Number of steam superheating channels	0	0	872
Uranium load, tons	192	189	226
Enrichment, %	1.8	1.8	1.8 to 2.2
Water circulation, t/h	37,500	29,000	39,300
Size of active zone, height, m	7	7	6
Size of active zone, diameter or length/width, m	11.8	11.8	7.75 by 24
Steam pressure before turbine, atm	65	65	65
Steam temperature before turbine, °C	280	280	450

SOURCE: N. A. Dollezhal, N. Ia. Emel'ianov, "Opyt sozdaniia moshchnykh energeticheskikh reaktorov v SSSR," *Atomnaia energiia,* vol. 40, no. 2 (February 1976), 124.

TABLE 7

VVER Nuclear Power Stations

Atomic Power Station	Number of Turbogenerators	Total Power (MW)	Date Providing Power to Grid
Novovoronezh 1	3 at 70 MW	210	September 1964
2	5 at 75 MW	365	December 1969
3	2 at 220 MW	417	December 1971
4	2 at 220 MW	417	December 1972
5	2 at 500 MW	1,000	May 1980
Kolsk 1	2 at 220 MW	440	June 1973
2	2 at 220 MW	440	December 1974
3	2 at 220 MW	440	March 1981
4	2 at 220 MW	440	December 1984
Armenia 1	2 at 220 MW	407.5	December 1976
2	2 at 220 MW	407.5	January 1980
Rovensk 1	2 at 220 MW	392	December 1980
2	2 at 220 MW	416	December 1981
3	2 at 500 MW	1,000	December 1986

(continued)

Table 7 *continued*

VVER Nuclear Power Stations

Atomic Power Station	Number of Turbogenerators	Total Power (MW)	Date Providing Power to Grid
South Ukraine 1	1 at 1,000 MW	1,000	December 1982
2	2 at 500 MW	1,000	January 1985
3	2 at 500 MW	1,000	December 1981
Balakovo 1	2 at 500 MW	1,000	December 1985
2	2 at 500 MW	1,000	October 1987
3	2 at 500 MW	1,000	December 1988
Zaporozhe 1	2 at 500 MW	1,000	December 1984
2	2 at 500 MW	1,000	October 1985
3	2 at 500 MW	1,000	December 1986
4	2 at 500 MW	1,000	December 1987
5	2 at 500 MW	1,000	September 1989
Khmel'nitskaia 1	2 at 500 MW	1,000	December 1987

SOURCES: G. A. Sharsharin, E. I. Ignatenko, V. M. Boldyrev, "Sostoianie i perspektivy razvitiia AES s VVER," *Atomnaia energiia,* vol. 56, no. 6 (June 1984), 354; and V. I. Bulatov, *200 Iadernykh poligonov SSSR* (Novosibirsk: Tseris, 1993), pp. 29–30.

TABLE 8

Hours of Operation of BR-5 Reactor at Different Power Levels

Year	Hours of Operation					
	< 100 kW	101– 1,000 kW	1,001– 4,000k W	5,000 kW	Total	Percentage of year
1959	574	167	342	48	1,222	27.4
1960	583	1,639	2,174	887	6,677	78.7
1961	498	78	864	2,709	4,380	75.4
1962	1,307	3,139	—	—	4,446	60.5
1963	529	3,771	990	—	5,290	61.6
1964	224	1,218	2,487	—	3,929	53.6
1965	271	240	281	1,586	2,457	46.5
1966	783	400	229	3,362	4,966	56.9
Total	4,769	10,652	7,367	8,592	33,367	—

SOURCE: A. I. Leipunskii et al., "Opyt ekspluatatsii reaktora BR-5 za period 1959–1966 gg.," *Atomnaia energiia,* vol. 23, no. 6 (December 1967), 504.

TABLE 9

Operating Parameters of the BR-5 and BR-10

Years	Fuel	Maximum Power (kW)	Na Temperature Entering Reactor	Na Temperature Exiting Reactor	Maximum Fuel Burn-Up
1959–1964	PuO_2	5,000	430° C	500° C	6.7
1965–1971	UC	5,000	430° C	500° C	6.1
1973–1979	PuO_2	7,000	350° C	470° C	14.1
1983–1989	UN	—	—	—	9.0
1990–1997	UN	—	—	—	9.7

SOURCES: Iu. E. Bagdasarov et al., "Obespechenie bezopasnosti pri ekspluatatsii AES s bystrymi reaktorami v SSSR," *Atomnaia energiia*, vol. 55, no. 6 (December 1983), 357; and communication from Oleg Kazachkovskii, March 1998.

TABLE 10

Specifications of the BN-350, BN-600, and BN-1600

Reactor	BN-350	BN-600	BN-1600
Thermal power, MW	1,000	1,500	4,000
Electrical output, MW	350	600	1,600
Sodium temperature			
at reactor inlet, °C	300	380	
at reactor outlet, °C	500	550	530–550
Sodium flow rate, t/h	14,000	6,800	
Steam generating capacity, t/h	300	1,840	
temperature, °C	435	505	~500
pressure, kgf/cm^2	50	140	140
Core length/width, cm	150/106	205/75	330/110
Fuel subassemblies	200	370	
Fuel rods per subassembly	169	127	
Fuel	UO_2 or $PuO_2 + UO_2$	UO_2 or $PuO_2 + UO_2$	
Maximum burn-up, %	5	10	10
Operating time between reloading, days	50–60	150	
Breeding ratio	1.5		

TABLE 11
Production of Cement in the Soviet Union, 1920–1980

Year	Thousands of Metric Tons*	Year	Thousands of Metric Tons*
1920	36	1955	22,500
1925	872	1960	45,500
1930	3,006	1965	72,400
1935	4,488	1970	95,250
1940	5,675	1975	122,100
1945	1,845	1980	125,000
1950	10,194		

*Figures have been rounded.

Sources: *Promyshlennost' SSSR. Statisticheskii sbornik* (Moscow: Gosstatizdat, 1957), p. 277; *Promyshlennost' SSSR. Statisticheskii sbornik* (Moscow: Statistika, 1964), p. 320; *Narodnoe khoziaistvo SSSR v 1973 g.* (Moscow: Statistika, 1974), p. 300; *Narodnoe khoziaistvo SSSR v 1973 g.* (Moscow: Finansy i Statistika, 1974), p. 178.

TABLE 12
Production of Pre-Fabricated Reinforced Concrete Forms

Year	Annual Production (in thousands of cubic meters)	
	Panels*	Total
1958	—	18,000
1960	143	30,200
1962	954	41,900
1965	3,000	56,100
1970	6,357	84,561
1975	11,580	114,161
1980	—	122,185

* Large-panel production figures no longer provided after 1975; cement factories moved to the serial production of more sophisticated forms.

Sources: *Promyshlennost' SSSR. Statisticheskii sbornik* (Moscow: Statistika, 1964), p. 332; *Narodnoe khoziaistvo SSSR v 1973 g.* (Moscow: Statistika, 1974), p. 301; *Narodnoe khoziaistvo SSSR v 1973 g.* (Moscow: Finansy i Statistika, 1981), p. 179.

TABLE 13

Atomic Ships of the Former Soviet Union

Name	Displacement (tons)	Length (m)	Width (m)	Power (1,000 s/hp)	Year Put in Service	Maximum Speed (knots)
Lenin	19	134	28	44	1959	20
Arctic	23	148	30	75	1974	12
Siberia	23	148	30	75	1975	21
Russia	23	150	30	75	1985	21
*Sevmorput'**	61	260	32	40	1988	20
Taimyr	20	150	29	50	1989	19
Soviet Union	24	150	30	75	1990	21
Iamal	20	150	30	50	1990	19
Vaigach	20	150	30	50	1990	19

* *The freighter* "Northern Shipping Lane"; *the others are icebreakers.*

SOURCE: B. I. Bulatov, *200 iadernykh poligonov SSSR* (Tseris: Novosibirsk, 1993), p. 37.

TABLE 14

Irradiation Pilot Plants and Experimental Facilities for Food Irradiation in Eastern Europe and the former Soviet Union

Location	Name/ Purpose	Source Strength kCi (date)	Source Strength kW	Product	Throughput Capacity t/h	Throughput Capacity Dose (Mrad)	Throughput Capacity Mrad/h
Novyi Krichim, Bulgaria	Multipurpose irradiator	34 (1975)	0.50	Potatoes, onions dried fruits	1.1– 12.0	0.01	0.077
Sofia, Bulgaria	Multipurpose irradiator	40 (1975)	0.59	Wheat, fruits, chicken, spices			
Budapest, Hungary	KEKI pilot food irradiator	60 (1974)	0.88	Potatoes, feed, spices	4.0	0.01	0.045
	Isotope institute	80 (1974)	1.18	Feed	0.03	2.5	0.075
Lodz, Poland	Multipurpose irradiator	20 (1973)	0.29	Spices, potatoes, grain			
Bogutsharovo, Tula, Russia	Multipurpose irradiator	136 (1971)	2.01		0.18	1.0	0.18
Kanibadam, Tajikistan	Dried fruit irradiator	35 (1971)	0.52				

(continued)

Table 14 *continued*

Irradiation Pilot Plants and Experimental Facilities for Food Irradiation in Eastern Europe and the former Soviet Union

Location	Name/ Purpose	Source Strength kCi (date)	kW	Product	Throughput Capacity t/h	Dose (Mrad)	Mrad/h
Dzerzhinskii, Moscow	Potato irradiator	50 (1971)	0.74	Potatoes	3.0	0.01	0.03
VNIIKOP, Moscow	Multipurpose irradiator	240 (1971)	3.55				
	On-board ship irradiator	91 (1971)	1.35	Marine products	0.10	0.25	0.025
VNIIZ, Moscow	Grain irradiator	35 (1971)	0.52	Grain	0.40	0.10	0.004

SOURCE: H. Goresline, in E. Josephson and M. Peterson (eds.), *Preservation of Food by Ionizing Radiation* (Boca Raton, FL: CRC Press, 1983), vol. 1.

TABLE 15

Irradiated Food Products Approved for Human Consumption in the USSR, 1958–1967

Product	Purpose of Irradiation	Dose (krad)	Date of Official Clearance
Potatoes	Sprout inhibition	10	March 1958
Grain	Disinfestation	30	1959
Dry fruits	Disinfestation	100	February 1966
Dry food concentrates	Disinfestation	70	June 1966
Fresh fruits and vegetables	Reduction of micro-organisms for shelf-life extension	200–400	July 1964
Raw meats, partially processed cuts of beef, pork, and rabbit, packaged in film	Shelf-life extension	600–800	July 1964
Eviscerated chilled chicken	Shelf-life extension	600	July 1966
Prepared meat products	Shelf-life extension	800	February 1967
Onions	Sprout inhibition	6	February 1967

SOURCE: L. V. Metlitskii, V. I. Rogachev, V. G. Krushchev, *Radiation Processing of Food Products* (Moscow: NCF, 1967), p. 81.

TABLE 16

Cyclic Accelerators Produced by NIIEFA

Year	Kind	Energy	Location
1949	Proton synchrocyclotron	680 MeV	Dubna
1957	Weak-focusing proton synchrotron	10 GeV	Dubna
1967	Strong-focusing proton synchrotron	76 GeV	Serpukhov
1967	Electron synchrotron	6 GeV	Erevan
1967	Synchrocyclotron	1 GeV	Gatchina
Under construction	Superconducting collider	3 TeV	Serpukhov

SOURCE: NIIEFA Promotional Brochure, no date, in Russian and English.

TABLE 17

Water-Water Research Reactors in the Soviet Union

Reactor	Location	Number of Experimental Channels
VVR-K	Almaty	41
VVR-Ts	Sbninsk	38
VVR-M	Gatchina	32
VVR-S	Tashkent	38
VVR-M	Kiev	39
IRT-2000	Tbilisi	26
IRT-2000	Riga	26
IRT-2000	Tomsk	26
VVR-2	Moscow	8
IRT-2000	Minsk	26

SOURCE: Zh. S. Takibaev, Sh. Sh. Ibramigov, G. A. Batyrbekov, B. N. Okolovich, "Modernizirovannyi reaktor VVR-K ii ego ispol'zovanie v narodnom khoziaistve Khazakhstana," *Vestnik Akademii Nauk Kazakhskoi SSR*, no. 2 (1972), 17.

TABLE 18

Research Reactors Built in Countries of Peoples' Democracies, 1957–1961

Country	Type of Reactor	Year of Operation	Power (MW)	Volumetric Power (kW/l)
Germany	VVR-S	1957	2	20
Czechoslovakia	VVR-S	1957	2	20
Poland	VVR-S	1958	2	20

(continued)

Table 18 *continued*

Research Reactors Built in Countries of Peoples' Democracies, 1957–1961

Country	Type of Reactor	Year of Operation	Power (MW)	Volumetric Power (kW/l)
Romania	VVR-S	1958	2	20
Hungary	VVR-S	1959	2	20
Korea	TVR-S	1959	10	8
Bulgaria	IRT-2000	1961	2	30

SOURCE: *Biulleten' tsentra obshchestvennoi informatsii po atomnoi energii,* no. 10–11 (1996), 69.

TABLE 19
Nuclear Power Stations Built or Forecast in Ukraine, 1988

Site	Type of Reactor	Number of Units	Megawatts per Unit	Total Megawatts of Station
Rovno	PWR	2	440	880
South Ukraine	PWR	5	1,000 +	6,200
Zaporozhe	PWR	4	1,000	4,000
Chernobyl	RBMK	4	1,000	4,000
Khmel'nitskaia	PWR	4	1,000	4,000

TABLE 20
Nuclear Explosions of the Five Original Nuclear Powers (as of January 1, 1991)

Country	Total	Atmospheric	Total Yield (megatons)
USSR	715	215	452
at Semipalatinsk	486	150	—
at Novaia Zemlia	132	87	—
United States	1,085	205	141
France	182	45	—
Great Britain	42	21	—
China	35	22	13
Total	2,059	508	629

SOURCE: B. I. Bulatov, *200 iadernykh poligonov SSSR* (Tseris: Novosibirsk, 1993), p. 13.

TABLE 21

PNEs in the Soviet Union

Location	Number of Tests	Purpose
Arkhangel region (not including Novaia Zemlia)[a]	3	Mining
Murmansk region[b]	2 (1972 and 1984)	
Perm[c]	10	
Kostroma region	1	Salt dome
Bashkiriia[d]	5	
Orenburg region	13 (1970–1974 and 1983–1984)	
Astrakhan region	15	Salt dome
North Caucausus	4	
Tiumen	~ 10	Oil/gas industry
Krasnoiarsk[e]	~ 10	
Iakutia-Sakha[f]	12	
Irkutsk region	2	
Kemerovsk region	1	
Zabaikal (Chitinsk) region	1	
Donetsk, Ukraine[g]	1	Coal mining
Kazakhstan[h]	38	
Other known[i]	41	
Central Asia	5	Well fires

a. *Includes unsuccessful 1981 attempt to put out fire in a well at Kumzha, Nenetsk national region.*

b. *One near Kirovsk, one with a radioactive gas release.*

c. *Two tests were in Osinovskoe Oil region in September 1969 (after 0.5 million tons of oil were lost; several years later radioactive water also flowed out). There were five tests in Krasnovisherskii region in the 1960s, where 5 million tons of oil above plan was extracted. One test each occurred near Kizel and Gremiachinsk. In March 1971 in Cherdynsk region near the Pechoro-Ilychsk Nature Preserve, the All-Union Scientific Research Institute of Industrial Technology carried out a nuclear test with three charges totaling 159 kt to build a channel for the Pechora-Kama Canal. A lake formed but was closed and patrolled to keep people out until 1989. Radioactive releases were high at 1 km from epicenter. Traces were found at 7 km. Two hundred other such explosions were planned. Between 1969 and 1987 in Perm region, there were eight underground explosions. See Bulatov, pp. 52–54.*

d. *At the Gracheskii Oil Site, including one on January 15, 1965.*

e. *Near Norilsk, Ermakovo, Tura.*

f. *Near Udachnyi, Aikhala, the Markha River Valley, and seven at Middle Botuobinsk Oil Site.*

g. *Enakievo Coal Mine.*

h. *In addition to PNEs at the Semipalatinsk weapons polygon, between 1966 and 1987 there were thirty-eight PNEs in twenty-seven areas of Gur'evskaia, Mangyshlakskaia, Akmolinskaia, Aktiubinskaia, and South Ukraine regions.*

i. *Small explosions to prove that an undergound explosion up to 15 kt at depth of 1.5 km at distance of 60–90 meters will close parallel wells and put out fires.*

SOURCE: B. I. Bulatov, *200 iadernykh poligonov SSSR* (Tseris: Novosibirsk, 1993), pp. 19–21.

TABLE 22

Radioactive Waste Storage Sites in Former Soviet Union, Excluding Military and Atomic Power Station Radwaste

Site Description	Number
Total	42
Still operating	35
in Russia	16*
in Ukraine	6
one each in other former republics	13

These facilities are located near Moscow in Sergiev Posad; in the Sverdlovsk, Kuibyshev, Rostov, Volgograd, Saratov, Lenigrad (Izhora), Murmansk (Ira Island), Gorkii, Novosibirsk (Chik), Cheliabinsk, and Irkutsk regions; in Khabarovsk, Bashkiriia, Tartarstan.

SOURCE: B. I. Bulatov, *200 iadernykh poligonov SSSR* (Tseris: Novosibirsk, 1993), pp. 33–35.

TABLE 23

Polygons: Major Closed Nuclear Cities of the Former Soviet Union

Arzamas-16	Krasnoiarsk-26	Stepnogorsk, Kazakhstan
Pensa-19	Krasnoiarsk-45	Kurchatov, Kazakhstan
Tomsk-7	Cheliabinsk-70	Priozersk, Kazakhstan
Sverdlovsk-44	Cheliabinsk-65	
Sverdlovsk-45	Zlotoust-26	

TABLE 24

Towns and Inhabitants in Regions of Russia at Radiation Risk Higher than 1 Ci/km^2

Region	Number of Cities, Towns, and Villages	Number of Inhabitants
Belgorod	37	4,200
Briansk	1,177	475,544
Voronezh	21	2,600
Kaluga	338	181,000
Kursk	171	408,500
St. Petersburg	44	5,600
Lipetsk	85	9,600
Orlov	525	455,400
Riazan	378	120,600
Smolensk	47	52,000
Tambov	11	1,600
Tula	1,447	936,200

SOURCE: "Chernobyl'skii sled v Rossii," *Ekho chernobylia*, no. 15–16 (May 1992), 13.

ABOUT THE SOURCES

I base this study on a series of published, unpublished, and archival materials, gathered in the course of a half-dozen visits to the former Soviet Union. The published sources include daily and weekly newspapers, some lengthy runs of which their editors gave me when I visited their offices (for example, *Ekho chernobylia*); scientific, popular scientific, and other journals (*Atomnaia energiia, Beton i zhelozobeton, Nauka i zhizn´,* et cetera); and Russian language books on the subject. The latter include a rich series of biographies, reminiscences, and published works that helped give depth to the personalities who appear in *Red Atom*. I also had the good fortune to work in the archives of the following institutions, which enabled me to get a sense of the institutional basis of big physics in the postwar USSR: in Moscow, the Kurchatov Institute of Atomic Energy, the Lebedev Physics Institute of the Academy of Sciences, the Institute of Physical Problems, and the Archive of the Academy of Sciences; in Novosibirsk, the Budker Institute of Nuclear Physics; in St. Petersburg, the Leningrad Physical Technical Institute, the Institute of Nuclear Physics in Gatchina, and the Leningrad division of the Archive of the Academy of Sciences; and in Kiev, the Institute of Physics, the Institute of Nuclear Research, and the Archive of the Ukrainian Academy of Sciences. Site visits to the Lenin Chernobyl Nuclear Power Station, the Ignalina Nuclear Power Station in Visaginas, Lithuania, the Physics Engineering Institute in Obninsk, and the Ukrainian Physical Technical Institute in Kharkiv completed my research.

A NOTE ON TRANSLITERATION

Throughout the text of *Red Atom,* for ease of reading Russian words and names, I have used a simplified system of transliteration based on the Library of Congress system, dropping diacritical marks and indications of soft and hard signs. In the endnotes, I employ these marks and signs.

Chapter 1

1. Leslie Dienes, Theodore Shabad, *The Soviet Energy System: Resources Use and Policies* (Washington: V. H. Winston, 1979), pp. 250, 259. The Don basin, a territory of more than 60,000 square kilometers, had reserves in 1968 of 128 billion tons of coal in 372 mines, which produced 193.4 million tons and 94 ore-processing and coke-producing factories. These produced 36 percent of the country's coal. See G. D. Bakulev, *Razvitie ugolnoi promyshlennosti Donetskogo basseina* (Moscow: 1955). The Kuznetsk Basin occupied second place in coal production by the same time. An area of roughly 70,000 square kilometers had 90 mines, which produced 119 million tons in 1972 but were more advanced from a technical perspective than most Donbas facilities. See also Z. G. Karpenko, *Kuznetskii ugol'nyi* (Kemerovo: 1971).

2. Paul Josephson, "Rockets, Reactors and Soviet Culture," in Loren Graham, ed., *Science and the Soviet Social Order* (Cambridge: Harvard University Press, 1990), pp. 168–191.

3. On Khrushchev, internationalism, and science, see Paul Josephson, "Nuclear Culture in the USSR," *Slavic Review,* vol. 55, no. 2 (Summer 1996), 297–324.

4. For discussion of the impact of nuclear weapons on Stalin's military policy, see David Holloway, *Stalin and the Bomb* (New Haven: Yale University Press, 1994), pp. 224–252.

5. "Vazhnaia vekha v razvitii mezhdunarodnogo sotrudnichestva uchenykh," *Izvestiia,* September 4, 1958, 1.

6. For example, Kurchatov addressed a plenary session of the Central Committee on June 24, 1958. The topic of his presentation was a narrow one, on the need to improve radically the production of radioisotopes. But his presence signaled how vital the cult of the atom had become. See Archive of the Kurchatov Institute (hereafter A KIAE), f. 2, op. 1, ed. khr. 27, ll. 1–9.

7. My thanks to Raissa Vasilievna Kuznetsova, who shared with me her candidate of science dissertation on archival sources available for the biography of Kurchatov's life, on which much of this narrative is based, and who showed such warm hospitality to me during my days in the Kurchatov House Museum; and to Igor Nikolaevich Golovin, who assisted me in gaining access to the Kurchatov Institute archive.

8. Paul Josephson, *Physics and Politics in Revolutionary Russia* (Los Angeles: University of California Press, 1991).

9. Archive of the Soviet Academy of Sciences (hereafter A AN), f. 411, op. 6, d. 184, l. 2.

10. Raissa Kuznetsova kindly showed me her typewritten rendition of the Kurchatov-Sinel'nikov correspondence, because in handwritten form the letters were nearly indecipherable.

11. A AN, f. 2, op. 71a, d. 5, l. 80.

12. Ioffe, "Tekhnicheskie zadachi sovetskoi fiziki i ikh razreshenie," *Vestnik Akademii Nauk. SSSR,* no. 2 (1939), 4. See also his "Problemy sovremennoi fiziki atomnogo iadra," *Pravda,* October 29, 1940.

13. Kurchatov, "Vsesoiuznoe soveshchanie po fizike atomnogo iadra, Noiabr´ 1940," *Uspekhi khimii,* vol. 10, no. 3 (1941), 350–358.

14. *Pravda,* June 22, 1941.

15. A AN, f. 2, op. 1, d. 5.111-13-18, ed. khr. 58a.

16. I. N. Golovin, Iu. N. Smirnov, *Eto nachinalos´ v zamoskvorech´e* (Moscow: KIAE, 1989). For the classic history of the Soviet atomic bomb project and its domestic and foreign policy aspects, see Holloway, *Stalin and the Bomb.*

17. A. P. Striganov, *Kratkaia istoriia razvitiia IAE im. I. V. Kurchatova i rabota partiinoi organizatsii za period s 1944 po 1960 god* (Moscow: KIAE, 1990), pp. 3–6.

18. A KIAE, f. 20, op. 1, ed. khr. 70/13, and Striganov, *Kratkaia istoriia,* p. 17. Only in October 1948 did laboratory 2 manage to get its library in order, as fears about spies and "ideologically harmful literature" limited circulation.

19. Striganov, *Kratkaia istoriia,* pp. 6–10, 22. By March 1949, they built another 62 apartment houses with even more spacious flats for 476 families. They planted 23,500 trees, 3,600 fruit tries, 111,000 bushes on the territory of the institute in October Field. A sauna, club, house of culture with 600 seats, stores, pioneers' camp, rest house, and sanitarium on the Black Sea followed.

20. Striganov, *Kratkaia istoriia,* pp. 11–19, 24–25. When they decided to build a huge synchrotron in Dubna, they suddenly had another 500 vacancies and no one to fill them. The laboratory directors got a special decree of the Council of Ministers and Central Committee enabling Kurchatov, Sobolev et al., to requisition any employee from industry, university, or research. They plugged these persons willy-nilly into the project, simultaneously throwing them into crash courses.

21. Ibid., pp. 37–40.

22. Ibid., pp. 56–57.

23. Ibid., pp. 43–44.

24. *XX s˝ezd KPSS. Stenographicheskii otchet,* vol. 1 (Moscow: Gosizdatpolit, 1956), pp. 595–600, and Kurchatov, "Nekotorye voprosy razvitiia atomnoi energetiki v SSSR," *Pravda,* May 20, 1956, 2.

25. L. A. Kochetkov, "Pervaia atomnaia—kak eto nachinalos´," *Izvestiia vuzov. Iadernaia energetika,* no. 2–3 (1994), 4–11.

26. Iu. K., "Leninskie premiii za sozdanie pervoi atomnoi elektrostantsii," *Atomnaia energiia,* vol. 3, no. 8 (1957), 87–90.

27. N. Il´inskii, "Ural´skaia atomnaia . . ." *Pravda,* August 29, 1959, 1.

28. N. Dubinin, "Beloiarskaia atomnaia," *Gudok,* October 8, 1960, 2.

29. V. Eremenko, "Ne dlia voiny . . ." *Ural,* no. 12 (1963), 128–140.

30. *Komsomol´skaia pravda,* August 9, 1963.

31. I. D. Morokhov, "K novym uspekham mirnogo atoma," *Atomnaia energiia,* vol. 17, no. 3 (September 1964), 164–166; and A. M. Petros´iants, "Desiatiletie iadernoi energetiki," *Atomnaia energiia,* vol. 16, no. 6 (June 1964), 482.

32. P. I. Aleshchenkov et al., "Beloiarskaia atomnaia elektrostantsiia im. I. V. Kurchatova," *Atomnaia energiia,* vol. 16, no. 6 (June 1964), 489–494.

33. A. M. Petros´iants, "Energeticheskie reaktory dlia atomnykh elektrostantsii," *Atomnaia energiia,* vol. 27, no. 4 (October 1969), 265–267.

34. Iurii Rytov, "Atomnaia energiia," *Literaturnaia gazeta,* October 2, 1958, 2; Iu. Klimov, "Atomnaia energiia v narodnom khoziastve," *Planovaia ekonomicheskaia gazeta,* November 19, 1958, 4; G. V. Ermakov, "Pervyi gigant atomnoi energetiki," *Izvestiia,* June 19, 1957, 1; N. A. Nikolaev, "Budushchie atomnye giganty," *Trud,* November 22, 1957, 4; V. Leshkovtsev, "Perspektivy razvitiia atomnoi energetiki," *Uchitelskaia gazeta,* July 9, 1964, 3.

35. Iu. Stvolinskii, "Sosnovyi bor LAES," *Neva,* no. 2 (1975), 144–146.

36. B. Konovalov, "Flagman atomnoi energetiki," *Izvestiia,* October 27, 1977, 6.

37. N. A. Dollezhal´, "Iadernaia energetika i nauchno-tekhnicheskie zadachi ee razvitiia," *Atomnaia energiia,* vol. 44, no. 3 (March 1978), 203–205.

38. A. Bogma, A. Kolesnik, "Tam, gde techet iuzhnyi bug," *Pravda,* April 10, 1978, 2.

39. V. Efimenko, "Konveier atomnykh gigantov," *Trud,* July 19, 1985.

40. http://www.iae.lt/ic/iae_eng.htm#RAD, 1–9.

41. http://www.iae.lt/iae/info/inf_e_13.html#new, ibid.,/inf_e_19.html, and ibid./ inf_e_31.html. This ranking scale is intended to keep the public informed about reactor safety but permits nuclear industries of any country to downplay safety concerns, for, after all, what is a "below scale event deviation" in any language?

42. N. A. Dollezhal´, N. Ia. Emel´ianov, "Opyt sozdaniia moshchnykh energeticheskikh reaktorov v SSSR," *Atomnaia energiia,* vol. 40, no. 2 (February 1976), 121–256.

43. E. V. Kulikov, "State-of-the-Art and Development Prospects for Nuclear Power Stations Containing RBMK Reactors," *Soviet Atomic Energy* (1984) as translated from *Atomnaia energiia,* vol. 56, no. 6 (June 1984), 359–365.

44. A. Chernyshov, "Atom na beregakh Dona," *Izvestiia,* August 14, 1959, 1; I. Vinogradov, "Eshche odna atomnaia elektrostantsiia," *Pravda,* August 14, 1959, 1; N. Pecherskii, "Rabochii atom," *Pravda,* September 12, 1967, 1.

45. N. M. Sinev, "Atomnyi gigant na donu," *Trud,* November 11, 1968, 3.

46. F. Ovchinnikov, "Atom nachal mirnyi trud," *Trud,* November 25, 1964, 1; N. Sinev, "Pervye milliony," *Izvestiia,* November 25, 1964, 4.

47. V. Golovachev, "Atom rabotaet na cheloveka," *Pravda,* November 24, 1964, 4; A. M. Petros´iants, "Desiatiletie iadernoi energetiki," *Atomnaia energiia,* vol. 16, no. 6 (June 1964), 482–483.

48. I. Vinogradov, "Eshche odna atomnaia elektrostantsiia," *Pravda,* August 14, 1959, 1; N. Pecherskii, "Rabochii atom," *Pravda,* September 12, 1967, 1; V. Sazhin, "Ia vernulsia iz 'zavtra'," *Smena,* no. 7 (1961), 29–31.

49. Petros´iants, "Atomnaia energetika na pod˝eme," *Atomnaia energiia,* vol. 20, no. 3 (1966), 202–205.

50. Iu. V. Vikhorev et al., "Reaktornaia ustanovka VVER-1000—osobennosti proketa, itogi puska piatogo bloka Novovoronezhskoi AES i puti dal´neishego sovershenstvovaniia ustanovki," *Atomnaia energiia,* vol. 50, no. 2 (February 1981), 87–93.

51. A. Piatunin, "Atomnyi ispolin," *Sovetskaia rossiia,* January 19, 1978, 2.

52. I. L. Sapir, "Potochnoe stroitel´stvo i montash AES s VVER-1000," *Atomnaia energiia,* vol. 55, no. 1 (July 1983), 3–9.

53. P. Neporozhnii, "Mirnyi atom piatiletki," *Pravda,* June 4, 1981, 2.

54. V. A. Siderneko, O. M. Kovalevich, "Obespechenie bezopasnosti atomnykh energoistochnikov," *Atomnaia energiia,* vol. 50, no. 2 (February 1981), 97–99; Iu. Soldatenko, "Atomgrad Kurskogo semirech´ia," *Krasnaia zvezda,* April 28, 1981, 4; N. A. Dollezhal´, "Iadernaia energetika i nauchno-tekhnicheskie zadachi ee razvitiia," *Atomnaia energiia,* vol. 44, no. 3 (March 1978), 208–209.

55. A. Starukhin, "Sogreet gorod," *Pravda,* July 8, 1983.

56. A. P. Aleksandrov, V. A. Legasov et al., "Struktura atomnoi energetiki s uchetom proizvodstva energii pomimo elektrichestva," *Atomnaia energiia,* vol. 43, no. 6 (December 1977), 427–432.

57. V. Dolgodvorov, "V zone povyshennoi sekretnosti," *Trud,* August 28, 1989, 2.

58. A. Piir, "Alternativnyi variant," *Trud,* February 28, 1990, 2, and *Sovetskaia rossiia,* April 1, 1990, 1.

59. V. I. Bobolovich, Iu. I. Koriakin et al., "Rol´ bystrykh reaktorov v strukture razvivaiushcheisia sistemy iadernoi energetiki," *Atomnaia energiia,* vol. 36, no. 4 (April 1974), 251–257.

60. N. Dollezhal´, Iu. Koriakin, "Atomnyi reaktor: svet i teplo," *Pravda,* July 14, 1976.

61. N. Dollezhal´, Iu. Koriakin, "Iadernaia elektroenergetika: dostizheniia ii problemy," *Kommunist,* no. 14 (September 1979), 19–23.

62. Ibid., 24–28.

63. A. M. Petros´iants, "Pervoprokhodets iadernoi energetiki," *Atomnaia energiia,* vol. 56, vyp. 6 (June 1984), 343.

64. Iu. Soldatenko, "Atomgrad Kurskogo semirech´ia," *Krasnaia zvezda,* April 28, 1981, 4.

65. "Ryvok v budushee," *Pravda,* January 15, 1980, 3.

66. A. M. Petros´iants, "Atomnaia energetika v piatiletke," *Kommunist,* no. 3 (February 1972), and "Budushchee iadernoi energetiki," *Pravda Ukrainy,* September 30, 1971.

67. "Iz materialov XXV s˝ezda KPSS," *Atomnaia energiia,* vol. 40, no. 5 (May 1976), 363–365; B. Troianovskii, G. Filippov, "Turbiny dlia atomnoi," *Sotsialisticheskaia industriia,* September 10, 1978.

68. A. M. Petros´iants, "60 let plana GOELRO," *Atomnaia energiia,* vol. 49, no. 6 (December 1980), 343.

69. G. A. Sharsharin, E. I. Ignatenko, V. M. Boldyrev, "Sostoianie i perspektivy razvitiia AES s VVER," *Atomnaia energiia,* vol. 56, no. 6 (June 1984), 354–356.

70. Dan Fisher, "Soviets' Nuclear Power Program Behind Schedule," *Los Angeles Times,* January 19, 1980, 2A.

Chapter 2

1. Hans Bethe, "Fast Reactors Are Essential to Future Atomic Power," *Nucleonics,* vol. 15 (April 1957), 4, 61–67.

2. Stephen Hilgartner, Richard Bell, Rory O'Connor, *Nukespeak* (New York: Penguin Books, 1983), pp. 110–112.

3. Gloria Duffy, *Soviet Nuclear Energy: Domestic and International Policies* (Santa Monica: Rand, 1979), pp. v–vii, 59–60.

4. A. I. Shal´nikov in B. F. Gromov, ed., *A. I. Leipunskii: Izbrannye trudy i vospominaniia* (Kiev: Naukova dumka, 1990), p. 140.

5. O. I. Leipunskii in Leipunskii: *Izbrannye trudy,* p. 138; A. N. Deriugin, in ibid., pp. 236–237.

6. Paul Josephson, "The Early Years of Soviet Nuclear Physics," *Bulletin of the Atomic Scientists,* vol. 43, no. 10 (December 1987), 36–39.

7. O. D. Kazachkovskii in Leipunskii, *Izbrannye trudy,* pp. 157–158.

8. Some of the details of Leipunskii's career, including his arrest, are in "Lichnoe delo. Leipunskii, Aleksandr Il´ich," Archive of the Academy of Sciences of Ukraine.

9. Kazachkovskii in Leipunskii, *Izbrannye trudy,* p. 163; Daniil Granin, *The Bison: A Novel About the Scientist Who Defied Stalin,* trans. Antonina W. Bouis (New York: Doubleday, 1990), pp. 171–191, 195–196.

10. My deep thanks to Tamara Belanova (Oleg Kazachkovskii´s wife) for sharing with me her, "S chego nachinalsia Obninsk," *Gorod,* April 1995, 52–59.

11. V. G. Kirillov-Ugriumov in Leipunskii, *Izbrannye trudy,* p. 229.

12. Iu. A. Prokhorov in Leipunskii, *Izbrannye trudy,* p. 232.

13. Kazachkovskii in Leipunskii, *Izbrannye trudy,* p. 153.

14. B. G. Dubovskii in Leipunskii, *Izbrannye trudy,* pp. 172–173.

15. Lichnoe delo Leipunskii; and Archive of the Institute of Physics of Ukraine (hereafter A IF AN UkSSR), f. 1, op. 3L-66. See also *Atomnaia energiia,* vol. 45, no. 5 (November 1978), 393–395, and N. S. Rabotnov and L. I. Kudinova, "Ocherk o zhizni i deiatel´nosti," in Leipunskii, *Izbrannye trudy,* pp. 56–57.

16. M. Novick, F. McGinness et al., *EBR-I and EBR-II Operating Experience* (Idaho Falls: Argonne National Laboratory, 1964). For extensive discussion of the United States breeder establishment, see Division of Research and Development, U.S. ERDA, *Liquid Metal Fast Breeder Reactor Program* (Argonne: ANL, 1975).

17. E. Eggen, D. Fulton, *Feasibility Study of a 1,000 MWe Sodium Cooled Fast Reactor* (Canosa Park, CA: Atomics International, 1966); S. Straus, "Our Fast Breeder Program . . .

Where It Stands, and Where It's Going," *Nucleonics,* vol. 24 (December 1966), 12, 41–47; A. Hammond, "Management of U.S. Breeder Program Draws Criticism," *Science,* 174 (November 19, 1971), 809; idem., "Complications Indicated for Breeder," ibid., 185 (August 30, 1974), 768.

18. Letter from Oleg Kazachkovskii to the author, March 26, 1998, and interviews with Kazachkovskii, March 26 and 27, 1998, Obninsk, Russia.

19. Kazachkovskii in Leipunskii, *Izbrannye trudy,* pp. 152–154.

20. "Oleg Dmitrievich Kazachkovskii," *Atomnaia energiia,* vol. 59, no. 4 (October 1985), 303–304.

21. Kazachkovskii, *Reaktory na bystrykh neitronakh* (Obninsk: IATE, 1995), pp. 5–6.

22. Ibid., pp. 7–11,

23. Ibid., pp. 5–6,11–12.

24. Ibid., pp. 12–13.

25. A. I. Leipunskii et al., "Eksperimental´nyi reaktor na bystrykh neitronakh BR-2," *Atomnaia energiia,* vol. 2, no. 6 (1957), 497–500.

26. Kazachkovskii, *Reaktory na bystrykh,* pp. 13–14.

27. Ibid., pp. 14–15.

28. "Laureaty Leninskikh Premii," *Atomnaia energiia,* vol. 8, no. 5 (May 1960), 407.

29. A. I. Leipunskii, O. D. Kazachkovskii, M. S. Pinkhasik, "Budushchee bystrykh reaktorov," *Atomnaia energiia,* vol. 11, no. 4 (October 1961), 372–376.

30. Ia. Golovanov, "Iadernoe ognivo," *Komsomol´skaia pravda,* July 7, 1962, 1, 2.

31. Leipunskii, Kazachkovskii, Pinkhasik, "Budushchee."

32. A. I. Leipunskii et al., "Opyt ekspluatatsii reaktora BR-5 za period 1959–1966 gg," *Atomnaia energiia,* vol. 23, no. 6 (December 1967), 503–511; Division of Reactor Development and Technology, U.S. AEC, *Soviet Power Reactors-1970,* (Washington, 1970), 46.

33. Division of Reactor Development and Technology, U.S. AEC, *Soviet Power Reactors-1970,* (Washington, 1970), 31; Kazachkovskii, *Reaktory na bystrykh,* p. 16. Over the long term, they built fast critical assemblies to follow on the footsteps of the BR-1, -2, and -5: the FBS-1 [1962] with a 3-meter active zone, and the BFS-2 [1972] with a 5-meter active zone in which they used hundreds of kilograms of enriched uranium and plutonium, and carried out measurement of breeding coefficients with different compositions of mixed fuel in the active zone.

34. Vladimir Orlov, "Neugasimoe plamia," *Pravda,* June 7, 1962, 4.

35. Golovanov, "Iadernoe ognivo."

36. V. N. Bykov, Iu. V. Konobeev, "Radiatsionnye povrezhdeniia konstruktsionnykh materialov bystrykh reaktorov," *Atomnaia energiia,* vol. 43, no. 1 (July 1977), 20–27.

37. Leipunskii, Kazachkovskii, Pinkhasik, "Budushchee bystrykh reaktorov," and O. D. Kazachkovskii, E. V. Kirillov, "Opredelenie tseny na plutonii, ispol´zuemyi v kachestve iadernogo goriuchego," *Atomnaia energiia,* vol. 22, no. 6 (June 1967), 439–444.

38. Iu. E. Bagdasarov et al., "Obespechenie bezopasnosti pri ekspluatatsii AES s bystrymi reaktorami v SSSR," *Atomnaia energiia,* vol. 55, no. 6 (December 1983), 357–358.

39. O. D. Kazachkovskii, "Bystrye reaktory," *Atomnaia energiia,* vol. 18, no. 4 (April 1965), 390–395.

40. Sinev in Leipunskii, *Izbrannye trudy,* pp. 167–168; O. D. Kazachkovskii, I. V. Krasnoiarov, E. P. Ostreikovskii, A. M. Petros´iants, "Atomnyi issledovatel´skii tsentr na rodine V. I. Lenina," *Atomnaia energiia,* vol. 28, no. 4 (April 1970), 287–290; V. A. Tsykanov and E. V. Kulov, "Nauchno-issledovatel´skii institut atomnykh reaktorov imeni V. I. Lenina v desiatoi piatiletke," ibid., vol. 48, no. 4 (April 1980), 211–215; V. A. Tsykanov, "25 let Nauchno-issledovatel´skomu institutu atomnykh reaktorov im. V. I. Lenina," ibid. vol. 50, no. 3 (March 1981), 222–228. The institute of atomic reactors grew out of an experimental station founded in 1956 to test the VK-50, a boiling water reactor; the GN-50, a reactor with a sodium coolant and graphite moderator; a somewhat smaller homogeneous reactor; and the BN-50, a fast sodium-cooled reactor. They abandoned the GN-50 because it just didn't fit in the national program, and the BN-50 because of the decision to build the BN-350. Then they gave up the

homogeneous reactor as too complex and unreliable, but had already half finished its building. They had a hard time convincing American delegates under Glenn Seaborg, who visited the facility, that a huge accident had not occurred, leaving a gutted structure. The institute soon became a leading center for the atomic energy industry in any event, pushing its own variants for power generation based on extensive research using experimental reactors and stands. Melekess physicists strove to optimize reactor operation, especially fast reactors for maximum utilization of uranium, and subjected reactor materials, fuel composition, and the radiochemistry of transuranic elements to close scrutiny. The institute possessed an impressive materials science complex with two reactors, the SM-2 and the MIR, and hot chambers. The SM-2, which came on line in 1961 and employed twenty-four experimental channels, was used primarily for irradiation of fuel rods used in both operating and projected atomic energy stations and materials. The radiochemical laboratory of the institute, founded in 1964, carries out research on the transuranic elements that are produced in the SM-2. The MIR was used for testing fuel assemblies, reactor materials, and coolants. Two such 10-MW MIR reactors were later built to expand this program. The institute also possesses an experimental boiling water reactor, the VK-50, which came on line in 1965.

41. M. M. Antipina et al., "Ispytanie opytnykh tvelov tipa BN-600 v reaktore BOR-60 do razlichnykh vygorani," *Atomnaia energiia,* vol. 40, no. 1 (January 1976), 16–22; Kazachkovskii, *Reaktory na bystrykh,* p. 19; and *Soviet Power Reactors—1970,* 49.

42. For a step-by-step description of the construction, see A. I. Leipunskii, O. D. Kazachkovskii et al., "Opyt sooruzheniia i puska reaktora BOR-60," *Atomnaia energiia,* vol. 30, no. 2 (February 1971), 165–168. See also O. D. Kazachkovskii et al., "Osnovnye rezultaty ekspluatatsii ustanovki BOR-60," ibid., vol. 38, no. 3 (March 1975), 131–134.

43. N. V. Krasnoiarov, "Vykhod gazovykh produktov deleniia iz defektnykh tvelov rekatora BOR-60," *Atomnaia energiia,* vol. 38, no. 2 (February 1975), 67–71.

44. V. D. Knizin et al., "Voprosy bezopasnotsi pri remontnykh rabotakh na AES BOR-60," *Atomnaia energiia,* vol. 48, no. 5 (May 1980), 291–294.

45. Kazachkovskii, *Reaktory na bystrykh,* p. 17.

46. R. Fedorov, "Bystrye neitrony Mangyshlaka," *Pravda,* July 19, 1973, 6.

47. B. Konovalov, "Atomnoe serdtse mangyshlaka," *Izvestiia,* July 18, 1973, 6.

48. Iu. I. Koriakin, A. A. Loginov, "Atomnaia energiia i opresnenie solenykh vod," *Atomnaia energiia,* vol. 20, no. 3 (March 1966), 232–243; V. Belov, "Stantsiia u moria," *Izvestiia,* August 14, 1974, 4; and *Soviet Power Reactors—1970, 77.*

49. I. S. Golovnin, Iu. K. Bibilashvili, T. S. Men´shikova, "Razrabotka teplovydeliaiushchikh elementov dlia energeticheskikh reaktorov na bystrykh neitronakh," *Atomnaia energiia,* vol. 34, no. 3 (March 1973), 147–153.

50. *Soviet Power Reactors—1970,* 62.

51. Ibid., 10–11, 18.

52. For greater detail on the design and safety features of the sodium technology for the BN-350, see A. I. Leipunskii et al., "Natrievaia tekhnologiia i oborudovanie reaktora BN-350," *Atomnaia energiia,* vol. 22, no. 1 (January 1967), 13–19.

53. Although the factory strove to keep the paraffin used in sodium manufacture to trace amounts, it turned out there was 0.1 to 3 kg in each container. Using a time-consuming but reliable system they had developed on the BOR-60, they heated each container to 230°–240°C, after which paraffin vapor evaporated and was caught in a special vacuum trap over several hours. The sodium was then purified with filters, cold traps, and by settling. They finally accumulated highly pure sodium with no more than 120 parts per million total of potassium, calcium, carbon, oxygen, hydrogen, nitrogen, and iron.

54. A. I. Leipunskii, F. M. Mitenkov, V. V. Orlov et al., "Opyt pusko-naladochnykh rabot i energopuska reaktora BN-350," *Atomnaia energiia,* vol. 36, no. 3 (February 1974), 91–97.

55. D. S. Iurchenko, "Itogi 10-letnei ekspluatatsii BN-350," *Atomnaia energiia,* vol. 55, no. 5 (November 1983), 269–272.

56. R. Fedorov, "Bystrye neitrony Mangyshlaka," *Pravda,* July 19, 1973, 6.

57. Iu. E. Bagdasarov et al., "Obespechenie bezopasnosti pri ekspluatatsii AES s bystrymi reaktorami v SSSR," *Atomnaia energiia,* vol. 55, no. 6 (December 1983), 355–356.

58. E. I. Iniutin, "Sostoianie rabot po bystrym reaktoram v SSSR na Aprel´ 1980 g.," Paper Presented at Thirteenth Annual Meeting of International Working Group on Fast Reactors of the International Atomic Energy Agency, April 9–11, 1980, Vienna, Austria, 10–11.

59. Kazachkovskii, *Reaktory na bystrykh,* p. 18.

60. L. Bobykin, "Kliuch k zavtrashnei energetike," *Izvestiia,* December 14, 1979, 2.

61. V. Danilov, " 'Bystry' reaktor daet tok!" *Pravda,* April 9, 1980.

62. *Soviet Power Reactors—1970,* 6, 18.

63. Ibid., 11, 81.

64. V. I. Nevskii, V. M. Malyshev, V. I. Kupnyi, "Opyt proektirovaniia, sooruzheniia i puska energobloka s reaktorom BN-600 na Beloiarskskoi AES," *Atomnaia energiia,* vol. 51, no. 5 (November 1981), 292–296; Kazachkovskii, *Reaktory na bystrykh,* pp. 18–20.

65. Kazachkovskii, *Reaktory na bystrykh,* pp. 20–21.

66. Bagdasarov et al., "Obespechenie bezopasnosti,", 356–357.

67. V. Gubarev, "Ural´skii bogatyr´," *Pravda,* March 13, 1980.

68. Sinev in Leipunskii, *Izbrannye trudy,* p. 168; A V. Zrodnikov et al., "State of the Art and Prospects of Fast Neutron Reactors," *Nuclear Engineering and Design,* vol. 173 (1997), 81; J. Moore, "International Progress with Liquid Metal Fast Reactors," *Mechanical Engineering International,* vol. 24, no. 278 (July 1979), 37–47.

69. Kazachkovskii, *Reaktory na bystrykh,* p. 21.

70. German Lomanov, "Bystrye reaktory mogut stat´ 'sanitarami' atomnoi energetiki," *Moskovskie novosti,* May 30, 1993; "Ural´tsy protiv rasshireniia AES," *Rossiiskaia gazeta,* July 13, 1993; A V. Zrodnikov et al., "State of the Art and Prospects of Fast Neutron Reactors," *Nuclear Engineering and Design,* vol. 173 (1997), 82.

71. A. Krasin et al., "Physical and Technical Principles of Creating Atomic Power Stations with Fast Neutron Gas Reactors," (Geneva, 1971), 2–12; A. Sal´nikov, *Mirnyi atom belorussii,* 2nd ed. (Minsk: Academy of Sciences, 1973), pp. 16–19.

72. Leipunskii, *Izbrannye trudy,* pp. 139–140, 220–222.

Chapter 3

1. A. A. Zvorykin, L. V. Zubkov, "Tekhnicheskoe perevooruzhenie narodnogo khoziastva SSSR," *Nauka i zhizn´,* no. 10 (1947), 22–34.

2. A. N. Komarovskii, "Puti ekonomii stali v reaktorostroenii," *Atomnaia energiia,* vol. 7, no. 3 (September 1959), 205–214.

3. R. S. Molchanov, "Sbornyi zhelezobeton," *Nauka i zhizn´,* no. 11 (1954), 9; V. V. Mikhailov, "Industrializatsiia stroitel´stva," *Nauka i zhizn´,* no. 4 (1955), 19–22; *Promyshlennost´ SSSR. Statisticheskii sbornik* (Moscow: Gosstatizdat, 1957), p. 281; and *Promyshlennost´ SSSR. Statisticheskii sbornik* (Moscow: Statistika, 1964), p. 324.

4. *Narodnoe khoziaistvo SSSR v 1980 g.* (Moscow: Finansy i statistika, 1981), pp. 178–179.

5. N. Vasin, "LAES—Kontsentratsiia energii," *Pravda,* October 2, 1971, 3.

6. Molchanov, "Sbornyi zhelezobeton."

7. V. B. Dubrovsky, *Construction of Nuclear Power Plants* (Moscow: Mir Publishers, 1981), pp. 204–207.

8. V. B. Dubrovskii, B. K. Pergamenshchik, "Vliianie oblucheniia na shamotnyi beton," *Beton i zhelezobeton,* no. 1 (1968), 29–31.

9. A. N. Komarovskii, "Sbornye betonnye i zhelezobetonnye konstruktsii v stroitel´stve iadernykh ustanovok," *Beton i zhelezobeton,* no. 8 (1959), 345–349.

10. V. V. Mal´kov, "Vliianie ob″emnogo vesa i vodosoderzhaniia betonov na razmery i stoimost´ radiatsionnoi zashchity uskoritelei vysokikh energii," *Beton i zhelezobeton,* no. 2 (1968), 28–30.

11. L. N. Zaitsev, B. S. Sychev, A. M. Tugolukov, "Betonnaia zashchita iadernykh reactorov," *Beton i zhelezobeton*, no. 1 (1964), 8–12.

12. A. N. Vorob´ev, V. B. Dubrovskii, Sh. Sh. Ibragimov et al., "Radiatsionnaia stoikost´ khromitovogo betona na portlandtsemente," *Beton i zhelezobeton*, no. 2 (1966), 11–13.

13. V. Chernikov, *Za zavesoi sekretnosti, ili stroitel´stvo no. 859 (stranitsy istorii IuUS)* (Cheliabinsk: Cheliabinskii dom pechati, 1995), p. 137.

14. Ibid., p. 73.

15. On Timofeeff-Ressovsky, see Granin, *The Bison*, op. cit.

16. Chernikov, *Za zavesoi*, pp. 73–74, 101, 126–133.

17. Ibid., pp. 76–83.

18. Ibid., pp. 99–101.

19. Ibid., pp. 48–53.

20. Ibid., pp. 84–86, 98.

21. Ibid., pp. 173–174, 212–213, 218–219, 236–241.

22. Leonard Bertin, *Atom Harvest: A British View of Atomic Energy* (San Francisco: W. H. Freeman and Company, 1957).

23. For detailed discussion of the construction of Windscale from the perspective of a proud civil engineer, see Stuart Sinclair, *Windscale: Problems of Civil Construction and Maintenance* (London: George Newnes Limited, 1960).

24. On DneproGES, see Anne Rassweiler, *The Generation of Power* (New York: Oxford University Press, 1988).

25. M. I. Moskovskii, "Zavod nachal novuiu zhizn´," in *Elektrosila*, vol. 27 (Leningrad: Energiia, 1968), 63; A. Ia. Berger, "Pervyi standart moshchnostei turbogeneratorov," in ibid., 71–72; R. A. Liuter, V. V. Romanov, G. M. Khutoretskii, "50 let sovetskogo turbogeneratorostroeniia," in ibid., vol. 31 (1976), 5–7.

26. Interview with G. K. Zherve, chief engineer, Elektrosila, St. Petersburg, January 9, 1993; "Ot volgi-k Angare," *Elektrosila*, vol. 14 (Leningrad-Moscow: Gosenergoizdat, 1956), 3–4; A. V. Mozalevskii, A. D. Molchanov, "Kurs na novoe," ibid., vol. 27 (Leningrad: Energiia, 1968), 20–21; N. P. Ivanov, R. A. Liuter et al., "Moshchnye gidrogeneratory," ibid., 5–11; and G. I. D´iachenko, G. M. Khutoretskii, "Turbogeneratory moshchnost´iu 800 i 1,200 Mvt," ibid., vol. 28 (Leningrad: LO Energoizdat, 1970), 22–24; and Iu. V. Aroshidze, "Turbogeneratorostroenie 'Elektrolsily' v XI piatiletke," ibid., vol. 33 (1981), 3–5. For testimony from another designer of huge turbines, see N. N. Kovalev, "Voploshchenie kommunizma," *Zvezda*, 1950 (12), 120–133.

27. M. Makhlits, M. Ovdienko, "Volgodonskii 'Atommash'," *Ekonomicheskaia gazeta*, no. 27 (July 1976), 24.

28. The Rybinskoe reservoir alone filled 4,550 square kilometers, once the largest artificial lake in the world, and covered 663 inhabited areas including six cities.

29. F. M. Loginov, "Velichaishee sooruzhenie stalinskoi epokhi," *Pravda*, September 5, 1950, 2; I. Grishin, "Na Stalingradskoi zemle," *Literaturnaia gazeta*, September 19, 1950, 2; "Glavnyi turkmenskii kanal," *Pravda*, September 12, 1950, 1; S. Babaev, "Velichaishee sooruzhenie stalinskoi epokhi," *Izvestiia*, September 15, 1950, 2; G. Mukhtarov, "Kanal schast´ia," *Sotsialisticheskoe zemledelie*, September 17, 1950, 2; I. Basalaev, "Pustynia budet sluzhit´ nam," *Zvezda*, 1951 (1), 141–145; L. Mel´nikov, "Po stalinskomu planu," *Pravda*, September 22, 1950, 2; A. Palladin, "Rodnoe delo nashego naroda," *Pravda*, September 26, 1950, 2; A. Kozlov, "Velichaishaia stroika sovremennosti," *Pravda*, September 23, 1950, 2.

30. Makhlits, Ovdienko, "Volgodonskii 'Atommash'"; F. M. Loginov, "Velichaishee sooruzhenie stalinskoi epokhi," *Pravda*, September 5, 1950, 2; Grishin, "Na Stalingradskoi zemle"; "Glavnyi turkmenskii kanal," *Pravda*, September 12, 1950, 1; Babaev, "Velichaishee sooruzhenie stalinskoi epokhi"; Mukhtarov, "Kanal schast´ia"; Basalaev, "Pustynia budet sluzhit´ nam"; Mel´nikov, "Po stalinskomu planu"; Palladin, "Rodnoe delo nashego naroda"; Kozlov, "Velichaishaia stroika sovremennosti"; M. M. Davydov, M. Z. Tsunts, *Ot volkhova do*

Amura (Moscow: Sovetskaia rossiia, 1958); G. V. Voropaev, D. Ia. Ratkovich, *Problema territorial´nogo pereraspredeleniia vodnykh resursov* (Moscow: IVP AN SSSR, 1985), pp. 252–253.

31. E. Riabchikov, *Volga-don* (Moscow: Geografgiz, 1954), pp. 44–50.

32. V. Kudriavchikov, ed., *Trudovye podvigi stroitelei volgo-dona* (Moscow: Gosizdatpolit, 1954), pp. 8–9. The Volga-Don Canal required thirteen locks to raise and lower water level with powerful pumping stations each equipped with the same pumps, thirteen virtually indistinguishable dams, two emergency repair stations, a large number of bridges and crossings, and a large port at Kalach.

33. Riabchikov, *Volga-Don,* pp. 201–207, and V. Talaktionov, *Doroga na okean* (Moscow: Molodaia gvardiia, 1952), pp. 56–58, 64. On the Tsimlianskii dam, see N. V. Pazin, *Tsimlianskii gidrouzel* (Moscow-Leningrad: Gosenergoizdat, 1954).

34. L. V. Timofeev, "'Atommash' stroitsia," *Atomnaia energiia,* vol. 13, no. 5 (November 1977), 419–421.

35. Ibid., and A. Anoshkin, "'Atommash'—perednii krai," *Sotsialiticheskaia industriia,* June 6, 1976, 1.

36. Viktor Muratov, "Donskoi reaktor," *Krasnaia zvezda,* March 14, 1981, 4.

37. "Komandirovka na 'Atommash'," *Komsomol´skaia pravda,* April 28, 1977, 2.

38. V. Pershin "Kadry dlia 'Atommasha'," *Trud,* February 9, 1979, 4.

39. S. Bogatko, M. Kriukov, "Atommash—solntse delaetsia v Volgodonske," *Pravda,* July 11, 1981, 2.

40. T. Makarova, "Sozdaetsia 'tokomak'," *Sotsialisticheskaia industriia,* July 14, 1983, 2.

41. A. Zornin, "Esli zaniat´sia vser´ez," *Sotsialisticheskaia industriia,* April 14, 1983, 2.

42. L. Shamardina, "Metso podviga—'Atommash'," *Ekonomicheskaia gazeta,* no. 4 (January 1979), 16.

43. S. Bagatko, M. Kriukov, "Atommash—delu venets," *Pravda,* July 12, 1981, 2.

44. N. Ivanitskii, "Programma 'Atommash'," *Sovetskaia rossiia,* October 18, 1976, 2.

45. See, for instance, A. Tiaglivyi, "Na stroitel´stve 'Atommasha'," *Partiinaia zhizn´,* no. 6 (March 1979), 27–31.

46. "Mismanagement at Atomic Reactor Plant," *Current Digest of the Soviet Press,* vol. 35, no. 29 (August 17, 1983), 1–2.

47. S. Sadowhenko, "Kar´er pretknoveniia," *Sotsialisticheskaia industriia,* January 6, 1983, 2.

48. Peter Hann, "An Assembly Line for Nuclear Reactors," *Business Week,* November 19, 1979, 511–512, and "Povyshat´ otvetstvennost´," *Pravda,* July 20, 1983, 2.

49. "Mismanagement at Atomic Reactor Plant." (See note 46.)

50. V. Ladnyi, "Atomnyi kotel v Kazach´em krugu," *Komsomol´skaia pravda,* April 7, 1993, 3; Iuriii Bespalov, "Tainstvennye manervy na rostovskoi AES," *Izvestiia,* November 11, 1993.

51. Ivan Kunitsyn, Aleksei Nikolaev, "Po Donu guliaet . . . 'mirnyi' atom," *Iunost´,* no. 4 (1990), 42–44.

52. Ibid.

53. A. Tiaglivyi, "Volgodonskii kompleks," *Sotsialisticheskaia industriia,* August 21, 1984, 2.

54. A. Baginskii et al., "Pustye smeny," *Sovetskaia rossiia,* August 10, 1983, 1; N. Gorshkov, "Privychka k otkloneniiam," *Sotsialisticheskaia industriia,* April 11, 1985, 2.

55. "Effektivnee ispol´zovat´ zhelezobetonnye konstruktsii," *Izvestiia,* January 15, 1977, 2; "Rasti zavodam i gorodam," *Pravda,* August 10, 1975, 1.

Chapter 4

1. N. M. Sinev, I. D. Kovalev, "Atomnaia elektrostantsiia TES-3," *Priroda,* 1965, no. 3, 114–117.

2. E. Maksimova, "Put´ k obninsku," *Izvestiia,* October 1, 1967, 5.

3. A KIAE, f. 2, op. 1, ed. khr. 72/3.

4. A. Syrmai, "Atomnaia energiia na transporte," *Atomnaia energiia*, vol. 2, no. 4 (1957), 395.

5. B. G. Pologikh, N. S. Khlopkin, "Sozdanie pervoi atomnoi energeticheskoi ustanovki dlia ledokola," in *Atomnaia energetika i transport XXI veka* (Moscow: Kurchatov Institute, 1993), pp. 70–76.

6. "K 75-letiiu A. P. Aleksandrova," *Atomnaia energiia*, vol. 44, no. 2 (February 1978), 107–109.

7. V. V. Regel´, "Eto byl porazitel´nyi uspekh," *Nauchnyi informatsioono-metodicheskii biulleten´. Iadernoe obshchestvo*, no. 1(5) (1993), 36–37.

8. K. A. Konoplev, "A. P. Aleksandrov i iadernaia energetika," in Zh. I. Alferov, ed., *K 90-letiiu Akademika Anatoliia Petrovicha Aleksandrov* (St. Petersburg: FTI, 1993), p. 20; A. P. Aleksandrov, "Gody s I. V. Kurchatovym," *Atomnaia energiia*, vol. 54, no. 1 (January 1983), 3–12.

9. A. P. Aleksandrov, "Budushchee energetiki," *Sovetskii fizik*, no. 5, February 11, 1976, 1–3.

10. A. P. Aleksandrov, "Tekhnicheskie aspekty iadernoi energetiki na grani vekov," *Atomnaia energiia*, vol. 56, no. 6 (June 1984), 340–341.

11. A. P. Aleksandrov, "Problemy atomnoi energetiki," *Vestnik Akademii Nauk SSSR*, no. 5 (1962), 20–32. This article was given high visibility; it was also published in slightly different versions with the same title in *Ekonomicheskaia gazeta*, March 19, 1962, 11–12, and *Atomnaia energiia*, vol. 13, no. 2 (1962), 109–122.

12. A. P. Aleksandrov, "Perspektivy energetiki," *Izvestiia*, April 11, 1970, 2–3; "Tekhnicheskie aspekty iadernoi energetiki na grani vekov," *Atomnaia energiia*, vol. 56, no. 6 (June 1984), 340–342. See also Aleksandrov et al., "Iadernaia energetika v SSSR," *Atomnaia energiia*, vol. 54, no. 4 (April 1983), 243–249.

13. A. P. Aleksandrov, "Ispolinskii atom," *Izvestiia*, December 31, 1964; "Atom vmesto uglia," *Izvestiia*, January 7, 1964, 5; "Oktiabr´ i fizika," *Pravda*, November 10, 1967, 2; "Iadernaia energetika i tekhnicheskii progress," *Atomnaia energiia*, vol. 25, no. 5 (November 1968), 357–360; "Rabotaet atom," *Trud*, November 28, 1974, 2; "Atomnaia energetika i ee rol´ v tekhnicheskom progresse," *Vestnik Akademii Nauk SSSR*, no. 11 (1968), 25–33 [also published in slightly different form in *Priroda*, no. 1 (1969), 14–24].

14. A. P. Aleksandrov, "Rech´ prezidenta AN SSSR Akademika A. P. Aleksandrov na xxv s˝ezde KPSS," *Vestnik Akademii Nauk SSSR*, no. 4 (1976), 3–8.

15. V. V. Lakhanin, "Atomnye dvigateli na sudakh," *Atomnaia energiia*, vol. 3, no. 9 (1957), 222–226.

16. Iu. I. Klimov, "Atomnyi ledokol," *Priroda*, no. 12 (1959), 35–40.

17. N. I. Afrikantov, et. al., "Opyt ekspluatatsii atmonoi ustanovki ledokola 'Lenin'," *Atomnaia energiia*, vol. 17, no. 5 (November 1964), 349–359.

18. A KIAE, F. 2, op. 1, ed. khr. 72/15.

19. Kendall Bailes, *Technology and Society Under Lenin and Stalin* (Princeton, NJ: Princeton University Press, 1978), pp. 381–406.

20. "Atomnyi ledokol 'Lenin' vstupil v stroi!" *Pravda*, December 20, 1959, 1.

21. A. Ermakov, "Atomokhod shvartuetsia v portu," *Trud*, March 3, 1960, 3.

22. I. Kovalkin, "Ekzamen vyderzhan!" *Izvestiia*, May 7, 1960, 12.

23. G. Edwin Brown, Jr., *Prospects for a Nuclear Powered Merchant Ship Program* (New York: Atomic Industrial Forum, 1974); British Nuclear Energy Society, *The Future for Nuclear Powered Ships* (London: British Nuclear Society, 1966).

24. V. S. Emelianov, "Atomnaia energiia v morskom transporte," *Vestnik Akademii Nauk SSSR*, no. 6 (1961), 57–66.

25. A. P. Aleksandrov et al., "Atomnyi ledokol 'Lenin'," *Atomnaia energiia*, vol. 5, no. 3 (September 1958), 257–276.

26. N. S. Khlopkin, "Sostoianie i perspektivy atomnoi energetiki na more," in O. V. Bazanov, G. Ia. Karmadonov, eds., *Materialy iubileinoi sessii uchenogo soveta tsentra* (Moscow: Kurchatov Institute, 1993), pp. 26–28.

27. Elena Sergeevna Knorre, *Atom sluzhit sotsializmu* (Moscow: Atomizdat, 1977), pp. 98–104; N. Klopkin, "Atomnaia energetika dlia severnykh morei," *Nauchnyi informatsioono-metodicheskii biulleten´. Iadernoe obshchestvo,* no. 1(5) (1993), 4–5; F. M. Mitenkov, "Ledokol *Arktika*—novoe dostizhenie sovetskogo atomnogo sudostroeniia," *Atomnaia energiia,* vol. 39, no. 3 (September 1975). For the technical specifications of Soviet nuclear icebreakers, see N. S. Khlopkin, "Atomnaia flota," *Sovetskii fizik,* no. 28 (July 1976), 2–3.

28. Valerii Iaroslavtsev, "Vreden li atomokhod 'Taimyr' dlia Taimyra?" *Rossiiskaia gazeta,* January 20, 1992.

29. For a discussion of these debates, see Gilbert Whittemore, "A Crystal Ball in the Shadows of Nuremberg and Hiroshima: The Ethical Debate over Human Experimentation to Develop a Nuclear Powered Bomber, 1946–1951," in Everett Mendelsohn, Merritt Roe Smith, Peter Weingart, eds., *Science, Technology, and the Military* (Dordrecht: Kluwer Academic Publishers, 1988), 431–462. See also W. Henry Lambright, *Shooting Down the Nuclear Plane* (Indianapolis: Bobbs-Merrill, 1967).

30. "U.S. A-Plane Progress on Four Fronts," *Nucleonics,* vol. 14, no. 5 (May 1956), 22; "Aircraft Reactor is Air-Cooled," ibid., vol. 14, no. 3 (March 1956), 94; "Atomic Plane Seen Flying by 1954–56," *Aviation Week,* vol. 55 (September 17, 1951), 16–17; "Atomic-Powered Aircraft—Development Measures," *Atomics,* no. 7 (March 1956), 77.

31. "The Truth About a U.S. Atomic Plane," *U.S. News and World Report,* December 12, 1958, 38–39.

32. Gerald Wendt, "The First Atomic Airplane," *Popular Science,* vol. 158 (October 1951), 98–102, and "Atomic Power for British Aircraft," *Atomics,* vol. 7 (1956), 173–174.

33. N. N. Ponomarev-Stepnoi, "Iadernaia energiia v letatel´nykh apparatakh," in O. V. Bazanov, G. Ia. Karmadonov, eds., *Materialy iubileinoi sessii uchenogo soveta tsentra* (Moscow: Kurchatov Institute, 1993), pp. 41–42.

34. Ibid., p. 43.

35. Ibid., pp. 43–45; V. Artamkin, "Ob atomnom samolete," *Atomnaia energiia,* vol. 4, no. 4 (1958), 389–391.

36. C. Bonestell, W. Ley, *The Conquest of Space* (New York: Viking Press, 1949), Chap. 2.

37. Erik Pedersen, *Nuclear Energy in Space* (Englewood Cliffs, NJ: Prentice-Hall, Inc., 1964), pp. 4, 18; R. W. Bussard, R. D. DeLauer, *Nuclear Rocket Propulsion* (New York: McGraw-Hill Book Co., Inc., 1958), pp. 2–3.

38. Pedersen, pp. 432–478.

39. Pedersen, pp. 4–9. See also William Beller, "Nuclear Spacepower Tug-of-War," *Missiles and Rockets,* February 19, 1962, 12–13, 38.

40. Pederson, pp. 4–9, Freeman Dyson, *Disturbing the Universe* (New York: Harper and Row, 1979), pp. 110–115, 129–130.

41. Ponomarev-Stepnoi, "Iadernaia energiia," pp. 45–46.

42. A. P. Petros´iants, "Atomnaia nauka i tekhnika k 50-i godovshchine velikoi oktiabr´skoi sotsialisticheskoi revoliutsii," *Atomnaia energiia,* vol. 23, no. 5 (November 1967), 388–390.

43. Ponomarev-Stepnoi, "Iadernaia energiia," pp. 48–49; Knorre, *Atom sluzhit,* 104–105. TOPAZ stands for *termoemissionnyi opytnyi preobrazovanie v aktivnoi zone.*

44. A. Romanenko, "Reaktory v kosmose," *Ekologicheskaia gazeta,* no. 11–12 (1992), 3.

45. "Falling Satellite Said to Pose Little Danger," *Current Digest of the Soviet Press,* vol. 35, no. 3 (February/April 1983), 10.

46. William J. Broad, "Radioactive Debris in Space Threatens Satellites in Use," *New York Times,* February 26, 1995, 12; idem., "Reactors in Space: U.S. Project Advances," ibid., October 6, 1987, C1, C12.

47. V. S. Emelianov, *S chego nachinalos´* (Moscow: Sovetskaia rossiia, 1979), pp. 253–255.

48. A. V. Bondarenko et al., "Opyt proektirovaniia, puska i ekspluatatsii Bilibinskoi ATETs," in L. M. Voronin, ed., *Atomnye elektricheskie stantsii* (Moscow: Energiia, 1980), pp. 39–45.

49. Iu. Balakirev, "'Kamelek' na vsiu chukotku," *Komsomol'skaia pravda,* December 2, 1973, 1.

50. R. Zviagel'skii, "Atomnoe sol'nste Chukotki," *Krasnaia zvezda,* December 22, 1976, 4.

51. V. M. Bramov et al., "Bilibinskaia atomnaia elektrostantsiia," *Atomnaia energiia,* vol. 35, no. 5 (November 1973), 299–304; A. A. Vaimugin et al., "Issledovanie fizicheskikh kharakteristik reaktora vo vremiia puska pervogo bloka bilibinskoi AES," ibid., vol. 39, no. 1 (July 1975), 3–8; A. V. Bondarenko et al., "Eksperimental'noe opredelenie plotnostnogo koeffitsienta reaktivnosti teplonositelia dlia reaktorov Bilibinskoi ATETs," ibid., vol. 46, no. 2 (February 1979), 75–78.

52. Iu. Balakirev, "Dobrovolets na udarnoi," *Komsomol'skaia pravda,* August 9, 1974, 2.

53. "Seminar 'Prospects for the Development and Improvement of Fuel and Energy Management in the Far North and Northeast of the USSR on the Basis of Nuclear Energy Sources'," translated from *Atomnaia energiia,* vol. 45, no. 2 (August 1978), 157–158; V. V. Dolgov, "Bilibinskaya Nuclear Power Plant," *Nuclear Engineering and Design,* vol. 173 (1997), 87–97.

54. Iu. Arkhangel'skii, I. Kovalev, "Pusk pervoi v mire AES s organo-organicheskim reaktorom," *Atomnaia energiia,* vol. 15, no. 5 (November 1963), 443; K. K. Polushkin et al., "Atomnaia elektrostantsiia 'Arbus' s organicheskim teplonositelem i zamedlitelem," ibid., vol. 17, no. 6 (December 1964), 439–448; I. D. Morokhov, "Sovetskii atomnye," *Pravda,* September 25, 1963, 4.

55. V. A. Tsykanov, "Opytnaia atomnaia stantsiia teplosnabzheniia na baze reaktora ARBUS," *Atomnaia energiia,* vol. 50, no. 6 (June 1981), 376–381.

56. N. M. Sinev et al., "Malogarabitnaia atomnaia elektrostantsiia TES-3," *Atomnaia energiia,* vol. 17, no. 6 (December 1964), 448–452; Sinev and Kovalev, "Atomnaia elektrostantsiia TES-3," 114–117.

57. A. I. Golovin et al., "Ispol'zovanie plavuchikh AES v raionakh severa," *Atomnaia energiia,* vol. 51, no. 2 (August 1981), 83–91.

58. Andrei Mirmovich, Dmitrii Latypov, "Reaktory s podlodok vsplyvaiut pod Khabarovsk," *Kommersant',* no. 4 (January 20–27 1992), 13.

59. A KIAE, F. 2, op. 1, ed. khr. 72/4.

60. Ibid., ed. khr. 72/22.

61. Klopkin, "Atomnaia energetika dlia severnykh morei," 5–6.

62. Khlopkin, "Sostoianie i perspektivy," pp. 28–30.

63. G. Chase, *The Military Engineer,* vol. 58, no. 382 (1966), 111.

64. Waldermar Kaempffert, "Next: The Atomic Locomotive," *Science Digest,* vol. 35 (May 1954), 4–6; "An Atomic Locomotive Could Be Built," *Popular Science,* vol. 164 (April 1954), 137–140, 276; "The Atomic Locomotive," *Life,* vol. 36 (June 21, 1954), 78–79.

65. On the development of the PWR for submarine proposal in the United States, the importance of the PWR for civilian power generation, and the role of Admiral Hyman Rickover in its development, see Richard G. Hewlett, Francis Duncan, *Nuclear Navy, 1946–62* (Chicago: University of Chicago Press, 1974). See also Craig Hosmer, "Nuclear Power for the Navy," *Proceedings of the United States Naval Institute,* May 1958, 57–64.

66. N. A. Dollezhal', *U istokov rukotvornogo mira* (Moscow: Znanie, 1989), pp. 163–169.

67. Ibid., pp. 168–170; S. Bystrov, "Reaktor dlia podlodki," *Krasnaia zvezda,* October 21, 1989, 3.

68. G. A. Gladkov, "Sozdanie pervoi sovetskoi atomnoi podvodnoi lodki 'Leninskii komsomol'," in O. V. Bazanov, G. Ia. Karmadonov, eds., *Materialy iubileinoi sessii uchenogo soveta tsentra,* (Moscow: Kurchatov Institute, 1993), pp. 9–13; Dollezhal', *U istokov,* pp. 168–173.

69. Gladkov, "Sozdanie pervoi," 13–15; *Boevoi put' sovetskogo voenno-morskogo flota* (Moscow: Voenizdat, 1967), p. 544.

70. V. P. Kilezhenko, V. N. Podymakhin, "Atomnyi vek i more," *Priroda,* no. 12 (1964), 39–43.

71. Khlopkin, "Sostoianie i perspektivy," pp. 21–25.

72. M. E. Vinogradova, A. M. Sagalevich, S. V. Khetagurov, eds., *Okeanologicheskie issle-dovaniia i podvodno-tekhnicheskie raboty na meste gibeli atomnoi podvodnoi lodki "Komsomolets"* (Moscow: Nauka, 1996); B. I. Bulatov, *200 iadernykh poligonov SSSR* (Novosibirsk: Tseris, 1993); Office of Technology Assessment ENV-623, *Nuclear Wastes in the Arctic: An Analysis of Arctic and Other Regional Impacts from Soviet Nuclear Contamination* (Washington, DC: USGPO, September 1995), pp. 33–35, 38.

73. *Nuclear Wastes in the Arctic,* pp. 27–30.

74. Bulatov, *200 iadernykh poligonov SSSR,* 39; Kim Smirnov, "Vse nashi radioaktivnye zakhoroneniia v moriakh rassekrecheny," *Izvestiia,* August 7, 1993, 15; Viktor Litovkin, "93 podvodnykh atomokhoda zhdut v rossii utilizatsii, no deneg na eto u gosudarstva net," ibid., August 9, 1993, 4; Igor´ Tsarev et al., "Skandal na iadernoi pomoike," *Trud,* October 22, 1993. The U.S. record at Hanford, Washington, Fernald, Ohio, and Aiken (Savannah River), South Carolina, is little better. See, for instance, Michele Stenehjem Gerber, *On the Home Front: The Cold War Legacy of Hanford* (Lincoln and London: University of Nebraska Press, 1992).

75. Yu. D. Baranov, V. V. Dolgov, Yu. A. Sergeev, "Activities in the Field of Small Nuclear Power Reactors," *Nuclear Engineering and Design,* vol. 173 (1997), 159–166.

Chapter 5

1. *Radiation Preservation of Foods,* Proceedings of International Conference, Boston, Massachusetts, September 1964 (Washington, DC: National Academy of Sciences, 1965); S. A. Allure, "Historical Development of Food Irradiation," in *Food Irradiation,* Proceedings of the International Symposium on Food Irradiation (Vienna: IAEA, 1966), pp. 3–17.

2. N. Teterin, "'Atomnye' kury," *Nedelia,* no. 8 (February 18, 1968), 5.

3. *Radiation Preservation of Foods;* Allure, "Historical Development of Food Irradiation."

4. Donald Streever, "Cost Benefit Analysis of Selected Radiation Pasteurized Meats," in *Eighth Annual AEC Food Irradiation Contractors' Meeting* (Washington: AEC, 1968), pp. 168–173; Kermit Bird, "Cost Benefit Analysis of Selected Agricultural and Fishery Foods," in ibid., pp. 196–200.

5. L. V. Metlitskii, V. N. Rogachev, V. G. Krushchev, in *Radiation Processing of Food Products,* Martha Gerrard, F. E. McKinney, P. S. Baker, eds., (Oak Ridge, TN: Oak Ridge National Laboratory, 1968), pp. 82–87.

6. The first industrial-scale grain irradiator pilot plant in the world was built in 1967 under IAEA auspices at the port of Iskenderun, Turkey. It had a capacity of 30 to 50 tons per hour for doses between 15 and 25 kilorads.

7. Edward Josephson, Martin Peterson, eds., *Preservation of Food by Ionizing Radiation* (Boca Raton, FL: CRC Press, Inc., 1983), vol. 1, pp. 15–26.

8. Metlitskii et al., pp. 82–84, 92–98.

9. E. S. Krasnitskaia, "Pishchevye otpravleniia v RSFSR za 1956 g.," *Gigiena i sani-tariia,* no. 3 (1958), 49–53.

10. V. P. Zotov, *Pishchevaia promyshlennost´ sovetskogo soiuza* (Moscow: Pishchepromiz-dat, 1958), pp. 23–25, 161–162; A. N. Anfimov, M. N. Vokov, *Pavil´on glavmiaso. Putevoditel´* (Moscow: Gosizdatselkhozlit, 1955).

11. Zotov, *Pishchevaia,* pp. 38–43; V. P. Zotov et al., *Pishchevaia promyshlennost´ SSSR* (Moscow: Pishchevaia promyshlennost´, 1967), p. 193.

12. Metlitskii et al., pp. 5–19, 101–103.

13. G. M. Egiazarov, "Posledeistvie ioniziruiushchei radiatsii na vitamin C i karotin, soderzhashchiesia v nekotorykh preparatakh i pishchevykh produktakh," *Voprosy pitaniia,* no. 5 (1958), 9–11. See also P. E. Kalmykov, G. M. Egiazarov, *Voenno-meditsinskii zhurnal,* no. 7 (1955), 59.

14. G. M. Egiazarov, "Vliianie nizkikh doz gamma-luchei na sokhrannost´ vitaminov v pishchevykh produktakh," *Voprosy pitaniia*, no. 4 (1960), 54–58.

15. K. I. Zhuravlev, "Vliianie ioniziruiushchei radiatsii na fiziko-khimicheskie i organolepticheskie svoistva podsolnechnogo masla," *Voprosy pitaniia*, no. 4 (1957), 60–64.

16. Metlitskii et al., pp. 67–68, 74; G. M. Egiazarov, "K voprosu bezopasnosti upotrebleniia v pishchu produktov, sterilizovannykh s pomoshch´iu ioniziruiushchego oblucheniia," *Voprosy pitaniia*, no. 1 (1960), 63–67. Proctor and Goldblith of MIT demonstrated that radioactivity could in no way arise in food products during irradiation with fast electrons and gamma rays with energies less than eight to ten megavolts, and that exclusion of atmospheric oxygen (a vacuum) accompanied by low-level irradiation at low temperatures was the way to go.

17. A. N. Liberman, "Primenenie ioniziruiushchikh izluchenii dlia konservirovaniia pishchevykh produktov," *Voprosy pitaniia*, no. 6 (1957), 52–56.

18. A. V. Bibergal et al., "Transportabel´naia gamma-ustanovka GUPOS-[137]Cs-800 dlia predposevnogo oblucheniia semian," *Atomnaia energiia*, vol. 12, no. 2 (February 1962), 159–160; A. V. Bibergal, E. S. Pertsovskii, M. E. Kuzin, "Gamma-ustanovka dlia oblucheniia zerna," ibid., vol. 16, no. 1 (January 1964), 84–86. To add to the effect of irradiation, the Americans also experimented with packaging grain in material, the outer wall of which was impregnated with insect repellents.

19. On the Canadian apparatus, developed by 1956, see E. Kulish, "Sovetskaia delegatsiia v Kanade," *Atomnaia energiia*, vol. 21, no. 5 (November 1966), 422–424. The English were not far behind with a gamma apparatus for sterilization of agricultural products, medical equipment, and other objects, developed from 1960. A pilot factory could handle 200 containers at a time. Several private firms followed in acquiring the technology. See R. A. Srapeniants, "Angliiskie–gamma-obluchatel´nye ustanovki," ibid., vol. 20, no. 1 (January 1966), 91–95.

In the United States, the Vitro Engineering Company developed a mobile cobalt facility in a tractor trailer that began field operation with fruits in May 1966 under the direction of scientists at the University of California, Davis. See Edward Ross, James Moy, "Dosimetry, Tolerance and Shelf Life Extension Related to Disinfestation of Fruits and Vegetables by Gamma Irradiation" in *Eighth Annual AEC Food Irradiation Meeting*, 110–115; E. C. Maxie, "Radiation Technology in Conjunction With Postharvest Procedures as a Means of Extending Shelf-Life of Fruits and Vegetables," in ibid., 123–126. Vitro Engineering also designed a large-scale ^{60}Co on-ship irradiator capable of processing 7,500 pounds of fish per hour at a dose of 100 kilorads. See *Radiation Preservation of Foods*, pp. 310–312. The Teledyne Corporation designed and operated a portable cesium irradiator, which, at 170,000 curies of [137]Ce, was the largest cesium irradiator in the world. AEC officials drove it around in a semi-trailer from parking lot to parking lot at dozens of private firms nationwide to demonstrate the benefits and commercial potential of the unit. See W. B. Grant, W. E. Erlebach, "Operation of the Portable Cesium Irradiator," in *Eighth Annual AEC Food Irradiation Meeting*, 214–217.

The French mobile IRMA-400-1 with applications for potatoes used ^{137}Cs source whose advantage was the 30 year half-life versus 5.3 years for cobalt, lighter shielding and weight, and higher efficiency. See Metlitskii et al., pp. 101, 106.

20. N. M. Berezina, A. M. Kuzin, D. A. Kaushanskii, "Vnedrenie prednosevnogo gamma-oblucheniia semian v sel´skoe khoziaistvo," *Atomnaia energiia*, vol. 37, no. 1 (July 1974), 43–51.

21. E. N. Vasil´eva, L. A. Okuneva, Iu. P. Kukel´, "Gigienicheskoe izuchenie zerna, obluchennogo radioaktivnym kobal´tom," *Voprosy pitaniia*, no. 5 (1960), 59–61.

22. G. I. Bondarev, "Vliianie obluchennykh pishchevykh produktov na funktsiiu vosproizvodstva krys i na ikh potomstvo," *Voprosy pitaniia*, no. 6 (1960), 18–22.

23. Arkhiv IIaF SO AN SSSR, f. 1, op. 1, ed. khr. 82, ll. 7–12; ed. khr. 30, ll. 1–8; ed. khr. 66, ll. 4, 6–7, 23; f. 1, op. 1, ed. khr. 123, ll. 8, 10, 16, 22; ed. khr. 122, ll. 4–7; ed. khr. 3, pp. 4–7; and Nauchnyi Arkhiv Sibirskogo otdeleniia AN SSSR, f. 10, op. 5, ed. khr. 524, ll.

6-10; and V. Konovalov, "Vygodno vsem: Novyi opyt finansirovaniia fundamental´nykh nauchnykh issledovanii," *Izvestiia*, February 22, 1969.

24. Iu. I. Shillinger, "Ob izuchenii khimicheskikh primesei i dobavlenii k produktam pitaniia, mogushchikh okazyvat´ kantserogennoe deistvie," *Voprosy pitaniia*, no. 5 (1959), 3-7.

25. A. A. Kudriasheva, I. G. Medvedskaia, "Pasterizatsiia svezhei maliny γ-luchami razlichnoi intensivnosti," *Voprosy pitaniia*, no. 3 (1963), 58-61.

26. V. I. Rogachev, "Sostoianie i perspektivy primeneniia ioniziruiushikh izluchenii dlia obrabotki pishchevykh produktov v sviazi s ikh khraneniem," in *Food Irradiation*, pp. 805-809.

27. Metlitskii et al., pp. 33-50.

28. On Chicago and the meat industry, see William Cronon, *Nature's Metropolis* (New York: W. W. Norton and Co., 1991), pp. 207-259.

29. Metlitskii et al., pp. 50-51.

30. I. M. Buznik, "K voprosu o gigienicheskoi otsenke kachestva miasa, obluchennogo ioniziruiushchimi izlucheniiami," *Voprosy pitaniia*, no. 2 (1960), 63-69. See also his work in *Tezisy dokladov 13-i nauchnoi sessii Instituta pitaniia AMN SSSR* (Moscow: Medgiz, 1969), p. 65.

31. V. I. Piul´skaia, "Vlianie g-luchei i termicheskoi obrabotki na razrushenie antiok- islitelei v svinom zhire," *Voprosy pitaniia*, no. 1 (1962), 65-68.

32. Iu. I. Shillinger, V. G. Kachkova, "Gigienicheskaia otsenka miasa kur, obluchennogo pasterizuiushchimi dozami g-radiatsii," *Gigiena i sanitariia*, no. 6 (1968), 44-49. In 1990, the Food and Drug Administration approved irradiation of chicken irradiated to prolong shelf life and prevent *Salmonella* and *E. coli* from growing. The FDA required any chicken so treated to be sold in a package marked with a small radiation symbol and explanation of the process. This has deterred consumers from buying the birds; the process remains underutilized.

33. Metlitskii et al., pp. 51-57.

34. A. V. Kardashev, "Rybnye konservy gamma-radiatsionnoi sterilizatsii," in *Food Irradiation*, pp. 561-566.

35. Iu. I. Shillinger, V. G. Kachkova, N. B. Maganova, "Vlianie na organizm sobak mias- nykh pishchevykh produktov, obluchennykh pasterizuiushchimi dozami g-radiatsii," *Voprosy pitaniia*, no. 1 (1965), 19-24; idem., "Izuchenie pokazatelei obmena nekotorykh vitaminov v organizme sobak, poluchaiushchikh miasnye produkty obluchennye pasterizuiushchimi dozami g-radiatsii," ibid., no. 2 (1965), 40-46; Shillinger, L. A. Okuneva, N. B. Maganova, A.V. Trufanov, G. M. Kiul´ian, V. N. Tretenko, "Obespechennost´ nekotorymi radio- labil´nymi vitaminami organizma obez´ian, nakhodivshikhsia na ratsione s rastitel´nymi produktami, podverguntymi g-oblucheniiu," ibid., no. 6 (1966), 60-64.

36. Iu. I. Shillinger, V. G. Kachkova, Z. M. Kamal´dinova, "Vliianie ratsiona iz pish- chevykh produktov, obluchennykh pasterizuiushchimi dozami g-radiatsii, na organizm belykh krys," *Voprosy pitaniia*, no. 3 (1967), 72-78.

37. M. S. Swaminathan, V. L. Chopra, S. Bhaskaran, "Cytological Aberrations Observed in Barley Embryos Cultured in Irradiated Potato Mash," *Radiation Research*, no. 16 (1962), 182-188.

38. M. J. Van Logten et al., "The Wholesomeness of Irradiated Mushrooms," *Food and Cosmetics Toxicology*, no. 9 (1971), 379-388.

39. Z. M. Kamal´dinova, "Vliianie kulinarno podgotovlennogo goviazh´ego miasa, radurizovannogo g-luchami na organizm belykh krys," *Voprosy pitaniia*, no. 2 (1970), 73-77.

40. I. A. Bronnikova, L. A. Okuneva, "K voprosu ob izuchenii mutagennykh i tsitotok- sicheskikh svoistva obluchennykh produktov pitaniia," *Voprosy pitaniia*, no. 4 (1973), 46-50.

41. Iu. I. Shillinger, I. N. Osipova, "Sovremennye dannye o mutagennykh i tsitotoksich- eskikh svoistvakh obluchennykh pishchevykh veshchestv i produktov," *Voprosy pitaniia*, no. 5 (1973), 7-14; I. N. Osipova, "Issledovaniia vozmozhnoi mutagennosti ekstraktov iz

obluchennogo kartofelia v zavisimost ot srokov ego kharnennia i kulinarnoi obrabotki," ibid., no. 1 (1974), 78–81.

42. Alla Iaroshinskaia, *Chernobyl´: sovershenno sekretno* (Moscow: "Drugie berega," 1992), pp. 447, 457.

43. I. Pyrkh, "Kolbasa s tseziem," *Sovetskaia rossiia,* September 12, 1989, 4.

Chapter 6

1. On Artsimovich, see B. B. Kadomtsev, ed., *Vospominaniia ob Akademike L. A. Artsimoviche* (Moscow: Nauka, 1981), and Archive LFTI, f. 3, op. 3, ed. khr. 121.

2. I would like to thank Igor Nikolaevich Golovin, for talking with me about the history of the Soviet fusion program, and for sharing his unpublished works on the subject, including "Rossiiskii Nauchnyi Tsentr—Kurchatovskii Institut" (1993?). On the Kurchatov Institute fusion program, see also *Order-of-Lenin I. V. Kurchatov Institute of Atomic Energy* (Moscow: Vneshtorgizdat, n. y.).

3. A. D. Sakharov, "Teoriia MTR. Chast´ III," A KIAE, 11/S-NT-39 (1951).

4. Andrei Sakharov, *Memoirs* (New York: Knopf, 1990), pp. 139–148.

5. L. A. Artsimovich, "O zapuske MTR," A KIAE, 11/S-NG-37 (1951). See also V. I. Veksler, "O vozmozhnosti isskustvennogo polucheniia iadernoi energii za schet sinteza legkikh elementov," A KIAE no. 5345 (1951) and I. E. Tamm, "O vzaimodeistvii izlucheniia s vysokotemperaturnoi plazmoi," A KIAE no. 5282 (1949).

6. A KIAE, no. 5285 (March 1950).

7. V. D. Shafranov, *Vklad sovetskikh uchenykh v issledovaniia po fizike plazmy i probleme upravliamogo termoiaernogo siteza* (Moscow: GKNT, 1987), p. 2.

8. n. a., "Ispol´zovanie atomnoi energii v mirnykh tseliakh i sovetskaia nauka," *Vestnik Akademii Nauk SSSR,* no. 7 (1955), 3–5, and n. a., "Ispol´zovanie atomnoi energii v mirnykh tseliakh," *Vestnik Akademii Nauk SSSR,* no. 8 (1955), 34–46.

9. The United States exploded a hydrogen "device" as big as a small house with massive refrigeration facilities for its deuterium on Eniwetok Island in the South Pacific in 1952, but its size made it "undeliverable" by airplane.

10. A KIAE, f. 2, op. 1, ed. khr. 14; I. V. Kurchatov, "Termoiadernaia energiia—osnova energetiki budushchego," *Pravda,* February 28, 1958, 3.

11. A. D. Sakharov, "O radioaktivnoi opasnosti iadernykh ispytanii," May 24, 1958, unpub. article, A KIAE. On Sakharov's efforts to gain a test ban, see Sakharov, *Memoirs,* pp. 197–204, 207–209, 215–218. Ovsei Leipunskii (the brother of Aleksandr, who directed the breeder reactor program) published a series of articles about the growing danger of radioactive fallout. He analyzed previously classified data to show that the growing megatonnage of nuclear weapons, even supposedly "clean" hydrogen bombs, produced significant amounts of radioactive strontium, cesium, carbon, and tritium upon explosion. Biologist Nikolai Dubinin and Andrei Sakharov, among others, read drafts of his articles in which he predicted tens of thousands of additional mutagenic and cancer deaths, primarily from leukemia, from the testing of these terrible weapons. See O. I. Leipunskii, "Radioaktivnaia opasnost´ vzryvov chistovodorodnoi bomby i obychnoi atomnoi bomby," *Atomnaia energiia,* vol. 3, no. 12 (1957), 530–539, and "O radioaktivnoi opasnosti nepreryvnykh ispytanii atomnykh bomb," ibid., vol. 4, no.1 (1958), 63–70. Leipunskii claimed no patience for Edward Teller and Albert Latter, whose books and writings on the nuclear world promoted the notion that the Soviet Union would cheat on any test ban, while underplaying the risk of weapons tests. See Leipunskii, "O knige E. Tellera i A. Liattera ´Nashe Iadernoe Budushchee´," *Atomnaia energiia,* vol. 4, no. 6 (1958), 608–610. In *Our Nuclear Future,* Teller and Latter ignored the risk from mutagenic consequences, argued that the dangers of disease and accidents in daily life were far greater than those from nuclear testing, and promoted the design of "clean" weapons.

12. On the history and politics of the peaceful atom, see Richard Hewlett, Jack M. Holl, *Atoms for Peace and War* (Berkeley: University of California Press, 1989).

13. n. a., "Atomnuiu energiiu—na sluzhbu miru!" *Atomnaia energiia,* vol. 1, no. 1 (1956), 3.

14. See for example, S. Malinin, V. Onushkin, *Mezhdunarodnoe sotrudnichestvo v oblasti mirnogo ispol´zovaniia atomnoi energii* (Moscow: Izdatel´stvo sotsial´no-ekonomicheskoi literatury, 1961).

15. n. a., "Ispol´zovanie atomnoi energii v mirnykh tseliakh," *Vestnik Akademii Nauk SSSR,* no. 8 (1955), 34–46, V. A. Leshkovtsev, "Sessiia Akademii Nauk SSSR po mirnomu ispol´zovaniiu atomnoi energii," *Fizika v shkole,* no. 6 (1955), 7–15.

16. n. a., "Mezhdunarodnoe nauchnoe sotrudnichestvo po mirnomu ispol´zovaniiu atomnoi energii," *Vestnik Akademii Nauk SSSR,* no. 9 (1955), 47–61; A. P. Vinogradov, "Atomnaia energiia i problemy geologii, khimii, metallurgii, tekhnologii," *Vestnik Akademii Nauk SSSR,* no. 11 (1955), 31–39.

17. There were also papers on agricultural, medical, and mining applications, on the biological effects of radiation based on animal experiments, on experience in clinical and diagnostic application of radioactive isotopes, and on worker safety measures. D. I. Blokhintsev, N. A. Nikolaev, "The First Atomic Power Station in the USSR and the Prospects of Atomic Power Development," *Proceedings of the First International Conference on the Peaceful Uses of Nuclear Energy,* vol. 3, 35–55; A. I. Alikchanow, W. K. Zavoisky et al., "A Boiling Homogeneous Nuclear Reactor for Power," ibid., vol. 3, 169–174; V. I. Veksler "Principles of the Acceleration of Charged Particles," ibid., vol. 1, 69–74; A. V. Kozlova, "Medical Application of Some Radioisotopes," ibid., vol. 10, 21–24; A. K. Guskova and G. D. Baisogolov on "Two Cases of acute Radiation Sickness in Man," ibid., vol. 11, 35–44; A. V. Palladin and G. E. Vladimirov, "The Use of Radioactive Isotopes in Studying the Function Biochemistry of the Brain," ibid., vol. 12, 402–408; I. A. Pigalyev, "Some Aspects of the Immunity of the Organism Exposed to Ionizing Radiation," ibid., vol. 11, 80–87; A. L. Kursanov, "Radioactive elements in the Study of Plant Life," ibid., vol. 16, 114–120; V. M. Klechkovski, "The Use of Tracer Atoms in Studying the Applications of Fertilizers," ibid., vol. 12, 109–117; I. N. Antipov-Karatayev, "Application of the Isotope Method to the Study of Adsorption of Electrolytes by the Soils in Connection with Land Improvement," ibid., vol. 12, 130–137; A. M. Kuzin, "The Utilization of Ionizing Radiation in Agriculture," ibid., vol. 12, 149–156.

18. I. V. Kurchatov, "Nekotrye voprosy razvitiia atomnoi energetiki v SSSR," *Atomnaia energiia,* vol. 1, no. 3 (1956), 3–10; ibid., "Polezhnyi obmen nauchnymi dostizheniiami," *Krasnaia zvezda,* May 27, 1958.

19. I. V. Kurchatov, "Ob upravlaiemykh termoiadernykh reaktsiiakh," *Pravda,* February 6, 1958, 3.

20. Gleb Anfilov, "Zvezdnaia spichka," *Iunost´,* no. 11 (1958), 111–118; M. Vasil´ev, "Okean energii," *Ekonomicheskaia gazeta,* August 1, 1964, 17; Kurchatov, "O vozmozhnosti sozdaniia upravliaemykh termoiadernykh reaktsii s pomoshch´iu gazovykh razriadov," *Pravda,* May 10, 1956, 3.

21. V. S. Emelianov, "Atomnaia energetika," *Krasnaia zvezda,* November 25, 1958.

22. M. A. Leontovich, ed., *Fizika plazmy i problema upravleiaemykh termoiadernykh reaktsii,* 4 vols. (Moscow: Izdatel´stvo Akademii Nauk SSSR, 1958). See also V. S. Emelianov, "Atom dolzhen sluzhit´ miru," *Izvestiia,* August 31, 1958, 3; "Atomnuiu energiiu—na sluzhbu miru i progressu," *Pravda,* August 31, 1958, 3; "Budushchee atomnoi energetiki v SSSR," *Atomnaia energiia,* vol. 5, no. 3 (1958), 217–222. The latter was published in slightly revised form in *Nauka i zhizn´,* no. 11 (1958), 23–26.

23. V. S. Emelianov, "Est´ chto obsuzhdat´, est´ chemu uchit´sia drug u druga," *Pravda,* January 10, 1960, 5; and "K tesnomu mezhdunarodnomu sotrudnichestvu v oblasti atomnykh issledovanii," *Vestnik Akademii Nauk SSSR,* no. 2 (1960), 3–11. On the exchanges between Soviet and American delegations to facilities, see Hewlett, Holl, *Atoms for Peace and War,* pp. 533–536.

24. Kurchatov, "Termoiadernaia energiia—energetika budushchego"; I. Podgornyi, "Energetika budushchego," *Trud,* November 27, 1958, 3; A. P. Striganov, *Kratkaia istoriia razvitiia IAE im. I. V. Kurchatova i rabota partiinoi organizatsii za period s 1944 po 1960 god* (Moscow: KIAE, 1990), pp. 71–76.

25. L. A. Artsimovich, *Upravlaiemye termoiadernye reaktsii,* 2nd ed. (Moscow: Gosizdat-fizmatlit, 1963).

26. L. A. Artsimovich, "Issledovaniia po upravliaemym reaktsiiami v SSSR," *Atomnaia energiia,* vol. 5, no. 5 (November 1958), 501–521.

27. V. D. Shafranov, *Vklad Sovetskikh uchenykh,* pp. 10–11; Lisa Jean Bromberg, *Fusion* (Cambridge, MA: MIT Press, 1982), pp. 110–111. The Salzburg conference involved over 500 delegates from 29 countries who presented over 100 papers, including keynote addresses from Artsimovich and Marshall Rosenbluth of the United States, a graduate student of Edward Teller and a Los Alamos employee who abandoned bombs for fusion pinches and the General Atomic Corporation. See E. I. Kuznetsov, E. P. Velikhov, "Mezhdunarodnaia konferentsiia po fizike plazmy i upravliaemym termoiadernym reaktsiiam," *Atomnaia energiia,* vol. 12, no. 2 (February 1962), 101–110.

28. On the Novosibirsk conference, see B. B. Kadomtsev, A. M. Stefanovskii, "III Mezh-dunarodnaia konferentsiia po fizike plazmy po upravliaemomu termoiadernomu sintezu," *Atomnaia energiia,* vol. 26, no. 1 (January 1969), 47–54.

29. Shafranov, *Vklad Sovetskikh uchenykh,* pp. 12–13.

30. L. Artsimovich, "Fizik nashego vremeni," *Novyi mir,* no. 1 (1967), pp. 190–203.

31. Shafranov, *Vklad Sovetskikh uchenykh,* pp. 6–7.

32. Personnel in the Institute of the Red Professoriat seem to have been behind the impetus for the institute. They justified it on the grounds that there were few physicists in the Academy of Sciences, save seismologists, and only through such an institute, they claimed, could the Marxist philosophers begin to have an impact on burning philosophical issues in physics. Such physicists of international renown as George Gamow, later author of the "Big Bang" theory in cosmology, supported the creation of theoretical physics institute within the Academy's walls. See A AN, f. 351, op. 1, ed. khr. 63, ll. 7, 32–37.

33. On L. I. Mandel´shtam, see N. D. Papleksi, "Leonid Isaakovich Mandel´shtam," in L. I. Mandel´shtam, *Polnoe sobranie trudov,* vol. 1 (Moscow: Nauka, 1948), pp. 7–66; S. M. Rytov et al., *Akademik L. I. Mandel´shtam. k 100-letiiu so dnia rozhdeniia* (Moscow: Nauka, 1979); L. I. Mandel´shtam, *Lektsii po optike, teorii otnositel´nosti i kvantovoi mekhanike* (Moscow: Nauka, 1972).

34. I. L. Rozental´, S. M. Rytova, B. B. Kadomtsev et al., "Mikhail Leontovich," *Nauka v SSSR,* no. 4 (1989), 20–27.

35. A. S. Sonin, "The Newspaper *Red Fleet* Versus Idealism in Physics," *Herald of the USSR Academy of Sciences,* vol. 61, no. 1 (1991), 70–75. See also FIAN Archive, Skobeltsyn letters of February 28, 1953, and June 12, 1953; and f. 532, op. 1, ed. khr. 232, ll. 9–19.

36. A AN, f. 532, op. 4, ed. khr. 105.

37. See Grigori Freiman, *It Seems I Am A Jew,* translated and edited by Melvyn Nathanson (Carbondale and Edwardsville: Southern Illinois University Press, 1980). On Nazi physics, see Alan D. Beyerchen, *Scientists Under Hitler: Politics and the Physics Commu-nity in the Third Reich* (New Haven and London: Yale University Press, 1977); Monika Ren-neberg, Mark Walker, "Scientists, Engineers, and National Socialism," in Monika Renneberg, Mark Walker, eds., *Science, Technology and National Socialism* (Cambridge, Eng-land: Cambridge University Press, 1994), pp. 1–29; Herbert Mehrtens, "Irresponsible Purity: The Political and Moral Structure of the Mathematical Sciences in the National Socialist State," in ibid., pp. 324–338. For the impact of anti-Semitic policies on the biological sciences in Nazi Germany, see Ute Deichmann, Benno Muller-Hill, "Biological Research at Universi-ties and Kaiser Wilhelm Institutes in Nazi Germany," in ibid., pp. 161–174; Robert Proctor, *Racial Hygiene: Medicine Under the Nazis* (Cambridge, MA and London: Harvard University Press, 1988).

38. A LFTI, f. 3, op. 1, ed. khr. 209, ll. 1–32, and A FIAN, F. 532, op. 1, ed. khr. 231, ll. 2–28, 42–54. Fock tried out several versions of his talk at Leningrad State University, including presentations on January 12, 1949, and April 27, 1950. See A AN LO, f. 1034, op. 1, ed. khr. 369 and ed. khr. 374.

39. M. A. Leontovich, "Liudi zazhgut na zemle svoe solntse," *Smena,* no. 17 (1960), 22–23.

40. For discussion of the history of fusion research at the Kurchatov Institute, see V. S. Strelkov, "Twenty-five Years of Tokamak Research at the I. V. Kurchatov Institute," *Nuclear Fusion,* vol. 25, no. 9 (1985), 1189–1194; B. B. Kadomtsev, V. S. Mukhovatov, V. D. Shafranov, "Magnetic Plasma Confinement . . . ," *Soviet Journal of Plasma Physics,* vol. 9, no. 1 (Jan.-Feb. 1983), 2–10; E. P. Velikhov, K. B. Kartashev, "Osnovnye rezul´taty issledovanii po UTS i fizke plazmy v SSSR za period s avgusta 1984 g. po avgust 1985 g.," *Voprosy atomnoi nauki i tekhniki. Seriia: termoiadernyi sintez,* no. 1 (1986), 3–24.

41. A. B. Berlizov et al., "Rezul´taty pervykh eksperimentov na ustanovke Tokamak-10," *Atomnaia energiia,* vol. 43, no. 2 (August 1977), 90–99. As of 1977, the machine operated at half-power with current of 0.4 megaamperes, and temperature in the center of the plasma cloud at 1–1.2 kiloelectronvolts for 40 to 70 milliseconds.

42. D. I. Ivanov et al., "Sverkhprovodiashchii toroidal´nyi solenoid Tokamaka-7," *Atomnaia energiia,* vol. 15, no. 3 (September 1978), 171–174.

43. n. a., *Ezhegodnik 77-78. Ordena Lenina Institut Atomnoi Energii im. I. V. Kurchatova* (Moscow: KAIE, 1979), pp. 32–45.

44. On the United States fusion program at Livermore, Oak Ridge, and Los Alamos national laboratories and at the Princeton Plasma Physics Laboratory, see Bromberg, *Fusion.*

45. *XXIV s´ezd KPSS, Stenograficheskii otchet* (Moscow: Politizdat, 1971), vol. 1, p. 270, and vol. 2, p. 103; I. M. Korolev, "General Meeting of the USSR Academy of Sciences Discusses Prospects for the Development of Power Engineering," *Current Digest of the Soviet Press,* vol. 26, no. 48, 9; E. P. Velikhov, B. B. Kadomtsev, "A Step Toward Thermonuclear Power," *Current Digest of the Soviet Press,* vol. 28, no. 10, 26–27; *XXV s´ezd KPSS, Stenograficheskii otchet* (Moscow: Politizdat, 1976), vol. 1, p. 136; A. Aleksandrov, "The Prospects for Power Engineering," *Current Digest of the Soviet Press,* vol. 31, no. 15, 4.

46. For example, in his entire speech before the twenty-sixth congress, A. P. Aleksandrov noted merely that "works on thermonuclear power are successfully being developed." See *XXVI s´ezd KPSS, Stenograficheskii otchet* (Moscow: Politizdat, 1981), vol. 1, p. 222. See also *Ekonomicheskaia gazeta,* no. 14 (March 1984), 13–14.

47. B. B. Kadomtsev, "Neustoichivost´ plazmy i upravlaiemye termoiaderny reaktsii," *Vestnik Akademii Nauk SSSR,* no. 2 (1967), 25–29.

48. "Evgenii Pavlovich Velikhov (On His Fiftieth Birthday)," *Soviet Journal of Plasma Physics,* no. 1 (1985), 83–84. Parallel with the problem of controlled thermonuclear synthesis, research on the dynamics of plasmas and charged particles was carried out and enabled the creation of MHD generators of electrical energy. An MHD plant generates electricity by sending a plasma perpendicularly into an intense magnetic field. Fuel, such as natural gas, oil, or coal, is burned in a combustor and seeded to produce an ionized gas. A plasma produced from the fuel travels down an electrode-studded generator at high speeds. This hot plasma then passes through a diffuser, a seed and heat recovery unit, and into a conventional steam power plant. Theoretically, MHD could achieve forty, fifty, or even sixty percent efficiencies. Soviet MHD research originated somewhat later than in the United States but became the world's largest program within a half-decade. The Soviet program was centered at the Institute of High Temperatures but much of its theoretical underpinnings came from Velikhov. See Paul Josephson, Jonathan Coopersmith, "Fundamental Science and National Security: Joint Soviet-American Research on Magnetohydrodynamics and Controlled Thermonuclear Synthesis," in Eric Stubbs, ed., *Soviet Foreign Economic Policy and International Security* (Armonk, NY: M. E. Sharpe, 1991), 185–208.

49. E. P. Velikhov, "Solntse zagoraetsia na zemle," *Trud,* August 24, 1982, 2; idem, "Podstupy k 'termoiadu'," *Literaturnaia gazeta,* January 1, 1981, 10; V. N. Veliakov, V. A. Glukhikh, B. B. Kadomstev, N. A. Monoszon, et al., "Ustanovka Tokamak-15," *Atomnaia energiia,* vol. 52, no. 2 (Feburary 1982), 101–108.

50. E. P. Velikhov et al., "Hybrid Fusion Reactor in a Nuclear Energetics System," *Soviet Journal of Plasma Physics,* no. 7 (1985), 525; E. P. Velikhov et al., "Gibridnyi termoiadernyi reaktor tokamak dlia proizvodstva deliashchegosia topliva i elektroenergii," *Atomnaia energiia,* vol. 45, no. 1 (July 1978), 3–9; I. N. Golovin, "O meste gibridnykh reaktorov v energeticheskoi sisteme mira," *Atomnaia energiia,* vol. 39, no. 6 (December 1975), 379–386.

51. E. P. Velikhov, "Dostizheniia fiziko-tekhnicheskikh nauk i zadachi nauchno-tekhnicheskogo progressa v narodnom khoziaistve," *Vestnik Akademii Nauk SSSR,* no. 5 (1984), 7–13; Interview with Dr. Stephen Knowlton, September 10, l986, MIT Plasma Laboratories, Cambridge, MA; P. R. Josephson, *New Atlantis Revisited* (Princeton, NJ: Princeton University Press, 1997), p. 131.

52. For detailed discussion of plasma fusion research at LFTI, see V. E. Golant, "Tokamak Experiments at the A. F. Ioffe Physico-Technical Institute," *Nuclear Fusion,* vol. 25, no. 9 (September 1985), 1183–1188; V. M. Tuchkevich, V. Ia. Frenkel´, *Plasma Physics* (Leningrad: Nauka, 1978); E. P. Velikhov, K. B. Kartashev, "Osnovy rezul´taty," op. cit., 8–10.

53. A. V. Zaitseva, L. A. Kolesnikova, V. Ia. Frenkel´, eds., *Akademik B. P. Konstantinov. Vospominaniia, Stat´i, Dokumenty* (Leningrad: Nauka, 1985), pp. 46–52. See also V. V. Afrosimov, V. A. Glukhikh, V. E. Golant, "Issledovaniia plazmy na ustanovke 'Alfa'," *Zhurnal tekhnicheskoi fiziki,* vol. 30, no. 12 (1960), 1381–1392. During experiments on the Tuman-3, the vacuum chamber ruptured, putting research well behind schedule.

54. My deepest thanks to Igor Golovin for sharing with me his "Dmitrii Vasil´evich Efremov," unpublished paper, March 1, 1987 (in Russian).

55. S. Iu. Gus´kov, "Tenth IAEA International Conference on Plasma Physics and Controlled Fusion," *Soviet Journal of Plasma Physics,* no. 6 (1985), 436; N. G. Basov, O. N. Krokhin, *Zhurnal ekspirimental´noi i teoreticheskoi fiziki,* vol. 46 (1964), 171. Basov, the director of FIAN during much of the Brezhnev period, describes the laser program in some detail in "Lazer i energetika budushchego," *Krasnaia zvezda,* July 2, l983, 3, and "Laser Controlled Fusion," *Soviet Journal of Plasma Physics,* no. 1 (1983), 10–14.

56. K. D. Sinel´nikov, ed., *Konferentsiia po fizike plazmy i problema upravliaemykh termoiadernykh reaktsii,* 2 vols. (Kharkov: UFTI, 1959).

57. Kadomtsev et al., "Magnetic Confinement," p. 5.

58. Interviews with Dr. Kurt Riedel, a theoretician at NYU's Courant Institute, who spent one year at KIAE, September 17, l986.

59. V. E. Ivanov, ed., *50 let Khar´kovskomu fiziko-tekhnicheskomu institutu AN USSR* (Kiev: Naukovo dumka, 1978), pp. 162–229.

60. I discuss the history of the Budker Institute and its fusion program in my *New Atlantis Revisited,* pp. 67–76, on which this discussion is based.

61. G. Budker, "Ukroshchenie plazmy," *Za nauku v sibiri,* September 14, 1964, 2.

62. R. Sagdeev, "K okeanu energii," *Izvestiia,* Janaury 4, 1969, 3.

63. D. Riutov, "I vnov´—o katstrofe na planete," *Pravda,* October 13, 1989, 3.

64. Interviews with Dr. Stephen Knowlton and Dr. Kurt Riedel.

65. Strelkov, "Twenty-Five Years," op. cit., 1194; *Izvestiia,* July 5, l975, 5, as cited in *Current Digest of the Soviet Press,* vol. 27, no. 27, 23; Interview with Dr. Riedel, September 17, l986; B. B. Kadomtsev, "Opytnyi termoiadernyi reaktor," *Voprosy atomnoi nauki i tekhniki. Seriia termoiadernyi sintez,* no. 2 (1984), 78–79; L. Zagal´skii, "Energiia budyshchego veka," *Komsomol´skaia Pravda,* April 21, l985, 4.

66. E. P. Velikhov, "Solntse zagoraetsia na zemle," *Trud,* August 24, 1982, 2; Zagal´skii, "Energiia"; Riedel, Trip Report, p. 6.

67. B. B. Kadomtsev, "Tokamak," *Soviet Life,* August l986, 13.

68. B. B. Kadomtsev, "Tokamak Is an Earthly Star," *Current Digest of the Soviet Press,* vol. 37, no. 48 (October 1986), 8, 15; "Tokamak," *Soviet Life,* 15.

69. Vanda Beletskaia, "'Iter'—2003. Prikonchit li khozraschet nauku?" *Ogonek,* no. 33 (August 11–18, 1993), 1–2.

70. Igor Golovin, "Upravliaemyi termoiadernyi sintez s magnitnym uderzhaniem plazmy," *Sovetskii fizik,* no. 5–6 (February 16, 1990), 3.

71. n. a., "V institute atomnoi energii," *Pravda,* February 22, 1989, 2.

72. Dmitrii Frolov, "'Atom u nas doma,'" *Nezavisimaia gazeta,* January 3, 1992.

73. I. F. Zhezherun et al., "Iskazhenie istorii IAE im. I. V. Kurchatova ne dolzhno prodolzhat'sia!" *Sovetskii fizik,* no. 3 (February 7, 1991), 2–4.

74. n. a., "Analiz, otvetstvennost', konstruktivizm," *Sovetskii fizik,* no. 1–2 (January 17, 1990), 5.

Chapter 7

1. See V. S. Kogan, *Kirill Dmitrievich Sinel'nikov* (Kiev: Naukova dumka, 1984), for the best biography of Sinel'nikov, which I consulted heavily for this section.

2. Eddie Sinelnikova, *I Married a Russian: Letters from Kharkov,* Lucie Street, ed. (New York: Emerson Books, Inc., 1947), pp. 39, 58, 65.

3. Archive Academy of Sciences of Ukraine, Anton Karlovich Valter, Lichnoe delo, 1–31, 41–59, 97, 144–160.

4. A KIAE, f. 2, op. 1, d. 5.11.13–18, 71.

5. Sinelnikova, *I Married a Russian,* pp. 40, 45, 59, 85, 87, 143, 152, 198, 275.

6. Ibid., pp. 39, 58, 65, 83–84.

7. A KIAE, f. 2, op. 1, d. 5.11.13–18, l. 54, and l. 57.

8. Ioffe, "Vorwort," *Physikalische Zeitschrift der Sowjet Union,* vol. 1, no. 1 (1932), 3–4.

9. A. P. Trofimenko, *Istoriia razvitiia iadernykh issledovanii na Ukraine,* candidate of science dissertation, (Moscow: Institute of History of Science and Technology, 1974), pp. 77, 98.

10. V. I. Bunimovich, "Opyty po razrusheniiu atoma," *Elektrichestvo,* no. 8 (1933), 4–9.

11. n. a., "Nachalas' novaia epokha v fizike," *Komsomol'skaia pravda,* October 24, 1932, p. 1; F. Kandlyba, "Chaipery atomnogo iadra," *Izvestiia,* November 11, 1932, 1.

12. Trofimenko, *Istoriia,* p. 109.

13. Ibid., pp. 80–81. As was standard for the country's scientists in the effort to raise the cultural level of the masses, the UFTI physicists also organized a cycle of public lectures in Kharkiv in workers' clubs on their achievements.

14. Ibid., pp. 111–113.

15. Ibid., pp. 114–119.

16. Sinelnikova, *I Married a Russian,* pp. 181, 237, 281.

17. L. B. Okun', ed., *Vospominaniia o I. Ia. Pomeranchuke* (Moscow: Nauka, 1988).

18. Sinelnikova, *I Married a Russian,* pp. 263–264.

19. A KIAE, f. 2, op. 1, d. 5.11.13–18, ll. 55, 58.

20. A KIAE, f. 2, op. 1, ed. khr. 71/8, ll. 1–4.

21. A KIAE, f. 2, op. 1, d. 5.11.13–18, ll. 61–68. My thanks to Raissa Kuznetsova for sharing her typewritten deciphering of these handwritten letters with me.

22. A FI UkrAN, op. 1, ed. khr. 185.

23. A FI ANUkr, op. 2, ed. khr. 153, ll. 14–15. A. S. Davydov, M. F. Deigen, I. M. Dykman, S. I. Pekak, K. B. Tolpygo, "Kvantovaia mekhanika i prichinost'," typewritten manuscript.

24. Trofimenko, *Istoriia,* pp. 131–136.

25. A. K. Valter et al., *Elektrostaticheskie uskoriteli zariazhennykh chastits* (Moscow: Gosizdat po atomnoi nauke i tekhike, 1963), pp. 171–173, 191–205. My thanks to A. A. Tsy-

gikalo, one of the authors of this volume, for his hospitality in showing me UFTI electrostatic generator facilities and for giving me a copy of this book.

26. V. V. Goncharov, V. F. Kuleshov, "Iadernofizicheskie tsentry v soiuznykh respublikakh," *Atomnaia energiia,* vol. 33, no. 6 (December 1972), 947–953.

27. L. I. Shtukaturova, *Prospekt NIIEFA* (Leningrad: NIIEFA, 1975); Interviews with Andrei Ivanov, Oleg Gennadievich Filotov, Oleg Aleksandrovich Gusev, Viktor Vasilevich Rumiantsev, NIIEFA, Leningrad, January 12, 1993. My thanks especially to Boris Zhukov for his informative exposition on the history of NIIEFA and for his hospitality during my brief visit to the facility.

28. A AN, f. 1683, op. 1, ed. khr. 1, ll. 137–142.

29. Sh. Esenov, "Razvitie nauki i rost nauchnykh kadrov sovetskogo Kazakhstana za 50 let soiuza SSSR," *Vestnik Akademii Nauk KazSSR,* no. 1 (1973), 8; V. Fesenkov, "O nekotorykh voprosakh razvitiia fiziko-matematicheskikh nauk v Kazakhstane," ibid., no. 11 (1947), 25–26; K. Satpaev, "Nauka v Kazkhstane za 25 let," *Vestnik Kazakhskogo filiala ANSSSR,* no. 6 (1945), 26.

30. V. Fesenkov, "Razvitie astronomicheskoi nauki v Kazakhstane," K. Satpaev, ed., *Nauka v Kazkahstane za sorok let sovetskoi vlasti* (Almaty: 1957), pp. 247–248; K. Satpaev, "Akademiia Nauk Kazakhskoi SSR," in ibid., pp. 38–46; I. G. Galuzo, "K otkrytkiiu AN KazSSR," *Vestnik Akademii Nauk KazSSR,* no. 6 (1946), 58–65; K. I. Satpaev, "Osnovnye itogi i zadachi nauchno-issledovatel'skikh rabot KazFANSSSR," *Vestnik Kazakhskogo filiala ANSSSR,* no. 1 (1944), 8–11; K. Satpaev, "Nauka v Kazkhstane za 25 let," *Vestnik Kazakhskogo filiala ANSSSR,* no. 6 (1945), 20–28; V. A. Ul'ianovskaia, "Iz istoriia sozdaniia AN KazSSR," *Vestnik Akdemii Nauk KazSSR,* no. 5 (1949), 43–53.

31. A. Kanapin, *Kul'turnoe stroitel'stvo v Kazkhstane* (Almaty: 1964), p. 142; *Kazakhstan za 50 let: statisticheskii sbornik* (Almaty: 1971), p. 173; and *Itogi vsesoiuznoi perepisi naseleniia, 1970* (Moscow: Statiszdat, 1972), pp. 13, 233.

32. I. G. Dem'ianikov, "Atomnyi tsentr Kazakhstana," *Nauka i zhizn',* no. 1 (1959), 33–35; V. A. Dobrotin, Iu. T. Lukin, "Fizika vysokikh energii i kosmicheskikh luchei v Kazakhstane," *Vestnik Akademii Nauk Kazakhskoi SSR,* no. 12 (1967), 12–23; O. A. Zhautykov, "Razvitie fiziko-matematicheskikh nauk v Kazakhstane," ibid., no. 1 (1973), 36–43; Sh. Sh. Ibragimov, "25 let Institutu iadernoi fiziki AN KazSSR," *Atomnaia energiia,* vol. 53 (December 1982), 405–410.

33. L. M. Nemenov, "Uskorenie ionov do nizkikh i srednikh energii i ikh primenenie v iadernoi fizike," *Vestnik Akademiii Nauk Kazakh SSR,* no. 10 (1965), 3–12; T. Elemanov et al., "O nekotorykh kharakteristikakh elektronnogo puchka lineinogo uskoritelia U-10," ibid., no. 6 (1967), 58–64.

34. G. A. Batyrbekov, B. N. Okolovich, Zh. S. Takibaev, "Rezul'taty eksperimentov po sozdaniiu tsental'nogo kanala bol'shogo diametra v aktivnoi zone reaktora VVR-K," *Vestik Academii Nauk Kazakhskoi SSR,* no. 8 (1969), 10–14; Zh. S. Takibaev, Sh. Sh. Ibramigov, G. A. Batyrbekov, B. N. Okolovich, "Modernizirovannyi reaktor VVR-K ii ego ispol'zovanie v narodnom khoziaistve Khazakhstana," ibid., no. 2 (1972), 15–26; "Kazakhstanskii reaktor—v stroiu," ibid., no. 11 (1967), 92–93.

35. V. P., "V institute iadernoi fiziki Akademii nauk Uzbekskoi SSR," *Atomnaia energiia,* vol. 6, no. 1 (January 1959), 79–80; P. K. Khabibullaev, "V institute iadernoi fiziki AN Uzbekskoi SSSR," *Vestnik Akademii Nauk SSSR,* no. 5 (1962), 61–66.

36. On the life and scientific activity of Konstantinov, see A. V. Zaitseva, L. A. Kolesnikova, V. Ia. Frenkel', *Akademik B. P. Konstantinov. Vospominaniia, stat'i, dokumenty* (Leningrad: Nauka, 1985), from which this account is largely drawn. My thanks to Dr. Kolesnikova for hosting my visit to the Leningrad Institute of Nuclear Physics and giving me a copy of this book.

37. B. P. Konstantinov, "Atom dolzhen sluzhit' miru," *Vechernii Leningrad,* September 18, 1958.

38. A AN, f. 1683, op. 1, d. 14, ll. 1–2, 13–16, 23, 79, 87; and ed. khr. 12, l. 10.

39. A AN, f. 1683, op. 1, ed. khr. 1, ll. 135–136.

40. Estonia has a population of 1.4 million with sixty-two percent Estonian and thirty percent Russian. It has a productive agricultural sector and the second largest oil shale industry in the world, as well as shipbuilding and phosphates industries. Lithuania, ethnically the most homogeneous of the Baltic states, has 3.6 million inhabitants with eighty percent Lithuanian, nine percent Russian, and eight percent Polish. Its economy is founded on agriculture, peat, machine building, metalworking, and food processing industries.

41. G. Gaile, "Ob opyte vnedreniia radioaktivnykh izotopov i iadernykh izluchenii na predpriiatiakh narodnogo khoziaistva Latviiskoi SSR," *Izvestiia Akademii Nauk Latviiskoi SSR*, no. 7 (1960), 163–171. An important aspect of diffusion of radioisotope technology was training for 400 enterprise workers, who continued to work full time while taking special courses.

42. V. Ia. Veldre, "Novyi iadernyi reaktor," *Vestnik Akademii nauk SSSR*, no. 11 (1962), 88–90; "Pervyi atomnyi v pribaltike," *Trud*, September 30, 1961, 4; V. Gavar, "Poleznaia radiatsiia," *Sovetskaia Latviia*, December 7, 1973.

43. A. A., "Belorusskii iadernyi reaktor," *Atomnaia energiia*, vol. 12, no. 6 (June 1962), 539–540; A. K. Krasin et al., "Razvitie issledovanii v Institute iadernoi energetiki," ibid., vol. 24, no. 4 (April 1968), 307–311; A. K. Krasin, "Atom sluzhit liudiam," *Sovetskaia belorussiia*, June 27, 1974, 2.

44. A. Kakosian, A. Pumpianskii, "Eshelony zashchity," *Komsomol'skaia pravda*, September 22, 1976, 4; "Vid s kholma metsamor," ibid., September 23, 1976, 4; "Atom Armenii," September 18, 1976, 2–3; "Shapka dlia nevidimki," ibid., September 19, 1976, 4.

45. D. T. Arshakian, "Armeniia bez AES," *Energiia*, no. 11 (1989), 2–3.

46. A. Sarkisian, "Vmesto atomnoi—teplovaia," *Pravda*, February 26, 1989, 1; Andrei Kolesnikov, "Est' li zhizn' na armianskoi AES?" *Moskovskie novosti*, no. 30 (July 25, 1993), 10–11.

47. A IF ANUkrSSR, op. 1, ed. khr. 710, l. 14.

48. Ibid., ed. khr. 440, ll. 1–5, 9, 14–21, 34.

49. Ibid., ed khr. 476, ll. 1, 30–32.

50. Ibid., ed. khr. 487, and ed. khr. 529, ll. 1–15.

51. Ibid., ed. khr. 613, ll. 1–41.

52. Ibid., ed. khr. 614, ll. 3–16.

53. Ibid., f. 1, ed. khr. 1070, "Perepiska po vypolneniiu postanovleniiu prezidiuma AN UkSSR, 1980," and "Perepiska po vypolneniiu postanovleniiu prezidiuma AN UkSSR, 1984."

54. Archive of the Institute of Nuclear Research of Ukraine (hereafter A IIaI AN UkrSSR), "Spravka po rezul'tatam proverki nauchno-organizatsionnoi deiatel'nosti instituta, 1980"; "Perepiska po vypolneniiu postanovleniiu prezidiuma AN UkSSR, 1984," ll. 1–3, 15, 18, 19, 36; "Otchet IiaI za 1970 g.," ll. 1–24; "Perepiska po bypolneniiu postanovlenii Prezidium AN USSR, 1982," Letter of Nemets of May 5, 1982, to OFIA AN Ukr SSR; A. P. Trofimenko, V. M. Pugach, *Institut iadernykh issledovanii* (Kiev: Naukovo dumka, 1981).

55. A IIaI AN Ukr SSR, "Perepiska po vypolnenii postanovlenii Prezidium AN USSR, 1982," Letter of Nemets of July 12, 1982, to President B. Paton, vice president F. S. Babichev, and others.

56. Ibid., "Perepiska po vypolneniiu postanovlenii Prezidium AN USSR, 1982," ll. 57–61, 91, and 1983, ll. 17–20; "Perepiska po vypolneniiu rasporiazhenii 1983, . . ." 1–2; "Svedeniia ob osnovnykh rezultatakh deiatel'nosti IIaI za 1983 g.."

57. On nuclear power in Ukraine, see in particular David Marples, *The Social Impact of the Chernobyl Disaster* (New York: St. Martin's Press, 1988). See also D. Marples, "Nuclear Energy in the Ukraine: The Wave of the Future?" *Radio Free Europe-Radio Liberty* Report 451/84 (November 27, 1984).

58. Nonna Chernykh, "Na postamente rozovoi mechty," *Vash Sputnik,* no. 11 (1998), 3.

59. Vladimir Shunevich, "V institute iadernykh issledovanii ostanovlen tsiklotron. Eto opasno dlia Ukrainskoi nauki," *Kievskie vedomosti,* June 26, 1993.

Chapter 8

1. V. S. Emelianov, *S chego nachinalos'* (Moscow: Sovetskaia rossiia, 1979), p. 256.

2. I. Dmitriev, "Mirnaia professiia iadernogo vzryva," *Sotsialisticheskaia industriia,* May 30, 1976, 4; M. D. Nordyke, "A Review of the Soviet Data on the Peaceful Uses of Nuclear Explosions," *Annals of Nuclear Energy,* vol. 2 (1975), 665–667.

3. Nordyke, "A Review of the Soviet Data," 662–663.

4. Vladimir Boreiko, "Izvestno, chto atomnyi zvryv v donbasse byl. Neizvestno bylo lish', kakovy ego posledstviia," *Kievskie vedomosti,* May 8, 1993, 9.

5. "Vzryvy v shtol'ne," *Ekho chernobylia,* no. 5–6 (February 1992), 7.

6. I. Dmitriev, "Mirnaia professiia iadernogo vzryva," *Sotsialisticheskaia industriia,* May 30, 1976, 4; Nordyke, "A Review of the Soviet Data," 663–664.

7. A. K. Kruglov, "Atomnaia nauka i tekhnika—narodnomu khoziaistvu strany," *Atomnaia energiia,* vol. 50, no.2 (February 1981), 82–84.

8. Dmitriev, "Mirnaia professiia iadernogo vzryva."

9. William Broad, "A Soviet Company Offers Nuclear Blasts for Sale to Anyone with the Cash," *New York Times,* November 7, 1991, A18.

10. Edward Teller with Allen Brown, *The Legacy of Hiroshima* (Garden City, NY: Doubleday and Co., Inc., 1962), pp. 81–92.

11. Ibid., p. 87.

12. Interview with Dr. Milo Nordyke, Lawrence Livermore National Laboratory, Livermore, California, January 10, 1993.

13. My deep thanks to Bart Hacker, for allowing me to read his "Project Plowshare, 1957–1973: Too Risky or Too Costly," unpublished paper, 1993, on which this section is based. See also Scott Kirsch, Don Mitchell, "Earthmoving as the 'Measure of Man': Edward Teller, Geographical Engineering, and the Matter of Progress," *Social Text,* vol. 16, no. 1 (1998), 101–134.

14. Glenn Werth, Philip Randolph, "The Salmon Seismic Experiment," *Journal of Geophysical Research,* vol. 71, no. 14 (July 15, 1966), 3405–3412.

15. Grigory Medvedev, *The Truth About Chernobyl* (New York: Norton, 1990), pp. 61–63.

16. Vladimir Boreiko, "Kto i kak 'poseial' Chernobyl'?" *Pravda Ukrainy,* April 24, 1993.

17. V. M. Chernyshenko, "Osnovnye itogi stroitel'stva chernobyl'skoi AES," *Energeticheskoe stroitel'stvo,* no. 11 (1984), 2–6.

18. Liubov Kovalevs'ka, "Ne privatna sprava," *Literaturna Ukraina,* no. 13 (March 27, 1986); Medvedev, *Truth,* pp. 44–49.

19. This technical summary of the accident is taken from Medvedev, *Truth;* V. G. Bar'iakhtar, ed., *Chernobyl'skaia katastrofa* (Kiev: Naukova dumka, 1995); and especially Victor G. Snell, "Introduction: The Cause of the Chernobyl Accident," in David Marples, *The Social Impact of the Chernobyl Disaster* (New York: St. Martin's Press, 1988), pp. 1–24.

20. Alla Iaroshinskaia, *Chernobyl': Sovershenno sekretno* (Moscow: Drugie Berega, 1992), p. 327.

21. Valerii Legasov, "Moi dolg rasskazat' ob etom . . ." *Pravda,* May 20, 1988, 3, 8.

22. Medvedev, *Truth,* pp. 138–139, 150, 167, 194–196.

23. Iaroshinskaia, *Chernobyl',* pp. 428–430.

24. Bar'iakhtar, *Chernobyl'skaia katastrofa,* pp. 18, 36–37; Legasov, "Moi dolg rasskazat'."

25. Medvedev, *Truth,* p. 154.

26. Iaroshinskaia, *Chernobyl',* pp. 512–517.

27. Ibid.

28. Legasov, "Moi dolg rasskazat´."

29. Iaroshinskaia, *Chernobyl´*, p. 514.

30. Ibid., p. 379.

31. P. Egiazarian, "Lopata . . . bez golovy," *Ekho chernobylia,* no. 15–16 (May 1992), 7.

32. S. Prokopchuk, A. Savain, "Pod pantsirem iz metalla i betona," *Trud,* September 28, 1986, 1.

33. S. Beliaev, A. Borovoi, A. Gagarinskii, "Chto delaiut liudi v 'sarkofage'?" *Pravda,* December 8, 1989, 4.

34. Leonid Zamiatin, "Golodovka chernobyl´tsev," *Pravda Ukrainy,* April 24, 1993; "'Atomnye soldaty' dobilis´ vypolneniia svoikh trebovanii," *Izvestiia,* October 1, 1993; S. Kosova, "Na mera nadeisia, a sam . . . ," *Ekho chernobylia,* no. 5–6 (Feburary 1992), 6; S. Feigina, "Kto pomozhet 'Chernobyl´tsam'—samoubiitsam?" ibid., no. 5–6 (February 1992), 5.

35. Iaroshinskaia, *Chernobyl´,* pp. 480–481.

36. Iaroshinskaia, *Chernobyl´,* pp. 292, 392, 415–416, 444; Bar´iakhtar, *Chernobyl´skaia katastrofa,* pp. 41–42.

37. I. A. Beliaev, *Beton marki 'Sredmash'* (Moscow: IzdAT, 1996); V. Demenev, "Ob˝ekt 'ukrytie'," *Ekho Chernobylia,* no. 18 (October 1993), 7; Aleksandr Naumov, "'Ukrytie', uvy, ne stalo sarkofagom dlia iadernogo dzhinna," *Kievskie novosti,* April 29, 1994, 5.

38. N. Semena, "Chernobyl´skaia katastrofa grozit novoi bedoi," *Izvestiia,* September 16, 1993.

39. Minchernobyl´ Ukrainy, Akademiia Nauk Ukrainy, *Opisanie ob˝ekta 'Ukrytie' i trebovaniia k ego preobrazovaniiu* (Kiev: Naukova dumka, 1992).

40. Larisa Kozik, "Konkurs 'ukrytie' podvodit pervye itogi," *Pravda Ukrainy,* June 5, 1993; Natalia Kurolenko, "'Sarkofag-2': Zhuri prinialo ikh proekt," *Kievskie vedomosti,* June 26, 1993; Stanislav Prokopchuk, "Budet 'sarkofag-2'," *Trud,* August 14, 1993.

41. N. M. Sorokin, General Director, Chernobyl Atomic Power Station, December 1, 1993, Unpublished paper, "Spravka ob osnovnykh tekhniko-ekonomicheskikh pokazateliakh Chernobylskoi AES, sostianii del i sushchestvuiushchikh problemakh (po sostoianiiu na konets 1992 g.)."

42. Marples, *Social Impact;* Viktor Demenev, "Liudi tozhe mogut vzryvat´sia," *Ekho chernobylia,* no. 3–4 (January 1992), 5.

43. n. a., "Chernobyl´skaia AES: Pozitsiia Minprirody," *Ekho Chernobylia,* no. 67 (May 1993), 2.

44. n. a., "Chernobyl´skaia AES: Techet voda iz basseina, gde khranitsia otrabotannoe toplivo," *Nezavisimaia gazeta,* June 16, 1994, 2.

45. Mikhail Kon´shin, "Cheliabinsk-Chernobyl´: dva kryla bedy," *Ekho chernobylia,* no. 1–2 (January 1992), 5. Among the studies published are V. A. Baraboi, *Ot khirosimy do chernobylia* (Kiev: Naukovo dumka, 1991); L. I. Frantsevich, V. A. Gaichenko, V. I. Kryzhanovskii, *Zhivotnye v radioaktivnoi zone* (Kiev: Naukova dumka, 1991), which explores the impact of radiation on lifestyle (of humans) and the radiobiology and genetics of other living things in the Chernobyl "nature preserve (zapovednik)"; Ia. A. Serkiz et al., *Radiobiologicheskie aspekty avarii na chernobyl´skoi AES* (Kiev: Naukova dumka, 1992), which examines the effect of small doses of radiation on living things (skin, organs, cells, etc.); E. V. Sobotovich, ed., *Radiogeokhimiia v zone vliianiia chernobyl´skoi AES* (Kiev: Naukova dumka, 1992), which examines the nuclear-physical aspects of the Chernobyl accident, including the impact of radioactivity on soils and their distribution throughout the area of pollution.

46. Iurii Dronzhkevich, "Ne esh´ kaban, Ivanushka," *Vestnik chernobylia,* no. 49 (June 1991), 3; n. a., "Radovat´sia poka nechemu," ibid., 2–3.

47. Simon Kordonskii, "Printsipy zony: luidi i vlast´ v chernobyle," *Vek XX i mir,* no. 9 (1989), 17–21.

48. Stepan Ignatov, "Nu, Nuklid, beregis´!" *Ekho chernobylia,* no. 2 (October 1991), 3.

49. S. Feigina, "Komu dozimetr?!" *Ekho chernobylia,* no. 21–22 (June 1992), 5.

50. Vitalii Romanov, "V zone chashche brodiat v chashchakh . . ." *Vestnik chernobylia,* no. 65 (October 1993), 2.

51. Iu. D. Abaturov et al., *Vlianie ioniziruiushchego izlucheniia na sosnovye lesa v blizhnei zone Chernobyl'skoi AES* (Moscow: Nauka, 1996); V. Demenov, "Chernobyl' ne znaet granits," *Ekho chernobylia,* no. 23–24 (July 1992), 3; "Chernobylskie pozhary," *Ekho chernobylia,* no. 29–32 (September 1992), 3.

52. Anatolii Panov, "Net nichego strashnee pozhara na AES," *Kievskie vedomosti,* November 12, 1993.

53. A. K. Mikeev, *Protivo-pozharnaia zashchita AES* (Moscow: Energoatomizdat, 1990).

54. Jane Dawson, *Econationalism* (Durham: Duke University Press, 1995); Roman Solchanyk, "More Controversy over Nuclear Energy in Ukraine," *Radio Liberty Research,* RL 231/88, May 26, 1988; Valentin Smaga, "Metastazy imperskikh mifov," *Vechernii Kiev,* May 27, 1993, 2.

55. Aleksandr Bolsunovskii, "Beskhoznyi plutonii," *Moskovskie novosti,* July 27, 1993.

Epilogue

1. Susan Gross Solomon, "Social Hygiene and Soviet Public Health, 1921–1930," in Susan Gross Solomon, John Hutchinson, ed., *Health and Society in Revolutionary Russia* (Bloomington: Indiana University Press, 1990), pp. 175–200.

2. Lewis Siegelbaum, "Okhrano Truda," in Solomon, Hutchinson, *Health and Society,* pp. 224–245.

3. F. G. Krotkov, "Osnovnye zadachi radiatsionnoi gigieny," *Gigiena i sanitariia,* no. 10 (1958), 3–4.

4. A. N. Marei, "Nekotorye voprosy sanitarnoi okhrany vodoemov ot zagriazneniia radioaktivnymi veshchestvami," *Gigiena i sanitariia,* no. 9 (1956), 7–11.

5. I. E. Mukhin, "K voprosy o neobkhodimosti opredeleniia radioaktivnosti vody pri vybore podzemnykh istochnikov pit'evogo vodosnabzheniia," *Gigiena i sanitariia,* no. 11 (1961), 9–13.

6. S. M. Gorodinskii, "Voprosy individual'noi zashchity pri rabote s otkrytymi radioaktivnymi veshchestvami," *Gigiena i sanitariia,* no. 1 (1956), 27–31. See also "New Pressurized Plastic Clothing," *Atomics,* September 1954, 263.

7. F. G. Krotkov, A. V. Bykhovskii, "Puti i itogi nauchnogo razvitiia sovetskoi radiatsionnoi gigieny," *Gigiena i sanitariia,* no. 11 (1967), 57–63.

8. A. N. Marei, "Radiatsionnaia kommunal'naia gigiena k-50 letiiu sovetskoi vlasti," *Gigiena i sanitariia,* no. 9 (1969), 6–10.

9. S. M. Gorodinskii, G. M. Parkhomenko, "Voprosy profilaktiki pri rabotakh s radioaktivnymi izotopami," *Gigiena i sanitariia,* no. 4 (1953), 22–28.

10. M. A. Nevstrueva, "O nekotorykh problemakh radiatsionnoi gigieny," *Gigiena i sanitariia,* no. 12 (1965), 3–6.

11. A. T. Avdonin, "Otvedenie stochnykh vod, zagriazennykh radioaktivnymi veshchestvami," *Gigiena i sanitariia,* no. 8 (1963), 14–19.

12. I. A. Sobolev, L. M. Khomchik, "Organizatsiia tsentralizovannogo udaleniia radioaktivnykh otkhodov s mest ikh nakopleniia," *Gigiena i sanitariia,* no. 5 (1965), 78–79.

13. B. I. Bulatov, *200 iadernykh poligonov SSSR* (Novosibirsk: Tseris, 1993), p. 14.

14. Liudmila Bogachevich, "Zhertvy 'kontseptsii'," *Ekho chernobylia,* no. 3–4 (January 1992), 12.

15. Zhores Medvedev, *Nuclear Disaster in the Urals* (New York: Vintage, 1980).

16. Murray Feshbach, Alfred Friendly, Jr., *Ecocide in the USSR* (New York: Basic Books, 1992), pp. 174–175; Bulatov, *200 iadernykh poligonov,* pp. 56–58.

17. "Zakon Rossiiskoi federatsii," *Rossiiskaia gazeta,* June 17, 1993, 5.

18. Thomas Cochran, Robert Norris, *Russian/Soviet Nuclear Warhead Production,* Nuclear Weapons Databook Working Paper 93-1 (Washington: Natural Resources Defense

Council, 1993), pp. 65–80; Bulatov, *200 iadernykh poligonov,* p. 55; Feshbach, Friendly, *Ecocide,* p. 175.

19. V. A. Vodianitskii, "Dopustim li sbros otkhodov atomnykh proizvodstv v chernoe more?" *Priroda,* no. 2 (1958), 46–52; V. G. Bogorov, E. M. Kreps, "Vosmozhno li zakhoronenie radioaktivnykh otkhodov v glubokovodnykh vpadinakh okeana," ibid., no. 9 (1958), 45–50; V. G. Bogorov, B. A. Tareev, "Glubiny okeana i vopros zakhoroneniia v nikh radioaktivnykh otkhodov," *Izvestiia Akademii Nauk SSSR. Seriia geograficheskaia,* no. 4 (1960), 10.

20. Leonid Veksler, " 'Pokhorony' radioaktivnykh otkhodov oboidutsia bolee chem v 200 mlrd rublei," *Moskovskie novosti,* May 16, 1993; Ivan Pyrkh, "Redaktiiu vyzyvaiut: ostanovka ne iskliuchena," *Rossiiskaia gazeta,* July 14, 1993.

21. Tamara Kariakina, "Tomsk-7: Tam stol´ko lzhi i podloga," *Rossiiskaia gazeta,* May 26, 1993; Aleksandr Chernykh, "Reaktory stanut mirnymi," *Rossiiskaia gazeta,* May 7, 1994.

22. "Tomsk-7: Pravitel´stvu priniat´ ischerpyvaiushchie mery," *Rossiiskaia gazeta,* April 16, 1993; Andrei Illesh, "Iadernaia vesna: chto obshchego mezhdu Chernobylem i Tomskom-7?" *Izvestiia,* April 27, 1993, 4, and "Tomsk-7: I zdes´ budet svoi 'sarkofag'," *Izvestiia,* April 22, 1993; Viktor Kostiukovskii, "Tomsk-7: Iadernye budni posle vzryva," *Izvestiia,* May 12, 1993.

23. V. Loginov, "Tomsk-7: otkrytyi gorod dlia bedy," *Komsomol´skaia pravda,* April 21, 1993.

24. D. Viktorov, "Iadernyi reket," *Ekho chernobylia,* no. 3–4 (January 1992), 9; Iurii Khots, "Reaktor — eto vam ne traktor," *Trud,* July 13, 1993. See also Michael Gordon, "Hard Times for Russia's Nuclear Centers," *New York Times,* November 18, 1998, A1, A12.

25. Vladimir Gubarev, "Atomnaia bomba bez prismotra," *Rossiiskaia gazeta,* June 29, 1993; Anatolii Ershov, "Iadershchiki 'Arzamas-16' mintinguiut i gotoviatsia k zabastovke," *Izvestiia,* June 29, 1993.

26. "Miting v iadernom tsentre 'Arzamas-16'," *Rossiiskaia gazeta,* June 25, 1993; "Korroziia v iadernom tsentre," *Moskovskie novosti,* July 4, 1993; Vladimir Gubarev, "Arzamas-16 gotov nachat´ zabastovku," *Rossiiskaia gazeta,* June 23, 1993, 1–2.

27. Sergei Smirnov, "Bomba zamedlennogo desitviia," *Komsomol´skaia pravda,* July 29, 1993.

28. Andrei Illesh, Valerii Iakov, "Vybros radioaktivnykh veshchestv v Cheliabinske-65 ne tak uzh bezopasen, kak zaiavliaet Minatom," *Izvestiia,* July 21, 1993; "Vybros est´. Ugrozy net," *Rossiiskaia gazeta,* July 21, 1993; "Obluchenie v norme," *Rossiiskaia gazeta,* August 4, 1993.

29. Aleksei Tarasov, "Prizrak Chernobylia brodit v Sibiri," *Izvestiia,* July 20, 1993, 1–2.

30. Vadim Petrasiuk, "Atomnoe kladbishche v stolitse Ukrainy," *Kievskie vedomosti,* April 18, 1993, 1, 8; Igor Osipchuk, "Radioaktivnaia vol´nitsa," *Vseukrainskie vedomosti,* no. 59 (July 9, 1994), 1l; Iurii Kril´, "Vnov´ pushchen ekspluatatsiiu radioaktivnyi mogil´nik," *Kievskie vedomosti,* June 24, 1993.

31. Kim Smirnov, "Vse nashi radioaktivnye zakhoroneniia v moriakh rassekrecheny," *Izvestiia,* August 7, 1993, 15; B. S. Kolychev, " 'Zola' atomnykh kotlov," *Trud,* March 3, 1966, 4; V. Serdobol´skii, "Rezul´tat atomnogo bezumstva," *Vestnik chernobylia,* no. 49 (July 1993), 1.

32. Nikolai Tsvetkov, "Rossiiskii sor v iaponskuiu izbu," *Komsomol´skaia pravda,* October 19, 1993; Igor Tsarev, Irina Nevinnaia et al., "Skandal na iadernoi pomoike," *Trud,* October 22, 1993; Craig Whitney, "Russia Halts Nuclear Waste Dumping in Sea," *New York Times,* October 22, 1993, A9.

33. Igor Stadnik, "Atomnyi shram," *Moskovskii novosti,* June 28, 1992, 18–19.

34. Sergei Eremeev, "Prezhdevremennye pokhorony," *Nedelia,* no. 49 (1991), 6–7.

35. A. V. Kurbatov, "Iskhody beremennostei v sem´iakh lits, podvergavshikhsia khronicheskomu professional´nomu oblucheniiu na predpriiatiakyh atomnoi promyshlennosti," *Meditsinskaia radiobiologiia i radiatsionnaia bezopastnost´,* no. 4 (1994), 32–35.

36. Evgenii Solomenko, "V epitsentre bedy," *Izvestiia,* September 11, 1993.

37. Aleksandr Emel´ianenkov, "Rossiia ukhodit iz pribaltiki . . . i vyvozit za soboi radioaktivnye otkhody," *Rossiiskaia razeta,* June 17, 1993, 5; Iurii Stroganov, "Radiatsiia na eksport," *Rossiiskaia gazeta,* June 29, 1993; Valerii Kul´bakov, "U berega Sakhalina—iadernaia 'bomba' zamedlennogo deistviia," *Izvestiia,* May 27, 1993; Vladimir Riabchinkov, "Sakahlin stoit na svoem Chernobyle?" *Pravda,* May 29, 1993, p. 4.

38. Oleg Zlobin, "Tuman nad atomnoi," *Rossiiskaia gazeta,* July 28, 1993.

39. Nikolai Lashkevich, "Trevoga na ignalinskoi AES: Litva provodit ucheniia," *Izvestiia,* June 1, 1993.

40. n. a., "Tsenoi svoei zhizni . . . vorona ostanovila atomnyi generator," *Kievskie vedomosti,* April 20, 1993.

41. *Current Digest of the Soviet Press,* vol. 11, no. 42 (November 16, 1988), 5–6.

42. "Pazhary na ZAES i v Zaporozh´e," *Nezavisimost´,* May 26, 1993; S. Kharchenko, "Radiofobiia v proshlom. Chto vperedi?" *Ekho chernobylia,* no. 29–32 (September 1992), 13; "Voronezhskaia statistika," ibid., no. 5–6 (February 1992), 7.

43. Veksler, " 'Pokhorony'," and Ivan Pyrkh, "Redaktiiu vyzyvaiut: ostanovka ne iskliuchena," *Rossiiskaia gazeta,* July 14, 1993.

44. Veksler, " 'Pokhorony'."

45. A. Kuziuk, "Chernobyl´skaia katastrofa: Prichiny iavnye, skrytye i ne vskrytye," *Ekho chernobylia,* no. 5–8 (February 1993), 14.

46. *Current Digest of the Soviet Press,* vol. 11, no. 42 (November 16, 1988), 1–5.

47. Svetlana Tutorskaia, "V Rossii sozdaetsia mezhdunarodnyi institut tekhnicheskoi bezopasnosti," *Izvestiia,* May 27, 1993.

48. On the opposition to the Tatar nuclear power station, see Dawson, *Econationalism.* See also *Rynochnaia ploshchad´,* June 29, 1994; Vladimir Katsman, "Zaporozhskaia AES, vidimo, ostanetsia bez shestogo energobloka . . ." *Kievskie vedomosti,* July 6, 1994, 1; V. Budianov, "Tsepnaia reaktsiia rastochitel´stva," *Sovetskaia rossiia,* December 24, 1989, 1; A. Pankratov, "Zhertv net, iasnosti—tozhe," *Komsomol´skaia pravda,* November 12, 1989, 3; Roostam Sadri, "Concern in Tatar ASSR About Nuclear Power Station to be Built on Kama River," *Radio Liberty Research,* RL 222/83, June 7, 1983.

49. Nikolai Efimovich, "Neizbezhen li novyi chernobyl´?" *Komsomol´skaia pravda,* May 29, 1993; N. V. Kniaz´kaia, *Obzor publikatsii sovetskoi tsentral´noi pressy po problemam razvitiia atomnoi energetiki za IV kvartal 1990 g.* (Moscow: Energiia and KIAE, 1991); S. M. Briushinkin, *Obzor publikatsii sovetskoi regional´noi pressy po problemam razvitiia atomnoi energetiki za IV kvartal 1990 g.* (Moscow: Energiia and KIAE, 1991).

50. Sergei Voronitsyn, "Atomic Energy in the USSR: The Lessons of Chernobyl´," *Radio Liberty Research,* RL 358/87 (September 10, 1987).

51. A. Vaganov, "Bezopasnyi iadernyi reactor—realnost´?" *Inzhenernaia gazeta,* no. 134 (November 1991), 2; Valerii Men´shchikov, Aleksandr Protsenko, Viktor Blinkin, "Iadernaia energetika: nas zhdut katastrofy ili blagopoluchie?" *Izvestiia,* August 28, 1993.

52. Vladimir Gubarev, "Iadernoe plamiia," *Rossiiskaia gazeta,* August 10, 1993, 2.

53. V. Demenev, "Ostanovit´ reaktor—eto eshche poldela," *Ekho chernobylia,* no. 5–8 (February 1993), 9.

54. *Fundamental´nye issledovaniia i sodeistvie nauchno-tekhnicheskomu progressu* (Moscow: Sovet federatsii federal´nogo sobraniia rossiiskoi federatsii, 1997), pp. 74–77; Richard Stone, "Russia's Last Shot at Space," *Science,* vol. 276 (June 20, 1997), 1780–1782.

55. Aleksei Tarasov, "Krasnoiarksu-26 vygodno ostavat´sia zakrytym ot mira," *Izvestiia,* September 28, 1993. See also "Russia's Secret Cities," *The Economist,* December 25, 1993–January 7, 1994, 65–68.

56. "Strasti vokrug AES," *NTR,* no. 7 (1989), 1.

INDEX